Best Places to Stay in the Mid-Atlantic States

THE BEST PLACES TO STAY SERIES

Best Places to Stay in America's Cities
Second Edition/Kenneth Hale-Wehmann, Editor

Best Places to Stay in Asia
Jerome E. Klein

Best Places to Stay in California
Third Edition/Marilyn McFarlane

Best Places to Stay in the Caribbean
Third Edition/Bill Jamison and Cheryl Alters Jamison

Best Places to Stay in Florida
Third Edition/Christine Davidson

Best Places to Stay in Hawaii
Third Edition/Bill Jamison and Cheryl Alters Jamison

Best Places to Stay in the Mid-Atlantic States
Second Edition/ Dana Nadel Foley

Best Places to Stay in the Midwest
John Monaghan

Best Places to Stay in New England
Fifth Edition/Christina Tree and Kimberly Grant

Best Places to Stay in the Pacific Northwest
Third Edition/Marilyn McFarlane

Best Places to Stay in the Rockies
Second Edition/Roger Cox

Best Places to Stay in the South
Second Edition/Carol Timblin

Best Places to Stay in the Southwest
Third Edition/Anne E. Wright

Best Places to Stay in the Mid-Atlantic States

SECOND EDITION

Dana Nadel Foley

Bruce Shaw, Editorial Director

HOUGHTON MIFFLIN COMPANY
BOSTON • NEW YORK

Second Edition

ISSN: 1061-7353
ISBN: 0-395-66616-3

Printed in the United States of America

Illustrations prepared by Eric Walker
Maps by Charles Bahne
Design by Robert Overholtzer

This book was prepared in conjunction
with Harvard Common Press.

VB 10 9 8 7 6 5 4 3 2 1

*To my husband, Patrick, who makes home
my favorite vacation*

Contents

Introduction

A vacation is a celebratory time, a skip in life's most regular beat. It might be a long-awaited romantic weekend, the knitting of schedules that unites friends separated by time and distance, a rare window when a family frees itself from school and work, or a well-deserved retreat from the stresses of the job. Whatever the occasion, a vacation is an exciting, luxurious, unpredictable event. In preparing this book, I am acutely aware of every bit of hope, anticipation, and money that we put into our vacations — an ominous responsibility.

It's a familiar drama: good wishes from co-workers, a final rush to the bank, stray phone calls, packing, making lists, losing lists, a vague feeling of butterflies as the taxicab meets traffic, picking out a magazine while watching the clock. Despite the recognizable emotions of travel, a vacation is often a blind act of faith. Will the weather hold up? Will this bed-and-breakfast be as charming as my twice-removed cousin's wife said it would (and now that I think of it, I never did like her taste)? What will we do at night? Will we make any friends?

Certainly, this book cannot guarantee a successful vacation, but it can alleviate some of those unsettling uncertainties. I have met nearly all the innkeepers you will meet and explored their rooms and grounds, sometimes with their pets in tow. I've been to the hotels and resorts, checked that what they advertise as a tennis court is not a paved driveway, that their swimming pool doesn't double as a fishing pond (which they also advertise).

While taking notes, interviewing, exploring, and snooping, I tried to envision each place as the special place in which you have invested your hopes and finances. I tried to imagine you here for that long-awaited respite. Will you be happy here? What could go wrong? Why is this place in the woods better than another on the shore? How professional is this innkeeper, and how warm is that hotel staff? I tried to predict who would like it here: a businessman, a businesswoman, a family, an amorous couple, a sophisticated couple, a shy couple, an older couple, a single person — in hopes of finding the best places to stay for every person with every imaginable need. It was a rewarding task: each beautiful hotel warmed my heart; each well-run inn lifted my spirits.

After months of research and 12,000 miles of driving in this unimaginably beautiful territory, having been hosted by hundreds of hoteliers and innkeepers, I was very taken with the concept of leisure. The eight Mid-Atlantic states comprise a fascinating gallery of Americana in a concentrated, accessible region smaller than Texas, home to more than 50 million people. Within its boundaries are some of the nation's most surprising geography and sophisticated culture, and the raw beginnings of American history. I envy you your travels.

Please keep in mind:

For the purposes of this book, I have defined a *bed-and-breakfast* as an intimate hostelry that serves a morning meal. An *inn* also serves dinner. Other lodging spots do not serve meals, unless otherwise stated, usually with the following terminology:

EP: European plan, includes no meals.
MAP: Modified American plan, includes breakfast and dinner.
AP: Full American plan, includes three meals.

Rates listed are double occupancy unless otherwise specified. Ask about single rates if you're traveling alone. Hotels and resorts have private baths unless otherwise specified.

While I am confident that the places in this book are wondrous and exceptional, there are several things that you can do to make your stay more comfortable. Do be specific about your needs when you make reservations, especially in smaller establishments, which often have smaller rooms and which may be booked months ahead.

Do request an update on anything that may be of importance to you: smoking policies, rates, proximity to restaurants, views, and facilities for adults as well as for teenagers, children, and infants. Though I tried to be as accurate as possible in my research, policies, rates, and owners change.

Please (and I implore you) do check in advance if you plan to travel with a pet and wish him or her to be as comfortable as you are.

Happy travels.

Dana Nadel Foley

Delaware

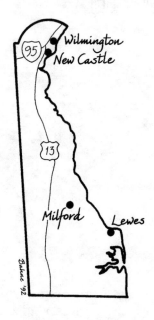

Lewes
New Devon Inn, 6
Milford
The Towers Bed and Breakfast, 8
New Castle
The David Finney Inn, 10
Wilmington
Guest Quarters Suite Hotel–Wilmington, 12
Hotel du Pont, 13

Best Romantic Retreat

Milford
  The Towers Bed and Breakfast

Best Village Bed-and-Breakfast

Lewes
  New Devon Inn

Best Village Inns

New Castle
  The David Finney Inn
Wilmington
  Guest Quarters Suite Hotel–Wilmington

Best for Metropolitan Magnificence

Wilmington
  Hotel du Pont

Unfortunately, most travelers simply zip through a 20-mile strip of Delaware's northern neck along Interstate 95, unaware of the rare beauty of its vast beaches, the rich history in its 17th-century settlements, and the quiet elegance of the Brandywine River Valley, which inspired generations of American painters.

The first of the original 13 states to ratify the Constitution in 1787, Delaware is also the second smallest state, with an area of 2,045 square miles. Just under 700,000 people live in Delaware. Wilmington and the northern part of the state hook under Pennsylvania's Brandywine Valley, separated from New Jersey by the Delaware River, which flows into the Delaware Bay. On its west and south, Delaware is bordered by eastern Maryland. From 3 to 35 miles wide, Delaware stretches 96 miles long, with 28 miles of beautiful Atlantic coastline beginning at Cape Henlopen State Park and shooting down to Fenwick Island State Park.

The Delaware Bay was first explored by Henry Hudson in 1609. It was named a year later for Sir Thomas West III, Lord de la Warr, Governor of Virginia. Delaware's history was a tug-of-war between the Dutch and Swedish, who succumbed finally to English rule in 1664. The Dutch first landed in Delaware in 1631 near Lewes and were quite trampled by the Lenni Lenape Indians. The country's first Swedish settlers alighted on Wilmington shores in 1638, followed closely by a second band of Dutch, who founded New Castle in 1651 and conquered their Swedish neighbors in 1655. The British ended the dispute by capturing all settlements in 1664.

Wilmington was crafted by a Frenchman named Eleuthère Irénée Du Pont, who landed in 1802 and whose black powder mill eventually emerged as one of the country's largest chemical plants. Now that the magnificent landmark Hotel du Pont has completed a massive restoration and renovation effort, Wilmington can once again accommodate even the most discerning travelers. Stroll along the five pedestrian blocks of Market Street Mall to Old Town Hall, a museum of Americana.

Wilmington's outskirts are home to beautiful countryside and a host of culturally refreshing activities. The Brandywine Museum houses three generations of paintings from the Andrew Wyeth family, as well as other well-known artists like Maxfield Parrish; the Delaware Art Museum has the country's largest public display of English pre-Raphaelite paintings and decorative arts and is the source for the works of Howard Pyle, known as the father of American illustration. The Chaddsford Winery is a bit north, as are the famous Longwood Gardens and Winterthur Museum, famous for its collection of decorative arts between 1640 and 1840. The Nemours Mansion and Gardens, on 300 acres, was the Louis XVI–style palace of Alfred I. Du Pont, quite worth a tour.

Historic **New Castle,** seven miles south of Wilmington, just below the Delaware Memorial Bridge, is one of the better preserved 18th-century communities in the Mid-Atlantic, with more than 50 18th- and 19th-century historic buildings in a wonderful cobblestone waterfront park called the Strand. It was bought from Native Americans in 1651 by Peter Stuyvesant, taken by the Swedes, and given over to the English, who gave the town its name. Try to plan a visit in the first week of May, when A Day In Old New Castle, a tradition for more than 65 years, welcomes visitors into the town's historic homes.

Heading south to Lewes and Delaware's beaches, you will drive through Dover. Those interested in history will want to see its historic State House, built in 1792 and the country's second-oldest state house in continuous use. Not so historic is the Dover Downs International Speedway, a big draw for this colonial town, particularly for the "500" races in early June and late September.

About 15 miles south is the town of **Milford,** the gateway to Delaware's beaches. Try to plan an overnight here at the Towers Bed and Breakfast, with a meal at the Banking House Inn. The next day, leave plenty of time to enjoy **Lewes,** a beautiful, unspoiled, preserved piece of history several miles off the well-beaten path of busy Route 1. The town is infinitely walkable and picturesque, best appreciated with a stay at the New Devon Inn. There are a handful of historic museums commemorating the Dutch settlers and Lewes's strategic involvement in several wars. At Front Street, the Lewes and Rehoboth Canal bisects the town, separating the historic section from modern development.

Across the canal is a spit of land that serves as breakwater for the Delaware Bay and the landing spot for the ferry. To the east are the 3,400 protected acres of Cape Henlopen State Park, which juts into the water like a hook. Its three miles of beaches are entirely windswept and protected, as untouched as they were when the first settlers arrived in the 17th century. There is hiking, camping, a nine-hole Frisbee golf course, and the Seaside Nature Center. Don't miss Shipcarpenter Square, a residential preservation project that saved and restored several historic homes. Closer to town is a similar civic project called the Complex, a two-acre site of colonial and 19th-century buildings open for guided and self-guided tours.

Below Cape Henlopen State Park are the Delaware Seashore State Park, a spit between the Atlantic and Rehoboth Bay, and Fenwick Island State Park at Delaware's base. Be sure to take the ferry to Cape May, across the Delaware Bay.

For Delaware travel information, call 800-441-8846 out of state, 800-282-8667 in Delaware.

LEWES

New Devon Inn

142 Second Street
P.O. Box 516
Lewes, DE 19958
302-645-6466
Fax: 302-645-7196

*A charmer
in historic Lewes,
near the ferry*

Proprietors: Dale Jenkins and Bernard Nash. **General Manager:** Barbara Lloyd. **Accommodations:** 24 rooms, 2 suites. **Rates:** $60–$105, $85–$125, $95–$145 depending on season. **Included:** Continental breakfast, turndown. **Minimum stay:** 2 nights on summer weekends, 3 nights on summer holiday weekends. **Added:** $20 additional guest, 8% tax. **Payment:** MasterCard, Visa, Diners Club, American Express. **Children:** Discouraged. **Pets:** Not allowed. **Smoking:** Not allowed in breakfast room. **Open:** All year.

On the western shores of the Delaware Bay across from New Jersey's southern tip is the town of Lewes, Delaware, often and unfairly remembered as the "other end" of the Cape May ferry. This surprisingly lovely fishing village was founded by Dutch settlers in 1631 and has boundless charm and historic import. It's easy to miss Lewes (pronounced "Lewis"), since the ferry access and Route 13 bypass the town by a quarter mile. However, it is certainly worth a detour if not a trip in itself to see this picturesque town and, on its fringes, Cape Henlopen State Park, which has some of the prettiest protected beachfront in the Delmarva peninsula.

The town looks like a movie set, and in the heart of it all is the New Devon Inn. The hotel sits on the corner of Market and Second streets. Second Street is the town's main thoroughfare, lined with elm trees, quaint shops, and good restaurants. The corner itself holds historic merit, having been the homestead of John Rodney from 1725 to 1792; Rodney's cousin Caesar was one of the three Delaware signers of the Declaration of Independence, and John's sons Caleb and Daniel both went on to govern the state.

The Caesar Rodney Hotel was built here in 1927 and served as the town's hostelry for years until it fell into disrepair

> **Not only is Lewes a wonderful destination in itself — home of the stunning beaches at Cape Henlopen State Park — it is an extremely convenient gateway from the west to the New Jersey shoreline. Stop here for a night; then take the ferry to Cape May for a complete weekend.**

during its tenure as a transient hotel. In 1987, Dale Jenkins, contractor and decorator, and her partner, Bernard Nash, bought the faded property, gutted the interior, and undertook a daunting renovation. The brick facade and old floors are the only testaments to the original structure. There are 24 rooms and two suites, all done in sophistication and splendor; six retail shops enliven the lobby and lower level. Owner Jenkins named the property rather touchingly for Devon Island, which disappeared from the Delaware Bay, an event chronicled by James Michener in his novel *Chesapeake*.

Upstairs are two floors of guest rooms; those overlooking Second Street are preferable. The rooms are decorated in Victorian antiques. A Market Street third-floor room has a double-size antique carved oak headboard, a petit-point Victorian chair, marble-top dresser, and old-fashioned floral linens. Others have similar period antiques and beds in oxford stripe linens or masculine paisleys. The bathrooms are new and sparkling, with black and white parquet linoleum, pedestal sinks with brass fixtures, thick towels, and a hair dryer. Nightly turndown brings sherry on a silver platter, glasses, and a filled ice bucket. Oriental runners and scatter rugs add color to the light wood flooring.

There are two common rooms: a downstairs television

room and a ground-floor Victorian parlor with a grand piano where guests partake of a generous Continental breakfast of fresh baked goods, juice, yogurt, and fruit.

No one knows the charms of Lewes better than General Manager Barbara Lloyd, who should be sought out in the unlikely event that she has not greeted guests herself. A source of enthusiasm and historical knowledge, Barbara represents the best of the New Devon Inn service.

MILFORD

The Towers Bed and Breakfast

101 Northwest Front Street
Milford, DE 19963
302-422-3814
302-424-0321
Reservations: 800-366-3814

> *One of the Mid-Atlantic's most beautiful B&Bs*

Proprietors: Dan and Sharon Bond.
Accommodations: 6 rooms (only 4 are used per night), 4 with private bath, including 2 suites. **Rates:** Rooms $95, suites $125. **Included:** Full breakfast. **Minimum stay:** Some weekends. **Added:** 8% tax. **Payment:** MasterCard, Visa. **Children:** Over age 12, welcome. **Pets:** Not allowed. **Smoking:** Not allowed. **Open:** All year.

The Towers is an incredibly beautiful bed-and-breakfast in the fairly uninspired working-class town of Milford, several miles inland from the Delaware Bay on the Mispillion River. A half hour's drive away are Rehoboth Beach, Lewes and the Cape May ferry, and two of the East Coast's major wildlife refuges, Bombay Hook and Prime Hook.

Listed on the National Register of Historic Places and part of North Milford's Historic District — some 30 historic houses are within walking distance — this fantastical house goes on forever, with turrets, towers, and 10 different kinds of gingerbread in a carnival of colors. The fabulous exterior is only a preamble to the lavish interior, filled with museum-quality French antiques.

The original house was built in 1783, long before the rise

of fanciful Victorian architecture, four years before Milford was founded. Dr. John Wallace was the proprietor; his stepson John Lofland, born here, became a poet of notable fame known as the Milford Bard; his friend and colleague Edgar Allan Poe often visited. In 1840, the house was bought by Delaware governor William Burton. Fifty years later, he gave the house to his granddaughter, who spent $42,000 on a complete Victorianization in 1895. She imported a master craftsman from Italy who supervised the installation of the lavish stained glass in every window of the house.

In 1985, Michael Real and partner Mark Springer were swept off their

> The original, extravagant stained glass windows throughout this historic house were the inspiration for the 12 exterior shades of the Towers — mauve, yellow, blue, pink, and mint, and more. Such is the extent of the aesthetic elaboration at this magnificent bed and breakfast, which is filled with exquisite French antiques.

feet by this property. Their restoration took two and a half years and included stripping plywood off walls to find traces of gold leaf. Dan and Sharon Bond were guests at the B&B, so charmed by the town that they bought and restored a Civil War Victorian four blocks down the street. In 1992, the Bonds bought the Towers from Michael and Mark; they are loving owners today.

The Music Room, to the right of the foyer and several steps down, has a coffered ceiling in a light variety of sycamore that had vanished, killed by a blight, by 1900. The parlor across the hall has cherry paneling; the mirroring dining room combines cherry with chestnut; and upstairs, the wainscoting combines these woods with walnut.

The Music Room has an 1899 Knabe grand piano, carved mantel, rose couches, and two lion-headed gilded French chairs from the turn of the 18th century. The room is separated from the hallway by thinly carved sycamore spindles that permit music to waft throughout the house. The formal dining room features an exquisite three-piece French dining set from the turn of the century; breakfast is served here, by the fire in cooler months.

Surely the third-floor Rapunzel Suite, named for its access to the turret tower in a screened porch, is the most magnificent. It has a 12-foot ceiling and a Louis XVI bed with a crown canopy that falls from a gilded Louis XV mantel. A Sun King double armoire stands in the corner of the room. Across the hall is the Victorian Bird's Nest Room, with a nine-foot carved walnut headboard. Both rooms feature sitting rooms and modern baths.

The second-floor rooms are all different, equal only in elegance. Only two of the four rooms are occupied at a time so everyone gets a private Victorian bath. The Tower Room has a delightful window seat in the turret. The Garden, Governor Burton, and John Lofland rooms are similarly decorated and filled with gorgeous Victorian furnishings.

The back gardens are highly groomed, with swirly high-backed white iron furniture. There are statues, a fountain, and a gazebo where guests may take breakfast — ricotta cheese pancakes are a specialty. Toward the back of the property is a swimming pool with a raised redwood deck.

Across from the Towers is the Banking House Inn, built in 1811, now one of Delaware's finest restaurants.

NEW CASTLE

The David Finney Inn

216 Delaware Street
New Castle, DE 19720
302-322-6367
800-334-6640

> *An 18th-century
> inn in wonderful
> New Castle*

Innkeeper: Judith S. Piser. **Accommodations:** 17 rooms, all with private bath. **Rates:** Rooms $75–$90, suites $120. **Included:** Continental breakfast. **Minimum stay:** 2 nights on some weekends. **Added:** 8% tax. **Payment:** Major credit cards. **Children:** Welcome. **Pets:** Not allowed. **Smoking:** Allowed in tavern only. **Open:** All year.

It seems unlikely, during a particularly congested seven-mile drive south from Wilmington, that anything as pure as historic New Castle exists so close to the Delaware Memorial Bridge. Thankfully, it does, and it's a joyful discovery for a weary traveler. The area was purchased from Indians by Peter Stuyvesant for Dutch settlers in 1651, but it was the English who named it New Castle in 1664.

Rent was a bushel of wheat per year on the land that Renere Vandercoolen bought in 1683 to build an inn where the David Finney stands today. Some of the inn's handmade bricks came from two other buildings that were erected here in 1713. Militia officer and attorney David Finney is noted to have joined the two buildings in 1757.

> **Visitors to historic New Castle will be charmed by this tiny, perfectly preserved town just south of Wilmington at the mouth of the Delaware Bay.**
> **The place to stay is the David Finney Inn, a relative latecomer (1757) to this 17th-century port town.**

The brick building is a handsome colonial: two large mullioned windows flank the Willliamsburg blue door on the first floor; five windows span the second floor; and three dormers cut into the saltbox shingled roof.

The seven second-floor rooms and 10 third-floor rooms are clean and sparely appointed with modest antiques and colonial reproductions. The trim is painted Williamsburg blue. Televisions and phones are available on request. Guests are welcomed with a basket that includes a split of wine and cheese and crackers.

But the David Finney is better known for atmosphere and food than for luxurious decor. Dinner starts with a choice of appetizers and salad; shellfish bisque with cream chantilly is a favorite. Roast rack of lamb is served with boursin cheese crust and Madeira wine; another specialty is the veal Oscar David Finney, with lump crabmeat, asparagus, and hollandaise sauce. Dinner entrées range from $16 to $25. The dining room is simply furnished with colonial spindleback chairs, but guests love the extensive patio, which stretches into the backyard and is furnished with wrought-iron chairs and tables. Common rooms, shared by dinner and overnight guests, are furnished with Williamsburg reproductions.

Five museums in town recreate Dutch and English colonial life. With more than 50 buildings from the early 18th and

19th centuries, New Castle is a walker's delight. A grassy
park faces the Delaware waterfront, bordered by the cobblestone Strand and the village commons, which are often enlivened by weekend activities.

WILMINGTON

Guest Quarters Suite Hotel–Wilmington

707 North King Street
Wilmington, DE 19801
302-656-9300
Fax: 302-656-2459
800-543-9106

> *The suite place
> for business
> travelers
> in Wilmington*

Proprietor: Christopher Pfohl. **General Manager:** Maryane Hill. **Accommodations:** 49 suites. **Rates:** $119, $89 on weekends. **Included:** Full breakfast buffet, morning newspaper. **Minimum stay:** None. **Added:** 8% tax, $10 additional person. **Payment:** Major credit cards. **Children:** Welcome; under 12 free. **Pets:** Not allowed. **Smoking:** Nonsmoking rooms available. **Open:** All year.

While the gorgeous beaux arts–style Hotel du Pont was under
renovation for several years in the early 1990s, this hotel,
then the Christina House, became the mainstay in Wilmington. Well, the du Pont is back in glorious business; but the
Christina House, now a Guest Quarters hotel, made a mark
for itself and is now the value option in Wilmington. The
two-room suites are configured with the business traveler in
mind, with separate work and sleep areas and mini- and wet
bars; a fine fitness facility is under the same roof.

The Guest Quarters is just around the corner from the
Hotel du Pont. As with any good piece of postmodern architecture, the space was developed from two existing brownstones — the former Braunstein's Department Store — now
connected and elaborated with a glass atrium and concrete
additions. It spans the full block between King Street to the
pedestrian mall behind called Market Street.

A triple-story atrium in the center is flooded with light that spills onto white walls and light wood floors covered with cushy Oriental rugs and filled with contemporary furnishings. Plants bask in the sunlight, and a fireplace is stoked on chilly nights.

The guest rooms border the atrium on three upper floors. There are 49 two-room suites, each configured a bit differently but all similarly furnished in deluxe hotel fashion. The unusually spacious suites feature two televisions hidden in contemporary or reproduction armoires, traditional wing chairs and camelback sofas, and enormous closets. The baths are luxurious, with

> **While the doyenne of Wilmington hotels, the Hotel du Pont, was being restored in the early 1990s, Guest Quarters became Wilmington's reliable mainstay. It has retained some loyal followers, who prefer its intimacy and reasonable rates.**

a third telephone and hair dryer. Service is prompt and friendly. The only drawback is the blameless dearth of views from most of the guest rooms.

Le Bistro offers reasonably priced lunch and dinner in a private, contemporary fireside setting. Entrées like pan sautéed crab cakes and baby rack of lamb range from $7 to $20.

Hotel du Pont

11th & Market Streets
Wilmington, DE 19801
302-594-3100, 800-441-9019
Fax: 302-656-2145

> *A Wilmington grande dame, resplendent once more*

Proprietors: Du Pont Co. **General Manager:** Jacques Amblard. **Accommodations:** 216 gust rooms and suites. **Rates:** $119–$209, suites $285–$385, packages from $159. **Included:** Use of fitness facilities, in-room fax and modem lines, three-language voice mail, golf privileges at the Du Pont Country Club. **Minimum Stay:** None. **Added:** 8% tax. **Payment:** All credit cards. **Children:** Welcome. **Pets:** Not welcome. **Smoking:** 3 of 10 guest floors nonsmoking. **Open:** All year.

In 1911, a 12-story Italian Renaissance monolith was constructed on the corner of 11th and Market streets in Wilmington for about $1 million. The brainchild — like many other early 20th-century innovations — of the Du Pont family, the hotel was meant to provide lodging for patrons of the burgeoning family business. In addition, the Hotel du Pont would be the pride of Delaware and the cornerstone of the Du Pont legacy. The palatial structure opened in 1913; two years later, its unheralded success called for expansions. In 1918, the fifth section of the Du Pont Building was constructed, nearly doubling the size of the hotel, adding 188 more guest rooms to the original 150 and grand public spaces including the breathtaking Gold Ballroom.

> **The only hotel in the region boasting two AAA four-diamond dining rooms, the Hotel du Pont emanates pure luxury. Its recent $40 million renovation afforded a renaissance not only to the grand hotel but to Wilmington itself, and provides a return to the wealth of the Roaring Twenties.**

The 1950s took their aesthetic toll on the hotel: among other affronts, its iron and opal glass marquee was replaced by a 127-foot aluminum and steel structure; the 37 balconies were removed; and the walnut reception desk with its bronze and iron grillwork was covered. The Hotel du Pont recently underwent its most major renovation: $40 million was spent to return the hotel to its original grandeur, focusing on the guest rooms, the main lobby, the Lobby Lounge, and the Brandywine Room. The results were magnificent, and the Hotel du Pont is once again the gem of Delaware.

Walking through the grand lobby, a visitor feels transported back to Wilmington's glory days. Not only is the hotel a work of art in itself, it houses an admirable collection of the Brandywine River School, featuring art from the brushes of three generations of Wyeths, McCoys, and Schoonovers.

Further superlatives apply: this is the country's only grand hotel with its own theater. The 1,200-seat first-run Broadway theater was a destination in itself for decades, as Sarah Bernhardt, the Barrymores, Lillian Gish, Ingrid Bergman, Helen Hayes, Bette Davis, and many others will attest.

While the renovation has revitalized the hotel's Old-World charm, it has also created new-world convenience. The guest rooms now number 216, down from 296. The American Hotel and Motel Association awarded its International Grand Prize Gold Key Award to the Hotel du Pont for most outstanding guest room design. The room palette is soft beige, peach, and mocha, and a built-in mahogany cabinet houses the mini-bar, television, and VCR. Three types of accommodations include large suites with separate boardroom areas, deluxe sleeping rooms with separate sitting areas, and traditional standard rooms. The work-friendly rooms have leather-inlaid desks large enough to accommodate a computer and fax (on request), two phone lines, trilingual voice mail, and an extra-large bath with a separate shower stall and oversize tub, dressing area and lighted vanity, and telephone. A new state-of-the-art fitness facility occupies the hotel's top floor.

The Hotel du Pont also offers extraordinary dining in two four-diamond restaurants. The Green Room has a lush interior with two and a half stories of luxurious oak paneling; its coffered ceiling has oak beams accented by gold leaf. Chef Daniel Bradway's French Continental cuisine may include a cake of fresh jumbo lump crabmeat and shrimp mousse, a salad of harvest greens with grilled quail and vegetable polenta, roast veal loin with sweetbreads, and wild mushrooms and truffles. Entrées range from $22 to $29. The Brandywine Room is a gallery of food and art: the works of Andrew Wyeth and other local artists are represented on the walls. A meal of classic American specialties might include grilled mushrooms with cilantro aioli and risotto; tomato bisque with avocado cream, and grilled filet mignon with truffled whipped potatoes in a Merlot sauce. Entrées here are from $18 to $23.

Be sure to get the full picture and visit other Du Pont attractions, including the more than 1,000 acres at Longwood Gardens and the historic Pierce Du Pont House and outdoor theater; Winterthur Museum and Gardens; Nemours Mansion and gardens, the 300-acre estate of Alfred I. Du Pont; and the Brandywine River Museum, which celebrates the opulence and culturalism the Du Ponts cultivated.

District
of Columbia

Washington, D.C.

Best Romantic Retreats

The Hay-Adams Hotel
The Jefferson

Best Gourmet Getaways

The Morrison-Clark Inn
The Watergate Hotel

Best for Metropolitan Magnificence

The Carlton
Four Seasons Hotel
The Henley Park Hotel
Hotel Washington
The Mayflower
Park Hyatt
The Ritz-Carlton, Washington, D.C.
The Willard Inter-Continental Hotel

The 69 square miles of the nation's capital are bordered on the southwest by Virginia and the Potomac River and are otherwise surrounded by Maryland. Deciding the site for our nation's capital was an early Congressional exercise in democracy, one that put today's Washington gridlock to shame. In 1783 it was proposed that a "federal town" was needed for the deliberations of the Continental Congress. By 1789, the First Congress was brimming with rivalry between southern and northern delegations about where to locate the federal seat. Another battle had been raging in the Congress about war debts. Then came the compromise: southerners gave in on the war debt vote, and the northerners conceded the capital to the Potomac's southern shores.

While 600,000 people call Washington home, more than 20 million visitors arrive annually. Since the bicentennial in 1976, about 50 new hotels have been added to this city, creating one of the highest concentrations of hotel rooms in the world.

Although the city is arranged in quadrants, a better orientation is by neighborhood: the Capitol Hill area and the Smithsonian Mall; the White House and the business district around Lafayette, Farragut, and McPherson squares; DuPont Circle and Embassy Row; Georgetown; Adams Morgan; and Foggy Bottom. Notable sites could keep a visitor occupied for weeks; the Visitor's Center publication called *Attractions* is a helpful guide.

The high point of a Washington visit, of course, is the 555-foot Washington Monument. Other highlights include a tour of the Capitol, the Lincoln Memorial, the Jefferson Memorial, Arlington Cemetery, the Vietnam Veterans and U.S. Marine Corps war memorials, the exceptionally comprehensive Holocaust Museum, and the Smithsonian Institution's 14 separate — and free — museums, including the National Zoo. One could spend an entire visit to Washington D.C. in art museums, so choose carefully among the National Gallery and its East Wing, the Freer, with its renowned Oriental collection, and the contemporary Hirshhorn, among many others. While you're in a cultural mood, you might want to arrange for tickets to an event at the John F. Kennedy Center for the Performing Arts. The Pentagon may be of interest to some; it's one of the largest office buildings in the world, with 23,000 employees in nearly 4 million square feet of office space.

In the summer, when the crowds and city heat get oppressive, take a day trip to Mt. Vernon, 16 miles south of town in northern Virginia, or to Old Town Alexandria, a lovely and authentic 17th-century port town.

For information, call the Washington, D.C., Conventions and Visitors Bureau, 202-789-7000, or visit their offices at 1455 Pennsylvania Avenue, N.W.

The Carlton

923 16th and K Streets, N.W.
Washington, D.C. 20006
202-638-2626
Fax: 202-638-4231
800-325-3535

> *A top choice among
> Washington's
> classic hotels*

Proprietor: ITT Sheraton Corp.
General Manager: Michel J. Ducamp. **Accommodations:** 197
rooms, including 13 suites. **Rates:** Rooms $240–$280, suites
$340–$875; seasonal weekend packages available. **Included:**
Complimentary shoeshine, newspaper, morning coffee/tea,
and a welcome amenity. **Added:** $25 each additional guest,
11% tax, $1.50 room tax, $15 for use of fitness facilities at the
University Club. **Payment:** Major credit cards. **Children:** Welcome; children under 17 stay free in existing bedding. **Pets:**
Small pets allowed. **Smoking:** 2 nonsmoking floors. **Open:** All
year.

The Carlton is a place you truly appreciate after you leave.
The serene and subtle elegance of this classic hotel lingers.
Two blocks from the White House, the Carlton was built in
1926 to resemble an Italian Renaissance palace, eight stone
stories high. Since the 1950s, it has been the flagship property of the Sheraton Corporation, which has returned the hotel
to its palatial origins. Between 1988 and 1990, $20 million
was invested in the Carlton's restoration and renovation.

The grand lobby is the hotel's treasure. Classic and intimate Louis XVI parlor settings cluster over an expansive Oriental carpet. Most breathtaking is the open-beamed, dark
wood ceiling, magnificently carved. Four mullioned arched
windows stretch to the ceiling, framed by heavy drapery.

Some grand architectural details are echoed in Allegro, the
Carlton's lovely restaurant. The dark beamed ceilings, with
less ornate carving, complement the mahogany bar. The original sconces and free-standing lamps, with their flower-
shaped smoky glass shades, are wonderful art deco speci-
mens. Allegro's atmosphere is a beautiful backdrop to the
contemporary continental cuisine of chef Greg Mengert.
Lunch, which ranges from $12 to $18, may feature blackened
ahi tuna with jalapeño ravioli; dinner, from $18.50 to $28,
may offer red snapper in a potato flake crust or boneless jerk-
style chicken.

The guest rooms are unusually elegant and comfortable. In addition to stocked mini-bars, in-room safes, terry bathrobes, and televisions hidden in armoires, the rooms have been decorated with a caring hand in several different schemes. The suites are especially nice, decorated to fit the original period of the hotel in neutral and pale blue shades. All the baths have marble walls and floors, makeup mirrors, hair dryers, and television speakers.

Special guest touches make the Carlton a kind place to stay. This city hotel is one of the few with a welcoming service for its younger guests, who are free (under 17) when they stay with parents in existing beds. In the Carlton Kids program, children are greeted with a variety of toys and games, including Nintendo, Trivial Pursuit, and board games. Nightly turndown service consists of milk and cookies. Infants receive a basket of Pampers and a stuffed animal.

> **Try to check in at the Carlton in the afternoon. This is the best time to see its wonderfully grand lobby, when afternoon tea is served to the music of a harpist. From the magnificently carved ceiling hang crystal chandeliers; you'll feel like a palace visitor.**

Four Seasons Hotel

2800 Pennsylvania Avenue, N.W.
Washington, D.C. 20007
202-342-0444
Fax: 202-944-2076
800-332-3442

> *A contemporary luxury hotel in Georgetown*

Proprietor: Four Seasons Hotels. **General Manager:** Stan Bromley. **Accommodations:** 197 rooms, including 30 suites. **Rates:** Rooms $295–$340, suites $825–$2,000; weekend and corporate rates available. **Included:** Shoeshine. **Minimum stay:** None. **Added:** $30 each additional guest, 11% tax, $1.50 room tax. **Payment:** Major credit cards. **Children:** Welcome. **Pets:** Allowed. **Smoking:** 4 of 6 floors nonsmoking. **Open:** All year.

22 • *District of Columbia*

Washington is teeming with elegantly refurbished grand old hotels that blend in with the embassies and beaux-arts government buildings of this landmark city. For those who have come to visit the White House — not stay in it — or for business travelers who appreciate contemporary comforts more than crown moldings, there is the Four Seasons. This chunky brick building nestles up to the edge of Georgetown, just over the C&O Canal and Rock Creek Park. It features one of the finest fitness facilities of any Washington hotel.

> While other D.C. hotels buddy up to the White House, the Four Seasons has its own territory, Georgetown, and this square brick monolith cuts quite a swath through the 18th-century neighborhood. It's a natural for business travelers.

The Four Seasons lobby is a majestic contemporary space, paneled with light wood, carpeted with a thick pile in geometric patterns. Geometry is a large part of the Four Seasons, with spaces feeling wider than they are tall, making the rooms expansive and relaxing.

Facing the woodsy C&O Canal at the end of the main corridor are several restaurants, including the formal Aux Beaux Champs, which serves classic modern French cuisine. Each waiter is responsible for only one table during the five-course meal. The Garden Terrace is a sunny, tiered area with myriad cozy sitting areas divided by lush plants, where guests enjoy light fare, cocktails, and afternoon high tea accompanied by piano music; the Plaza Café courtyard is yet another option. Downstairs, the Desiree nightclub is a 12-year Washington veteran of nighttime entertaining, with banquettes and living room seating.

The Fitness Club features state-of-the-art equipment as well as business facilities including a fax machine, computer station, and messenger service. The three levels have sweeping views of the canal and greenery through large picture windows. Among the facilities are a heated skylit lap pool, whirlpool, sauna and steam baths, massage, aqua aerobics, personal trainers, and fitness evaluations. The exercise bikes and Stairmasters are equipped with VCRs and stereo cassette recorders, for which the hotel has a full library. Guests receive complimentary workout attire and next-day dry cleaning. A nice alternative to treadmill workouts is running on the towpath to the C&O Canal.

The guest rooms are furnished in unsurprising luxury hotel themes, with views of Rock Creek, the M Street Canal, or the courtyard. Baths feature nice amenities like a telephone and a scale. Rooms are serviced twice daily and are given a full turndown. With children's packages, kids are loaned Nintendo games for their stay. The rates reflect not the unusual aspects of the guest rooms but the emphasis on impeccable service.

The Hay-Adams Hotel

16th and H Streets, N.W.
One Lafayette Square
Washington, D.C. 20006
202-638-6600
Fax: 202-638-2716
800-424-5054

> *An elegant boutique hotel with a great location*

General Manager: Urs Aeby. **Accommodations:** 143 rooms, including 20 suites. **Rates:** Rooms $210–$360, suites from $475. **Minimum stay:** None. **Added:** $25 each additional guest, 11% tax, $1.50 room tax. **Payment:** Major credit cards. **Children:** Welcome. **Pets:** Not allowed. **Smoking:** Nonsmoking rooms available. **Open:** All year.

Arguably Washington's most beautiful hotel — and assuredly so when its $12 million renovation is completed by 1995 — the Hay-Adams certainly has the city's best location, facing the White House and Lafayette Square. Although this grand old building looks as if it has held a position of prominence since it was built in 1928, its glory days really began in 1983, when previous owner David H. Murdock undertook a massive restoration and renovation of the formerly mediocre hotel.

The history of the hotel predates the building and rests on this landmark site. In 1885, world-renowned architect Henry Hobson Richardson designed adjoining homes on a lot across from the White House for John Hay and his longtime friend and Harvard classmate Henry Adams. Adams, the descendent of two presidents, and Hay, a millionaire who was at one time the private secretary to President Lincoln, were great friends and the hub of Washington's inner circle. Their houses, done in a classic, heavy Richardson Romanesque style, served as the gathering spot for the country's most important guests, including President Roosevelt, who often stopped by for lunch.

> **The best views in the country are at the Hay-Adams, directly overlooking the White House. (On the fourth floor, you get cherry blossoms, too.) If your party is not in office, request a view of St. John's church. Note the intricate plaster moldings around your ceiling, a wonderful detail in every guest room.**

After the houses' heyday, they were purchased by Washington developer Harry Wardman in 1927 for $600,000. With an additional $900,000 investment, Wardman erected an eight-story, 200-room hotel. Turkish architect Mirhan Mesrobian designed the building after the river elevation of the Farnese Palace in Rome. Faced in Indiana white limestone, the hotel featured intricate plaster moldings on nearly every ceiling and balconies accessible by French doors; it paid tribute to John Hay by copying the Tudor detailing and coffered paneling from the foyer of his home.

But the hotel fell into the lurches of the Great Depression, and after only four prosperous years, the Hay-Adams was sold at public auction. The Manger Hotel Company owned the property for nearly 40 years, operating it as a transient hotel, followed by several other owners.

Today the hotel is breathtakingly beautiful. The rich walnut paneling of the lobby is adorned by gilded pilasters, above which are light-hued molded arches and an elaborately coffered ceiling with 16th-century motifs, from which hang several brass chandeliers.

Up half a flight of stairs, guests have breakfast, lunch, and dinner in the Lafayette Room, which yields White House views through seven floor-to-ceiling windows. Lighter fare and high tea are taken in the John Hay Room, a surpassingly magnificent public space. Heavy carved walnut paneling is brightened by a gilded and light plaster coffered ceiling. Brass sconces decorate walls, echoed in large chandeliers hanging from ceiling medallions. Tea is a beautiful event in the John Hay room. Tea master Charu, who has graced the Hay-Adams for years, presents a spectrum of delicacies and teas, impeccably served.

The guest rooms are decorated with the feel of a lavish private residence. Nearly all have intricate plaster moldings and ceiling designs. The reproduction furnishings vary from room to room — some Queen Anne, some Chippendale — with an occasional antique chair or mirror. Some have canopy beds reached by wood steps. Rooms facing the White House have the best views in the city. Some of these feature balconies through French doors, and some have carved mantels.

The service at the Hay-Adams is formal, discreet, and high quality, and the concierge service rises to every challenge.

The Henley Park Hotel

926 Massachusetts Avenue, N.W.
Washington, D.C. 20001
202-638-5200
Fax: 202-638-6740
800-222-8474

> *A small European-style hotel*

Proprietor: RB Associates. **General Manager:** Michael A. Rawson. **Accommodations:** 96 rooms, including 6 suites, all with private bath. **Rates:** Rooms $185–$235, weekend packages from $89, suites from $295. **Added:** $25 each additional guest, 11% tax, $1.50 room tax. **Payment:** Major credit cards. **Children:** Welcome. **Pets:** Not allowed. **Smoking:** Nonsmoking rooms available. **Open:** All year.

The Henley Park is an understated, small-scale hotel, with intimate public spaces that include a romantic restaurant,

Coeur de Lion. While 16th Street serves as the gallery for grand old Washington hotels, the Henley Park sits apart like a quiet foreigner at an embassy party, in a rather wanting area near the Convention Center, brightened by the Morrison-Clark across the street.

The Henley Park's owners have restored many of the original elements of its 1918 Tudor architecture, including some 119 gargoyles. The eight-story limestone and brick building has a straightforward neo-Gothic exterior, but the low-ceilinged foyer set with Mercer tiles shows its Tudor influence.

> **The Henley Park is elegant and understated, a hop away from the Convention Center. Its lobby looks like a medieval foyer; and Coeur de Lion is reputed to have one of Washington's most romantic dining rooms.**

The Wilkes Room is an intimate common room and library where guests lounge in leather wing chairs and tapestry sofas. Draperies fall from crown moldings over floor-to-ceiling French windows.

Through an archway is Marley's, where the afternoon sun filters through thick leaded glass windows while guests take high tea of eight varieties, complemented by scones and clotted cream, finger sandwiches, sweets, ports, and sherries. Nighttime jazz and cocktails are enjoyed at the marble-top bar or in tapestried banquettes and chairs.

The Coeur de Lion, named for Richard the Lionhearted, whose crest hangs above the threshold, is reputed to have one of Washington's most romantic dining rooms. The three separate spaces begin in the Atrium, laced in greenery, with exposed brick and a beamed glass ceiling hung with a crystal chandelier. French doors open to a bilevel dining area with stained glass windows, mirrored pillars, and lavish crystal sconces. Chef Jon Dornbusch's American-Continental cuisine may feature lamb chops with balsamic tomato relish or crab cakes with tomato coulis; entrées range reasonably from $14 to $22.

On the upper floors, the guest rooms feel like apartments, with about 12 rooms per floor along a winding corridor. The suites have interesting configurations, and some have kitchens. Rooms are furnished traditionally, with reproduction Queen Anne and Chippendale furniture. Among the niceties are nightly turndown, complimentary newspaper, and a stocked mini-bar. Service is quiet and helpful, as is every aspect of the Henley Park.

Hotel Washington

15th Street and Pennsylvania
  Avenue
Washington, D.C. 20004
202-638-5900
Fax: 202-638-1594
800-424-9540

> *A classic hotel
> with good rates
> and great views*

Proprietor: Gal-Tex Corp. **General Manager:** Muneer Deen. **Accommodations:** 350 rooms, including 37 suites and 7 junior suites, all with private bath. **Rates:** $147–$204; reduced rates July–early September. **Minimum stay:** None. **Added:** $18 each additional guest; 11% tax; $1.50 room tax. **Payment:** Major credit cards. **Children:** Welcome. **Pets:** Cats and dogs welcome. **Smoking:** 2 of 10 floors nonsmoking. **Open:** All year.

Among the attractive aspects of the Hotel Washington are its location overlooking the White House, its relatively low rates, and the wonderful 11th-story rooftop café, one of the best places from which to view this well-planned city.

The Hotel Washington was built in 1918 and has been owned for the last half century by the Gal-Tex Corporation. Maintaining its reputation as the oldest continually operating hotel in the city, the Washington remained open during its two-year $12 million renovation. One of the most costly projects was the restoration of the colored facade, one of the few examples of Italian *sgrafitto* in North America. An Austrian artisan painstakingly restored the arabesque designs around the perimeter and between the upper windows, medallion portraits of Washington, Jefferson, and Lincoln, emblazoned in bold red and white on the brick and limestone exterior.

The two-story lobby features fabulous arched floor-to-ceiling windows that run the entire length of the building, decorated with white Roman shades and framed by dressy pink tasseled drapes. Lit by lavish chandeliers, the wooden molding is richly carved with friezes, columns, and capitals, themes that are reproduced in the lobby's Corner Bar.

The Two Continents restaurant on the lobby floor is a lovely room of historic merit. Murals above the windows feature not-so-pithy quotes from George Washington that once served as incentive when the room was used as the Bache Stock Exchange: "Timely disbursements to prepare for danger frequently prevent much greater disturbances to repel it." The Empire chairs and geometric carpeting are made formal by the Corinthian columns supporting the ceiling.

> **Every visitor to Washington ought to visit the Hotel Washington, at least for an afternoon or evening at the Sky Terrace. From here you can see not only the nearby White House but the entire city in all its glory.**

Any Washington visitor ought to whisk up to the 11th floor to have a bite or a drink on the Sky Terrace, which runs the length of the building. From period reproduction wicker chairs, guests can gaze at the lovely city panorama. Ceilings in the Sky Room are 15 feet high, and enormous windows display views across the Potomac. Three wall murals were painted by Jardin d'Armide in the mid-19th century.

The guest rooms retain their original doorbells and are now decorated with 18th-century reproduction mahogany furnishings. The pretty baths are appointed in Italian marble.

The Washington Hotel offers special packages for families.

The Jefferson

Sixteenth and M Streets, N.W.
Washington, D.C. 20036-3295
202-347-2200
800-368-5966

> *A romantic and gourmet retreat in a grand hotel*

Proprietor: Lancaster Group Hotels. **Managing Director:** Elmer Coppoolse. **Accommodations:** 100 rooms, including 32 suites. **Rates:** Rooms $220–$275, suites from $275; weekends $160 and up. **Added:** $25 each additional guest, 11% tax, $1.50 room tax. **Payment:** Major credit cards. **Children:** Allowed. **Pets:** Small pets allowed. **Smoking:** Nonsmoking rooms available. **Open:** All year.

The Jefferson is not only one of Washington's great grand old hotels — with its plush, individually decorated rooms and intimate, nearly residential scale — it is a true gourmet getaway featuring the new Virginia cuisine of its very young award-winning chef Will Greenwood.

Four blocks from the White House, next to the National Geographic Society, the Jefferson is the height of Washington sophistication imbued with European grace. Built as a residence in 1923, the U-shaped beaux-arts building is eight stories of light stone. It holds one of the most beautiful reception halls in Washington, the Grand Foyer. The long,

> **Even if you can't stay overnight, try to visit the Jefferson for a meal. The intimate restaurant, with tufted leather banquettes and wood floors, is an elegant and serene setting in which to enjoy the new Virginia cuisine that has many critics cheering.**

single-story, barrel-vaulted corridor, the open part of the U shape, looks rather like a lost wing of the National Gallery. This main breezeway is flanked by two cool, airy atriums with fountains, where guests may have breakfast. The elaborate plaster moldings and trim, from the Doric columns to the arched vaulting, are painted a soothing ecru. Three formal Federal parlor sets divide the Grand Foyer into separate areas. Over a faux marble fireplace is a portrait of Lafayette. The marble floors are covered with Oriental rugs.

Each of the 100 guest rooms is decorated in surprisingly different and boldly successful colors and patterns, all with unusual antiques and classic reproductions. Some beds have upholstered headboards matching their linens, and others have rich wood sleigh beds. Some have French doors leading to bedrooms, others have working fireplaces or whirlpool baths. Televisions and VCRs are in each room, and the suites also have armoires housing mini-bars and CD players. Among the amenities are robes and hair dryers in the baths, which have charming flowered porcelain fixtures. Guests are greeted with a half bottle of red wine, and service includes nightly turndown.

The Jefferson Lounge, to the right of the Grand Foyer, is a clubby place, with leather chairs, red walls, and a fireplace under a nautical oil painting. The intimate restaurant is quite striking, with wood floors and tufted leather banquettes. The walls are graced with historic 18th-century prints, some of which once hung in the White House and Blair House.

Will Greenwood's menu changes daily. A choice of appetizers might include plantation corncake with smoked salmon and chive cream, wild rice and pheasant cakes with shiitake mushroom essence, or crab hush puppies with red pepper marmalade. Entrées, averaging $20, could include venison escalops with lingonberry sauce and chestnut spoonbread or smoked pork chop roasted with cider honey glaze served with sweet potato hotcakes. The desserts are highly acclaimed, as is the extensive wine list.

Service is impeccable. Beyond the formality, the staff is genuinely friendly, personable, and solicitous.

The Mayflower — A Stouffer Hotel

1129 Connecticut Avenue, N.W.
Washington, D.C. 20036
202-347-3000
800-468-3571

A grand revival of a truly historic hotel

Proprietor: Stouffer Hotels. **General Manager:** Bernard Awenenti.
Accommodations: 680 rooms, including 68 suites. **Rates:** Weekdays, rooms $210, suites $375; weekends, rooms $135, suites $185. **Included:** Coffee and newspaper with wake-up call. **Added:** 11% tax, $1.50 room tax. **Payment:** Major credit cards. **Children:** Welcome. **Pets:** Small pets allowed. **Smoking:** 1 of 9 floors nonsmoking. **Open:** All year.

Two weeks after its opening in 1925, the Mayflower hosted 6,000 guests at Calvin Coolidge's inaugural ball. This event exemplifies the massive scale and rich history that the Mayflower represents in Washington. This historic property completed its most recent, $10 million renovation in 1991, focusing on accommodations.

When it was built at a cost of $12 million, the block-long neoclassic Mayflower had 1,057 guest rooms, furnished with 25,000 pieces of furniture that took three months to install. The 10-story brick building was designed by Warren and Wetmore of New York, who also designed Grand Central Station. A promenade one-tenth of a mile long served as a public hallway between blocks, with Oriental rugs, sculpture, and more gold leaf than any building in the country outside the Library of Congress. The hotel had its own upholstery and carpentry shops, as well as a clinic for its 1,000 employees.

In the 1950s, the Mayflower entered a self-conscious era during which it scaled down its glories to appeal to the masses: the 24-karat details were covered by paint, wood paneling replaced the lobby's marble pillars, the chandeliers were taken down, and the big bronze doors were traded for stainless steel and glass. A group of Washingtonians bought the Mayflower in 1965

> **The recent refurbishment of this grand hotel has done a service for the town, for the Mayflower was once an important player in Washington society life. Today it once again fulfills its role as a great capital host, its grand proportions evocative of Washington itself.**

and invested $65 million in its resurrection. By 1985, the hotel was once again the grande dame it was born to be, and the capitals and ceiling glimmered in gold once again. Most recently, Stouffer Hotels bought the Mayflower and completed its refurbishments.

Taking up the entire block of Connecticut Avenue between L and M streets, in the center of businesses and shops, the Mayflower seems to urge guests not to leave. Its famous promenade holds an arcade of shops, as well as the formal Nicholas restaurant offering new American and Mid-Atlantic cuisine, the informal Café Promenade, the Town & Country Lounge for entertainment, and the Lobby Lounge. The two-story lobby has the grandeur of a ballroom, with marble flooring, plaster pillars topped by gilded capitals and crown molding, observed from a second-floor balcony that wraps around the room.

The guest rooms needed a facelift and are lovely today, with custom-made Henredon reproduction furnishings and upholstery and fabrics consistent with the Federal period. For such a large property, service is surprisingly available at every turn.

The Morrison-Clark Inn

Massachusetts Avenue and
  Eleventh Street, N.W.
Washington, D.C. 20001
202-898-1200
Fax: 202-289-8576
800-332-7898
Restaurant: 202-289-8580

> *Washington's beautiful inn and lauded restaurant*

Proprietor: R.B. Associates. **Innkeeper:** Michael A. Rawson. **Accommodations:** 54 rooms, including 13 parlor suites in the inn's addition and 12 Victorian suites in the historic section. **Rates:** $135–$185; weekend and seasonal packages available. **Included:** Expanded Continental breakfast, use of fitness center, morning paper, shoeshine. **Minimum stay:** None. **Added:** 11% tax plus $1.50 occupancy, $20 for additional guest. **Payment:** Major credit cards. **Children:** Welcome. **Pets:** Not allowed. **Smoking:** Nonsmoking rooms available, no smoking in restaurant. **Open:** All year.

In a town dominated by large hotels, the Morrison-Clark stands apart as a boutique inn of unusual refinement and luxury, featuring exceptional food. The reasons for its outstanding nature are twofold: the creativity of Albert Massoni and his partner Royce LaNier, who masterminded the project of saving a crumbling piece of history in a marginal part of town; and the talents of chef Susan McCreight-Lindeborg, who oversees lunch and dinner every day but Sunday.

The historic property was built in 1864 by business partners David Morrison and Reuben Clark. The twin three-story brick houses served for years as the Soldiers and Sailors Club. Its following grew, and the property was enlarged in 1876. In

1917, the distinctive verandah was sewn onto the front; and to tone down the levity of the place, the club was used as the Woman's Army and Navy League gathering spot from 1923 to 1980. The houses fell into sad disrepair over the next years until preservationist Albert Massoni came to the helm in 1987 and undertook a massive and laudable restoration effort.

Today, the inn nearly gleams with pride, the old part renewed to its former glory and a new addition with 42 guest rooms complementing the historic lines in postmodern understatement; the inn is on the National Register of Historic Places and a member of the Historic Hotels of America.

> **The Morrison-Clark Inn is a unique offering in Washington: sophisticated accommodations in a gorgeous historic property — built in 1864, with a distinctive Chinese-influenced verandah added in 1917 — and a showcase for the talents of chef Susan McCreight-Lindeborg.**

The original mansion has 12 Victorian suites on the second and third floors, with wonderful high ceilings, enormous windows, colorful reproduction Victorian wallpaper borders, some stunning armoires containing remote televisions and stereos, and beautiful period furnishings including antique chairs, writing desks, marble-topped dressers, and lavish carved wood headboards. The baths are elegantly appointed with marble and sophisticated amenities. Some of these rooms have porches. The artwork on display in the hallways and guest rooms is notable.

The rooms and parlor suites in the new L-shaped wing have two strikingly different decor schemes: simple country French and neoclassical, with clean-lined, custom-designed furniture and Roman shades. Service is exceptional, with nightly turndown, twice-daily maid service, morning newspaper, room service, and in-room movie rentals.

The common rooms and dining rooms at the Morrison-Clark are simply beautiful. The foyer is a parquet marble, with a huge floral centerpiece on a round table, set off by deep rust-colored walls. Heavy mahogany doors lead to the breakfast room and bar, one of five dining areas, with floor-to-ceiling windows and carved marble fireplace mantel. An intimate dining room has a circular banquette, high ceilings, and enormous windows covered in diaphanous white curtains. Other dining areas are in the exterior courtyard, on the Chinese verandah, and in the sunny solarium.

Dinners in this eclectic and elegant setting are orchestrated by Susan Lindeborg, a noted pastry chef whose talents have expanded to great acclaim. Her vegetables and side dishes have been called sensational, memorable, and luscious by local reviewers. A dinner might begin with an appetizer of goat cheese and roast garlic flan with tart tomato fondue, or stuffed quail with grilled polenta and ancho chili sauce. Warm leek salad with pommery mustard and honey dressing might follow; or perhaps a salmon chowder with tomato and ginger. Entrees may include grilled rabbit loin stuffed with spinach and bacon in a bourbon sauce; or Maryland crab in lemon-herb crepes. The setting is a lovely backdrop to the gorgeous meal. Entrées are quite reasonably priced for the capital, from $16.75 to $22; lunches from $11.50 to $15.

Although an overnight stay is highly recommended, a meal at the Morrison-Clark is a Washington necessity.

Park Hyatt

1201 24th Street, N.W.
Washington, D.C. 20037
202-789-1234
Fax: 202-457-8823
800-922-7275

A contemporary marvel of exceptional luxury

Proprietor: Hyatt Hotels. **General Manager:** Allan Farwell. **Accommodations:** 224 rooms, including 130 suites. **Rates:** Rooms $255–$350, suites from $595; weekend rates $169–$194, $190–$215 with breakfast. **Added:** $25 each additional guest, 11% tax, $1.50 room tax. **Payment:** Major credit cards. **Children:** Welcome. **Pets:** Allowed. **Smoking:** Several nonsmoking floors. **Open:** All year.

While 16th Street is the bastion of grand old Washington hotels, a cluster of grand new hotels has opened on the corner of 24th and M streets. Its finest offering is the Park Hyatt, which opened in 1986. Its first two stories of stone and plentiful glass house the public spaces and Melrose restaurant. The 10 higher stories for guest rooms rise above in stone, culminating in a green copper roof.

Guests enter a massive double-height lobby, with floors in two-toned herringbone marble, walls in softer beige and brown marble decorated with contemporary paintings from the Washington Color School and Oriental sculpture, and several precious works by Pablo Picasso and Frank Stella. This grand contemporary space is best enjoyed during afternoon high tea, when visitors listen to piano music and muse over French pastries, finger sandwiches, and individual pots of tea over candle warmers. A palm reader circulates on Wednesdays and Thursdays; her most certain prediction is that evening caviar and champagne will be served in this setting several hours hence.

> A leader among Washington's new hotels, the Park Hyatt is an exciting property of the highest standards. Designed in 1986 by the prestigious architecture firm of Skidmore, Owings, and Merrill, the Park Hyatt has a dramatic, airy lobby filled with glass, marble, and magnificent contemporary art.
> And there's a rooftop pool.

On the ground floor, in two stories of enclosed glass, is Melrose restaurant. Chef Kenneth Juran prepares contemporary American cuisine, in a $34 prix fixe or à la carte menu (ranging from $19 to $25), which could include an appetizer of angel hair pasta with fresh Maine lobster, mascarpone cheese, tomato, and herbs; or an entrée of Lake Superior whitefish with olive paste and wild mushroom risotto. Best of all, children dine for half price. Melrose overlooks the outdoor café, where guests may enjoy light fare to the sounds of the fountain and scents of surrounding flowers as late as 3 A.M. on weekends.

The rooms at the Park Hyatt are larger than average, with a majority of suites to which all guests are upgraded on availability. Contemporarily furnished with light pecan wood and pastel fabrics, all rooms have at least a separate dressing area as well as a sitting area and full writing desks. The baths are quite luxurious in marble with brass and chrome fittings, a phone and television, hair dryer, and terry robes. In addition to evening turndown, guests receive a morning newspaper. Among other amenities are complimentary shoeshine and foreign currency exchange.

Guests have full use of the health club, with Nautilus weights, sun roof pool and Jacuzzi, and massage, steam, and sauna rooms. In addition, the mezzanine level of the Park Hyatt has a full business center, the Write Choice.

The Ritz-Carlton, Washington, D.C.

2100 Massachusetts Avenue, N.W.
Washington, D.C. 20008
202-293-2100
Fax: 202-293-0641
800-241-3333

> *A classic hotel,*
> *recently revived,*
> *on Embassy Row*

Proprietor: Newfield Enterprises.
General Manager: Cheryl O'Donnell. **Accommodations:** 206 rooms, including 32 suites; deluxe services on the Ritz-Carlton Concierge Club floors. **Rates:** Rooms $195–$380; suites from $500; special weekend rate $195. **Added:** $30 each additional guest, 11% tax, $1.50 room tax. **Payment:** Major credit cards. **Children:** Welcome. **Pets:** Small pets welcome. **Smoking:** Nonsmoking rooms available. **Open:** All year.

It hardly seems possible, but the Ritz-Carlton, Washington, D.C. was recently improved. A multimillion-dollar facelift, begun after President Clinton's inauguration, resulted in a new fitness facility, refurbished guest rooms and suites, and much more.

Inspired by the legendary service and taste of the London Ritz Hotel, the Old World sophistication of the Ritz-Carlton Hotel Company first landed on American shores in1983. The Washington property was transformed from the grande dame Fairfax Hotel. The lovely Fairfax had been a sophisticated Washington fixture since it was built in 1927 and home to the famous Jockey Club restaurant for more than 20 years.

Sister Parish was brought from Great Britain to redecorate the entire property in the style of an English country manor house, with dark wood, library-style parlors and formal Federal hallways. The extensive art collection begs a guest to meander through the hallways gazing at the 18th- and 19th-century oil paintings. In true Anglophile fashion, the themes are often nautical or equestrian — of the races, the hunt, or portraits of beloved hunting dogs poised at attention.

The Fairfax Bar is a wonderful lounge and gathering spot

that is the setting for afternoon high tea. Sweets and scones, salmon, and cucumber and tomato sandwiches are served in front of the wood-burning fireplaces. The neighboring Potomac Room is plush with tapestried pillows, banquettes, and leather wing chairs.

Ever since it opened in 1961, the familiar Jockey Club has been an insider's restaurant with the atmosphere of an English tap room. The restaurant recently welcomed back from California Hidemasa Yamamoto, the Jockey Club chef from 1986 to 1990. His menu still features Chesapeake Bay

> **The Ritz-Carlton is Washington's veteran incumbent: since 1927 it has been the home and home-away-from-home of Washington insiders. It's also been the locale for the Jockey Club, a favored eating spot since President Kennedy's inauguration in 1961.**

crab cakes but also lighter, more contemporary dishes. A new favorite is Poele Lobster, with avocado, mango, and beets.

The guest rooms received much of the attention in the recent renovations. Guests can expect such luxuries as 24-hour room service, nightly turndown, and terry robes. The seventh and eighth floors are the Ritz-Carlton Club, with special concierge service, use of the Federal parlor, and five complimentary food presentations, including Continental breakfast, a midday snack, tea, cocktails and hors d'oeuvres, and chocolate and cordials at night.

The staff is reliably professional and highly trained in Ritz-Carlton etiquette at this classic property.

The Watergate Hotel

2650 Virginia Avenue, N.W.
Washington, D.C. 20037
202-965-2300
Fax: 202-965-1173
800-424-2736
800-225-5843

> *A beautiful back-drop to the city's finest dining*

Proprietors: Forte Hotels. **Managing Director:** Ibrihim Fahmy. **Accommodations:** 235 rooms, including 160 suites. **Rates:** $285–$310, suites from $410; weekend and holiday rates available. **Included:** Use of health club facilities. **Minimum stay:** None. **Added:** $25 each additional guest, 11% tax, $1.50 room tax. **Payment:** Major credit cards. **Children:** Welcome; children under 18 stay free. **Pets:** Small pets allowed. **Smoking:** Nonsmoking rooms available, no smoking in restaurant. **Open:** All year.

Everyone recognizes the Watergate Hotel. The landmark building has changed little on the outside — it's still a modern collection of scalloped buildings trimmed with balconies. The interior, however, is impressively improved. Forte Hotels acquired the landmark hotel in the spring of 1990 and redecorated all the guest rooms to their current state of elegance. In addition, the hotel was given a fantastic new health club, one of the few and certainly the plushest in Washington hotels.

With half of its guests coming from overseas, the hotel's staff prides itself on its linguistic versatility. The lobby is a glistening display of polished marble, the setting for afternoon high tea. About half of the guest rooms have balconies and views of the Potomac River, on whose banks the hotel sits, next to the Kennedy Center. The rooms are furnished with dark wood furniture and chintz fabrics. Period reproduction highboys contain remote televisions, videos, and tape decks, and all rooms have stocked mini-bars. The baths are appointed in light marble.

In its fairly glamorous marbled setting, the health club is equipped with a Nautilus gym, a 25-by-30-foot lap pool, a whirlpool, and saunas. Massages are available.

Chef Jean-Louis Palladin's dining room is an incredible spot, with only 12 tables in a mystical, dim setting. The menu is boldly handwritten by the chef in French, with a typed English translation, and it changes like the palette of a working artist. Jean-Louis offers two fixed-price selections at $85 or $95. The meal might include a crab soup with crab cakes and quenelles; a salad of fresh seaweed with sesame, smoked salmon, and ginger; roasted saddle of rabbit with herbs and marrow flan, a julienne of celery root and truffles; followed by tiramisu with coffee coulis and cacao ice cream.

> The Watergate has a name, yes; but it also has a great location that no other city hotel has, right on the Potomac, next to the Kennedy Center. Most importantly, it has chef Jean-Louis Palladin, who has won two stars from Michelin and five from the Mobil guide for his culinary mastery, the city's only chef to have done so.

The plusher menu offers six courses, proceeding as follows: celery root soup with rabbit sausage, truffle quenelle, and fresh truffle; Santa Barbara abalone served with enoki mushrooms; fresh American duck *foie gras* with rhubarb; salmon wrapped with a leaf, concassée of tomato and black olives; followed by mignon of Pittsburgh lamb with cheese ravioli and spices; finishing with a symphony of pears.

The Watergate also features all-day dining in Palladin by Jean-Louis. Its extensive wine list and river view are lovely complements to the masterful menu.

The Willard Inter-Continental Hotel

1401 Pennsylvania Avenue, N.W.
Washington, D.C. 20004
202-628-9100
800-327-0200
Fax: 202-637-7326

> *The classic and
> regal residence
> of presidents*

Proprietor: Willard Associates. **General Manager:** Graham K. Jeffrey. **Accommodations:** 365 rooms, including 65 suites. **Rates:** Rooms $285–$345, suites from $500; special weekend rates. **Added:** $30 each additional guest, 11% tax, $1.50 room tax. **Payment:** Major credit cards. **Children:** Welcome. **Pets:** Dogs and cats allowed. **Smoking:** Three smoking floors. **Open:** All year.

The Willard is basking in the relatively new limelight of its third incarnation. After sitting vacant and boarded up since 1968, the Willard received $74 million worth of attention and was reintroduced to Washington society in 1986 with great fanfare. But despite its new image, the Willard is a grand old hotel, with a history as rich as that of the town it so well represents.

The site on which the glorified Willard sits, catercorner from the White House, has been occupied by hostelries since 1816. In 1850, the land was bought by Henry Willard, who with the help of his brothers Edwin and Joseph turned the property into a 100-room hotel.

The Willard sat at the focal point of political activity. After receiving death threats, Abraham Lincoln lived secretly at the Willard from February 23 until his inauguration on March 4, 1861. The same year, Julia Ward Howe wrote the "Battle Hymn of the Republic" in her Willard guest room.

When the Willards decided to expand their accommodations, they hired famed architect Henry Janeway Hardenbergh, who had designed such treasures as the Waldorf-Astoria, the Plaza, and the Dakota apartments in New York. Completed in 1904, the Willard was one of Washington's first skyscrapers, 12 stories of lavish French Second Empire beaux-arts architecture, reinforced in steel. The hotel prospered, although a gradual decline came after World War II, when the Willard family sold the property for $5 million. Under its new ownership, the hotel survived until 1968. Just several months before the hotel closed its doors, Martin Luther King wrote his "I Have a Dream" speech in his room.

> An ambassador to Washington history, the Willard has experienced triumph and tragedy. Designed by famed Henry Janeway Hardenbergh in 1904 as a Washington icon, the French Second Empire beaux-arts masterpiece was saved from abandonment in 1978 and restored to its present glory, reopening in 1986.

In 1976, the Pennsylvania Avenue Development Corporation hired the Oliver Carr Company to restore the property, and in 1983 Inter-Continental Hotels was asked to oversee hotel operations. Since it had been abandoned for 15 years, nearly all of the interior work had to be reconstructed, a job that required three years of intensive research.

The restored public spaces included the lobby, the 189-foot Peacock Alley, the Willard dining room, the F Street Lobby, and the Crystal Room. The 7,000 square feet of flooring in the lobby and Peacock Alley, tiny mosaic tiles set by hand, were laboriously replaced after several trips to Italy to locate the original marble. Layers of paint were scientifically matched to contemporary hues. Archival photos of the interior were used as documentation to replace millwork, marble flooring, chandeliers, plaster molding, and the grand lobby carpet. The intricate craft of scagiola, an elaborate faux marbling, was restored and matched in the columns of the lobby and the Willard dining room. Replicas of the 12 original chandeliers were handmade by the grandson of the original craftsman.

Eclectic antiques carefully decorate the Willard's lobby, but the true treasure lies overhead, in the 48 state seals adorning the coffered ceiling; Hawaii and Alaska have been added. Other public spaces include the exquisite Willard Room, which features regional American food prepared by chef Guy Reinbolt (from $19.50 to $32 — try the crème brulée). The Round Robin Bar is a popular, clubby space with green fabric walls lined with portraits of well-known guests such as Charles Dickens, Warren Harding, Walt Whitman, Nathaniel Hawthorne, John Philip Sousa, Calvin Coolidge, and Alice Roosevelt Longworth, daughter of Teddy, who created a stir by smoking publicly in the dining room. The ladies' lounge was once above this room; it's now the Nest, where high tea is served daily.

Compared to the lavish public areas, the accommodations are subdued. The suites, done in Federal simplicity, are quite nice and worth the upgrade. All rooms have a mini-bar and a bath with a telephone, hair dryer, and television speaker.

Maryland

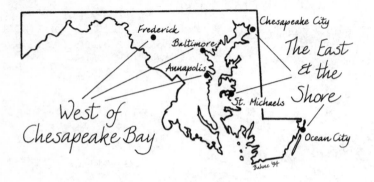

With its major city, Baltimore, and its 17th-century capital, Annapolis, and from its western panhandle in the Allegheny mountains to its elegant eastern shore bordered by the Chesapeake Bay and the Atlantic ocean, Maryland is a wonderfully rich state.

The seventh of the 13 original states to ratify the Constitution, in 1788, Maryland was settled a century and a half earlier, in 1634, by Lord Baltimore's brother Leonard Calvert. He sailed into the mouth of the Potomac River and proclaimed the southernmost stretch of land St. Mary's City, after Henrietta Maria, wife of King Charles I. In 1694, the capital was moved to Annapolis and remains there today.

Maryland is a beautiful, diverse state, with a Rorschach ink blot shape. The top of Maryland borders entirely on Pennsylvania and the Allegheny Mountains; the rest is a ragged-edged land mass that creeps into the Virginias in the west, wraps around Washington, D.C., and at its eastern point borders Delaware.

Maryland comprises four areas: western Maryland, a narrow peninsula that hosts the main vein of Route 40, America's first National Pike, to West Virginia; the main chunk of the state, including Frederick, landlocked between Washington and Baltimore; the western shore, including Annapolis, which undulates between the Chesapeake Bay and the Potomac River on the south; and — as one of the trio of states that make up the Delmarva peninsula — the tony eastern shore of the Chesapeake, which also sees a breathtaking bit of the Atlantic Ocean around Ocean City and Assateague Island National Seashore.

Maryland has nearly 5 million inhabitants, and more than 3,000 of its 10,460 square miles are tidal shoreline. For Maryland tourist information, call 800-543-1036.

West of
Chesapeake Bay

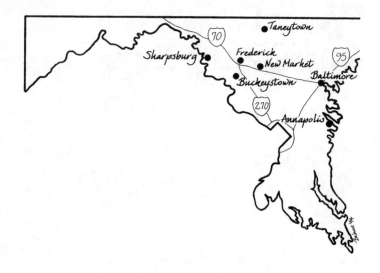

Best Romantic Retreat

Taneytown
  Antrim 1844

Best for Urban Intimacy

Baltimore
  Admiral Fell Inn
  Ann Street Bed and Breakfast
  Celie's Waterfront Bed and Breakfast
  Government House
  Henderson's Wharf

Best for Metropolitan Magnificence

Baltimore
  Harbor Court Hotel
  The Doubletree Inn at the Colonnade
  Peabody Court

Best Country Bed-and-Breakfast

Sharpsburg
  Inn at Antietam

Best Village Bed-and-Breakfasts

Annapolis
  Prince George Inn
Frederick
  Tyler Spite House
New Market
  National Pike Inn

Best Village Inns

Annapolis
  Historic Inns of Annapolis

Buckeystown
  The Inn at Buckeystown

One out of every six Marylanders — more than 730,000 people — lives in **Baltimore,** an exciting, revitalized city whose
Inner Harbor on the Patapsco River is not only a major tourist
attraction but one of the country's busier working ports.
There are 45 miles of waterfront in Baltimore, culminating in
the Inner Harbor, a major attraction for the 20 million who
visit Baltimore each year. Harborplace was built in 1981, with
a panoply of shops and restaurants on the docks of Inner
Harbor. The National Aquarium shares its waterfront locale,
as does the Baltimore Maritime Museum and the Maryland
Science Center and Davis Planetarium. Cultural diversions
include the Edgar Allan Poe House and the Baltimore & Ohio
Railroad Museum; Baltimore was the launching spot for
America's first passenger train. Just east of Inner Harbor is
Fells Point, Baltimore's first settlement. This magnificent
gallery of Federal and colonial architecture has been wonderfully revived and now includes 350 original residential buildings. It's a great place for a walking tour. One of the most
exciting Baltimore activities is a trip to Camden Yards, the
magnificent new home of Baltimore's nine — so plan ahead
for Orioles tickets.

Less than an hour's drive southeast from Baltimore brings a
visitor to the state capital, the country's oldest. **Annapolis**
has 1,500 period buildings and is an ideal place for walkers,
with its sidewalks illuminated by glowing lanterns at night.
Annapolis is very much a planned town, organized by British
Governor Francis Nicholson in 1695. The focal point is the
state capitol building and its State Circle, which winds
around groomed lawns, and the lesser Church Circle to the
west. Around these two hubs, narrow streets radiate like
spokes on a wheel, pointing toward the water, home of the
17th-century British settlers. The expansive U.S. Naval Academy, founded in 1846, rests on the waterfront east of town,
and venerable St. John's College, from 1697, sits contempla-
tively to the northeast.

An hour's drive west of Baltimore takes a traveler to lovely
farmland, horse country, historic sites, and eventually the Allegheny mountains. **Frederick,** the birthplace of Francis Scott
Key, and **New Market** are about an hour's drive north of
Washington, havens for antiques lovers. Frederick, founded in
1745, is a particularly charming town, a tremendous display

of Federal and colonial architecture. In the distance are the Catoctin Mountains and Camp David. The fulcrum of the Cumberland Valley is Hagerstown; beyond is Harper's Ferry, **Buckeystown,** and **Sharpsburg,** site of the Antietam battle-field. Cumberland marks the wild westernmost part of the state bordering West Virginia and western Pennsylvania, home of Mount Savage, the Savage River, Green Ridge, and Potomac state forests. It's also the home of the state's largest freshwater lake, Deep Creek, which covers nearly 4,000 acres.

ANNAPOLIS

Historic Inns of Annapolis

16 Church Circle
Annapolis, MD 21401
410-263-2641
Fax: 410-268-3813
800-847-8882

> *A quartet of colonial houses*

Proprietor: John Greco. **General Manager:** Gerard Boismain. **Accommodations:** 136 rooms, including 10 suites, all with private bath: 44 in Maryland Inn, 29 in Robert Johnson House, 9 in State House Inn, 54 in Governor Calvert House. **Rates:** $90–$155, $125–$250 (seasonal). **Minimum stay:** None. **Added:** $10 each additional guest, 12% tax. **Payment:** Major credit cards. **Children:** Welcome. **Pets:** Not allowed. **Smoking:** Limited. **Open:** All year.

Annapolis is a town with a rich past, and these accommodations are a part of it. The Historic Inns of Annapolis offer the amenities of a larger hotel in four properties within walking distance of each other, all set in historic homes.

Of the four, the Maryland Inn is the best known, for its façade, which looks like a colonial version of the Flatiron Building, and for the popular Treaty of Paris Restaurant. Built in 1776 in a panoply of brickwork, the Maryland Inn sits on the angular corner of Main and Duke of Gloucester streets on Church Circle. Where the two streets come together, the building narrows to a five-sided turret on the corner. Porches and windows protrude at odd angles, and the dark-tiled mansard roof is topped by a Victorian cupola. Guests enter a parquet marble foyer to the hotel or through the separate entrance below to the renowned Treaty of Paris Restaurant — if you can fit in a meal, sample chef Kevin Frederick's crab and lobster meat cakes in corn meal and beurre blanc. The property is also the home of the original 1784 King of France Tavern, the only and highly popular jazz club in the area. The 44 guest rooms recently received an expensive and much-needed renovation.

> **Annapolis is a living museum of 17th- and 18th-century America, and you'll feel like part of the exhibit when you stay in one of the four Historic Inns of Annapolis. There's an intriguing sense of independence about staying across town from the reception desk where you checked in: you'll feel like a real Annapolitan.**

The remaining three buildings are a block away on State Circle. The finest is the 1727 Governor Calvert House. There are 54 rooms here, most of which are in a new annex in the back that also houses a conference center. If possible, request one of the historic front rooms, with highly polished original floors and tall, narrow windows looking out to the Capitol. All rooms are different, with much antique furniture, Victorian curtains, armoires, and reproduction rice beds or Queen Anne headboards.

Across State Circle from the Calvert House, the 1820 State House Inn has nine rooms on three floors. From State Circle, the house is a three-story early Federal, with a Victorianized porch at the ground level; guests may descend a narrow set of stairs beside the house to Main Street and the Maryland Inn to view the four-story back of the building.

The Robert Johnston House, built in 1765, sits on the corner of School Street, which connects State and Church circles, with views of the Governor's Mansion and gardens from most of its 29 rooms. The facade of the regal brick four-story building is a convex curve aligning with State Circle.

The staff is noticeably happy, helpful, and enthusiastic about their beautiful town.

Prince George Inn

232 Prince George Street
Annapolis, MD 21401
410-263-6418

*A homey B&B
in the heart
of Annapolis*

Proprietors: Bill and Norma Grover-
mann. **Accommodations:** 4 rooms
with 3 baths. **Rates:** $75–$95.
Added: 12% tax. **Included:** Full buffet breakfast. **Minimum
stay:** 2 nights on weekends. **Payment:** Visa, MasterCard. **Children:** 12 and older welcome. **Pets:** Not allowed. **Smoking:** In
restricted areas. **Open:** Mid-April–December.

Annapolis is full of history and students. The town was
named for Princess Anne (who later reigned as queen) in 1694.
The following year, Francis Nicholson laid out the British-
named city streets. In 1696, St. John's College was founded,
a beautiful, introverted place of architectural purity where
students study only the classics. The United States Naval
Academy was founded in 1845, on 300 acres on the banks of
the Severn River. For a complete history lesson, however, one
can turn to the host and hostess of the Prince George Inn,
Annapolitans for a quarter century. Their charming bed-and-
breakfast is steps from the shady lawns of St. John's College
and two blocks from the Naval Academy.
    Norma and Bill Grovermann opened Annapolis's first B&B
in 1983. Before that, Norma was the president of the Tourism
Council for the City and County for eight years, started the

tour service for the Historic Annapolis Foundation, and co-founded Three Centuries Tours. Bill was involved in historic preservation throughout Maryland, including that of the 37-room William Paca House, built in 1763.

The Grovermanns' own house is a meticulously restored narrow brick Italianate built in 1884. Once through the Texas tiled foyer, guests may be lured upstairs by fascinating relics found during the Grovermanns' restoration and now displayed on the wall. A right turn takes a visitor to the common areas and to the breakfast porches added in 1910. The living room is papered in a rust-colored William Morris pattern. A grand wall mirror once belonged to President William McKinley;

> **Your hosts at the Prince George Inn are devoted to Annapolis history: Norma co-founded Three Centuries Tours, whose staff conducts city tours in authentic colonial dress; Bill is a historic preservationist. And the B&B is just lovely.**

Bill's grandfather was the jeweler for the McKinley administration, and he so admired the piece that the president gave it to him at the end of his tenure. Other artifacts from the Grovermanns' extensive travels fill the room: tapestry on the mantel, original paintings, interesting prints, and sculpture.

There are four guest rooms on two upper floors, all plushly decorated. The beautiful antique beds are brass, Gothic Revival, or Victorian carved wood, and the linens complement the deep tones of the decor. The back second-floor room has a narrow Victorian armoire, a crewel chair, and a bath decorated in black and white nautical designs inspired by a model of the *Mayflower* made by Norma's father. The third-floor back room has a Persian theme, with wonderful tapestries, a ceiling fan, and on the wall a fascinating Indian mosque decoration of carved wood. The front room has a Gothic Revival bed, an armoire, and a dresser that Norma sponge-painted in green.

The Grovermanns are wonderful people whose love for their city and home is quite evident and easily shared.

BALTIMORE

Admiral Fell Inn

Fells Point, 888 South Broadway
Baltimore, MD 21231
410-522-7377
800-292-INNS
Fax: 522-0707

*An intimate inn
in historic
Baltimore*

General Manager: Dominik Ecken-
stein. **Accommodations:** 38 rooms, 3 with Jacuzzi. **Rates:**
$125–$155; seasonal discounts. **Included:** Continental breakfast, free off-street parking nearby. **Minimum stay:** None.
Added: $15 each additional guest, 12% tax. **Payment:** Visa,
MasterCard, American Express, Discover. **Children:** Welcome; under 16 stay free with parents. **Pets:** Permitted on a
limited basis; check with the manager. **Smoking:** Nonsmoking rooms available. **Open:** All year.

With the intimacy and originality of a bed-and-breakfast and
the sophistication of a luxury hotel, the Admiral Fell Inn is a
unique property that epitomizes the rich history of its Fells
Point neighborhood. The inn sits on the oblique corner of
South Broadway and Thames Street, with an unobstructed
view of the historic waterfront docks. A microcosm of its
eclectic neighborhood, the Admiral Fell comprises four joined
buildings, built between 1720 and 1910: the northernmost is
the oldest, the former home of Baltimore's first mayor; the

second is a three-story red brick building with a cast-iron Victorian facade; and the middle two are four stories tall, with Georgian detailing in red brick. In former lives, parts of the property have been a hotel, a YMCA, and a vinegar-bottling plant. The buildings remained vacant between the mid-1970s and 1984, when the property was bought with the intent of creating a deluxe country inn.

> **The Admiral Fell is a neighborhood in itself, comprising four historic properties built between 1720 and 1910. Inside, despite the Inn's odd-angled configuration, the atmosphere is seamless, united by lovely Williamsburg decor.**

The inn is undergoing a major expansion, scheduled to be completed in 1995, that will add 12 guest rooms, including a suite with a loft bedroom and Jacuzzi. Until then, guests will be more than pleased with the present rooms, decorated with period reproductions and occasional antiques in an intriguing array of shapes and sizes. Be sure to inquire thoroughly about your room when booking. Some are large and have harbor views; others are small or have odd, intriguing angles. The double beds have fishnet canopies on four-poster rice beds; king-size beds have crown canopies that fall from ceiling moldings. There are always two telephones and a writing desk, ample lighting, and often a television hidden in an armoire. The colors are traditional Williamsburg rusts, yellows, or greens.

Guests can relax in the pleasant foyer, where a green faux marble fireplace reaches to the crown molding; in the quiet brick courtyard behind the inn; or in the heart pine–floored library, where Continental breakfast is served.

The restaurant (closed during the renovations) has several rooms, including a cozy pub, a dining room with exposed brick walls, and another with stone walls. The low ceiling lends romance.

The Admiral Fell is a busy place with surprisingly friendly service, in the heart of a busy neighborhood that gets quite lively on weekends.

Ann Street Bed and Breakfast

804 South Street
Baltimore, MD 21231
410-342-5883

*A B&B in a
colonial home*

Proprietors: Joanne and Andrew Mazurek. **Accommodations:** 3 rooms, including 1 suite, all with private bath, 2 with fireplace. **Rates:** $75–$85. **Included:** Full breakfast. **Minimum stay:** None. **Added:** $15 each additional guest, 12% tax. **Payment:** No credit cards. **Children:** Check with innkeeper. **Pets:** Not allowed. **Smoking:** Not allowed. **Open:** All year.

Ardent B&Bers who hunger for a taste of history cannot do better than the Ann Street Bed and Breakfast in Baltimore's Fells Point. Just around the corner from harborfront Thames Street is the Mazurek home, which opened to guests in 1988. It is a beautiful marriage of two colonial houses, mirror images in brick, four windows across, with dormer windows peeking out from the fourth-floor roof. In the center is a chimney that serves an incredible 12 working fireplaces.

On Ann Street in historic Fells Point, on cobblestone roads, a pair of brownstones built in the 1790s stand side by side. This is the Mazurek home, and it can be yours for the night, too. Beautiful Williamsburg decor makes this home a warm and fitting way to experience historic Baltimore.

The houses were built in the 1790s, and Joanne and Andrew have stayed faithful to the period, using Williamsburg trim colors, pewter light fixtures, wreaths of dried flowers, candles on the windowsills, and 18th-century reproduction furniture where they could not find antiques. Unseen from the street but accessible to guests is a charming backyard garden with patio furniture.

One house is devoted entirely to guests. The dining room is the fireside setting for the large breakfasts, which include a hot entrée. The common room is furnished in primitive country decor and also is warmed by the fireplace. The accommodations are on the second floor. The suite has a sitting room including a blue-checked sofa bed and blue wing chairs, and the wall is enlivened by an antique quilt. The trim is traditional green and maroon. The other guest room is furnished with a crewel wing chair and a four-poster curved canopy bed.

The second house is also the Mazureks' home. It has one large guest room with an antique rope bed and an impressive bath, which has a working cast-iron fireplace and white-washed brick walls. The room is strikingly clean, right down to the wide-planked original pine floors and the original mantels in deep Williamsburg colors. Flannel sheets and antique quilts dress up the beds.

While the accommodations in the Mazurek home might seem intimate, the other house offers a great deal of independence. The young couple is ever-present to answer questions and recommend activities, yet they are respectful of their guests' privacy.

Celie's Waterfront Bed & Breakfast

1714 Thames Street
Baltimore, MD 21231
410-522-2323

> *A cheerful and comfortable Baltimore B&B*

Proprietor: Celie Ives. **Accommodations:** 7 rooms, all with private bath, 4 with whirlpool, 2 with fireplace. **Rates:** $95–$140; handicapped-accessible room $85. **Included:** Continental breakfast. **Minimum stay:** 2 nights in some rooms on weekends. **Added:** 12% tax. **Payment:** Visa, MasterCard, Discover, American Express. **Children:** Age 10 and over welcome. **Pets:** Not allowed. **Smoking:** Not allowed indoors. **Open:** All year.

Celie Ives opened a single room in her private home to overnight guests several years ago and liked the bed-and-breakfast business so much that she decided to expand. Around the corner from her Fells Point home, she built an old-looking new Federal rowhouse on cobblestone Thames Street, separated from the water only by the Fells Point Recreation Center. Her three-story inn, opened in February 1990, is gray brick with wine-colored trim and old detailing, quite a complementary addition to its historic neighbors.

Celie is a gregarious hostess who heartily enjoys her guests and sharing her knowledge of Baltimore and the historic neighborhood of Fells Point.

Many a bed-and-breakfast is characterized by old moldings, Victoriana, and slanted wood floors, but Celie's is a fresh haven of clean lines, cream-colored walls, low-pile carpeting, and traditional antiques and furnishings. There is some historic detailing: three fireplaces, built-in bookshelves, small-paned windows, French doors, and window seats; but these are done crisply and tidily, in contemporary comfort.

> **One might not guess from its traditional exterior that this pretty building is a newcomer to old Fells Point. Once inside, you'll welcome the immaculate, crisp, and refreshing aura of the B&B's interior design, which feels like a summer cottage.**

The first floor includes the neat-as-a-pin living room and a tiled breakfast room where guests enjoy a Continental breakfast of freshly squeezed orange juice and several baked goods. In warmer months, the French doors of the breakfast room open to the brick patio, furnished with wrought-iron café tables and walled in with weathered wood. A handicapped-accessible room is also on the first floor, with three rooms on each of the two upper floors.

Celie is adamant about down comforters, cotton linens, full bath sheets (not towels), and fresh flowers. The finest room is the third-floor king suite, with a fireplace and whirlpool bath, which overlooks the harbor from three large mullioned windows topped by chintz swags and underscored by a long window seat filled with cushions. The king-size bed has a crown canopy. The room directly below shares the same view; two rooms have views of the back gardens, and two more rooms look into the atrium in the middle of the house. All these guest rooms are decorated in light colors and have sparkling new baths and alcoves with refrigerators and coffee-makers.

The Doubletree Inn at the Colonnade

4 West University Parkway
Baltimore, MD 21218
410-235-4100
Fax: 410-235-5572
800-456-3396

A cosmopolitan hotel steps from Johns Hopkins University

Proprietor: Uptown Hotels. **Director of Sales:** Teri Agosta. **Accommodations:** 125 rooms, including 34 suites. **Rates:** Rooms $115–$125, suites $135–$450. **Included:** Morning newspaper and evening cookies. **Minimum stay:** None. **Added:** $10 each additional guest; 12% tax. **Payment:** Major credit cards. **Children:** Welcome. **Pets:** Small pets welcome. **Smoking:** Second floor is nonsmoking. **Open:** All year.

For convenience to Johns Hopkins University with Inner Harbor elegance, Baltimore visitors stay at the Inn at the Colonnade. This property opened in early 1990 and has already received several Four Diamond Awards from AAA. A tall brick condominium building with two floors for hotel guests, the inn devotes special attention to overnighters.

As if airlifted from Baltimore's Inner Harbor and dropped in the freshman quad, the Doubletree Inn at the Colonnade brings sophistication to a college campus, with its Beidermier-inspired furnishings, marble baths, a fitness facility, and an acclaimed restaurant.

Across the street from Johns Hopkins's lacrosse field, the inn sits behind an elegant portico supported by two-story pillars, introducing the colonnade concept echoed throughout the property. The main sitting room is a lovely octagonal room, its walls paneled with satinwood. A round mural overhead, hand-painted by local artist Janet Pope, suggests an open-air rotunda and a classic architectural influence. The handmade octagonal carpet covers a mahogany floor inlaid with redwood, and the columns that support the rotunda and the subsequent hallway are a burnished maple with painted capitals. To one side of the rotunda are several gift shops, a salon, and the Polo Grill.

The 18th-century Beidermier-inspired furnishings of the guest rooms result in a commanding decor. The headboards look like pediments trimmed in black, flanked by bedside tables supporting neoclassic lamps. Televisions and VCRs are tucked into Beidermier armoires, and each room has two telephones, with a third in the bath. Luxury services include nightly turndown, room service until 1 A.M., and same-day valet. The baths are grandly appointed with floor-to-ceiling marble and brass fixtures. Some have Jacuzzis. Original artwork and architectural drawings are a high point of the decor.

In the back courtyard is the glass-domed poolhouse, with Italian marble walls interrupted by picture windows, sparkling Tivoli lights, and two hot tubs. Guests may use exercise equipment and rowing machines in the newly appointed fitness room, walled in pink marble.

The favorably reviewed Polo Grill offers eclectic American cuisine from Chef Harold Marmelstein in an intimate setting. Entrées range from $15 to $30 and may include interesting dishes like penne pasta with blackened chicken with pine nuts and tomatoes or fried lobster tail.

Government House

1125 North Calvert Street
Baltimore, MD 21202
410-539-0566
Fax: 410-539-0567

*A stay here
is a treat
and a pleasure*

Proprietor: Baltimore International Culinary College. **Managing Director:** Mariana G. Palacios. **Accommodations:** 20 rooms, all with private bath, including 1 suite. **Rates:** $100–$125. **Included:** Continental breakfast, high tea. **Minimum stay:** None. **Added:** 12% tax. **Payment:** MasterCard, Visa, American Express. **Children:** Welcome. **Pets:** Check with manager. **Smoking:** Not allowed. **Open:** All year.

Government House, for years the leading property in the Society Hill Hotels, is now home to the Baltimore International Culinary College, which has another branch in Ireland, founded in 1991. Not only do guests have the privilege of staying at this magnificent house, they are also treated to elaborate afternoon high tea and, in the morning, fresh-baked croissants and sticky buns, studiously and creatively prepared by the students.

> Being a guest at Government House is like being a stowaway in a fine arts museum: you may find yourself tiptoeing around in the evening when no one's around, viewing the original lithographs with awe. But soon you'll feel right at home — particularly with treats prepared by the culinary students.

Government House is composed of three connecting townhouses in the elite Mount Vernon district. Dating to the 1880s, the grand corner Government House, with its three-story turret, was built for William Painter, inventor of the bottle cap. Today, the Government House is where political royalty often stays or entertains. In addition to being furnished with beautiful period antiques, the house has been impeccably restored, with faux wood graining on original millwork and wood flooring patterns unique to each room. The Anglo-Japanese sitting room has a Renaissance Revival parlor set and such treasures as Ming Dynasty temple jars on bookcases. The dining room has a stunning Renaissance Revival chandelier, an electrified gasolier from 1843 with original glass shades. The ceiling paper is elaborate Victorian decoupage in 17 patterns. Guests may explore the Edwardian library with its unusual paneling, original marble fireplace, and stained glass windows.

The guest rooms, accessible by a luscious wood elevator or a walk up a light-filled atrium staircase, are blessed with original stained glass, woodwork, and molding, some marble mantels, and unusual spaces. Two of the finer rooms are in the turret, with lush fabrics and window treatments. Reproduction Victorian wallpapers decorate each room. The baths are nicely updated, with bonuses like hair dryers. The Government House is notably stocked with a beautiful collection of original lithographs.

Mariana and Meg are consummate, gracious hostesses who revere this wonderful building. Guests receive a museum-type tour of the house upon check-in. The innkeepers are quite enthusiastic about the school and its sister property, the Park Hotel in County Cavin, 50 miles northwest of Dublin.

Harbor Court Hotel

550 Light Street
Baltimore, MD 21202
410-234-0550
Fax: 410-659-5925
800-824-0076

> *The most elegant
> and best located
> hotel in Baltimore*

Proprietors: David H. Murdock.
Managing Director: Werner R. Kunz. **Accommodations:** 203 rooms, including 25 suites. **Rates:** Rooms $220–$260, suites from $375. **Added:** $15 each additional guest, 12% tax. **Payment:** Major credit cards. **Children:** Welcome, no charge for children under 18. **Pets:** Not allowed. **Smoking:** 1 of 8 floors nonsmoking. **Open:** All year.

Since the summer of 1985, Baltimore's premier hotel has been the Harbor Court. It was built shortly after owner David Murdock completed the restoration of the gorgeous Hay-Adams Hotel in Washington, D.C. Not only is this hotel stunningly appointed with unusual Old World antiques and beautiful accommodations, but the Harbor Court is magnificently located. The hotel shares its Inner Harbor waterfront location with the Baltimore Science Center, shop-filled Harborplace, and the National Aquarium, within a short walk of the business district and the Baltimore Convention Center.

The seven-story brick building has a dignified, postmodern exterior, its second floor an array of floor-to-ceiling arched windows, under which billowing flags mark the entrance. Cars drive into a courtyard, centered around a fountain.

Through the entrance is the sweeping lobby, its marble floor inlaid with red and green geometric marble. Circular tables and urns are adorned with floral arrangements, between over-stuffed armchairs.

Two stories above, a brass chandelier hangs from a round mural of ivy. Follow the grand red-carpeted curving staircase to the second-floor Explorer's Lounge and the Harbor Court's fine restaurants, Hampton's and Brighton's. The Explorer's Lounge decor was inspired by safari and African themes. Huge murals of an elephant and monkeys grace the walls, and lush plants suggest the tropics, though the overwhelming elegance rests largely in the classic furnishings.

> **Generally, only large chain hotels, backed by corporations, can afford the sums needed to open a grand-scale property. Amazingly, the Harbor Court Hotel is a privately owned treasure, built in 1985 right on the beautiful harborfront. Its individualism and elegance put it above all the rest.**

Taking great advantage of the floor-to-ceiling arched windows trimmed in combed wood, Hampton's restaurant provides postcard views of the Inner Harbor. Columns, exposed ceiling beams, and crown moldings are done in rich wood. Rust-colored damask silk wallcoverings complement the heavy drapes. Guests dine in modified wing chairs in a room that feels overwhelmingly English. Also the setting for a brunch that has been touted as Baltimore's best, Hampton's is the home of chef Michael Rork, who prepares American dishes that begin at $25. Upwards of 200 wines are available from Hampton's cellar.

For high tea, lunch, and casual dinner there is the exceptionally cheerful garden room of Brighton's, which shares the arched window view of the Inner Harbor. Lunch ranges from $10 to $12, dinner from $15 to $25.

The Harbor Court guest rooms are reminiscent of an English country home with creative touches. Those rooms blessed with a harbor view have enchanting floor-to-ceiling windows in a keyhole shape, offering nonpareil views. The furnishings are classic Chippendale reproductions. Most beds are king-size. Rooms have televisions in armoires and mini-bars. The lovely baths are the height of luxury, with marble vanities, telephones and televisions, and five-foot bathtubs. Fluffy robes are hung on satin hangers.

Configured like an open square, with guest rooms around the perimeter, the Harbor Court has a third-floor atrium garden atop the two-story lobby. Four floors up, on the seventh-floor rooftop, the Harbor Court Fitness Center has a heated indoor swimming pool and saunas, whirlpool, racquetball, and a tennis court. Cruises on the *Lady Baltimore* and the sailboat *Clipper City* leave from the dock in front of the hotel daily.

Service is outstanding at this rare, glamorous property. A stay at the Harbor Court is worth a trip in itself to experience such sophisticated elegance.

Henderson's Wharf

1000 Fell Street
Baltimore, MD 21231
410-522-7777
800-522-2088

A contender for Baltimore's finest harbor views

General Manager: Ken Callihan. **Accommodations:** 38 rooms, including 2 studios with kitchens. **Rates:** $89–$135. **Included:** Continental breakfast. **Minimum stay:** 2 nights on some holiday and event weekends. **Added:** $15 each additional guest, 12% tax. **Payment:** Major credit cards. **Children:** Welcome. **Pets:** Not allowed. **Smoking:** Designated areas only. **Open:** All year.

Nestled into Baltimore's Harbor, Fells Point is a curving bite of shoreline lined with historic brick-faced buildings that date to the early 18th century. However watery this district may be, no property in Fells Point has views like Henderson's Wharf's. Half of the 38 guest rooms look out over the water to the planked boardwalk that scurries around the harborfront.

The end of cobblestone Fell Street looks as if it might tip right into the harbor, as a huge and heavy brick building sits at its peninsular tip. This is Henderson's Wharf, a seven-story pentagonal brick structure trimmed with blue wood-plank shutters. Built as a tobacco warehouse in the 19th century, Henderson's Wharf was restored in 1990–91 and placed on the National Register of Historic Places.

There are two faces to its entrance, and three more sides complete the pentagon. Visitors enter a large, long, traditionally appointed lobby dressed like a comfortable living room, with Oriental rugs thrown over the highly polished wooden floors. One entire side is walled with French doors overlooking the formal English garden and brick patio, allowing light to sweep into the long, narrow lobby.

Set in historic Fells Point, away from the business district and literally on the water, Henderson's Wharf remains a well-kept secret. Here you can experience the poetry of this port by walking right out of your room onto a dock that floats over Baltimore's harbor.

The guest rooms radiate from the center corridor of the lobby in several wings. Half rest around the perimeter, with views of the water through sliding doors behind floor-to-ceiling plantation shutters set in a brick archway; the other half have views of the English garden or of Fell Street. Decorated in nonhistoric formal or country schemes, all the rooms have televisions hidden in armoires. The beds are brass and black wrought iron or oak spindle sleighs, and the wing chairs complement the spreads, in tapestries or in black chintz; some rooms have blanket chests and dressers painted with historic murals. Baths are elegant.

Guests take a Continental breakfast to their rooms or eat in the lobby or gardens. Service is that of a deluxe hotel, discreet and formal. Because Henderson's Wharf is largely a condominium complex, overnight guests have a feeling of independence and privacy. Active guests may consider visiting the exercise studio, the marina, or nearby Camden Yards. Courtesy van or water shuttle service to the business district is provided.

Peabody Court

612 Cathedral Street
Baltimore, MD 21201
410-727-7107
800-732-5301

The second oldest hotel in historic old Baltimore

Proprietors: Grand Heritage Metropolitan. **General Manager:** Russell Conoglio. **Accommodations:** 104 rooms, including 20 suites. **Rates:** Rooms $132–$152, suites from $158. **Added:** $20 each additional guest, 12% tax. **Payment:** Major credit cards. **Children:** Welcome. **Pets:** Not allowed. **Smoking:** 1 of 12 floors nonsmoking. **Open:** All year.

The clear choice in Baltimore for Old World elegance is the Peabody Court in the historic Mt. Vernon district. The neighborhood, marked by a 178-foot monument to George Washington, was established in 1827 and reigned as the city's most fashionable for years, evidenced today by the charming rows of restored townhouses, the world-renowned Peabody Conservatory of Music, and the Walters Art Gallery.

The hotel is Baltimore's second oldest, built in 1927–1929. It served as an apartment house for years before it was reintroduced as a grand hotel in 1985. The highly polished marble floors and elevators, the six-foot, 500-pound Baccarat crystal chandelier, and the valuable French antiques and hand-loomed carpets throughout the public spaces suggest the intimate luxury of a European boutique hotel. In addition, the Conservatory, with its top-floor, panoramic city view, offers some of Baltimore's finest food and has one of the loveliest dining rooms in the region.

The first four stories of this 13-story brick edifice are brightened with light stone and maroon awnings. Guests are welcomed to a small, dimly lit lobby, plush with antiques, artwork, and tapestries. Elevators whisk guests to rooms or to the Conservatory, or guests might glide up a curved set of marble stairs to the clubby Bistro, with green marble walls, dark-stained paneling and floors, elaborate crown molding, and forest green tooled-leather chairs.

The guest rooms are decorated with European and Empire reproduction furnishings in strong, neutral colors and patterns. Remote cable televisions are hidden in dark wood armoires, and all rooms have stocked mini-bars. Though the suites have separate parlors, even the standard guest rooms have plush sitting areas. Imported lamps on marble-top bedside tables were hand-painted to complement the room's hues. All guest rooms are blessed with great bathrooms with marble floors and walls, towel warmers, hair dryers, and separate vanities with makeup mirrors.

> **The Peabody Court is a symbol of Old World elegance. Its 13th floor is home to the Conservatory, one of Baltimore's finest restaurants offering the city's finest views. It feels like a Victorian greenhouse; its marble pillars, brass gasoliers, and sweeping velvet and tasseled drapes are the perfect backdrop to elegant French fare.**

Thirteen stories above the city is the glass-enclosed atrium of the Conservatory restaurant. Victorian patterned carpeting muffles one's steps past green faux marble pillars, lit by winged brass gasoliers. Black wrought-iron trellises entwined with ivy curve gracefully along the ceiling, and live plants line the sills and fill the corners. Sweeping drapes are ingeniously let down or gathered up the curving glass depending on the time of day, filling the room with light or enclosing it with warmth in the evening. The food is elegant French, with dinner entrées from $26 to $30. A $32 prix fixe menu is available weekdays.

When the service is not invisibly discreet, it is friendly and softspoken. Guests at the Peabody Court have complimentary passes to the Downtown Athletic Club.

BUCKEYSTOWN

The Inn at Buckeystown

General Delivery
3521 Buckeystown Pike
Buckeystown, MD 21717
301-874-5755
800-272-1190

*A quaint place of
culinary delight*

Proprietors and Partners: Daniel R. Pelz and Chase Barnett.
General Manager: Rebecca E. Smith. **Accommodations:** 7
rooms, all with private bath, including the Parson's Cottage
and a 2-bedroom suite in St. John's Cottage. **Rates:** Rooms,
$167–$230 MAP Monday–Thursday, $209–$272 MAP Friday–Sunday; cottage $230–$272 MAP. **Included:** 5-course dinner, full breakfast; tax; gratuities. **Minimum stay:** 2 nights in
October and on holiday weekends. **Added:** $75 additional
guest, MAP (includes dinner, breakfast, tax, gratuities). **Payment:** MasterCard, Visa, American Express. **Children:** Over
16 welcome. **Pets:** Not allowed. **Smoking:** Allowed only in
parlors. **Open:** All year.

An evening at the Inn at Buckeystown is like a reunion with
old friends. Innkeepers Dan Pelz and Chase Barnett are unusually warm-hearted and take great pride in their celebrated
dinners. The MAP rates remind guests that food is an integral
part of a stay at the inn, the real highlight of the occasion.

Buckeystown was named for John Buckey, village tavern-
keeper during the late 18th century. A Nationally Registered
Historic Village — though it feels more like a hamlet —
Buckeystown has changed little since then, but for the additions of some wonderful buildings here and there, among

them a magnificent 18-room Italianate white clapboard structure that sits on the main Pike. This is the Inn at Buckeystown, with its large wraparound porch, slate gable roof,
and black shutters, built
in 1897 by the influential
Keller family.

> **Though guests come for the countryside, for the local history, antiques, and architecture, and for bed-and-breakfast romance, they'll leave remembering the food. Meals — and the atmosphere of hospitality that surrounds them — are the centerpiece at the Inn at Buckeystown.**

Inside, the house has a
very large scale, with 12-
foot ceilings on the first
floor, 10- and 8-foot ceilings on the remaining
floors. The woodwork is
chestnut and golden oak,
with cherry-stained heart
pine floors. The two par-
lors have fireplaces, and
the two dining rooms are
large and airy. Dan and
Chase have filled the
house with their eclectic
collections: Dan's pictures and figurines of clowns, antique
china and glass, and American art pottery, and Chase's toy
collection.

The five second-floor rooms have private baths and fine antiques. The Love Room has a cottage Victorian bedroom
suite, its appellation woven whimsicaly into the carpet's pile.
Fresh flowers and sherry are provided in every room. All
rooms have crystal chandeliers, and the Winter Suite has a
fireplace with a Victorian oak bedroom suite.

For special occasions, book the St. John's Cottage down the
Pike a quarter of a mile. In 1985, then-partners Dan Pelz and
Marty Martinez bought tiny St. John's Reformed Church, an
1884 brick Georgian structure, which they converted for
guests. This wonderful space is great for romantics seeking
seclusion; it has magnificent pointed vitrine windows on
three sides, a kitchenette, a piano, a fireplace, high cathedral
ceilings, and a redwood hot tub on the private porch. The adjacent Parson's Cottage has a fireplace and plenty of privacy.

As with any reunion, the heart of the evening is around the
dinner table. Guests sit down at 7:30 to a table set with fine
china, antique lace, and crisp linens, in formal family style. A
sample winter menu might go as follows: "Inn" toast, curried
emerald soup, an antipasto salad platter, stuffed manicotti;
for the main course, Osso Bucco Milanese served with yellow

rice and garlic bread; and for dessert, Italian pound cake with peaches and cream, coffee and tea. Daniel has many specialties, including paella and also German duck with sweet and sour red cabbage. The innkeepers have a passion for fine dining and will tailor a special menu for their guests; make arrangements in advance for a holiday meal, cocktail party, brunch, or high tea.

FREDERICK

Tyler Spite House

112 West Church Street
Frederick, MD 21701
301-831-4455
800-417-3264

The only hostelry in Frederick's historic district

Proprietors and Innkeepers: Andrea and Bill Myer. **Accommodations:** 6 rooms, including 2 suites, 4 with private bath. **Rates:** $100–$175. **Included:** Full breakfast, high tea. **Minimum stay:** 2 nights on major holidays. **Added:** 20% gratuity, 5% tax. **Payment:** Visa, MasterCard. **Children:** Not allowed. **Pets:** Not allowed. **Smoking:** Not allowed. **Open:** All year.

Hood College was born about a hundred years ago, by the time most of Frederick had been well established. In the heart of Frederick's 33-block historic district, the Tyler Spite House is a fine representative of the town's rich history. The Federal mansion was built in 1814 by Dr. John Tyler in a plan to "spite" the town zoning commission, which planned to extend Record Street into a thoroughfare. The whitewashed three-story mansion sits like an exclamation point at the end of Record Street.

Bill and Andrea Myer bought the Tyler Spite House in 1989, and after a year of restoration they opened their second bed-and-breakfast — their first was the Castle in Mt. Savage. Three stories high and three green-shuttered windows across, the Tyler Spite House is quite grand inside. The first floor has 13-foot ceilings, Georgia pine woodwork with raised paneling, and the original plaster moldings. Many of the mantels of the eight working fireplaces are the original imported marble. Five chandeliers hang throughout the house, the grandest set in its original medallion in the center of the three-story winding staircase. Among the large-scale common rooms are the formal music and dining rooms and a library. An addition was built onto the back of the house in 1850, providing a wall of privacy for the pool and the brick garden patio, where guests dine around wrought-iron tables and chairs in warmer months.

> **Akin to Georgetown and New Castle, Frederick is an enchanting historic town, and a stay at the Federal Tyler Spite House will take you back about 150 years. You'll feel convinced you're a Federalist — until you take a swim in the Tyler Spite's pool.**

Most of the guest rooms have working fireplaces, and the decor is dressy but uncluttered. The third-floor Parsons Room has a wicker sleigh bed and a pair of mahogany rockers inlaid with mother-of-pearl. The Page Room overlooks the pool through tall windows framed in yellow Federal swags. The floors are covered with Oriental rugs, and if the furnishings are not antiques they are fine-quality reproductions. Beds are covered in down comforters and white cotton linens. Guests are greeted with fresh flowers and sherry upon arrival.

Bill's high tea is equaled in lavishness only by his breakfasts, which might feature Belgian waffles, chipped beef, and always a hot fruit compote like baked apples. The Tyler Spite House is the only bed-and-breakfast in the historic district — a blessing given the town's dearth of parking. The inn offers, for $10, horse-drawn carriage rides for guests who want to forget their car entirely.

NEW MARKET

National Pike Inn

9 West Main Street, Box 299
New Market, MD 21774
301-865-5055

*An authentic
stop in antiquers'
heaven*

Proprietors: Tom and Terry Rimel.
Accommodations: 5 rooms, 3 with
private bath. **Rates:** $75–$125. **In-
cluded:** Full breakfast. **Minimum stay:** 2 nights on some
weekends in September and December. **Added:** 5% tax. **Payment:** MasterCard, Visa. **Children:** Over 10 welcome. **Pets:**
Not allowed. **Smoking:** Not allowed. **Open:** All year.

New Market is an adorable little one-street town 10 minutes
from Frederick. Its name is a misnomer: this isn't a New
Market but rather a very old one, founded in 1793. It's about
40 miles north of Washington, D.C. and 30 miles west of
Baltimore, a perfect weekend spot for urbanites who don't
want to get lost in the country but who want a relaxed retreat.
For weekend antiquers looking for a place of some historic
merit without having to dust themselves off at every turn, the
National Pike is just the place.

Named for the nation's first federally funded highway, the
National Pike Inn was built at the turn of the 18th century.
The house is two and a half stories of stucco over brick,
painted brown with red shutters and ivory trim, with a cupola
built into the center of the steep shingle rooftop. Tom and
Terry Rimel lived in New Market for 13 years before they

bought the house in 1986 and restored it. The Rimels make good use of the two-family construction, using one side for their home and the other side for guests.

The Federal living room was built in 1802 and is furnished with period reproductions. The room that is now the dining room was built in 1796. It contains family heirlooms such as a 200-year-old tea cart, set on the well-cared-for wide-plank original floors.

> Built just after the town itself was founded at the turn of the 18th century, the National Pike Inn puts a guest in the mood for antiquing. It's neat as a pin, spare, and warmly accommodates the guest who's traveled 200 years back in time to get here.

Upstairs are two rooms that share a bath. The wide floor boards here are nearly hilly. One room has an antique oak bedroom set, the other has cherry furniture and a brass bed. The pretty and simple Federal Room is in the middle of the house above the living room, with a small, nonworking fireplace, fireside bench, steps up to the four-poster canopy bed, and a view of the 1820s smokehouse. Its hall bath is a creative black and white. The front Victorian Room has a four-poster spindle bed, a carved cherry dresser with a matching nightstand, and a new bath with a sit-shower.

The half acre of groomed backyard is quite pretty and sociable. From the brick patio, guests enjoy the azalea gardens, a bird bath, and a fountain that trickles on the vast lawns — a grassy haven for a village bed-and-breakfast. Terry is the full-time innkeeper, a warm hostess who is glad to welcome guests to her pretty home. As natives, both Terry and Tom have a lot of good advice about the goings-on of New Market and Frederick, home of Hood College.

SHARPSBURG

Inn at Antietam

220 East Main Street, Box 119
Sharpsburg, MD 21782
301-432-6601
Fax: 301-432-5981

> *A neighbor of*
> *Antietam Battlefield*

Proprietors: Calvin R. and Betty
N. Fairbourn. **Accommodations:** 4 suites, all with private
bath. **Rates:** $95, $105 weekends and holidays. **Included:** Full
breakfast. **Minimum stay:** 2 nights on holidays and weekends. **Added:** $25 each additional guest, 8% tax. **Payment:**
American Express. **Children:** Over 6 welcome. **Pets:** Not allowed. **Smoking:** Allowed in designated areas only. **Open:**
Year-round; closed December 23–January 5.

The Antietam National Battlefield marks the decisive point
at which the Confederates failed in their effort to conquer the
North. Eighty-seven thousand federal soldiers fought 41,000
southerners on this field in one of the bloodiest battles of the
Civil War: on September 17, 1862, more than 20,000 men
were killed. On this 12-square-mile setting, the National Park
Service leads detailed tours and maintains a cemetery. After a
day on the battlefield, historians will appreciate a peaceful
place to stay right on the property.
    The Inn at Antietam is a serene, relaxing, lovely bed-and-
breakfast with generous and knowledgeable hosts, Cal and
Betty Fairbourn. Bordering on historic property, the acreage of
the Inn is well-groomed, and the flowers around the property
are quite lavish, tended to by the owner and his trowel. In
1983, the Fairbourns bought this white clapboard house,

which was built in 1908 and served for years as a horse farm. They restored it over the course of a year and had it decorated professionally. The Fairbourns have also added plenty of their own sincere, personal touches.

Each of the four guest rooms is actually a two-room suite, with perfect antiques and traditional, lovely, spotless decor. A favorite is the Smoke House, a masculine room with light blue plaid wing chairs, wide-planked heart pine floors and wall paneling, a beamed cathedral ceiling, and a huge brick fireplace. Up narrow stairs is the loft bedroom. At the front of the house is another first-floor room, the Master Suite, which has an 1880 queen-size four-poster pineapple bed with a crown canopy, pink floral wallpaper matching the linens, and a lovely bay window permitting extra sunlight overlooking the front porch and sloping front lawn. Its sitting room is quite large. Above this on the second floor is the Blue Bird Suite, with a queen-size iron and brass bed; and across the hall is another favorite, the Queen Suite, done in pink and green. All guests may use the sun porches around the house, furnished in antique wicker. The preppy elegance of the decor came from the hand of Keith Knost, whose work can also be seen at the Greenbrier in West Virginia.

> The war was right next door, but peace now reigns at the Inn at Antietam. From a rocker on a sun porch, overlooking gardens and acres of fields, one can't help but be filled with a sense of tranquility at this lovely bed-and-breakfast.

Guests are pampered here, thanks to the excellent, professional hosting of the Fairbourns. They can spend time privately in their large rooms or gregariously in the three common spaces — the dining room, living room, and sun porch. Cal has the sociable air of a retired senator; and if she announced that her surname was Crocker, those who tried Betty's peanut butter cookies or large breakfasts wouldn't blink an eye.

TANEYTOWN

Antrim 1844

30 Trevanion Road
Taneytown, MD 21787
410-756-2744

> *A fantastically romantic Maryland plantation*

Proprietors: Dorothy and Richard Mollett. **General Manager:** Amy Angerer. **Accommodations:** 14 rooms, all with private bath, most with fireplace; 4 deluxe accommodations. **Rates:** Weekends $150–$250, deluxe accommodations $175–$300. Weekdays, all accommodations $150. **Included:** Wake-up tray and full breakfast; champagne and hors d'oeuvres; turn-down service. **Minimum stay:** 2 nights on weekends and holidays. **Added:** 5% tax. **Payment:** Visa, MasterCard, American Express. **Children:** Allowed. **Pets:** Restricted. **Smoking:** Restricted. **Open:** All year.

Antrim is an exciting property set on 25 acres of rural farmland about 40 minutes north of Washington, D.C., and 12 miles south of Gettysburg. Only a few years old, this stunning property is being brilliantly developed by its owners and is a real up-and-comer for travelers from Baltimore and Washington. The mansion is genteel and impressive, from its preserved architecture to its 11 fireplaces, its lovely accommodations and luxurious baths, and the gourmet dinners and stunning collection of antiques. In 1988, Dort and Richard Mollett rescued this brick plantation home from 50 years of vacancy and undertook an extensive, year-long restoration that included installing electricity.

Antrim was built in 1844 by Andrew Ege, a wealthy Irish immigrant who fondly named his home after the county in which he was born. In 1860, Antrim was bought by George Washington Clabaugh and expanded to 2,800 acres; it remained in the family until 1965. The house was used at one time by Union General Meade during the Civil War, who observed Confederate troops from the widow's walk.

> **Twelve miles south of Gettysburg, Antrim stands in all its glory, a regal combination of Greek Revival, Federal, and Italianate architecture. It offers a memorable historic experience, luxurious guest rooms, and wonderful dining, as well as beautiful grounds that include a clay tennis court, a competition-style croquet court, and even a bowling lawn.**

The house has a single-story verandah running the length of the facade and wrapping around one side. The other side of the building faces the formal gardens, with a fountain in a fish pond and gravel walkways illuminated by lanterns leading to the tennis court and the croquet and bowling lawns. Past the yellow clapboard Ice House, with one luxurious guest room, is the black-bottom swimming pool. Farther on, the green barn contains two luxurious guest rooms, the Sleigh Room and the Carriage Room. Also on the grounds is the admirable Smith House. These deluxe accommodations in the outbuildings offer fireplaces, steam showers, Jacuzzis, and canopy beds.

Visitors enter from the verandah to a magnificent foyer on whose heart-pine floor is laid a great Oriental carpet and a Scottish case clock from 1830. At either end of the double parlor are grand pocket windows, French doors that disappear into the wall above the threshold. Among the vast treasures here are two marble mantels carved by sculptor William Rinehart, an 1880 Knabe piano, a Queen Anne highboy from 1780, and an 1840 Chinese Chippendale settee with a tapestried base. All the plaster moldings are original, including the magnificent rose medallions, from which hang a pair of brass chandeliers.

Opposite the parlors across the foyer is the blue-walled formal dining room, where breakfast might include Belgian waffles, fried tomatoes, grilled scrapple and bacon, and poached pears. (This is in addition to your silver wake-up tray, which is delivered to your room.) Adjacent is the Hunt Room den, with a pair of tufted leather sofas, a full stereo system, and polished granite working fireplace.

Four rooms fill each of the following two floors above, decorated by Dort, a former interior designer. Most notable are the museum-quality canopy beds. The Clabaugh Room has a 19th-century rosewood half-tester bed covered in tapestry linens, with the original gas sconces attached on the headboard, now electrified for night reading. Across the hall is the chintz-papered Boyd Room, named for the colonel who owned the magnificent 1790 canopy bed. The Meade Room has access to the side balcony through a weighted window in its marble bath. Its 1820 canopy bed is Honduras mahogany, and the walls are done in a masculine blue and white stripe. Among the other accommodations are the four third-floor rooms and the Room with a View from its verandah on the second floor. Guests are treated to port and chocolates at nightly turndown.

Antrim's dining has been a tremendous success; manager Stewart Dearie no doubt can take credit, having honed his skills at Baltimore's exquisite Conservatory restaurant. Beautiful five-course Continental meals are orchestrated by celebrated chef Sharon Ashburn, formerly of Baltimore. For a fixed price of $50, you will be treated to a memorable feast, which may include salmon with feta and spinach in phyllo with saffron beurre blanc; or perhaps fillet of beef with tarragon cognac cream. In the former Summer Kitchen and Smokehouse adjacent to the mansion, this romantic brick-floored room is enchanting: guests sit in soft wool plaid wing chairs and dine fireside by a stone hearth on distinctive gold-trimmed Antrim china.

The East
and the Shore

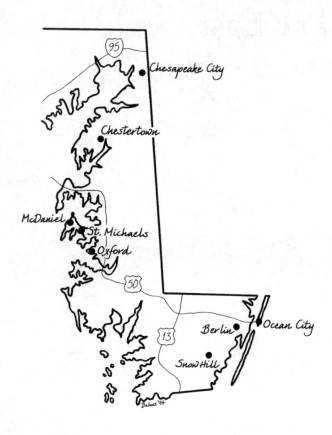

Best Romantic Retreats

Berlin
  Atlantic Hotel
Chestertown
  Brampton Bed and Breakfast
  The White Swan Tavern
Ocean City
  Lighthouse Club Hotel
Oxford
  Robert Morris Inn

Best Gourmet Getaways

Chestertown
  Imperial Hotel
St. Michaels
  Inn at Perry Cabin

Best for Metropolitan Magnificence

Ocean City
  Coconut Malorie

Best Country Bed-and-Breakfast

St. Michaels
  Wades Point Inn on the Bay

Best Village Bed-and-Breakfasts

Chesapeake City
  Inn at the Canal
St. Michaels
  Victoriana Inn
Snow Hill
  Chanceford Hall Inn

The Bay Bridge is an introduction to another world of Maryland. The pace slackens, the land spreads out in a leisurely stretch. The Eastern Shore is Maryland's retreat, and while there is a good deal of farming and fishing, much of this land is used for private recreation, for boating, swimming, and pleasantries. Flat, green, and low, this landscape is fed by the Chesapeake Bay. On a map, this portion of Maryland looks like an incomplete puzzle, as the water reaches into the land from all sides.

Just north of the Bay Bridge on the eastern side is **Chestertown,** on the Chester River, a historic village that features some of the Eastern Shore's finest dining at the Imperial Hotel. If you keep traveling north toward Wilmington, you will certainly want to pass through the enchanting town of **Chesapeake City,** in the corner of Maryland that abuts Pennsylvania, where the Chesapeake & Delaware Canal makes an island out of the Delaware-Maryland-Virginia peninsula.

South of the Bay Bridge, you'll drive through Easton, the gateway to the southern towns, including sleepy Oxford and bustling **St. Michaels.** The landscape becomes rural and windswept as one continues toward Tilghman Island, a quiet, moorlike refuge. While on the Chesapeake side of the Eastern Shore, continue south on Route 50 past Cambridge, taking Route 13 to southernmost Crisfield, the launch point for the ferry to Tangier Island. The land is wonderfully remote here; the only towns are fishing communities off the main roads.

Rich farmland separates the Chesapeake from the Atlantic. En route to the eastern Eastern Shore, stop off at **Snow Hill** for rafting on the Pocomoke River and dinner in **Berlin** at the Atlantic Hotel; then on to Maryland's brief exposure to the Atlantic Ocean. **Ocean City** appears to be the Miami Beach of the north; it may host as many as 200,000 beachgoers on a busy summer day. Its 10 miles of populous beach are between the havens of Delaware's Fenwick Island State Park and Assateague National Seashore — worth the trip in itself, and providing at least a full day of hiking, birding, and watching the herds of wild ponies who live here.

BERLIN

The Atlantic Hotel

2 North Main Street
Berlin, MD 21811
410-641-3589
Fax: 410-641-4928

*A Victorian inn
flanked by farms
and beaches*

Proprietors: The Partners. **General Manager:** Stephen Jacques. **Accommodations:** 16 rooms, all with private bath. **Rates:** $55–$110 low season, $65–$135 high season. **Included:** Continental breakfast. **Minimum stay:** 2 nights in high season. **Added:** $20 additional guest, 8% tax. **Payment:** Visa, MasterCard. **Children:** Welcome, under 12 free. **Pets:** Not allowed. **Smoking:** Ground floors only. **Open:** All year.

The din of Ocean City will quickly fade into memory at the Atlantic Hotel, seven miles west of the beach in Berlin amid the lush, flat fields of Eastern Shore farmland. The hotel sits at an odd intersection of three streets in the middle of this charming small town, slightly askew on the sidewalk, with a pretty, tiny park as its front lawn.

For years, this tidy Rockwellian working-class town was subjected to the prominent sight of the crumbling 1895 Atlantic Hotel, exacerbated by a lousy 1946 addition. A group of local businessmen rescued the property from demolition in 1986. After stabilizing the older structure, they tore down the ugly addition, and, as their journal cites, "the swan arose." The Atlantic Hotel opened in August 1988, a faithful period restoration.

The porch of the Atlantic stretches along its entire front, supported by a row of pillars. Guests enter an elegant foyer decorated with sepia-toned photographs of the hotel and antiques, wallpapers, and rugs from the Victorian era. To the right is a highly polished lounge and elegant period bar. Green wainscoting complements maroon stools and handsome upholstery, all warmed by a carved mahogany fireplace.

The dining room has received excellent reviews. Appetizers might be coconut shrimp, wild mushrooms in pastry, or crab bisque en croûte. Entrées are upwards of $19, for unusual dishes such as locally raised quail stuffed with cornbread, crab, shrimp, and tomato finished with garlic glaze, or chicken and scallops with orange almond cream. The meals are presented in a sophisticated setting of two rooms divided by a wide archway. Victorian prints decorate the walls.

> **A terrific find, the Atlantic Hotel is a genteel launching point from which to enjoy dozens of Eastern Shore activities — in one direction, the stretch of beach at Ocean City and wild ponies at Assateague; in another, the joys of the Pokomoke River.**

A landing on the wide stairway is the site of an elegant sitting area just for overnight guests, with nicely restored antiques and a detailed journal that chronicles the hotel's restoration. The rooms on the upper two floors vary in shape and size, all generous but for two budget rooms. The beautiful rugs are all Victorian reproduction patterns of latticework and floral swirls. The rooms display eclectic, high-quality antiques, including brass lamps and unmatched end tables, and carved wood and marble bedroom suites. The corner rooms are particularly nice, with bay windows and tasseled drapery. The bathrooms are surprisingly tasteful for a renovation, with old fixtures or brass reproductions.

For all its elegance, the Atlantic Hotel is a friendly place with a happy, helpful staff. A long list of local activities can keep guests forever busy — if they decide to leave their romantic rooms.

CHESAPEAKE CITY

Inn at the Canal

104 Bohemia Avenue
P.O. Box 187
Chesapeake City, MD 21915
410-885-5995
Fax: 410-885-3585

*A Victorian stop
on the 150-year-
old C&D Canal*

Proprietors: Al and Mary Ioppolo.
Accommodations: 6 rooms, all with private bath, including a
3-room suite with kitchenette. **Rates:** $75–$105. **Included:**
Full breakfast, afternoon refreshments. **Minimum stay:** 2
nights on holiday weekends. **Added:** $25 each additional
guest, 5% tax. **Payment:** Major credit cards. **Children:** Over
10 welcome. **Pets:** Not allowed. **Smoking:** On porches only.
Open: All year.

The Chesapeake & Delaware Canal makes an island out of
the Delaware-Maryland-Virginia peninsula. A pretty tourist
town teeming with antiques shops, Chesapeake City sits at
the peninsula's western neck, under the arching narrow
bridge that straddles the canal. Everything from oil tankers to
pleasure boats passes slowly through the 13-mile-long channel, originally completed in 1829.

The Inn at the Canal has a front-row seat to all the action,
several houses from the end of the main street in town, its
back lawn floating right on the water. The house was built in
1868 by the prominent Brady family, a reward of sorts when

Mrs. Brady presented her husband with a son, their third child. In those days, houses were taxed by their width facing the street, so the two-and-a-half-story front is quite modest, while the house stretches forever toward the waterfront.

The owners of the bed-and-breakfast, Al and Mary Ioppolo, love the old town and its history. They bought the Victorian house in 1989 and set about restoring the fanciful creamy white exterior with its celery-colored shutters and gabled slate roof. The gingerbread front porch with white wicker chairs faces the busy street.

> **What a surprising place: just off I-95 past Wilmington at the narrowest, northern-most part of Maryland is South Chesapeake City, a port for the Chesapeake & Delaware Canal. The Inn at the Canal has terrific water views and a convenient setting on the town's funky main street.**

The first-floor common rooms have looming 12-foot ceilings, with windows nearly as high. It's believed that Mrs. Brady herself painted and stenciled the elaborate ceilings in the parlor and the breakfast room on either side of the foyer. They are being restored, along with the faux marble fireplaces. Al and Mary collect antiques — their shop is at the rear of the inn — and some of their best finds are on display throughout the house: antique door stops rest on every other step of the stairways, Peter Pan prints decorate the walls, and antique quilts are draped on an old sled on the second-floor landing.

Two rooms with water views rest in the back wing of the house. Mary made the black and pink quilt in the farthest room, which inspired the colors of the two wing chairs and the needlepoint rug. At the front of the house are four more rooms, one with a water view. An especially sweet room here features an antique white linen counterpane on a white brass and iron bed and diaphanous drapes. All rooms have small, unobtrusive televisions, often hidden in cabinets. The successful baths are the result of the renovation, with Mexican tile and sinks in old oak dressers.

The kitchen features Al's extensive collection of antique cast-iron muffin pans — which could also be featured in Al's antique shop, housed in the adjacent, restored milking room. The great common porch at the back of the house overlooks the canal. Guests can sit here in rockers, watch the boats, and listen to the jazz band that plays on Sunday evenings in the warmer months in a tiny old wooden band shell on the water. Al and Mary will prepare a crab feast for groups of eight or more.

CHESTERTOWN

Brampton Bed and Breakfast

25227 Chestertown Road
Chestertown, MD 21620
410-778-1860

A nonpareil experience in bed-and-breakfasting

Proprietors: Michael and Danielle Hanscom. **Accommodations:** 10 rooms, including 2 suites, all with private bath, some with whirlpool bath, 8 with fireplace. **Rates:** $90–$140. **Included:** Full breakfast, afternoon tea. **Minimum stay:** 2 nights on weekends. **Added:** $25 each additional guest, 8% tax. **Payment:** Master-Card, Visa. **Children:** Allowed in suite only. **Pets:** Not allowed. **Smoking:** Not allowed. **Open:** All year.

This is one of the most beautiful homes along the back roads of the Mid-Atlantic, a regal Greek Revival built in 1860 of classic red brick, three stories high and five black-shuttered windows wide, complete with a pair of porch swings on the white-trimmed portico. Even the grounds are welcoming: a short mile drive from the charming, ageless village of Chestertown brings one to the circular drive, bordered by bushes and groomed lawns and flowers throughout the 35 acres.

The Hanscoms, a refreshing young couple, opened Brampton as a bed-and-breakfast in December 1987. Built in 1860 by peach farmer Henry Ward Carville, the house has inspired generations of care and love and was first restored in 1937. Brampton is now on the National Register of Historic Places and was at one time a stop on the Underground Railroad. The walnut woodwork on the doors, trim, and stairway is all original, as are the old slate mantels, plaster walls, and grand ceil-

ing medallions. The interior is majestic on a large scale —
ceilings 12 feet high on the first floor, 11 feet on the second
floor, and nine feet on the third floor. In the living room, a fire
blazes most months of the year and immense floor-to-ceiling
windows line three sides of the room. The dining room has a
1930s Waterford crystal chandelier and wonderful wide-planked floors. The Hanscoms cook breakfast by the blazing fire, a full meal with several courses with a choice of two entrées such as buttermilk waffles.

> **Brampton is kind on the senses: a magnificent example of Greek Revival architecture; 35 acres of groomed fields; a classic interior space with working fireplaces in nearly every romantic bedroom. The Hanscoms' passion for bed-and-breakfasting is evident throughout the house.**

The guest rooms have queen-size beds (in a rare compromise with modern times) and down duvets, good reading chairs, and very fluffy towels. Seven rooms are in the Manor House. While the choice rooms are in the front, consider the two-story suite above the original 1860 kitchen. The two second-floor rooms, Yellow and Blue, have old fireplaces; and the two third-floor rooms have Franklin stoves on marble platforms. Michael put in the new bathrooms on the third floor. Across from the Red Room, the third-floor Green Room has a fishnet canopy with Martha Washington chairs and displays some of Danielle's grandfather's sophisticated artwork. Throughout are some wonderful antiques from Danielle's family in Switzerland. Other accommodations are in the 1860 Smokehouse and in the former horse barn, the latter the Sunrise and Sunset cottages with fireplaces, whirlpool baths, and private gardens.

Be sure to make dinner plans at the magnificent Imperial Hotel in Chestertown.

Imperial Hotel

208 High Street
Chestertown, MD 21620
410-778-5000
Fax: 410-778-9662

A sensory and culinary treasure on the Eastern Shore

Proprietors: Albert and Carla Massoni. **Accommodations:** 13 rooms, including 2 suites, all with private bath. **Rates:** Rooms $95 weekdays, $150 weekends; Parlor Suite and Carriage House $150 weekdays, $200 and $250 weekends. **Included:** Continental breakfast. **Minimum stay:** 2 nights on holiday weekends. **Added:** $35 additional guest, 8% tax. **Payment:** MasterCard, Visa, Discover. **Children:** Welcome. **Pets:** Small pets in Carriage House suite only. **Smoking:** Allowed. **Open:** All year.

Albert and Carla Massoni are people of passion. They love food, wine, art, and a great old building in need of revival. They were welcomed into elite Washington food circles with the Morrison-Clark Inn, applauded by travelers insightful enough to stay there. Next, in the fall of 1990, the Massonis turned their energies to their beloved Eastern Shore home of Chestertown and the neglected town hotel.

The Massonis wanted the Victorian restoration of the Imperial Hotel to serve as a backdrop to a restaurant of highest repute, with the talents of chef Rodney Scruggs. Their wine list has received the Award of Excellence from *Wine Spectator* magazine every year since 1990. Their monthly wine-maker dinners match the talents of the finest vintners to those of their chef — to the delight of guests lucky enough to get a reservation. Just 175 couples are members of the Imperial Wine Society, an educational club founded in 1992.

A trip to the Imperial Hotel is an extremely rewarding experience. It's a pretty and easy drive from Washington, Baltimore, Philadelphia, or Wilmington, and a destination unto itself. Historic Chestertown is north of the Chesapeake Bay Bridge in Kent County, on the Chester River — an ideal weekend destination. On charming High Street, near the river, the Imperial Hotel is a three-story brick building with a generous white gingerbread porch to match its height. Built in 1903 by Wilbur W. Hubbard to rule the town, it was placed on the National Register of Historic Places in 1984 and then fully restored. Al found a picture of the hotel from 1910 and had the sign reproduced as exactly as possible, so look for the "Hotel Imperial."

> The Massonis love art — be it visual, architectural, musical, edible, or bottled. They have made the Imperial Hotel, next to their art gallery in Chestertown, a gallery itself for a lovely historic restoration, jazz concerts, romantic rooms, and outstanding food complemented by an extraordinary wine list.

An impressive Audubon print collection is displayed on the first floor, as well as some of the original elevations of Hotel Imperial. The Victorian beauty of the restaurant lounge is equaled only by that of the second-floor guest lounge, which opens onto the wide porch overlooking town. The Parlor Suite is the loveliest accommodation: two rooms dressed in high Victorian antiques and a porch, taking up the third-story front of the building. Other rooms have similar levels of elegance on a smaller scale, appointed with antique end tables, armoires holding televisions, and king-size reproduction brass beds. The bathrooms are new and spotless. Interesting prints and antique quilts decorate the walls.

Behind the inn is the garden patio, where guests may dine and enjoy jazz concerts in summer. Behind the patio is the Carriage House, with a one-bedroom suite featuring a cathedral ceiling and American country antiques and art.

Though an overnight stay is highly recommended, a meal is mandatory. Chef Rodney Scruggs creates a beautiful menu for lunch and dinner; the former ranges from $5 to $17, the latter from $12 to $24. Of 650 restaurants in the Washington-Baltimore area, the 1993 Zagat Restaurant Survey deemed the food of the Imperial Hotel third best in American Regional cuisine. Chef Scruggs is awarded free rein and boundless respect. His domain includes two intimate, elegant dining rooms. The darkly lit tartan room has the feel of an English supper club, with tufted Queen Anne chairs, candle lamps and flowers on the tables, and hunt scenes on the walls. The Leighton Room, named for Carla's uncle (a New York restaurateur) is more decorative, with black and claret chintz, and on the nine tables silver chargers and fringe lamps.

The award-winning crab bisque is worth the trip (from anywhere); and an entrée of crab cakes is nonpareil, served with watercress, mustard, and tomato cream. Other masterpieces include an appetizer of smoked salmon, shrimp, and bay scallops with cucumber salad in fresh dill, horseradish, and mustard cream, and entrées of grilled lamb chops with lemon and lime *jus*; grilled breast of chicken with corn custard, roasted tomatoes, and cilantro *jus*; or roasted semi-boneless quails stuffed with wild mushrooms and sage in shallot butter. Lisa Scruggs's pastry is the perfect completion to the meal.

A separate light-fare menu is offered in warmer months in the back garden, amid wooden Jefferson furniture and umbrella tables. It faces the Geddes-Piper House, built in the 18th century, recently restored to perfection, and often the location for receptions hosted by the Imperial Hotel. On the Patio, the Massonis host a jazz concert series in summer.

Aside from the artistic food and decor, the Massonis have created two additional gallery spaces at the Imperial. A shop called the Cellar in the lower level of the hotel features all of the 150 wines and gourmet food products used in the award-winning restaurant. Next door is the Massoni-Sommer Gallery, with an extensive collection of art, American contemporary crafts, jewelry, and wearable art. Monthly exhibitions feature local and nationally known artists — in celebration of the many forms of true art.

Special events can be hosted in the 1780 Geddes-Piper House. Should a guest have the unusual wish to leave the Hotel, they may swim at neighboring Washington College pool, secure golf and tennis privileges, or bike around the beautiful Chestertown area.

The White Swan Tavern

231 High Street
Chestertown, MD 21620
410-778-2300

A museum-quality colonial restoration in Chestertown

Proprietors: The Havemeyers. **Innkeeper:** Mary Susan Maisel. **Accommodations:** 2 suites, 4 rooms, all with private bath. **Rates:** $85–$135. **Included:** Continental breakfast. **Minimum stay:** On college weekends. **Added:** $25 each additional guest, 5% tax. **Payment:** No credit cards. **Children:** Welcome. **Pets:** Not allowed. **Smoking:** Allowed. **Open:** All year.

This museum-quality restoration of a 1733 house has its own museum about the restoration process itself. The two-story brick structure with a sweeping overhanging first-floor porch was originally built as a private home but served as a tavern from 1760 through the 1850s. The restoration brings the house back to these hospitable days, roughly 1795.

Among the relics found in the White Swan's restoration were pieces of 1790 square graywacke sandstone pavement and pre-1750 treasures such as iron fire tongs from England, a triangular clock key, a bridle bit, a glass decanter stopper, a pipe bow with the seal of royal arms, and a large ale glass.

After a perusal of history, guests may be either exhausted or excited, but either way they will be glad to retire to one of the six pristine accommodations, furnished with beautiful and noteworthy antiques. The White Swan is a cartologist's treasure trove, decorated with maps of Maryland and the Eastern Shore dating from the mid-18th century. The living room contains primitive colonial tables, a 1797 map of Maryland, and Federal swags over the windows. The breakfast room, formerly a game room for the tavern, features an incredible reproduction of an Evans desk made in colonial Williamsburg, a William and Mary walnut secretary from the 1600s, and many fascinating maps and prints on the walls.

With a private entrance at the back of the house is a guest room called the Thomas Lovegrove Kitchen, named for a shoemaker who worked here in a tannery that predated the house. The room was used as the kitchen of the original tavern and has brick flooring, an open-beam ceiling, thick plaster walls, and a five-foot-wide fireplace. Antique rope twin and double beds furnish the sleeping area, along with an ancient pew table and chairs.

> **Preservationists and historians will be thrilled with the White Swan Tavern. An exhaustive restoration that brought the inn back to 1795 produced 7,000 shards, making it one of the most interesting archaeological finds in colonial Maryland. In addition, the guest rooms are just beautiful.**

The romantic Sterling Suite is at the front of the house on the first floor. The bedroom has white floral linens over a queen-size bed and a wonderful canopy. Through double red doors is the living room, with a wing chair and huge windows overlooking Chestertown's High Street.

The Bordley and Wilmer rooms in front on the second floor are decorated in spare colonial furnishings, the latter with a 1755 French map of Maryland. At the back is the smallest, the Peacock Room, with a wonderful curved fishnet canopy bed nestled perfectly under the eaves. Last, the Eliason Suite has a hint of Victorian decor in its two rooms.

Innkeeper Mary Susan Maisel is highly enthusiastic about the inn and serves a wonderful afternoon tea open to the public. Afterward, guests will want to stroll the wonderful brick sidewalks of Chestertown, visit the river, and surely dine at the Imperial Hotel across the street, known for its exceptional food and epic wine list.

OCEAN CITY

Coconut Malorie

60th Street in the Bay
Ocean City, MD 21842
410-723-6100
Reservations: 800-767-6060

The most luxurious hotel on the Maryland shore

Proprietors: John and Denise Fager. **General Manager:** Angela Reynolds. **Accommodations:** 85 suites. **Rates:** 1-bedroom and studio suites $59–$199, penthouse suites $149–$199, presidential suites $180–$350. **Minimum stay:** 2 nights on weekends, 3 nights on holidays. **Added:** $15 each additional guest, including children; 8% tax. **Payment:** Major credit cards. **Children:** Welcome. **Pets:** Not allowed. **Smoking:** Allowed. **Open:** All year.

The Coconut Malorie, the sister property of the Lighthouse Club Hotel, is the premier luxury hotel in Ocean City, a nine-mile peninsula of beach on Maryland's brief Atlantic shore, sandwiched between Delaware to the north and Virginia to the south. Due west several hundred yards from the Atlantic are the Isle of Wight and Assawoman bays. Perched on these calm shores, the Coconut Malorie sits on a bit of marshland developed by John and Denise Fager. It's the closest thing to a Caribbean vacation this far from the islands.

The Coconut Malorie is a rectangular blue-gray building, identified tersely by the word "Hotel," a grave understatement in a town teeming with undistinguished properties. This 85-suite luxury hotel was modeled after the Grand Hyatt in the Cayman Islands. The owners have invested much research, care, and money in the extensive collection of Haitian art that thoroughly decorates the hotel.

Though the outside bespeaks Miami, the hotel's interior is in luxurious good taste, filled with impressive original art, cool, contemporary decor, and wonderful marble. The two-story lobby has a terraced fountain; Greek blond marble offers fine acoustics for the grand piano played nightly. A pair of 18th-century Manchurian sculptures loiter on stairs that lead up to the great deck and pool overlooking the bay. The elevators are especially lovely, with green marble and mirrored mahogany walls.

> **Modeled after the Grand Hyatt in the Cayman Islands, the Coconut Malorie has a distinctly Caribbean feel. The Fagers' passion for Haitian art fills the public space with color and life, and rich marble, wood, and brass make an elegant and gleaming backdrop to their extensive collection.**

There are five floors of studios and one-bedroom suites, all with observation terraces, some with views of the ocean, most with views of the bay. The decor, as at the Lighthouse Club, was designed to give a sandy, beachy, Caribbean feel: fresh, clean, neutral colors for linens and drapes and either light or dark rattan furniture and tile floors in clean white or Spanish red. All rooms have televisions, wet bars, microwaves and kitchens, telephones, and luxurious marbled baths with phones, hair dryers, plush terry robes, and Jacuzzi tubs. The cathedral-ceilinged penthouse suites offer all this plus nightly turndown, Continental breakfast, and newspapers. Room service is available from Fager's restaurant.

Be sure to ask about the configuration of the rooms: the upper-floor rooms have a thorough view of Ocean City, one side facing the ocean, the other bay. The first-floor rooms have only a bay view from the living room and an oddly placed window to the hallway in the bedroom. New tower additions of the library and art gallery provide wonderful views of the city and ocean.

Lighthouse Club Hotel

56th Street In-the-Bay
Ocean City, MD 21842
410-524-9327
Reservations: 800-767-6060

A romantic retreat modeled after a century-old lighthouse

Proprietors: John and Denise Fager. **General Manager:** Angela Reynolds. **Accommodations:** 23 rooms with deck, including 8 suites with fireplace. **Rates:** $69–$229. **Included:** Continental breakfast. **Minimum stay:** 2 nights in summer, 3 nights on holiday weekends. **Added:** $15 each additional guest, 8% tax. **Payment:** Major credit cards. **Children:** Welcome. **Pets:** Not allowed. **Smoking:** Allowed. **Open:** All year.

Eastern Maryland has a short, 30-mile stretch of gorgeous beach along the Atlantic Ocean, below Delaware and above Virginia, most of which is the pristine Assateague Island National Seashore, home of the wild ponies. Just north of this is nine miles of similar beachfront open to the public, which ends busily at Ocean City. The stretch in Ocean City is about five miles long and several hundred yards wide, flanked on one side by the Isle of Wight and Assawoman bays and on the other by the Atlantic Ocean. The city looks more like Miami Beach than the Maryland shore, a four-lane, five-mile stretch of highway sandwiched between walls of motels.

There are two deluxe properties here amid all the clamor, both on the Isle of Wight Bay on a spit of wetland owned by John and Denise Fager: the Lighthouse Club and Coconut Malorie, separated by the well-attended Fager's Island restaurant. Though surf people might be discouraged, the bay is absolutely lovely and serene, a retreat from the bustle of the city, with sunsets spilling picturesquely onto calm and marshy waters.

The Lighthouse Club is an intimate, romantic spot, a 23-room luxury inn built in 1989 to replicate the historic octagonal lighthouse, part of the Chesapeake Bay Maritime Museum, in St. Michaels. Its three white clapboard stories have a cheerful red roof topped by a cupola in true lighthouse fashion. The lobby is the first floor; 15 studio suites radiate around the second floor of the octagon like pieces of a pie, each with a semiprivate deck and whirlpool tub; the third floor has eight deluxe one-bedroom suites twice the size of the second-floor rooms, with entirely private balconies, fireplaces, and heart-shaped double Jacuzzis. The rooms make guests feel pampered and secluded. Thanks to the octagonal shape, the rooms are angled, widening out to the water views.

The fresh decor is the same in both sister properties. Lawrence Peabody designed the contemporary furniture for the Lighthouse Club and Coconut Malorie to give the feel of light and air: rattan headboards on beds dressed in cool off-white linens, modern rattan armoires holding a television and wet bar (with coffeemaker and fridge with icemaker), nightly turndown, and sitting area with the great view of the bay.

> So many wonderful surprises greet guests at the Lighthouse Club: Caribbean decor in a historic Eastern Shore lighthouse; romance in a town of motels flanking a highway strip; and the sound of the surf on a serene bay.
> You wake up and wonder where you are.

Baths have hair dryers, phones, and fluffy terrycloth robes. The Lighthouse Club shares the luxury of its sister property but also has an intimacy that makes it truly unique.

Room service is available from 11 A.M. to 10 P.M. from the popular Fager's Island restaurant, where dinners range from $16.50 to $24.

OXFORD

Robert Morris Inn

Morris Street on the Tred Avon
   River
Box 70
Oxford, MD 21654
410-226-5111
Fax: 410-226-5744

> *A tranquil haven
> on the banks of
> the Tred Avon*

Proprietors: Ken and Wendy Gibson. **Innkeeper:** Jay Gibson.
Accommodations: 34 rooms, all with private bath (14 rooms
in main inn, others in Sandaway Lodge, Sandaway Hideaway,
River Rooms, River House). **Rates:** $70–$160. **Included:** Continental breakfast in mid-winter. **Minimum stay:** 2 nights on
high-season weekends. **Added:** 8% tax. **Payment:** Visa, MasterCard. **Children:** Over age 10 welcome. **Pets:** Not allowed.
Smoking: Allowed in some rooms. **Open:** All year; restaurant
closes in mid-winter.

The puzzle-piece shoreline and low-lying farmland of tony
Talbot County is filled in by strands of the Chesapeake from
all directions. The sleepy 18th-century port of Oxford is
where the Tred Avon and Choptank rivers meet and float
imperceptibly to the Chesapeake. At the ferry crossing from
Oxford to Bellevue is the Robert Morris Inn, the kind of con-
templative place where people come to fall back in love. It's
the setting that is most conducive to romance: long walks,
vivid sunsets on the rippling waters of the Tred Avon River,
and dining over candlelight at the inn's restaurant, famous for
its fresh seafood.

    Ken and Wendy Gibson bought the Robert Morris Inn in

1971 when they began their family. Today, Ken's brother Jay is the hospitable innkeeper. The Gibsons are sociable, effortless hosts who love their inn and enjoy seeing others captivated by its restful and romantic setting.

The inn is two stories of sunny yellow clapboards with white trim, topped by a third story of weathered shingle with dormer windows peeking out of a mansard roof. An overhanging porch spans its length. The main inn was built by ship carpenters in the early 1700s with wooden pegged paneling, ship nails, and hand-hewn beams. The original Georgia white

> **The serenity of the Chesapeake still lives in this tiny port town. In fact, about 200 years ago, time just came to a halt in Oxford. The Robert Morris Inn is all about this calm: bare feet, a book plopped spine up in the grass, wave-lapped shores, and soothing tranquility.**

pine lines the second-floor hall. The building was bought in 1730 by an English trading company for its Oxford representative, Robert Morris. His son, Robert Morris, Jr., invested wisely and helped finance the American Revolution; became fast friends with George Washington, for whom he served as superintendent of finance; and went on to sign the Declaration of Independence, the Articles of Confederation, and the Constitution.

The 14 rooms on two floors in the main inn (as well as the two in the adjacent River Cottage) are simply furnished in reproductions and some period antiques. Though they are quite interesting for their place in history, far more desirable and private rooms are located down the block on the brief peninsula that juts into the Tred Avon.

The Sandaway Lodge is a rambling Victorian built in 1875, a cream-colored clapboard with black trim and wraparound porches. The rooms here have been newly redecorated, with floral papers and lovely tiled baths. Adjacent are two new structures hidden in the foliage, home of the four River Rooms. These are capacious, with large screened porches, picture-perfect views of the river, king-size beds, sitting areas, and large wainscoted baths with clawfoot tubs in the middle of wood floors, showers, and separate vanity areas. Farther down the shore is the contemporary River House. And facing the sunset at the riverfront is the Sandaway Hideaway, a romantic cabin with a king-sized waterbed and television.

Evocative fishing and nautical scenes by local artist John Moll are displayed throughout the public spaces. The wallpaper murals in the dining room are identical to those chosen by Jacqueline Kennedy when she redecorated the White House in 1962, made in France in the early 19th century and depicting indigenous American scenes: West Point, Winnipeg Indian Village, Natural Bridge of Virginia, and Boston Harbor.

The dinner menu ($14 to $20) offers a generous selection of seafood, including expert ideas with crab: crab Norfolk, with butter and sherry; crab imperial, in a seasoned white sauce; and three varieties of the crab cakes — baked, fried, and with cheese and shrimp — of which even James Michener, king of the Chesapeake, has spoken highly.

ST. MICHAELS

The Inn at Perry Cabin

308 Watkins Lane, on the
  Miles River
St. Michaels, MD 21663
410-745-2200
Fax: 410-745-3348
800-722-3427

> *Maryland's most luxurious inn*

Proprietor: Sir Bernard Ashley. **General Manager:** Tom Ward. **Accommodations:** 41 rooms, all with private bath, including 6 suites. **Rates:** $175–$500. **Included:** Breakfast, afternoon tea. **Minimum stay:** None. **Added:** $50 for additional guest, 8% tax. **Payment:** Major credit cards. **Children: Age** 10 and over welcome. **Pets:** Not allowed. **Smoking:** Allowed. **Open:** All year.

The British have again touched ground on American shores, more specifically on Maryland's Eastern Shore, via the Chesapeake Bay. With the Inn at Perry Cabin, Sir Bernard Ashley has created a tribute to his late wife, Laura, the fabric designer of legendary repute. He sought to replicate the genteel life of the English country house using Laura Ashley wallpapers, fabrics, and furniture, in the form of a country inn. Not only is Perry Cabin a thoroughly elegant and romantic experience, it is an exciting setting for the culinary creations of chef Mark Salter.

During his extensive travels, Sir Bernard found international accommodations a bit lacking. As a result, he sought to realize his own ideas of hospitality in the United Kingdom (Wales) and the United States. Perry Cabin was the first of several planned American inns — next came Keswick, just outside of Charlottesville, which opened in the fall of 1993.

> **Straight out of the English countryside, floating on the Chesapeake, the Inn at Perry Cabin is a mastery of exquisite taste, both in its decor and cuisine. Because discretion abounds at Perry Cabin, Sir Bernard Ashley's first English country house in America is still being discovered.**

Sir Bernard searched for a suitable property of historic merit and found exactly that in tony St. Michaels, part of Maryland's wealthy Talbot County. Just outside the charming township, Perry Cabin sits tranquilly at the end of a formal drive, a three-story white clapboard Federal house built in 1820. The front of the house, with its two-story Greek Revival portico supported by four Ionic columns, faces the Miles River. The grounds are immaculate and elegant and include one of Maryland's largest holly trees. The work of the full-time gardening staff is very much evident throughout the 25 acres.

The main house dates to 1820 and contains the four common rooms and three dining rooms. Sir Bernard added two complementary wings with guest rooms stretching out from either side. The new architecture displays carefully crafted wainscoting, wide arched doorways, chair rails, and moldings to match those in the original house. Yet the new influences add an interesting depth to the classic aspects, with some duplex guest rooms with hand-carved jointed spiral stairs in odd angular spaces.

The rooms were elegantly designed in consistent Laura Ashley style, overseen by Nick Ashley, Sir Bernard's son. Most rooms have an outdoor patio through French doors with an oblique or direct view of the water. Antiques, unusual artwork of England or the Eastern Shore, lots of books, and fresh flowers lend an elegant but personal touch to each room. The baths are traditional but quite luxurious, with a towel warmer and fluffy bath sheets.

Guests may take an elaborate, traditional afternoon tea in the many public rooms that open airily to the front patio and grassy lawns. Sir Bernard's extensive art collection decorates the elegant halls and walls, setting the tone for the exquisite meals at Perry Cabin. The prix fixe menu is $50 for four or five courses and changes seasonally. A sample menu might include an appetizer of tartare of local oysters or house-made *fromage blanc* with pesto aspic and marinated artichoke hearts, a consommé between courses; an entrée of tempura fried softshell crab with creamed corn and braised leeks, or Atlantic salmon fillet in potato crust with *foie gras* and clear tomato broth. The creativity and presentation are overwhelmingly artistic, served on Ashley china by Spode. Service, as with every aspect of life at Perry Cabin, is discreet, elegant, and simply flawless.

With a pool, fitness facilities, sauna and steam rooms, and a croquet lawn on the property, and golf, fishing, and boating steps away, a visit to the Inn at Perry Cabin is like a stay at a luxury resort with the intimacy of a country inn.

Victoriana Inn

Box 449, 205 Cherry Street
St. Michaels, MD 21663
410-745-3368

> *The finest view*
> *of the Maritime*
> *Museum*

Proprietor: Janet Bernstein. **Accommodations:** 5 rooms, 1 with fireplace, 2 with private bath, 3 rooms share two baths. **Rates:** $95–$135. **Included:** Full country breakfast. **Minimum stay:** 2 nights on weekends. **Added:** 8% tax. **Payment:** Visa, MasterCard. **Children:** Over 13 welcome. **Pets:** Not allowed. **Smoking:** Limited to the sun porch and parlor. **Open:** All year.

Whether the octagonal Chesapeake Bay Maritime Museum is the state's most recognizable piece of architecture is arguable; but surely the best place to ponder the question is the porch at the Victoriana Inn. This mansard-roofed, two-story Victorian sits right on the channel and near the bay in St. Michaels. It was built by army officer Dr. Clay Dodson during the Civil War and underwent renovations in 1910 by a family who sold the house to present owner Janet Bernstein in 1988.

There are several particularly nice aspects to this B&B: it's private, but only a half block from busy Talbot Street, with serene water views, lovely

> A pretty bed-and-breakfast in a busy tourist town, the Victoriana Inn is set on the water's edge, with nothing between its front lawn and the historic Chesapeake Bay Maritime Museum. Set off from the main road, it offers privacy, fine linens, and a fantastic view.

linens, and generous common space. Guests enter the house from the wide verandah; to the right is the living room with a fireplace leading to an enclosed sun porch with that great view of the Maritime Museum. There is also a breakfast room, where the full meal is always served with two home-baked coffee cakes and a main dish such as strawberry pancakes, eggs Benedict, or creamed chipped beef.

The only guest room on the first floor is also the largest. The Tilghman Island Room has a wood-burning brick fireplace, pink-hued walls, a four-poster bed with a curved fishnet canopy, a daunting triple armoire, and windows with a view of the cove and the little bridge across the canal. Of the four second-floor rooms, Solomon Island is quite pretty, with a four-poster queen-size bed showing off a lovely presentation of triple Laura Ashley sheeting, ample pillows, and a tiny sachet placed on a pillow. The Poplar Island Room has an impressive French Victorian bedroom suite. Three of the rooms have water views. While they share two baths, the second-floor rooms all have a sink and vanity.

Janet is devoted to her home and is a well-informed hostess. The little shops and restaurants of St. Michaels are all within walking distance; and back from a walk, guests have nothing better to do than sit on the wicker porch chairs or the Adirondack lawn chairs overlooking the little canal and the Maritime Museum.

Wades Point Inn on the Bay

Box 7
St. Michaels, MD 21663
410-745-2500

A secluded estate jutting into Chesapeake Bay

Proprietors: John and Betsy Feiler. **Accommodations:** 24 rooms (3 in Main House, 6 in Summer Wing, 12 in Mildred T. Kemp house, 2 in Guest Cottage); 10 rooms have shared baths. **Rates:** $69–$165. **Included:** Expanded Continental breakfast. **Minimum stay:** 2 nights on weekends and holidays. **Added:** $10 each additional guest, 8% tax. **Payment:** Visa, MasterCard. **Children:** Welcome, cribs available with notice. **Pets:** Not allowed. **Smoking:** Not allowed. **Open:** All year except January and February.

Following bucolic Route 33 for five miles from St. Michaels toward the tip of the peninsula at Tilghman Island, an Eastern Shore visitor happens upon a sign for Wades Point Inn. A long, straight drive leads to the 1819 farmhouse, a graceful brick and white clapboard building set on 120 acres of pastures and fields. The waters of the Chesapeake Bay lap against the stone seawall surrounding the property.

Wades Point was named for Zachary Wade, who received a land grant for the property in 1657. The Main House was built a century and a half later, in 1819, by Baltimore shipwright Thomas Kemp. In 1890, he added the Summer Wing, completing the longer part of the T that stretches out toward the waters on the Wades Point peninsula. The Kemp family operated the inn for nearly a hundred years before the Feilers arrived in 1984. Most recently, the Feilers added modern comforts in the 1990 Mildred T.

> On this 120-acre point, a guest has the sense of being on a private island. Three sides of the main house at Wades Point Inn are treated to water views of the Chesapeake Bay — and if views aren't enough, there's fishing and crabbing off the inn's dock.

Kemp wing, a two-story building with postmodern gingerbread.

The accommodations are quite varied at Wades Point. The six rooms in the Summer Wing were built for a growing Victorian family, with in-room sinks and three shared full baths. They are furnished with double beds, and the walls are painted a summery white with a pink hue warmed by diaphanous gauzy curtains, lending a glow to the breezy interior. On either side of a hall leading to a generous second-floor porch, all rooms have water views. Four additional guest rooms in the Main House are more traditionally appointed. Across the lawn is a white clapboard cottage with a rustic interior, a good choice for a family.

In the new Mildred T. Kemp wing, named for the estate's hostess of 53 years who retired at age 91, the deluxe rooms have angled balconies overlooking the bay, the breakwater, and sweeping lawns furnished with Adirondack chairs. The white clapboard exterior is trimmed in forest green and stained wood, with sky blue porch ceilings. The 12 guest rooms in this wing have traditional reproduction furniture, with one or two queen-size beds, white spreads punctuated with colorful comforters, and sparkling new baths with peach towels. Four rooms have kitchenettes.

Below the Summer Wing is the enchanting dining room, with three sides of windows providing water views. The tables and chairs are white wicker, set in three rows separated by two colonnades. Guests enjoy a Continental breakfast here of fresh-baked muffins, French rolls, cheese, and fruit. The formal dining room and common room are furnished traditionally with antiques and lead to screened porches on all sides of the house.

While the interior is beautiful, keep in mind that nary a guest spends much time inside with grounds as magnificent as these. Around the property's perimeter is a one-mile nature and jogging trail; Adirondack chairs dot the sprawling lawns; and a fishing dock beckons just past the stone seawall at the property's edge. If the prospect of fishing in the Chesapeake Bay doesn't grab you, then crabbing will. Golf and tennis are also nearby.

SNOW HILL

Chanceford Hall Bed and Breakfast Inn

209 West Federal Street
Snow Hill, MD 21863
410-632-2231

> *A pretty and convenient home in Snow Hill*

Proprietors: Michael and Thelma C. Driscoll. **Accommodations:** 5 rooms, all with private bath, 4 with fireplace, including 1 suite. **Rates:** $110–$125. **Included:** Full breakfast; evening hors d'oeuvres. **Minimum stay:** None. **Added:** $25 each additional guest, 8% tax. **Payment:** No credit cards. **Children:** Over 12 welcome. **Pets:** Not allowed. **Smoking:** Restricted. **Open:** All year.

The small town of Snow Hill is one of Maryland's southernmost, on its Eastern Shore below Delaware and 12 miles east of Virginia's eastern peninsula and Chincoteague Bay. Owned by Thelma and Michael Driscoll, Chanceford Hall is truly memorable because of Michael's skill in making fine furniture. Anyone with an interest in woodwork ought to make a pilgrimage to this gallery of handmade furniture, all designed and created by the owner.

> One of the most memorable aspects of a stay at Chanceford Hall is the handmade furnishings of innkeeper Michael Driscoll. The Williamsburg furnishings are elegant and classic; but when a guest learns the extent of the craftsmanship that has gone into the furnishings, one can't help but feel privileged.

The house is an immaculate, elegant colonial of brick and white stucco with black shutters, built around 1759, with 10 working fireplaces. It's set back from the residential street by a pretty lawn and a walkway lined with old English boxwoods, leading to a bright red front door. The Driscolls moved into the house in October 1986 and opened the inn after two years of restoration. Most of the color is applied in faithful Williamsburg hues, but some of the woodwork, like the stairs and gorgeously carved mantels, has been stripped and exposed throughout the house.

Centered on a vivid antique Oriental rug in the large formal dining room is the gleaming dining room table, mahogany with ebony and holly inlay. It is perhaps Michael's finest work. The yellow pine dentil-carved mantel complements the carved crown moldings, as do the mantels throughout the house. The formal living room has a traditional sitting area in front of another fireplace and a tea table made by Michael that cleverly expands.

The Chanceford Room is the only first-floor guest room, with Williamsburg gold trim, crewel drapes, and a private bath. Directly above is the Chadwick Room, where Michael made the quilt rack (as he did in all rooms), the trestle schoolmaster desk, and the dark pencil-post queen-size bed. Tapestry swags — which Michael also made — cover the original windows. Two more rooms are accessible from the back stairway: the Cliveden Room and the Carrington Suite, larger than the rest with a sitting area in front of a fireplace, windows on three sides, a dark-stained pencil-post bed, and an antique cannonball twin bed. All beds have down comforters.

On the first floor, the wonderful kitchen, a nice gathering spot, was crafted entirely by Michael. At the back of the house is the only addition, built in 1970, an informal common room that runs the width of the house, with a turretlike ceiling and engulfing sofas from which guests can see the 200-year-old walnut tree that nearly touches the window and the acre and a half of groomed lawns on three sides of the house. In the backyard, under a covered trellis, is a small lap pool.

Snow Hill is an ideal hub from which to explore the diverse landscape of Worcester County on Maryland's Eastern Shore: from the beaches at Chincoteague, Assateague, and Ocean City, to fishing and canoeing on the Pocomoke River, to dozens of historic sites. Thelma and Mike are extremely friendly, love their business, and are pleased to help guests with their day-trip plans. The Driscolls moved to Maryland from Milwaukee in search of a perfect bed-and-breakfast and work tremendously hard to keep guests contented and returning. While the Driscolls are happy to prepare private gourmet dinners with advance notice, the in-town option is the Snow Hill Inn, for great seafood.

New Jersey

Northern & Western
New Jersey

Hope

Short Hills

Princeton

South Belmar

Absecon

The Shore

Cape May

New Jersey is the most concentrated Mid-Atlantic state, with more than 1,000 people per square mile and a population of nearly 8 million. Despite these figures and its reputation as an industrial highway, New Jersey has 40 state parks and 11 state forests, 11 wineries, a huge amusement park, several racetracks, and 127 miles of coastline, making it a recreational haven in the Mid-Atlantic. The state stretches 166 miles from the New York border to Cape May.

There are two scenic avenues to New Jersey: its vast, straight Atlantic coastline from Sandy Hook National Recreational Area, past Long Beach Island and Atlantic City down to Cape May, with towns ranging from ticky-tacky to quaint to Victorian elegant; and the western edge, bordered by the Delaware River, from the Killchohook National Wildlife Refuge up into the mountainous New Jersey Highlands.

The telephone number of the New Jersey Tourism Authority is 1-800-JERSEY-7.

Western and
Northern
New Jersey

Best Romantic Retreats

Frenchtown
  The Hunterdon House
Lambertville
  Chimney Hill Farm Bed and Breakfast

Best for Metropolitan Magnificence

Short Hills
  Hilton at Short Hills

Best Village Bed-and-Breakfasts

Milford
  Chestnut Hill on the Delaware
Stanhope
  The Whistling Swan Inn

Best Village Inns

Hope
  Inn at Millrace Pond
Lambertville
  The Inn at Lambertville Station
Princeton
  Peacock Inn
Stockton
  Stockton Inn

A pleasant visit to New Jersey's western face begins north of Trenton, west of Princeton, in Mercer County. Just across the Delaware from the cultural enclave of **New Hope,** Pennsylvania, is **Lambertville;** you'll travel north along the Delaware's calmer New Jersey banks through Hunterdon County to **Stockton, Frenchtown,** and then **Milford** for quaint antiquing towns, fine foods, and historic homes. A short jaunt east brings a shopper to Flemington, an outlet heaven for bargain-hungry shoppers.

  Farther north, toward the Delaware Water Gap, you may want to stop in historic **Hope,** en route to **Stanhope,** which lends convenient access to New Jersey's largest lake, Lake Hopatcong. Eventually, you will find the magnificent Delaware Water Gap, with more than 30 miles of lovely wild landscape that culminates at High Point State Park.

FRENCHTOWN

The Hunterdon House

12 Bridge Street
Frenchtown, NJ 08825
908-996-3632
800-382-0375 outside New Jersey

An Italianate mansion at the foot of the Frenchtown bridge

Proprietors: Karen Johnson-Amritt and Clark Johnson. **Innkeeper:** Gene Refalvy. **Accommodations:** 7 rooms, including 2 suites, all with private bath, 2 with fireplace. **Rates:** $80–$100 weekdays, $110–$145 weekends. **Included:** Full breakfast. **Minimum stay:** 2 nights weekends and some holidays. **Added:** 6% tax, $15 additional guest. **Payment:** Major credit cards. **Children:** Not allowed. **Pets:** Not allowed. **Smoking:** Not allowed. **Open:** All year.

Along the series of narrow metal bridges spanning the Delaware River connecting Pennsylvania and New Jersey is the latter state's Frenchtown. Named for a Swiss soldier who retreated here to escape death threats during the French Revolution in 1794, Frenchtown is a most charming stop along the Delaware's calmer banks, good for antiquing, cycling, and food. It's also home to the extremely romantic Hunterdon House, a stunning 1865 Italianate and Gothic brick mansion.

A stone's throw from the bridge, behind an elaborate wrought-iron gate, the formidable house is a trick-or-treater's dream: scary at night, evocative during the day. Its two stories are made of brown bricks with a third-story cupola crowning the flat roof. The facade has a wrap-around gingerbread porch and is punctuated with floor-to-ceiling clerestory, arched, and rounded windows. The Hunterdon House has undergone major revitalization since the Johnsons bought the property in the spring of 1992. The new owners are enchanted with their B&B, and the sentiment is contagious.

The breakfast and common rooms flank the

> In the adorable town of Frenchtown on the Delaware, a breathtaking piece of architecture prompts passersby to stop in their tracks. Its magnificence is carried past the threshhold into the interior of the Hunterdon House, appointed with lovely Victorian antiques.

foyer, both with original faux marbling on their respective coal fireplaces. The rooms have interesting period antiques and lavish floor-to-ceiling windows arched inches below the 14-foot crown moldings. The William Apgar Room, one of the seven guest rooms, is here to the left, on the first floor. Its working fireplace and Eastlake carved cathedral-style bed make it a favorite.

Rooms are named for previous owners of the home. The second-floor rooms feature such attractions as a step-up sleeping area, a wrought-iron bed, and a decorative fireplace. The Ruth Apgar Room has a huge carved mahogany Renaissance Revival headboard and a wainscoted bath with a marble-top sink, from which one sees the gingerbread through lace curtains.

Third-floor rooms are especially wonderful. The Daisy Apgar Suite is the most luxurious, with a rosewood double bed, circular clover-rosette window, and dormer skylight. The James Agee Room has a tartan couch and a burl bed under a tapestry spread. The beds are especially wonderful at the Hunterdon House, with thick sheets and pretty presentation.

Guests enjoy a full breakfast — perhaps eggs Benedict, crêpes, or made-to-order omelettes — fireside in the dining room or in warmer months, on the wraparound porch, overlooking the lawn and Bridge Street. The adventurous must view the town from the cupola's window seats. Make dinner reservations at the Frenchtown Inn for a memorable four-star meal, or at Evermay on the Delaware in Erwinna across the bridge.

HOPE

Inn at Millrace Pond

Route 519
Hope, NJ 07844
908-459-4884

A country inn in a Moravian village

Proprietors: Cordie and Charles Puttkammer. **General Manager:** Dirck J. Noel. **Accommodations:** 17 rooms, including 1 suite, all with private bath (9 in Gristmill, 2 in Wheelwright's Cottage, 6 in Millrace House). **Rates:** $85–$150. **Included:** Hearty Continental breakfast. **Minimum stay:** 2 nights on weekends. **Added:** 6% tax, $20 additional guest. **Payment:** Major credit cards. **Children:** Welcome in some rooms. **Pets:** Not allowed. **Smoking:** Permitted. **Open:** All year.

The town of Hope is about 10 miles east of Delaware Water Gap. The building that now houses the Inn at Millrace Pond was the first built for the Moravian village founded here in 1769. During its heyday in 1774, the town peaked at a prosperous 147, but it quickly shrank to 84 people by 1799, was abandoned in 1807 and sold a year later for $48,000.

> The town of Hope, in the northwest corner of New Jersey, was one of the country's first planned communities. About 20 original houses remain from the Moravian heyday that created Hope in the late 1700s, including the one that is now the Inn at Millrace Pond.

Today, the Inn at Millrace Pond is again the keystone of its community. During a two-year project that began in 1985, the abandoned mill was restored, the adjacent miller's house and wheelwright's cottage were improved, and the 23 acres of grounds and pond were grooomed — including the thousand-foot millrace, which the Moravians carved by hand through slate.

The inn is a huge fieldstone block resting heavily at the bottom of a hill. The restaurant, on the ground floor of the mill, has colonial Windsor chairs, hardwood flooring, and colonial green tablecloths accented by candlelight. Hearty entrées, prepared by Andrew Tomko and Jack Rudewick, range from $16 to $21 and might include trout in parchment, roast duckling with raspberry balsamic vinaigrette, or New York sirloin with bourbon sauce. After dinner, guests can venture downstairs, past the trickling millrace and the wine cellar, to the tavern room. Cooled by brick flooring, heated by a brick fireplace, the tavern is filled with relics of the working mill, including a 15-foot wood drill and the original grain chute.

Rooms in the Gristmill are on the second and third floors, decorated successfully in spare Shaker and colonial style with reproduction queen-size pencil post beds, televisions hidden in antique reproduction armoires, Williamsburg colors on the walls, and all with new, simple private baths, some with whirlpool tubs. All rooms have wing chairs, telephones, clock-radios, dried flower arrangements, and some original exposed wood from the old mill. Some upper rooms have cathedral ceilings with sleeping lofts tucked under eaves.

Across a brick patio from the dining room is the Millrace House, built in the late 1700s. Its six rooms are more decorative than those in the Gristmill, featuring formal Queen Anne, Chippendale, and Sheridan antiques and Oriental rugs. The first floor has a nice common room with books and sitting areas in period decor. The Wheelwright's Cottage next door is a good choice for families or couples traveling together. Its duplex accommodations can also be taken separately. The adorable building has some lovely pre-1835 antiques, original wide-plank floors, and charming deep dormer windows on three sides of the upstairs suite.

The lovely grounds are often the setting for weddings. The lawns behind the inn are mildly hilly and rambling, leading from the millrace to a tennis court, Beaver Brook, and a pond. A hearty Continental breakfast is served in the main dining room.

LAMBERTVILLE

Chimney Hill Farm Bed and Breakfast

207 Goat Hill Road
Lambertville, NJ 08530
609-397-1516

*A romantic retreat
on a hill above
the Delaware*

Proprietor: Kenneth M. Turi. **Accommodations:** 8 rooms, all with private bath, 2 with fireplace. **Rates:** $55 weekdays, $100–$125 weekends. **Included:** Continental breakfast. **Minimum stay:** 2 nights on weekends. **Added:** 6% tax. **Payment:** Visa, MasterCard. **Children:** 16 years and older. **Pets:** Not allowed. **Smoking:** Not allowed. **Open:** All year.

Just before the Delaware River widens and becomes congested toward the bay, it serenely divides two charming towns: New Hope, Pennsylvania, and Lambertville, New Jersey. The former is a popular tourist spot, madly busy at certain times of the year, and the latter, just across a bridge, is often overlooked in the shadow of its Bucks County neighbor. Locked in the 19th century, Lambertville is a great place for antiquing as well as cycling along the flat scenic roads beside the Delaware.

> **Try to come to Chimney Hill Farm in the warmer months to enjoy the wonder of its 10 groomed acres, including a boxwood maze. A stroll around these majestic grounds affords a generous view of this 1820 stone farmhouse and its 1927 wings, gables, dormers, and chimneys.**

Chimney Hill Farm is set atop steep Goat Hill, half a mile from Lambertville. The 10 acres of grounds include lovely perennial gardens, old Adirondack chairs, two huge and ancient holly trees, and white and pink azaleas.

The farmhouse was built in 1820 as a small two-story stone box. In 1927, an international attorney named Edgar Hunt bought the farmhouse as his summer retreat during the Bucks County Round Table days and contracted architect Margaret Spencer, MIT's first architecture grad, to put three stone wings onto the building, creating most of the structure as we see it today. The house lay vacant for a year and a half until the present owner bought and restored it, opening it as an inn in 1988.

Chimney Hill, highly and exactingly decorated, borders on formal elegance. The federal living room has some exceptional antiques, including an 18th-century English secretary and a 17th-century William and Mary chest of drawers. Two steps down to the right is a great stone sun porch with flagstone floor, front and back views of the lawns through six wide-paned windows, and two floral wicker sofas. The dining room, in the 1820 section of the house, is lovely, with an embroidered rug over wide-plank floors, colonial tables, low beamed ceiling, window seat, and the owner's Blue Willow china collection. Full breakfast may include a specialty such as Grand Marnier French toast or pancakes with home-grown raspberries, which are highly acclaimed. The three common rooms have fireplaces, as do two of the guest rooms.

The only first-floor room has one of the two guest room fireplaces and a black and white toile ceiling canopy over the bed. There are five rooms on the second floor: one in red chintz with a queen-size canopy bed; a second room has the other guest fireplace and is decorated with a black rose duvet and linens; another room has unicorn tapestry fabric; and the fifth, exotic room has marbleized wainscoting and a bed entirely enclosed by curtains. Chimney Hill is a very romantic spot, with an overwhelming sense of elegance and privacy.

The Inn at Lambertville Station

11 Bridge Street
Lambertville, NJ 08530
609-397-4400
Fax: 609-397-9744
800-524-1091 out of state

One of the few inns featuring the Delaware River

Proprietor: Daniel Whitaker. **General Manager:** Charles Kroekel. **Accommodations:** 45 rooms, all with private bath, including 8 suites with fireplace and whirlpool and 22 deluxe rooms. **Rates:** Rooms $80–$115, suites $125–$150; corporate rates available. **Included:** Continental breakfast, newspaper. **Minimum stay:** None required, but Saturday-only stays have higher rates from April through December. **Added:** $15 each additional guest, 6% tax. **Payment:** Major credit cards. **Children:** Welcome (12 and under free). **Pets:** Not allowed. **Smoking:** Allowed. **Open:** All year.

The Inn at Lambertville Station rests on the calmer banks of the Delaware River across from bustling New Hope, Pennsylvania, via a narrow two-lane bridge. It is one of the few places in Bucks County (Pennsylvania) and Hunterdon County (New Jersey) that enjoys a Delaware River location, with river views from some rooms and an unobstructed view from the breakfast room.

> In a county of Victorian B&Bs, the Inn at Lambertville Station has carved out a different niche for itself. While antiques abound, homespun quaintness has been replaced with modern comforts, spacious rooms, plenty of privacy, fine dining, and great views of the water.

Unlike most area properties, the Inn at Lambertville Station is new, just completed in August 1985. It's certainly not an intimate bed-and-breakfast, which may be a relief to those who are sated with the quaintness of Bucks County. Rather, it aspires to be a small luxury hotel with formal, discreet service. There are two unfortunate aspects to this otherwise ideal spot: the blacktop landscape of a parking lot separating the inn from Lambertville Station and the town and the placement of the rectangular building, with its shorter side on the river. Of its 45 rooms, only four suites take advantage of this beautiful view, which others may see obliquely.

With the look of a contemporary barn, the inn has brown siding with white trim. The lobby is three stories of dramatic open beams with some interesting antiques, a huge fireplace, and one wall filled with lovely and unusual old paintings. Past the fireplace, through French doors, is a shaded deck over a babbling brook that spills into the Delaware.

There are 15 rooms on each of three floors, named for cities around the world with representative decor: the Miami Room has light wood furniture; the Salzburg Suite has European antiques. The standard rooms are more spacious than elaborate, with either queen-size or two twin beds, telephones and televisions, and separate vanity areas next to the new baths. The London Suite is one of four overlooking the Delaware and is quite representative of the eight suites, with a dark wood headboard on a king-size bed, a large sitting area with antique marble-top tables, and a gas fireplace. Guests have breakfast in the Riverside Room, graced with glorious river and bridge views through arched windows.

A great draw for the inn is its affiliation with the renowned restaurant at Lambertville Station, a restored 19th-century train depot. Chef Fred VanDuyne creates American dishes like chicken walnut salad and shrimp and scallop Creole. In winter, VanDuyne prepares wild game dishes.

On Sundays, the Black River and Western Railroad train leaves from the front doors of Lambertville Station for a ride through the countryside. There is a leisurely ride or a direct one to Ringoes, where shoppers can catch a train to the Flemington clothing outlets.

MILFORD

Chestnut Hill on the Delaware

63 Church Street
P.O. Box N
Milford, NJ 08848
908-995-9761

> *A beloved B&B with the Delaware in the front yard*

Proprietors: Linda and Rob Castagna. **Accommodations:** 5 rooms and a 1-bedroom cottage. **Rates:** Rooms $75–$100, cottage $130. **Included:** Full breakfast. **Minimum stay:** 2 nights on weekends. **Added:** 7% tax. **Payment:** No credit cards. **Children:** Check with innkeeper. **Pets:** Not allowed. **Smoking:** Not allowed. **Open:** All year.

Thornton Wilder could have written *Our Town* about Milford. In an area of the Delaware River Valley where much has been given over to the traveling public, Milford remains seemingly untouched by tourism. Chestnut Hill on the Delaware is nestled in this charming, nearly minuscule town, just over a narrow bridge from Upper Black Eddy, Pennsylvania. It's about a half hour from New Hope and a world away but a short drive to Flemington's shopping outlets.

> **People who like B&Bs will love Chestnut Hill.** It's got a classic Victorian parlor with a pump organ and pretty antiques; the bedrooms are adorable; breakfasts are bounteous; and the front porch has river views and rockers.

The town began as a small hamlet called Burnt Mills in honor of its first mill, destroyed by fire soon after it was built in 1760. The town grew, and its name was changed to Milford in 1820. Small, subtle changes have been made ever since: mandatory dog licensing in 1911, the purchase of its first town fire hose cart in 1912, laws against street ball in 1926, the paving of Bridge Street in 1929, and installation of a traffic light in 1954.

The bed-and-breakfast sits just across some rickety train tracks separating Chestnut Hill from the abrupt grassy banks of the Delaware. It's a neat old house, a white Victorian with dark green wrought-iron pillars. The Castagnas have undertaken a laborious several-year project to remove 25 layers of paint and restore the original colors of the house: cranberry, gold leaf, and three shades of green. The Country Cottage just across the drive mimics the design of the house and shares the view of the river and the bridge. Anyone with a sense of romance will appreciate the porch rockers and the river views from both houses.

This is a very Victorian home. The common rooms are elegant, with lovely Victorian antiques such as a working pump organ, a mannequin wearing a satin wedding dress, reupholstered period settees, and Bradbury and Bradbury wallpaper.

The guest rooms are playful and decorative, with some modern touches. The three rooms on the second floor are as pretty and sweet as their names: Bayberry, Peaches and Cream, and Pineapple. The third floor is called Teddy's Place, named for the 166 bears who live up here.

The Country Cottage, with the advantage of independence without the cluttered homeyness of the main house, is furnished with pine furniture, including an antique Norwegian armoire. It also has a generous kitchen, good for longer stays.

Full breakfasts are served at a lovely dining table. Specialties include German apple pancakes and fresh muffins. As with many long-standing bed-and-breakfasts, it's the owners who make this place memorable — proud, involved professionals who care about the needs of their guests.

PRINCETON

Peacock Inn

20 Bayard Lane
Princeton, NJ 08540
609-924-1707

An intimate inn with fine French food

Proprietors: Michael Walker and Candy Lindsay. **General Manager:** Michael Walker. **Accommodations:** 17 rooms, 10 with private bath. **Rates:** $90–$125. **Included:** Continental breakfast. **Minimum stay:** None. **Added:** $10 each additional guest, 6% tax. **Payment:** American Express, Visa, MasterCard. **Children:** Welcome. **Pets:** Allowed. **Smoking:** Allowed. **Open:** All year.

Princeton parents, alumni, and friends have a nice alternative to the sprawling, uninspired Nassau Inn. The Peacock Inn has been a sophisticated hostelry since 1912, having hosted guests of such repute as F. Scott Fitzgerald, Albert Einstein, and Bertrand Russell. Its 17 guest rooms are quaintly decorated in antiques, and its excellent Le Plumet Royal serves lunch, dinner, and Sunday brunch.

> **The Peacock Inn is the place for parents and alumni who prefer old houses and family heirlooms to color televisions and plastic room keys. Its first floor is devoted to Le Plumet Royal, a fine French restaurant that is the place to go when you've just made the Dean's List.**

The white fieldstone mansion dates to 1775, built for John Deare — not the tractor maker but a Princeton scholar. The three stories are topped by a gambrel roof punctuated by three dormers and two chimneys. A single-story porch spans the front of the house, supported by six pillars. Inside, the first floor is dominated by the restaurant, which consists of several separate dining areas warmed by peach walls, green carpeting, and Queen Anne chairs with upholstered seats. Several choice dining spots are near the many bay windows of the house or in the sunny enclosed back porch. Guests may choose from an à la carte menu ($20–$27) or a special four-course $20 prix fixe menu. A meal might include an appetizer of sautéed ravioli filled with duck confit and caramelized onions in balsamic vinegar; a lobster bisque with cream and brandy; and a salad, a timbale of smoked chicken, radicchio, pancetta, and fontina cheese on a bed of greens with bacon and sherry vinaigrette. An entrée may be a choice of sautéed medallions of tuna, wrapped with smoked salmon, served atop a soy-accented *beurre blanc*; or sautéed medallions of venison on wild rice and green onion pancakes, finished with *grand veneur* sauce and lingonberries. The wine list is extensive.

There are ten guest rooms on the second floor and seven on the third under the sloped roof, of varying luxury and decor. The sloping floors hint at the great age of the house, as do the moldings. Some rooms have televisions or fireplaces, but all have some pretty French, American, or English antiques, and always some image of a peacock. Room 5 has a wonderful art deco bedroom suite with an inlaid wood dresser, half sleigh bed, and matching end tables. The antique brass bed in Room

8 rests in a five-windowed bay, with a tufted blue wing chair nearby. While not dressed in formal elegance, the Peacock Inn is comfortably decorated, as might be the homes of well-to-do Princeton parents.

Guests are treated to a Continental breakfast in the sunny dining rooms. A common room downstairs is an informal gathering spot, as is the old-fashioned bar on the first floor.

SHORT HILLS

Hilton at Short Hills

41 John F. Kennedy Parkway
Short Hills, NJ 07078
201-379-0100
800-HILTONS

> *The only
> five-diamond inn
> in New Jersey*

Proprietors: Hilton Hotel Group. **General Manager:** Eric Long. **Accommodations:** 300 rooms, including 37 suites and 70 Tower rooms; 2 floors with special services. **Rates:** Rooms $155–$190, suites $215–$425. **Included:** Tower rooms have extra amenities, including evening cocktails, hors d'oeuvres, and Continental breakfast. **Added:** $20 each additional guest, 6% tax. **Payment:** All credit cards. **Children:** Welcome. **Pets:** Not allowed. **Smoking:** 3 of 7 floors nonsmoking. **Open:** All year.

That the Hilton at Short Hills has received the first AAA five-diamond award in New Jersey merits some congratulations — and some awe, since it opened only in February 1988. Despite its interior beauty, this bastion of elegance seems rather misplaced, anchored in a concrete landscape of the Short Hills mall — like a swan in a parking lot.

Once through the squat red brick exterior, a guest experiences a sense of calm enveloping the lobby. The rich wood walls are hung with oil paintings. Overstuffed gray couches match classic chairs in similar shades. The ubiquitous floral arrangements are designed for the hotel by Emiko Marouka.

The acclaimed Dining Room offers highly reputed American cuisine under the direction of Chef Spost. Offerings from the seasonal menu might include an appetizer of scallop seviche and smoked salmon with couscous and lime, followed by an entrée of lobster and sweetbreads parmentier. The prix fixe menus are $48 and $58 for three or four courses, enjoyed in this classic setting of mahogany paneling, china-filled breakfronts, and art deco chairs, with strains of a harp in the background.

The Terrace dining room is meant to be casual, but with its garden atmosphere, pine chairs and trelliswork, and banquettes under a painted dome ceiling, it too feels luxurious. Adjacent is the living room Retreat, featuring piano and harp music during afternoon high tea or evening cock-

> **Don't be dissuaded by the fresh-off-the-highway setting: the Hilton at Short Hills is a luxurious, cosmopolitan hotel. In fact, it's more like a resort, with fine dining, a full fitness facility and pool, and a European spa.**

tails. Later, guests in a sociable mood might venture to the Club Short Hills and try out the sunken dance floor.

The guest rooms are impressively decorated, with formal, masculine furnishings specially made for the hotel. The two-poster beds, side tables, writing desks, and chairs are designed in a lovely burlwood, with black accents. The thick pile carpets are in jade or rose, accenting chintz colors in the drapery. The baths have marble-top sinks, a hair dryer, a green marble vanity area, and two terry robes. French doors divide the two rooms in the suites. The 70 rooms on the top two floors of the Towers have a concierge and a private lounge and receive complimentary Continental breakfast, afternoon tea, and evening cocktails with hors d'oeuvres. These rooms also have scales and pants pressers.

In a sublime setting under a vaulted ceiling, the ground-floor Spa has a three-lane 50-foot lap pool, with a Jacuzzi at its feet, Keiser weight machines, rowing machines, Stairmasters, wind racers, aerobics classes, and a full-time trainer. Its European salon offers herbal wraps and mud treatments, facials, hair care, and beauty treatments, as well as Swedish and shiatsu massage.

An extensive business center provides copying, fax transmission, word processing, secretarial and transcription services, personal computers, and more — as well as a personal shopper.

STANHOPE

The Whistling Swan Inn

Box 791, 110 Main Street
Stanhope, NJ 07874
201-347-6369
Fax: 201-347-3391

> *A sweet but grand house in the New Jersey Highlands*

Proprietors: Paula Williams and Joe Mulay. **Accommodations:** 10 rooms, including 1 suite, all with private bath. **Rates:** $75–$100. **Included:** Full breakfast buffet. **Minimum stay:** 2 nights on holiday weekends. **Added:** 6% tax, $20 additional guest. **Payment:** Major credit cards. **Children:** Over 12 welcome. **Pets:** Not allowed. **Smoking:** Not allowed. **Open:** All year.

The town of Stanhope is quite representative of the northwest New Jersey Skylands, characterized by old rolling mountains and a sprinkling of lakes and reservoirs, just a half hour east of the Delaware Water Gap. Several blocks from downtown Stanhope is the Whistling Swan, a gray and white Queen Anne Victorian with black shutters and welcoming wrap-around porch, topped by an octagonal turret.

The house was built in 1900 by Stanhope's justice of the peace, Daniel Best, for his wife and seven children. Paula Williams and Joe Mulay bought the mansion in December 1985 and worked nonstop to open their six-room bed-and-breakfast on Memorial Day. They have since expanded to 10 rooms, with the newest rooms on the third floor.

The innkeepers are creative scavengers. In nearby Hackettstown, Paula and Joe found the charming "Whistling Swan" sign that hangs out front, and the authentic brass bathroom fixtures were rescued from demolition at the great Essex-Sussex Hotel in Spring Lake.

Upon entering, a visitor will quickly become enamored of the old house. The first floor has rich tiger oak molding and fireplaces with vivid green Moravian tile in the foyer. The thick carpeting and pink and red hues in the common rooms, however, mark a lapse in the traditional decor. The tiger oak continues up the stairs, in the boxy fashion of American shingle Victorians. While all of the rooms have new private baths, the original shared bath has been whimsically transformed into Tubs for Two, with a pair of old clawfoot tubs painted a cheery cornflower blue (one tub is six feet long).

> Half an hour west of the Delaware Water Gap, in the lush green Highlands, is the pretty town of Stanhope. One of its most regal houses is a Queen Anne Victorian, topped by an octagonal turret, built in 1900. Lovely both inside and out, the Whistling Swan is an ideal B&B.

Highlights of the six second-floor guest rooms are the Harmony Room, with Oriental and Thai antiques collected by Paula's great-uncle; the Waterloo Village Room, with antiques from Paula's Oklahoma grandmother, including her great-grandmother's marriage license; and the Great Meadows Room, with an art deco theme, including a Lindbergh *Spirit of St. Louis* tapestry and Paula's grandmother's beautiful four-piece oak bedroom set.

The third-floor High Point Suite is the feature attraction of the house, its bedroom in the octagonal turret, which has an 18-foot ceiling and cedar wainscoting and is furnished with a three-piece carved oak bed, dresser, and washstand with a brass sink. Three tall windows welcome light. The sitting room is furnished in summery wicker, and the private bath, with a clawfoot tub, sits at an amusing angle. Also striking is the 1940s Stillwater Room, set under steeply pitched gables, with a period bedroom suite.

The owners are generous people, devoted to the concept of bed-and-breakfasting. They are extremely well informed and enthusiastic about the area, which is near Lake Hopatcong (the state's largest lake), ski areas, and historic Waterloo Village. In addition, Joe and Paula are good cooks, and the full breakfasts might include broccoli and cheese pie, farmhouse corn pancakes, frittatas, apple-cheese muffins, or cold fruit soup.

STOCKTON

The Stockton Inn

One Main Street
P.O. Box C
Stockton, NJ 08559
609-397-1250

The small hotel with the wishing well

Proprietor: Andy McDermott. **Accommodations:** 11 rooms with 8 fireplace, including 8 suites, in the Main, Carriage, Wagon, and Federal houses. **Rates:** $60–$110 weekdays, $85–$145 weekends. **Included:** Continental breakfast. **Minimum stay:** 2 nights on weekends, 3 nights on some holidays. **Added:** 6% tax, $20 additional guest. **Payment:** Major credit cards. **Children:** Limited facilities. **Pets:** Not allowed. **Smoking:** Allowed. **Open:** All year except Christmas Day.

Though the Stockton Inn was founded around 1796, the place became a cultural haven in the 1930s and 1940s. Words from the Rodgers and Hart musical *On Your Toes* were inspired by the Stockton Inn: "There's a small hotel with a wishing well. I wish that we were there . . . together." Secret meetings during the Lindbergh trial were held here in 1935. Bandleader

Paul Whiteman signed off his radio show by saying that he was going to the Stockton Inn for dinner. Other regulars included F. Scott Fitzgerald, Clark Gable, Helen Hayes, Dorothy Parker, George S. Kaufman, and S. J. Perelman.

Today, the former three-story stone hostelry is a complex of five buildings in a charming town on the banks of the Delaware. One of this inn's most outstanding features is its hospitable dining rooms. Three of the six share magnificent, brightly colored primitive murals depicting colonial scenes of a courtship, a fox hunt, a fair, and a local schoolhouse. The murals were painted by three artists in the 1930s in exchange for room and board; one of the artists went on to illustrate the book *Bambi.* A fourth room in the 1930s addition is done in clubby, masculine plaids, with an

> **Conviviality, a charming town, and the wish to rub elbows with the ghosts of bandleader Paul Whiteman, F. Scott Fitzgerald, Clark Gable, Helen Hayes, Dorothy Parker, George S. Kaufman, S. J. Perelman, and the literati of the 1930s and 1940s: these are reasons to visit the Stockton Inn.**

intimate alcove curtained off in paisley tapestries. At the back of the inn is a slate garden room with a wood trellis and piano, used for weekend entertainment; the room extends into a modest private dining area. In the warmer months, people dine outside on the slate patio to the sounds of the waterfalls set into the landscape.

Dinners range from $14 to $24; offerings might include veal with lemon, sun-dried tomatoes, and capers; shrimp and mussels in chardonnay with fresh dill cream sauce over sweet red pepper fettucini; or roasted rack of lamb crusted with Dijon and herbed bread crumbs with minted apricot chutney.

The two suites in the main house have wide-planked, creaky floors and fireplaces, and two have access to the front porch that runs the length of the building, looking straight ahead into town to Centre Bridge. The furnishings are comfortable and traditional, in colonial simplicity. The adorable 1832 Carriage House is steps from the slate porch dining room, which has parquet flooring and dramatic black and pink chintz decor. Just beyond are two loft suites in the stone

Wagon House, also built in 1832. Across the street is the recently redecorated Federal House, built in 1850, which has a fresh, crisp feel about its rooms. Three suites have wood-burning fireplaces and access to a charming garden in the back with wrought-iron outdoor furniture. The Victorian Smith House just south of the inn is currently being restored.

Innkeeper Andy McDermott adopted the property in 1989. His primary concern as a former restaurant manager was to renew its reputation as a fine dining establishment, and he has also added a formidable wine list. He deserves much credit for redecorating and refreshing the Stockton Inn's accommodations. He and his staff are extremely kind and are proud of the way they have rejuvenated this historic property.

The Jersey Shore

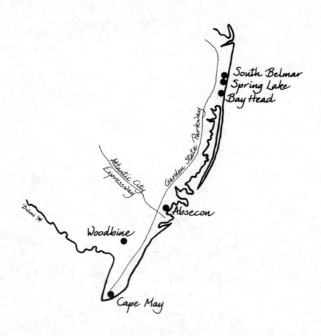

Best Romantic Retreats

Cape May
   The Mainstay Inn
   The Virginia Hotel

Best Resort

Absecon
   Marriott's Seaview Golf Resort

Best Country Bed-and-Breakfast

Woodbine
   Henry Ludlam Inn

Best Village Bed-and-Breakfasts

Bay Head
   Conover's Bay Head Inn Bed and Breakfast
Cape May
   The Abbey Bed and Breakfast
   The Queen Victoria
Spring Lake
   Hollycroft
   The Normandy Inn
   Sea Crest by the Sea

Best Village Inns

Cape May
   The Chalfonte Hotel
Spring Lake
   Hewitt Wellington

The 50 beach communities along the Atlantic coastline stretch from Sandy Hook National Recreation Area to Cape May. Each town's personality is entirely different from that of its neighbors.

There are terrific books detailing the different towns, culture, and history (see "Recommended Guidebooks," page 643). Briefly, the breakdown is as follows: from Sandy Hook to Asbury Park; from elegant Spring Lake and Belmar to Long Beach Island, including Island Beach State Park; Atlantic City; Ocean City down to the Wildwoods; and Victorian Cape May.

Cape May is a most wonderful Victorian enclave on the southernmost tip of New Jersey, truly a world unto itself. Be sure to visit the Emlen Physick House and the Cape May Point Lighthouse. Ferry service goes daily to Lewes, Delaware, across the bay.

ABSECON

Marriott's Seaview Golf Resort

US Route 9, Absecon
Galloway Township, NJ 08201
609-652-1800
800-228-9290

> *A golfers'*
> *paradise on*
> *Reeds Bay near*
> *Atlantic City*

Proprietor: Marriott Corp. **General Manager:** Richard Fetter. **Accommodations:** 299 rooms, including 18 executive suites and 19 suites. **Rates:** For up to 4 people per room, March–October $189, November–February $115; golf packages available. **Minimum stay:** None. **Added:** 6% tax. **Payment:** Major credit cards. **Children:** Welcome. **Pets:** Not allowed. **Smoking:** Allowed. **Open:** All year.

Marriott's Seaview Resort is a premier spot for golfers. Its Bay Course was planned by utility mogul Clarence H. Geist, who vowed to build his own course as he waited in frustration to tee off during a leisurely day on the links in 1912. He did just that, in 1914, with the help of Scottish designer Donald Ross.

The course begged for a country club, which soon followed, a graceful three-story manor house with a generous porte-cochere and a circular dining room. The Pines Course was added in the 1940s, designed by William Flynn and Howard Toomey and rated as one of New Jersey's best. The property remained a private country club until Marriott came along in 1983 with the intent of creating a premier golf resort. The corporation bought the property, added a wing toward the back of the original building, redecorated the rooms in 1986, introduced the John Jacobs Practical Golf School in 1989, and opened a new fitness center in 1990. The 670-acre property

> **Two championship courses would fulfill many a golfer's dream, but Seaview promises much more. Set on 22 acres, the John Jacobs Practical Golf School is the largest of 20 such programs around the country, offering putting, chipping, and teeing greens, a driving range, and at least one instructor for every five students.**

sits on Reeds Bay, six miles northwest of Atlantic City. While the Seaview still has the feel of a tony country club, it's a full-scale resort, with indoor and outdoor pools, two Har-Tru and six all-weather tennis courts, two paddle tennis courts, a marked jogging trail on the golf courses, sauna and steam baths, hydrotherapy pool, and exercise facilities.

The new wing was built when Marriott acquired the property in 1983, with 150 rooms throughout four floors; the original wing has about the same number of rooms on three floors. They are decorated unsurprisingly, with traditional reproduction furniture and luxury hotel style, with two phones, remote cable televisions, and king-size beds with triple sheeting and nightly turndown.

The formal oval main dining room with its rotunda ceiling looks out over the putting green with panoramic views. The Grill Room has the woody air of an English men's club. There is a pro shop in the lobby, and outdoors a pool, gazebo, and gardens.

The Seaview still feels like a country club, a refreshing change of pace from the hype of Atlantic City and a great place to concentrate on golf. The staff is respectful, understated, and solicitous. Though the glitz of Atlantic City is a safe distance away, it is close enough for an evening's fun.

BAY HEAD

Conover's Bay Head Inn
Bed and Breakfast

646 Main Avenue
Bay Head, NJ 08742
908-892-4664, 800-956-9099

A model B&B, immaculate and charming

Proprietors: Carl, Beverly, and Timothy Conover. **Accommodations:** 12 rooms, all with private bath, including Carriage House suite. **Rates:** $85–$150 low season, $90–$195 summer. **Included:** Full breakfast. **Minimum stay:** 2 nights on weekends, 3 nights on holidays. **Added:** 6% tax. **Payment:** Visa, MasterCard, American Express. **Children:** Check with innkeepers. **Pets:** Not allowed. **Smoking:** Not allowed. **Open:** All year.

One of the oldest bed-and-breakfasts on the Jersey shore looks like its newest thanks to the perpetual work of its proprietors, the Conover family, who opened their home to the public way back in 1970. Because the owners are always improving, painting, and redecorating, Conover's seems — every year — as if it had just opened its doors for the first time.

Beverly is responsible for the 12 splendid guest rooms. The antique beds here look like they are from a decorator's showroom, their matching linens from Ralph Lauren, Waverly, Laura Ashley, Mario Buatta, and Jennifer Moore — all, amazingly, hand-ironed. Lovely antiques decorate the rooms with different results: a matching oak bedroom set in one, pineapple twins in another, a dominating armoire in a third, light summery wicker in yet another. Beverly's taste in wallpapers is traditional yet bold. The third-floor rooms are particularly sweet, with deep dormers inset with odd-shaped triangular windows, and the rooms only accent these charming eccentricities.

> **For a quarter of a century, the Conover family has welcomed guests into their home. The dedication they bring to innkeeping is nothing short of remarkable. Rooms are redecorated every three years, plush designer linens are hand-ironed, stenciling enlivens many rooms, and care is evidenced at every step.**

The new baths are spotless and fit cleverly into small spaces. Some rooms have garden views; several have beach views. Above all else, the rooms are immaculate, and Beverly's stencil work adds a wonderful personal touch.

Bay Head is just south of Spring Lake, a calm village of summering families. Like most things in Bay Head, Conover's was built at the turn of the century, a three-story weathered shingle with white trim, two blocks from the town beach. While the common room space is limited to one room, it is charming, with a cut stone fireplace and generous chintz sofas surrounded by walls of books. Beverly serves a very full breakfast in the sunny dining room, perhaps featuring homemade waffles or eggs Benedict. Afternoon tea is served in the colder months.

Bay Head is a relaxing beachfront retreat, without the tourist frenzy of neighboring Spring Lake or southern Cape May, yet within a short drive of both. Birders will enjoy the area and nearby Twilight Lake.

CAPE MAY

The Abbey Bed and Breakfast

34 Gurney Street at Columbia
  Avenue
Cape May, NJ 08204
609-884-4506

> *A classic Victorian
> in the heart
> of Cape May*

Proprietors: Jay and Marianne Schatz. **Accommodations:** 14 rooms (7 in Villa, 7 in Cottage), all with private bath and refrigerator. **Rates:** $90–$150 spring and fall, $90–$190 summer. **Included:** Full breakfast, afternoon refreshments. **Minimum stay:** 2–4 nights on weekends, depending on season. **Added:** 6% tax. **Payment:** Visa, MasterCard, Discover. **Children:** Over 12 welcome. **Pets:** Not allowed. **Smoking:** Not allowed. **Open:** April–mid-December.

Cape May, on New Jersey's southern tip, is a glorious seaside town with the largest concentration of Victorian architecture in the Mid-Atlantic outside Chautauqua, New York. One of the most whimsical buildings here is the Abbey, a mint-colored, three-story Gothic Revival structure decorated profusely with gingerbread and clerestory windows, rarified by a four-story, 60-foot tower at its corner entrance. It was built in 1869 for a wealthy Philadelphia coal baron named John McCreary.

The Abbey main house, or Villa, was bought in 1979 by Jay and Marianne Schatz when they retired from careers in chemistry to start a bed-and-breakfast. In 1986, the Schatzes acquired the adjacent property, the Cottage, built in 1873 by McCreary's son George as a family summer home. The narrow Second Empire house, with a convex red mansard roof on its third story, doubled the seven rooms of the Villa and echoes its colors.

Jay and Marianne have collected beautiful antiques over the years and display them throughout the two houses. In addition to antiques, the owners use ornate and impressive period reproduction wallpapers from Bradbury and Bradbury, which hang like artwork on the walls and even the ceilings of the formal parlors and dining room. Some of the plaster medallions are original to the house, and the brass gasoliers and fixtures are from the period. In the front parlor is a Herter Brothers–style parlor set of gilded rosewood from 1860. Musicians will appreciate the square mahogany grand piano from 1850 and the Swiss harp. In the back parlor is a highly crafted Renaissance Revival parlor set in inlaid satinwood and fruitwood.

> **Cape May is a museum of Victorian homes; but even in such a gallery, the Abbey is an architectural masterpiece. With turrets, gables, gingerbread, a widow's walk, and a four story tower topped by a cupola, the Abbey is a fanciful, fantastic place.**

The guest rooms, on the second and third floor of the Villa and throughout three floors of the Cottage, are named for cities. The rooms are vastly different, yet all contain an impressive variety of showroom antiques. Some of the baths are nearly bedroom-sized, unusual in a Victorian house; others are cleverly created from tiny closets. The second floor of the tower has a charming nook of a room with tall, double arched windows on two sides. Those wishing extra privacy might like one of the Cottage rooms; a favorite is the Nantucket Room under the third-floor eaves with a many-sided bathroom with a shower and clawfoot tub.

Afternoon tea is a grand tradition in Cape May. Jay and Marianne like to take this opportunity to chat with guests. Their long tenure in Cape May has made them familiar with the town's history and local events. Breakfasts are full, featuring quiches, stratas, and baked French toast. The town center is just two blocks away, and the beach is a block in the other direction.

The Chalfonte Hotel

301 Howard Street
P.O. Box 475
Cape May, NJ 08204
609-884-8409

> *A family hostelry
> featuring
> home-cooked
> southern dinners*

Proprietors: Anne LeDuc and Judy Bartella. **Accommodations:** 103 rooms, most with shared baths. **Rates:** From $72–$165 per couple MAP. **Included:** Full breakfast, full dinner. **Minimum stay:** 2 nights on weekends, 3 nights on holidays. **Added:** $25 each additional guest, $3–$15 each child in room with parents, 6% tax, $6 gratuity. **Payment:** Visa, MasterCard. **Children:** Welcome; added fees for cots and meals. **Pets:** Not allowed. **Smoking:** Allowed in public rooms. **Open:** May–October.

The Chalfonte is renowned for two reasons: it's the best deal in Cape May, and the meals are legendary. Don't expect the glamour of the other Cape May bed-and-breakfasts. The Chalfonte is bare-bones boarding, with shared baths along long hallways, sparely decorated rooms with a double bed or two, an in-room sink, with very little chintz or lace. Though it may seem uncharacteristic for a Cape May hostelry not to have museum-quality antiques, Chalfonte fixture Eldred Morris explains that when the Victorians came to the shore, their customs were closer to the Chalfonte way than to the luxurious elegance of other local bed-and-breakfasts. The gleaming furniture and ceiling papers belonged in their Philadelphia and New York City homes; their vacation houses were spare and functional.

From the outside, the Chalfonte looks as regal as its Cape May neighbors. Colonel Henry Sawyer, a Civil War hero, built the Chalfonte in 1876 and oversaw its daily activities for 17 years. The hotel was bought by Virginian Susan Satterfield in 1910 and remained in her family until 1980, when the present owners took over. Its three stories of white clapboard are shuttered in green, with its first two levels covered in elaborate gingerbread porches and verandahs. It even has an accessible cupola with four views from arched windows looking to town and to the ocean. Inside, the Chalfonte is spare, simple wood. It is the home of the popular King Edward Bar.

> There are New York, Baltimore, and Philadelphia families for whom the Chalfonte has been a tradition for generations. No doubt the traditional home-cooked southern dinners have worked their way into the fabric of their lives, the spoonbread and buttermilk biscuits calling them back summer after summer.

For more than 70 years until 1990, the meals were orchestrated by the saintly Helen Dickerson, who proudly presided over the Chalfonte's kitchen. Her daughters Dorothy and Lucille have inherited her silver spoon, and Helen's spirit lives on through their cooking and the large, bustling dining room that came into its own during her reign. Included in the rates are a huge Virginia breakfast of spoonbread, buttermilk biscuits, muffins, eggs, fish, and fruit and a hearty southern dinner with a choice of three entrées. The four-course dinner is accompanied by homemade relishes, soups, rolls, vegetables, salads, fruit compotes, and desserts. The menu changes with the day of the week: Monday's menu may include turkey with Virginia ham and oyster dressing or fried scallops with cornmeal breading; Tuesday is roast leg of lamb with mint sauce or deviled crab à la Chalfonte; Thursday could include seafood Newburg or roast pork with apple dressing. Children six and under eat in their own supervised dining room.

The Chalfonte hosts a wonderful tradition each year: volunteer work weekends in exchange for room and board, at the beginning and end of the season. Other in-season themes have prevailed over the years, including quilting, rug hook-ing, and watercolor workshops, two weeks in July and August devoted to children's activities, a mystery weekend, and a Gilbert and Sullivan weekend. There is a lighthearted friendliness about the Chalfonte, like a college reunion or similar convivial event. Those who warm to the rustic informality of the Chalfonte return for generations. Families can book rooms in the Annex and the Howard Street Cottage. The Franklin Street Cottage is good for groups.

The Mainstay Inn

635 Columbia Avenue
Cape May, NJ 08204
609-884-8690

> *Cape May's most authentic, elegant, and original B&B*

Proprietors: Tom and Sue Carroll. **Accommodations:** 16 rooms: 4 rooms and 2 suites in the inn; 5 rooms and 1 suite in the cottage; 4 1- and 2-bedroom suites in Officer's Quarters. **Rates:** $95–$190 weekdays fall–spring; $130–$195 weekends and in summer. **Included:** Full breakfast, afternoon tea. **Minimum stay:** 3 nights in season and on spring and fall weekends. **Added:** 6% tax, $20–$25 for additional guest. **Payment:** No credit cards. **Children:** Welcome in the Officer's Quarters. **Pets:** Not allowed. **Smoking:** Not allowed. **Open:** All year, with limited accommodations in the winter.

The most elegant bed-and-breakfast in a most elegant town, the Mainstay is a legendary place. Tom and Sue Carroll have been the owners and innkeepers of this museum-quality property for more than 20 years, making the Mainstay one of the country's first bed and breakfasts and the Carrolls pioneers in the bed and breakfast industry. To their credit, the Mainstay has maintained its status as the premier property in the region ever since. And they keep innovating: in the summer of 1994 they introduced four new suites in a separate building, with aesthetic links to the Mainstay but modern comforts as well.

The beauty of this bed-and-breakfast starts with the magnificent architecture of Stephen Decatur Button. Built in 1872 as an exclusive entertainment and gambling club for men, the house was designed to represent the height of the era's luxury. Above the two stories of butter yellow clapboards, a cupola crowns the flat roof. The first-floor windows are nearly as high as the 14-foot ceilings, shuttered in forest green with white trim.

> **The consummate Victorian bed-and-breakfast, the Mainstay is a wondrous refuge for sophisticated people who know that travel and compromise need not go hand-in-hand. Every element of this nonpareil property is perfect: from the antiques, to the breakfasts and teas, to the amenities, right down to the gracious hosts. This is how it should be done.**

A deep, lavish single-story porch wraps around three sides of the building, supported by gingerbread pillars, in true Italianate elegance. Inside, the glory continues, with wide plaster moldings, crystal chandeliers, marble mantels, and 12-foot mirrors all designed for the house. Some of the majestic original furnishings are still here, but owners Tom and Sue Carroll have contributed their own finds to this palatial interior in appropriate splendor.

The Carrolls are true professionals. Despite their seasoned ways, they are young, creative, sophisticated, and quite gregarious. It's therefore necessary to take a tour of the house to understand the thoroughness of Tom and Sue's endeavor, from the elaborate wallpapering to the choice of antiques and upholstery to the carefully chosen relics around the house. While the ceiling decorations are a composite of 19 period papers, the walls are hand-painted in a period stencil motif.

The elegant front parlor is filled with Tom and Sue's antiques and lit by the original brass-plated chandelier; the formal drawing room has a collage of ten different period papers specially designed by Bradbury and Bradbury. Many original pieces are displayed throughout the room, including the mirror above the mantel, which matches that in the dining room; a marble-top table and desk; and several sitting pieces. The 1886 Chickering and Sons grand piano is in working order, as is the turn-of-the-century mahogany grandfather clock, which belonged to Tom's grandfather — one of the most recent pieces in the house.

Across the hallway is the dining room, a gathering spot for formal breakfast and afternoon tea. Its large pieces are original, including the 300-pound mirror that hangs above the 500-pound marble-top buffet illuminated by a solid brass Cornelius and Baker chandelier.

Upstairs, the General Grant and Stonewall Jackson suites rest at the back of the house. Of the four front rooms, the Cardinal Gibbons, with an original walnut bedroom suite, is the most often requested. The nimble should climb the steep set of stairs to the cupola.

Fortunately, there is more to the Mainstay. The Carrolls bought the neighboring Cottage in 1980, built a century earlier by the same architect who built the main house. The tall, narrow three-story villa has a double-story porch running the width of the building. The yellow clapboard echoes its sister property, but the maroon shutters and celery trim are distinctive. A parlor features wicker furniture and period magazine drawings of Cape May. Several of the six guest rooms have porches.

The newest but still historic addition to the Mainstay is the Officer's Quarters, which celebrated its first summer in 1994. Across the street from the main house, the Officer's Quarters is the former home of a World War I Navy officer, offering a living room with a gas fireplace, a kitchenette, a color television and VCR, and a whirlpool tub and shower.

The food is as elegant as the decor at the Mainstay, with endless cookies and cakes at teatime and beautifully prepared full breakfasts. Tom and Sue are some of the most gracious and intelligent hosts in the business. Be sure to reserve months ahead for a perfect sojourn here.

The Queen Victoria

102 Ocean Street
Cape May, NJ 08204
609-884-8702

*A Victorian B&B
with modern
comforts*

Proprietors: Dane and Joan Wells. **Accommodations:** 23 rooms, including 6 deluxe suites, in Queen Victoria, Prince Albert Hall, and 3 cottages; all with private bath, some with whirlpools. **Rates:** Rooms $75–$208, suites $115–$250. **Included:** Full breakfast, full afternoon tea. **Minimum stay:** 2 or 3 nights on holidays and weekends. **Added:** $20 each additional guest, 6% tax. **Payment:** Visa, Master-Card. **Children:** Welcome. **Pets:** Not allowed. **Smoking:** Allowed on porches. **Open:** All year.

The Queen Victoria is one of the prettiest and most professional of Cape May's bed-and-breakfasts. It stands out among its colleagues for two reasons: it welcomes children and is fully open all year. While filled with precious antiques, the Queen Victoria is not a velvet-rope property. Here, modern convenience meets Victorian splendor; whirlpool baths, in-room refrigerators, and electric blankets happily coexist with 19th-century oak bedroom sets, marble-top dressers, and rare Stickley mission furniture.

Dane and Joan worked in Philadelphia, he as manager of the Main Street revitalization program and she as executive director of the Victorian Society of America, jobs that well prepared them for restoring and running a B&B. Their gregarious, warm-hearted natures further qualified them for their new life, which they began in 1980 in Cape May.

The Queen Victoria was built in 1882 on a site one block from the beach; Prince Albert Hall was built six months later. In addition to these are three cottages. Together they add up to a surprisingly large property that retains the intimacy of a much smaller B&B.

> **Dane and Joan Wells have carved a unique niche for themselves in Cape May. Their home and three cottages feature lovely Victorian antiques, creative and elegant afternoon tea; but the Wellses also supply creature comforts including whirlpool tubs, televisions, refrigerators, and accommodations for kids, and they are open all year.**

The Queen Victoria is a light jade color, with a cedar shingle red mansard roof. Two double-story bay windows flank the entrance. The porch holds some of the inn's 50 trademark green rockers with yellow caning and leads to the adjacent Prince Albert Hall, a buttery yellow with jade and red accents. On its third-floor roof at the back of the house, a generous sun deck provides great views of the town and ocean.

All the rooms have traditional B&B decor, with handmade Mennonite quilts, Oriental rugs, canopy beds, and decorative Victorian antiques such as a tufted slipper chair or an Eastlake settee. The rooms are serviced twice daily, with custom-made chocolates at turndown. Electric blankets are provided in winter, and some rooms have refrigerators and whirlpool tubs. Pantries in the two guest houses provide a bottomless supply of popcorn, ice, snacks, and drinks.

Dane and Joan are justifiably proud of the breakfasts over which they preside, when guests gather and chat about Cape May and their plans. The meal can go on for hours in each of two houses around the expansive antique dining tables. Unfinished stories will continue at afternoon tea, where home-baked sweets and savories are served. To work off the meal, guests may borrow bicycles at no charge.

The Virginia Hotel

25 Jackson Street
Cape May, NJ 08204
609-884-5700
Fax: 609-884-1236

> *A luxurious
> inn-sized hotel
> on Cape May*

Proprietors: Curtis Bashaw. **General Managers:** Margie Rovira. **Accommodations:** 24 rooms, all with private bath. **Rates:** $80–$180 standard, $100–$250 premium. **Included:** Continental breakfast, morning newspaper. **Minimum stay:** 2–3 nights on weekends and some holidays. **Added:** $20 each additional guest, 6% tax. **Payment:** Major credit cards. **Children:** Welcome. **Pets:** Not allowed. **Smoking:** Allowed. **Open:** Year-round.

For those who love Cape May but not the intimacy of bed-and-breakfast travel, the Virginia is an ideal place to stay. Though its 24 guest rooms make it the size of some of the larger bed-and-breakfasts, the Virginia is a small luxury hotel, with cosmopolitan, sophisticated service. In addition, its Ebbitt Room is one of the finest restaurants in this seaside resort town.

The Virginia even looks like a Victorian bed-and-breakfast. A flat-roofed, three-story structure in white clapboard, it boasts a magnificent double-story verandah covered in gingerbread. Built in 1879 by Alfred and Ellen Ebbitt as a hotel, this property was Cape May's first to be open year-round, with steam heat. It's a half block from town and a block to the beach in the other direction. It remained an active hotel until the 1980s, when it lay vacant for seven years.

Curtis Bashaw bought the dilapidated building in 1988 and undertook an extensive restoration. All the artwork of history had been stripped from the hotel's exterior in the 1950s, and Bashaw and his architect pieced it back together, reconstructing the lattice and gingerbread from a 1912 postcard of the hotel. The 112-year-old stained glass casts colorful light on the interior stairwell. Three of the baths are original to the hotel, on stilts at the side of the building, and renovated to modern standards. When the Virginia reopened in 1989, its exterior had been faithfully restored to its 19th-century days, and its interior had become an elegant full-service hotel.

> **Couples come to the Virginia Hotel to get to know each other — not innkeepers and fellow travelers. From the street, it looks like the other elegant Victorian homes throughout town, and it has an excellent Victorian dining room. But the rooms are sophisticated, contemporary, and sublime.**

The guest rooms are all slightly different, decorated in chic postmodern cleanliness. The walls are a sedate beige, often papered in a Bradbury and Bradbury Victorian reproduction sponge print in similar soothing hues of beiges and creams. The custom-made cherry beds are covered in down comforters with raw silk duvets and thick cotton sheeting. The armoires, housing televisions and even VCRs, are a sandwashed light wood. Terry robes are provided in gleaming compact baths. The standard rooms have queen-size beds, and the larger, better-located premium rooms have kings, three of which open onto the graceful verandah. Room service and nightly turndown are available.

Dinner in the Ebbitt Room is an elegant affair offering new American cuisine ranging from $16.50 to $23 a plate. Chef Christopher Hubert might prepare rack of lamb in a honey thyme *jus*, with white bean cassoulet; or pan-roasted lobster tail in a sauce chinoise, with braised red cabbage and ginger confit.

SPRING LAKE

Hewitt Wellington

200 Monmouth Avenue
Spring Lake, NJ 07762
908-974-1212
Fax: 908-974-2338

> *A luxury property
> in Spring Lake*

Proprietors: Hewitt Wellington Condo-Hotel Association. **General Manager:** Cindy Woolley. **Accommodations:** 29 rooms, including 12 suites. **Rates:** Low season $70–$120 weekdays, $90–$150 weekends; high season $110–$200 weekdays, $140–$220 weekends. **Included:** Continental breakfast, beach passes in season. **Minimum stay:** 2 nights on summer weekends. **Added:** $10 each additional guest, 6% tax. **Payment:** Visa, MasterCard, American Express. **Children:** Over 12. **Pets:** Not allowed. **Smoking:** Limited. **Open:** April 1 through October, weekends only in November and December.

The Hewitt Wellington Hotel, thoroughly facelifted in 1988, is a great example of the Old World wealth that has defined Spring Lake for the last century. In 1875, a development group called the Spring Lake Beach Improvement Company set out to build some grand hotels. They built the Hewitt Wellington at the south end of the lake from which the town took its name. In fact, there are a number of grand hotels around town as a result of these turn-of-the-century development plans, most of which have gone bankrupt over the years, palatial mansions faded like Tara after the Civil War. Fortunately for the Hewitt Wellington, CT Investments, Inc. bought the property in 1987 and saved it from demise.

The hotel is a marriage of two houses connected by a newly constructed breezeway, one facing east, the other facing south, both in fresh white clapboards in the Queen Anne style, with turrets, wraparound porches, and some subtle gingerbread, topped by a green shingle roof.

> **They don't make places like this anymore. Bigger than a mansion, more like a beachside castle with turrets and porches, the Hewitt Wellington represents Spring Lake at the turn of the century. Inside, however, are all the comforts of a modern hotel.**

The hotel has an elegant and pristine atmosphere, much like a country club; the service is formal and elite. In fact, the property is a condominium hotel, though transient guests make up a large percentage of the hotel's business. The rooms are decorated with reproduction furnishings, with four-poster beds and wing chairs in traditional dark woods, televisions, telephones, and luxurious marble baths. Some rooms have balconies overlooking the lake or the ocean. The Hewitt Wellington has the elegance of a large hotel but the intimacy of a country inn, as there are only four to six rooms per floor.

Aside from beach activities, Spring Lake is a historic town worthy of an extended stay, its Victorian railroad depot recently restored and used by the Jersey Shore Coast Lines. Nearby is the Garden State Arts Center for music, Monmouth Park and Freehold racetracks, several golf courses and public tennis courts, and the Great Adventure amusement park and Allaire State Park.

Hollycroft

P.O. Box 448
Spring Lake, NJ 07762
908-681-2254

> *A beach cottage
> and Arts and
> Crafts log cabin*

Proprietors: Linda and Mark Fessler. **Accommodations:** 7 rooms, all with private bath, 2 with fireplace, 2 with balcony. **Rates:** $95–$135 May–September, $85–$125 rest of year. **Included:** Expanded Continental breakfast. **Minimum stay:** 2 nights on weekends, 3 nights on holidays. **Added:** 6% tax. **Payment:** American Express. **Children:** Over 12 welcome. **Pets:** Not allowed. **Smoking:** Not allowed. **Open:** All year.

The New Jersey coastline is full of pleasant surprises. Here, on the cusp of South Belmar and Spring Lake, still above Atlantic City, is a wonderful bed-and-breakfast called Hollycroft. Several blocks from the lovely beach on an inlet called Lake Como, Hollycroft is an enchanting piece of architecture, built in 1908 as a log cabin in the Arts and Crafts style.

While the towns along the Jersey shore sit amid flat, scrubby beach growth, Hollycroft's is a wooded setting of bramble, bushes, and trees. Its first floor is tightly stacked ironstone, and the second story is Tudor.

It seems fitting that a rare Arts and Crafts house would belong to an architect, but Mark Fessler was lucky. The house was built in the turn of the century by the Ripleys as a summer retreat and remained in the family until Linda and Mark

Fessler bought it in 1985. The house is built of cedar and pine, with exposed ceiling beams, creating a rustic Adirondack feel. The ironstone was quarried from what is now neighboring Allaire State Park, home of Allaire historic village. The interior space is a fascinating collection of low-ceilinged areas separated by open-beamed doorways, with the particular intimacy of a mountain log cabin.

> You'll be pleasantly surprised when you arrive at Hollycroft. Where other area houses are clapboard and shingle cottages, your bed-and-breakfast is an architectural treasure in the true Arts and Crafts style: a log cabin near the beach.

The common room is an enclosed brick patio with pretty green velvet couches and chintz chairs with full views of the woods outside. The dining room is a concert hall of cedar and pine. The mantel of the large stone fireplace is adorned with an enormous English porcelain delft bowl that was on display at the Philadelphia Exhibition in 1876. Two mirroring stairways embrace the fireplace and meet above on a landing. One side of the second-floor hallway overlooks the stairs like a balcony; the other side leads to four guest rooms.

The rooms were given English names, contributing to the feel of an English country house. The Ambleside and Windsor Rose have breezy porches. All rooms have antique beds — some canopied — with pretty linens, lovely European lace window treatments, and several important antiques as focal points. The Grassmere and Somerset rooms have their own fireplaces. Linda made a lot of the crafts in the house: the quilts, the stenciled washstands, and throw pillows. The baths are immaculate and lovely, and rooms are sweetened by chocolates and graced with a gift of Perrier and sherry.

Linda, a former New York City copywriter, loves her job as an innkeeper. In or out of beach season, there are other activities besides the shore, which is just a few blocks away: a freshwater lake across the street; Allaire State Park and Sandy Hook/Twin Lights National Park; nearby Englishtown has the largest flea market on the East Coast, and there's an antique center at Red Bank; and the Great Adventure amusement park is a short drive away.

The Normandy Inn

21 Tuttle Avenue
Spring Lake, NJ 07762
908-449-7172
Fax: 908-449-1070

*A Victorian
choice in
Spring Lake*

Proprietors: Michael and Susan Ingino. **Innkeeper:** Anne Marie Boyle.
Accommodations: 17 rooms, all with private bath, including 2 suites. **Rates:** $102–$235 Memorial Day weekend, weekends in June and September, and from July through August; $82–$185 rest of year. **Included:** Full breakfast. **Minimum stay:** 3 nights on July and August weekends; 2 nights midweek July and August. **Added:** $20 each additional adult guest; children under 10, $10; 6% tax. **Payment:** Major credit cards. **Children:** Welcome. **Pets:** Not allowed. **Smoking:** Limited. **Open:** All year.

While most of the large houses in elegant Spring Lake are of the conservative grand Queen Anne style, with wide calm porches, a turret or two, and cool white clapboards, one in particular makes a stunning contrast, as if swept from the southern shores of high Victorian Cape May. The Normandy Inn is a three-story olive clapboard with a square wraparound porch on the first floor, another inset porch on the second floor, and a series of grand, puzzling, round and arched windows punctuating its exterior, culminating in a fourth-story square cupola. The two porches and many levels to the house give a large role to the red shingled rooftop, which reappears at different stories.

The Normandy Inn was built before 1889 and moved to its

present location near the beach around 1906, shortly before it became a guest house. The tradition continued, albeit informally, for more than 70 years, until Michael and Susan Ingino bought the property in 1982 to satisfy their loves for innkeeping and for antiques. Over the years, they have continued to add to their vast collection, searching for period wallpaper, furniture, light fixtures, and decorative pieces — right down to the Victorian urn on the front lawn. The only reproductions found at the Normandy Inn are the period wallpapers from Schumacher and the lovely flowered rug that traipses through the halls.

> While rooms feature some outstanding antiques, there is a common link at the Normandy Inn: lighting fixtures. Michael and Susan Inigo are avid antique collectors, but their passion is lighting. Here, a good lamp, chandelier, sconce, or globe can make a room.

Michael and Susan redo about three rooms every year. There are eight rooms each on the second and third floors, with a wonderful, creative tower room in the cupola. While those at the front are larger than those in back, all the guest rooms have unusual pieces: an 1850 four-poster bed in southern style with a gathered silk canopy; a four-piece 1870 Renaissance Revival bedroom set including a nine-foot headboard of walnut and burl; two brass French twins, with a German regulator clock. Throughout, every room has a lavish Victorian chandelier or globed lamps or sconces. The wallpapers are deep paisleys and patterns or boldly bordered in complementary patterns. Commendably, the baths are large and useful — an accomplishment in an old Victorian.

Breakfasts are a popular occasion at the Normandy Inn and are open to the public by reservation. In the large, convivial dining room, several full courses are served on fine china. Specialties include hot Irish porridge, chocolate chip pancakes, and, for the adventurous, Mexican omelettes with homemade salsa. Of the two common rooms, the front parlor is decorated with a rare six-piece 1870 Renaissance Revival set in the Jeliffe style, surrounded by artifacts, sculpture, clocks, and curios. Guests relax here or on the sweeping, wicker-filled wraparound porches, which are within a minute's walk of the beach.

Sea Crest by the Sea

19 Tuttle Avenue
Spring Lake, NJ 07762
908-449-9031
800-803-9031

> *A B&B enlivened by pampering and special themes*

Proprietors: John and Carol Kirby. **Accommodations:** 12 rooms, including 1 suite, all with private bath. **Rates:** $115–$239 mid-May–September, $92–$189 rest of year. **Included:** Full breakfast and afternoon tea. **Minimum stay:** 3 nights on July and August weekends and holidays; 2 nights midweek in July and August and low-season weekends. **Added:** 6% tax. **Payment:** Visa, MasterCard. **Children:** Not allowed. **Pets:** Not allowed. **Smoking:** Not allowed. **Open:** All year.

Though Spring Lake's two finest bed-and-breakfasts are neighbors, the Normandy Inn and Sea Crest by the Sea don't really overlap. While the former is a more formal setting for seasoned bed-and-breakfasters and antiques lovers, Sea Crest has a pampered intimacy and playful elegance. Most of the rooms have themes: Casablanca has a rattan bedroom set and a curtain of beads at the doorway, Mardi Gras has masks decorating the walls, and Yankee Clipper is a tribute to the owner's days in the Merchant Marines. Though theme rooms often result in a certain cuteness, here it means a thoughtful decor. All is done in the finest of taste: exceptionally memorable bedding, chocolates at turndown, and, throughout, interesting family heirlooms and lovely Victorian French and English antiques.

The Kirbys were determined to make bed-and-breakfasting

a second career and searched along the Jersey shore for the perfect place. They found the Sea Crest, a well-worn 35-room hostelry of 50 years, several houses from the two-mile-long boardwalk on Spring Lake's beachfront. This 1885 Victorian house was perfect, and they bought it on Valentine's Day 1990 and have invested much work in its restoration. Today, it stands as a white clapboard inn with peach shutters, three stories topped by a center turret flanked by a pair of cozy dormers, with a blue and white striped awning shading the length of the first-floor porch.

> The Kirbys really love what they do; very likely, their guests will come to feel the same way during a stay at Sea Crest by the Sea. Their secret is in the bedding, the stunning centerpiece of every room. The linens could not be more sumptuous, more luxurious.

The comfortable library is complemented by a formal living room, with elegant tapestry chairs set around the gas fireplace, where afternoon tea — and the inn's specialty of white chocolate cheesecake — is served to the tunes of a player piano. The dining room, where guests have a full breakfast, is centered on an 1870s French table. The menu changes daily but may include fresh fruit and homemade granola, buttermilk scones with marmalade and clotted cream, banana bread, cinnamon raisin bread, baked honey walnut French toast, and special Scandinavian blend coffee.

The seven guest rooms on the second floor and five on the third have private baths and the best-quality queen-size beds draped in down quilts with fine cotton duvet covers. Tiny televisions are hidden in each guest room. The Victorian Rose and the Sleighride have gas fireplaces, the former with an 1880s American walnut bed. Family heirlooms throughout the house include John's family's deed from West Virginia in the George Washington Room, a window in which is draped with a flag swag.

The Kirbys are joyous owners, enamored of Spring Lake and their new duties as innkeepers.

WOODBINE

The Henry Ludlam Inn

1336 Route 47
Woodbine, NJ 08270
609-861-5847

*An ideal spot
for birders
and B&Bers*

Proprietors: Marty and Ann Thurlow. **Accommodations:** 5 rooms, 3 with private bath. **Rates:** $75–$110. **Included:** Full breakfast, wine and sherry on arrival. **Minimum stay:** 2 nights July and August. **Added:** $20 each additional guest, 6% tax. **Payment:** MasterCard, Visa, American Express. **Children:** Over 12 welcome. **Pets:** Not allowed. **Smoking:** Not allowed. **Open:** All year.

Five miles inland between Atlantic City and Cape May is a quaint, romantic bed-and-breakfast characterized by creative cooking and antique beds dressed in featherbeds and handmade quilts. Though set on busy Route 47, the Henry Ludlam Inn is rooted in the country, with its lovely grounds, Adirondack chairs, proprietary geese, and a gazebo overlooking 56-acre Henry Ludlam Lake. Parts of this sweet old house were built in 1740 and still have the old wide-plank floors. The Federal three-story front was added in 1800, and today the house is a smart-looking gray with maroon trim.

Ann and Marty Thurlow bought the house in 1983, realizing their lifelong dream of opening a bed-and-breakfast. They restored and decorated the house themselves, naming the property after an area lawyer who was one of the social founders of Cape May County. Victoriana was left in nearby

Cape May; this bed-and-breakfast leans more toward Pennsylvania country colonial. The common room is in the charming 18th-century part of the house, used as a sitting room with wooden banquettes. In the Federal part of the house is a pretty breakfast area where colonial tables are warmed by one of the original fireplaces.

> At its southernmost point, New Jersey has a tail 20 miles long and 10 miles wide that dangles into the ocean. The Henry Ludlam Inn splits the difference between the Atlantic on its east and the Delaware Bay to the west, with beaches, bird sanctuaries, museums, and history in all directions.

While most travelers neglect the New Jersey coastline in the colder months, the Henry Ludlam is highly desirable at this time of year, especially for guests who take Ann's six-course gourmet dinners on autumn and winter Saturday nights ($37). Featherbeds adorn antique beds, and three of the five guest rooms have fireplaces, including the first-floor Wicker Room and, on the second, the Pine and Oak rooms, with lovely views. Though they have no fireplaces and share a small bath, the cozy third-floor rooms are adorable, set under the eaves, their walls of exposed brick from the fireplaces downstairs. The pitched ceiling in the Linden Room is of pickled pine; its window seat overlooks the lake with the help of a telescope, also used for birding.

Upon arrival, guests are greeted with a tray of two splits of wine and glasses. Marty also makes picnic baskets for $25, filled with wine, sandwiches, cheese, fruits, and dessert — a romantic meal, especially when taken in a canoe on Ludlam Lake or fireside in winter. Morning is announced by the smells of a hearty and healthy breakfast that may feature cardamom French toast, honey rum syrup, and poached pears.

Guests may fish in Ludlam Lake, and they don't have to venture far for other activities. Some of the many attractions include the beach in Stone Harbor; Victorian walks in Cape May and its County Zoo, Historical Society, and the Physick Estate; 50-acre Leamings Run, an arboreal sanctuary; bird-watching in Stone Harbor's Bird Sanctuary and Wetlands Institute; historic sights in 18th-century Cold Spring Village and Bridgeton; Belle Plain State Park; and Wheaton Village, for a history of glassmaking.

New York

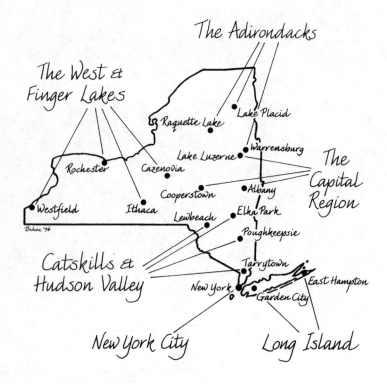

The Adirondacks

The West &
Finger Lakes

The
Capital
Region

Catskills &
Hudson Valley

New York City

Long Island

Raquette Lake

Lake Placid

Lake Luzerne

Warrensburg

Rochester

Cazenovia

Cooperstown

Albany

Westfield

Ithaca

Lewbeach

Elka Park

Poughkeepsie

Tarrytown

East Hampton

New York

Garden City

Bahme '94

The country's second most populous state has more than 18 million people, spread over 47,000 square miles; yet more than half its occupants live in a handful of square miles around New York Harbor at the base of the Hudson. In 1609, Henry Hudson discovered his river, and Samuel de Champlain discovered his lake. The Dutch followed, settling Albany in 1614 and Manhattan in 1626. New York offers the best of all the Mid-Atlantic states in one state: the largest city and several great smaller ones; the longest stretch of the finest beaches; the Adirondacks and Catskill mountains, unsurpassed in wilderness beauty; vineyards in the Finger Lakes as well as on Long Island as fine and varied as those in Virginia; access to two Great Lakes and, of course, Niagara Falls; and more lakes than any other Mid-Atlantic state.

For New York travel information, 800-CALLNYS, or 518-474-4116.

The Adirondacks

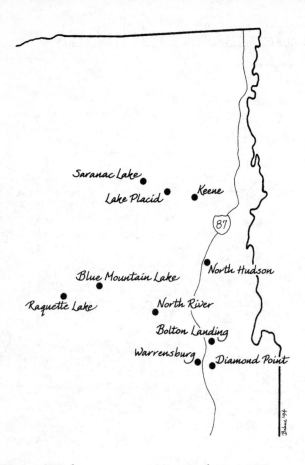

Best Gourmet Getaways

Lake Placid
Lake Placid Lodge
Saranac Lake
The Point

Best Resort

Bolton Landing
The Sagamore, an Omni Classic Resort

Best Remote Refuges

Blue Mountain Lake
The Hedges
Hemlock Hall
North Hudson
Elk Lake Lodge
North River
Garnet Hill Lodge
Raquette Lake
Sagamore Lodge

Best Country Inns

Diamond Point
Canoe Island Lodge
Keene
The Bark Eater

Best Village Bed-and-Breakfast

Warrensburg
Bent Finial Manor

Best Village Inn

Lake Placid
Mirror Lake Inn

The Adirondacks are the state's most precious and uninvaded refuge, 6 million acres of wilderness with more than 2,000 lakes and 45 mountains over 4,000 feet tall. In addition to the incredible beauty of its forests, the Adirondacks have one of the state's finest museums, the Adirondack Museum in **Blue Mountain Lake.** The Adirondacks begin at Glens Falls, stretch up to Plattsburgh to the north, and are introduced by Old Forge in the west, famous for its Hardware Store, a cultural enclave in the wilderness.

The azure waters of Lake George begin shortly after Glens Falls, reaching about 40 miles to Fort Ticonderoga and its restored 18th-century military complex, which sits on the lower waters of Lake Champlain. Lake George Village is quite touristy, but several miles north, grace returns in **Diamond Point** and at the famous Sagamore Resort in **Bolton Landing.** The drive along the lake is magnificent, and at its end, at Fort Ticonderoga, the drive north continues with gorgeous scenery, all the way to Westport. A trek westward plunges immediately from water to mountains, past **Keene** to **Lake Placid** and its abundance of winter and water sports.

Lake Placid introduces a traveler to the Great Camps along Route 30, which bends west and then south. At the turn of the century, with the increased leisure and wealth provided by the enlightened industrial age, New York City financiers and magnates conquered the northern wilderness. They built, with lavish abandon, the rustic, highly crafted Adirondack Great Camps, playgrounds of the opulent, where the pampered "roughed it" in a most civilized manner. Route 30 is the best avenue from which to see some of these estates. The architecture is abundant, recognizable, beautiful, and entirely specific to the area. The drive takes one from Lake Placid to Lower and **Upper Saranac Lakes,** past Tupper Lake, down to Blue Mountain Lake and the Adirondack Museum, west to **Raquette Lake** and Sagamore Lodge, the great camp of the Vanderbilts. West of Racquette Lake is Old Forge, the western gateway to the Adirondacks.

Quite a distance, though well worth the trip, is a visit to the Thousand Islands at Alexandria Bay, dotting the St. Lawrence River across from Canada. Boldt Castle, on Heart Island in the bay, was only partially built by magnate George C. Boldt when his wife died in 1904. He was too heartbroken to complete the mansion, and it remains today a sad tribute to his love. About a half hour's drive south is the Frederic Remington Museum, in his home town of Ogdensburg.

BLUE MOUNTAIN LAKE

The Hedges

Blue Mountain Lake, NY 12812
518-352-7325
518-352-7672

> *The historic,
> formal side of
> Blue Mountain
> Lake*

Proprietors: Dick and Cathy van Yperen. **Accommodations:** 6 rooms in Stone Lodge, 4 rooms in Main Lodge, 14 1- to 4-bedroom cottages.
Rates: $58–$70 per person MAP; seasonal and midweek discounts. **Included:** Two meals, use of all boats and facilities.
Minimum stay: One week in July and August. **Added:** $40 each additional adult, $20–$30 each additional child; 7% tax.
Payment: No credit cards. **Children:** Welcome. **Pets:** Not allowed. **Smoking:** Allowed in rooms only. **Open:** June 14–Columbus Day.

Set on the lapping shores of Blue Mountain Lake, the Hedges is a pristine, rather formal family retreat. The elegant architecture of the Main Lodge and dining room is thoroughly faithful to an Adirondack Great Camp, and the lakeside cottages are picture-perfect log cabins. The Hedges sits at eye level with Blue Mountain Lake, with a tiny beach and 1,500 feet of grassy lakefront. The 12 acres of grounds are well groomed, consistent with the air of formal rusticity.

The Hedges has an interesting history. The Main Lodge was built as a retreat for Colonel Hiriam B. Duryea, who after a highly successful career in the Civil War made his fortune as president of the National Starch Company, with the help of his brilliant son Chester, who invented cornstarch. Duryea had this upstate estate built by 1892 and several years later added the Stone Lodge for another son. Duryea's demise was tragic: he was murdered by his son Chester.

> **There are two great inns on Blue Mountain Lake. Hemlock Hall is the place to go with young kids. Although children are welcome at the Hedges, this is a good place to go when the kids and the parents are traveling together as friends.**

In 1920, the estate was sold for $22,000 at auction to Richard Collins, a caretaker for the Vanderbilt family at their nearby great camp, the Sagamore in Raquette Lake. Collins built the dining room in 1924 for his guests, and the cottages followed in the 1930s. The Hedges remained in the Collins family until 1972, when the van Yperens began their long and successful tenure here.

The Stone House, made from hand-cut stone, topped with a roof of imported cypress shingle, has beautiful interior woodwork, coffered light wood ceilings, and several working terra cotta fireplaces. The first floor is home to an unusual three-room suite with a private porch. Upstairs are five guest rooms, two with wonderful water views.

The Main Lodge is an enchanting, rambling Adirondack camp structure, a masterful gallery of woodwork, with elaborate wall and ceiling paneling. Its large wraparound porch is characteristic of the architecture, with unfinished pillars supporting the heavy second floor, the rail, wrapped in its original bark, just feet from the lake, and curved lawns undulating around its banks flecked with white Adirondack chairs. Upstairs, the grandest of the four lovely rooms is the Colonel Duryea Room, with a stunning original window seat nestled into carved woodwork in a bay window.

The cabins that line the lakefront are charming: the first three are cut log; the following two are knotty pine; the last three are shingle with sleeping lofts, two bedrooms, and a living area and are situated around a little beach.

The dining room is a wonderful structure in itself, consisting of two large rooms with tin walls, a 10-foot tin ceiling, and a polished wood floor underfoot, all warmed by a huge stone fireplace. One entrée is served nightly, in formal service, with waitresses and white linens. On view is the original oak breakfast table and a 19th-century Adirondack guideboat strapped to the wall.

Guests can use any of the large number of canoes and boats or play on the clay tennis court. Nearby is the Adirondack Museum, an upstate cultural mecca, and 60 miles of trails including a hike up 3,800-foot Blue Mountain. Daily tours are led through Sagamore, a short, lovely drive away.

Hemlock Hall

Blue Mountain Lake, NY 12812
518-352-7706
518-359-9065

The informal, family side of Blue Mountain Lake

Proprietors: Paul and Susan Provost. **Accommodations:** 8 rooms in main house, 5 with private bath; 14 cottage and motel units. **Rates:** $93–$123 per couple MAP, June 16–September; rest of year $80–$111 per couple. **Included:** Breakfast and dinner, use of boats. **Minimum stay:** 3 nights preferred. **Added:** $30 each additional adult, $20 each additional child age 2–8, 7% tax. **Payment:** No credit cards. **Children:** Welcome. **Pets:** Not allowed. **Smoking:** Limited. **Open:** May 15–October 15.

Where the Hedges, across Blue Mountain Lake, is somewhat formal in its rusticity, Hemlock Hall is entirely without pretension — a place where kids let loose and parents don't worry. This informal setting is ideal for small children and active families. The tone of the Adirondack lodge is camp, set by owner Paul Provost, a self-admitted overgrown child, who loves life, his family, and this property.

Paul vacationed at Hemlock Hall with his family from age three and had always wanted to own the place. In 1986, he and his wife, Susan, were able to buy this Adirondack camp, which had been welcoming guests since 1949. Paul is simply thrilled, expressing glee at times with his loon call, reportedly one of the best in the area.

> **Hemlock Hall is the kind of place that kids remember all their lives: Blue Mountain Lake, family dinners, and sheer freedom. Paul Provost spent summers here as a child and decided to buy Hemlock Hall as an adult, so he'd never have to leave.**

Dinner is announced by a big outdoor bell, and because every kid gets a chance to ring the bell, the process may go on for five minutes. Guests eat family style on Blue Willow china, sitting on twig chairs at one round table in the older part of the house and around five tables in the 1960 wooden addition, which overlooks the backyard streams to the lakefront. Freshly baked bread accompanies the evening's single entrée: lamb on Monday, roast pork on Tuesday, chicken and biscuits on Wednesday, corned beef on Thursday, cured ham with haddock fillet on Friday, a turkey dinner on Saturday, and a big roast beef on Sunday afternoon. There is no alcohol at Hemlock Hall.

The Adirondack Victorian Main House was built in 1890. From the original twig rockers on the wraparound porch, guests look out over carved paths and green lawns to Blue Mountain Lake. Inside are two lovely cedar- and pine-paneled common rooms. Pretty window seats are tucked in several bay windows. The granite fireplace is the house's center, opening in three directions: to the round table in the dining room, to the entry foyer, and to the sitting room, which contains its only working hearth.

The upstairs rooms work well for couples. The rooms have the original French diamond-paned leaded windows, some of which open to the pleasant sounds of the brook beside the house. Set under lovely gables and pitched eaves, each room is different, cheerful and rustic, some with canoe canvas for walls painted in artistic pastels.

The cabins scattered throughout the property are fun and informal. They have one to several bedrooms, and some have fireplaces. Those nearer the lakefront are more desirable and best suited to families. The lakefront offers a pretty, narrow beach, with many canoes, rowboats, and sailboats and a swimming dock.

Fishing is highly rewarding at Blue Mountain Lake, excellent for large- and smallmouth bass and rainbow and brown trout. Sixty miles of hiking trails are etched throughout the area, including an exciting walk to Blue Mountain's 3,800-foot summit. Well worth a visit is the Adirondack Museum, within a short walk of Hemlock Hall, sure to take up the entirety of a rainy day.

BOLTON LANDING

The Sagamore, An Omni Classic Resort

110 Sagamore Road, On Lake
   George
Bolton Landing, NY 12814
518-644-9400
Fax: 518-644-2851
800-358-3585 or 800-THE-OMNI

> *The most breathtaking resort
> in the state*

Proprietor: Green Island Associates. **General Manager:** W. Robert McIntosh. **Accommodations:** 100 in hotel, including 46 suites; 240 in lodge units, including 120 suites with fireplaces and the 10 bi-level lakeside suites of Hermitage Executive Retreat. **Rates:** Rates are EP; MAP also available. Hotel rooms $79–$300, lodge rooms $79–$170; hotel suites $119–$295, lodge suites $149–$400. **Minimum stay:** None. **Added:** $4 per person service charge; 7% tax or 12% tax over $100; $99 MAP for adults over 19, $36 MAP for children 6–18. **Payment:** Major credit cards. **Children:** Welcome. **Pets:** Not allowed. **Smoking:** Allowed. **Open:** All year.

The Sagamore has one of the most breathtaking resort settings in the East. It sits on an island in the middle of azure

Lake George, across a causeway from the village of Bolton Landing. There have been several incarnations of the graceful Sagamore resort, though all recall an Old World magnificence from the days of Pullman cars and sojourns lasting months. The first was built in the English Tudor style in 1881–1882 and accommodated about 300 guests, including *New York Times* publisher Adolph Ochs and photographer Alfred Stieglitz. When it burned to the ground a decade later, the Sagamore was quickly replaced with a modern structure outfitted with electricity, Western Union wires, steam elevators, and private baths. This time, the hotel managed to elude destruction by fire for 20 years, until Easter Sunday 1914.

> **The Sagamore floats on Lake George as if in a dream. High above the azure waters on a 70-acre island, the whitewashed grand resort hotel was built in 1922 for the wealthiest people in the East. Its shape is winged — a wonderful symbol of hospitality that makes it seem as if the Sagamore is embracing its guests.**

The present structure was built in 1922, a 100-room clubhouse. In 1981, the hotel underwent a major expansion. The classic 1930 white clapboard building looks as it always did, facing downlake from its perch on a tiered grassy hill, shaped like a bow tie. The three stories of white clapboard are trimmed in black, with several lower levels trenched into the hill. One hundred guest rooms remain in the refurbished 1930 hotel, and 240 new units were added in seven contemporary lodges along the tree-lined shore behind the hotel. An exciting addition was the transformation of the nightclub into extensive spa facilities in 1991.

The common areas at the Sagamore are just beautiful, offering views of the lake through an endless number of windows from different angles. The appointments are classic and traditional, and every cornice, chair rail, and archway seems to be gleaming with a fresh coat of paint. There are six restaurants: from the pool and golf eateries, to Mister Brown's pub setting, to the large Sagamore Dining Room and the ladylike Veranda for high tea and early evening hors d'oeuvres, to the elegant Trillium.

Above the main hallway and in the four-story wings, the guest rooms in the hotel are done in classic or Adirondack style; the latter are fewer but more interesting. The rooms are quite smart and new-looking, with a touch of Omni-ubiquitous decor that is, thankfully, enlivened by the magnificent views. Families and groups may prefer the Lodge units, done in contemporary or Adirondack decor, half with living rooms, wet bars, wood-burning fireplaces, and terraces.

At the new Spa and Fitness Center, guests look out over the lake while working out on the 10-station Keiser Training Circuit, stairmasters, Lifecycles, windracers, rowers, and treadmills. The heated indoor-outdoor pool is open year-round. The spa offers many therapeutic treatments including Moortherapy, a mud wrap used in full-body, masks, and scalp treatments. Other offerings include European facials, salt-glo and loofah scrub, herbal wraps, seaweed body mask, foot reflexology, hydrotherapy, and salon services. Therapists offer four types of massage; saunas, steam rooms, whirlpools, and hot and cold plunge pools complete the facilities.

Several miles from the Sagamore is the par 70 Donald Ross golf course: 18 holes, 6,950 yards on 188 acres, overlooking the lake, and offering breathtaking views all year, especially in the fall when the leaves turn. By the Lodge units, the Tennis Club has two indoor and five outdoor courts of Har-Tru or hard surface and a racquetball court. Winter activities abound: cross-country skiing, ice skating, ice fishing, sledding, and daily shuttle service to the Gore and West mountains. For a fee, guests enjoy water skiing, surfing, sailing, and parasailing. A thorough summer children's program provides a plethora of activity for kids from 3 to 13.

DIAMOND POINT

Canoe Island Lodge

Box 144
Diamond Point, NY 12824
518-668-5592
Fax: 518-668-2012

*A place of grace
on Lake George*

Proprietors: Jane and Bill Busch.
Accommodations: 65 rooms, including 7 2-room suites and 7
luxury lakeview suites, in 15 buildings, chalets, and log cabins; most have decks or patios, many have fireplaces. **Rates:**
$77–$140 per person, MAP (FAP spring and fall); weekly rates
available. **Included:** Breakfast and dinner, or three meals
spring and fall; extensive boating facilities, tennis. **Minimum
stay:** 3 nights in season. **Added:** 7% tax, three-quarters of full
rate for each additional adult, children $1 per year of age. **Pay-
ment:** No credit cards. **Children:** Welcome. **Pets:** Some pets in
some accommodations; please inquire in advance. **Smoking:**
Permitted. **Open:** Mid-May–mid-October.

For a classic lake setting, one can hardly do better than Canoe
Island Lodge, which sits on 16 acres on the southern part of
32-mile-long Lake George. The legendary owners are Jane and
Bill Busch, who have made Canoe Island Lodge their home
and livelihood for more than 40 years and are among the kindest and proudest innkeepers in the region.

Mr. Busch bought the property in 1946, and his new bride
joined him in his endeavors two years later. Carving out the
steep, rocky landscape on Lake George's shores and doing his
own logging, Mr. Busch built every one of the 15 buildings on
the property, including four log cabins and some small houses
and chalets. The property includes four-acre Canoe Island on
Lake George. It is named for the American Canoe Federation,
which was founded in a log cabin on the island in 1882 (ask
Mrs. Busch to show you pictures). Several weekly events are
planned on Canoe Island, including Thursday barbecues,
Tuesday breakfasts, and sand castle contests.

From Route 9N, the buildings of Canoe Island Lodge tum-
ble down the tiers of slate to the sandy beach on Lake George.
The Main Lodge has an enchanting lobby, made of dark pine
logs cut on the property. Sitting areas encourage cozy chats

by the huge stone fireplace. Many items have sentimental significance, including a pair of clarinet lamps atop a piano made by a frequent guest and the braided oval rugs handmade for the Busches 30 years ago by a friend. Steps from the main common area is the oak bar with views of Lake George through a picture window.

The views from the dining room are spectacular, looking to the lake from the 40-foot height of the lodge down the slate hill. The Busches are very proud of their homemade and hearty food, served family-style, with entrées like beef Stroganoff, roast beef, chicken breast, and sea scallops, served with steamed vegetables from their own garden. The house favorite is steak,

> **Canoe Island Lodge is many things to many people: a wonderful family find, with home-cooked meals lifted (piping hot) out of a Rockwell painting; or a romantic retreat complete with fireplaces and a deck overlooking Lake George. It's a happy, healthy inn filled with goodness top to bottom.**

cooked outside over a hickory wood fire. Their baker makes breads and desserts daily. Finally, the ground level is also the dancing and activities room, built right on the ledge rock. Two fun mealtime outings to Canoe Island are a Tuesday morning breakfast picnic and a Thursday evening chicken and corn barbecue.

Throughout the property is an astounding variety of accommodations — in luxurious chalets, rustic log cabins, traditional lodge rooms, and family houses. Almost all guest rooms have a patio or deck as well as a wood-burning fireplace, and most have lake views. Rooms vary in extent of luxury: the most deluxe rooms are in Chalet Erika — which has fireplaces, European appointments, and Italian tiles — and in the mini-chalets and Chalet Edelweiss, with its bright stencil colors and decor and large patios. Some of the cabins are more rustic; the upper log cabin, for instance, has a huge cathedral ceiling and stone fireplace, a little patio, and a picture window onto Lake George. The staff is treated like extended family at Canoe Island Lodge, happy to help, lighthearted, and enamored of the beautiful environment.

Below Chalet Edelweiss is a common area covered in green

all-weather carpeting, where guests indulge in light fare and watch the lake's activities. The boating facilities are exceptional, among them three 31-foot sailboats, a 24-foot sailboat, two cruise boats, Windsurfers, plenty of rowboats, a Ski-Nautique for waterskiing, and the *Ark*, a 40-foot passenger boat that takes guests on cruises to a private island. Landlubbers might enjoy the three tennis courts (two are clay), a great hiking route to a high vantage point called the Ledges, and a visit to the nearby magnificent Omni Sagamore for high tea.

KEENE

The Bark Eater

Alstead Mill Road
Keene, NY 12924
518-576-2221
Fax: 518-576-2071

A High Peaks inn for polo and cross-country skiing

Proprietor: Joe Pete Wilson. **General Manager:** Jodi Downs. **Accommodations:** 7 rooms in main house, 6 sharing 2 baths; 4 rooms in carriage house, all with private bath; 2 rooms with private bath and 2 3-room suites in log cabin. **Rates:** $90–$110 per person; 5-day MAP and B&B packages available. **Included:** Full breakfast; breakfast and 5-course gourmet dinner with MAP. **Minimum stay:** 2 nights on weekends, 3 nights holiday weekends. **Added:** $22.50–

$27.50 each additional adult, $6.50 each child, 13% gratuity, 7% tax. **Payment:** Major credit cards. **Children:** Welcome. **Pets:** Not allowed. **Smoking:** Not allowed. **Open:** All year.

The Adirondacks are literally defined in a country inn called the Bark Eater, halfway between Lake Placid and Lake Champlain. "Bark Eater," or Adirondack, was the pejorative epithet given to the Algonquin Indians by their Mohawk neighbors. White surveyors, having often heard the term, began referring to the wilderness area by this name as early as the 1830s. At around the same time, a 1780 farmhouse in the town of Keene was transformed into a stagecoach stop. The family of the present owner, Joe Pete Wilson, bought the farmhouse-inn in the 1930s, and they adopted the name Bark Eater as a tribute to the first tenants of the land.

The two-story white clapboard house is an architectural collage of additions, from 1780 to the present. It encompasses

> **There are few places where polo is played; fewer still where the horsepower thunders across a green plateau 2,000 feet up in the mountains. When the green is covered by white, half the year, skiers grace the fields and miles of trails throughout the 200 acres of Bark Eater.**

the neighboring 1890 spruce clapboard carriage house, renovated in 1985 to provide four guest rooms, and, a five-minute walk into the woods, a fairly luxurious log cabin with two rooms and two suites. Only one of the seven guest rooms in the main house has a private bath; the other six share two baths. The guest rooms are comfortably informal, decorated with eclectic well-worn antiques.

For deluxe and more private accommodations, guests might prefer the Carriage House, with cut pine interior walls, new private baths, and more contemporary sitting areas. Even more deluxe are the recently redecorated rooms and suites in the nearby Log Cabin, some with fireplaces, with a huge wraparound deck set into the woods.

The Bark Eater is a place for the informal and the active, reflecting the varied outdoor interests of owner Joe Pete, a former Olympic Nordic skier. In addition to its bed-and-breakfast rates, the Bark Eater offers special instructional packages for cross-country skiing, horseback riding (the 55 horses are trained in both English and western style), Hudson River Gorge whitewater rafting, and Adirondack climbing. Guests explore the 200 acres of Bark Eater land on horseback or on cross-country skis, rented on premises. The adventurous might like to try their hand at polo, played seasonally on the grand fieldlike front lawn.

Yet another appreciated aspect of the Bark Eater is the cooking of chef James Metzger. Guests eat at a family table in the low-ceilinged colonial dining room. His five-course dinner might feature marinated grilled lamb chops with apple and basil chutney or baked trout with warm sherry and onion vinaigrette. The next morning, guests eat a full breakfast of homemade granola and baked goods, at the same table or in the pretty, informal sun porch in the front of the house.

LAKE PLACID

Lake Placid Lodge

Whiteface Inn Road
Box 550
Lake Placid, NY 12946
518-523-2573
Fax: 518-523-1124

*A great
Adirondacks
discovery*

Proprietors: David and Christie Garrett. **General Manager:** George Shattuck. **Accommoda-**

tions: 24 rooms, including 4 suites, most with fireplaces and outdoor decks, 7 rooms and 1 suite in the lodge, 8 rooms and 2 suites in the Lakeside building, 2 rooms and 1 suite in the Cedar building, 3 rooms in the Pine building. **Rates:** $175–$375. **Added:** $25 each additional guest, 12% tax. **Payment:** Major credit cards. **Children:** Welcome. **Pets:** Check with innkeeper. **Smoking:** Not allowed in dining room. **Open:** All year except in April.

On this ski mountain, equipped with complete Olympic facilities and an inn run by David and Christie Garrett, remarkable vacations happen.

Hidden in admired obscurity, Lake Placid Manor was for decades a pleasant, unusual retreat, with loyal patrons, a wonderful view, classic Adirondack camp architecture, and — most importantly — great potential. David and Christie Garrett spotted this potential. In 1993, the Garretts bought Lake Placid Manor and undertook six months of intensive renovations to produce their new masterpiece and Adirondack lodge in the summer of 1994.

> This is the property they'll be talking about for the rest of the decade. A turn-of-the-century Adirondack camp, Lake Placid Lodge was all but forgotten until Bill and Christie Garrett bought it in 1993. The Point, arguably the country's finest country inn, was the Garretts' last project, so all eyes are on Lake Placid Lodge.

The property consists of the classic Adirondack great camp Main Lodge and four satellite cottages carved into a precipitous landscape that tumbles to the lakefront. Guests check in at the Hillside Building at the top of the hill. A covered walkway leads down to the Main Lodge. This enchanting chocolate clapboard building was built in 1895 and still has its original diamond-paned leaded windows and bare bark railings on its long porch, which loftily overlooks the lake. The tap room is a warm, wooded Adirondack room decorated with rich fabrics and classic Adirondack twig furniture. It is adjacent to the gorgeous living room, with exposed yellow birch and wainscoting, warmed by a huge stone fireplace over which hangs a moose under a cathedral ceiling. A yellow birch banister leads upstairs to two Main Lodge rooms, one suite, and a game room; there are also five rooms on the ground level below. But ahead, the dining room features cozy dining areas, scatter Orientals, and magnificent water views. Beyond are steps that climb the hill to cottages and descend to the beachfront.

The outbuildings are just as wonderful. The Cedar Building hovers above the Main Lodge, with two rooms and a suite, all with fireplaces and porches. Below the Hillside Building is the Pine Building, with three rooms; and below, at beachside, is the Lakeside Building, with eight rooms and two suites, all with fireplaces and inspiring views of Lake Placid. Each room is individually decorated with artistic, authentic, beautiful pieces, fabrics, and taste.

The service is just as nonpareil. Led by Manager George Shattuck, who made an outstanding reputation for himself at Rhinebeck's Beekman Arms Hotel on the Hudson, the staff at Lake Placid Lodge is helpful, unpretentious, and discreet.

Tennis and golf on the PGA course are right next door at the Whiteface Inn; fishing, skating, and cross-country skiing are steps from one's room; and of course, the luge, the bobsled, downhill skiing, and ski-jumping are a quick ride away at the Olympic facilities.

Chef Robert Atkins prepares French-American dinners, ranging from $19 to $28. The Garretts have a history of choosing chefs who have first been chosen by Michelin, so dinner will surely be a highlight of a stay at Lake Placid Lodge. One may, for example, have the difficult choice between fillet of poached wild Scottish salmon with fresh garden vegetables and braised quail stuffed with wild mushrooms served with huckleberry *jus* — all this while gazing up at Whiteface Mountain and right over Lake Placid.

Mirror Lake Inn

Mirror Lake Drive
Lake Placid, NY 12946
518-523-2544
Fax: 518-523-2871

> *An intimate
> hotel, an
> expansive inn*

Proprietors: Ed Weibrecht. **Accommodations:** 128 rooms, including 11 suites; 52 rooms in Mountain View, 36 rooms in Terrace, 5 rooms in Colonial Cottage, 8 rooms in Lake Cottage. **Rates:** $72–$258 high season, $92–$326 low season. **Minimum stay:** 2 nights on winter weekends. **Added:** $34 for MAP; $15 additional guest; 7% tax, 12% tax over $100. **Payment:** Major credit cards. **Children:** Welcome. **Pets:** Not allowed. **Smoking:** Nonsmoking rooms available. **Open:** All year.

On Mirror Lake, just yards south of Lake Placid, the Mirror Lake Inn looks like one of the grand old hotels that occupied this resort town in the early part of the century; and until 1988 it was. Destroyed by fire, the hotel was immediately reconstructed as closely as possible to its original state through the grand efforts of its current owners, Ed and Lisa Weibrecht. Today it looks much as it did in 1926, when Rufus Wikoff, better known as the Fuller Brush Man, expanded a grand lakeside home into a grand hotel and shortly thereafter winterized it for the 1932 Olympics. Historic pictures of the hotel and its guests from these days are displayed on the public walls and in guest rooms. Still, the Mirror Lake Inn offers sophisticated accommodations and the amenities of a luxury hotel.

The white clapboard mansion sits on eight acres above Mirror Lake, wedged into a steep hill. The lobby successfully imitates its ancestor, with deep mahogany paneling, traditional sitting areas in front of a green marble hearth, and a 1902 Knabe piano. It abuts a clubby library, with a huge buck above the grand stone hearth, opening to a porch permitting wonderful breezes from the lake. At the other end of the building, across from the reception area, is the dining room, along an entire windowed wing overlooking Mirror Lake. Front porches with lakefront views are good spots for quiet reading or sociable gathering.

> **Facing Mirror Lake, this property has a wonderful small-town charm about it. One might almost forget that grand Lake Placid is just around the bend; that the Olympic facilities are only a luge run away; or that people come to Lake Placid for sights other than the Mirror Lake Inn.**

There are five types of rooms, nearly all with a balcony and water view, throughout the inn, which expands up the hill to a newer section and across the street in the Colonial and Lake cottages on the banks of the lake. Most preferable are those in the Mountain View; those in the Terrace building are less distinctive. All are generously sized, decorated with reproduction furniture, some with cathedral ceilings and modern conveniences like televisions and phones. The new bathrooms are spotless and spacious. For a bed-and-breakfast feel, some guests may prefer the Colonial and Lake cottages. The Lake Cottage has four rooms on each of two floors, each room with a large balcony right on the lake — be sure to ask for the front rooms for the best view. The Colonial Cottage has no balconies and is decorated in English country style.

The charming Cottage Café neighbors the Lake Cottage, with wonderful light fare on an outdoor porch and an informal indoor setting. On the ground floor of the Main Inn is the fitness center, with an indoor pool, hair salon, and exercise equipment, whirlpool, and sauna. Service is sophisticated though friendly. The abundance of outdoor activities, winter and summer, is exhilarating, and the staff is happy to provide information.

NORTH HUDSON

Elk Lake Lodge

North Hudson, NY 12855
518-532-7616

> *A remote
> fishing lodge
> wedged between
> glacial ponds*

Proprietors: Elk Lake Lodge, Inc. **Innkeeper:** Peter Sanders. **Accommodations:** 6 rooms in main lodge, 6 in Emerson lodge, 6 1–4-bedroom cottages. **Rates:** $90–$100 per person per day, FAP. **Included:** Three meals, use of all canoes and boats. **Minimum stay:** 2 days. **Added:** 15% gratuity, 7% tax. **Payment:** No credit cards. **Children:** Welcome. **Pets:** Not allowed. **Smoking:** Allowed. **Open:** Early May–mid-November.

Off the lonely North Hudson exit on the Northway, with the highest Adirondack peak, Mt. Marcy, looming in the distance, a visitor travels five miles toward the heart of the wilderness, then five miles on a private, mostly unpaved road. Only when one feels undoubtedly lost do the gates of Elk Lake Lodge appear. Within the private preserve lie two lakes: Elk Lake, dotted with islands and comprising 600 acres of inlets, bays, and open water, and Clear Pond, a 95-foot-deep glacial pond covering 200 acres.

Hopeful fishermen come for landlocked salmon, lake trout, and a strain of speckled trout that Elk Lake Lodge has worked to develop since 1971 with Cornell University. Elk Lake empties into the Branch River, a favorite haunt for fly fishing. While there is a limited game hunting season in early November, most come simply to enjoy the tranquility of the magnificent wilderness at Elk Lake Lodge, its 40 miles of walking trails, and five mountain views of the High Peaks area that surround the lodge. Naturalists delight in the variety of wildflowers, birds, and the occasional black bear.

The two-story weathered shingle main lodge was built in 1904 by a logging company in the Adirondack and Arts and Crafts style. The rustic interior shows off exposed logs and knotty pine paneling. The common room has a huge stone fireplace surrounded by Adirondack twig and leather Mission-style furniture, the blanched corner hutches built by a man in Schroon Lake.

Hearty country meals are taken family-style in the dining addition to one side of the lodge, with frames supporting a cathedral ceiling. A free-standing round stone fireplace is the room's centerpiece, with one wall devoted to picture windows providing breathtaking lake and mountain views.

> **Five miles down a gravel road surrounded by Adirondack forest are the gates of Elk Lake Lodge, an Arts and Crafts outpost built in 1904. Within the 6 million acres of the Adirondacks, Elk Lake sits on a 12,000-acre private forest preserve between two glacial ponds, home to landlocked salmon and lake and speckled trout.**

The Elk Lake dam creates an audible and pleasant waterfall between the Main Lodge and three cottages, and between Emerson Lodge and three other cottages. The cottages all have views of the lake from their porches outfitted with rockers. The interior furnishings are rustic, with starburst quilts and simple, tidy decor, some with fireplaces and sitting rooms.

Adirondack chairs on the lawn overlook the little docks lining the lakefront. Eight canoes and about 20 rowboats are available. Mr. Sanders has been the innkeeper since 1975, following in his father's footsteps. He and his staff are true pioneers of the area, used to the ways of the wilderness.

NORTH RIVER

Garnet Hill Lodge

13th Lake Road
North River, NY 12856
518-251-2444

A place for fishing, canoeing, and skiing

Proprietors: George and Mary Heim. **General Manager:** Peter Fitting. **Accommodations:** 16 rooms in Log House, 4 in Birches, 2 in Tea House, 7 in Big Shanty.

Rates: $55–$80 per person MAP; 4- and 7-night packages available. **Included:** Gratuities and sales tax. **Minimum stay:** Some weekends. **Added:** $40 each additional guest, MAP; $28 each child under 10, MAP. **Payment:** No credit cards. **Children:** Welcome. **Pets:** Not allowed. **Smoking:** Limited. **Open:** All year.

Garnet Hill Lodge is a sophisticated Adirondack refuge for lovers of the outdoors. George and Mary Heim have happily presided over their 600 acres since 1977.

The two-story Adirondack lodge, built in 1936, is tucked on a scenic plateau a mile's hike above Thirteenth Lake, four miles into an intricate web of dirt roads from North River. Since 1879, garnet mining has been the mainstay of this tiny mountain community, which once produced the world's greatest supply of garnets, the ruby of the Adirondacks. The Log House was built by mining magnate Frank Hooper in 1936, in which he and his son-in-law Charles Tibbits opened a guest house and restaurant. Today, the Heims carry on their tradition in this and several buildings,

> **North River was the North American capital for garnet mining. Now it's the capital for trout fishing on Thirteenth Lake, fly fishing on the Hudson River, cross-country skiing on Garnet Hill's 35 miles of groomed trails, and downhill skiing on Gore Mountain.**

including Frank Hooper's original classic Adirondack mansion, Big Shanty.

The Log House is a long two-story building of dark-stained wood trimmed in traditional red, its first floor finished in stacked logs, the second in rough-hewn clapboards with an overhanging balcony with log rails. Inside, the first floor consists of an impressive common area, dark with varnished wood, supported by bark-clad yellow birch pillars and beams. Classic Mission couches rest around the enormous stone fireplace, which sparkles with hunks of garnet. Outside on an enclosed porch, guests dine overlooking the groomed front lawn and the wonderful sunsets provided by the western view.

Upstairs, the guest rooms retain the richness of exposed wood. The rooms facing the back have pine walls and ceilings, though the front rooms are preferable for their larger size and furnished balconies, which peer over the trees to the lake at the bottom of the hill. The rooms are furnished in rustic comfort, with new baths. Down the hill, groups enjoy the Big Shanty's rustic accommodations, wonderful Adirondack living room, and great front porch on the large lawn. The Birches and Tea House have more contemporary furnishings.

Meals at Garnet Hill are hearty and plentiful, always accompanied by fresh breads and pastries by Mary Jane Freeburn, who has been at Garnet Hill since before the Heims. Guests also ought to visit Highwinds Country Inn for a spectacular view, intimate setting, and French food prepared by Scott Aronson at the Barton family house.

Garnet Hill Lodge offers guests mountain bikes, canoes, sailboats, cross-country ski equipment, and two tennis courts. Its kind, warm staff is headed by innkeeper Peter Fitting, who offers knowledgeable and enthusiastic advice about all these activities and more.

RAQUETTE LAKE

Sagamore — Historic Adirondack Great Camp

Sagamore Road
Raquette Lake, NY 13436
315-354-5311
Fax: 315-354-5851

The former Vanderbilt great camp on Raquette Lake

Proprietor: Sagamore Institute. **Director:** Beverly Bridger. **Innkeeper:** Bobbie Hawks. **Accommodations:** 26 rooms sharing 10 bathrooms in 5 buildings; 7 rooms with private bath. **Rates:** $100 per person AP; weekend programs, added rates. **Included:** Three meals daily. **Minimum stay:** 2 nights, Friday dinner through Sunday lunch; 5 nights, Sunday dinner through Friday lunch. **Payment:** Visa, MasterCard. **Children:** Welcome. **Pets:** Not allowed. **Smoking:** Not allowed. **Open:** All year except April.

Sagamore is an Indian word for "wise chief," a fitting name for a place that has since 1973 served as a unique intellectual retreat. This National Historic Site is in the resortlike setting of Raquette Lake in the western part of the Adirondack Forest Preserve. The Sagamore Lodge is one of the few remaining great camps built at the turn of the century by William West Durant, and one of an even smaller number accessible to the public. Not to be confused with the Sagamore Resort owned by Omni Hotels in Lake George, this Saga-more was built in 1897 for the Vanderbilt family, a recreational home for up-scale "roughing it."

Raquette Lake is half-way between Old Forge, the westernmost access into the Adirondack Forest Preserve (and famous for its hardware store), and Blue Mountain Lake, home of the renowned Adirondack Museum. A four-mile dirt road from main Adirondack Route

> **Not until you are sur-rounded by the 6 million acres of Adirondack wilderness can you fully appreciate the beauty and significance of the region's crafts and architecture. Nowhere is this atmos-phere more fully experi-enced than at Sagamore, an authentic Adirondack great camp.**

28 brings a visitor to Sagamore Lodge. On its vast acreage are 27 buildings erected between 1897 and 1930. Sagamore is set up like a plantation, with each building serving a single pur-pose: a blacksmith shop, a woodshed, an icehouse, a school house, a men's chalet, and even a bowling alley. Nearly half the land is devoted to service buildings and servant quarters, not surprising when one learns that servants outnumbered guests six to one.

A Sagamore weekend is spent in accomplishment. Guests enroll in specific programs: an Adirondack weekend, moun-tain biking, women in the wilderness, Adirondack geology, gilded age film festival, rustic furniture, north country wild-flowers, fly fishing, fly tying, or llama trekking. There are craft programs, like tapestry weaving, blacksmithing, and wood carving. There are storytelling and landscape photogra-phy weekends, as well as Adirondack history weekends, with a great estates tour. Most wonderful is the grandparents' and grandchildren's camp. Weekend rates include three meals daily in the beautiful dining hall, as well as full use of the Sagamore facilities.

The classic Adirondack architecture is characterized by rough-looking logs still clothed in bark, bent-twig railings and support beams, wide, low-pitched roofs sturdy enough to hold heavy snow, and fireplaces of large stones. There are no great creature comforts here except in the intellectual satisfaction of residing in unaltered history and aesthetic beauty. Accommodations are authentic but rustic, in several lodges. The rooms are furnished with original Adirondack furniture, twin beds covered with thick red wool blankets, and shared hall baths.

Tours are conducted twice daily (except Wednesdays) in summers, weekends only through Columbus Day. Twenty miles of skiing and hiking trails lace through the property, and canoeing and fishing are offered on Raquette Lake.

SARANAC LAKE

The Point

HCR 1, Box 65
Saranac Lake, NY 12983
518-891-5678
800-255-3530

An inn that forever changes your expectations

Proprietors: David and Christie Garrett. **Innkeepers:** Bill and Claudia McNamee. **Accommodations:** 4 rooms in Main Lodge, 3 in Eagles Nest, 3 in the Guest House, 1 in the Boathouse, all with fireplace and private bath. **Rates:** $775–$925 per couple, AP. **Included:** Three meals daily with wine and open bar. **Minimum stay:** 2 nights on weekends, 3 nights on holidays. **Added:** 12% tax, $150 additional guest. **Payment:** American Express. **Children:** Under 18 not allowed. **Pets:** Allowed with prior approval. **Smoking:** Allowed. **Open:** Closed mid-March through mid-April.

The miles of dirt road flanked by looming trees that lead up to the gates of the Point are a gift: use the time to prepare yourself for what you are about to behold. The Point is one of the most glorious travel experiences to be had and one never to be forgotten. A model of great camp architecture in the heart of Adirondack wilderness, a gallery of culinary art, a showcase of decorating showmanship, a lesson in impeccable service, the Point is the ideal country inn.

In 1932, William Avery Rockefeller, nephew of John D., commissioned architect William Distin to built a great camp on Upper Saranac Lake, in the untrodden reaches of the 6-million-acre Adirondack wilderness. Camp Won-undra has since been re-named the Point, the only great camp standing to-day that sustains the ex-traordinary level of lux-ury of the period in which it was built. Guests of the Point experience one of the most thoroughly ro-mantic and elegant vaca-tions a traveler can have in this country: from the

> **The finest country inn in the area — likely in the region, possibly in the country — the Point surpasses all superlatives. Set high enough upstate to approach heaven, this 12-room coun-try inn is a masterpiece.**

food overseen by three-star Michelin chef Albert Roux and executive chef and innkeeper Bill McNamee, to the unusu-ally beautiful rooms, which seem lifted from the pages of *Ar-chitectural Digest*, to the nonpareil great camp Adirondack architecture, to the breathtaking remote lakeside setting, to the etiquette-perfect service orchestrated by innkeeper Clau-dia McNamee.

The Point was sold in 1980 by the Rockefeller estate to Ted Carter, who began the tradition of elegant hostmanship, and subsequently went to the present owners David and Christie Garrett in 1986. To upgrade the food to national renown, the Garretts asked Bill and Claudia McNamee to join them at the Point in 1987 as innkeepers. While Claudia lends a tasteful touch to the design and manages the administrative aspects, Bill brings to the Point his experience as an accomplished chef. He has received accolades for his work at Le Pavillon in Washington, D.C., Le Chardon d'Or at the Morrison House in Alexandria, and Le Gavroche in London under chef Albert Roux.

The resort consists of nine buildings on a 10-acre peninsula called Whitney Point. The architecture is intriguingly en-demic to the Adirondacks, a varied collection of luxurious Canadian pine log cabins with the original slate roofs and Queen Anne gables. The rich wooden interiors have open-beamed cathedral ceilings, formidable stone hearths, and traditional twig furniture and museum-quality antiques. The walls are enlivened by beautiful original art. The decor of the common and guest rooms is a successful, eclectic combination of Ralph Lauren ease and sophistication; colorful Aztec and Indian patterns on wall hangings, heavy draperies and bedding; and hunting and wilderness themes, evidenced by lumberjack plaids and moose heads, antlers, and zebra and bearskin rugs. The king-size beds are triple-sheeted and turned down nightly, and several have inventive canopy treatments, like the diaphanous scarf wrapped around the bed in the Boathouse. The baths are of a grand old scale, large and traditionally luxurious, with thick terry robes, slippers, and hair dryer.

Set around a groomed drive are the three main buildings for guests: the Guesthouse, with three rooms; the Eagles Nest, with three rooms and a Pub, a pool table, and a common room; and the Main Lodge, with two guest rooms in each wing, astride the Great Hall, where guests dine and socialize around two enormous fireplaces. A great slate porch rests outside, facing Upper Saranac Lake. Down a path is the Boathouse, with a second-floor guest room above the dock and a small fleet of boats for guests' use. These include a 30-foot launch for nightly predinner excursions, a ski boat, smaller outboard motorboats, canoes, and a vintage mahogany touring boat that cost more than the nice Porsche that brought you here.

The three meals served daily are gorgeously presented, whether on a silver tray to one's room, in a picnic basket taken to an island, or around the polished round wood tables gleaming with candlelight in the Great Hall. Under the guidance of Albert Roux, James Byars is the chef who works with Bill McNamee, organizing the elaborate kitchen staffed with protégés of the master chef from London. The dinners are especially memorable under the dramatic 25-foot ceilings of the Great Hall, flanked by blazing fires. The four-course meal might begin with a terrine of pheasant with wild mushrooms and truffle sauce and move on to a salad of goat cheese and walnuts, followed by roasted fillet of salmon on coulis of leek with *pommes fondants* and bouquets of spinach and carrots in champagne butter sauce, and ending with chocolate truffle cake served with rum *crème anglaise.* Wines are presented with each course, and appropriate liqueurs are introduced after dinner.

Claudia and Bill are ever-present when needed, invisible when privacy is preferred. Every whim and fancy is answered, from fishing to golf to tours of the great camps of Saranac Lake on the Hacker boat, led by Bill with utmost acuity. Every aspect of a stay is at the height of elegance and sophistication, as the Rockefellers or the Vanderbilts or the Whitneys intended life to be in the Adirondacks.

WARRENSBURG

Bent Finial Manor

194 Main Street
Warrensburg, NY 12885
518-623-3308

A Victorian bed-and-breakfast in the Adirondacks

Proprietor: Patricia Scully. **Accommodations:** 5 rooms, all with private bath, including 1 suite with fireplace and garden. **Rates:** $85–$95. **Included:** Full breakfast. **Minimum stay:** 2 nights in season. **Added:** 7% tax, $20 for children under 12 in parent's room. **Payment:** No credit cards. **Children:** Welcome. **Pets:** Not allowed. **Smoking:** Limited. **Open:** All year.

Bed-and-breakfasters disenchanted with the kitsch of Lake George and the expense of the impressive Omni Sagamore resort in Bolton Landing will love the Bent Finial Manor over the mountain in nearby Warrensburg. The interior of this lovely Queen Anne Victorian uses a memorable 23 types of wood, mainly cherry on the first floor, in the form of paneling, wainscoting, coffered ceilings, and the elaborate Corinthian columns and carved stairs decorating the foyer and the stairwell.

Built in 1904 by wealthy cattle rancher Lewis Thomson, this house is three grand stories of white clapboard, with a stone portico and a curved wraparound porch. The gabled third floor ascends to a lovely candle-snuffer turret topped by a copper rod finial — bent, of course.

The vast front porch wraps to the left, and from this guests enter the foyer. In the living room, a fabulous alcove game room is tucked into the turret space, and elaborate columns support the ceiling. There is a marvelous terra cotta fireplace here, one of many in the house. In the dining room, guests have candlelight breakfast under coffered ceilings. Pat cooks generously: soufflés, crêpes, and fresh baked goods are served on silver and crystal. Behind the dining room is a glass-enclosed conservatory that is original to the house.

> When you're driving through the hamlet of Warrensburg, just before the mountains that plummet down to Lake George, you'll spot the Bent Finial Manor and hope it's the place. Nothing, however, will prepare you for the grandeur inside.

The rooms are furnished with antiques Pat found at estate sales and had nicely reupholstered, with lovely variety within the Queen Anne and Victorian period, albeit a little sparse in the common rooms. Halfway up the magnificent stairs is a bench built into the landing overlooking the porte-cochere.

Turn-of-the-century family portraits decorate the second-floor landing. The incredible stained glass in the house is original and extremely colorful — there are 104 windows in all — used by Pat as the guidepost for decorating the rooms. The lovely Turret Chamber is easily the room of choice, with a sitting area in the turret and bright floral wallpaper. Its private bath is playful, designed by Pat to have all the gingerbread that this later Victorian is missing from its austere exterior. The Eastlake Chamber is named for its lovely bedroom set. The Master Chamber has another terra cotta fireplace and is decorated with an odd brown and mauve color scheme inspired by its stained glass window.

Breakfasts are grand here: possibly apple-walnut French toast, ham and cheese soufflé, or Belgian waffles, there will always be homemade biscuits and cinnamon buns. Though there's not much to do in tiny Warrensburg but eat at the Merrill Magee House and fish in a narrow branch of the Hudson River, there is plenty to do nearby. Lake George is a short scenic drive away, and skiing and boating abounds in this southeast corner of the Adirondacks.

The Capital,
Saratoga Springs,
and Cooperstown

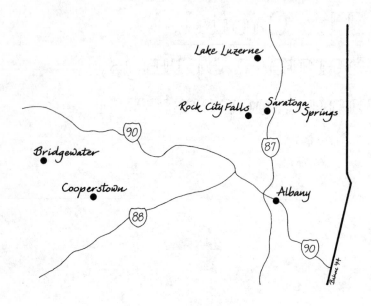

Best Romantic Retreats

Cooperstown
  J. P. Sill House
Rock City Falls
  The Mansion
Saratoga Springs
  The Adelphi Hotel

Best Resorts

Cooperstown
  The Otesaga Hotel and Cooper Inn
Saratoga Springs
  Gideon Putnam Hotel

Best for Urban Intimacy

Albany
  Mansion Hill Inn

Best Country Bed-and-Breakfasts

Cooperstown
  Toad Hall
Lake Luzerne
  The Lamplight Inn Bed &Breakfast

Best Country Inn

Bridgewater
  The White House Berries Inn

Albany is a tiny city, the state's government seat, that received some much-needed revitalization around its tricentennial in 1986. The downtown capital district is easily walkable and is best viewed from the 42nd story of Corning Tower at the Empire State Plaza, near the visitors' center. From here, visit the New York State Museum on the Empire Plaza's south end. After a tour of the capitol, visit the Albany Institute of History and Art several blocks away.

Less than an hour's drive north of Albany is the state's premier Victorian and Roaring Twenties resort, **Saratoga Springs.** People think of horse racing, extraordinary wealth, and frivolity when they think of Saratoga — the racing season is about six weeks long around August — though its first attraction was its natural mineral springs, and they are still very much a part of this privileged community. The beautiful town is the home of Skidmore College. One mile south of the charming Victorian downtown is culturally rich Saratoga Spa State Park, on 1,500 acres. In addition to housing the Saratoga Performing Arts Center and the Roosevelt Mineral Baths, the park is the home of the Gideon Putnam Hotel, which has full use of the park's generous array of activities.

As well as providing the stage for fine theater, the Saratoga Performing Arts Center is home to the New York City Ballet and Opera and the Philadelphia Orchestra during its August season. The Roosevelt Baths offer mineral baths, massages, and hot packs in the original turn-of-the-century setting. Also within the park are a PGA 18-hole golf course, a 9-hole par three course, three outdoor swimming pools, eight tennis courts, ice skating, and cross-country skiing.

Among the sights to see in Saratoga are the National Museum of Racing and Hall of Fame, the artistic retreat Yaddo, and the National Museum of Dance.

A 70-mile drive west of Albany, **Cooperstown,** on the southern banks of Lake Otsego, is true paradise for any fan of America's favorite pastime. The Baseball Hall of Fame was built in the town where Abner Doubleday is said to have invented the game in 1839. A man named William Cooper founded the town in 1786 and also sired a son named James Fenimore Cooper, a great American novelist. Do take a cruise on the wonderfully picturesque lake.

ALBANY

Mansion Hill Inn

115 Philip Street at Park Avenue
Albany, NY 12202
518-465-2038
518-427-7358
800-477-8171

> *The B&B*
> *experience*
> *in Albany*

Proprietors: Steve and Maryellen Stofelano. **Accommodations:** 2 rooms above restaurant, 5 at 45 Park Avenue, 5 on Philip Street; including 3 with kitchens. **Rates:** $105–$145. **Included:** Full breakfast, depending on rate. **Minimum stay:** None. **Added:** $10 each additional guest, 7% tax. **Payment:** Major credit cards. **Children:** Welcome; under 12 free. **Pets:** Check with manager. **Smoking:** Allowed. **Open:** All year.

The Albany Hilton sits several blocks below the capitol building, the Albany Marriott a short hop from the airport — plush, contemporary, and unsurprising. City travelers who prefer the smaller scale of a bed-and-breakfast will be glad for this relative newcomer in a town with a paucity of alternatives. Mansion Hill Inn sits south of Empire State Plaza and the Governor's Mansion. In addition to housing seven comfortable rooms, the inn has a pleasant, bistro-style restaurant that serves three good meals daily.

The Mansion Hill Inn toes the neighborhood line between trendy, restored Victorian brick rowhouses and those in need of a little attention. Steve and Maryellen Stofelano bought a condemned three-story clapboard townhouse in 1983 in the Mansion neighborhood and worked for nearly a year restoring its 1861 frame. Here, two rooms hover above the small restaurant. The Stofelanos rescued the adjoining property on Park Avenue, providing five more guest rooms. The five additional rooms in the Philip Street rowhouse are the newest, connected to the Mansion Hill Inn by outdoor garden dining.

> The 1861 brownstone is a fine representative of the charm of the Mansion Hill neighborhood, which sits just south of the Governor's mansion. It's a personable place, with fine rooms set up for the business traveler; if you lived in Albany, you'd be a regular at the Mansion Hill Inn restaurant.

The guest rooms vary in size, providing comfort to a transient guest as well as for those who plan a longer stay in Albany. All rooms are furnished with dark wood Queen Anne reproduction furniture including queen-size beds, private telephones, remote cable televisions tucked in cabinets, and serviceable desks. Two suites have a living room and a den, a fully stocked kitchen, bedroom, and a terrace. A third, smaller suite has a stocked kitchen. The remaining rooms have unusual alcoves providing separate work areas, some with stained glass windows, and bright new baths with pedestal sinks, fluffy towels, and a second telephone. Fresh flowers and Saratoga water greet arriving guests.

The dining room is a small, friendly spot with a brick fireplace, green wainscoting, and blue floral paper above the chair rail. David K. Martin is the dinner chef. His entrées range from $12 to $21 for various pasta dishes, shrimp Madagascar with Pernod cream sauce, or perhaps veal sauté with smoked Canadian bacon, avocado, and tomato.

The Stofelanos and other staff are friendly, informal, and helpful about Albany activities.

BRIDGEWATER

The White House Berries Inn and Restaurant

Box 78, Route 8
Bridgewater, NY 13313
315-822-6558

A northern out-post for southern home-cooked meals

Proprietors: Juanita and Crystal Bass. **Manager:** Juanita Bass. **Accommodations:** 3 rooms sharing 2 baths. **Rates:** $65. **Included:** Full breakfast. **Minimum stay:** Check with innkeeper. **Added:** 8% tax. **Payment:** Visa, MasterCard. **Children:** Welcome. **Pets:** Not allowed. **Smoking:** Not allowed in rooms. **Open:** March 1–December 31.

Halfway between Cooperstown and Utica, Bridgewater holds a southern treasure. Since it was built in the mid-19th century, a lavish Italianate house outside of Bridgewater had remained an elegant fixture known simply as the White House, for its color. Several years ago, a sign appeared in front of the house advertising fruit from the owner's garden: "White House Berries," the sign said. When Juanita Bass bought the house in 1986, she restored the house and a bit of its lore as well, recreating the sign for her country inn when it opened in January 1989. It's still technically a white house, somewhere under the green, mint, and mauve gingerbread.

Juanita Bass is so well loved by patrons and local residents that she is a bit of a legend. Bridgewater, about 12 miles north of Cooperstown, has been her home for generations: her father made history here when he became New York State's first black mayor in 1972. Juanita's experience as an antiques dealer is evident throughout. All is done with a fine eye for collecting Victoriana and a sense of humor. In the Rest Room, for example, the huge clawfoot tub with beautiful Wedgwood blue tiling is a planter filled with greenery. Her dining rooms are an eclectic mix of mismatched chairs and silver settings, individually interesting pieces that together create a beautiful ensemble. The wallpaper is a vivid red damask, a dramatic backdrop for her dinners, where the fun begins.

On the left side of the menu are "Soul Food Dinners." Juanita is helped in the kitchen by her sister, Arlene Bellamy. The family's famous sauce is the reason so many come back for baby back ribs. Stuffed pork chops, fried catfish, southern fried chicken, and honey glazed ham are among the other choices, all served with black-eyed peas, macaroni and cheese, collard greens, and potato or rice.

> **People come here for the cooking: southern fried chicken, stuffed pork chops, shrimp gumbo, barbecued ribs, catfish; cornbread, hush puppies, and hot syrup; collard greens and black-eyed peas. For dessert, there's peanut butter, sweet potato, and chocolate porch pie.**

On the right side of the menu are "Yankee Dinners," including rosemary chicken, fresh fish, and strip steak, served with baked potato or rice and vegetables. All dinner entrées are served with cornbread, hush puppies and hot syrup, and fresh-squeezed lemonade. A choice of five pies stymie the sweet-toothed: sweet potato, banana cream, pecan, peanut butter, and chocolate porch pie. Dinners range from $17 to $21 and are served Thursday through Saturday from 5 to 9, Sundays from 2 to 6:30.

The three guest rooms upstairs are showcases of Victoriana, sharing two very pretty baths. While the first two rooms are adorable, one with a three-piece teardrop oak bedroom set, the third is the prettiest, done in contrasting patterns of black and pink chintz, from the wallpaper to the needlepoint rug to the lampshades; there's a brass double bed. The common room for guests on the second floor has a television, viewed from the pretty settee.

Expensive Cooperstown is just a short drive away. Shoppers who don't want to venture that far can visit Juanita's Berry Patch antiques and gift shop behind the inn — it's a good excuse to spend more time with a delightful hostess.

COOPERSTOWN

J. P. Sill House

63 Chestnut Street
Cooperstown, NY 13326
607-547-2633

> *A most romantic place, next to the Hall of Fame*

Proprietors: Laura and Angelo Zucotti. **Accommodations:** 5 rooms, all with private bath. **Rates:** $70–$95; $5 less October–May. **Included:** Full breakfast. **Minimum stay:** On some weekends. **Added:** 8% tax. **Payment:** American Express, Visa, MasterCard. **Children:** Teenagers welcome. **Pets:** Not allowed. **Smoking:** Not allowed. **Open:** All year.

Baseball is a wonderfully romantic sport: full of nostalgia, long afternoons in the park, loyalty, heroism, celebration, and heartbreak. Cooperstown is the home of the Baseball Hall of Fame, and those who know the poetry of the sport might want to complete the romance at the J. P. Sill House, an elegant, sophisticated bed-and-breakfast in the heart of town.

Painted a warm yellow with deep red trim, the J. P. Sill House is a pristine Victorian restoration on the National Register of Historic Places, set back from the road by a groomed lawn and colorful flowers. Sill was the wealthy president of a Cooperstown bank who had this house built between 1862 and 1864 to mirror his own residence across the street.

Although the former owners of this B&B did much of the restoration work in the 1980s, the Zucottis have made the property a first-class bed-and-breakfast since they bought it in 1990. Former owners of El Morocco Club in Manhattan, from Italy and England, the couple are worldly, gracious hosts. Laura insists on three dressings for every bed: a light woven European cotton as well as summer- and winter-weight comforters.

> **Baseball diamonds are a girl's best friend in Cooperstown. Next on the list is the J. P. Sill House, which will surely make the Romantic Hall of Fame. This beautifully presented bed-and-breakfast, generous with plush linens, teacakes, and luxuries, is a sophisticated retreat after a day at the ballpark.**

The walls are covered in Victorian reproduction wallpapers designed by William Morris and Audsley Brothers of London. The doors are faux grained pine; the ceiling moldings are elaborate tiger oak. In the formal parlor, where afternoon tea is served, Laura's china collection is housed in shelves and the original carved window valances are echoed in the mirror above the fireplace. A television is hidden in a cabinet. The dollhouse replica of the Sill House was made by local artisans at Toad Hall, a Cooperstown crafts and antiques shop.

The Bridal Room, the only first-floor accommodation, is the most luxurious. The valuable brass and white wrought-iron bed is from the Roebling estate. In the corner of the room is a large Jacuzzi and bath area that was photographed for a Laura Ashley catalog. Linen robes are provided in summer and terry robes in winter. The armoire holds a television, VCR, and stereo. Lace curtains fall from ceiling to floor, topped by silk balloon curtains. A private front porch enjoys views of the gardens and Chestnut Street. The original brass door poles, hung with heavy damask Chinese silk, were used to deter drafts. They are found throughout the house.

The four upstairs rooms have equally lovely and varied displays of Laura Ashley linens, elegant window treatments, and Victorian wallpapers. Rooms are graced with magnificent antique armoires fragranced by sachets. All rooms have private baths, one of which has a pewter tub in oak casing.

Guests take breakfast on the sun porch or in the formal dining room, framed by Scalamandre silk curtains and bordered in golf leaf paper. Tea is dispensed from a silver samovar from the Ottoman Empire, and the full meal is served on antique china and silver accompanied by antique linens. Breakfast may feature a soufflé or egg custard, with chocolate or lemon bread.

The Otesaga Hotel and Cooper Inn

60 Lake Street
P.O. Box 311
Cooperstown, NY 13326
607-547-9931
Fax: 607-547-9675
Cooper Inn: 800-348-6222,
607-547-2567

> *A classic resort
> on Lake Otsego*

Proprietor: The Leatherstocking Corp. **General Manager:** Frank J. Maloney. **Accommodations:** 124 rooms, including 6 parlor suites, 6 deluxe combination bedrooms, and 8 2-bedroom suites with connecting bath, plus 20 rooms in Cooper Inn. **Rates:** $230–$335 per couple MAP in hotel; $104–$114 in the inn. **Included:** Breakfast and dinner in hotel, Continental breakfast in inn. **Minimum stay:** 2 nights weekends. **Added:** $60 each additional adult MAP; $15–$45 each child age 3–18 MAP, $9 per person per day gratuity, 7% tax plus 7% bed tax on room rate only. **Payment:** Visa, MasterCard, American Express. **Children:** Welcome. **Pets:** Not allowed. **Smoking:** Allowed. **Open:** Late April–late October; Cooper Inn is open all year.

A great way to see America's greatest sport is to stay at the Otesaga Hotel while visiting the Baseball Hall of Fame in Cooperstown. The town itself is a picture-perfect vision of Americana, with small 19th-century brick buildings on quaint straight and narrow streets. Founded in 1786 by William Cooper, father of author James Fenimore Cooper, the town is better known as the laboratory in which Abner Doubleday invented the game of baseball in 1839. The southern shores of Lake Otsego are just a block or two from town, its lazy waves falling in the lap of the Otesaga Hotel.

The Otesaga was built in 1909, a fine Georgian structure of solid brick that is highly reminiscent of the Gideon Putnam in Saratoga. Shaped like a flattish H, the Otesaga has a grand Greek Revival three-story portico in the center at the front entrance supported by four columns; behind is the trademark curved verandah overlooking the lake. Flanking the center portion are two four-story wings. The common rooms are grand and regal, with original moldings, soft-hued plaster walls, classic and elegant furniture, and chintz curtains framing views of the lake. Less magnificent are the guest rooms: clean, traditional, standard, and unsurprising, with television and reproduction furnishings.

> Those who have been to Cooperstown will remember Doubleday Field first, and then the view of Lake Otsego from the curved verandah at the Otesaga Hotel. Its memorable setting at the base of this magnificent lake makes the resort a destination in itself.

The 18-hole Leatherstocking par 72 championship golf course — quite an attraction in itself — is a short walk from the Otesaga. The 6,324-yard course was designed by Devereux Emmet in 1909. On the property are two tennis courts and a heated swimming pool. The ACC Sport Center of Cooperstown offers racquet sports and a host of other athletic opportunities, including technical climbing. The adventurous or the romantic might want to embark on a lake cruise.

Guests who prefer more intimate accommodations might try the Cooper Inn around the corner, also owned by the Otesaga. Built in 1816 by Henry Phinney as Willowbrook, the gracious Italianate house became the Cooper Inn in 1936. Guests here are treated to Continental breakfast and use of the facilities at its sister property. Some of the furnishings are nice antiques, and several guest rooms have black marble fireplaces and the original plaster ceiling medallions and moldings.

The hotel is rather bustling when open, as it is often the choice for groups. While the guest rooms are uninspired, they are clean and comfortable. The elegant common spaces, glorious lake views, and fine dining make for an exciting stay in Cooperstown.

Toad Hall

RD1, Box 120
Fly Creek, NY 13337
607-547-5774

A gallery of exquisite hand-made furniture

Proprietors: Randy Van Syoc and Allen Ransome. **Accommodations:** 3 rooms, all with private bath. **Rates:** $80. **Included:** Full country breakfast. **Minimum stay:** None. **Added:** 9% tax; $10 additional guest. **Payment:** Major credit cards. **Children:** 12 years and older. **Pets:** Not allowed. **Smoking:** Not allowed. **Open:** All year.

Many people come to Cooperstown for baseball; a sophisticated few come just to pay homage to Toad Hall, a magnificent furniture and craft shop sitting modestly on a Cooperstown side street. Devotees of this glorious shop, filled with the masterful work of furniture maker Allen Ransome as well as local crafts and folk art, will be thrilled to know that Toad Hall's talented owners operate a three-room B&B in their home, four miles outside of town.

That they chose an upstate New York location for their gallery is evidence that the owners of Toad Hall prefer understatement in everything — especially in the home they open up to guests. It's a low-profile place.

> Those who admire interior design have all entertained the same fantasy of living in a home furnishings display, where pillows are ever plump and fabrics fall in tresses. It's really like that at Toad Hall, a breathtaking home decorated with the owners' own masterful handmade creations.

Before they moved across the country from California to Cooperstown, Allen had a rich history in furniture and interior design, and Randy owned a fabric company. They transplanted themselves in 1985, bought a near-to-falling-down 1820 stone farmhouse outside Cooperstown, and undertook a three-year restoration effort. The house is a magnificent stone structure, with four large columns across a sweeping verandah. On their 80 acres of farmland, Randy keeps two horses and breeds Newfoundland dogs.

The common rooms are on the second floor, the three guest rooms on the third floor. The living room is decorated with American, 18th-century English, and 19th-century Japanese antiques. The house is a gallery of interesting antiques, including pre-Columbian, Thai, and Cambodian pottery, folk art, and handmade quilts.

The guest rooms are generously sized, each with a private bath. Allen built the furniture, including the four-poster beds of rare tiger maple in two rooms and a low-country queen-size and twin bed in the third. Handmade quilts adorn the beds, and artwork decorates the walls.

Guests enjoy a full country breakfast in the dining room furnished entirely in Allen's work, which is derivative of primitivism and folk art.

LAKE LUZERNE

The Lamplight Inn Bed & Breakfast

2129 Lake Avenue
Box 70
Lake Luzerne, NY 12846
518-696-5294
800-262-4668

*A picture-perfect
bed-and-breakfast*

Proprietors: Gene and Linda Merlino. **Accommodations:** 10 rooms, all with private bath, including 5 rooms with gas fireplace. **Rates:** $85–$150 (seasonal). **Included:** Full breakfast.

Minimum stay: 2 or 3 nights on weekends. **Added:** 7% tax, 12% tax over $100; $25 additional guest. **Payment:** Visa, MasterCard, American Express. **Children:** Over 12 welcome. **Pets:** Not allowed. **Smoking:** Not allowed in bedrooms or dining area. **Open:** All year.

Eleven miles south of Lake George, across the street from the azure, still Lake Luzerne is the Lamplight Inn, the highest point in town. Inngoers will be hard pressed to find a more devoted and hardworking couple than Linda and Gene Merlino, who bought this large Victorian in 1984 and opened on Memorial Day 1985 after laborious restorations, including winterizing. Though their work in the inn would exhaust most people, it energizes this friendly couple. Linda decorated the rooms and made the curtains and bed coverings, while Gene built the new sun porch and four rooms above with utmost respect for the grandeur and craftsmanship of the

> Halfway between Saratoga Springs and Lake George, the countryside begins to turn into Adirondack wilderness. The air is crisper, the woods thicken, lakes pop up at every bend, and there, on the top of a hill, is the Lamplight Inn — a study in charm and perfection.

original 1890 Victorian. He also cooks breakfast for the inn's guests while Linda serves. The meal features crêpes, waffles, popovers, homemade granola, and Gene's famous home fries.

The Lamplight Inn is a cheerful and rambling wooden house, yellow with blue and white trim, with an extensive wraparound porch, lots of hanging flower baskets, and hilly lawns. It was built in 1890 by a bachelor named Howard Conkling as a summer party house. He was in the lumber business and imported the chestnut molding and elaborate wainscoting from England, as well as the wonderful unique carved keyhole staircase. (When Gene built the sun porch in 1989, he made sure to match the windows and wood to the original moldings and framing downstairs.) The house remained with Conkling until the 1920s, when it was bought by the Ketchum family, who owned it until the 1980s.

Guests enter to a double parlor, each room with a fireplace of carved chestnut inlaid with colorful tiles. The first parlor has two Victorian sitting areas and wainscoted walls; the second parlor is less formal, with the air of a game room. Guests take breakfast on the back sun porch, with an almost double-height ceiling, its windows overlooking the sloping lawns.

On the second floor are 10 guest rooms, five of which have gas fireplaces. Rooms not furnished with Victorian antiques have convincing reproductions. The Canopy and Rose rooms are exceptionally pretty, with mahogany and brass beds and tiled fireplaces. Four smaller rooms in the adjacent wing lead to the larger new rooms with fireplaces. Of these, the Victoria Room is especially lovely, with a lace-covered Henredon canopy bed and art deco bedroom suite. Bathrooms are tidy and small. Linda is an immaculate housekeeper as well as a creative one.

With equestrian influences from Saratoga Springs (20 miles south), Lake Luzerne is home to one of the oldest rodeos in the country, and many trail rides are available in the area. The town is also the summer home of a music camp for gifted students run by the Philadelphia Philharmonic.

ROCK CITY FALLS

The Mansion

801 Route 29
Box 77
Rock City Falls, NY 12863
518-885-1607

*A stunning
stopover
outside Saratoga*

Proprietors and Innkeepers: Tom Clark and Alan Churchill. **Accommodations:** 5 rooms, including 1 suite, all with private bath; 1 2-bedroom guest cottage. **Rates:** Rooms $95, suite $110; $165 July 15–August. **Included:** Five-course breakfast. **Minimum stay:** On some weekends and in high season. **Added:** 8% tax, 13% tax over $100. **Payment:** No credit cards. **Children:** Teenagers welcome. **Pets:** Not allowed. **Smoking:** Limited. **Open:** All year, except two days at Christmas.

Saratoga Springs comes alive in the summer, with events at the Performing Arts Center and the racing season. Find some rest at an idyllic retreat seven miles west. The Mansion is an exceptional beautiful bed-and-breakfast that has all the finery of Saratoga Springs without the traffic, crowds, and unreasonable rates.

In 1866, George West, best known as a philanthropist and the inventor of the folding paper bag, built a Venetian-style villa across from his paper mill in Rock City Falls to use as a summer home. The Italianate house was bought in 1986 by Tom Clark, who spent months restoring it to its former grandeur. The three-story peach-colored clapboard house was built of chestnut, trimmed in white, and topped by a cupola. A half dozen tiger tail spruce trees tower over the house. Nearly all of the house is original, from the brass and copper chandeliers with Waterford shades found in nearly every room, to the carved brass hardware and doorknobs, to the parquet flooring and chestnut and walnut moldings, to the six elaborately carved wood and marble fireplaces. Even the wooden shutters in the long, narrow windows are from the era.

> **A breathtaking restoration of an 1866 Venetian-style villa, the Mansion is romantic and relaxing, upscale and down-to-earth, intimate and sociable, sophisticated and countrified. Who would believe that the inventor of the folding paper bag could surround himself with such luxuries?**

To the left of the foyer is an informal library, lined with ample reading material in a comfortable setting. Two floor-to-ceiling windows look out to the front lawn, and in a three-windowed bay facing west stands a 300-pound sculpture of St. Francis carved of solid mahogany. To the right of the foyer are two parlors separated by arched pocket doors. One has Empire furnishings, with a black marble mantel and a carved wood mirror 13 feet high. The second parlor has Eastlake furniture, a white marble fireplace, and a hand pump organ.

At the back of the house is the dining room, with five intimate tables. Alan is quite proud of his breakfasts of French toast, omelettes with fresh herbs, or maybe eggs Benedict, served fireside with a special blend of coffee and fresh fruit breads. Just outside, Dutchman's pipe vine clings to the 60-foot porch, decorated with wicker furniture and flower boxes.

Of the five bedrooms, the first-floor suite has a little sitting room brightened by a pink marble fireplace and the original parquet flooring of oak, maple, and rosewood. A set of Currier and Ives racing prints appropriately decorates the walls. The antiques that fill the four second-floor rooms include a bird's-eye maple chest, a chestnut and walnut Renaissance Revival bedroom suite, and faux marble fireplaces in green and black. Here, a plant-filled sitting room features six Winslow Homer wood engravings and bentwood rockers that overlook the front lawns and river through arched windows. Before strolling the four acres, scan the grounds from the cupola.

Innkeeper Alan Churchill strives to immerse his guests in luxury and elegance. Many activities are a short drive away, including day trips to the Hudson River and the Adirondacks.

SARATOGA SPRINGS

The Adelphi Hotel

365 Broadway
Saratoga Springs, NY 12866
518-587-4688

An artistic enclave and Victorian wonderland

Proprietors: Gregg Siekfer and Sheila Parkert. **Accommodations:** 35 rooms, all with private bath, including 17 suites. **Rates:** $80-$185 May–October; $140-$290 August. **Included:** Continental breakfast; swimming pool. **Minimum stay:** 3 nights on racing weekends, 2 nights on some other weekends. **Added:** 11% tax, 16% tax over $100. **Payment:** MasterCard, Visa, American Express. **Children:** Allowed. **Pets:** Not allowed. **Smoking:** Allowed. **Open:** May weekends; June–October.

Visiting the Adelphi is like following Alice through Wonderland. At every turn, there is something magical, otherworldly, and illusory. The Adelphi, built in 1877 and restored to its former glory, stands as a reminder of Victorian opulence and the lavish beginnings of Saratoga Springs. The landmark hotel is the quintessence of sophistication during the exuberant summer months of racing season and cultural events at the Performing Arts Center and at Yaddo, the artists' retreat. However, the Adelphi leaps beyond a simple period restoration with boundless creativity and humor within its three stories and behind its brick walls.

> A drive down Broadway in Saratoga Springs is like a drive through Newport, with majestic mansions at every turn. Even in this company, the Adelphi causes a visitor to stop and gape. This architectural wonder is a living reminder of why Saratoga was the resort town of the Victoria era; its interior is even more magnificent.

The Adelphi had been abandoned for 10 years when Gregg Siekfer and Sheila Parkert bought it in 1979. Sheila is a painter and interior designer, and Gregg is an artistic carpenter: their marriage has produced a wondrous work in progress that attests to their talents. They are also inspired collectors, finding pieces at local antiques shows and trips abroad. Furniture is reupholstered to fit a room or a mood, mirrors are regilded, lamps refringed, old photographs rematted and framed — and the eclectic pieces in every room come together beautifully. Crafting and tailoring two or three rooms yearly, they have arrived at the present 36, each a unique world in itself.

More important than the innumerable treasures within the hotel is the sensory rapture a guest feels at the Adelphi. The three-story brown brick building, one of Broadway's most elegant, has creamy yellow trim and deep red highlights, with wood columns climbing the full height, adorned with gingerbread. Through the doors, guests enter an imaginary world. Eclectic Victorian parlor sets huddle together amid lush greenery, separated by faux marble pillars supporting the coffered ceiling. The walls are colorfully stenciled from Victorian patterns. Underfoot, the floors are stained dark and covered with Oriental rugs. A straight walk brings a guest to the Café Adelphi, decorated with tasseled drapery, upholstered banquettes, wall murals, and pillars, lending the air of a European hotel or even a movie set. The gardens are through French doors, with fountains, trellises, and wrought-iron furniture shaded by awnings. Gregg and Sheila recently added a wonderfully landscaped and private outdoor swimming pool.

A Victorian trellis-patterned carpet leads a guest upstairs to two floors of rooms, and, for common use, a formally appointed double parlor leading to a wicker-filled sun porch overlooking Broadway. Here guests can take breakfast and watch the crowds. Sheila designed each room around a specific era, piece of furniture, or carpet. The Neoclassic Suite has faux granite walls, faux black marble pillars, a gold and white silk Empire couch, and murals on the living room walls depicting a Roman landscape. With the same attention to detail and *trompe l'oeil* brushwork, the other rooms successfully make sweeping statements: the French Room, the Hungarian Room, the Adirondack Room, the Victorian Room, and the Dorothy Draper Room. The smaller rooms are less overwhelming, but they still have gorgeous wallpaper with playful borders, Sheila's handmade crown canopies, window treatments, and crocheted bedding. The baths are new and clean, sometimes wedged into confounding spaces. Rooms all have phones, televisions, and air conditioning. Breakfasts are a treat, brought to the room in a basket with home-baked muffins and fruit.

For all their whimsical creativity, Gregg and Sheila are surprisingly friendly and accessible, and their staff is extremely enthusiastic.

Gideon Putnam Hotel

Box 476
Saratoga Springs, NY 12866
518-584-3000
800-732-1560
Fax: 518-584-1354

A historic resort in Saratoga Spa State Park

Proprietor: TW Recreation Services, Inc. **General Manager:** Kenneth G. Boyles. **Accommodations:** 132 rooms, including 12 parlor suites and 6 porch suites. **Rates:** $94–$147 EP November–April, add $35 per person for AP; $236–$443 EP August, add $40 per person for AP; $115–$165 EP rest of year, add $35 per person for AP; $89 B&B December–March. **Included:** Up to three meals. **Minimum stay:** None. **Added:** $15–$30 EP each additional person; 11% tax, 16% tax over $100. **Payment:** Major credit cards. **Children:** Welcome. **Pets:** Not allowed. **Smoking:** Nonsmoking rooms available. **Open:** All year.

Only in Saratoga Springs can a state park represent the height of luxury. The Gideon Putnam Hotel sits in the middle of the 1,500-acre Saratoga Spa State Park, which is a mile south of downtown Saratoga Springs. Hotel guests are welcome to use all the park facilities, including a PGA 18-hole golf course, a nine-hole par three course, three outdoor swimming pools, eight tennis courts, ice skating, and cross-country skiing. Sharing the grounds is the Saratoga Performing Arts Center, summer home of the New York City Ballet and Metropolitan Opera, the Philadelphia Orchestra, and the Roosevelt Mineral Baths, in a turn-of-the-century setting.

> **Every state should have a park like this one. The Saratoga Spa State Park is the sophisticates' campground — summer home of the New York City Ballet, Metropolitan Opera, and, since 1934, to the wonderful Gideon Putnam resort hotel and the Roosevelt Mineral Baths.**

Built in 1934, the classic red brick hotel is trimmed in white in high Georgian style. A three-story portico supported by eight pillars shades the long inset verandah, topped by a balcony across the fourth floor and balanced on either side by five-story wings. A circular drive is carved into the sweeping front lawn of the Gideon Putnam. Guests enter the grand reception hall under a green and white striped awning covering bright flowers in window boxes.

The hotel was bought in 1988 by TW Services, which undertook a two-year redecorating project. The result is a toned-down version of the classic Williamsburg Inn in Virginia: Old World elegance and hospitality, formal sitting areas with floral arrangements atop side tables, cream-colored walls, classic moldings, high and wide archways, and Palladian windows opening to patios and gardened walkways. While the Williamsburg Inn was done in exacting, formal Regency style, the grand Georgian nature of the Gideon Putnam stops a bit short of museum-perfect elegance.

Guests dine in several rooms: the Georgian Room, whose walls were gloriously painted with landscape murals in 1935 by an Irish artist; the Garden Room, with lighter murals on a wall textured with plaster vines; and the smaller Estate Room, a classic room with a working marble fireplace. The Saratoga Room bar is enlivened by a mural depicting Saratoga scenes; and the Arches Room offers jazz in the summer, in a setting of sunlit archways. The Victoria pool is quite lovely, set in a Georgian palazzo with covered brick archways.

While the common areas are elegant, the guest rooms, throughout the five floors of the hotel, are rather predictable. Decorated traditionally in reproduction Queen Anne furniture, they are comfortable and spacious and have televisions and phones, but the colors and patterns are uninspired. Preferable are the six porch rooms that take advantage of the lovely scenery surrounding the hotel.

Service at the hotel is friendly and prompt, though the summer high season is assuredly hectic. The remarkable park setting and lovely Georgian architecture are quite worth the trip, especially in the off-season.

Western New York
and the
Finger Lakes

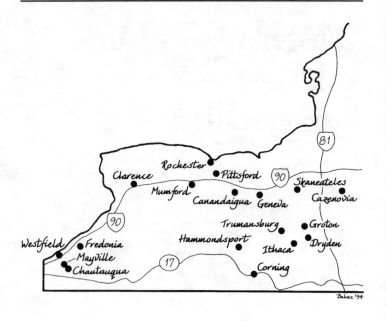

Best Romantic Retreats

Geneva
Geneva on the Lake
Ithaca
Rose Inn

Best for Metropolitan Magnificence

Rochester
Strathallan

Best Country Bed-and-Breakfasts

Canandaigua
Morgan-Samuels Inn
Chautauqua
Plumbush
Westfield
The William Seward Inn

Best Country Inns

Geneva
Belhurst Castle
Trumansburg
Taughannock Farms Inn

Best Village Bed-and-Breakfasts

Corning
Rosewood Inn
Dryden
Sarah's Dream
Hammondsport
The Blushing Rosé
Mumford
Genesee Country Inn

Best Village Inns

Cazenovia
  Brae Loch Inn
  Lincklaen House
  The Brewster Inn
Chautauqua
  Athenaeum Hotel
Clarence
  Asa Ransom House
Fredonia
  The White Inn
Groton
  Benn Conger Inn
Skaneateles
  The Sherwood Inn
Pittsford
  Oliver Loud's Inn

The western stretch of New York below Lake Ontario is reached via the dull Route 80, from Utica to Buffalo. A scenic stretch along this route is from Syracuse to Rochester, the northernmost border of the Finger Lakes. The parallel access road to the Finger Lakes, Route 20, is often quite congested. The lakes bleed south from Route 20, truly like fingers on an outstretched hand, ranging from a few miles in length to more than 40 miles: Skaneateles, Owasco, Cayuga, Seneca, Keuka, Canandaigua, and some smaller ones. The area was conquered with horrific force in 1779 by General John Sullivan, who ravaged the many outposts of Iroqouis Indians. There is much for a visitor to do, from museums to wineries and historic sites. Each lake has its focal town: **Ithaca,** for example, at the southernmost point of Lake Cayuga, **Hammondsport** at the base of Lake Keuka, and car-racing hub Watkins Glen at the base of Seneca Lake.

  Corning, below the Finger Lakes near Pennsylvania, has one of the state's largest tourist attractions. The Corning Museum of Glass, which welcomes millions of visitors yearly, is divided into three different sections: historical aspects of glass through changing exhibits, glass in the making at the Steuben Glass Factory, and displays with an eye to the future at the Hall of Science and Industry. The town is also home to the highly acclaimed Rockwell Museum, located in the restored 1893 city hall, which also offers one of the country's most comprehensive exhibits of American western art and Indian artifacts. A town replete with history, Corning's boom began in 1868, when the Flint Glass Company moved here from Brooklyn. At that time, Corning was a sleepy railroad depot about 40 years old. The main venue, Market Street, was restored and put on the National Register of Historic Places in the 1970s. It is lined with brick sidewalks and many Victorian buildings from the town's heyday.

Rochester is removed from Lake Ontario by several miles of the Genesee River. There is a great deal of history attached to this small city: Susan B. Anthony was arrested here en route to the ballot box, and Frederick Douglas's bold periodical *The North Star* was printed here. Rochester is still a formidable corporate hub, the largest resident of which is Eastman Kodak. The interesting sites include the International Museum of Photography, in the former mansion of Kodak founder George Eastman, and Kodak Park. Other museums include the Memorial Art Gallery, with ancient and European art; the Rochester Museum & Science Center, with one of the world's best collections of Iroquois Indian artifacts; and the Strong Museum, with one of the world's most extensive doll collections, upwards of 20,000, and domestic artifacts. The annual Festival of Lilacs is held in May at Highland Park.

Aside from visiting the falls, there is little to do in the tourist town of Niagara Falls, though a visit to the Canadian side is quite recommended. Be sure to have a meal at the Red Coach Inn, a Tudor house on the rapids that is one of the town's oldest buildings. It's famous for its prime rib.

In Buffalo, cruise the waters of Lake Erie, which is filled by the waters from Niagara and its river. Among the notable sights is the Buffalo and Erie County Historical Society, featuring archaeological history of the Niagara frontier, Indians, and the Erie Canal. The Albright-Knox Art Gallery has some great contemporary art. Be sure to stop at the Buffalo Zoo, laid out by Frederick Law Olmsted more than a century ago.

Driving south along Route 90, a traveler eventually reaches **Chautauqua,** a sleepy Victorian haven on a lake that shares its name. For nine weeks in summer, the town hosts the famed Chautauqua Institution, gifted with an infusion of art, dance, music, and academic performances. The abundance of adorable Victorian architecture is a testament to the Institution's beginnings — in 1874, a band of Methodist Sunday school teachers came here to create a cultural and intellectual refuge.

CANANDAIGUA

Morgan-Samuels Inn

2920 Smith Road
Canandaigua, NY 14424
716-394-9232
Fax: 716-394-8044

*A farmhouse B&B
in the
Finger Lakes*

Proprietors: John and Julie Sullivan. **Accommodations:** 6 rooms,
all with private bath, including 1 suite. **Rates:** $99–$195. **Included:** Full breakfast, afternoon tea. **Minimum stay:** 2 nights
on weekends, May–November. **Added:** $25 each additional
guest; $15 each child; 7% tax, 12% tax over $100. **Payment:**
MasterCard, Visa, Discover. **Children:** Under 4 and over 12.
Pets: Not allowed. **Smoking:** Not allowed. **Open:** All year.

The "Morgan" of this inn's name was the poor cousin of the
better-known tycoon J. P. Morgan. Having recovered from the
mild disappointment that it's not the magnate's mansion, a
visitor quickly admits that this is a lovely home by any standards. Two miles from the tip of one of the westernmost
Finger Lakes, Lake Canandaigua, and a short drive from its
charming and surprisingly bustling town, this bed-and-breakfast has a tranquil setting, removed from the country road
junction by two long gravel driveways. The unusual stone and
brick house was built in 1810 by a farmer, and present owners John and Julie Sullivan retain 46 acres of lovely flat corn-
fields and hay fields.

The farmhouse was expanded in 1930 to become a long,
narrow composite of two buildings, thick stone and brick,
nearly engulfed in ivy vines, with a kind of cottage-in-the-
woods feel.

The Sullivans opened their bed-and-breakfast in January
1989, escaping a corporate environment and seeking a serene
place for their young family. The rooms are on three floors: a
favorite is the Antique Rose Room, furnished with a smash-
ing, rare 19th-century five-piece bedroom set with hand-
painted green wood and gold trim and offering two views of
the farm. The master suite is large, in muted white and beige,
with a stunning 1749 serpentine French bedroom set and a
room-size dressing area. A rope banister takes visitors to the

third floor, with the charming Gothic Room and its pointed high windows, and to the spectacular Victorian Room, which has a barrel cathedral ceiling, a king-size bed fitted with dark and heavy tapestry linens, and floral trellised wallpaper. Some people think the bath is this room's finest feature: one wall has been exposed to reveal the stone chimney, marble lines the floor and walls, and a Jacuzzi lies under the pitched ceiling. Some of the rooms have porches, and all have peaceful farm views. A tennis court is framed by the stone foundation of an old barn.

The outskirts of Canandaigua quickly dissolve into corn and hay fields. Bisecting the main Route 20 — often, and then occasionally — are farm roads, straight, flat, and eventually unpaved. This is the setting of the Morgan-Samuels Inn, secluded and serene, on six acres of fields and fresh air.

Breakfasts are ample, served in the formal dining room or the enclosed slate porch overlooking the fields through enchanting wrought-iron doors. An outdoor slate patio sits amid the groomed gardens. Those who love the full breakfast — buckwheat pancakes, blackberry muffins, double cheese omelettes — will be pleased to know that John will cook dinners by prior arrangement for eight (or more) guests. For $27.50 to $50, visitors may enjoy a romantic and sybaritic treat at the elegant candlelit dining table.

CAZENOVIA

Brae Loch Inn

5 Albany Street, Route 20
Cazenovia, NY 13035
315-655-3431
Fax: 315-655-4844
800-722-0674

> *A Scottish enclave
> across from
> Lake Cazenovia*

Proprietors: H. Grey and James Grey Barr. **Accommodations:** 15 rooms, 13 with private bath. **Rates:** $75–$125. **Included:** Continental breakfast. **Minimum stay:** Some weekends. **Added:** $15 each additional guest; 10% tax, 12% tax over $100. **Payment:** American Express, Master-Card, Visa. **Children:** Welcome; under 12 free. **Pets:** Not allowed. **Smoking:** Allowed. **Open:** All year.

Owned by the same family since 1946, the Brae Loch is one of the few inns in this book with a theme. The Barr family is of Scottish descent, and their ancestry is heralded throughout the rambling home as if pumped in by bagpipes. A gift shop on the first floor sells Scottish items such as wools, kilts, and crystal; and the family is always there to greet guests with convivial, proud smiles. All guests are Scottish under this friendly roof.

Best known as a large family-style restaurant serving Scottish-American food, the Brae Loch has an extensive dinner menu, which ranges from $12 to $18. In addition to tournedos of lamb Athena, wrapped in phyllo pastry in a Madeira herb sauce, or mustard-fried Delta catfish with Cajun mayonnaise, there are Scottish salmon, rack of lamb, steak and kidney pie, the royal Scot (a mixed grill of veal, lamb, beef, and pork), and the Brae Loch Inn's specialty: prime rib minister. From September through Father's Day (a big holiday at this family place), the restaurant offers an extensive Sunday brunch. A plaid rug runs throughout most of the dining rooms, which ramble through the first and the ground floors that were dug out by Grey and his brother more than 40 years ago.

> **Family pride and national pride are the resounding themes at the Brae Loch Inn. In 1946, the Barr brothers began to reconfigure the 1805 mansion into a New Scotland; today the old and the new generations of the same family run this festive property together.**

Much to their credit, the Barr family is constantly updating the inn. The original house on the site was built in 1805, and there are four rooms in this section around a center stairwell, decorated in a respectful Victorian style. Room 11 has a beautiful striped cherry and pine floor, Oriental rug, and marble sink top, and it's the only room with the Scottish themes echoed in its tartan rug and chair. Room 12 is the prettiest in the old section, with a king-size fishnet canopy, unusual purple tiles with a religious theme on the fireplace, and a large window seat flanked by carved wood columns. The fireplace in Room 13 also has fancy tilework.

Four rooms in the back addition are deluxe, with king-size canopy beds, traditional reproduction furniture, large new baths, and a complimentary bottle of wine. Those who don't mind sharing a small but elegant marble bath may want one of the two third-floor rooms, with high ceilings that open to a skylight, exposed brick walls, and a brick fireplace. There are also two rooms on a private stairwell above the gift shop, good for families, with two three-quarter-size beds and new marble-tiled baths under a pitched roof. All rooms have televisions, phones, and coffeemakers.

Brae Loch is across the street from Lake Cazenovia in a parklike setting. Half a block in the other direction is the charming town. Chittenango Falls State Park is a short drive away, and within a half hour's drive are several colleges, including Colgate, Hamilton, Syracuse, and Cazenovia College.

The Brewster Inn

6 Ledyard Avenue
Cazenovia, NY 13035
315-655-9232
Fax: 315-655-2130

*An oil magnate's
mansion on
Lake Cazenovia*

Proprietors: Richard and Catherine Hubbard. **Accommodations:** 17 rooms, including 2 suites, all with private bath, 4 with Jacuzzis. **Rates:** $60–$195. **Included:** Continental breakfast. **Added:** $10 each additional guest plus 10%; 10% tax, 15% tax over $100. **Payment:** Visa, MasterCard, Diner's Club. **Children:** Welcome. **Pets:** Not allowed. **Smoking:** Not allowed in dining rooms. **Open:** All year.

One of three unique and complementary lodging spots in the charming town of Cazenovia, the Brewster Inn is the only one to sit right on the village lake. Guests enter at the back driveway but can look forward to walking two and a half lovely acres of lawn fronting glassy Lake Cazenovia.

The 1890 stone mansion was designed in the Richardson style by New York architect Robert Stevenson, built for his cousin William Brewster, one of the country's wealthiest men. The Hubbards have spent several years redecorating the nine guest rooms and restoring and maintaining the grande dame; most recently, they restored the neighboring Carriage House and added eight terrific rooms. Dick is a proud host who cares particularly about his wine — which has won the Wine Spectator Award for Excellence since 1992 — and about his seafood, which is flown in daily from Boston. Chef Brian Shore's specialties include tournedos of beef on artichoke hearts with a sauce of shallots, red wine, and cream; and veal Atlantis, sautéed veal cutlets with a lobster and tarragon beurre blanc sauce. Entrées range from $12 to $18. The three dining rooms have spartan decor but lovely architecture — two rather traditional spots in the original house have coffered ceilings of mahogany and working fireplaces — and wonderful views. One room glimpses the lake through a five-windowed bay; another is set in a rounded glass atrium over-looking the water.

The rooms are exceptionally large, as befits the home of a millionaire, and some have decks and porches. The master bedroom is one of several decorated in antiques. It has a spectacular three-piece 1890 Eastlake bedroom set with a grand carved headboard. The room is upholstered in boudoir red and carpeted with Oriental rugs. The bath features a three-and-a-half-foot-wide pedestal sink. The room has a porch that descends to the front lawn.

Other rooms are done in reproductions, including the Harden Room, with a four-poster cherry queen-size canopy bed, a modern bath, and a large deck through a sliding glass door. The third-floor Stickley Suite is more than a thousand square feet, with semicircular window views to the lake. Its fabulous bath has a sunken Jacuzzi overlooking the lake. Two third-floor rooms with lovely views need some attention.

> An impressive stone mansion with grand proportions, the Brewster Inn is Cazenovia's only lodging right on the village lake. Entering from the back, guests do not see the sweeping lawns that embrace the gentle banks of the lakefront: this wonderful view is reserved for the dining room.

Original blueprints of the mansion are displayed in some of the halls. The second-floor landing features a lovely Horace Waters square piano from around 1870 with mother-of-pearl inlay. The elegant entry has an impressive coffered ceiling, quarter-sawn oak walls, and a gilded mirror over the mantel of a working fireplace. Don't let the interior beauty distract you from the charms of the outdoors, including Chittenango Falls State Park.

Lincklaen House

79 Albany Street
Cazenovia, NY 13035
315-655-3461
Fax: 315-655-5443

> *The state's oldest continuously operating inn*

Proprietors: The Tobin family. **General Manager:** Howard M. Kaler. **Accommodations:** 21 rooms, all with private bath, including 3 suites. **Rates:** $70–$130. **Included:** Continental breakfast, afternoon tea. **Minimum stay:** 2 nights some college weekends. **Added:** $8 each additional guest; 7% tax, 12% tax over $100. **Payment:** Visa, MasterCard. **Children:** Welcome. **Pets:** Allowed. **Smoking:** Allowed. **Open:** All year.

On Cazenovia's main corner is the Lincklaen House, an unusually sophisticated small hotel that recently underwent a much-needed renewal. It's said to be the oldest continuously operating hotel in New York, having kept it doors open since 1835, even when fire marred its walls in the early 1900s.

The lobby restoration resulted in a stunningly elegant formal entrance with diagonal black and white parquet tiles. The house sits on the corner, so two entrances converge in front of the old reception desk. Some of the elaborate wood paneling was reproduced, painted over with thick white paint. A waiting area has lovely formal Federal antiques, high coffered white ceilings, and an elaborate carved mantel warmed by a gas fireplace. Through French doors away from the reception area is a formal double parlor with traditional couches and chairs. Cheerful but elegant floral swags decorate the huge windows. The lines throughout are clean and

white, and there is a formal air about the entire place.

The serenely beautiful dining room is reached through French doors. The floors are a light wood parquet. Four Corinthian columns separate the three rows of tables and support the coffered ceiling. At the end of the room, an elaborate fireplace warms the soft white walls. The tables are decorated in snowy linen cloths; the chairs are Windsor. Chef Robert Fasce, Jr. prepares Continental cuisine, with entrées ranging from $13 to $20. The seafood bisque is highly acclaimed, as are the popovers served with every meal. The Tap Room in the lower level is a woody Ivy League enclave whose walls bear witness to visitors of the last century and a half — including quite a lot of college students, who come from nearby Hamilton, Syracuse, Colgate, and local Cazenovia.

> There is a tremendous sense of history at this establishment. For a century and a half, people have been coming here for lodging, food, and conviviality. The longevity of this inn reminds a visitor — as few places do — that we are stewards of our buildings, and that they may carry on much longer than we will.

The renovations married some of the smaller rooms, bringing the number down from 28 to 21 on two floors. Though the remaining twin rooms are very small (unless you're traveling alone, try to avoid these), the larger rooms are wonderful, with Hitchcock furniture, a Martha Washington chair, a writing desk, a reproduction highboy, and lovely wallpapers and window treatments — some in chintz, some more masculine. There is some clean and spare stencilwork in and around the borders and bathrooms, usually of flowers and vines. All rooms have televisions and phones. The bathrooms are the most recent beneficiary of the improvements, with ceramic faux marble black and white tiles and new fixtures.

Devoted host Howard Kaler is sure to greet guests. His staff is warm and enthusiastic about the recent changes in the Lincklaen House. There is an elegant gentility about this place, a bit of nobility in a charming small town. Be sure to visit Lake Cazenovia at the end of the street and Chittenango Falls State Park.

CHAUTAUQUA

Athenaeum Hotel

Box 66, Chautauqua Institution
Chautauqua, NY 14722
800-821-1881

*A Victorian
monolith in a
Victorian enclave*

Proprietor: W. Thomas Smith. **Accommodations:** 160 rooms, all with private bath. **Rates:** $104–$148 per person, double occupancy, AP. **Included:** Three meals daily. **Minimum stay:** None. **Added:** $25–$29 for Chautauqua gate ticket; 7% tax, 12% over $100. **Payment:** No credit cards. **Children:** Welcome. **Pets:** Allowed. **Smoking:** Not allowed in public areas. **Open:** Mid-June–August.

Squeezed into the southwest corner of New York's 47,400 square miles is Lake Chautauqua and the cultural enclave that bears its name, a sleepy community of fewer than 500 that swells to thousands in summer. Methodist Sunday school teachers first sought intellectual refuge here in 1874, and the tradition of cultural enrichment continues today from late June through August with programs at the Chautauqua Institution. The village is cluttered with teetering, gingerbreaded, brightly colored houses on narrow streets meant more for strolling than for driving.

It is fitting that the place to stay here is the grandest piece of Victorian architecture within the Chautauqua gates, the palatial Athenaeum Hotel, built in 1881 and commendably restored in 1984 by the present manager, W. Thomas Smith. The exterior is one of the grandest in the region. From the lakefront, the lawns sweep up to a double staircase embracing a fountain, which reaches a two-story portico, outfitted with green wicker rockers, spanning the length of the grand building. Atop it all is an immense mansard-roofed cupola with floor-to-ceiling Palladian windows on four sides, topped by a flag. The Chautauqua amphitheater is steps behind the hotel.

The two-story lobby is lit by Victorian brass chandeliers with etched globes, diagonal wainscoted wood, and rich exposed flooring. The ballroom-size common room is full of creamy wicker furniture, with double floor-to-ceiling windows shaded in lace overlooking the lake, all complemented by a latticework floral Victorian area carpet. The dining room is brightened by grandmotherly floral paper with white linen cloths covering tables, Queen Anne chairs, and polished wooden floors. At the Athenaeum, everyone is on the full American plan and is treated to its hallmark of two desserts with lunch and dinner.

The second- and third-floor rooms all have very high ceilings, twin beds, Victorian antiques and wallpapers, and now, private baths. They are simple and tidy, with accommodations appropriate for families, doubles, and singles. The rooms are configured in a square, in the center of which is an outdoor patio on the second floor, with wicker furniture, slatted flooring, latticework, and a gazebo, as well as an abundance of plants.

> A grande dame of painted ladies (brightly colored Victorian houses), the Athenaeum is a stunning edifice that rests on the banks of Lake Chautauqua. It serves as a mascot for this quirky little town, devoted to the arts and probably featuring more Victorian homes per square mile than anywhere else in the world.

Most of the staff and guests are Chautauqua veterans, happy and relaxed. No visit is complete without a visit to the institution's bookstore.

Plumbush

Chautauqua-Stedman Road
Box 332, RD 2
Chautauqua, NY 14722
716-789-5309

*A sweet and
private B&B near
Chautauqua*

Proprietors: Sandy and George Green. **Accommodations:** 5 rooms, all with private bath. **Rates:** $80–$95; off-season rates available. **Included:** Buffet breakfast. **Minimum stay:** 2 and 3 nights in peak season and on some weekends. **Added:** 7% tax. **Payment:** MasterCard, Visa, American Express (add $2). **Children:** Over 12 welcome. **Pets:** Not allowed. **Smoking:** Not allowed. **Open:** All year.

If one wants a more private or romantic place to stay in Chautauqua than the famous and very busy Athenaeum, there is no better choice than Plumbush. This glorious 1867 Italianate Victorian mansion is a minute's drive from the Chautauqua gates, painted in mauve and trimmed with plum, pale pink, and greens. Propped on a little hill, Plumbush is neat as a pin, and its rooms are just as pristine. The 125 acres of grounds are gently groomed. Only a turret pokes above the two stories of the house, with its arched windows, corner bays, a little corner porch where guests enter. To the left is the living room with a bay window, to the right a music room with a bay window, a piano, and an organ. The dining room has a spectacular cherry and hard maple floor in a striped pattern, highly polished, with a handmade quilted tiger maple table. Past the kitchen is the sun porch, an addition to the old house, with brick flooring, large windows, and sliding doors to the lawns.

The carved walnut banister leads guests upstairs to the

landing. From here, a white iron spiral staircase leads to the third-floor turret, with views all around of the property and the maple trees outside.

The two larger of the five guest rooms, Pipestone and Bleufre (they're named for plums) face the front of the house. These rooms have lovely antiques and cheery new baths. Pipestone has two large curved windows, a queen-size iron and brass bed, and white wicker chairs with green chintz cushions. Bleufre features an incredible double rope bed and a rare chest of tiger maple. Greengage, down the hall, is the smallest room, with a little Victorian pine dresser and a nice little bath.

> Chautauqua explodes with activity for nine cultural weeks in the summer. Set on 125 acres of fields, the pretty Victorian Plumbush is the perfect place for those who want to enjoy the season while retaining their privacy and quiet time.

Bradshaw, in the back of the house, has twin beds. Victoria overlooks the back fields through three windows; its best feature is a *trompe l'oeil* headboard painted on the wall behind the queen-size bed.

Innkeepers Sandy and George are quite knowledgeable about the area and are happy to offer advice over a buffet breakfast, served in the dining room or on the sun porch.

CLARENCE

Asa Ransom House

10529 Main Street, Route 5
Clarence, NY 14031
716-759-2315
Fax: 716-759-2791

> *A pretty inn celebrating farmhouse cooking*

Proprietors: Robert and Judith Lenz. **Accommodations:** 9 rooms, including 2 suites, all with private bath, 7 with fireplaces or balconies. **Rates:** $85–$145; $140–$195 MAP on Saturdays. **Included:** Full breakfast; breakfast and dinner with MAP. **Minimum stay:** None. **Added:** $15 each additional guest; 11% tax, 13% tax over $100. **Payment:** MasterCard, Visa, Discover. **Children:** Welcome. **Pets:** Not allowed. **Smoking:** Not allowed. **Open:** All year except January; restaurant closed Fridays.

The area surrounding Buffalo and Niagara Falls was settled as late as the turn of the 19th century. The oldest town in Erie County is Clarence, founded in 1803. Several years before this, in 1799, the Holland Land Company offered plots of land ten miles apart to anyone who would build a tavern for the area. Asa Ransom, a Lake Erie fur trader, was the first to take up the offer. He built a log cabin and tavern on the site that now bears his name, as well as Erie County's first gristmill in 1803. Parts of today's Asa Ransom House date to 1853.

The rest of the inn, including the two large dining rooms and two of the guest rooms, was built by Robert Lenz in 1975. It's beige clapboard with red trim, to complement the historic brick home. An addition with five guest rooms was built in

1991. Lenz and his wife, Judy, opened the Asa Ransom House in 1976 as young newlyweds and have been attracting a large dinner crowd from Buffalo ever since.

A large brick fireplace warms two dining rooms: one is traditional and overlooks the street through bay windows; the second has views of the woods behind the house. This latter room is walled with bookshelves and has several wonderful maps from an 1875 atlas of Erie County, showing all the old towns and original family tracts. The common room is furnished with antiques in cozy sitting areas, and the convivial Tap Room is papered with an impressive collection of wine bottle labels.

> **Country inns must strike a balance between food and lodging; more often than not, scales swing in favor of dining. At the Asa Ransom House, however, the Lenzes have managed to do both very well. People come from all over for the farmhouse cooking and the lovely rooms.**

The two rooms on the second floor of the 1853 house have a distinctly older feel. The Green and Lavender Room has an unusual Chippendale broken arch king-size bed and a matching antique armoire. Two much larger rooms in the 1975 wing are of note: the Gold Room has an exposed brick wall —the exterior of the original house — and a queen-size iron and brass bed with a fireplace; the Green Room is a favorite, with dentil molding around the fireplace echoed in crown canopies over two double pine beds. The new wing has five rooms that equal or better this large scale, four with gas fireplaces.

Breakfasts are generous at the Asa Ransom House, with a choice of two hot entrées: perhaps an egg and cheese soufflé, a breakfast pie, pecan French toast, quiche, or crêpes with berries. A three-course afternoon tea is served on Thursdays, a full lunch on other days. Dinners ($11 to $20) are served nightly except Friday and Saturday. Chef Robb Perrott specializes in New York farmland hearty fare, including smoked corned beef with apple raisin or horseradish sauce or salmon pie with tomato and vegetables, topped with cheese pastry. From greetings to good-byes, Bob and Judy are very good neighbors, kind hosts, and informed area guides.

CORNING

Rosewood Inn

134 East First Street
Corning, NY 14830
607-962-3253

> *The best B&B
> in Corning*

Proprietors: Stewart and Suzanne Sanders. **Accommodations:** Seven rooms, all with private bath, including 2 suites. **Rates:** $68–$100. **Included:** Full breakfast, afternoon tea. **Minimum stay:** None. **Added:** $15 each additional guest, 9% tax. **Payment:** Visa, MasterCard, Diners Club. **Children:** Welcome. **Pets:** Permitted in one suite. **Smoking:** Restricted. **Open:** All year.

The Rosewood Inn was built as a Greek Revival in 1853 and was given a Tudor face in 1917. Since 1980, it has been a special place in Corning for devoted B&Bers. The double-sized living room opens to a sun porch at the side of the house and, toward the back, to an elegant, family-style dining room. Around the dining room's oversize mahogany table, a full breakfast is served, beginning with home-baked goods, pineapple French toast, and baked dishes such as strata and quiche.

The second floor has five rooms. The Charles Dana Gibson Room has six prints of Gibson girls from the turn of the century and a lovely quilt on a Victorian faux grained burl bed. The Rockwell Gallery Room has western art and a queen-size canopy bed; the Frederick Carder Room, named for the artisan who began the Steuben Glass works in 1903, has a glass solarium and wicker furniture; the Herman Melville Room has whaling memorabilia, walnut beds, and a marble-top dresser; and the Jenny Lind Room has a bed constructed shortly after the soprano's American tour in 1851. The second-floor landing serves as an informal common room, with room for a television and rockers.

For 80 years, the house was also a doctor's office. The examining rooms are now a pair of ground-floor suites with private entrances, phones, and televisions. The George Pullman kitchen suite, with stocked kitchen, is simply furnished with a pair of twin pineapple single beds; the Benjamin Patterson parlor suite has a cherry queen-size canopy bed in the bedroom and a sofa bed and a fireplace in the sitting room.

> **With friendly new owners devoted to innkeeping, the Rosewood Inn once again reigns as the best bed-and-breakfast option in Corning. It's a much-needed homespun offering in a town that hosts a great deal of corporate activity — and a nice place for romantics as well.**

Guests receive a welcome basket with fruit, cheese, and crackers and as much interaction as they desire with their gregarious hosts. Nearby are vineyards at Hammondsport and its Lake Keuka, and auto racing at Watkins Glen. The Rosewood Inn is less than a mile from the Corning Glass Museum and two blocks from the Rockwell Museum of Western Art.

DRYDEN

Sarah's Dream

49 West Main Street
Dryden, NY 13053
607-844-4321

> *A tea-lovers'*
> *haven*
> *outside Ithaca*

Proprietors: Judi and Ken Morusty. **Accommodations:** 6 rooms, including 2 2-room suites, 1 with fireplace. **Rates:** $65–$120; weekday discounts. **Included:** Full breakfast and refreshments. **Minimum stay:** Some weekends. **Added:** Afternoon tea Tuesdays–Thursdays, dinner with advance notice, 7% tax. **Payment:** Major credit cards. **Children:** Over 10 welcome. **Pets:** Not allowed. **Smoking:** Not allowed. **Open:** All year.

A nine-mile drive east from Ithaca through rolling farmland brings one to Dryden, a small agricultural town in the valleys beyond the Finger Lakes. On the town's main street is Sarah's Dream, an 1828 Greek Revival home listed on the National Register of Historic Places, named for the owner's mother, who always wanted such a hospitable home.

While it is a charming bed-and-breakfast, Sarah's Dream is best known throughout the area as a refuge for takers of high tea. Three sittings daily during the middle of the week bring guests from all over to choose among nine kinds of tea that accompany the endless menu of scones, shortbread, walnut pie, lemon bars, gingerbread, cucumber sandwiches, quiche, Welsh rarebit, watercress sandwiches, chocolate torte, cream puffs, and madeleines. The delicacies are gorgeously presented on Judi's heirloom china, silver, and linens.

While most proprietors choose a house as a vehicle for innkeeping, Judi and Ken always wanted this particular house. They are both in real estate, and they had an eye on the house for years until it was put on the market in 1987. The three-story gray clapboard house sits on a well-tended village lot on the corner of Main and Mill.

> **Judi is an overachiever. Because she likes to bake, she thought it would be nice to serve afternoon tea for her guests. Word of her talents spread, and now it's an event for which people come from all over to sample her cakes, her watercress sandwiches, madeleines, cream puffs, and nine kinds of tea.**

There are two rooms on the first floor: the Garden Room is charming and simple, with a brass bed under a crocheted spread and its sink in a dresser in the closet, a quirky but successful touch. Facing front is the Porch Suite, with a brick fireplace, a queen-size brass bed, a sitting area with a television and VCR, a wall full of books, and a private sitting porch.

The second floor has a pretty two-room suite with damask rose walls, a sitting area with a daybed and television, and a bedroom with a king-size bed and porcelain lamps like Staffordshire figurines. The Rose Room is also quite pretty, with a queen-size canopy bed in heavy carved oak and a wicker sitting area. The baths are new and extremely clean; Judi's obsession is a fresh, full bar of soap for every guest. There are bathrobes in every room.

Those who miss Judi's afternoon tea will be grateful for the opportunity to sample her elaborate cooking at breakfast. A perpetual baker, Judi serves fresh scones and muffins, casseroles, quiche, and fresh fruit in an old-fashioned presentation. This classic bed-and-breakfast is near Lake Cayuga and Lake Owasco, a hop from Greek Peak in Virgil for skiing and Ithaca's Sapsucker Woods for renowned birding.

FREDONIA

The White Inn

52 East Main Street
Fredonia, NY 14063
716-672-2103
Fax: 716-672-2107

> *A beacon of hospitality on the western shore*

Proprietors and Innkeepers: Robert Contiguglia and Kathleen Dennison. **Accommodations:** 23 rooms, all with private bath, including 11 suites, some with whirlpool and fireplace. **Rates:** $59–$159; MAP $149 weekdays, $159 weekends. **Included:** Full breakfast. **Minimum stay:** None. **Added:** $5–$10 service charge; $5–$10 for cots; 7% tax, 12% tax over $100. **Payment:** Major credit cards. **Children:** Welcome, under 12 stay free. **Pets:** Not allowed. **Smoking:** 5 nonsmoking rooms available. **Open:** All year.

Halfway between Buffalo and Erie, just south of the region's Great Lake, is the town of Fredonia. Passersby can't miss the White Inn, an imposing structure on Main Street. The three-story building is painted white, named coincidentally for the family who built it in 1811, some of the county's first settlers. The house was expanded to its present mansion size in 1868. The Greek Revival facade, added in 1919, greatly dresses up the rectangular structure, its two-story portico supported by six looming pillars and flanked by a single-story porch, making the verandah an endless hundred feet in length. The White Inn was one of the country's first motor inns, transformed into an overnight hostelry with 40 rooms in 1919, and it remained such until 1980.

> **A regal place — the largest building in Fredonia — the White Inn opened in 1919. The hostelry was reviewed in the 1930s by Duncan Hines (yes, the baker), a frequent traveler and writer of some of our earliest lodging and dining books.**

Underfoot in the grand foyer is a pretty green and pink trellis rug that leads into a huge wood-paneled bar to the left and into the dining rooms to the right. Guest rooms are on the second and third floors. They are all decorated differently, some furnished with traditional reproductions, others with Victorian antiques. The baths are all new and sparkling.

While the rooms are large and comfortable, people flock from all over for the food (lunch and dinner) at the White Inn. American country entrées range from $10 to $20 on a large and creative menu prepared by chef Richard Orloff. A specialty is buffalo steak.

There is a festive quality about the White Inn, with informal, friendly service in a formal atmosphere. There is a busy gift shop in a barn at the back of the lot, full of local products, artwork, and crafts. Chautauqua Institute is a half-hour drive, and Lake Erie is a hop away.

GENEVA

Belhurst Castle

Lochland Road
Route 145, Box 609
Geneva, NY 14456
315-781-0201

A Romanesque castle on the banks of Lake Seneca

Proprietor: Duane R. Reeder. **Innkeeper:** Kevin Reeder. **Accommodations:** 13 rooms, all with private bath, including 2 suites. **Rates:** Rooms $90–$125, suites $175 and $225; rates lower in winter. **Included:** Continental breakfast. **Added:** $15 each additional guest; 7% tax, 12% tax over $100. **Payment:** MasterCard, Visa. **Children:** Welcome (under 8 free). **Pets:** Not allowed. **Smoking:** Allowed. **Open:** All year.

Without reminders of the modern world or evidence of place, a visitor can easily picture Belhurst Castle in the Loire Valley, home of royalty, subject of fairy tales. It was built, however, high on the northern banks of Lake Seneca beginning in 1885 for Carrie Harron Collins, daughter of the founder of Dun and Bradstreet. Her picture, painted on porcelain, greets guests at the foyer. Fifty men built the castle, for an overwhelming cost of $475,000, with materials imported from Europe. It was built of red Medina stone in the heavy Richardson Romanesque style, with small windows and witch-hat turrets wrapped in ivy.

> With its gothic proportions, the Inn at Belhurst Castle is a stunning sight, a place from the mind's landscape. Its dark and impressive image high above Lake Seneca looks as if it were lifted from the pages of a fairy tale, evoking fantasy, romance, sorcery, and mystery.

The interior of the castle is an impressive display of carved and highly varnished wood paneling and coffered ceilings of cherry, golden oak, and mahogany. To the right of the foyer is a masculine library, walled in rich mahogany. The elegant restaurant has two pretty rooms paneled in cherry and a porch dining room on the first floor. Chef Casey Belile may prepare veal Clarissa, with artichoke hearts and Alaskan crab in sherry; or salmon Kelsey Lea, a boneless fillet baked with a honey-pecan crust in champagne mustard. Entrées range from $11 to $22.

Because of the busy nature of Belhurst's restaurant, guests may not receive intimate attention from the innkeeper and hosts. Romantics might not care, however, once shown up the formidable carved golden oak stairway to their grand room. Some rooms have original stained glass windows, toile and damask wallpaper, and elaborately carved mantels. Four rooms have working fireplaces. The furniture is mostly reproduction, but the rooms have interesting high ceilings with oddly pitched angles, wainscoted walls, and alcoves tucked into turrets. The finest room is the Tower Suite, with little stairs leading to the tower turret, including a huge wainscoted bathroom with a double Jacuzzi.

As the hub of New York's wine country, the Finger Lakes offer wonderful day trips for romantics. The public Seneca Country Club is a mile away, as are Hobart and William Smith colleges.

Geneva on the Lake

1001 Lochland Road
P.O. Box 929
Geneva, NY 14456
315-789-7190
800-3-GENEVA

*An Italian villa
on the banks of
Lake Seneca*

Proprietors: Norbert H. Schickel, Jr.
Accommodations: 30 suites (studios and 1- and 2-bedrooms).
Rates: $178–$440 summer, $113–$318 winter. **Included:** Bottle of wine, fresh fruit, Continental breakfast. **Minimum stay:** 2 nights May–October, with Saturday stay. **Added:** Additional guests age 4–9 $17, age 10–15 $29, adults $52; 12% tax. **Payment:** Major credit cards. **Children:** Allowed; 12 and under stay free. **Pets:** Not allowed. **Smoking:** Not allowed in public rooms. **Open:** All year.

On the shores of Seneca Lake, a bit of Italy exists in the inn called Geneva on the Lake. A replica of the Villa Lancellotti in Frascati, Italy, this palatial white stucco building with a red Mediterranean tiled roof transports a visitor to Italian shores. Throughout the ten acres, formal gardens are connected with walkways peopled by Greek and Roman sculptures. Near the hill that descends steeply to Seneca Lake, gilded Italian urns border a 70-foot swimming pool that approximates the azure of the Mediterranean.

The mansion was built as a private home for the Nester family from 1910 to 1914 and served as a Capuchin monastery from 1949 to 1974, relics of which remain throughout the inn. When Norbert Schickel bought the property in 1979, it had been vacant for five years. He accomplished extensive restoration as well as some renovations with apartments in mind. Involved in the project were some of his 13 children as well as his brother, a prominent designer and artist. As the phoenix rose from the ashes, the family decided that the mansion was better suited to resort living.

> With its wineries and rolling hillsides, the landscape of the Finger Lakes region is the Italy of the New World. Geneva on the Lake celebrates this relationship, in its Mediterranean-influenced architecture, groomed and sculptured gardens, and European antiques.

The suites show the influence of the short-lived apartment idea. They are equipped with full kitchens, including refrigerators stocked with a bottle of Finger Lake wine. All but two have lake views. There are six groups of suites, furnished with reproductions, traditionally decorated with curtains and rugs, and equipped with new baths. While some rooms have a traditional yet contemporary feeling as a result of the renovations, others, like the Classic Suite and the Library, retain the original plaster moldings, medallions, wall paneling, and outward-opening French windows.

The common rooms and grounds are truly exceptional. Mr. Schickel commissioned reproductions of significant sculptures to decorate the grounds. The two intimate original dining rooms are breathtaking, tiled in marble, overlooking the formal gardens through French doors. Some of the rare antiques include a 17th-century Bible box, a tiled Portuguese 18th-century planter, Italian Renaissance church candlesticks, and gold carved panels from an 18th-century French carriage.

Mrs. Schickel hosts a wine and cheese party every Friday on the outdoor piazza. Dinner is served on weekends only, in a careful presentation of five entrées ranging from $18 for chicken Jacqueline with port wine cream sauce, sliced apples, and almonds to $32 for Australian lobster tail with brandy cream sauce. Elaborate desserts may include baked Alaska or strawberries Romanoff in Grand Marnier. A pianist and singer enhance the romance of the setting. Sunday brunch is a popular event here.

A strong sense of family unites the staff and creates a warm, pleasant atmosphere throughout the formal property.

Among the activities on the immaculate grounds are croquet, swimming, and sailing. Only a short drive away are the public Seneca Lake Country Club and tours of the magnificent wine country.

GROTON

Benn Conger Inn

206 West Cortland Street
Groton, NY 13073
607-898-5817

> *A wine and food lover's treasure*

Proprietors: Peter and Alison van der Meulen. **Accommodations:** 3 suites, 1 room. **Rates:** $75–$125, fireplace suite $150. **Included:** Full breakfast. **Minimum stay:** 3 nights on holidays and university weekends. **Added:** $25 each additional guest; 10% tax, 15% tax over $100. **Payment:** Major credit cards. **Children:** Check with innkeeper. **Pets:** Will consider. **Smoking:** Allowed in common room and library. **Open:** All year.

Peter and Alison van der Meulen bought this 12-year-old, well-reputed country inn in the heart of the Finger Lakes in 1990 with grand ambitions. They are a young cosmopolitan pair from the downstate city, Peter a former operations producer for "Nightline" and "World News Tonight," Alison in magazines and fashion. During their tenure in New York City, they restored several brownstones to period status. They wanted to buy a country inn to display Alison's flair for decorating and Peter's skills as a trained chef.

The Greek Revival house is a magnificent structure built in 1921 by industrialist Benn Conger, a founder of Smith Corona who later became a state senator. The two-story facade of white clapboard and green shutters has a portico of equal height, topped by a true mansard roof with dormers. The inn sits on a hill on 18 acres, a short walk from the adorable town of Groton.

At present, the inn is best known for its extensive, award-winning wine list and Peter's Mediterranean-inspired cuisine, ranging from $14 to $22. Guests await dinner in the library, with a cherry bar and a working fireplace with a marble mantel, one of three originals in the house. The common areas and three dining rooms have recently been redecorated by Alison, with beautiful results. The most spectacular is the small Conservatory dining room with green tile and trim, floor-to-ceiling Palladian windows on three sides, and Pierre Deux linens. The inn's menu changes with the seasons but might include Cornish game hens with apricot and Grand Marnier stuffing, or medallions of pork de la Touraine with a red wine demiglace.

> A few memorable properties are defined by the personalities of their owners; the Benn Conger Inn is such a place. To this Greek Revival in the Finger Lakes countryside, Peter has brought a passion for Mediterranean food and wine, and Alison has contributed a great sense of taste and design; together, they bring a refreshing energy to innkeeping.

There are four rooms on the second floor of the main house and eight rooms in a complementary addition behind. Alison has decorated all the accommodations in the height of elegance, with the quality and style of the finest country inn, including 350-thread-count designer linens and decorator wallpapers in bold but traditional colors and patterns. The small Cornell Suite has a blue and white comforter and French doors to a balcony over the porte-cochere. The Dutch Schultz Suite (Conger's proper political family had a scandalous 20-year friendship with the famous mobster) is a massive 16-by-30-foot room, with a balcony over the Conservatory. Its sleigh bed sits grandly in the middle of the room, and its huge Old World tiled bath has a walk-in closet.

The four rooms in the main house encircle a private hot tub. The eight guest rooms in the addition each have a private verandah that looks out to the pergola and the groomed acreage of the estate.

The elaborate breakfasts are prepared by Alison, perhaps a pancake ball stuffed with glazed apple, eggs Benedict, frittata, or soufflé.

HAMMONDSPORT

Blushing Rosé

11 William Street
Hammondsport, NY 14840
607-569-3402, 800-982-8818

*A charming home
at the edge
of Lake Keuka*

Proprietors: Ellen and Bucky Laufersweiler. **Accommodations:** 4 rooms, all with private bath. **Rates:** $75–$85. **Included:** Full breakfast. **Minimum stay:** 2 nights Memorial Day–October. **Added:** $15 each additional guest, 10% tax. **Payment:** No credit cards. **Children:** Will consider; $10 additional. **Pets:** Not allowed. **Smoking:** Not allowed. **Open:** All year.

Lake Keuka is one of the westernmost Finger Lakes, and Hammondsport is the endearing town on its southern shore. The old town is a good base for visiting the Finger Lakes, auto racing in nearby Watkins Glen, the Corning glass works, and especially the wine country, with the Taylor vineyards just minutes away. This is the heart of wine country — even back in 1843, when grape growers built a sweet two-story house at the end of William Street, known today as the Blushing Rosé.

With only four rooms, the Blushing Rosé is reserved for those who love the bed-and-breakfast concept. Ellen and Buck are gregarious hosts who moved here from the Catskills in 1986 and restored the house. The pretty pink clapboard house with deep red trim, topped by a tiny cupola, is a cozy place. Full breakfasts made by Ellen are sociable events where guests linger over zucchini quiche, baked French toast, and Belgian waffles. Buck built a wing in the back of the house that has two lovely new rooms.

The living room is a busy place, full of the lives of its own-ers. Upstairs in the original section of the house are rooms called Magnificent Walnut, for its bed, and Moonbeams, for its skylight. Ellen stitched the pink and mauve quilt on the Magnificent Walnut bed. Buck did the charming stenciling in Moonbeams, a preferable room set under the eaves with a blue iron and brass bed covered in white eyelet linens and a clever slim bathroom.

> For those who want a homey base in the Finger Lakes, the Blushing Rosé is just the place. It has all the classic qualities bed-and-breakfast devotees require: sociable owners, accessibility, personal touches, pretty decor, informality, and of course, great big breakfasts.

The two new rooms are the large Burgundy, with a king-size bed covered with a log cabin quilt and a lace canopy, a wicker-furnished sitting area, and dried eucalyptus wreaths on the walls. Buck skillfully refinished the floors to look like pine. The Queen Room is more feminine, with a dark Bennington bed. Given her guests' penchant for early fishing on Lake Keuka, Ellen has considerately put a cof-feemaker in each room.

The boat launch is half a block away, and the lovely town square of Hammondsport, offering wonderful shops, is half a block in the other direction.

ITHACA

Rose Inn

Route 34 North, Box 6576
Ithaca, NY 14851-6576
607-533-7905
Fax: 607-533-7908

> *One of the country's finest country inns*

Proprietors: Charles and Sherry Rosemann. **Accommodations:** 15 rooms, including 5 suites, all with private bath, 4 with Jacuzzi, 3 with fireplace. **Rates:** Rooms $100–$160, suites $185–$250. **Included:** Full breakfast. **Minimum stay:** 3 nights on holidays and some university weekends. **Added:** Dinner (by prior arrangement) $50 per person, 16% tax, $25 additional guest. **Payment:** Visa, MasterCard. **Children:** Over 10. **Pets:** Not allowed. **Smoking:** Not allowed. **Open:** All year.

The Rose Inn is New York's only four-star, four-diamond country inn — with a half-decade history of such accolades — offering exceptionally decorated rooms and, with prior reservations, gorgeous meals in a rare, romantic setting. What's more, the Rose Inn is architecturally magnificent, an 1840s Italianate mansion painted a subtle pink with dark green shutters and white trim, with a stunning spiral staircase made of Honduras mahogany that ascends three floors to a cupola from which one can view the countryside. The Rose Inn is the only country inn in New York to have received four stars from Mobil and four diamonds from AAA for several years running, thanks to a decade's hard work from owners Charles and Sherry Rosemann.

In the early 1980s, Charles, a German hotelier, and Sherry, a Dallas native, agreed that their skills were well suited to innkeeping. They realized a lifelong dream when they bought this house on Lake Cayuga's eastern shores, ten miles north of Ithaca in the heart of the Finger Lakes. After months of restoration, they opened the inn in 1983 with five rooms and four baths. It was so successful that they expanded with a first-floor addition in 1986 and a second in 1988, a commendably sensitive structure that Sherry herself designed. The Rosemanns are a rare breed: Sherry a creative soul who has found her calling, and Charles a true romantic who has found his muse.

> **The Rose Inn is a masterpiece of superlatives that will exceed a traveler's loftiest expectations. Why? Because Charles and Sherry Rosemann have set for themselves the highest standards in the innkeeping business. From the food and wine to the decor, from the apple-orchard setting to the architectural mastery, the Rose Inn is perfection.**

The house, high on a hill, sits on 20 parklike acres of groomed gardens, distinguished trees, and an apple orchard in the back fields. Though most of the five first-floor and 10 second-floor rooms are in the new part of the house, guests really don't notice. When Sherry designed the addition, she specified classic molding and wall paneling to match the original structure, as well as matching windows and exterior trim. The Honeymoon Suite, for example, looks out back through three Palladian windows to the orchards from a solarium with a Jacuzzi sunken in marble flooring. The bedroom is Neoclassic in design with clean lines in strong taupe, black, and cream. The Perry Ellis linens complement an upholstered gilded headboard, and ornate brass sconces are set into the paneled walls beside Victorian prints.

Each room is as thoroughly decorated as the next, and all are different, with lush damask wallpapers and impeccable French and 19th-century American antiques throughout. The baths are sophisticated, some with parquet tiling in classic patterns. Sherry provides the finest quality bedding, down comforters, fine cotton linens, and oversize bath sheets; and she executes an elegant evening turndown. Two rooms have working fireplaces, but all are romantic boudoirs.

At the time of reservation, guests may choose to dine here

and are wise to do so. Guests dine intimately at separate tables in the living room, library, dining room, and the base of the circular stairway, which feels like a conservatory. It's a romantic experience that lasts several hours. Sherry selects the wines and tailors the meal to the desires of guests. Appetizers might be smoked oysters in beurre blanc, artichoke heart strudel on puréed tomato with fresh dill, or stuffed ravioli quartet of lobster, Gorgonzola, salmon, and mushrooms. A hearts of palm salad dressed in edible flowers might follow. Entrées might include Châteaubriand with béarnaise sauce, rack of lamb, veal chasseur with a creamy Madeira sauce, or shrimp flambéed in brandy with tomato, curry, and cream. Breakfast is equally sumptuous. The several-course meal is elegantly presented, perhaps including German apple pancakes with homemade jams and jellies.

From here, guests may enjoy a day trip to local wineries. Ithaca College and Cornell University are ten miles south.

MUMFORD

Genesee Country Inn

948 George Street
Mumford, NY 14511-0340
716-538-2500
Fax: 716-538-4565

> *A pleasant
> stone inn over
> a bubbling stream*

Proprietor: Glenda Barcklow. **Innkeeper:** Kim Rasmussen. **Accommodations:** 9 rooms, all with private bath, 3 with fireplace. **Rates:** $85–$125. **Included:** Full breakfast, afternoon refreshments. **Minimum stay:** 2 nights on some weekends May–October. **Added:** 7% state tax, 4% county tax. **Payment:** Visa, MasterCard. **Children:** Check with innkeepers. **Pets:** Not allowed. **Smoking:** Allowed. **Open:** All year, but closed Sunday–Tuesday, November–March.

Where some bed-and-breakfasts stand out for one or two fine details, Glenda Barcklow's has myriad memorable aspects. Rochester is a half hour's drive and a world away. Not only is this owner one of the most professional innkeepers in the business, she is infinitely warm-hearted, as is kindred soul Kim Rasmussen. The inn has a unique setting; it was built in 1833 as a plaster mill right above Spring Creek. The creek wends its way across a road to a waterfall that empties at the inn's front lawn, a pleasant greeting for guests checking in. The water flows audibly around and behind the inn, calming on flat rocks to the delight of the family ducks. It's a great spot for fly-fishing, as the county fish hatchery is just one town upstream from the little hamlet of Mumford.

> For businesspeople weary of nondescript travel, and for romantics who want a convenient weekend getaway, the Genesee Country Inn is a wonderful discovery. This pretty property has all the amenities of a classic B&B, such as Amish quilts and four-poster beds, with some added comforts including telephones and televisions.

A stone house with two-and-a-half-foot-thick walls, the Genesee Country Inn looks smallish from the road — two stories and six windows across — but there is another floor at creek level, for a total of 18 rooms. The walls of the cheery common room were stenciled by local artist Ruth Flowers from authentic 19th-century patterns. The airy breakfast room has diagonal wood paneling and a pitched roof. Breakfasts are ample and interesting, with entreés like cream cheese–filled French toast, Cheddar egg bake, and pancakes with cinnamon vanilla cream sauce.

The Genesee Country Inn has a dual face. During the weekend, the inn is a romantic spot for couples retreating to the countryside who love the New York Amish quilts and canopy beds, the creative breakfasts, the six wooded acres, and the bubbling stream. On weekdays the inn changes pace, becoming a haven for businesspeople grateful for the desk in every room, direct-dial phones, televisions hidden in pine armoires, new private baths, oversize towels, and thoughtful amenities (such as razors and hair dryers in some rooms).

Though all rooms are charming, the three downstairs rooms are a bit newer and more spacious than the six upstairs rooms and each has a private entrance. Of these, the Skivington is preferable, with a four-window view of Spring Creek and the back porch, the hilly back lawn, and ducks. The McGinnis is one of three with a gas fireplace and a little sun porch. All the rooms are immaculate.

Be sure to bring your tackle for the top-rated trout fishing. Those who venture out will want to visit the Genesee Country Museum and Nature Center, home of a 19th-century crafts village just down the road.

PITTSFORD

Oliver Loud's Inn

1474 Marsh Road
Pittsford, NY 14534
716-248-5200
Fax: 716-248-9970

An upscale and intimate choice in Rochester

Proprietor: Vivienne Tellier. **Accommodations:** 8 rooms, all with private bath. **Rates:** $125–$155, seasonal. **Included:** Welcome tray, Continental breakfast basket. **Added:** $25 each additional guest, 17% tax. **Payment:** Major credit cards. **Children:** Over 12 welcome. **Pets:** Not allowed. **Smoking:** Restricted. **Open:** All year.

The group of buildings at Bushnell's Basin, ten miles east of Rochester, is a restoration of an 1820s hamlet including Richardson's Canal House Restaurant, Oliver Loud's Inn, and several shops. In 1978, Vivienne Tellier and her husband, Andrew Wolfe, happened upon a historic building destined for demolition. Dating to 1818, it was the oldest tavern on the

373-mile-long Erie Canal, which reached the Rochester area in 1821. The tavern served as a stagecoach stop between Rochester and Canandaigua for nearly a century and survived various other incarnations including tenure as a nudist colony in the 1930s, but it had been abandoned since 1968. The couple bought the building and undertook a full restoration, resulting in the highly acclaimed Richardson's Canal House Restaurant, which has consistently earned four stars from the *Mobil Guide*.

> **Vivienne Tellier is passionate and smart. At Bushnell's Basin, she saved several historic buildings, relocated them on the Erie Canal just outside Rochester, and teamed up top-notch overnight accommodations with a terrific restaurant, locating them in neighboring buildings.**

The couple saved yet another abandoned building from demolition in 1985, a formidable inn that belonged to Oliver Loud, dating from 1812. The Wolfes moved it four miles to Bushnell's Basin. The inn is a two-story mustard yellow clapboard with black shutters and trim. It sits on a nice grassy plot of land with views of the canal, across a parking lot from Richardson's Canal House. The first-floor porch extends like a hat brim beyond the house and wraps around the entire structure, supported by square pillars, and has lots of hanging flower baskets and wicker furniture.

Vivienne documented the interior design to remain faithful to the 1820s. The brick-face hall paper was a common theme, as were the ornate borders, their subjects the names of the guest rooms: Feathers, Boxwood, Garland, St. Cloud. The inn's original moldings were reproduced, and an artist was hired to do the faux mahogany graining on all the doors. The common room features a silver service from 1825, Wedgwood china, and a wonderful mantel done in elaborate faux marble and gold leaf panels. The guest rooms, four on each floor, are furnished in Stickley reproductions, immaculate and generously sized, with creative swags and window treatments. About half the rooms have views of the canal. While romantics enjoy the canopy beds and antique quilts, business travelers appreciate the modern baths and private telephones.

Guests are greeted by a bountiful display of refreshments

upon arrival: spring water, crackers, cheese, fruit, and cookies, on a pretty European tray. A breakfast basket is presented in the mornings like a country picnic, with fresh muffins, an egg, and fruit. Lists of local activities, from shopping to museums, are provided in the inn's common room.

Richardson's Canal House remains easily accessible but somewhat independent, though Oliver Loud guests booking dinner receive a $10 deduction from their room rate and a complimentary dessert. Richardson's is an extremely popular restaurant, with a series of small, intimate dining rooms. The captivating colonial and folk art interior is decorated with stencilwork by Ruth Flowers and primitive murals by Edith Lunt Small. Chef Jeff Coon prepares four-course dinners at a fixed price of $32 that might start with dill-cured gravlax with brown bread and dill mustard sauce. After salad, guests have a choice of nine entrées: perhaps roast tenderloin of beef with wild mushroom sauce, duckling with rhubarb-raspberry glaze, or Cajun broiled sea scallops. There is a lighter pub-fare menu on weekdays, ranging from $5 to $9.

ROCHESTER

Strathallan

550 East Avenue
Rochester, NY 14607
716-461-5010
800-678-7284

*A private
luxury hotel
in Rochester*

General Manager: Barbara Ruocco.
Accommodations: 151 suites, studios to 2 bedrooms. **Rates:** $115–$205; $10 less on weekends. **Included:** Weekend breakfast buffet, weekday Continental breakfast on two-floor Executive Level. **Minimum stay:** None. **Added:** 11% tax, 16% tax over $100. **Payment:** Major credit cards. **Children:** Welcome. **Pets:** Not allowed. **Smoking:** 1 of 8 floors nonsmoking. **Open:** All year.

As a thriving business hub, Rochester has several fine chain hotels. However, these don't have the personal and unique qualities of the Strathallan, a distinctive luxury hotel several blocks from downtown. Unfortunately, its facade is an uninspired eight-story rectangular chunk of balconies and concrete. Rest assured, things get better inside. While not glamorous and gleaming with marble, the Strathallan is a comfortable refuge in a lovely neighborhood on Rochester's Museum Trail. Within walking distance are dozens of charming Victorian homes and a park; the Memorial Art Gallery, with ancient and European art; the Rochester Museum and Science Center, with one of the world's best collections of Iroquois Indian artifacts; the International Museum of Photography in the former mansion of Kodak founder George Eastman; and the toy-filled Strong Museum, with one of the world's most extensive doll collections.

> One of the Strathallan's finest features — and what separates it from Rochester's other luxury chain hotels — is its location. It is in a very walkable part of downtown Rochester, near a park, Victorian homes, the former Eastman mansion, and dozens of offerings along Museum Trail.

The Strathallan was built in the 1970s as an apartment building but sat empty for four years when the project went bankrupt. Ambitious new owners remodeled the Strathallan and turned it into a hotel in 1980.

The guest rooms are decorated with traditional if predictable cherry or mahogany reproduction furnishings. Most accommodations are one-bedroom suites, but there are a few two-bedroom suites, and the standard rooms have large sitting areas. All have televisions in armoires, refrigerators, and coffeemakers, and most have balconies. Guests can pay an additional $20 for Executive Level privileges such as complimentary breakfast, newspaper, robes, hair dryers, two balconies, and use of a private lounge with sweeping city views.

Sabrina's restaurant serves three meals daily in a businesslike setting, leaning toward French food later in the day. The top floor has a nice cocktail lounge called Hattie's with a fabulous view of the Rochester skyline, enlivened by weekend jazz. The hotel also has fitness facilities, with a sauna, Lifecycles, and exercise equipment in a solarium setting.

SKANEATELES

The Sherwood Inn

26 West Genesee Street
Skaneateles, NY 13152
315-685-3405
Fax: 315-685-8983

A classic offering atop Lake Skaneateles

Proprietor: William B. Eberhardt. **Innkeeper:** Claire O'Boyle Downey. **Accommodations:** 18 rooms, including 6 suites, all with private bath. **Rates:** $70–$120. **Included:** Continental breakfast. **Added:** 12% tax, $10 additional guest. **Payment:** Major credit cards. **Children:** Welcome. **Pets:** Not allowed. **Smoking:** Discouraged. **Open:** All year; restaurant closed Christmas Eve and Christmas Day.

The classic Sherwood Inn sits in the heart of one of the Finger Lakes' prettiest towns at the north end of Lake Skaneateles. Isaac Sherwood, a successful stagecoach businessman, built this inn and tavern in 1807, and it has been run nearly continuously as such ever since. The only thing that has changed is its name, which has had seven incarnations.

> **The Sherwood Inn is just what you hoped for: a beautifully preserved historic hostelry built in 1807, its decor a creative and authentic colonial, with fine food taken on a breezy enclosed porch — with the best location in town at the top of the lake.**

The Sherwood Inn is a beautiful slate-blue shingle building, three stories tall, with black trim. The first floor is enclosed by a porch, lined with dozens of windows, that wraps around the sides and front and overlooks the lake. It's a breezy, memorable place in warmer months, a quaint and cozy enclave in the winter. Visitors enter through the central foyer, with a generous hearth and a piano. To the left are formal and informal dining rooms; to the right, a tap room.

Upstairs are two floors of rooms that remain as they were

when the Sherwood Inn was built. It's up here that the history of the place emerges with the feeling of a colonial refuge. The halls are unusually wide, with light random-width planking.

The wallpapers vary throughout the guest rooms: sometimes a floral or heavy chintz, a stencil print, or a stripe. There is some variety in the size of rooms, but none is too cozy, and the suites are quite roomy. Each room features some nice antiques, including armoires, highboys, and marble-top tables and vanities and is done in Williamsburg, Stickley, or sometimes a playful Victorian style, as in the Red Room, which has a red-fringed chandelier and a brass bed. About half the rooms have lake views, and these are highly preferable. All have clean, modest baths with tub shower.

Meals are a great event here, quite reasonably priced from $11 to $17. Guests might try sea scallops in red pepper and caper cream sauce over linguine, crabmeat au gratin in white wine cream sauce over rice, or pork loin medallions in a mustard cream sauce.

The warmer months are a great time to visit, with lakeside band concerts, sailing regattas, and polo; fall is especially picturesque. The Finger Lakes have an easy hospitality, their beauty still relatively undiscovered, and the staff at the Sherwood Inn is always immensely helpful and proud.

TRUMANSBURG

Taughannock Farms Inn

2030 Gorge Road at Taughannock Falls State Park
Trumansburg, NY 14886
607-387-7711

A crow's-nest view of Lake Cayuga from the falls

Proprietors: C. Keith and Nancy A. Le Grand. **Accommodations:** 7 rooms, including 2 2-bedroom guest houses, 1 with fireplace; 5 with private baths, 2 rooms share a bath in guest house. **Rates:** $85–$100; guest houses $150–$175 for four persons. **Included:** Expanded Continental breakfast. **Minimum stay:** College weekends and some fall weekends. **Added:** 8% tax, $20 additional guest. **Payment:** Major credit cards. **Children:** Welcome. **Pets:** Not allowed. **Smoking:** Not allowed. **Open:** Easter–Thanksgiving.

Best known as a restaurant for the past half century, Taughannock Farms is a lovely country inn that teeters over Lake Cayuga's western shores on Point Goodwin, about eight miles north of Ithaca. The landscape is beautiful, characteristic of the Finger Lakes, with precipitous cliffs and sweeping water views in the rolling landscape of wine country.

> Its few rooms are pretty and pleasant, but the most memorable aspect of Taughannock Farms Inn is its restaurant. The dining room has several levels whose focal point is the dramatic view from 20 floor-to-ceiling windows overlooking Lake Cayuga as if from cliffs.

The rambling Victorian was built in 1873 by Philadelphian John Jones, who donated much of the rest of his 600-acre farm to New York State, creating Taughannock Falls State Park. In 1945, the Jones family sold the house to the Agards, who started the country inn. Since 1973 their granddaughter Nancy and her husband, Keith, have been maintaining the tradition. Pleasing details are everywhere: the first floor is covered by an overhanging porch, the third floor is hidden under gingerbread gables, a fourth-floor cupola pops out of the roof like a chef's hat.

The large dining room is known for its spectacular views. Of the three areas, the uppermost is the smallest, quite pretty, with a bay window. The two-tiered main dining room spills past dramatic square pillars to the lower level, where about 20 floor-to-ceiling windows look out across the front of the house to the park and lake.

Taughannock Farms has a reputation for hearty country dinners, prepared by chef Daniel Wright, ranging from $17 to $27, always including homemade rolls, relish, and a signature orange date bread. Specialties are roast loin of pork with sautéed apples, sole stuffed with crabmeat, rack of lamb, and prime rib, served with brandied apples. A daunting selection of 14 desserts completes dinner: diners can choose from the likes of double chocolate mousse torte and bittersweet ice cream pie in almond crumb crust. The wine list is a creative blend of local vineyards' offerings.

The second floor has five quaint rooms — three with lake views, two with views of the woods. All are furnished in a tasteful mixture of antiques and an occasional reproduction. Perhaps the most sought-after room is the Garden Room at the end of the hall, with a curved fishnet canopy bed reached via old-fashioned steps, pretty period wallpaper, an antique desk and marble-top dresser. In a touch reminiscent of a summer boarding house, the rooms have slatted doors to welcome a hilltop breeze. The guest parlor has some lovely Victorian antiques, such as an 1883 music box, most of which are original to the mansion.

The two guest cottages have rooms decorated more in family style than in high Victorian. The property's seven acres provide quick access to the park and falls. Keith and Nancy, lifelong natives, are the informal, kind hosts who orchestrate this rare family environment.

WESTFIELD

The William Seward Inn

South Portage Road, Route 394
Westfield, NY 14787
716-326-4151
Fax: 716-326-4163
800-338-4151

A remote, convenient, romantic stop in western New York

Proprietors and Innkeepers: Jim and Debbie Dahlberg. **Accommodations:** 14 rooms, all with private bath, 4 with double Jacuzzis. **Rates:** $90–$155. **Included:** Full breakfast. **Minimum stay:** 2 nights most weekends. **Added:** $20 each additional guest; 5-course dinners mid-September–mid-June, $35 per person; 7% tax, 12% tax over $100. **Payment:** Visa, MasterCard, Discover. **Children:** Over 10 welcome. **Pets:** Not allowed. **Smoking:** Not allowed. **Open:** All year.

In February 1991, Jim and Debbie Dahlberg bought the well-known but faded William Seward Inn, which had been a bed-

and-breakfast since 1983. Through devotion, hope, and much personal investment from Jim and Debbie, the hostelry has markedly improved, from the decor to the grand breakfasts to the four deluxe rooms in a new addition.

Jim was formerly a vice president of a Buffalo bank, and Debbie was a fair-housing advocate. Jim does the cooking and the finances, and Debbie is redecorating with promising taste. The Dahlbergs have refurbished several guest rooms and the common rooms, adding a gas fireplace, and completed the delightful four-room addition perpendicular to the main house — a clever complement to the 1837 Greek Revival front, echoing the Palladian themes.

> With Lake Erie and Westfield's wineries and antique shops in one direction and Chautauqua a 20-minute drive in another, the William Seward Inn offers a great deal for its country-inn goers. To owners Jim and Debbie, it's a dream come true.

The two-story white clapboard home has two faces: the original 1821 cottage front, built by Asa Farnsworth, which faces the side of the property, and the roadside Greek Revival face added in 1837. The later addition was built by William Seward, an agent of the Holland Land Company who took on the governorship of New York just a year later and eventually went on to serve as Abraham Lincoln's secretary of state. The grand Greek Revival front, three pillars and four Palladian arched windows across, looks out over Route 394 and, in the distance, Lake Erie. In 1966, expansions at the nearby Welch Corporation threatened the Seward home in its original location, and owner Lucille Owens moved the house to its present site, about three miles west of Westfield, on a hill with glorious views of Lake Erie.

Two front rooms in the main house (ask for one of the second-floor rooms off the porch) and all four rooms in the addition are blessed with lingering views of sunsets on Lake Erie. The latter rooms are the finest, featuring double Jacuzzis and queen-size canopy beds; the second-floor rooms have the additional advantages of vaulted ceilings and a shared porch. The rooms in the main house do need the work that Debbie is undertaking, but all have some lovely antiques.

The living room and library are charming, comfortable sitting areas. Debbie used creamy paint and yellow chintz fabrics to brighten the library, which is enhanced with long Palladian windows, original shelves, paneled walls, and a working coal fireplace.

Jim is up early preparing a multi-course breakfast, which will perhaps include Amaretto French toast or scrambled eggs with tarragon and four cheeses. Plan ahead for dinner: the $36 fixed-price meal may begin with baked mushrooms with French garlic sausage or a seafood crêpe and might feature fillet of salmon with pinot noir sauce or sliced tenderloin beef with wild mushroom sauce. Jim's wonderful meals are served for guests only; you'll feel especially catered to.

The intriguing town of Chautauqua is a 20-minute drive away, and little Westfield on Lake Erie is a hub for antiquers and vintners.

The Catskills and Hudson Valley

Best Romantic Retreats

Cold Spring
  Pig Hill Bed and Breakfast
Dover Plains
  Old Drovers Inn
Purdys
  The Box Tree

Best Gourmet Getaways

Amenia
  Troutbeck
Lewbeach
  Beaverkill Valley Inn

Best Remote Refuge

Bear Mountain
  Bear Mountain Inn

Best Resort

New Paltz
  Mohonk Mountain House

Best Country Inn

Elka Park
  The Redcoat's Return

Best Village Bed-and-Breakfasts

Poughkeepsie
  Inn at the Falls
Rhinebeck
  The Village Victorian Inn at Rhinebeck

Best Village Inns

Millerton
Simmons Way Village Inn
Rhinebeck
Beekman Arms

Visitors to the Hudson Valley may want to take the Henry Hudson Parkway on the river's east banks, or the refuge of the Palisades Parkway and cross the Hudson at Tarrytown, or proceed up to West Point for a visit and cross the Hudson at the Bear Mountain Bridge. **Cold Spring** is the first wonderful refuge of note, and after a long day of antiquing and romancing along the picturesque banks of the Hudson, a hungry traveler has two good choices for dinner, the Bird and Bottle Inn in nearby Garrison or Plumbush. Just past **Poughkeepsie** are the sites for which the Hudson Valley is best known: Hyde Park and a 16-mile historic district that lines the Hudson's eastern shore. Before you do anything — several months before — make reservations at the Culinary Institute of America for dinner. Activities for a busy day include the Vanderbilt Mansion National Historic Site, the Franklin D. Roosevelt Library Museum, Val-Kill, Eleanor Roosevelt's one-time retreat, and the Mills Mansion.

On to **Rhinebeck,** where summer and early fall visitors can watch the air shows at the Rhinebeck Aerodrome or spend time antiquing in the historic village.

A must in this area is a special trip to the Mohonk Mountain House, a world unto itself in the Shawangunk Preserve. A Mohonk visit can be embellished with a dinner at the DePuy Canal House in High Falls, an eclectic colonial tavern. The Hudson Valley Wine Company in Highland is a great diversion on the way back to New York City.

While best known for the boisterous family resorts of the 1950s and the bad comics who worked them, the Catskills are actually a beautiful, protected landscape that inspired painters like Thomas Cole and George Inness with its rough beauty.

Despite the reputation of the old resorts, the Catskills are remote and unspoiled, and the protected Forest Preserve, about 100 miles from New York City, measures 50 miles across at its widest. Aside from its fine ski resort, Hunter Mountain, with 17 lifts and a 1,600-foot vertical drop, the Catskills are home to gentle mountains and lovely scenery, as well as the artistic enclave of Woodstock, which hosted the famous concert. A scenic drive across the preserve brings a visitor to Beaverkill Valley in **Lewbeach,** birthplace of American fly-fishing.

AMENIA

Troutbeck

Leedsville Road, Box 26
Amenia, NY 12501
914-373-9681

An English manor two hours north of Manhattan

President and Innkeeper: Jim Flaherty. **General Manager:** Karen Sargent. **Accommodations:** 36 rooms, most with private bath. **Rates:** $595–$825 per couple per weekend, AP. **Included:** Six meals daily, open bar. **Minimum stay:** 2 nights in season. **Added:** 12% gratuity, 7.25% tax. **Payment:** American Express, Visa, MasterCard. **Children:** Over 12 welcome. **Pets:** Not allowed. **Smoking:** Allowed in public rooms only. **Open:** All year.

Because Troutbeck has been such a success with corporate groups, couples are limited to weekend visits at this 442-acre estate. But it's a full weekend, with swimming in indoor and outdoor pools, tennis, fishing, walking — and glorious food, the real attraction at Troutbeck.

A weekend here is more like a stay at an English lord's manor house than at a country inn two hours from Manhattan. Since the 1920s, Troutbeck has been a gathering spot for literati and intellectuals; the NAACP was begun within the walls of this grand fieldstone Tudor mansion. Owners Jim Flaherty and Bob Skibsted encourage the same exciting, sophisticated atmosphere today in their private corporate meetings and couples weekends.

> **Troutbeck is a full-service resort for, at most, several dozen people. Visitors will never have to leave the property, which provides tennis courts, a swimming pool, enchanting gardens, and rambling grounds. And six fine meals a day will keep guests well sated.**

Most of the indoor activity at Troutbeck takes place in the Tudor house. Guests wander through the rambling mansion as room spills into room, from the formal to the informal living rooms, to the oak-paneled library, to the dark woody conference room, and finally to the Winter Garden dining rooms with an entire wall of small-paned windows overlooking the brook for which the estate was named. The decor is befitting an English country house: the traditional wing chairs and camelback sofas are suitable for novels and intimate conversations, chintz curtains decorate the leaded windows, walls are boldly painted and hung with shelves of books or intriguing prints and maps.

The rooms are comfortable, filled with antiques and curios that are both valuable and well worn, as in the New England house of a wealthy Mayflower-descended aunt. Some rooms have sleeping porches, others are set cozily under pitched roofs; some are grand, and others more modest. An additional 18 guest rooms are in the pale mauve clapboard Guesthouse, which sits at the beginning of the Troutbeck drive. Part of the house was built in the mid-18th century, and a recent addition was done in a complementary fashion. The Guesthouse affords a bit more privacy than the main house, with a large, airy living room and two wings of guest rooms, four of which have working fireplaces.

Meals are lengthy and glorious events at Troutbeck, created by brilliant Chef Paul Bernal. A five-course spring menu might consist of an appetizer of sautéed escargots with pernod, then gorgonzola and pears, followed by a mesclun salad with hearts of palm and roasted red peppers and balsamic vinaigrette. A Troutbeck sorbet prepares one for an entrée of broiled Norwegian salmon served with braised fennel, four-grain pilaf and lobster brandy sauce; or perhaps a roasted rack of lamb served over a provencale bean stew with a port-mint sauce and roasted garlic new potatoes. One of the five desserts offered may be the favorite chocolate ganache tarte with raspberry coulis.

The object of this kind of estate living, strolling these overgrown or highly groomed grounds, is to work up an appetite for the next culinary creation.

BEAR MOUNTAIN

Bear Mountain Inn

ARA Leisure Services
Bear Mountain, NY 10911
914-786-2731
Fax: 914-786-2543

> *An array of accommodations in Bear Mountain State Park*

Proprietor: New York State. **General Manager:** Charles Willis. **Accommodations:** 60 rooms in 6 lodges. **Rates:** $59 weekdays, $84 weekends and holidays. **Added:** $10 each additional guest, 7.25% tax. **Payment:** Visa, MasterCard, American Express, Discover. **Children:** Welcome. **Pets:** Not allowed. **Smoking:** Allowed. **Open:** All year.

The 38-mile Palisades Parkway serves as a great and scenic driveway from the George Washington Bridge to Bear Mountain's front door. The state park comprises 5,067 acres and is most unusual for its winter offerings, including a skating rink, sledding, and ski-jumping competition hosted during Winter Carnival. The land was formally incorporated as Bear Mountain State Park in 1908–1910, when construction of Sing Sing Prison threatened the environs.

> **Less than an hour's drive from Manhattan is a fine state park that offers a host of activities. Within its 5,000 acres, set around Hessian Lake, are varied accommodations at the Bear Mountain Inn, from the magnificent Adirondack lodge to convenient contemporary rooms to cabins in the woods.**

The magnificent Adirondack inn was built in 1916, three stories handcrafted from native rock and chestnut. Most spectacular is the enormous two-story common room, with a beamed ceiling and a vast stone fireplace that flickers off the highly varnished, rich wood, revealing two views of the park. Guests may have a formal dinner in quaint Wildflowers, where dinners range from $10 to $17, or a lavish and extremely popular Sunday brunch in the larger dining hall, for $17.25.

ARA Leisure Services, which also runs the concessions on Skyline Drive, has managed the historic inn since the mid-1970s. While the 12 rooms above the inn are comfortable, those across Hessian Lake are preferable for their setting. Of these, the Stone Cottages are the more charming, built in the 1940s, with six rooms in each of the foursquare single-story structures. Each cottage has a common room with a large stone fireplace. Off this are six private rooms, decorated in the same modest French country style found in the inn rooms, with pine furniture, thick pile blue carpets, and queen-size beds. The rooms in the Overlook Lodge are contemporary and rather dormlike, though the magnificent locale, on the rocky, steep banks above Hessian Lake, is quick to distract.

Square dancing is an extremely popular activity at Bear Mountain. Hessian Lake, 200 feet deep, offers pedal and row boats and is one of seven area lakes that host fishermen, who also may try their lines in the Hudson River. The park maintains more than 30 trails, measuring more than 200 miles.

The Trailside Museum and Zoo was founded in 1927 under the sponsorship of John D. Rockefeller, Jr. and the American Museum of Natural History. It is visited by more than half a million people annually, who participate in walks and treks to learn about geology, zoology, history, and botany of the Bear Mountain area.

The inn is an informal place, especially wonderful for families. Kids will no doubt love the 94-by-224-foot pool.

COLD SPRING

Pig Hill Bed and Breakfast

73 Main Street
Cold Spring on Hudson, NY 10516
914-265-9247

> *The finest B&B
> on the
> lower Hudson*

Proprietor: Wendy O'Brien. **Accommodations:** 8 rooms, 4 with private bath, 6 with fireplace. **Rates:** $85–$140. **Included:** Full breakfast. **Added:** $25 for cot or crib in room, 12.25% tax. **Payment:** Major credit cards. **Children:** Welcome. **Pets:** Not allowed. **Smoking:** Not allowed. **Open:** All year.

Pig Hill Bed and Breakfast, one of the prettiest B&Bs along the far-reaching Hudson River, receives an unqualified recommendation. It's a cosmopolitan place with sophisticated, expensive decor, most of which is for sale through the ground-floor antiques shop. The house feels like a transplanted New York City brownstone decorated by an expensive designer, in a humble version of Manhattan's SoHo with antiques shops and chic boutiques.

The bed-and-breakfast sits toward the bottom of Cold Spring's Main Street on a hill that barrels right through town, ending abruptly at a delightful gazebo that offers nonpareil views of the town marina, the Hudson River, and the precipitous banks on the other side. The three-story brownstone was built in the 1830s and later became a booming Civil War foundry that produced several thousand cannonballs for the Union. Wendy, whose family summered here in Cold Spring for decades, bought the building in 1986, gutted and worked on it for six months, and opened it as a bed-and-breakfast that fall. The first floor houses an upscale antiques store, which also serves as a common area to guests — a bit disconcerting when weekend browsers traipse through. Even the dining room table on which guests eat breakfast is for sale. A sweet back garden with flagstone steps and a brick patio is perfect for warm-weather breakfasting.

> One of the most attractive aspects of Pig Hill is its convenience to Manhattan. Travelers can take a train to Cold Spring and walk to the B&B from the station. Because Cold Spring is so charming and walkable, you won't want for a car; and because Pig Hill is so wonderful, you might not even leave your room.

Pig Hill has eight guest rooms on the second and third floors, in a creative and intimate architectural space. The two outside rooms share the hall bath, and the two inner rooms have private baths. The decor changes constantly, as guests may choose to bring their rooms home with them, but the high level of luxury and design remains. All but two rooms at the front have colorful Franklin stoves, and the back rooms have nice views of the overgrown yard and patio.

The Adirondack Room has some enchanting examples of twig furniture, a bed and settee, and a pair of antlers above the fireplace. One room with a private bath has a blue iron and brass bed, a blue Franklin stove, and green damask wallpaper with a Victorian feather border. The shared baths are clean and clever, one with a clawfoot tub enclosed in wainscoting and all with new sinks with brass or painted fixtures. Plentiful original art decorates the walls, including Wendy's collection of old windows into which mirrors have been installed. The bedding is especially lovely, with thick designer sheets and down-filled duvets.

Pig Hill is well known for breakfasts such as egg pot pie, spinach soufflé roll, and shirred eggs. Be sure to eat at Hudson House, for the best water views along the Hudson, or at Wendy O'Brien's restaurant, Henry's, up the road a piece.

DOVER PLAINS

Old Drovers Inn

Old Route 22
Dover Plains, NY 12522
914-832-9311
Fax: 914-832-6356

Romance abounds in a 265-year-old house

Proprietors: Alice Pitcher and Kemper Peacock. **Innkeeper:** Alice Pitcher. **Accommodations:** 4 rooms, all with private bath, 3 with fireplace. **Rates:** $130–$225. **Included:** Full breakfast on weekends, Continental breakfast on weekdays; tax; service charge. **Minimum stay:** 2 nights on October weekends. **Added:** $25 each additional guest. **Payment:** Visa, MasterCard, Diners Club. **Children:** Over 12. **Pets:** Small dogs allowed with prior approval. **Smoking:** Allowed. **Open:** All year.

While the Old Drovers Inn has been around for some time — nearly 60 years — it's recently come into its own, the object of rave reviews and top ratings, thanks to owners Alice

Pitcher and Kemper Peacock. It has most recently joined the ultra-exclusive ranks of Relais & Chateaux properties. Visit now and you can say you stayed here when it was still relatively undiscovered.

> Few places in the Mid-Atlantic states stand out as remarkable houses from history, at once ancient and well-preserved, but none is as romantic as Old Drovers. The rooms are authentically colonial and cozy; the dining room feels like a place where the Revolution was planned.

Old Drovers Inn is east of Poughkeepsie, shouldering Kent, Connecticut, and the Berkshire foothills. It sits on 12 acres neighboring Old Route 22, which at one time was the main thoroughfare between Bennington, Vermont, and New York City. The inn was named for its clientele, rowdy drovers who herded cattle and swine down the main thoroughfare to market downstate.

Restored as an inn as early as 1937, Old Drovers' reputation has fluctuated greatly. Its latest incarnation is the finest in years. Alice Pitcher and Kemper Peacock were summoned by the charms of the 260-year-old house from Nantucket and Westport, Connecticut, in 1989. As innkeepers, they are consummate emissaries of history.

The dining room on the ground floor of the inn is an enchanting spot, one of the most romantic eating spaces in the region. The ceiling of the dark Tap Room is of exposed logs, the walls of original stone. Two rooms are separated by a huge hearth with brass guards, one room with chairs in aristocratic tooled leather, the other with elegant banquettes. Charlie Wilbur has stooped in the six-foot space for nearly 30 years as the host of the restaurant, which serves lunch and dinner. The contemporary American menu changes every six weeks but always includes the inn's famous cheddar cheese soup. Chef Jeffrey Marquise deserves knighthood for his lobster hash with Benedictine and Brandy corn sauce. Entrées range from $17 to $35 for double cut rack lamb chops with Charlie's tomato chutney, pepper-crusted sirloin with potato blue cheese gratin, or sautéed paillards of duck with fresh mango and red onion jam.

Upstairs, the inn's floors are endearingly buckled with age. The main sitting room has a marble and stone fireplace over which hangs an old musket. A second common room has Lafayette green paneling. One of a pair of original inset shell cabinets is here; the other is now on display at the Metropolitan Museum of Art. The library has three walls filled with volumes of wonderful reading and accommodating down chairs and sofas.

Three of the four guest rooms upstairs have working fireplaces. The Meeting Room, which functioned as such for the town until 1840, has an incredible barrel-vaulted ceiling arching high over two double beds, a fireplace, chintz-covered wing chairs, and dark wide-plank flooring. The Sleigh and Cherry rooms have authentic colonial paneling, fireplaces, and clawfoot tubs.

Guests take breakfast in the fabulous Federal Room on the first floor surrounded by four walls of hand-painted murals done in 1941 by Edward Paine, depicting Old Drovers, West Point, Hyde Park, and a Dover Plains barn. There is also a patio with wrought-iron furniture for outdoor dining.

ELKA PARK

The Redcoat's Return

Platte Clove Road
Elka Park, NY 12427
518-589-6379 or 518-589-9858

A trusty old chum in the Catskills

Proprietors: Thomas and Margaret Wright. **General Manager:** Tom Wright. **Accommodations:** 14 rooms, 6 with private bath. **Rates:** $80–$95. **Included:** Full breakfast. **Minimum stay:** Some holiday weekends. **Added:** $15 each additional guest, 7% tax. **Children:** Age 4 or older. **Pets:** Dogs permitted with prior approval. **Smoking:** Limited. **Open:** All year except April–mid-May.

Halfway between Sugarloaf and Roundtop mountains, in the heart of the Catskill Game Preserve, is a British sanctuary. Tom Wright is the English half of the proprietary staff. He and his wife, Peggy, retreated to the Redcoat's Return in 1972.

In 1910, potato farmer Willie Dale transformed his 1840

farmhouse into a summer boarding house called the Grenoble and built an addition. The result was a looming but elegant white clapboard structure four stories high, with a wrap-around porch. A week's vacation at the Grenoble cost a Catskill vacationer $25, with three meals daily. After World War II, the inn faded, closed, and reopened in 1955. Tom and Peggy Wright bought the place in 1972 with the intent of creating an English country retreat. The grand old house looks much as it did when the Dales hosted their hayrides at the turn of the century. The Wrights themselves seem a bit of that era — worldly, knowing, as if they just emerged from a thatch-roofed cottage in the Hebrides.

> For more than 20 years, the Redcoat's Return has been a bit of Britain in the Catskills. It's the rugged — not the precious — England that the Wrights have brought to New York, with hearty food, warmth, and conviviality.

The inn is at 2,200 feet, enveloped by 18 acres laced with hiking trails. Cheerful plants hang between the porch columns. Guests enter through rickety doors. To the right are the dining rooms, to the left the wonderful antique mahogany bar that Peggy and Tom found in an abandoned tavern. Worn leather couches rest in front of a large stone hearth. Decorated with lovely pieces of art, Redcoat's seems more like the home of particularly interesting people than a hostelry.

The 14 guest rooms are split between the second and third floors and are decorated similarly in small floral print cotton comforters, oak dressers, wrought-iron double beds, rocking chairs, tiny flowered wallpaper in rust and green, and terra cotta–colored rugs. Though the rooms could use some new paper and better lighting (the baths are harshly lit with fluorescent fixtures), Redcoat's Return remains exactly what it was designed to be: a cozy country inn, a genial refuge from the city.

Tom is a wonderful chef. Many guests return for dishes such as English sherry trifle, grilled quail with polenta and roasted peppers, breast of chicken stuffed with goat cheese and eggplant purée, and prime rib with Yorkshire pudding on Saturday night. The menu is seasonal, and entrées range from $13 to $20. Guests dine in one of two rooms equipped with

graceful Hitchcock chairs — a formidable library that looks
as if it might be Oscar Wilde's study and an enclosed porch
that opens to the back lawns, home of an interesting sculpture of an empty suit that Peggy bought in Europe.

Woodstock is only a 15-minute drive, Schoharie Creek on
the property is stocked aplenty with trout, and Hunter Mountain is a hop away for skiing.

LEWBEACH

Beaverkill Valley Inn

Lewbeach, NY 12753
914-439-4844

> *The fly-fishing capital of the Catskills*

Proprietor: Laurance Rockefeller.
Manager: Christina L. Dennis. **Accommodations:** 20 rooms, 11 with
private bath; annex house has 5
rooms with 1 shared bath. **Rates:** $260–$330 per couple; children ages 3–12, $110–$145, AP. **Included:** 3 meals a day, afternoon tea. **Minimum stay:** 2 nights on weekends, 3 nights on
holidays. **Added:** 7.75% tax. **Payment:** Visa, MasterCard,
American Express. **Children:** Welcome. **Pets:** Not allowed.
Smoking: Allowed in Card Room and outdoors. **Open:** All
year.

Teddy Roosevelt missed the Catskills when he deemed part of
upstate New York State "forever wild." Larry Rockefeller,
however, did not. In 1978, this environmental lawyer bought

up parcels of land that he thought were perilously close to development in the historic Beaverkill Valley in the 50-mile-wide Catskill Forest Preserve. One of the area's most precious resources is the Beaverkill Valley River, known to those who practice the art as the home of American fly-fishing, born here around 1865.

> **Restored by conservationists Larry and Wendy Rockefeller, the Beaverkill Valley Inn is a reverent tribute to outdoor life and the 50-mile-wide Catskill Forest Preserve. Despite its hearty demeanor, the inn is luxurious, featuring elaborate and elegant dining.**

The former Bonnie View Inn was built in 1893 to house the increasing number of fly-fishermen and was one of the earliest boarding houses on the Beaverkill River. When Larry Rockefeller bought the inn in 1983, it was barely standing. A thorough renovation and restoration have established this boarding house as an informally elegant, privileged retreat for anglers and moguls alike who want to relax and fish in the wilderness.

The Rockefellers are well represented by Christina Dennis, the hardworking young innkeeper who maintains the Beaverkill Valley Inn somewhere between an exclusive private retreat and a country inn. The house and its 60 surrounding acres, outside the hamlet of Lewbeach, are far removed from civilization. The nearest town, Livingston Manor, is about 10 miles away. The inn looks rather like a grand Newport cottage, a square three-story white clapboard building with green shutters and trim and dormer windows peeking out from a red shingled roof. A porch wraps around the perimeter, filled with green-painted swings and wicker furniture looking out from three sides onto a croquet lawn. Inside, the cherry staircase, oak millwork, and hardware are original, though the rest of the house is the result of recent renovation. Comfortable, traditional chairs and sofas decorate the large parlor to the right of the foyer; clubby leather furnishings fill the informal Card Room to the left. Downstairs are pool and Ping-Pong tables and tabletop soccer in three rooms with rich wainscoted walls, decoy lamps, wing chairs, and settle benches. Throughout, Larry Rockefeller has selected wonderful original artwork of nature, wildlife, and Catskills landscapes, most by watercolorist David Armstrong.

Upstairs there are nine guest rooms with private baths on the second floor and ten around the perimeter of the third floor that share five baths in the center. Simply decorated, as if by the hand of a fisherman with ample funds and fine taste, the rooms have handmade quilts, useful dressers, and comfortable wing chairs. Half the rooms have queen-size beds, half have twins. The clean, new bathrooms have Mexican tile floors and framed maps of the Beaverkill. Reading is a major activity here, and the rooms are stocked amply with books and current wildlife and outdoor magazines.

Despite its rather informal decor of square oak tables, the dining room is the setting for elegant American regional cuisine. The day begins with a full buffet breakfast. Guests usually have two entrée selections at lunch and again at dinner, a four-course meal prepared by chef and innkeeper Christina, joined by chef Timothy Rogers. Using local products, they might serve the following meal: a green pea and mint soup, a cherry tomato and artichoke heart salad, perhaps filet of beef with bleu cheese sauce or poached Norwegian salmon with ginger lime *beurre blanc,* and a dessert of chocolate Kahlua mousse with hazelnuts.

Inn guests have private access to three miles of the Beaverkill River and many more miles of ten-foot-wide cross-country ski trails laid out by Rockefeller himself. Several tennis courts are carved into a plot above the inn. In the former dairy barn is a conference center that doubles as a square-dance hall, an indoor pool with an atrium ceiling and Mexican tiles, and a self-serve ice cream bar.

MILLERTON

Simmons Way Village Inn

Route 44 East, Box 965
Millerton, NY 12546
518-789-6235

> *A village inn
> nestled in the
> Berkshire foothills*

Owners and Innkeepers: Richard
and Nancy Carter. **Accommodations:** 10 rooms, all with private
bath, including 1 suite. **Rates:** $125–$150. **Minimum stay:** 2
nights on weekends May–November, 3 nights on holiday
weekends. **Added:** $30 each additional guest, 10.25% tax.
Payment: American Express, Visa, MasterCard. **Children:**
Welcome. **Pets:** Not allowed. **Smoking:** Restricted. **Open:** All
year.

South of the Taconic State Park near the Berkshire foothills,
Millerton is closer to Connecticut than to its nearest New
York neighbor. This small lumber town is nearly level with
Rhinebeck on a map, in a narrow farmland valley along scenic
Route 22. Simmons Way Village Inn is a wonderful attraction
in this rarely traveled area, offering congenial dinners and
lovely overnight accommodations.

The rambling white clapboard building sits on a sweeping
hill overlooking Millerton's main street. Eddie Collins, the
exonerated ninth man of the Chicago Black Sox, was born
here. The three-story house was built by industrialist E. W.
Simmons in 1854 and Victorianized in 1888 with its present
array of gingerbread and porches. Ninety years later, the
house was transformed into a country inn and was bought in
1987 by its present owners, Richard and Nancy Carter. This
warm, interesting couple has traveled all over the world, lived

in Vienna for years during Dick's tenure with the United Nations, and happily decided to settle in Millerton.

The roofline undulates with gabled peaks that render the interior spaces interesting and unpredictable. Guests enter a common room that opens onto the breakfast room, illuminated by a large bay window. Throughout are some fascinating pieces from the Carters' travels, including the handmade table where guests enjoy a breakfast of homemade granola and goat's milk yogurt from the nearby Coach Farm.

To the right of the foyer is a tea room and verandah of white wicker where the Carters host high tea on summer Saturdays. At the back of the house is the dining room,

> **What makes Simmons Way such a classic village inn are its kind-hearted and well-traveled hosts, Dick and Nancy Carter. Sensitive to the needs and interests of travelers, they'll be the reason you enjoy your stay and come back for more. (Pretty and immaculate rooms are an added incentive.)**

a rather contemporary addition with large gabled skylights that allow moonlight to reflect off the oil lamps and antique silver chargers. Chef Michael Myers might prepare an appetizer of smoked salmon terrine with dill sauce and red caviar, followed by a main dish of seafood ragout with miniature vegetables in goat's milk yogurt cream, or sautéed quail with bitter orange and currant sauce, and ending with white chocolate mousse cake. Entrées range from $14 to $23. The wine list is selective, chosen to complement particular items on the menu.

The carved and paneled oak staircase leads to 10 rooms on two upper floors. Some, like numbers 2 and 4, are unusually large, with private porches through which guests can appreciate some of the original stained glass. While some rooms are feminine, with circular crown canopies, some, like room 7 on the third floor, with king-size duck comforter, are more masculine. Room 3 is a particularly lovely room with an off-pink Italian linen damask coverlet draped on a pine four-poster queen-size bed under a two-sided pink canopy, with a sitting area tucked under a gabled window. The baths are newly appointed with generous amenities but retain an Old World elegance with antique sinks and tubs, Old World octagonal tiling, and brass fixtures. All beds are antiques lengthened for modern sleepers, and all the rooms are unusually clean.

The Housatonic River and Appalachian Trail are four miles away in Connecticut, near twin lakes Wononpakook and Wononskopomuc by Salisbury. Nearby Hotchkiss offers tennis, great cross-country skiing, and trout fishing.

NEW PALTZ

Mohonk Mountain House

Lake Mohonk
New Paltz, NY 12561
914-255-1000
Reservations: 914-255-4500,
  800-772-6646

*A castle on a
lake in the sky*

Proprietors: Albert and Alfred Smiley. **Accommodations:** 276 rooms, most with private bath, many with fireplace. **Rates:** $171–$369 per couple AP. **Included:** 3 meals a day and afternoon tea. **Minimum stay:** 2 nights on weekends, 3 nights on holidays. **Added:** $60 each additional guest over age 12 AP, $50 each child age 4–12 AP, 15% service charge, 7% state tax, 2.5% occupancy tax, $1 county tax. **Payment:** Visa, MasterCard, American Express. **Children:** Welcome. **Pets:** Not allowed. **Smoking:** Allowed. **Open:** All year.

One of the region's most magical places was discovered during a picnic in 1869, when Alfred H. Smiley was captivated by the beauty of Lake Mohonk in the Shawangunk Mountains. He spent the night in a ten-room tavern on the property and soon began discussions with its owner to buy the surrounding 300 acres. He and his twin brother, Albert, had long hoped to own a country house and they saw this as an early and ideal opportunity.

Such were the modest beginnings of the Mohonk Mountain House, which grew from 10 to 276 rooms, from 300 acres to 7,500. The brothers built their dream together, based on their Quaker belief that nature and humans can live in harmony. Mohonk remains in the Smiley family today and looks most certainly as it did at the turn of the century, focused around "the lake in the sky."

Though it's only 90 miles from New York City and just barely off the Hudson, Mohonk is secluded on its acreage. The setting, several miles up a mountain drive and overlooking an azure lake, seems truly out of a fairy tale. Freshwater Lake Mohonk is a half mile long and 60 feet deep. Conjuring up images of European castles, the Mohonk Mountain House is an elegant architectural collage of Romanesque, Richardson, and Adirondack styles. In 1870, the house was expanded to accommodate 40 guests. The large central building was built in the late 1880s, followed by the seven-story stone lodge in 1899. Transoms conduct the ever-present breezes through the venerable doors to the wide, rocker-filled verandah overlooking the lovely lake that so inspired the Smiley brothers. The eye floats across the mirrorlike lake to the craggy heights of Sky Top and its stone tower. This scene is painted in the minds of those who have been to Mohonk, always remembered with a smile.

> **This hundred-year-old resort in the Shawangunk Mountains, 100 miles north of New York City, is an eclectic, dramatic, fantastic dream. Generations have been raised at Mohonk, romantics have courted at Mohonk, outdoorspeople have communed with nature at Mohonk — and all who have been here will never forget its majesty.**

There's an Old World sociability here that recalls the days when people vacationed for months at a time, content with company and natural surroundings. Throughout the house are 151 working fireplaces, 200 balconies, six parlors, and three verandahs. Almost all the guest rooms have porches, and all porches have caned rockers, a good many of which are original to the house.

The rooms themselves are all different. Some are quite luxurious, like a Ritz-Carlton gone Gothic; some are nearly ascetic, with a sink in the corner or closet. All have antiques, old dressers, and ceiling fans.

The rooms, however, are a small part of the Mohonk experience. Quite telling of times gone by are the abundance and variety of public places that somehow remain so private: little libraries with dusty leatherbound classics, a nook in a wraparound porch untrespassed for hours. The dining room is one of the glories of the place: a wonder of open space that draws the eye across the pine wainscoting to the large picture windows overlooking the mountains — the sunsets are the most delectable part of the meal, viewed in a panorama of 30 feet of window.

Throughout the 2,000 acres of the Mohonk Mountain House and 5,500 acres of the Mohonk Preserve, today's guests can choose among more activities than any of the five presidents who visited here would ever have had in a daily schedule. Romantics enjoy a picnic in one of the 115 Adirondack gazebos that dot the landscape; kids love the daily cookouts at the Granary. An astounding 85 miles of hiking trails are maintained. There is a nine-hole rambling Scottish-style golf course, a putting green on the front lawn, a bowling green, croquet, six tennis courts (four clay and two Har-Tru), horses for western and English and pony riding, rowboats, paddleboats, canoes, carriage and sleigh rides, cross-country skiing, fishing, ice skating, horseshoes, platform tennis, shuffleboard, snow tubing, softball, volleyball — and countless other activities, including storytelling, a grand tradition at Mohonk. Mohonk offers an extensive children's program during the weekends, holidays, and summers for kids aged 2–17.

POUGHKEEPSIE

Inn at the Falls

50 Red Oaks Mill Road
Poughkeepsie, NY 12603
914-462-5770
800-344-1466
Fax: 914-462-5943

A luxurious, contemporary B&B near Vassar College

Proprietors: Arnold and Barbara Sheer. **Manager:** Gerry Roth. **Accommodations:** 36 rooms, all with private bath, including 2 mini-suites and 12 large suites. **Rates:** $110–$150. **Included:** Continental breakfast. **Minimum stay:** None. **Added:** 15%

state and local tax, $10 additional guest. **Payment:** Major credit cards. **Children:** Welcome. **Pets:** Not allowed. **Smoking:** Nonsmoking rooms available. **Open:** All year.

The Inn at the Falls is a unique property on the outskirts of Poughkeepsie, several miles from Vassar College. It's not quite an inn, since no dinners are served; it's not quite a bed-and-breakfast, since it has the amenities, decor, and service of a small luxury hotel; and it's certainly not historic, having been built in 1985 for $2.5 million by Arnold and Barbara Sheer, a hardworking, sincere couple whose most recent endeavor is a cumulative effort of their several decades in the hotel industry.

> On the outskirts of Poughkeepsie, the Inn at the Falls is a unique creation, a hybrid between a luxury hotel and a bed-and-breakfast. Business travelers will appreciate the contemporary conveniences; romantics will enjoy the plush decor and privacy.

The Inn at the Falls is a wonderful place for excellent service and comfort in an area that sorely lacks fine and unusual accommodations. Arnold Sheer wanted to build an intimate property devoted to excellence in accommodations — so much so that he avoided adding a restaurant for fear that it would detract from the emphasis on overnight guests.

The inn is set on three and a half acres of relatively quiet countryside, just alee of a heavily congested area. The contemporary brick building sits on the banks of some busy little rapids called Wappinger Creek, which spill over at the foot of Red Oaks Mill Road to a tiny waterfall at the entrance to the inn. The L-shaped inn borders the creek, takes a left, and bridges the driveway. Guests enter to a marble foyer that leads to a sunny common area overlooking the creek through two stories of mullioned windows.

The guest rooms on the first- and second-floor wings flare out from the center point at reception; half the rooms have views of the rapids. Rooms have phones and televisions, and the suites have mini-refrigerators. Arnold conceived four decorating schemes — contemporary, English, country, and Oriental — hoping to please as many guests as possible. Original artwork was commissioned for the inn. The English rooms have fishnet canopy beds and chintz window treatments; the contemporary rooms have sectional couches, mauve textured walls, and black lacquered furniture; the country rooms have wicker headboards and caned chairs. All have fluffy robes in large, luxurious baths with telephones and hair dryers; some baths have whirlpool tubs. There's always a little treat at night, perhaps fine chocolates or port wine.

The full Continental breakfast may be taken in the common room or delivered on a silver tray with a pot of coffee, juice, home-baked muffins and breads, and jams. This ought to sustain a visitor through a day at Vassar or touring the mansions of the Hudson, until it's time for dinner at the Culinary Institute of America, a short drive away.

PURDYS

The Box Tree

Route 22 & Route 116
Purdys, NY 10578
914-277-3677
Fax: 914-276-3376

> *A romantic refuge*
> *50 miles from*
> *New York City*

Proprietor: Augustin V. Paege. **Manager:** Alain Pirony. **Accommodations:** 3 suites, all with private bath, 2 with fireplace. **Rates:** $165 weekends, $65 weekdays. **Included:** Continental breakfast. **Minimum stay:** None. **Added:** 12% tax. **Payment:** American Express. **Children:** Not allowed. **Pets:** Not allowed. **Smoking:** Limited. **Open:** All year.

The romance at the Box Tree, which recently celebrated its 20th anniversary, is due to the lavish work of decorator Heinz Simon, who has draped and swagged luxurious Waverly fabrics around museum-quality French and English antiques. Also responsible for the experience is chef Ken Lindh, whose French cuisine is served in three intimate candlelit rooms fitted with muted tapestry chairs, crystal, and china.

A weekend at the Box Tree is transporting. The 48-mile drive from Manhattan into upstate New York's horse country brings a couple to a 1775 colonial house two and a half stories high, set in front of pastures and ponies. The white clapboard building has an enclosed porch across its facade, walled in mullioned windows.

The three dining rooms are colonial refuges, decorated in plush French and English antiques. The Aubusson tapestry chairs are reproduction Louis XIII, surrounding gleaming wood tables. Chef Ken Lindh prepares entrées from a French menu, ranging from $22 to $29. A dinner might start with a timbale of pasta, herbs, and ragout of lobster, shrimp, and scallops, or perhaps snails gratiné in Pernod butter; followed by roast duck in ginger and pinot noir sauce or quail stuffed

A place of romance and fantasy, the Box Tree has a dreamy quality. While antiques abound, they share not a common nationality or heritage or period, but simply grand-scale drama. This eclectic elegance pervades the historic house, its dining rooms, and its boudoirs.

with wild rice and truffle sauce. Ending the meal is a selection of seven desserts that may feature a terrine of dark chocolate with hazelnut cream or apples in pastry with mango coulis. The wine list is admirable.

Two of the three guest suites are above the dining room, and a third has a private porch on the ground level at the back of the house. The finest room is the François Premier Room, with a carved canopy bed from 1665 draped elaborately in black chintz. This room also has the finest bath, done in black and white parquet, with plush towels and terry robes, a bidet, and hair dryer. King Ludwig's Room has a carved Renaissance Revival suite. The Florentine Suite at the back has a stunning canopy bed, its four posters gilded and interestingly gnarled. Here the bath is done in pink marble. The guest's lounge between the two second-floor rooms has a green silk-covered Regency parlor set against a backdrop of peach moiré walls, linked by Waverly chintz drapes. Elaborate gilt ormolu candelabras are used as wall sconces.

David Bennett is the conscientious innkeeper who serves as full-time butler. The high level of luxury is intriguing in this modest colonial house. Service is quite solicitous, yet guests are left very much to themselves.

RHINEBECK

Beekman Arms

4 Mill Street, Route 9
Rhinebeck, NY 12572
914-876-7077 (also for fax)

An inn that offers two centuries of hospitality

Proprietor: Charles LaForge. **Manager:** Eve Diaz. **Accommodations:** 59 rooms, 22 with fireplace, in inn and several outbuildings. **Rates:** $70–$140. **Included:** Continental breakfast. **Minimum stay:** 2 nights May–October. **Added:** $10 each additional guest, 10.25% tax. **Payment:** Major credit cards. **Children:** Welcome. **Pets:** In the motel unit only. **Smoking:** Nonsmoking rooms available. **Open:** All year.

Reputed to be the country's oldest continuously operating inn, the Beekman Arms opened its doors in 1766. It is a composite of ten buildings, with its history concentrated in the main inn. Rhinebeck was settled in the early 18th century by German religious refugees. They named the town for their beloved Rhine, which looked so like the Hudson River. Halfway between Albany and New York City, Rhinebeck became a major commercial center. In 1766 Arent Traphagen constructed an inn — two stories tall, with three-foot-thick stone walls, 8-by-12-inch oak beams, and 14-inch-wide floor planks — as a stagecoach stop. The Bogardus Tavern, as it was then known, was quickly caught in the throng of the Revolutionary War and often served as a meeting spot for generals and soldiers. In 1777, the entire town of Rhinebeck sought refuge in the tavern when given word of an impending British attack — word that later proved to be false.

A gathering spot for dignitaries ever since, the Beekman Arms is a living piece of history. The common rooms and five dining areas in the main house are filled with lore, colonial pewter collections, a 1795 deed, Civil War muskets, a 1760 tavern table, and an 18th-century Hudson Valley corner cupboard. Adjacent to the reception area is a Federal addition with a library furnished in comfortable couches and wing chairs. Old pictures of the inn and area decorate the walls, including an ancient ferry ticket from Fishkill to Newburgh across the Hudson (fare for a man and a horse: two shillings).

Despite a rather daring proximity to the renowned Culinary Institute of America, the on-site restaurant has recently made quite an impression with its creative American cuisine. The restaurant is leased to Larry Forgione, who runs it independently as the Beekman 1766 Tavern. Its five dining areas include a sunny brick-floored atrium, a paneled Tap Room with banquettes, and two colonial rooms. The tavern, under chef Tony Nogales, is open every day for lunch and dinner, and a lavish brunch is served on Sundays. Entrées range from $16 to $24; choices may include cedar-planked Atlantic salmon atop soft corn pudding and a toasted pumpkin seed vinaigrette; or honey–glazed roast Adirondack free-range duck with wild rice, cranberries, and shiitake mushrooms.

The lower Hudson Valley teems with history, and there is no better place to celebrate that than at New York's oldest inn. While dining and guest rooms in the main inn are convincingly colonial, accommodations elsewhere on the property are Victorian and even contemporary.

The second-floor rooms in the main house vary in size from smallish to pretty large, with traditional furnishings, antiques, and modest private baths. The variety of other accommodations have telephones and televisions, and most are decorated with traditional reproduction pine furnishings. The prettiest is the 1844 Gothic Revival Delamater House, two stories of vertical cream clapboard with much gingerbread and dozens of diamond-paned Tudor windows (of the seven rooms, choose the first-floor south room with a settee in the three-sided bay). The Delamater House is on a grassy commons, around which sit the similarly decorated courtyard buildings flanking the Federal Germand House. The single-story Carriage House, with five deluxe rooms for business travelers, was built on the site a century earlier, across the lawn from the new patio. Behind the inn adjacent to the Rhinebeck Antiques Center are the Fire House, built in the 1800s, and the Guest House, for the budget-minded.

The Village Victorian Inn at Rhinebeck

31 Center Street
Rhinebeck, NY 12572
914-876-8345

> *A model B&B*
> *in the heart*
> *of Rhinebeck*

Proprietor: Judy and Rich Kohler.
Accommodations: 5 rooms, all with private bath, 1 with fireplace.
Rates: $175–$250. **Included:** Full breakfast, afternoon tea.
Minimum stay: 2 nights on weekends, 3 nights on holiday weekends. **Added:** $50 each additional guest; 12.25% tax.
Payment: American Express. **Children:** Not allowed. **Pets:** Not allowed. **Smoking:** Not allowed. **Open:** All year.

A picture-perfect bed-and-breakfast with luxury resort rates, the Village Victorian is a wonderful place for guests who care about romance and privacy and not a whit about budgets. Rhinebeck is a wonderful weekending town just an hour from New York City, best known for its antiques and surrounding history and for being the home of America's oldest inn, the Beekman Arms. It's a very walkable town with much to do, and within a short drive are Hyde Park, the Vanderbilt Mansions, and the Culinary Institute, for which one ought to make reservations months in advance.

The Village Victorian is just a block from the center of this bustling and charming town. There are some spectacular antiques here, which owner Judy Kohler has assiduously collected, refinished, and reupholstered with great care. Many of these pieces are for sale. The house is rather modest-looking on the outside, its facade painted a buttery yellow, with black shutters and white trim, set behind a picket fence. Only two stories, the house has a sweet overhanging porch at its front entrance, furnished with white wicker settees. It was built around 1860, an early, none-too-ornate Victorian. Judy Kohler rejuvenated it to its pristine state in 1987 and had it placed on the National Register of Historic Places. The formal living room, with its wide-plank dark-stained floors, period Victorian furniture, Oriental carpet, and lace-covered bay window, is also the setting for an ornate tea.

> **The formidable antiques and sumptuous linens at the Village Victorian are highlights, but what stands out at this property is the excellent service. Judy Kohler's staff is polite, discreet, thoughtful, and creative.**

The one guest room on the first floor has two antique brass twin beds pushed together to make a king, a huge double armoire with two mirrors, and a settee positioned in the bay window. The four guest rooms on the second floor have elegant and formal antiques, such as brass or heavily carved Victorian headboards, fishnet canopy beds, delicate writing tables, formidable armoires, and slipper chairs and settees done in thick tapestries. The fireplace room has a curved fishnet canopy over a king-size bed, an antique fainting couch, and a gilded oak French armoire. Perhaps the most lavish aspect of the inn — aside from its breakfasts — is the linens, with heavy, fine cotton sheets and duvets topped by myriad pillows. The wallpapers and curtains have equal attention to detail and pattern; the baths are simple, new, and clean.

New York City

New York City

Best for Urban Intimacy

The Algonquin
The Box Tree
The Carlyle
The Lowell
The Mark
The Mayfair Hotel Baglioni
The Michelangelo
The Pierre
Hôtel Plaza Athénée
The Royalton
The Hotel Wales
Westbury Hotel

Best for Metropolitan Magnificence

Essex House
Four Seasons Hotel
Paramount
The Peninsula
Radisson Empire Hotel
Rihga Royal Hotel
The Ritz-Carlton Hotel
The St. Regis
U.N. Plaza-Park Hyatt
Waldorf Towers
Waldorf-Astoria

The best way to see New York City is on a walking tour, and several good books describe wonderful routes (see "Recommended Guidebooks," page 643). A walk in Manhattan can take one through ethnic neighborhoods of Little Italy, Chinatown, Delancey Street, or Yorkville; shopping tours of Madison or Fifth Avenue or SoHo's West Broadway; around the theater district; past the bulls and bears of Wall Street; several days' work along Museum Mile of Upper Fifth Avenue; jazz clubs of the West Village; or architectural archives of the avenues.

Though it's quite touristy, the three-and-a-half-hour Circle Line tours are a great way to get a sense of the island and its architecture and history. The guides are well trained and knowledgeable, and amid the one-liners and puns a passenger will glean some good stories.

The Algonquin

59 West 44th Street
New York, NY 10036
212-840-6800
800-548-0345
Fax: 212-944-1419

> *Home of the*
> *Round Tablers*
> *of the 1920s*

Proprietors: Caesar Park Hotel America, Inc., Aoki Corp. **General Manager:** Mr. Dai Zenno. **Accommodations:** 165 rooms, including 23 suites. **Rates:** Rooms $215, suites $300; lower rates on weekends. **Included:** Continental buffet breakfast. **Added:** $25 each additional guest, 19.25% tax plus $2 room tax. **Payment:** Major credit cards. **Children:** Welcome. **Pets:** Not allowed. **Smoking:** 1 nonsmoking floor. **Open:** All year.

In August 1991 the Algonquin completed a several-year, $20 million restoration, the most thorough effort since it was built in 1902. The history of this institution and the Round Table for which it is famous did not commence until several years after the red brick and limestone building opened, when Frank Case, a former employee, bought the hotel in 1907. (During his years as an employee, Case suggested changing the hotel's name from Puritan to Algonquin to denote strength and pioneerism.)

Case extended hospitality and credit to his favorite patrons, writers, and actors including Douglas Fairbanks, Sr., and H. L. Mencken. The group grew, and Case accommodated them at a round table found originally in the Oak Room, providing celery and popovers to fuel the intellectual fires. By the mid-1920s, the Round Tablers included about 30 literati, including such nobles as Dorothy Parker, George S. Kaufman, Edna Ferber, Ring Lardner, Robert Benchley, and Harold Ross, later the editor of *The New Yorker*. Evidence of these halcyon days is seen in Al Hirschfeld's drawings found throughout the hotel and copies of *The New Yorker* in every guest room.

The reverence displayed by Ben and Mary Bodne during their 30 years of ownership was equaled by the new owners during the recent renovation, begun in 1987. The original oak woodwork of the Edwardian lobby, including the arched doorways, supporting beams, and Corinthian capitals, has been restored to its former luster, as have the plaster dentil moldings, the painted glass sconces, and even the furnishings.

Today the lobby is a renowned landmark as well as a favorite place for afternoon tea, cocktails, and entertainment. The Rose Room, the feminine alternative for afternoon and evening dining, features rose-colored damask walls and banquettes under an Austrian crystal chandelier. The clubby Oak Room, with its traditional lamp sconces and dark paneled walls, is a bastion of New York cabaret life that is matched only at the Carlyle.

The 12 guest room floors are intimately configured and are decorated with original art depicting scenes of old New York, the Round Tablers, and Algonquin legends. Because of the hotel's landmark status, the new owners were allowed to retain the original open staircase that ascends the center of the building, of white wrought iron and marble.

> **The Algonquin's public spaces are some of the most beloved of all New York City hotels. The Edwardian lobby is a marriage of eclectic tradition and comfortable formality; the Rose Room is the feminine complement to the clubby Oak Room, a celebrated stage for the city's cabaret and jazz talent.**

Accommodations are fresh and immaculate. While the standard rooms are quite small and the smaller rooms cramped, the suites are a nice size and well worth the investment. Or try the center standard rooms with window seats below curved bay windows. Most of the Algonquin's original Edwardian furnishings have been either refinished or reproduced, set into schemes of peachy rose, mint green, or light blue, with high ceilings, and floral spreads matching structured drapes. The baths are gleaming white, with a hair dryer and prints of flowers.

The Box Tree

250 East 49th Street
New York, NY 10017
212-593-9810

> *The city's most
> romantic B&B*

Proprietor: Augustin V. Paege. **General Manager:** Nina Fuenmayor.
Accommodations: 12 suites, all with private bath. **Rates:** $270–$300, including $100 credit toward dinner. **Included:** Continental breakfast. **Minimum stay:** None. **Payment:** American Express. **Children:** Allowed. **Pets:** Allowed. **Smoking:** Not allowed in rooms. **Open:** All year.

Manhattanites have been preparing for the urban Box Tree for years. Its 20-year-old relative in Purdys, 40 miles north, is a romantic guest house and culinary refuge. Since 1982, the Box Tree restaurant has prepared wondrous dinners, but it began welcoming guests only in 1989. The Box Tree experience is a stunning surprise: romantic, fantastic, whimsical.

Guest pick out the nattiest brownstone on East 49th Street, between Second and Third Avenues, marked by a verdigris marquee and a scripted sign adorned with gold leaves. Inside is an interior landscape created by Mr. Paege, the result of a lifetime of collecting and impeccable, eclectic, wondrous taste. Guests enter a patterned brick foyer. Among the curiosities are a Louis XIII tufted leather wing chair with a hooded back. Two 18th-century Italian porcelain figures support a mantel designed for the setting.

A series of intimate dining rooms on the lower two floors creates a sense of evolution at the Box Tree; each scene captures the imagination and then proceeds into another realm. The Music dining room has reproduction Louis XIII chairs covered in Aubusson muted tapestry, backlit by a turn-of-the-century stained glass window. The magnificent mantel is supported by wide terra cotta columns inset with colored glass. The Marie Antoinette dining room seems to have been lifted from Versailles, with lavish gilded millwork and molding as well as candelabras and chandelier. Most masterful is the Gaudi-inspired staircase sculpted by collaborator David Mills, which connects the two levels of dining rooms.

Each of the 12 suites on floors above and in the adjacent brownstone is a world unto itself, diminutive versions of palaces in China, Egypt, or France. The *trompe l'oeil* doors re-

flecting each room's decor were painted by decorative artist
Heinz Simon, who crafted much of the Purdys Box Tree.

Each suite has a sitting area facing a working gas fireplace.
The topmost suite has a
high ceiling and a green
malachite fireplace. The
Chinese Suite has lac-
quered tables and chairs
and Chinese porcelain ac-
cents. The Japanese Suite
has Mackintosh English
antiques. The King Boris
of Bulgaria Room is filled
with Louis XVI gilt furniture. Gilded molding dec-
orates the walls in the
Consulate Suite, which
also has a green marble
fireplace.

> **New York City hotels are
> generally a serious
> business, and none is so
> frivolous and purely
> pleasurable as the Box
> Tree. Its bedrooms are
> boudoirs, each a whimsical
> fantasy created around a
> different country theme.
> The dining room is no less
> magical, an experience
> devoted to romance.**

Guests can focus on
the individual treasures
or revel in the whirlwind
of changes from room to room. It's a wondrous, magical
place. Be sure to come back from shopping in time for high
tea, a tradition seemingly invented for this lavish setting.

The Carlyle

Madison Avenue at 76th Street
New York, NY 10021
212-744-1600
800-227-5737
Fax: 212-717-4682

> *The champion of
> New York City
> hotels*

Proprietor: Carlyle Management
Co. **General Manager:** Daniel Camp. **Accommodations:** 190
rooms and suites. **Rates:** Rooms $275–$350, suites $500–
$1,200. **Added:** $25 each additional guest, 19.25% tax. **Payment:** Major credit cards. **Children:** Welcome. **Pets:** Allowed.
Smoking: Allowed. **Open:** All year.

The Carlyle has consistently offered the best in overnight
accommodations longer than any other New York City hotel.

It has received the Mobil Five Star award for more than 20 consecutive years. Yet the Carlyle has kept up nicely with its modern competitors, with a gorgeous new state-of-the-art fitness center, as well as constant refurbishment — the rooms are redecorated every three years.

The Carlyle is just a block from Central Park and Museum Mile and Madison Avenue's finest art galleries. It was completed in 1931 by architects Bien & Prince, a square building culminating in a blanched-brick, 35-story tower with a recognizable gilded crown. Inside, it is a world unto itself. One of its most wonderful features is Bemelmans Bar, a gallery of murals painted by Austrian artist Ludwig Bemelmans, author and illustrator of the Madeline books that have charmed generations of children. Bemelmans painted the murals when he and his wife, Madeline, lived in the Carlyle in 1946–47.

> **Artistic talent abounds at this hotel. Mark Hampton has lent a hand to the guest rooms' interior design; author and illustrator of the Madeline books, Ludwig Bemelmans painted the murals at the enchanting Bemelmans Bar (his models were the playful monkeys in the Central Park Zoo); and of course Bobby Short graces the halls of the Cafe Carlyle.**

Bemelmans spills into the Gallery, a space as intimate as a genie's bottle, a plush recreation of the Turkish Topkapi Palace where guests have tea and champagne suppers. The Café Carlyle is the forum for the much-loved music of Bobby Short, who has charmed audiences here for 26 years, as well as other cabaret entertainers. It is a lavish environment for the mural of French artist Vertes. The Carlyle restaurant is a beautiful setting for highly rated food. The wine cellar has an astounding 25,000 bottles.

Guests enter at 76th Street and descend to the lobby, rich with Gobelin tapestries and black and white marble flooring, topped in cool months by magnificent Aubusson antique carpets. Elevator operators politely take guests to their floors. Each room is unique in configuration and design. Dorothy Draper was the hotel's original decorator, and today Mark Hampton and his team follow in her footsteps. Some rooms have the original wood flooring, covered with needlepoint and Oriental carpets. Audubon prints, architectural Piranesi engravings, hunt pictures, and English country scenes decorate the walls. The rooms have quite different looks: some in traditional chintz, others in bold orange or hunter green. The beds have wood or upholstered headboards, the antique marble-top dressers may support Chinese porcelain lamps — all in the classic style of the Carlyle's residential neighbors. All rooms have televisions, VCRs, stereos, and CD players. The marble baths include phones, and all have whirlpool tubs. Every room is equipped with its own fax machine.

The Carlyle's new fitness center is intimate, private, and beautifully appointed, with Lalique crystal doors, an atrium skylight, serene Canadian maple walls, French limestone, and English green slate tiles. In addition to cardiovascular equipment, there are saunas and steam rooms as well as private massage.

Despite its stature as perhaps the city's most famous grand old hotel, the Carlyle is a welcoming, nonstuffy place. Service is impeccable but friendly, unobtrusive without being cold, elegant but not pretentious.

Essex House

160 Central Park South
New York, NY 10019
212-247-0300
800-645-5687

Art deco revival on Central Park South

Proprietor: Nikko Hotels International. **General Manager:** Wolf Walther, Vice President. **Accommodations:** 591 rooms, including 61 suites. **Rates:** Rooms $265–$315, $185–$235 weekends; suites $285–$850. **Added:** $25 each additional guest, 19.25% tax. **Payment:** Major credit cards. **Children:** Welcome, under 18 free. **Pets:** Not allowed. **Smoking:** Nonsmoking floors available. **Open:** All year.

Originally built in 1931 as the city's largest and tallest hotel, Sayville Towers, as the Essex House was called, opened with 1,286 rooms and such luxurious, modern amenities as a radio and private bath in every room. Over the years, the Essex declined sadly. Nikko Hotels bought the dowager in 1989 and undertook a $75 million renovation, completed in September 1991.

The Essex House was redesigned to evoke a nostalgia for the New York City of the 1930s: the days of big bands, black and white balls, glamorous movie stars, and art deco extravagance. Even the location conjures up images of old New York, as the shoppers and hansom cabs whisk by on Central Park South.

> **The Essex House has been warmly received into the city's social scene since it put its newest face forward in 1991. Two restaurants are doing quite well: Les Célébrités is a showcase for French cuisine and celebrity artwork; the charming Café Botanica, with views of the Park, has also made quite a splash.**

There is a great deal of gilt at the Essex House, both outside and inside. Guests enter to a grand-scale lobby of brown and white parquet floors and coffered ceilings that are supported by heavy black pillars. To the left is Café Botanica, serving three meals and light California fare. The wonderful room has a terrace area facing Central Park South through floor-to-ceiling Palladian windows, with wicker and rattan chairs and verdigris sconces. Ben Kay offers fabulous traditional Japanese breakfasts. Journeys is an Old World bar with the feel of an English club.

The high point of the public spaces is Les Célébrités, showcase for the French cuisine (with Japanese influences) of chef Christian Delouvrier and a gallery for the artwork of celebrities such as Pierce Brosnan, James Dean, Gene Hackman, Elke Sommer, and Billy Dee Williams, among others. The paintings are proudly displayed on the walls, viewed from tapestried banquettes and comfortable chairs in a plush, patterned environment.

Guests proceed up to rooms on 41 floors via original etched brass elevator doors, which open to a painted foyer on each floor. The decor here is as traditional as that in the rest of the hotel is art deco, though the colors are bright and fresh, if predictable. Fine features are extremely large closets, pristine gray marble baths with large soaking tubs, phones, scales, eyelet curtains, and tassel tiebacks. Chintz and stripes and bold carpets brighten the rooms, against a backdrop of traditional Chippendale furniture.

Nikko thought of its guests at work and at play. They designed a full business center, including computers and even a Japanese word processor. The private health club and spa features a good amount of cardiovascular equipment and two types of massage overseen by a full staff.

The staff are extremely enthusiastic about their new place in New York and respectful of the Nikko's Japanese roots.

Four Seasons Hotel

57 East 57th Street
New York, New York 10022
212-758-5700, 212-758-5711
800-332-3442

The city's newest luxury hotel, glamorous and exciting

Proprietors: The Hotel Investment Corp. **General Manager:** Thomas Gurtner. **Accommodations:** 367 rooms, including 60 one- and two-bedroom suites; 23 rooms with terraces. **Rates:** Rooms from $390, suites from $695, weekend packages available. **Included:** Complimentary shoe shine. **Minimum Stay:** None. **Added:** 19.25% city and state tax, plus $2 occupancy tax. **Payment:** Major credit cards. **Children:** Welcome. **Pets:** Welcome. **Smoking:** 25 nonsmoking floors. **Open:** All year.

New York City is larger than life, and its newest luxury hotel takes this message very much to heart. Those of us who happened along 57th Street between 1989 and 1993 can well recall the thrill associated with the construction site: it was the setting for a modern-day cathedral-in-creation. In short, the new Four Seasons is a spectacular thing to behold: a monolith rising 682 feet in 52 floors, both classic and futuristic, both familiar in its towering presence hovering over the city skyline and eerily strange, with its luminescent limestone facade and empty oculus, or hole, above the front entrance. As the city's tallest hotel, it offers eye and ear-popping views of Central Park and midtown Manhattan. Between 57th and 58th Street, and between Madison and Park avenues, steps from Tiffany, Barney's, Trump Tower, Carnegie Hall, Steuben Glass, the Museum of Modern Art, Bergdorf Good-

man, the Plaza, F.A.O. Schwarz, and so much more, the new
Four Seasons is at the very center of the city's pulse.

The Four Seasons is not only a new New York City landmark but an interesting
comment on the chang-
ing shape of the grand
hotel. Architect I. M. Pei
designed the hotel, his
only hotel design in the
Western Hemisphere. His
design is breathtaking,
both a tribute to the era
of the grand hotel and a
singular vision for the future of this architectural
phenomenon. The grand
hotel had its heyday in
the 1920s and 1930s in
the form of romantic
towers like the St. Regis,
the Pierre, and the Wal-
dorf-Astoria. In the real

> A monument to the classic
> grand hotel of the 1920s
> and 1930s, the new Four
> Seasons is a spectacular
> thing to behold: a mono-
> lithic tower, both classic
> and futuristic, both
> familiar in the city skyline
> and eerily strange, with
> its luminescent limestone
> facade and empty hole
> above the front entrance.

estate boom of the 1980s, grand became grandiose: hotels
were opulent, glitzy, showy, replete with marble, brass, and
chrome. Reactionists reacted, and the understated boutique
hotel was born. The Four Seasons is a wonderful compromise — some would say advancement. It is both a monument
of grandeur, a towering monolith of classic proportions, and
an understated sanctuary of respite and calm.

The Grand Foyer, a 23-foot stone and glass entryway at
57th Street, is a breathtaking setting: from the marble floor,
limestone walls stretch 33 feet upward, supported by weighty
octagonal columns, to a back-lighted ceiling of onyx. Terraced conversation and dining areas radiate around the Grand
Foyer — I.M. Pei described his intent that the Grand Foyer be
a stage for gathering travelers, contributing to the sense of
urban theater that is a grand hotel. At the rear, Danish beech-
wood is a backdrop to the registration area, both a beautiful
and ominous shrine, which looks as if St. Peter might be in
the wings, deciding if you may be checked in.

Artwork of Le Corbusier, Kandinsky, and Léger, among
others, underscores the modernist approach of the architecture. Neutral tones like honey, gray, and beige complement
the limestone, onyx, and marble, and woods like sycamore,

beech, and maple. The Lobby Court folds around the building's trunk to the 58th Street grand staircase. Fifty Seven Fifty Seven, the contemporary American Bar and Grill of the Four Seasons, was designed to conjure up images of a brasserie with American traditional cooking. The restaurant's interior design was born of the I. M. Pei architecture; 22-foot coffered ceilings, maple and walnut floors, and bronze chandeliers create a soothing serenity, continued from the Grand Foyer. In addition to Fifty Seven Fifty Seven, the Four Seasons offers all-day dining at the Lobby Lounge, and lunch at the Bar.

The configuration of the guest tower, which begins on the fourth story, is interesting. Seven vertical setbacks make the tower progressively narrower and maximize the views of the city. Thus, there are 12 rooms per floor up to the 30th floor; 6 rooms per floor to the 49th floor; four rooms on the 50th floor; and then one or two luxury suites on the uppermost floors. At night, the tower is a dramatic face on the skyline, as the setbacks are home to 46 twelve-foot lanterns, lending a warm glow to the limestone facade.

The guest rooms are dominated by the soothing tones of English sycamore wood, a favorite in the era of the grand hotel. From window moldings to bedroom furnishings and cabinetry, the sycamore forms the foundation for the two color schemes of the guest rooms, caramel and light green. Tables, desks, nightstands, and chairs are oval or round, lending a sense of softness and spaciousness to the rooms, which are an average of 600 square feet. Every room has a dressing room, also paneled in sycamore. Large bathrooms complement the soft hues with a triad of marble, in peach, beige, and grey. Guests can pre-set the water temperature and pressure in the shower; and tubs fill in 60 seconds. Notably, half of the guest rooms at the Four Seasons feature full Central Park or city views.

If guests are not energized enough by the very fact of their visit, they may enjoy the Four Season's Fitness Center, with 12 workout areas, steam rooms, saunas, whirlpools, and spa services.

Hôtel Plaza Athénée

37 East 64th Street
New York, NY 10021
212-734-9100
800-223-5843
Fax: 212-772-0958

*A Parisian
luxury hotel
in New York City*

Proprietor: Forte Hotels. **General Manager:** Bernard Lackner. **Accommodations:** 153 rooms, including 36 suites. **Rates:** Rooms \$320–\$400, suites \$590–\$900; single rates \$35 less. **Added:** \$35 each additional guest, 19.25% tax. **Payment:** Major credit cards. **Children:** Welcome. **Pets:** Not allowed. **Smoking:** 1 of 16 floors nonsmoking. **Open:** All year.

With its bright red awnings flagging every window, the New York Hôtel Plaza Athénée pledges allegiance to its inspiration, the Paris Athénée, one of the world's finest hotels since it was built more than a century ago. Despite its Old World appearance, the New York Plaza Athénée opened in September 1984, a transformation of the former 1927 Alrae Hotel with a redesign by architect John Carl Warnecke. It is surely the ritziest of the Madison Avenue boutique hotels and caters to an elegant European crowd.

Guests enter on 64th Street between Madison and Park avenues, under a portico draped with French and American flags, through polished brass doors. Through the lobby, appointed in Italian marble and luxurious French antiques, registration is at an 18th-century desk by the concierge in a room of green silk-covered walls and antiques.

A few steps down from the lobby is the restaurant Le Régence. The restaurant serves Continental food with a French flair at the hand of chef Marcel Agnez. The ornate room has gold millwork, green walls, leather chairs, and crystal sconces and chandeliers under a mural of clouds. Dinners range from \$20 to \$30. The neighboring piano lounge is a clubby, intimate place for drinks and cocktails, under Brazilian mahogany millwork, with walls covered in dark green fabric and oil paintings.

The elevator banks in the lower lobby are surrounded by three walls of a lavish hand-painted mural of pastoral scenes. Guest rooms occupy 17 floors on intimate, hushed hallways appointed with Old World moldings. Irish Navan carpets quiet the step. Headboards are upholstered velvet. There is no chintz or clutter here but classic silk and velvet in complementary colors or paisleys in handsome tones. The furnishings were handmade for the hotel, from the Directoire night tables to the desks and television cabinets in dark wood. The bathrooms are beautiful, with stunning Portuguese Aurora Rose marble on the floors and walls. Italian Frette terry robes add to the elegance. Eight suites have terraces or solariums. The rooms do not have mini-bars, as the hotel places such emphasis on its full service.

> **The Upper East side hosts a handful of the City's finest hotels, but only one derives from French hospitality. Having found this niche, the Hôtel Plaza Athénée is elegant, formal, and exclusive. It's also home to the highly regarded French restaurant, Le Régence.**

The staff is reserved and solicitous, emphasizing the aura of formality that pervades the Plaza Athénée.

Hotel Wales

1295 Madison Avenue
New York, NY 10128
212-876-6000

> *A classic and affordable choice on the Upper East Side*

Proprietor and Manager: Henry Kallan. **Accommodations:** 92 rooms, including 50 suites and 1 penthouse suite. **Rates:** Rooms $145, suites $175–$225, penthouse $375. **Included:** Continental breakfast. **Minimum stay:** None. **Added:** 19.25% tax, $2 occupancy tax. **Payment:** Major credit cards. **Children:** Welcome. **Pets:** Not allowed. **Smoking:** Allowed. **Open:** All year.

As daunting and impersonal as New York City can be for an out-of-towner, the Hotel Wales is just as comforting and friendly. This oasis on Manhattan's Upper East Side is as much country inn as city hotel, with surprisingly rural rates.

The Hotel Wales is located on Madison Avenue between 92nd and 93rd streets. It's a relatively peaceful part of town, referred to by New Yorkers as old-moneyed Carnegie Hill. This high up on Madison Avenue, fashionable boutiques are outnumbered by posh private schools, as close as you'll get in Manhattan to suburbia.

> Many travelers come to New York to see the sights and museums and are mired in the business and traffic of midtown. And many pay a great deal for this inconvenience. The Hotel Wales offers solutions: set in a lovely neighborhood on Museum Mile, it's both pretty and economical.

The Wales was built in 1901 as a lovely brown-stone hotel, designed as a leisurely place of respite for busy travelers who would stay for weeks at a time. Many of the suites have kitchenettes. The configuration is beneficial for nearly every room (except the smallest of singles): the suites are on the corners of the building, looking either southwest or west, but with a guaranteed view of glorious Central Park and the lakelike reservoir at 90th Street. Even if the pastoral setting is slightly obscured by the block between Madison and Fifth avenues, such obliqueness is a luxury: this is the highest-rent view in the city.

In early 1990, the hotel underwent a $6 million renovation that revealed ubiquitous oak woodwork: transoms, molding, trim, French doors, and mantels have been stripped of decades of paint. The rooms are furnished with English antiques or credible reproductions in mahogany and oak, often matched with original artwork. Each room is different, more in the style of a turn-of-the-century mansion than a hotel: a fine writing desk, a fireplace, or a canopy bed are pleasant surprises in some of the rooms. The bathrooms are nearly sparkling thanks to the renovation, with touches of marble here and there, and any native would say they are bigger than a city studio.

A word of advice: Make sure a crowded weekend does not leave you with one of the smaller singles, which are small even by city standards. Conversely, the penthouse is magnificent, a full one-bedroom apartment attached to 1,000 square feet of terrace overlooking Central Park.

Although there is no room service at the Hotel Wales, handsome Busby's is next door. Also nearby is one of the chic-elite brunch locales in the city, the immensely popular

Sarabeth's Kitchen, which boasts a 45-minute wait on weekends and no hope of reservations. Service at the hotel is hushed, reverent, and near to invisible. Continental breakfast is served in the recently finished salon, 1,600 square feet of grandeur, also the pleasant setting for Friday night classical concerts.

The Lowell

28 East 63rd Street
New York, NY 10021
212-838-1400
800-221-4444
Fax 212-319-4230

> *The city's most intimate and elite luxury hotel*

General Manager: Martin Hale. **Accommodations:** 61 rooms, including 48 suites. **Rates:** Rooms $320, suites $420–$1,500. **Minimum stay:** None. **Added:** $20 each additional guest, 19.25% tax, $2 occupancy tax. **Payment:** Major credit cards. **Children:** Allowed. **Pets:** Check with manager. **Smoking:** Allowed. **Open:** All year.

Though it was built in 1928 as a residence hotel, the Lowell was purchased by its present owners in 1984. They recently invested $25 million in its renovation, returning it to the glory days when Scott and Zelda Fitzgerald, Dorothy Parker, Eugene O'Neill, and Noel Coward were regular guests.

The Lowell is the only full-service New York City hotel with fewer than 100 rooms. It has the largest number of working fireplaces in any city hotel, with 33 in its suites. While others scramble to establish unique identities, the Lowell is comfortable in its exclusivity. As a member of the elite Relais & Châteaux, the hotel is necessarily privately owned, since 1984. A recent $25 million renovation on this boutique property established it as an elite Manhattan hideaway.

The 17-story art deco landmark in patterned brick sits on 63rd Street between Madison and Park avenues, its exterior so understated as to be mistaken for a private apartment building. Guests, laden with packages from Givenchy and Ungaro around the corner, enter the formal lobby, with faux marbling and Empire parlor sets, Scalamadre window treatments, and upholstery in regal gold silk. The concierge sits attentively behind his Edgar Brandt desk next to the modestly sized reception desk. Behind is a faux pediment-topped book-case, actually a door to offices.

Guests are escorted up black lacquer elevators to their rooms, in a wide assortment of layouts and variety, though assuredly appointed in the height of good taste. Thirty-three suites have wood-burning fireplaces, and 56 accommodations have kitchens supplied with china and silver. Ten suites have private terraces. The Gym Suite also has a private exercise room with a treadmill, Stairmaster, weights, and even a ballet barre with a wonderful view of the Upper East Side.

> Another major player in the Upper East Side's boutique hotel row, the Lowell is the smallest and by far the most exclusive. The guest rooms have been designed to feel like private New York City pieds-à-terre, the concierge is devoted to guests' needs, and many suites have working fireplaces.

The rooms are as elegant as they are under-stated, with an overall relaxing feel amid precious antiques. The French and Oriental furnishings include leather chairs, ormolu mirrors, 18th- and 19th-century prints, and Chinese porcelain. The original mantels and fireplaces have been restored. Every room has its own library of leatherbound books. Umbrellas are provided. The baths are done in rich brown Italian marble with brass fixtures and provided with terry robes and fresh flowers. All rooms have mini-bars, televisions, and VCRs.

Service at the Lowell is hushed, discreet, and extremely personable, as if the staff is working for the guests rather than for the hotel.

The Mark

25 East 77th Street
New York, NY 10021
212-744-4300
800-843-6275
Fax: 212-744-2749

> *A chic and re-*
> *freshing presence*
> *on the*
> *Upper East Side*

Proprietors: The Rafael Group Hoteliers. **General Manager:** Raymond
N. Bickson. **Accommodations:** 180 rooms, including 60
suites. **Rates:** Rooms $275–$325, suites $525–$2,200. **Minimum stay:** None. **Added:** $20 each additional guest, 19.25%
tax plus $2 room tax. **Payment:** Major credit cards. **Children:**
Welcome. **Pets:** Not allowed. **Smoking:** Allowed. **Open:** All
year.

The Mark is a nice addition to the traditional row of elite
Upper East Side hotels, with unique neoclassic decor and a
highly regarded restaurant. Built in 1926 and known over the
years as the Hyde Park Residence and the Madison Avenue
Hotel, the building was bought by the Rafael Group, transformed for about $35 million, and opened in April 1989. The
Mark stands proudly as the American flagship property of the
group headed by hotelier Georg Rafael, who spent a decade
mastering the trade with Regent International Hotels.

The entrance is on 77th Street between Madison and Fifth
avenues. While the building is a classic Upper East Side brick
monolith, the brightly lit glass and brass doors promise something new. The intimate black and white marble lobby is a
transitional space with Beidermier furnishings, inviting a visitor to relax in the library setting of Mark's Bar or to have tea
or a lavish meal at the restaurant.

The restaurant is a wonderful gallery of tufted circular
banquettes and gossipy groups of chairs around low tables
under a backlit greenhouse ceiling, separated from an upper
dining tier by tapestried screens and a wrought-iron rail. The
cuisine of Normandy native Philippe Boulot is described as
French-inspired cuisine moderne and has been widely praised
as one of the finest among New York hotel restaurants. Dinners range from $20 to $30.

Architect Pennoyer Turino and designer Mimi Russell are
responsible for the neoclassic and Italian Renaissance elements of the interior spaces. Among the pieces setting the

tone are original Piranesi prints, Gundolt wool carpeting, and plentiful neutral tones of Italian marble. The hallways are serene spaces with classic molding in muted gray and white, lit by classic sconces. The standard rooms have an odd, modernish scheme of rose lacquer; all have mini-bars, VCRs, and televisions. The suites are well worth the upgrade, with handsome furnishings and lovely neoclassic art. All rooms feature Belgian cotton linens and down pillows.

> **The Mark took the New York Hotel scene by storm in 1989, boldly reopening its doors across the street from the Carlyle. Its unique contribution to the Upper East Side's boutique hotel row is a fresh and young mystique and a restaurant that has received raves from even the toughest critics.**

The bathrooms at the Mark accounted for about a quarter of the restoration's budget. Done in black and white ceramic tile or in several tones of Italian marble, they are deluxe, with Kohler soaking tubs and free-standing showers and fresh flowers. Most of the suites' baths have bidets.

The Mark has valiantly and gracefully risen to the competition of the Carlyle across the street — it's an exciting and tasteful addition to the new New York hotels.

The Mayfair Hotel Baglioni

610 Park Avenue at 65th Street
New York, NY 10021
212-288-0800
800-223-0542
Fax: 212-737-0538

> *A hotel with the air of a private Park Avenue residence*

Managing Director and Vice President: Dario Mariotti. **Accommodations:** 201 rooms, including 105 suites. **Rates:** Rooms $275–$410, suites $440–$1,700. **Added:** $30 each additional guest, 19.25% tax plus $2 room tax. **Payment:** Major credit cards. **Children:** Welcome. **Pets:** Small pets permitted. **Smoking:** Allowed. **Open:** All year.

The Mayfair Hotel Baglioni is one of the few city hotels with wood-burning fireplaces — 28 of them throughout the hotel. It has been the home of Le Cirque restaurant since 1974, one of the city's culinary treasures. Its Lobby Lounge is a sublime place, famous for its business breakfasts and afternoon teas and cocktails. Another unique touch is the Mayfair's Pillow Bank, offering guests 12 kinds of pillows in addition to the four down pillows in each room — neck rolls, water pillows, facial pillows, reading wedges, and so on. Other extras include free local telephone calls, complimentary chicken soup to guests with colds, and a putting green in the fitness center. Aside from these unusual offerings, the Mayfair is a picture of a traditional hotel.

> **That the Mayfair Hotel Baglioni is the home of Le Cirque — one of the city's top restaurants — gives an indication of its import in New York hotel society. Its Lobby Lounge is one of the loveliest of the city's hotel public spaces, a genteel and romantic meeting spot.**

Guests enter from 65th Street between Park and Madison avenues. The reception area is thoroughly elegant with a hint of Tudor influence in the arched thresholds, Palladian windows, and mirrors under painted coffered wood ceilings. The Lobby Lounge was a convivial gathering spot when the hotel opened, and this tradition continues today. Guests step down to the sunken inner sitting area with tufted couches, lifted by a series of arches and colonnades.

The rooms have traditional, plain decor in ecrus and pastels, with reproduction Queen Anne furnishings and some interesting prints on the walls. While the decor is uninspired, the rooms are generously sized and bright, with VCRs and televisions. The baths are pretty; among the usual features of robes, dryers, and phones are linen hand towels and fresh flowers. Umbrellas are placed in every room.

The two rooms of the fitness center have bright views of Park Avenue, cardiovascular equipment, and a professionally designed putting green.

Service at the Mayfair is friendly and eager, under the watchful gaze of active director Dario Mariotti. The staff is happy and helpful and easily approachable.

The Michelangelo

152 West 51st Street
New York, NY 10019
212-765-1900
800-338-1338
Fax: 212-581-7618

> *A quiet, elegant hotel, one of midtown's best-kept secrets*

Proprietor: StarHotels, Italy. **General Manager:** Laurence Jeffrey. **Accommodations:** 178 rooms, including 52 suites. **Rates:** Rooms $195–$265, suites from $395. **Included:** Morning newspaper. **Added:** $25 each additional guest, 19.25% tax. **Payment:** Major credit cards. **Children:** Welcome. **Pets:** Not allowed. **Smoking:** Permitted. **Open:** All year.

This elegant theater-district hotel has the tony feel of an Upper East Side property, with one of the prettiest lobbies in Midtown Manhattan. Built in 1926 as the Taft Hotel, it hosted a bohemian, eclectic theater crowd for nearly 40 years. The property was closed for four years as it underwent a $100 million renovation, reopening to rave reviews in October 1987 as the Grand Bay Hotel at Equitable Center. The property transferred to the hands of Park Lane Hotels in 1990 — which called the hotel the Parc Fifty-One — and even more recently, to Italian hoteliers who have renamed the doyenne once again. Despite all the ownership difficulties, the Michelangelo is a bastion of elegance and dignity.

Guests enter on 51st Street on the corner of Seventh Avenue, through a well-lit portico. By the time they reach the reception desk at the lobby's far end, they have forgotten the blaring horns and madding crowds of this neighborhood. The marbled setting is lovely and serene, with floors a rosy pink hue and walls a cocoa brown. Oil paintings hang above the French antiques and bergères and gilded-leg glass coffee tables. The main lobby reaches two stories upward, culminating in a gilded, pressed tin ceiling from which hangs a crystal chandelier. Huge floral arrangements dress polished antique tables. The original brass elevator doors were restored from the Taft's Roaring Twenties days.

Throughout five floors of guest rooms, the hallways are lined with plush neutral carpeting, made residential in feel by right-angled turns, antiques, and original art. Rooms have light-colored marble foyers and are unusually large, with an average of 500 square feet. The doubles are done with geometric pastels and solids and traditional wood furniture with black and gold accents; the suites are done in French country and art deco. French country rooms have beautiful pine furnishings, a king-size sleigh bed, and a large Empire sofa. Dividing the living room from the bedroom is a floor-to-ceiling armoire containing a television, stereo, and bookshelves (all rooms have several classic novels and other books). The duvets, carpeting, and upholstery are done in neutral solids. The art deco rooms are surprisingly different, furnished in black lacquer and mauve accents. A unifying theme is the bottled mineral water offered in every room next to trademark green marble ice buckets.

A sumptuous hotel, the Michelangelo suffers from a bit of an identity crisis, having undergone three name changes since its coming out in 1987. Despite this, the hotel has developed a loyal patronage, thanks to capacious rooms, general elegance, and proximity to Radio City, the theater district, and Sixth Avenue's financial houses.

All rooms, regardless of their size, have magnificent baths, including five-foot tubs and cotton bath sheets, towels, and robes, hair dryers, televisions, and phones. The floors and walls are done in blond marble, and the separate sinks and vanities are finished in green marble.

The Lobby Lounge near the reception area is a living room setting of muted tapestried chairs and plush down-filled sofas, featuring piano music and finger food in the afternoon and evening. Guests are served complimentary Continental breakfast in the hotel's restaurant, Bellini by Cipriani, an affiliate of the famous Harry's Bar in Venice, the hotel restaurant. Northern Italian lunch and dinner entrées ranging from $15 to $45 are served to the public in this light setting of leather chairs and verdigris sconces.

Paramount

235 West 46th Street
New York, NY 10019
212-764-5500
800-225-7474
Fax: 212-354-5237

> *A happening,*
> *chic, affordable*
> *city hotel*

Proprietors: Ian Shrager and Philip Pilevsky. **General Manager:** David Miskit. **Accommodations:** 610 rooms, including 13 suites. **Rates:** $155–$205, weekends $99–$165. **Added:** $25 each additional guest, 19.25% tax plus $2 room tax. **Payment:** Major credit cards. **Children:** Welcome. **Pets:** Not allowed. **Smoking:** 2 of 17 floors nonsmoking. **Open:** All year.

In the heart of the theater district, Paramount is the stage, and its guests are the players. This showcase of daring design was reborn in August 1990 after a three-year, $75 million investment. Predicting the recession, noting the abundance of unaffordable hotels in New York, owner Ian Shrager invented overnighting on a shoestring in the height of style.

The Century Paramount Hotel was designed by Thomas Lamb in 1927, architectural author of the Ziegfeld and the Pierre. The Paramount declined into dowdiness over the years until Ian Shrager and partners bought it in 1986. While Shrager's Royalton is an example of the high art of hotel design, the Paramount is performance art with a sense of humor, designed by Philippe Starck.

The formidable exterior looks like the grandest of grand old hotels, its Carrara marble facade restored by Rockwell Newman, fresh from restoring Carnegie Hall and the Statue of Liberty. A marble breezeway is the transition where the fun begins. Like guests at a potluck dinner, Europe's best designers showcase their signature pieces: odd couches, a silver chair, and weird lamps, under a ceiling inspired by Joan Miró. Those in the lobby gaze up at framed duets of diners in the Mezzanine restaurant, which wraps entirely around the perimeter. From their second-floor balcony, diners observe the lobby players, reached by a platinum leaf staircase. Very happening.

Much is conceptual at the Paramount. The 18 floors of guest rooms are reached by elevators lit in primary colors. A wide weather mirror posts the day's weather on a stark wall along white hallways lined with rope rails, reminiscent of the ocean liners of the '20s and '30s.

Though the public spaces are playful galleries of design, the rooms, though chic, were designed to be restful and welcoming. All rooms have a black and white parquet rug, a stark, Brancusi-style chandelier, clean-lined white cabinets for televisions and VCRs, and a brightly colored Starck armchair. Headboards in the single rooms are oversized replicas of Vermeer's masterpiece *Lacemaker:* a maternal figure hovers over the bed, a smooth, white platform dressed with a long cylindrical pillow. The immaculate baths retain their Old World tiling but also have New Age charm, with Philippe Starck's trademark stainless steel sink.

The public spaces include a room derivative of PeeWee's Playhouse, done by the same designer, Gary Panter; a 24-hour exercise club; a sunny breakfast room off the Mezzanine; a Dean & DeLuca espresso/pastry bar; and an incredibly chic supper club that draws lines most evenings.

Despite the overwhelming chicness of the Paramount, it is a down-to-earth, friendly, accessible place. The theatrical staff literally auditioned for their respective roles as bellmen and concierges.

> **Paramount is one of the theater district's greatest shows. A bastion of chic-elite and high design, the Paramount attracts directors and producers, actors and models, agents and influential up-and-comers, be it in the stage of the Mezzanine restaurant or the Whiskey Bar. But the Paramount is also attractively affordable and low-key.**

The Peninsula

700 Fifth Avenue at 55th Street
New York, NY 10019
212-247-2200
800-262-9467
Fax: 212-9034-3949

A midtown classic with the city's best hotel health club

Proprietor: The Peninsula Group.
General Manager: Niklaus Leuenberger. **Accommodations:** 242 rooms, including 42 suites.
Rates: Rooms $295–$415, suites $550–$1,100. **Added:** $20 each additional guest, 19.25% tax. **Payment:** Major credit cards; no personal checks. **Children:** Welcome. **Pets:** Not allowed. **Smoking:** 4 of 17 floors nonsmoking. **Open:** All year.

This grand old property is actually quite a new property, Peninsula Group's first American hotel. Built as the Gotham Hotel in 1905 by Hiss and Weekes for $2.25 million, the hotel was designed to complement its neighbor, the University Club. It sits across Fifth Avenue from the masterpiece St. Regis, completing quite an astounding trio of beaux-arts Italian Renaissance architecture.

The 23-story limestone structure lived a long life before a renovation was undertaken in 1979. But when those plans were disrupted, the hotel sat boarded up for seven years. The property was renovated to its present grandeur by the Pratt Corporation and opened in the spring of 1988. The Peninsula Group bought the hotel that year for $127 million.

While renovations have become as common as pillow mints in New York hotels, two outstanding features separate the Peninsula from its cousins: a state-of-the-art, 35,000-square-foot health club and spa and the wonderful PenTop Bar & Terrace, with panoramic city views from terraces peering over a copper cornice.

Guests enter from 55th Street into the two-story lobby, flanked by cozy parlors that are furnished in art nouveau antiques. A sweeping staircase of Italian marble ascends five steps and divides to Adrienne restaurant and Le Bistro d'Adrienne to the left and to the reception area and the Gotham

> There are many outstanding aspects of the Peninsula — from its dramatic opulent lobby to its admired restaurant, Adrienne, to its art deco rooms dotted with antiques. But its full-service health club is fantastic, with a spa and indoor pool. Also, there's the PenTop bar, still a secret, with the best views in town.

Lounge for high tea and cocktails to the right. The ornate plaster ceiling and faux pink marble under Corinthian capitals are striking. The armoire on the landing was featured at the 1904 Exposition des Beaux-Arts in Paris. Other original pieces throughout the public spaces, including bergères, tables, and a sofa, were designed by art nouveau master Louis Marjorelle. The Palm Court features the astounding legerdemain of Ben Strauss, who painted the faux limestone walls.

The guest rooms are furnished with original art nouveau antiques and lighting fixtures and custom-designed furnishings, in masculine understated decor. The futuristic telephone consoles control temperature, lighting, and the television and offer assistance in seven languages. The baths have dignified brass fixtures, bidets, and phones. Compared with the lavish public space, however, the rooms are plain and muted, and a number have poor views of the interior air shaft.

The fabulous trilevel spa occupies the top floors, a blessed contribution of the Peninsula Group. The facilities include

• *New York City*

Cybex circuits and extensive cardiovascular machines in several windowed rooms with city views. Under an atrium roof is a 17-by-42-foot pool and whirlpool. The salon offers massages, facials, and beauty services. Guests enjoy a carpeted wraparound sundeck.

Chef Nicholas Rabelais is a wonderful contribution to Adrienne, and his fine contemporary American and European cuisine is complemented by the restaurant's pretty salmon-colored decor. All is softspoken and decorous at the Peninsula — the guests as well as the staff elegant and hushed in these grand-scale public spaces.

The Pierre

Two East 61st Street
New York, NY 10021
212-838-8000
800-332-3442

*A leader
of the elite
on Central Park*

Proprietor: Four Seasons Regent Hotels. **General Manager:** Herbert Pliessnig. **Accommodations:** 203 rooms, including 57 suites. **Rates:** Rooms $310–$490, boudoir $630, suites $630–$2,500. **Added:** 19.25% tax, $25 additional guest. **Payment:** Major credit cards. **Children:** Welcome. **Pets:** Welcome; special pet amenities. **Smoking:** 9 nonsmoking floors. **Open:** All year.

In the spring of 1992, the Pierre completed a two-year renovation effort, resulting in the beautification of all its guest rooms and public spaces. The result is simply lovely, not an embellishment of an earlier Pierre but an affirmation of how we have always thought of it — as one of New York's few and finest grandes dames.

Charles Pierre, raised by a European hotelier, was invited into the fashionable set when he arrived in New York in 1904. After several years, he was able to open his own restaurant. By the 1920s, Pierre's Park Avenue was one of Manhattan's chicest eateries. Through a venture with Wall Street magnates like Otto Kahn, E. F. Hutton, and Walter Chrysler, Pierre embarked on a dream of building a grand hotel on Fifth Avenue. For $15 million, architects Schultze and Wener built a palatial Georgian monolith, its 40 stories topped in copper.

The Pierre Hotel took a year to build and opened in October 1930; but after only two years, the Depression took hold of the hotel, Pierre filed for bankruptcy, and he died disappointed in 1934. The Four Seasons Hotels signed on to manage the Pierre in 1981, and the hotel has since reclaimed its upstanding place in New York's high society.

> **The Pierre is a classic personality that is quintessentially New York.**
> **A fixture on the southeast corner of Central Park for decades, the Pierre is not only one of New York City's finest and most elegant overnight experiences but also the pinnacle for private parties. And if you're not hosting one, it's always fun to watch.**

The perfection of the Pierre starts with its location. On 61st Street and Fifth Avenue, the Pierre has all the glamour and scenery of Central Park South without the tourists and horses. Guests enter from Fifth Avenue via a scenic and rather famous hallway, which playfully and elegantly toys with window shopping as art: well-known, upscale boutiques show off displays behind glass. Or guests can enter from the subtle 61st Street side, which brings them immediately to the reception area to the left, with a restful sitting area half a tier removed from the public space. The decor is formal and classic, with Edwardian antiques and glorious floral arrangements.

At ground level, beside the 61st Street entrance, is the Café Pierre, a quiet, formal dining spot decorated in neoclassic grays and golds. This is the setting for Chef Joel Somerstein's Continental fare. Ranging from $24 to $31, entrees may include black bass in artichoke broth with fricassee of wild mushrooms, asparagus, and gnocchi.

The magnificent Rotunda lounge, beneath a French garden of murals, is a glorious spot for afternoon tea and cocktails. This splendid oval space is one of the Pierre's finest attributes. Intimate tables cluster on a brightly patterned carpet. Two wings of an ornately carved marble staircase ascend to a second floor, under the floor-to-ceiling murals with clouds painted overhead.

Like many old hotels, the Pierre has some oddly configured rooms, many with large closets. While the furnishings are nice but uninspired Chippendale or Queen Anne reproductions, the fabrics are wonderful. The rooms are decorated in several schemes with bold colors and an unusual marriage of patterns. One room might be octagonal, with drapery and bedding in an oversized chintz on a bright yellow background, with a plaid bedskirt. Another room might have twin two-poster beds with fabulous blue toile spreads and drapery. Such unpredictability is refreshing in a large, traditional Old World hotel. The baths are glorious, some with wonderful wide old-fashioned sinks, others with plain pedestal sinks, all with terry towels and robes as well as linen towels. The walls and floors are black and white marble, and all have hair dryers and phones.

The grand opening of Barney's — the city's newest and fanciest department store — just steps away on Madison Avenue at 61st Street has increased the level of elegance in the neighborhood; you may not even have to leave 61st Street. While professional and helpful, the Pierre staff are not overly solicitous — they are quite confident in their Old World stature.

Radisson Empire Hotel

44 West 63rd Street
New York, NY 10023
212-265-7400
800-333-3333
Fax: 212-315-0349

An easy choice for Lincoln Center-goers

Proprietor: Metromedia Hotels. **General Manager:** Val Reyes. **Accommodations:** 371 rooms including 25 suites. **Rates:** Rooms $135–$200, suites from $210. **Included:** Use of health club. **Added:** 19.25% tax plus $2 room tax, $20 additional guest. **Payment:** Major credit cards. **Children:** Welcome. **Pets:** Not allowed. **Smoking:** Nonsmoking rooms available. **Open:** All year.

The Empire is a fabulous value in a city of inflated hotel rates. Guests here sacrifice space as a result, but this brings them closer to the way native New Yorkers live — or so say Empire devotees. A stay at the Empire is highly recommended for value and for its location opposite Lincoln Center — as long as guests don't have a lot of luggage, and as long as they confirm that they don't have one of the smallest rooms.

Though the existing building was erected in 1923, the original Empire Hotel was built in the 19th century. The decor reflects its Old World origins, thanks to a two-year, $30 million renovation completed in 1990. Look for this landmark building's recognizable art deco copper and red neon sign high above its eleventh floor. The building is on the oblique corner between Broadway and Columbus Avenue, with its brightly lit entrance on 63rd Street. The large brick building sits at odd angles on the site, making for some intriguing room configurations.

A low breezeway leads to reception and a grand double-story lobby, overlooked by a second-floor balcony. The room has English Tudor influences, with somber dark wood chairs upholstered in royal red and heavy wrought-iron sconces matching a chandelier. A dark red Oriental rug rests on the marble floor. A lavish tapestry hangs from the wall of the staircase, carpeted in red. The creamy colors of the stone walls and plaster pediments lighten the pleasant room.

> **Accommodations at the Empire are a blessing in disguise — albeit a very small disguise, because if the Empire has any faults, it's the diminutive (but pretty) nature of its guest rooms. Other than that, you can't beat the location — right at Lincoln Center, a block from Central Park and the Visitor's Bureau — and the very reasonable rates.**

Try to get a room overlooking one of the major streets, preferably Broadway, with sweeping, dramatic views. The Empire is configured like a misshapen E, and about half of the interior rooms look onto a courtyard and one another. The furnishings are traditional Chippendale reproductions, on a dark low-pile rug, with yellow walls and bright chintz fabrics. Rooms have VCRs and CD players. The best features are the baths, small but neat as a pin. The fixtures are nice and old, and the generous amenities include phones and hair dryers.

In the same building on the ground floor directly opposite Lincoln Center is Iridium, just about the most happening restaurant and bar in the city at press time. Somewhere on the design scale between the Flintstones and Le Cirque, Iridium is what you'll be talking about when you get home.

Rihga Royal Hotel

151 West 54th Street
New York, NY 10019
212-307-5000
800-937-5454
Fax: 212-765-6530

*An all-suite
business hotel
with great
park views*

Proprietors: Royal Hotels. **General Manager:** Frank Arthur Banks. **Accommodations:** 476 1- and 2-bedroom suites, including 6 Grand Royal suites. **Rates:** $290–$2,000. **Added:** 19.25% tax. **Payment:** Major credit cards. **Children:** Welcome. **Pets:** Not allowed. **Smoking:** 5 of 52 floors nonsmoking. **Open:** All year.

In November 1990, the Rihga Royal opened its doors, issuing a challenge to all business-oriented New York City hotels. It runs like a clock and was planned well by its Japanese-owned company. There are only 10 or 12 rooms per floor, creating an unusual amount of privacy and quiet for a 500-room property. The rooms are exceptionally large, averaging 572 square feet, with at least one bedroom set apart from a living room. The fitness facilities are extensive and brand new. The hotel offers a nice business center to guests, with a fax machine, a copier, a computer, and typewriter. Half the guest rooms have fairly good views of Central Park, others have views of the Hudson or East River.

At 54 stories, the Rihga is one of the city's tallest hotels, designed by Frank Williams and Associates in the classic form of the soaring skyscrapers of the 1920s and 1930s. The tower of rose-beige brick and granite teeters above 54th Street, narrowing toward its top. Porters flock to the revolving doors. The lobby is quite small for such a large hotel, decorated in two tones of polished marble two stories high.

Guest rooms line an intimate hallway on each upper floor. With either one or two bedrooms, they are decorated similarly, with sofa beds and bay windows in the living rooms. Remote cable televisions are hidden in built-in corner cupboards. Mirrored French doors close or open to the bedroom, most with a king-size bed. Though a bit lacking in warmth, the rooms are immaculate, colorful, and utilitarian — some with wondrous views. The mini-bars have ice makers, the rooms have safes, and there are two televisions, one with a VCR. The baths are small but quite nice, with marble floors, a separate bath and shower, a telephone, a hair dryer, and a scale.

The big Fitness Center, open 24 hours and staffed with a daytime personal trainer, has new equipment including treadmills, Lifecycles, universal weights, and two saunas, with views to a small garden outdoors.

On the ground floor beside the lobby is Halcyon, the hotel's restaurant. The decor is classic, with Empire chairs and green banquettes under a lovely Italian mural. The sommelier is quite justly proud of Halcyon's 140-wine list, which makes a nice complement to Chef John Halligan's American

> **The Rihga Royal Hotel is an inspiring postmodern skyscraper that fits right into the classic landscape of midtown. It lurches skyward in vertical splendor, with only about 10 guest rooms on each of 50 floors. As a result, the views are remarkable: of Central Park, the Hudson River, and glorious midtown.**

cuisine. Visitors have drinks and enjoy piano music in the living room setting of the Halcyon Lounge, open for light fare until 2 A.M. Halcyon also provides guests with 24-hour room service.

The Ritz-Carlton, New York

112 Central Park South
New York, NY 10019
212-757-1900
212-757-9620
800-241-3333

> *A noble giant on Central Park South*

Proprietor: The Ritz-Carlton Hotel Co. **General Manager:** Edward A. Mady. **Accommodations:** 214 rooms, including 30 suites. **Rates:** Rooms $260–$350, luxury rooms $450, suites $550–$3,000; Ritz-Carlton Club rooms, add $30. **Included:** Morning newspaper, use of fitness center. **Added:** $50 each additional guest, 19.25% tax. **Payment:** Major credit cards. **Children:** Welcome. **Pets:** Not allowed. **Smoking:** Nonsmoking floors. **Open:** All year.

330 • *New York City*

With its ideal location right on Central Park South, offering some of the city's finest views, the Ritz-Carlton had been a sleeper for a number of years. But having recently completed a multimillion-dollar renovation, the Ritz-Carlton is once again one of New York's top hotels.

> A scant few hotels have a Central Park address; fewer still live up to it. And while Ritz-Carlton properties pop up around the country, this particular hotel represents the best in this luxury chain and is most suited to its tony location. An exciting renovation was recently completed.

The Navarro Hotel was built in 1928, and the Ritz-Carlton moved into its shell in 1982. This New York property embodies all the aspects of a Ritz-Carlton to a tee: the Old World flavor of its Central Park South address and regal brick facade convince a passerby or even a long-term guest that this is one of New York's grand old hotels — especially in the understated elegance displayed by the solicitous staff and at its new restaurant, Fantino. Here chef Gennaro Villella prepares Northern Italian meals in a beautiful setting, ranging from $21 to $29. You may be treated to Norwegian salmon and chicken liver roulade, with celery fondue and Liguria olive oil, or perhaps roasted lamb chops in oregano.

The guest rooms have been entirely redone in pleasing, bold schemes: heavy drapery in Wedgwood blue laced with gold, matching linens, and classic sofas. Televisions and mini-bars are fixed in lovely custom-designed armoires, wood with brass accents. The baths remain in pristine condition, with light marble on the walls and floors, classic fixtures, hair dryers, vanity mirrors, scales, phones, and two robes. A Ritz-Carlton umbrella is provided in every room. Be sure to request a park view.

While a trademark of the Ritz-Carlton properties is faultless and unobtrusive service, the staff at the New York hotel has a bit of a spring in its step after the new renovations. The Ritz is still a quiet refuge in the midst of Manhattan glitz.

The Royalton

44 West 44th Street
New York, NY 10036
212-869-4400
800-635-9013

> *The city's
> most chic retreat
> is a gallery
> of superlatives*

Proprietor: Ian Shrager. **General Manager:** Terry Ford. **Accommodations:** 168 rooms, including 28 suites, 40 with fireplace. **Rates:** Rooms $235–$350, suites $370. **Added:** $25 each additional guest, 19.25% tax. **Payment:** Major credit cards. **Children:** Welcome. **Pets:** Not allowed. **Smoking:** Allowed. **Open:** All year.

The Royalton is first a phenomenon, then a hotel. It looks like an art deco retrospective during the 21st century, like Alice in Wonderland in corporate America, as if the Algonquin's Round Table suddenly went elliptical under the hands of a space-suited Dorothy Parker.

Although it was built in 1898 as the Hotel Royalton, only the name remains remotely the same since its reintroduction to the New York chic elite in 1988 by the late Steve Rubell and Ian Shrager — a Hollywood-type producer of sophisticated Manhattan hotels. There is nothing to introduce the hotel from the street — no signs or flying flags — except the name modestly carved in stone on the pediment of the Greek Revival portico and the unearthly glow of the polished mahogany doors that signify importance.

The interior design of Philippe Starck transports a guest into the Royalton world. A cobalt blue carpet, bordered on one side with a line of white dancing ghosts, stretches nearly the block-long distance of the hotel's granite floor. A gleaming bank of highly varnished mahogany doors lines one side of the corridor, topped by wall sconces with a peculiar horn shape repeated throughout the hotel.

Down several steps are dining and sociable tables. The walls are decorated with such oddities as four large glass bowls inhabited by fighting fish and a huge beveled mirror hung with two purple tassels. Occasional lines of bright color emerge from the neutral backdrop of gray slate, stone, and carpet. Shrager and Rubell had this in mind: what nightclubs were to the '70s and restaurants were to the '80s, hotel lobbies will be to the '90s.

Visitors must be sure to visit the Round Bar for a drink. Its entirely round celery-colored tufted velvet walls give the feeling of being in a genie's bottle. Traditional black and white parquet floors are distorted in a dizzying round design. Like all things at the Royalton, the Round Bar has classic origins, designed after Ernest Hemingway's favorite bar, the Paris Ritz.

> **The Royalton remains the scene to be seen. This is the property that shifted New York's social life from the clubs to hotels, that redefined the concept of the hotel lobby from a glitzy marble showcase to a playful theater and art gallery.**

Emerging from the elevator on one of 16 floors of guest rooms, a visitor is left in a hallway as if dropped in the sea at midnight. The hallways are painted the same cobalt blue of the specter carpet. The round room numbers glow eerily from the mahogany doors like portals from a ship's hull. The halls feel claustrophobic, but once inside the guest rooms, one feels a sense of calm.

The palette is a simple one of slate gray, stainless steel, and white light from the lamps and bedding, warmed by the glow of mahogany, plus a midnight blue velvet easy chair. Cool Vermont slate floors are covered in a thick-pile gray carpet. The low bedding is an oasis of creamy white brushed cotton down comforter with seven down pillows perfectly arranged. Nightstands are inset portals cut into the mahogany wall on either side of the bed, with one fresh flower, a notepad, and a pencil. Tiny round stainless steel tables are placed just so. A candle is replaced at nightly turndown. Many of the rooms feature working fireplaces.

The spacious baths are the highest of high tech, a panoply of slate, steel, glass, and mirrors, warmed slightly by plush white terry robes and towels. A stainless steel basin rests on one wall and a vanity mirror on another. The room may have either a five-foot-diameter tub or a tub with glassed-in shower.

The rooms all contain mini-bars without liquor but with pastries made by Dean and DeLuca in black lacquer boxes designed for the hotel. All rooms are outfitted with a television, a VCR, and stereo cassette player, and tapes available at the front desk will be delivered to one's room with a bowl of warm popcorn.

The black-suited model types at the reception desk also serve as concierges, ever efficient and highly trained. Among other things, they will make reservations at the highly reputed 44, which serves a nouvelle Continental cuisine. Odd-hour diners will be glad for the Sushi Bar Without the Sushi, which serves light fare around the clock.

The St. Regis

Two East 55th Street at Fifth
  Avenue
New York, NY 10022
212-753-4500
800-759-7550
Fax: 212-787-3447

> *A royal
> experience
> in overnighting*

Proprietor: The ITT Sheraton Corp. **Managing Director:** Rick Segal. **Accommodations:** 313, including 91 suites. **Rates:** Rooms $350–$450, suites $575–$3,000. **Added:** 19.25% tax. **Payment:** Major credit cards. **Children:** Welcome. **Pets:** Not allowed. **Smoking:** 4 of 19 floors nonsmoking. **Open:** All year.

When it was completed in 1905, the St. Regis was New York's tallest building. While it no longer holds that honor, it does bring to mind other superlatives as one of the city's newest, most expensive, and most upscale new hotels. After three years and $100 million of restoration and renovation, the St. Regis reopened in September 1991 to a glorious reception.

The 18-story building was constructed as a hotel for $5.5 million by Colonel John Jacob Astor IV, between 1902 and 1905, designed by Trowbridge and Livingston, who also designed the Hayden Planetarium and B. Altman's. The beaux-arts masterpiece was intended to be the world's finest hotel, with crystal chandeliers, antique tapestries, Oriental rugs, and antique Louis XV furnishings. One of the hotel's most noted treasures is the Maxfield Parrish mural *King Cole*, which was installed in the hotel in 1932. While today's hotels boast of large video libraries, the original St. Regis had a 3,000-volume library of gold-tooled books for guests to check out. The restoration project was intended to replicate that turn-of-the-century majesty. Throughout the hotel are 600 handmade crystal chandeliers. Nearly 200 miles of wood molding and 23 miles of plaster molding were installed. The restoration involved the second largest gold leafing project ever undertaken in this country.

When Colonel Astor died on the *Titanic* in 1912, the St. Regis went to his son Vincent. In the '30s, the hotel became the center of New York social life. When the Iridium Room opened in 1938, it was an immediate success for dining and dancing, with a skating rink that pulled out from under the stage.

> Every floor at the St. Regis has its own butler, a measure of the hotel's remarkable commitment to luxury and service. Surely this exciting revival is one of the city's finest.

The guest rooms on the upper floors were greatly enlarged during the renovation, their number reduced from 557 to 313, all with 12-foot ceilings and crown moldings. While they are furnished similarly, there are nearly 70 different room configurations. Decorated with reproduction Louis XV furnishings, the rooms are exquisitely done in soothing gray silks and damasks. The beds have upholstered headboards and featherbeds. The beautiful wood armoires with brass fittings were custom-designed to house the television and mini-bar, and the contents of the latter are complimentary. The large baths are exquisite in white marble, with large tubs and free-standing showers, with linen and terry towels and robes.

There is a full-service business center, as well as a fitness center on the lower level with ample cardiovascular equipment and saunas.

Guests will want to enjoy high tea in the Astor Court, with its hand-painted murals in a French setting. For a clubbier experience, the King Cole bar is a smoky, woody room featuring the romantic landscape of Maxfield Parrish. Lespinasse is the setting for formal French cuisine. Executive chef Michael Carrer and chef Gary Kunz received three stars from the *New York Times* shortly after the hotel opened. The china and flatware were designed for the St. Regis by Tiffany.

Expect solicitous service at every turn. The staff is exceptionally attentive at the St. Regis, as the hotel tries to live up to all the expectations the renovation prompted.

U.N. Plaza–Park Hyatt

One United Nations Plaza
44th Street at First Avenue
New York, NY 10017-3575
212-758-1234
212-702-5051
800-233-1234

> *A contemporary
> luxury hotel
> on the East River*

Proprietors: U.N.D.C. **General Manager:** John F. Power. **Accommodations:** 428 rooms, including 110 with kitchenette and 45 suites. **Rates:** Rooms $260–$280, suites $325–$1,100. **Included:** Use of health club and swimming pool; overnight shoeshine. **Added:** $20 each additional guest, 19.25% tax. **Payment:** Major credit cards. **Children:** Welcome. **Pets:** Not allowed. **Smoking:** 8 nonsmoking floors. **Open:** All year.

One of a handful of New York City hotels with a pool and the only one with a tennis court, the U.N. Plaza also has the bonus of wonderful views from most of its rooms. This gleaming glass tower across First Avenue from the United Nations is a change of pace from the beaux-arts revivals in midtown Manhattan.

The interior of the building is a bold, contemporary play between deep green marble and smoky mirrors. The hotel comprises two separate towers flanking an octagonal, brightly lit double-height lobby. In addition to the lobby lounge, with leather and muted tapestry seating, the Wisteria lounge off the reception area is an intimate space with trellised walls and gilded arches, where guests take breakfast and afternoon high tea. Most exceptional is the hotel's lovely and interesting art collection displayed throughout the public spaces: framed textiles representing United Nations countries, such as batik, tapas, tapestries, silks, and embroidery.

> **Three outstanding elements of this hotel create a loyal following: stunning views of the East River; a First Avenue midtown address (most hotels are half a mile west); and an indoor pool on the 29th floor. These plus a dedication to service make the U.N. Plaza a contemporary classic.**

Rooms begin on the 28th and 29th floors of either tower and soar to 40 stories, providing wonderful views of the East River and three city views. Because of the irregularly shaped exterior, many of the rooms have interesting angles and exceptional views through the oversized windows. Sensitive to these dramatic details, the rooms are simple, bright, contemporary, in pastels or warm, lemony color schemes, with nice bright marble baths. Each suite is decorated differently: some are contemporary, others lavishly feminine.

Three meals daily are served in the Ambassador Grill, prepared under the supervision of chef Walter Houlihan. Specialties may include lemon soy grilled shrimp with succotash salsa or grilled rack of lamb with goat cheese tequila sauce over chestnut spaetzle. American grill entrées are about $25.

The 29th floor of the East Tower houses a fitness room, with Cybex and cardiovascular equipment, which looks onto the East River and north over the open space of the United Nations park. Each pink-marbled locker room has its own sauna and teak locker. The swimming pool also has two views of the East River and downtown through floor-to-ceiling windows. The ceiling is draped in a reflective cloth, so the room is flooded with sunlight. The regulation tennis court, on the top floor, is staffed with a full-time pro.

Besides the usual amenities of morning newspaper and complimentary shoeshine, guests are treated to daily limousine service to Wall Street and the garment district and evenings to the theater district. The staff speaks a total of nearly 50 languages, and its members are extremely accommodating , as befits their international exposure and setting.

The Waldorf Towers
The Waldorf-Astoria

The Waldorf Towers
100 East 50th Street
New York, NY 10022
212-872-4635
800-HILTONS
Fax: 212-872-4799

> *Two distinct properties at one prominent address*

Executive Director: Peter O. Wirth.
Accommodations: 191 units, including 106 1- to 4-bedroom suites. **Rates:** Rooms $350–$375, suites $500–$4,000. **Added:** $25 each additional guest, 19.25% tax. **Payment:** Major credit cards. **Children:** Welcome. **Pets:** Check with manager. **Smoking:** Permitted. **Open:** All year.

The Waldorf-Astoria
50th Street and Park Avenue
New York, NY 10022
212-355-3000
800-HILTONS
Fax: 212-421-8103

General Manager: Per Hellmann. **Accommodations:** 1,410 rooms, including 150 suites. **Rates:** Rooms $250–$325, suites $375–$800. **Added:** $25 each additional guest; 19.25% tax. **Payment:** Major credit cards. **Children:** Welcome. **Pets:** Check with manager. **Smoking:** Nonsmoking floors. **Open:** All year.

There are two distinct properties within the massive walls of this New York landmark. The Waldorf-Astoria is an enormous hotel occupying floors 1–27; and the Waldorf Towers is an intimate, luxurious hotel with a separate entrance and concierge, on floors 28–42. The more luxurious property is the Towers, offering perhaps the most elegant accommodations in the city. Yet the Waldorf-Astoria has its own charm, an excitement that mirrors that of being in New York: the expansive common areas bustling with people, some of whom are probably famous; the grand old art deco architecture; the feeling that something is going on that you're not a part of (the Waldorf has 25 meeting rooms); and that exciting feeling of being lost that often accompanies a visit to New York.

The Waldorf-Astoria and the Towers opened in 1931. Conrad Hilton acquired the management rights to the legendary hotel in 1947, and then the Hilton Corporation bought the hotel in 1977. An incredible $180 million renovation was completed in the late 1980s, which revived the mosaics, the bronze doors and elevators, the guest rooms, and all public spaces to their current splendor.

> The Waldorf hotels are a microcosm of the city they so well represent. It's the place where you can pass royalty in the hall, and then pass for royalty in the lounge. The Waldorf is the hotel for the city that never sleeps.

Staying at the Waldorf Towers is like visiting a palace and staying in the king's quarters. Guests have access to the public spaces and restaurants of the Waldorf-Astoria and can retreat to their privileged sanctuary, where every possible wish is anticipated. Guests enter through the private side entrance of the hotel on 50th Street to an impeccable lobby and are escorted to their rooms on the original bronze and burlwood elevators, which have been brought up to futuristic standards. Every room is different and individually decorated in flawless, classic taste. Every detail is perfect, from the antiques to the beautiful and precious fabrics and linens to the amenity-filled baths. A stay at the Towers is like playing king for a day — and a king from some country or another will probably be a fellow guest.

While the Towers are hushed and discreet, the Waldorf-Astoria is busy and grand-scale — though the magnitude does not imply lackluster service. The Waldorf-Astoria staff is savvy and professional, an attentive army matching guests on a one-to-one basis. In an ongoing refurbishment plan, 300 rooms are redecorated each year at the Waldorf, so be sure to ask for as new a room as possible. These will assuredly be nice, with lots of chintz, some pretty pieces like marble-top dressers, and nice baths: either gracefully Old World, like those in the Towers, with arched molding and wide old sinks and fixtures, or new and marbleized.

A wonderful new feature of the Waldorf-Astoria is the Plus-One Fitness Center. Visits are complimentary to Tower guests and available to regular guests for $15 (much less than the usual $25 for outside club use at city hotels). With terrific views looking north on Park Avenue, the club has an airy feel, appointed in beautiful light sycamore. Several staffers are always available for fitness evaluations and personal training. Cardiovascular equipment is extensive, and treadmills and bikes are equipped with headphones and televisions. Five types of massage are available by appointment.

The lavish public spaces include all-day dining at Peacock Alley, with floral decor; clubby, elegant fare at the Bull & Bear; Oscar's coffee shop; and Inagiku, the country's first outpost of Japan's best restaurant, for lunch and dinner. After-dinner drinks can be had in a safari setting at Harry's Bar and Restaurant or at Cocktail Terrace overlooking the Park Avenue art deco lobby — also a perfect setting for afternoon tea.

Westbury Hotel

15 East 69th Street
New York, NY 10021
212-535-2000
800-321-1569
Fax: 212-535-5058

> *The English enclave on the Upper East Side*

Proprietor: Forte Hotels. **General Manager:** Stefan Simkovics. **Accommodations:** 231 rooms, including 51 suites. **Rates:** Rooms $265–$295, suites $2,000–$2,200. **Included:** Morning newspaper, use of fitness center. **Added:** $30 each additional guest, 19.25% tax. **Payment:** Major credit cards. **Children:** Welcome. **Pets:** Allowed. **Smoking:** 2 of 16 floors nonsmoking. **Open:** All year.

The Westbury was built in the Gatsbyesque days of 1926 by the family of an American polo player. It has been a hotel since, run today in the same privileged fashion by the gentle hand of the Forte Group since 1978. It represents a bastion of quiet Old World elegance, housing the Polo Restaurant in a gallery of Ralph Lauren paisleys and equestrian prints amid intimate banquettes along street-front windows. With its Madison Avenue location, the Westbury, along with the Plaza Athénée and the Lowell, is in the heart of the country's finest and most exclusive boutiques. Sharing the same beautiful city block is the Frick Museum.

The limestone entrance is on 69th Street between Fifth and Madison avenues, marked by an elaborate art nouveau portico. As with most elite New York properties, the entrance is small, like a mansion's foyer, leading to a modest-sized double-height lobby with a second-floor balcony.

A stay at the Westbury wouldn't be complete without dining at the Polo Lounge. The American Continental cuisine, by the hand of Kerry Heffernan, is superb.

> **Another boutique hotel on the Upper East Side, the Westbury has carved out its own niche. Tony and British, it's no wonder that the Westbury is the preferred hangout for the crowd from Sotheby's, the art auction house. Its lobby seems like the entrance of an English castle, tapestried, marbled, but warm and intimate. The Polo Lounge is one of its finest offerings.**

The guest rooms lie on 16 floors along a long, straight hall that parallels Madison Avenue. Though most rooms have a view of Madison Avenue, some overlook the back of a building. The rooms have been recently redecorated in warm, wonderful, busy schemes of boldly striped wallcovering and large-print chintz fabrics. The feeling is that of an English country home, with high ceilings and welcoming interior space. An upholstered bench rests at the end of the Chippendale Drexel reproduction headboard. Rooms or suites have several extremely comfortable club chairs or sofas with tasseled dust ruffles separated by tables with delft-type ginger jars or plants. Lovely prints and architectural drawings grace the walls, and Oriental scatter rugs enhance the low nap carpet. All rooms have televisions and VCRs; the suites have CD players. The pristine baths are clean and lined with marble; those in the smaller rooms are fitted into cozy nooks, those in larger rooms have separate vanity areas.

The third-floor fitness center was a relatively recent addition, with views of Madison Avenue and ample cardiovascular equipment in a gray-carpeted room, with separate sauna and steam facilities.

The staff is letter-perfect at this long-standing property, gracious and softspoken.

Long Island

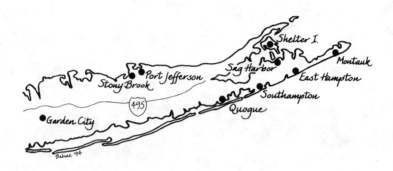

Best Romantic Retreat

East Hampton
  Centennial House

Best Gourmet Getaways

East Hampton
  East Hampton Point Cottages
Quogue
  The Inn at Quogue

Best Resorts

Montauk
  Gurney's Inn Resort & Spa
  Montauk Yacht Club Resort and Marina

Best for Metropolitan Magnificence

Garden City
  The Garden City Hotel

Best Country Inn

Shelter Island
  Ram's Head Inn

Best Village Bed-and-Breakfasts

East Hampton
  The Pink House
Southampton
  The Village Latch Inn

Best Village Inns

East Hampton
  Maidstone Arms

Port Jefferson
   Danfords Inn on the Sound
Sag Harbor
   The American Hotel
Shelter Island
   The Chequit Inn
Stony Brook
   Three Village Inn

Like Mercury, Long Island has two night-and-day faces: one watches the rough surf of the Atlantic, and the other sees the quiet, lapping Long Island Sound. These two sides of the island are entirely different in character. The south shore starts out as Long Beach and Jones Beach. The miraculous refuge of Robert Moses Beach and the Fire Island National Seashore follow, 30 miles of protected beachfront with about 20 tiny communities that do without cars in the summer, accessible by various ferries from the mainland.

The exclusive beaches of the Hamptons pick up where Fire Island's long sandy stretch ends. If you're extremely lucky, you have a house in the Hamptons; if you're lucky, you know someone with a house in the Hamptons; if you're average, you tan in Central Park — but every New Yorker ought to make the trek to the Long Island beaches at some hot and sticky point in the summer. Westhampton Beach comes first, then **Quogue,** then **Southampton,** the first English colony established in the state. **East Hampton** follows, then Amagansett and **Montauk.**

Compared with its western neighbors, Montauk remains curiously undiscovered on Long Island's exposed southern fork. The surf beats down on expansive, sparsely populated beaches; the crowds stop just west of here at East Hampton and Amagansett, before Hither Hills State Park. Easternmost Route 27 is the only main road out to the peninsula, though it digresses at a certain point as the scenic Old Montauk Highway, laid out in the 1700s. The landscape is unusual here: scrubby, windswept dunes, rough undulating rock with stubborn, thick shrubs growing low to the ground — in fact, the Indian name Montauk means "hilly country."

Backtracking a bit, an explorer goes back to East Hampton and heads north on Route 114 to the charming and subdued town of **Sag Harbor.** From this fishing village — actually one of the island's most exclusive escape towns — take a five-minute ferry to **Shelter Island,** perfectly wedged between the north and south forks of Long Island alee of the Sound and the Atlantic. New England Quakers sought refuge here from persecuting Puritans in 1652. There is no surf, but there is water everywhere, and both sandy and rocky beaches. Unlike the other Long Island shore towns, Shelter Island remains relatively unvisited, and its generations of blue-blooded summer families prefer it this way. About a quarter of its land is protected as the Mashomack Preserve.

A ferry to Greenport brings a visitor to the north shore. Among the sites and estates to see on the Gatsby side of the island are the Museums at **Stony Brook,** the Vanderbilt Museum Eagles Nest in Centerport, the Guggenheim estates at Sands Point Preserve, Cold Spring's Whaling Museum, Planting Fields Arboretum and Teddy Roosevelt's summer house Sagamore Hill in Oyster Bay, Old Westbury Gardens and its Georgian Revival mansion, and the antebellum restoration of Old Bethpage Village.

EAST HAMPTON

Centennial House

13 Woods Lane
East Hampton, NY 11937
516-324-9414
Fax: 516-324-2681

The toniest B&B in Long Island's most elite town

Proprietors: David Oxford and Harry Chancey, Jr. **Innkeeper:** Bernadette Meade. **Accommodations:** 6 rooms, all with private bath; 3-bedroom cottage. **Rates:** $150–$200 low season, $150–$225 mid-season, $175–$250 high season, cottage $300–$375. **Included:** Full breakfast except in cottage. **Minimum stay:** 4 nights on summer holidays, 3 nights on summer weekends, 2 nights on other weekends. **Added:** 7.5% tax. **Payment:** Visa, MasterCard. **Children:** Welcome in cottage. **Pets:** Not allowed. **Smoking:** Not allowed. **Open:** All year.

For an island with the densest population in this country, there are surprisingly few places to stay on Long Island. The paucity is quickly felt in the beach communities, so exclusive that residents don't want or need tourism. So would-be Hamptonites were especially pleased in 1988 when attorney David Oxford and television executive Harry Chancey, Jr., unveiled their treasure, Centennial House, one of the most elegant bed-and-breakfasts in the region.

The house sits on the corner of Montauk Highway and East Hampton's Village Pond, half a mile from town and the gorgeous beach, in opposite directions.

The weathered shingle house was built in 1876 by Thomas E. Babcock, a celebrated local craftsman, and David and Harry spent nearly a year restoring the house. They are avid antique-hunters and have fascinating stories about nearly every piece in the house. When the neighbors are among the country's wealthiest, a yard sale can produce some treasures: brass sconces acquired at auction at a millionaire's mansion; breakfast china bought for $85 because the owner paid "about that" for the set in the early part of the century; padded Schumacher wall fabric and Scalamandre silk in the dining room rescued from estate sales.

Like any moneyed East Hampton house, the rooms feel relaxed and rambling, but the individual pieces that furnish them are extraordinarily valuable and lovely. The formal parlors have matching Czechoslovakian crystal chandeliers, a green marble hearth, and a four-windowed bay that softly lights the antiques, the chintz couches, and the grand piano. The formal dining room is the setting for bountiful meals of pancakes, French toast, and meat, while dishes like buttermilk pancakes and cheese grits reflect David's Alabama roots.

Of the four second-floor rooms, the Rose Room has a four-poster canopy corkscrew bed. The baths are all beautifully decorated, and here a heavy tapestry curtains a clawfoot tub. The Bay Room is David's favorite because of its size and the wonderful bathroom with brass fixtures, wainscoting, claw-

foot tub, and pine washstand — a former pulpit found in England. The Lincoln Room has a beautiful Victorian bedroom
set and green walls hung with oval brass frames. Its black and
white marble bath is two
steps down.

The Loft is the only
third-floor room, for the
nimble or the romantic,
up impossibly steep stairs
to a wonderful space un-
der the eaves with thick
rose carpeting, a king-size
bed with a down duvet,
and views through high,
curved-top windows. Its
bath is cleverly placed
under the steep roof. All
rooms are provided with
lush terry robes; a split of
wine and chocolate truf-
fles are special treats in
every room.

> **From the sumptuous fabrics
> to the luxurious baths, from
> the antiques to the artwork
> that has been so carefully
> selected, every inch of
> the Centennial House is
> an aesthetic pleasure.
> The sublimity continues
> outdoors to the pool,
> set against a backdrop
> of lovely gardens and
> willow trees.**

The three-bedroom cottage in the backyard is tasteful and
private, about a hundred years older than the house itself.
The colors are intriguingly fresh, the walls and wide floorboards a mint and ecru lending a breezy, summer-house feel.
The cottage features a kitchen, a gas fireplace, and a lovely
front porch teeming with flower boxes.

A highlight of Centennial House is the acre and a quarter of
groomed grounds, overseen by Harry. The 40-foot pool is set
among pink and white rose bushes, near formal gardens and a
rambling English garden with rhododendrons. A legendary
weeping birch and a bench swing on another tree overlook
the grounds.

David and Harry are elegant and gracious hosts, dissolving
the mystique of East Hampton. Visitors here feel a magical
combination of being invited weekend friends and guests at
an elegant resort.

East Hampton Point Cottages

295 Three Mile Harbor Road
P.O. Box 847
East Hampton, NY 11937
516-324-9191
Fax: 516-324-3751

*A magnet
for gourmets
on Long Island*

General Manager: Dominique Cummings. **Accommodations:** 13 cottages including two 2-bedroom duplexes. **Rates:** Low/high season: 1-bedroom cottages $125–$175/$175–$225, deluxe 1-bedroom cottages $225–$250/$275–$300, deluxe 2-bedroom cottage $275/$325. **Included:** Use of tennis courts and swimming pool, transportation into East Hampton. **Minimum Stay:** 2 nights May and September, 3 nights June–August, 4 nights on summer holiday weekends. **Added:** Tax and service. **Payment:** Major credit cards. **Children:** Welcome. **Pets:** Welcome. **Smoking:** Yes. **Open:** All year.

Advertising mogul Jerry Della Famina made headlines when he opened his restaurant in East Hampton several years ago; to his credit, his restaurant also made headlines — and these were rave reviews. The Island was buzzing with Della Famina's life transition: was it a crazy or brilliant move to trade in a world-famous advertising career for a seafood restaurant? But with the same self-made success that had gotten him so far on Madison Avenue, Della Famina struck it rich again on Long Island. His new restaurant was an advertiser's dream.

Four miles north of town, when the beach is all but a faint memory, the landscape becomes cool and wooded. One feels most certainly inland; but then, water reappears, and this time, it's Shelter Island Sound. On this narrow southern fork of Long Island, Jerry Della Famina and his partners anchored his East Hampton Point Waterfront Restaurant, Marina and Boat Yard, and Country Cottage Inn. While many a visitor is expecting East Hampton's wide beaches, the remote and woody setting and calm waters are a big surprise.

Looking very much like a country club, the restaurant is a rambling clapboard expanse, with mullioned windows, a cupola, bright blue awnings, sweeping porches, and a nautical theme. But while the restaurant is bold and sociable on the water's shores, the cottages are hidden back from the main strip, behind bushes and trees along a maze of brick walkways. Weathered clapboard with white trim, the 13 cottages are all different yet similar, complementary and unique. With their individual porches, dormers, trellises, and patios, each one a home unto itself, the cottages look like homes in a little fishing village.

Inside, the home-away-from-home motif is carried out successfully. Spacious, immaculate, and contemporary, the cottages feel like little luxury homes. The country design is airy and bright, elegant and practical. Tile floors, open beamed ceilings, and pine wainscoting and abundant windows enhance the cottage feel. Fully stocked kitchens lend a further sense of independence. The bathrooms are wonderful and huge, with skylights, Jacuzzis, and tiled showers.

> **This collection of charming cottages nestles in the woods on East Hampton Bay. While the Atlantic and the wide picturesque beaches of East Hampton are only about four miles south, East Hampton Point Cottages feel as if they are several hundred miles north, on the wooded coast of Maine. The seafood only confirms the fantasy.**

Porches and patios, large and small, poke off the cottages in unexpected places, with charming results.

No trip to East Hampton Point is complete without a meal in the fine restaurant; many have made this a destination in itself. Inside, the restaurant has the distinct feel of a ship's deck: dark varnished floors, vaulted beams, and panoramic views of the water. Sunsets are breathtaking, especially when enjoyed with the specialty, seafood. From lobster to salmon to swordfish, the catch is prepared with a Continental flair, with entrées ranging from $20 to $34.

Maidstone Arms

207 Main Street
East Hampton, NY 11937
516-324-5006

*A recently
revived classic
brightens the
island*

Proprietor: Ms. Coke Anne Saunders. **Manager:** Christophe Bergen.
Accommodations: 19 rooms in inn,
including 6 suites; 3 cottages with
fireplace. **Rates:** $165–$290, cottage $1,460–$1,530 per week.
Included: Continental breakfast. **Minimum stay:** 3 nights on
summer weekends, 2 nights other weekends. **Added:** $25 each
additional guest, 14.25% tax. **Payment:** Visa, MasterCard,
American Express. **Children:** Welcome. **Pets:** Not allowed.
Smoking: Allowed. **Open:** All year.

East Hampton is the most exclusive of the Hamptons, and the
most exclusive place to stay here has long been the Maidstone
Arms. Devotees will be thrilled and newcomers will be rapt
with the new and improved Maidstone Arms,
which made its debut in
1992. A recent thorough
refurbishment has made
it exactly what one would
hope a beachside inn
would be — sophisticated
yet unpretentious. It's a
much-needed contribution to Long Island.

> **The Maidstone Arms spent
> decades as a reliable
> mainstay in East Hampton.
> But thanks to creativity
> and generous investments,
> the Maidstone Arms is in
> tip-top shape — a beacon
> on the southern shore and
> better than ever.**

The decor changes with
the seasons: in summer,
a beachy atmosphere is
conveyed through blue
and yellow stripes and a light, willowy feel. In fall, the furnishings are slipcovered in plaids, reds, and rusts for a cozy atmosphere.

The white clapboard inn is shaded by blue and white
striped awnings and blue shutters and sits across from the
Town Pond and Village Green on the sleepy corner of Routes
114 and 27. The building was erected between 1800 and 1830
and is in pristine condition, the exterior much as it always
was. The furnishings are mostly American antiques and

wicker, with nautical themes. There are novels and coffee table books in every room, along with fresh flowers. The baths have been entirely renovated in bright white tile.

The cottages offer wonderful, albeit expensive, accommodations for families or couples traveling together. They are cute clapboard reiterations of the main inn with similar decor, complete with immaculate, stocked kitchenettes.

Most impressive is the Maidstone's impressively upgraded cuisine. General Manager Christophe Bergen, formerly of Blantyre, the Relais & Châteaux property in the Berkshires, was just the soul to lead the effort. Open all year, the inn's restaurant serves three bountiful meals daily, orchestrated by chef Jim Litman, who serves real American food with a magic touch: pan-seared fish with wilted greens and couscous; or perhaps rack of lamb with thyme-mashed potatoes and ratatouille. Dinner entrées range from $16 to $30.

The beach is a 15-minute walk away, and the inn thoughtfully provides bicycles, beach passes, and towels for guests and will make picnic lunches on request. Winter is also an active time at the Maidstone Arms, with flower-arranging classes, lecturers from Sotheby's, and painting classes among the scheduled events.

The Pink House

26 James Lane
East Hampton, NY 11937
516-324-3400

A low-key, tasteful find in East Hampton

Proprietors: Ron Steinhilber and Sue Calden. **Accommodations:** 5 rooms, all with private bath. **Rates:** $185–$235 high season, $145–$195 low season. **Included:** Full breakfast, afternoon tea. **Minimum Stay:** July, August, and holiday weekends. **Added:** Tax. **Payment:** Major credit cards. **Children:** Discouraged. **Pets:** Discouraged. **Smoking:** Discouraged. **Open:** All year.

East Hampton, regardless of image or preconception, is a summer town, informal and friendly. While money and power may bring people here, three hours east of Manhattan, the relaxed atmosphere keeps them coming back. These are the qualities of the Pink House, a casual, comfortable, yet elegant bed-and-breakfast that sits just behind the town's pond, hidden behind a thicket of trees and flowers. What makes this property unique is that is offers the intimacy of a B&B without fussiness or preciousness. The decor is simple, bare but beautiful: clutter-free but comfortable; elegant but not extravagant.

> **No frills — nor ruffles, nor teddy bears. A hint of the Southwest and a touch of Idaho fishing cabin combine with friendly informality to make the elegant Pink House a good offering in East Hampton.**

The house itself is understated, a lovely clapboard of classic New England proportions, with undulations that resulted from practical expansions over the years. Built in the mid-1880s by a sea captain, the Pink House has had many additions and is now on the National Register of Historic Places. Its setting in the bramble and its modest size make the house nearly unremarkable from the outside but for its color. It's not a shocking magenta, nor a deep rose, nor a neon glow, but an easy-on-the-eyes pastel. The gravel drive at the side of the house leads to the cheery porch, with its overflowing window boxes of flowers and wicker chairs. Inside are an informal living room, with facing couches and an admirable stereo system, and a more formal dining room that conveys a sense of hospitality.

The most attractive feature of the Pink House is its guest rooms, and their immaculate marble and brass baths with fresh flowers. The Blue Room offers an understated Southwest motif on slate gray floors, with sumptuous Sheriden sheets on a pencil-post canopy bed draped in lace. The Twin, the Green, and the Garden rooms offer simple, spare elegance. For the adventurous, the place to stay is the spacious third-floor Elk Room, an Idaho fishing cabin perched atop the house and reached by a set of impossibly narrow stairs.

Breakfast includes freshly baked muffins, fruit, and possibly banana-walnut pancakes or sautéed pears with sourdough French toast. After breakfast, you might want to prepare for a day at the beach with a swim in the pool in the landscaped backyard.

GARDEN CITY

The Garden City Hotel

45 Seventh Street
Long Island, NY 11530
516-747-3000
800-547-0400 out of state
Fax: 516-747-1414

> *A luxury hotel
> on Long Island*

General Manager: Michael Graziosa. **Accommodations:** 275 rooms, including 16 suites. **Rates:** Rooms $220, suites from $400; $169 weekends. **Included:** Breakfast on weekends. **Added:** $20 each additional guest, 13.5% tax. **Payment:** Major credit cards. **Children:** Welcome; under 12 free. **Pets:** Small pets welcome. **Smoking:** Nonsmoking rooms available. **Open:** All year.

In a corporate community about 35 minutes east of Manhattan, the Garden City Hotel reopened in May 1983 as Long Island's finest full-service hotel. The first Garden City Hotel was a great Georgian structure that reigned on the island from 1874 to 1971 and hosted such notables as the Vanderbilts, the Astors, the Cushings, the Morgans, and Charles Lindbergh on the eve of his historic flight to Paris.

The building is now a lovely modernization of its former Georgian self, nine stories of brick and scalloped bay windows, centered on a bell tower topped by a gilded cupola. The lobby is appointed with French antiques, including a Louis XIII marble-top bombé chest under a gilded mirror and French provincial reproduction furnishings and bergères. The polished marble floors and rich mahogany walls gleam under the light of the chandeliers and brass sconces. Guests may proceed to the lower lobby to the café, Health Club, and shops.

The guest rooms are on floors 2–9, with moderate to penthouse rooms that ascend in rate as they do by floor. The 15 penthouse rooms on the ninth floor have private patios. All of the rooms are traditionally decorated with good reproduction furnishings. The creamy marble baths have telephones.

> **Though you've driven a half hour east of Manhattan, once you step inside the Garden City Hotel, you feel like you're back in the city again. This luxury hotel is the island's finest, complete with spa facilities.**

At the G.C. Spa, guests enjoy a 32-foot pool as well as whirlpool, sauna and steam rooms, fitness equipment, massage therapy, and facials.

The Polo Grill serves American contemporary cuisine in three meals daily; in addition, guests may venture to the Market Street Grill for seafood specialties at dinner. The Polo Lounge offers tea, cocktails, and hors d'oeuvres; the G Club is for dancing and socializing.

The staff is friendly and professional at this busy, well-run hotel, which attracts a curious mix of weekend shoppers and weekday corporates.

MONTAUK

Gurney's Inn Resort & Spa

Old Montauk Highway
Montauk, NY 11954
516-668-2345
800-445-8062
Fax: 516-668-3576

> *A resort with the ocean out front*

Proprietors: Lola and Nick Monte. **General Manager:** Paul Monte. **Accommodations:** 109 units, including 5 cottages. **Rates:** $240–$320, cottages from $320. **Included:** Breakfast and $23 credit toward dinner. **Minimum stay:** 2 nights on summer weekends. **Added:** $65 each additional guest, 15%

gratuities, 13% tax. **Payment:** Major credit cards. **Children:** Welcome; cribs available. **Pets:** Not allowed. **Smoking:** Non-smoking dining area. **Open:** All year.

The main access to Montauk, Long Island's easternmost town, is Route 27, though it digresses at one point as the scenic Old Montauk Highway, laid out in the 1700s. Along this sometimes desolate road, 2.6 miles west of Montauk's town center, is Gurney's Inn Resort and Spa, the only marino-therapeutic spa in North America.

Without the modest sign at the entrance, Gurney's could go unnoticed, its many buildings terraced into the hill that tumbles from the historic road down to the beachfront. Gurney's is one of the few Long Island properties open to the public right on the south shore's glorious beach.

> A wonderful, unique resort set in the lonely dunes of Montauk, Gurney's is the only spa in North America that offers marino-therapeutic spa treatments using seawater and seaweed extracts from Europe.

The resort was built in 1926 by developer Carl Fisher, who wanted to make Montauk the Miami of the North. The original parts of the inn remain today, an unobtrusive row of weathered shingled buildings. Nick and Joyce Monte bought Gurney's in 1956 and have infused a warm-hearted generosity to this place over the years. Unlike the nearby Montauk Yacht Club, a new, luxurious corporate venture, Gurney's is a retreat for generations of repeat guests and families. The staff is very much a part of the continuity here, friendly and enthusiastic.

Anticipating a boom in fitness and health consciousness in the 1970s, Nick Monte decided that Gurney's needed a spa. To make it unique and complementary to his beloved seaside setting, he decided the spa should concentrate on marinotherapeutic treatment, using seawater and seaweed extracts available only in Europe. After much research, the spa opened in February 1979, the only one of its kind on the North American continent. Unique to the spa is an indoor heated saltwater pool (84 degrees) less saline than the ocean; there are also massage rooms, fango packs, seaweed wraps, Thalasso tubs, Swiss showers, and a beauty salon.

The premises are uniquely tiered and carved into the hillside, with no structure above the tree line. Wooden walkways connect the six guest houses and four cottages to the ample public spaces, resulting in an ever-changing perspective on the waterfront. Among the public spaces are two dining rooms, an outdoor dining area, an entertainment lounge, and an outdoor walking track.

Montauk stands fast by its dune preservation laws. The guest houses abut the dune growth without disruption, though over the years several noticeably new buildings have been added to Gurney's. Included in these are the deluxe sand-colored Forward Watch, with porches right on the sand. Four cottages line the beachfront by the prominent Foredeck, with 20 rooms. Guest rooms all have balconies, some at beach level, some with higher views, and even the less desirable rooms behind the parking lot have water views. All rooms are decorated in contemporary style, with televisions and phones in the room and the bath. From studios to two-bedroom suites, rooms are done in summery pastel colors, each with a sitting area and queen-size sofabed.

Be sure to visit Hither Hills and Montauk State Parks and the historic lighthouse erected in the 1790s.

Montauk Yacht Club Resort and Marina

Star Island
Montauk, NY 11954
516-668-3100
800-832-4200

An oceanside resort on New York's easternmost point

Proprietors: Brock Associates Management. **General Manager:** Bruno Brunner. **Accommodations:** 107 rooms, including 4 suites and 22 rooms in 5 villas. **Rates:** Low season $119–$150, mid-season $179–$205, high season $249–$285. **Included:** Continental buffet breakfast. **Minimum stay:** 2–4 nights on weekends. **Added:** $25–$50 each additional guest, 18% service charge, 13% tax. **Payment:** Major credit cards. **Children:** Welcome. **Pets:** Not allowed. **Smoking:** Allowed. **Open:** All year except January to mid-March.

Just north of town on Star Island, in the northern bite of Montauk Bay, is a glimpse into the days of Jay Gatsby. The Montauk Yacht Club was bought, in faded condition, by Brock Associates in 1988 and renovated through 1990. The marina resort's impressive history began in the Roaring Twenties, when it was built as a private club with founding members like J. P. Morgan, Marshall Field, Vincent Astor, and William K. Vanderbilt, Jr. The Yacht Club bordered the Ziegfeld estate, which was later incorporated into the club property.

> **This reputable luxury resort is tucked so far away from civilization that it feels like an island unto itself — and technically it is. Anchored on a spit of land in Montauk Bay, Montauk Yacht Club seems to float on the water.**

The Yacht Club centers around the original 1929 hexagonal lighthouse, a structure of whitewashed concrete that now serves as the Lighthouse Bar, overlooking the 247-slip marina. The shingled saltbox buildings to the south of the lighthouse are original; those to the north, including Ziegfeld's restaurant and adjacent buildings, are additions designed to replicate the old architecture. The original lobby has floors of dark-stained wood, with a compass underfoot six feet in diameter. An elaborate model of the 1883 *Atalanta* yacht is encased in glass, one of the club's many nautical treasures.

Most rooms have an oblique water view or are directly on the marina's boardwalk; all have balconies decorated with flower planters. The saltbox buildings provide two floors of rooms along a paneled hallway, up or down a half flight of steps. The rooms are finished in several different pastel color schemes, some with wicker headboards and bedroom sets, some with a rose toile spread, some with a beautiful crown canopy in a weedy print complemented by a plaid inlay and bed skirting. The remote television and refrigerator are hidden in a bleached wood corner cupboard, topped by a handmade decoy or a cherubic weathervane. Bathrooms are large and contemporary, with a separate vanity area, pedestal sink, and plentiful closet space.

Guests who don't mind a short walk to the main hotel may prefer the 22 rooms in the five Ziegfeld Villas, all individually decorated. The stucco, green-shuttered villas at the north edge of Star Island look like fairy-tale Tudor cottages set around a little commons made fanciful by four trampolines on the lawns. There are some nice art deco antiques in these rooms, amid the original architecture of nonworking marble fireplaces and heavy square-paned leaded Tudor windows with some whimsical triangular portals. The dark-stained walls and floor have the feeling of an old library on a north shore estate.

On the property are two outdoor pools, waterskiing, horseback riding, boat rentals, and an indoor pool with a fitness area and sauna. Golf is available at nearby Montauk Downs. Dinners at Ziegfeld's range from $17 to $26, with fresh fish cooked on an outdoor grill. A short drive away is the Montauk State Park and the historic lighthouse, constructed in the 1790s.

PORT JEFFERSON

Danfords Inn on the Sound

25 East Broadway
Port Jefferson, NY 11777
516-928-5200
800-332-6367 outside New York
Fax: 928-3598

> A terrific
> destination in
> fun Port Jefferson

Proprietor: James McNamara. **General Manager:** Kathy Passafiume. **Accommodations:** 85 rooms in 7 buildings, including 10 suites and 3 apartments. **Rates:** Rooms $110–$160, suites $180–$280. **Included:** Buffet breakfast on weekdays. **Added:** $10 each additional guest, 13.5% tax. **Payment:** Major credit cards. **Children:** Welcome; under 18 free. **Pets:** Not allowed. **Smoking:** Nonsmoking rooms available. **Open:** All year.

Port Jefferson is a working fishing town and also the terminus for the Bridgeport ferry, halfway out on Long Island's north shore. This old port and historic whaling town is more or less dominated by the phenomenon of Danfords Inn and Marina, an overwhelming presence in the heart of town. Though its seven sweeping white clapboard buildings were completed only in 1983, Danfords looks convincingly seasoned. In addition to housing a large number of lovely guest rooms, Danfords is home to numerous gift shops and a reputable restaurant that is beloved by locals and travelers alike for its extensive seafood selections, as well as a full-service marina.

Five of the seven buildings are three-story white clapboards with red trim lining the harborfront. Except for the main building, these are linked by a brick walkway decorated

> Travel sometimes yields welcome surprises, and Danfords is one of them. Perched on the calm northern shores of Long Island Sound, right at the ferry from Bridgeport, Port Jefferson is a quaint working town. Danfords is its convivial hostelry: pretty, creative, and nicely done.

with hanging geraniums in front of first-floor shops. Their facade is a medley of second- and third-floor balconies, dormers, and porches that seem like a haphazard collection of New England home facades. Two without water views include one brick building behind the main inn and another around the corner with a historic stone facade.

The success of the interior spaces is due largely to owner James McNamara's passion for art and antiques. The main building has a great lobby, with a knotty pine wide-planked floor covered with antique Oriental rugs. Worn leather wing chairs and sofas comfortably fill the room, decorated with a wondrous eclectic collection of Victoriana, colonial Americana, and seafaring memorabilia. Of the five dining rooms, some have great water views, others are ensconced in greenery, and the sail loft is tucked in the A-frame of the second floor. Three meals are served daily by a bustling, friendly wait staff. The dinner entrées range from $10 to $25, possibly for Châteaubriand or almond-crusted chicken prepared by chef Stephen Meade.

Even the lowest of the eight room categories is impressive, with a minimum of 400 square feet. Each room is decorated differently, and while most have reproduction furniture, the more deluxe rooms have glorious antique treasures like a

Mission bookcase, an imposing armoire, or a tufted fainting couch. Mahogany television cabinets were made for the inn. Artwork in hunt or nautical themes decorates the walls.

Danfords is a luxurious but friendly and informal place. Visible owner James McNamara is wholeheartedly involved in the inn's daily activities. His happy and helpful staff seems to enjoy his attention and accessibility. Be sure to plan for a yacht excursion in season.

QUOGUE

The Inn at Quogue

Quogue, NY 11959
516-653-6560
800-628-6166

Fine dining in an enchanting town

Manager: Stephanie Winters. **Accommodations:** 70 rooms, including suites and cottages. **Rates:** June 15–Labor Day, rooms $117–$140, suites $170–$225; off-season, rooms $95–$110, suites $139–$149. **Minimum stay:** 3 or 4 nights on weekends in high season; 2 nights off-season. **Added:** $25 each additional person, 13% tax. **Payment:** American Express. **Children:** Allowed. **Pets:** Allowed. **Smoking:** Allowed. **Open:** All year; restaurant closed in winter.

While the Hamptons bustle in the summer like Wall Street in the bear market or Bloomingdale's at Christmas, the hamlet of Quogue has escaped all signs of tourist intrusion. A visit here reveals the unspoiled, historic Hamptons before the crowds discovered the island, with regal clapboard and weathered shingle houses used as summer retreats for the country's wealthiest and most influential hidden on shady lanes a short, barefoot walk from some of the East's most beautiful beaches.

The Inn at Quogue is the town's only licensed establishment for food, drink, and board. While such a monopoly might suggest indifference, the result is quite the opposite — as if the inn auditioned for the privilege of representing Quogue. Its restaurant has received a daunting two stars from the *New York Times,* a rating that should please patrons who dine during the week at Le Cirque and Le Bernardin.

This is the way the Hamptons used to be, about 50 years ago. Now, however, Quogue is just about the last outpost of undiscovered shoreline on the southern shore. While the setting gives little hint of civilization, the food is quite the opposite: sophisticated and exceptional.

The Inn is a 200-year-old white clapboard paragon of Hamptons sophistication, set on landscaped grounds attended by an exacting gardener. In addition to the classic old building are the Civil War–era Weathervane Cottage and private cottages from this century. Recently redecorated by the skilled hand of Marsha Fox-Martin, the rooms are comfortable, airy, and immaculate, befitting a summer cottage of impeccable taste. The rooms vary from small to spacious, some with fireplaces and original wide-planked floors. In the tradition of the true summer cottage, where the precious furniture is saved for the city house, the Inn at Quogue has spare, clean furnishings mixed and matched in perfect taste. The place has a freshly swept look reminiscent of summertime.

The Inn has a 20-by-40-foot outdoor pool, but for those who prefer the gorgeous surf here, beach passes are provided to the village's private beach, a mile's walk. Guests may also use the facilities at the Quogue Racquet Club and Hampton Athletic Club, offering tennis, racquetball, aerobics, Nautilus, and an outdoor pool and spa. Facials and massages are also available. The best way to explore Quogue is on bicycles provided by the inn.

SAG HARBOR

The American Hotel

Main Street
Sag Harbor, NY 11963
516-725-3535

*An acclaimed
inn in an
enchanting town*

Proprietor: Ted Conklin. **Accommodations:** 8 rooms, all with private bath. **Rates:** $75–$130 per person. **Included:** Continental breakfast. **Minimum stay:** 2 nights on weekends, 3 nights on holiday weekends. **Added:** 8% tax. **Payment:** Major credit cards. **Children:** Not allowed. **Pets:** Not allowed. **Smoking:** Restricted. **Open:** All year.

The population of Sag Harbor reached its peak in the early to mid-19th century, when whaling was the port's mainstay. Today, the streets are less populated than they were in Melville's day, though doubtless as charming, with Federal and Victorian houses flanking narrow streets that join at Shelter Island Harbor. This is the one tony Hampton resort town without surf, a refuge for the rich and famous who don't want to be seen. The understated wealth is best typified by a Sag Harbor landmark, the American Hotel.

Built in 1846 as a hotel during Sag Harbor's heyday, the three-story brick edifice was bought by its present owner, Ted Conklin, in 1972. Over the years, the hotel had served as a boarding house for businessmen in rather nonluxurious quarters, small and boxy. During his renovations, Ted Conklin broke through walls and expanded the rooms. The eight guest rooms today spread throughout a space that once held 20 rooms, expanding into odd corners and ells. The beds represent the different periods: simple sleighs, rare twin brass beds, pre-Victorian wood headboards, and even an art deco suite. Some walls are papered in deep paisleys and stripes, others in light peach or floral patterns. The antiques and wonderful prints are the result of Ted Conklin's 20 years of collecting.

From the wicker-filled porch lined with planters spilling with flowers, guests enter to a living room with a working fireplace and Empire couches under the original pressed tin ceiling. A double parlor dining room is to the left, with pretty floral paper over wood wainscoting. Ahead is a smaller dining room with café tables and the magnificent original bar with its wood wainscoting and enormous moose head hovering above. A sunny atrium dining area is a last alternative.

While the French menu changes, entrées range from $16.50 for shepherd's pie to $28.50 for tournedos Rossini. Other entrées might include exotic sautéed sweetbreads, baby pheasant with fresh black truffles, antelope paillard au poivre vert, or brace of quail Véronique. The creative chef also offers appetizers like terrine de lapin au porto and sautéed foie gras with fennel. The wine list is extensive and well researched.

The American Hotel is one of Long Island's most sophisticated hostelries; except for the tans and the easy smiles, it could easily be mistaken for a midtown Manhattan gathering spot for the chic-elite.

> **Sag Harbor is wedged between East Hampton and Shelter Island but feels hundreds of miles north, perhaps somewhere on Nova Scotia. The 19th-century fishing town couldn't be more charming, and the American Hotel is its ambassador.**

SHELTER ISLAND

The Chequit Inn

Grand Avenue
Shelter Island, NY 11965
516-749-0018

> *A convenient inn in Shelter Island Heights*

Proprietors: Alice Klaris, Guy Gorelik, Mindy Goodfriend-Chernoff, Harry Chernoff. **Accommodations:** 32 rooms. **Rates:** $75–$150. **Included:** Continental breakfast. **Minimum stay:** 2 nights on weekends. **Added:** $20 each additional guest. **Payment:** Visa, MasterCard, American Express. **Children:** Welcome. **Pets:** Not allowed. **Smoking:** Not allowed. **Open:** May 15–October 31.

In January 1990, two creative couples bought the neglected Chequit's on Shelter Island. They knew better than to try to compete with the two nonpareil local properties, the Ram's Head Inn and Sag Harbor's American Hotel. Instead, the owners have made Chequit's a spare, clean, postmodern inn, a place for art directors, architects, and designers. While some may find it lacking in warmth, others will enjoy the stark, bold furnishings and cottage-white floors.

> Manhattanites are an immobile species, often carless, and frustratingly stranded in the summer. The Chequit is a much-appreciated solution, just a few train hours to Greenport, then the ferry to Shelter Island, and presto: vacation.

The Chequit Inn is a landmark in Shelter Island's village, up a steep hill from the ferry dock. It was built around 1870, roughly the same time as the rest of the island's architecture. Of the three buildings that constitute the inn, the Main House offers the most rooms and activity. Dining is on the wide wraparound porches and outdoor patio, as well as indoors in a lovely dining room reminiscent of a SoHo warehouse loft, its tin ceiling supported by rows of seven pillars, painted an airy pink and white.

The hand-written menu features entrées ranging from $13 to $21. Dinners are artistic and eclectic, perhaps roast Muscovy duck breast with raspberry-rhubarb relish or grilled New York shell steak with potato, leek, and onion pancake. Appetizers might include yellowfin tuna salad on cold noodles with sesame dressing, or crab cakes with corn and tomato relish. Downstairs is a local hangout with a pool table and bar.

The guest rooms are decorated sparely, as if by a New England–style Georgia O'Keeffe. The walls and floors serve as a white canvas to offset dramatic colors; a tiny night table is checkered with red and yellow; the beds are dressed in blue chambray; a piece of driftwood holds a reading lamp. Fresh flowers and original art enliven the spareness. Each piece was decidedly placed by owner Alice Klaris.

Service is understated and casual, like the rest of Shelter Island. More than one third of the island is set aside as the Mashomack Nature Preserve, which provides a full range of activities including hiking and birding.

Ram's Head Inn

108 Ram Island Drive
P.O. Box 638
Shelter Island Heights, NY 11965
516-749-0811
Fax: 516-749-0059

*A cottage
on an island on
an island*

Proprietors: James and Linda Eklund. **Accommodations:** 17 rooms, 8 with private bath; 4 2-bedroom suites have adjoining baths. **Rates:** $65–$140 low season, $90–$195 high season. **Included:** Expanded Continental buffet breakfast, tennis court, sauna, boats. **Minimum stay:** 2 nights on weekends, 3 nights on holiday weekends. **Added:** $15 each additional person, 9% tax. **Payment:** MasterCard, Visa, American Express. **Children:** Welcome. **Pets:** Not allowed. **Smoking:** Allowed only in lounge. **Open:** All year; restaurant has seasonal hours.

Settled in 1652 by Quakers seeking refuge from persecution by the Puritans, Shelter Island remains a peaceful retreat. Only three hours by train from Manhattan, plus a ten-minute ferry ride from Greenport, Shelter Island nevertheless seems isolated. Even more remote is Ram Island, several miles from town and attached to its mother isle by a causeway. It is home to an idyllic, romantic country inn, often the setting for summer weddings.

Built in 1929, the Ram's Head Inn is a traditional weathered-shingle building on a grassy hill above the water. A long porch spans the length of the building, and third-floor dormer windows poke out from the green shingled roof. As young newlyweds, natives James and Linda Eklund bought the inn in 1979 and have invested a great deal of work over the years to get it to its current pristine condition. Common rooms include an informal living room and bar and a lovely dining room, with pillars supporting the high ceiling.

> A great place for a retreat, an excursion, or a wedding, the Ram's Head Inn is a regional tradition that has never looked better. Its refreshing, simple cottage rooms, wide porches dressed with wicker, sloping lawns, and wonderful food seem to work together to celebrate summertime.

The Eklunds are quite proud of their creative chef, John Barton. His changing menu of American Continental cuisine might include an appetizer of poached shrimp with sushi and pickled ginger; seviche of scallops in vinaigrette over shoestring potatoes; or corn chowder with mussels. A salad might be grilled leeks with radicchio and Gorgonzola. The entrées, ranging from $14 to $22, might include breast of chicken with cilantro and lime, sweet corn and black bean sauté, and potato-crusted red snapper. An artistic dessert chef presents a eight delicacies nightly.

While not luxurious, the guest rooms have the informal charm of a summer cottage. Each room is supplied with a new, firm mattress covered in soft white linens, a wing chair, and a white bureau. The windows overlook sloping lawns, the tennis court, the little bay with a beach and moorings, the sandbox under the big oak tree, croquet, and volleyball.

The staff at the Ram's Head Inn is extremely kind, relaxed, and happy under the friendly leadership of the Eklunds. Guests are free to use the bicycles and boats — the 13-foot O'Day sloops, Sunfish, paddleboats, and kayaks.

SOUTHAMPTON

The Village Latch Inn

101 Hill Street
Southampton, NY 11968
516-283-2160
800-54-LATCH

> *An eclectic place
> in a tony
> community*

Proprietors: Marta Byer and Martin White. **General Manager:** Chris Stanley. **Accommodations:** 25 rooms in inn, 12 in motel (6 duplexes and 6 singles), 3 in Potting Shed, 10 in Terry Cottage, 9 in Homestead East, 6 in Homestead West. **Rates:** Rooms $95–$160 midweek (from $85 low season), $140–$195 weekends ($95–$125 low season); suites and duplexes $150–$250 midweek, $175–$300 weekends (from $125 low season). **Included:** Continental breakfast. **Minimum stay:** 3 nights in high season. **Added:** $50 each additional guest, 8% tax, 13% tax over $100, 10% service charge. **Payment:** MasterCard, Visa, American Express. **Children:** Welcome. **Pets:** Not allowed. **Smoking:** Allowed. **Open:** All year.

A small estate of five acres, the Village Latch Inn consists of five buildings and just under 70 rooms, with wild variations in style and decor. It's hard to call it a bed-and-breakfast, but it's even harder to call it anything else. Some may find it a relaxing, informal resort; others think of it as a beachside cottage; still others as a fitting place for corporate retreat or a wedding. The Village Latch is simply unique, a dizzying combination of artifacts, playful decor, and architectural whimsy in one of New York's wealthiest towns.

The eclectic set of buildings is the creation of owners Marta Byer and Martin White, she a former actress and theater director, he a former fashion photographer. They travel several months a year, sending back oddities and necessities from faraway lands the way other people send postcards. Half a block or so from Southampton's main street, the Village Latch is set back from the road by a lovely front lawn made private by a privet hedge. There is a tennis court and a swimming pool and a little golf cart to transport guests around the property.

> What do you get when you combine the talents of a former fashion photographer and a theater director? The Village Latch Inn, of course. This unique property is a panoply of styles, filled with artifacts and whimsy, all in one of the East Coast's most exclusive villages.

The three-story white clapboard Latch was an elegant annex to the famous old Irving Hotel across the street, demolished a quarter century ago. The main inn has 25 rooms, some comfortable and homey, some decisively decorated. Marta tries to match the guests to the rooms — "typecasting," as she aptly calls it. Room 60, for example, is a suite with windows on two sides, black chintz curtains, a fireplace and refrigerator, and a wicker sitting area. Nearby Room 52 is simpler, with yellow walls and two twin beds. The third-floor rooms have skylights; some have patios, some fireplaces. The common rooms are in the inn; they teem with scary international dolls, throw pillows, mannequins, and artwork from the Whites' travels. A sunny porch breakfast room has green slatted chairs that give the room a cottage feel.

The motel units across the parking lot are much more imaginative than their appellation would suggest. The six duplexes and six singles all have private brick patios and interesting decor with toile curtains, antique Oriental rugs, South American wall hangings, and Guatemalan pillows.

In the middle of the great lawn of the property, the Potting Shed is an ideal place for couples or families traveling together, with two bedrooms and a studio, which can also be rented singly. The living room has a huge A-frame ceiling of deep-hued woods, next to a full kitchen. The eclectic decor includes Indian pillows, Mexican painted pigskin chairs, a wood-burning fireplace, and a nine-foot carved stone statue.

The Homestead, on the edge of the great lawn, is made of weathered shingle. It consists of two buildings (the western one is Southampton's oldest) with 15 bedrooms, joined by a Victorian greenhouse that was moved onto the site. The western house has an Adirondack-type common area, woody and low-beamed, with worn leather couches and chairs, wood pillars, and a huge stone hearth. The eastern house has more of an arts and crafts feeling — geometric, with a beamed ceiling and brick fireplace. The greenhouse is enchanting painted iron, with a hot tub in the center and porch furniture.

Try to seek out Marta and Martin, two fascinating people who seem like characters from a movie, cast as New York City expatriates who start an arts colony in a wealthy beach community — they're perfect for the part.

STONY BROOK

Three Village Inn

150 Main Street
Stony Brook, NY 11790
516-751-0555
Fax: 516-751-0593

A friendly gathering spot in a historic town

Proprietors: Jim and Lou Miaritis. **Accommodations:** 27 rooms in house and annex, 6 cottages. **Rates:** $110. **Minimum stay:** None. **Added:** $10 each additional guest, $20 for cot, 9.25% tax. **Payment:** Major credit cards. **Children:** Welcome, under 16 free. **Pets:** Not allowed. **Smoking:** Allowed. **Open:** All year.

After immigrating from Greece as a young man, Jimmy Miaritis worked for 30 years in the hotel business on Long Island. In 1989, he and his son Lou took over the lease of a historic landmark called the Three Village Inn, about halfway out Long Island's north shore in Stony Brook. One of the kindest souls to set foot in the house since it was built in 1751, Jimmy keeps his staff smiling, and his guests leave with the promise that they will see him again on their next visit.

Three Village Inn was saved from disrepair by Jennie Melville in 1921. It became a popular place for tea and welcomed its first overnight guests in 1939. Ward Melville inherited his mother's love for this town and sought to rebuild its colonial history. The Museums at Stony Brook were the result of his efforts, with varied exhibits that include the country's largest display of horse-drawn vehicles as well as several restored 19th-century buildings.

The inn sits behind a sweeping lawn shaded by large trees. The rambling, comfortable hostelry is a composite of the original two-story colonial clapboard house, plus additions over the years that reach out like branches from a family tree. Behind the main house and its many dining rooms are six cottages built at the turn of the century by a Presbyterian retreat group.

> **Because it's a historic property in a historic town, the Three Village Inn is virtually obliged to be a bastion for conviviality. Owner Jimmy Miaritis more than lives up to this obligation, and his warmth is contagious. Every Sunday he demonstrates the extent of his hospitality by providing a Thanksgiving feast.**

While the cottages do have privacy, fireplaces, and porches that scan the harbor over tidy lawns, the six rooms in the main house are wonderful for ambience and romance. Laura Ashley decorators recently redid the rooms, tucked under the low-ceilinged eaves and reached by slanted stairs and narrow passageways. Floral wallpapers cover the thick stone walls, and Williamsburg trim frames the old-paned windows covered with lace curtains.

The dining rooms are attended by a staff dressed in colonial attire. Jenny Melville's sugar bowl collection is displayed in a case for guests to admire before being seated in the sunny Old Field, Setauket, and Stony Brook dining rooms or the colonial tavern. To the right of the old foyer, in the original house, common rooms reveal the pre-Revolutionary beams, hearth, and wood paneling, trimmed in Williamsburg colors.

Lunch and dinner are served daily, with dinner entrées priced from $20 to $30. Guests might start with cold plum soup, followed by old-fashioned Yankee pot roast with potato pancake, lobster pie, or roast prime rib with popovers. The dessert menu is extensive.

Pennsylvania

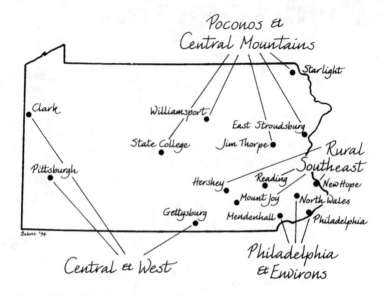

Pennsylvania is the country's fifth largest state, with more than 12 million people living in 45,000 square miles, a good deal of it forestland. The state was settled first by the Swedish in 1643 but became an official place of religious tolerance when William Penn established his Quaker state here in 1682. It was here that the Declaration of Independence was signed and the Constitution was drafted.

For visitor information, call 800-VISIT-PA.

The Poconos and Central Mountains

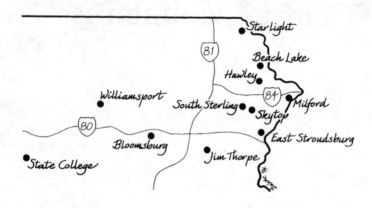

Best Romantic Retreat

Jim Thorpe
  Harry Packer Mansion

Best Gourmet Getaway

Hawley
  The Settler's Inn at Bingham Park

Best Resorts

Hawley
  Woodloch Pines
Skytop
  Skytop Lodge
Somerset
  Hidden Valley

Best Country Inns

Beach Lake
  Beach Lake Hotel
Bloomsburg
  The Inn at Turkey Hill
East Stroudsburg
  The Inn at Meadowbrook
Milford
  Cliff Park Inn
South Sterling
  French Manor
Starlight
  The Inn at Starlight Lake
Williamsport
  The Thomas Lightfoote Inn

Best Village Inn

State College
  The Nittany Lion Inn

Derived from the Indian word *pocohonne,* the Poconos describes the stream between the mountains — between the New Jersey Highlands and the low old mountains of Pennsylvania's northeast corner. The Poconos are the most popular vacation spot in the state and have a rather unfortunate reputation for heart-shaped tubs and nightclub hotels. Aside from low-level skiing, the area offers wonderful outdoor activities; the Delaware Water Gap, with spectacular hiking along its 35 miles; 13-mile-long manmade Lake Wallenpaupack at **Hawley,** the state's largest recreational lake; and **Jim Thorpe,** a cozy town that served as the country's railroad capital during the late 19th century.

Past the western edge of the Poconos, beyond Scranton and Wilkes-Barre, Pennsylvania dissolves to farmland. **Bloomsburg** is another transition point into the Central mountains of the state, introduced by the Susquehanna River. Then, on to **Williamsport,** once one of the world's wealthiest towns during the heyday of the logging industry a century ago. It was also the birthplace of Little League Baseball, with a popular museum today to prove it. Right in the state's geographic and spiritual center is the town of **State College.**

BEACH LAKE

The Beach Lake Hotel

Box 144
Beach Lake, PA 18405
717-729-8239
800-382-3897

An antiques lover's haven hidden in the Poconos

Proprietors: Roy and Erika Miller. **Accommodations:** 6 rooms, all with private bath. **Rates:** $95; $75 per night for 3 weeknights. **Included:** Full breakfast. **Minimum stay:** 2 nights on holidays and on weekends May–October. **Added:** 6% tax, $40 additional guest. **Payment:** MasterCard, Visa, American Express. **Children:** Not allowed. **Pets:** Not allowed. **Smoking:** Not allowed in rooms. **Open:** All year.

The village of Beach Lake, in a quiet part of the Poconos, is separated from New York by only a few miles and the Delaware River. The modest Beach Lake Hotel sits in the heart of town — a few buildings and a post office — marked with a quaint sign. It's a quiet area in Pennsylvania's lake district, with its own lake, for which the town was named, several miles uphill from the magnificent Lake Wallenpaupack in Wayne County.

A rewarding discovery, the Beach Lake Hotel is only several miles from New York State, fenced into a remote part of the Pennsylvania lake country by the Delaware Water Gap. Roy and Erika's passions for antiques and wonderful food are evident.

Built in the 1830s, the three-story clapboard hotel was christened the Beach Lake Hotel in the Civil War. Throughout its many lifetimes, the house has served as a tavern, a general store, and finally as a post office from 1879 to 1936. Roy and Erika Miller resurrected the property in 1987 and rejuvenated its beautiful wainscoted walls and ceilings.

In keeping with their respect for history, the Millers have filled the house with antiques, which are all for sale. Antiques dealers in previous careers, the Millers are avid collectors and have made the house a living gallery. Not only are the guest rooms and dining rooms filled with wonderful furniture and artwork from the 18th and 19th centuries, but part of the inn serves as an antiques shop. Among the treasures are an 1840 English cabaret piano with mahogany inlay, a set of delft plates, an art deco leather screen, an 18th-century Sheraton field bed, and several unusual dioramas from a renowned taxidermy artist.

With Victorian reproduction fabrics as background, the rooms recede into history, with antique full beds and lavish draperies and canopies designed by Erika. Armoires, marble tables, writing desks, and chairs complete the picture — yet the decor is ever-changing, as guests often leave with a painting, a pillow, a lamp, or even their bed. The two third-floor rooms are charming, set under the eaves, with pretty yellow pine floors. A great asset is the common porch at the front of the house on the second floor.

There are two dining areas, one with wicker chairs at seven tables, the other with couches and banquettes. The dinner menu, prepared by Erika, is varied, eclectic, and creative. The meal may begin with oysters wrapped in prosciutto and poached in champagne sauce. Entrées might include fettucini d'hotel with lobster, scallops, cream sauce, and prosciutto; quail in brandy sauce; sea scallops in bourbon mustard; or veal Rockefeller.

If you can find an appetite the next morning, you will feast on several courses, including possibly eggs Benedict, a baked dish, pancakes, and home-baked goods.

BLOOMSBURG

The Inn at Turkey Hill

991 Central Road
Bloomsburg, PA 17815
717-389-1500
Fax: 717-784-3718

*A pleasant place
in a country
college town*

Proprietor: Babs Pruden. **Innkeeper:** Andrew Pruden. **Accommodations:** 18 rooms, including 2 suites (2 in main house, 16 in newer section). **Rates:** Rooms $84, suites $130–$170. **Included:** Continental breakfast. **Minimum stay: Added:** $15 each additional person, 6% tax. **Payment:** Major credit cards. **Children:** Welcome. **Pets:** Allowed. **Smoking:** Not allowed in main house. **Open:** All year.

Bloomsburg State College was founded in 1839, the same year that a family farm called Turkey Hill was begun on the edge of town. Progress was kind to Bloomsburg; the university expanded to about 6,000 students, and Turkey Hill became a popular country inn in an idyllic setting near I-80. Babs Pruden is the present owner of the Inn at Turkey Hill, and she is quite devoted to the property which her parents bought in 1942. Her son Andrew is the innkeeper, a young and enthusiastic influence.

In 1983, Babs Pruden decided to transform her childhood home into a country inn as a tribute to her father. A greenhouse was added to the back of

> **Three generations of Prudens have been the proud proprietors of this Pennsylvania farmhouse. The wonderful original work of a local artist is prominently featured throughout the inn and on the walls of two dining rooms. All else is comfortable, tasteful, and traditional.**

the white clapboard farmhouse providing one of three dining areas, from which guests can look up to the stars at night and to the groomed back lawns, a duck pond framed in daffodils, and a trellised gazebo by day. A new single-story clapboard wing perpendicular to the farmhouse contains 16 guest rooms.

The entrance foyer at the side of the farmhouse is elegantly and traditionally furnished in the style of a library, with wing chairs and sofas, a fireplace, and a tiny nook where guests may buy bath goods and powders from a Bloomsburg shop. Displayed in the inn is lovely original artwork as well as some furniture painted by local artist Fran De Ballas.

The two indoor dining areas are the Mural Room and the Stencil Room. The Stencil Room has painted ivy above the chair rail and pineapple designs between windows. The Mural Room was named for a magnificent painting by De Ballas, which was destroyed in a fire and is being slowly recreated by a local artist. The greenhouse dining room is bright and contemporary. Entrées range from $14 to $20. Among chef David Maclachlan's specialties are shrimp with crabmeat stuffing and chicken with raspberry Chambord cream sauce.

While the two guest rooms in the main house are pretty, guests might prefer the newer units for privacy and comfort, with duck pond and gazebo views. The traditional country furnishings are reproductions from Habersham in Georgia. Four-poster king-size beds in rich wood are covered in duvets of either blue or forest green. De Ballas's paintings hang in every room, which are further enlivened by plants and flowers. All rooms have phones, televisions, and roomy private baths. Guests enjoy a Continental breakfast in their rooms, the garden, or the greenhouse.

EAST STROUDSBURG

The Inn at Meadowbrook

Cherry Lane Road
RD 7, Box 7651
East Stroudsburg, PA 18301
717-629-0296

*A classic
country inn
in the Poconos*

Proprietors: Robert and Kathy Over-man. **Accommodations:** 16 rooms (5 in Mill House, all with private bath; 11 in Manor House, 6 with private bath, 5 sharing 2 baths). **Rates:** Manor House $55–$90, Mill House $75. **Included:** Full breakfast. **Minimum stay:** 2 nights on weekends. **Added:** 6% tax. **Payment:** Visa, MasterCard, American Express, Discover. **Children:** 12 and over welcome. **Pets:** Not allowed. **Smoking:** Allowed in common rooms. **Open:** All year.

In the Poconos just west of the Delaware Water Gap is this pleasurable country inn, a welcome change from the clutter of hotels scattered through the area. The Inn at Meadowbrook looks like a New England farmhouse and was built as such by a farmer in 1842 of white clapboards. As every tireless patriarch dreams of doing, he later built an extension on the manor house for his grandchildren to stay in when they visited.

The six original guest rooms in the main house are of average size, but the five for the grandchildren are rather small, with tiny sinks in each room and a shared hall bath (good for the budget-minded). There are lovely pieces of furniture: a brass bed, a leather tufted wing chair, oak washstands, and nice touches of original artwork. Kathy did the bold decor, with walls in surprising colors or vivid floral paper. Across the narrow street is the Mill House, built as a gristmill in the 1930s, offering more interesting and more private accommodations. The rooms were all designed creatively by Kathy with interesting crown canopies and a fabulous painted log cabin room.

> **The best way to experience the outdoors at Meadowbrook is from indoors, in the dining room, which has views in three directions to the fields and Meadowbook Pond. The equestrian influence of the fields and neighboring farms is continued indoors throughout the inn.**

The Manor House's most elegant attribute is a 1930s addition, a wonderful space that is now the dramatic setting for the dining room overlooking the country, the stream, and Meadowbrook Pond. Three forest green walls have windows to the countryside, and a fireplace rests along the fourth wall. A lovely area at the foot of the dining room has pillars separating three open archways in a classic, clean-lined style. Bob Overman is the chef; his dinners range from $17 to $21, including veal Valdastana stuffed with proscuitto and fontina cheese, and chicken and shrimp Milano, served in a creamy champagne sauce over pasta.

The house has a nice common area with a fireplace, but if crowds at dinner are invasive there is a lounge downstairs, with two sitting areas, a game closet, a television, and a mural of the homestead painted by Kathy.

A full equestrian facility, including a tack shop, is next door, and guests may take lessons and explore trails for a cost. The equestrian theme throughout the house includes riding hats, crops, and boots in unexpected corners, and even a polo-styled room. Other diversions at the Inn at Meadowbrook include two tennis courts, shuffleboard, a large sundeck, and a 20-by-40-foot pool.

HAWLEY

The Settler's Inn at Bingham Park

4 Main Avenue
Hawley, PA 18428
717-226-2993
Fax: 717-226-1874
800-833-8527

A feast of Pennsylvanian, German, and Asian foods

Proprietors: Grant and Jeanne Genzlinger and Marcia Dunsmore. **Accommodations:** 17 rooms, including 3 2-bedroom suites and 2 suites, all with private bath. **Rates:** $75–$110. **Included:** Full breakfast. **Minimum stay:** 2 nights June to October and on holiday weekends. **Added:** 6% tax, $15 additional guest. **Payment:** Major credit cards. **Children:** Welcome. **Pets:** Not allowed. **Smoking:** Restricted. **Open:** All year.

Settler's Inn is a great gathering and dining spot in the pretty Victorian town of Hawley, on the shores of manmade Lake Wallenpaupack. While the rooms at Settler's are sweetly decorated, the emphasis is clearly on the dining experience. However, the informality of the guest rooms adds to the general ambience of sociability, good cheer, and familial friendliness created by Settler's owners. Grant Genzlinger is the talented chef; his wife, Jeanne, is a member of the Chamber of Commerce; and family friend Marcia Dunsmore is the notable baker.

The large three-story Tudor building with leaded windows rambles in several angles. Across the street is Hawley's town park, with basketball and tennis courts. The inn is a mile and a half from beautiful Lake Wallenpaupack. Settler's Inn was begun in 1927 but not completed until after World War II, serving as a hotel, a boys' school, a nightclub, and a senior citizens' home.

The owners bought the property in 1980 as a forum for Grant's culinary skills, an unusual blend of Asian and German cooking. Grant and Jeanne are touchingly loyal to their community: their cheese comes from neighboring Amish farms, their meats are all cured and smoked in-house, and their produce is grown locally, if not on the property. The menu is hearty and interesting, providing suggestions from the large list of Pennsylvania wines and beers. Appetizers might include applewood smoked trout with

> **Lake Wallenpaupack is a wondrous natural resource in Pennsylvania's Poconos. Visitors will work up a tremendous appetite fishing, boating, hiking, and basically recreating — in preparation for the creative cuisine of Grant Genzlinger at Settler's Inn.**

apple horseradish cream or wild mushrooms and walnuts in armagnac sweet cream. Entrées could include roast chicken breast stuffed with cornbread and *bauern schinken* (German country ham); or scallops, shrimp, and flounder in Asian sauces. The desserts are all made fresh each day by Marcia, and might include apple cobbler or maple crème brulée. She also bakes four or five breads for dinner, for which a garlic boursin cheese is provided. Entrées range from $12 to $20. Sunday brunch is a famous event, summoning hungry diners from all over for full meals from $9 to $11.

The Genzlingers have made some tasteful and much-needed upgrades in the guest rooms, increasing the comfort of a stay at Settler's. The rooms are clean, cheerful, and old-fashioned, with queen-size beds, wicker furniture, antique dressers, and clean baths.

Guests ought to consult Jeanne for advice about numerous local activities, including boat tours, train excursions from Honesdale (the birthplace of the American railroad), hiking, birding, or museum-going.

Woodloch Pines

RD1, Box 280
Hawley, PA 18428
717-685-7121
Fax: 717-685-1205

*A timeless
family tradition
in the Poconos*

Proprietors: John Kiesendahl and Russell Kranich. **Accommodations:** 158 rooms in 4 main buildings and smaller houses. **Rates:** $60–$150 per person AP (seasonally), also summer weekly rates from $855. **Included:** 3 meals a day, all activities. **Minimum stay:** 3 nights during the summer. **Added:** Children age 13–19 half adult rate, age 7–12 $45, age 3–6 $23, 6% tax. **Payment:** Visa, MasterCard, Discover. **Children:** Welcome; under 3 free. **Pets:** Not allowed. **Smoking:** Allowed. **Open:** All year except Christmas week.

This family resort, set on Lake Teedyuskung in the Poconos, is a secret, rarely advertised. Difficult to find on a map, it's nine miles east of Hawley and Lake Wallenpaupack. Its original structures were built as a summer estate in 1918 by the wealthy Lochwood family.

In the 1950s, two young couples, a foursome of friends — Harry and Mary Kiesendahl and Don and Margie Kranich — decided to open a business together. They were thrilled to find Woodloch for sale, on the lake where Mary had spent childhood summers. A new generation of Kiesendahl and Kranich families runs Woodloch Pines today, with love and respect for the lake, the traditions of Woodloch, and their generations of returning guests. The staff is an extension of their families, a wholesome, dependable, happy bunch, numbering about 400 for as many guests in warmer months.

Woodloch Pines borders the southern end of Lake Teedyuskung, fed by underground springs and named for a majestic Indian chief known as the King of the Delawares. The 65-acre lake is a mile and a half long and a half mile wide, with an average depth of 15 to 20 feet. At 1,500 feet above sea level, the lake offers magnificent winter activities such as tobogganing, skating, ice fishing, skiing, and sleighing; in warmer months there's water skiing as well as boating and swimming.

The original shingled house is surrounded by several rambling cottages

> If your family hasn't been coming to Woodloch Pines for generations, you're in for a nice surprise. For many, Woodloch Pines is a legacy, and no wonder: the beauty of Lake Teedyuskung gets into your blood, it's felt in your bones and sung in your heart.

and contemporary lodges. While some buildings may be new and not necessarily beautiful, they remain hidden in the foliage and natural landscape. In addition to the resort characteristics of well-appointed rooms in the larger buildings, Woodloch Pines can also feel like a camp, with smaller cabins tucked off pathways, areas for go-carts, volleyball, basketball, handball, and horseshoes.

The rooms are decorated with a clean American-country feel, in traditional light pine, reproduction cherry, or contemporary furnishings. Meals are served family-style in the large dining rooms, with all the wholesome, hearty food you can eat. Everything is made fresh in the Woodloch kitchens; they even make their own ice cream.

Joey Ranner and Randy Barnes mastermind a dizzying number of activities for every imaginable group, from toddlers to senior citizens. In addition to lakeside activities, there is an outdoor pool, a new fitness complex with an indoor pool, and, a mile from the resort, an 18-hole golf course that opened in 1992.

JIM THORPE

Harry Packer Mansion

Box 458, Packer Hill
Jim Thorpe, PA 18229
717-325-8566

*A dramatic
mansion of
monumental
proportions*

Proprietors: Pat and Robert Handwerk. **Accommodations:** 13 rooms, including 1 suite (7 rooms in main house, all but 2 with private bath; 6 rooms in Carriage House, all with private bath). **Rates:** Rooms $75–$95, suite $110, murder mystery weekends $320–$410 per couple. **Included:** Full breakfast. **Minimum stay:** 2 nights on weekends. **Added:** 6% tax. **Payment:** MasterCard, Visa. **Children:** Not allowed. **Pets:** Not allowed. **Smoking:** Not allowed in guest rooms. **Open:** All year.

The Harry Packer Mansion was built in 1874 by Harry's father, Asa Packer, who at the time was the third wealthiest man in the country, having made his fortune as the founder of the Lehigh Valley Railroad. Asa built the mansion next to his own (now a museum) as a wedding gift for his son Harry, who died several years later from kidney failure at 34. Much to his father's dismay, he left no heirs but an illegitimate daughter.

The town of Jim Thorpe, named for the Olympic track star born here, sits on the Lehigh River in the western hills of the Poconos. The salmon-colored, three-story brick house rests on an impossibly steep cliff above town. The gothic porch is framed in a colonnade of carved sandstone laced with ivy. Third-floor dormer windows poke out from the undulating lines of the mansard roof, which follows the bayed exterior. The present owners bought the house in 1984, and they have elaborately restored it. The Tiffany windows, English Minton tiles, brass and bronze chandeliers, carved wood mantels, a few antique furnishings, and hand-painted ceilings are all original.

Guests wanting special privacy should know that tours are conducted from Sunday through Thursday and on some Saturdays. Also, on most weekends the house is the setting for a well-written murder mystery involving the Packer family and their fortune.

> **The Harry Packer Mansion is larger than life and almost otherworldly in its beauty and high drama. Its grand scale feels more like a theater set than a bed-and-breakfast. In this house it's easy to assume the role of a romantic Victorian traveler.**

The scale of the mansion is massive: the exterior doors weigh 500 pounds, the etched-glass doors to the foyer a mere 400. The first-floor ceilings are 15 feet high, with gilded mirrors soaring to the ceilings. There is a ladies' and a gentlemen's parlor, the latter's walls papered in a reproduction of the original pattern. The library has mahogany-paneled walls and some with the original blue silk wallcovering, images of Shakespeare and Byron in the stained glass windows, and 18-karat gold paint on the chandelier globes.

You may feel remarkably as if you just removed a velvet rope while visiting a museum, undressed, and retired to bed, especially in the seven rooms of the main house. The six rooms in the Carriage House don't impart this feeling of time travel. The present owners have made these rooms traditional and cheery, on the smallish side, with queen-size beds, reproduction Queen Anne furniture, tufted wing chairs, settees, and clean new baths in a hunt theme.

The must-see Asa Packer Museum next door is open from spring through fall. For the full Packer experience, be sure to ride the trains. Hickory Run State Park and several ski mountains are a short drive away.

MILFORD

Cliff Park Inn

Milford, PA 18337
717-296-6491
Fax: 717-296-3982
800-225-6535

> *A golfer's and walker's paradise on the Delaware*

Proprietors: Harry Buchanan III. **Manager:** Patricia O'Connor. **Accommodations:** 18 rooms (11 rooms in main house, 3 in Garden Cottage, 4 in Clubhouse Cottage). **Rates:** European Plan $85–$120, B&B $100–$145, MAP $140–$195. **Included:** Half the greens fees on 9-hole golf course for MAP guests. **Minimum stay:** On some weekends. **Added:** $15 each additional guest, 6% tax. **Payment:** All major credit cards. **Children:** Welcome. **Pets:** Not allowed. **Smoking:** Allowed. **Open:** All year.

On the upper reaches of the Delaware River, across from New Jersey's northwest corner, George Buchanan built a regal three-story farmhouse in 1820 on the fields outside Milford. The house remained a family home until the new century, when Annie Buchanan, wife of the patriarch's grandson, decided to open a small summer hotel. In 1913, a family friend who happened to be a golf course architect offered to transform some of the surrounding fields into a 9-hole golf course, overlooked today from high-backed rockers on the vast front verandah. The tradition of golf and hospitality remains today at the fifth-generation Buchanan estate, on 560 acres encircled by the Delaware River National Recreation Area and seven miles of hiking trails.

The spacious old farmhouse has rambling common rooms and sloping original wide-planked floorboards. Narrow, worn stairs lead to the second- and third-floor guest rooms, which are furnished with family antiques. While not luxurious, these rooms are heartwarmingly comfortable, quaint, and clean, some with wonderful sun porches overlooking the links at different angles.

> **The fifth-generation Buchanan estate comprises 560 acres within the Delaware River National Recreation Area.**
> **The 1820 farmhouse has its own 9-hole golf course, constructed in 1913. For golfers, skiers, walkers, and diners, Cliff Park is memorable and unique.**

The Garden and Clubhouse cottages are more daringly furnished, the latter with a high cathedral ceiling and fieldstone fireplace.

Scottish is most certainly the theme in the Grill Room, one of two Cliff Park dining rooms. The wallpaper, tablecloths, curtains, and even the rugs are cheerily done in the Buchanan family tartan. The other dining area is quaintly decorated in the style of a traditional country inn, with lace tablecloths, wooden chairs, peach walls, and a crackling fire. Chef Chad Gasiorek serves fine American French cuisine, with dinner entrées priced reasonably from $6 to $10. A prelude to dinner might be hickory-smoked salmon gravlax with capers, onions, and cream cheese, or perhaps snapping turtle soup with sherry. Entrée choices might include rabbit and spring vegetable fricassee; charred baby lamb chops with eggplant and leeks; roast fillet of beef Wellington with bordelaise sauce; or baked game pie, with venison, pheasant, grouse, wild boar sausage.

In season, guests pay half price for greens fees on the 9-hole course and enjoy seven miles of walking trails in and around the glorious palisades bordering the Delaware River. The golf course and trails are popular with cross-country skiers in the winter.

SKYTOP

Skytop Lodge

Skytop, PA 18357
717-595-7401
Fax: 717-595-9618
800-345-7SKY

> *A magnificent Old-World resort isolated in the Poconos*

General Manager: Eugene Yacuboski. **Accommodations:** 166 rooms in main lodge, including 16 mini-suites, 3 VIP suites; also 9 4-bedroom cottages. **Rates:** Seasonal rates apply. Rooms $231–$280, suites $240–$315, cottages $215–$285, all AP; special family plans available. **Included:** Three meals a day, use of all facilities. **Minimum stay:** None. **Added:** $70 each additional guest, $15 each additional child younger than 13, 15% gratuities, 6% tax. **Payment:** Visa, MasterCard, American Express, Diners Club. **Children:** Welcome. **Pets:** Not allowed. **Smoking:** Nonsmoking rooms available. **Open:** All year.

Skytop was christened in the mid-1920s, with a name borrowed from the highest peak on the property surrounding the Mohonk Mountain House in New Paltz, New York — which tells a visitor a great deal about this mountaintop haven. That Skytop is the least known of the grand old resorts is either a grave oversight or a blessing. In any case, many travelers arrive unprepared for the Old World magnificence of this four-story stone lodge. Skytop sits atop a 5,500-acre mountain plateau three miles north of Canadensis in an untouched area of the Poconos. While the exterior looks a bit like an English stone castle, the high-ceilinged great hall and elegant dining room invoke the feeling of Gatsby-era wealth.

The lodge was successfully designed to look as if it rose out of the mountain, which is made up mostly of red shale and sandstone. The stone has the blanched, weathered look of exposure to many a hard winter. While the enclosed North Porch has an elevation of 1,576 feet, the property reaches above 2,000 feet on West Mountain. Everything in sight, within eight square miles, belongs to Skytop.

The Pine Room, the great reception hall, has rich paneled walls warmed by an enormous fireplace. It's classically furnished with comfortable reading chairs and gregarious sitting areas, lit by large windows hung with crewel drapes. In the clubby library, guests read at fireside. In the west wing is the formal dining room with Palladian windows; in the east wing are the fitness area and indoor pool. The guest rooms are furnished in classic pine, with four-poster pineapple beds, wing chairs, and a television tucked into an armoire.

One of Skytop's finest and rarest features is its resident naturalist. In 1983, Patrick Fasano became Skytop's first on-staff naturalist and wrote an excellent primer of the land called *The Nature of Skytop*, available at the lodge. He has since been

> There's nothing to see but trees and distant peaks from the 5,500-acre plateau on which Skytop reigns. Those who revere this incredible place count their blessings in whispers, hoping fervently that Skytop remains undiscovered.

replaced by wondrous John Serrao, who watches over the nine miles of hiking trails, the forests, the Leavitts and Indian Ladder waterfalls, the five miles of streams, and the meadows, including their 265 species of wildflowers.

Robert White designed the golf course in 1926, a year before ground was broken for the lodge. The 18-hole, 6,220-yard course offers beautiful scenery and suffers little from the mountainous terrain. Twenty bluebird houses are strategically stationed throughout the links.

In addition to golf, guests enjoy trout fishing along a mile and a half of private stream, paddle tennis and tennis on seven courts, and lawn bowling, miniature golf, shuffleboard, nightly deer spotting, and other activities. There is downhill skiing and instruction on West Mountain with two poma lifts, as well as cross-country skiing. Skating is offered indoors in the Pavilion or on the lake (alas, the skating waiter who carried coffee and hot chocolate is gone now). The health club and fitness room has exercise equipment, a sauna and whirlpool, and an indoor pool in a lovely atrium setting. An outdoor pool rests below the lodge. Skytop offers a children's program, Camp-in-the-Clouds, during the summer months.

The staff at Skytop is unpretentious, gracious, and unusually pleased that visitors had the insight to find the place. Just 100 miles from New York City and Philadelphia, with intimate service and resort amenities, Skytop feels like a blue-blooded family secret.

SOMERSET

Hidden Valley

1 Craighead Drive
Somerset, PA 15501
814-443-6454
800-458-0175

*Great skiing
in the
Laurel Mountains*

Proprietors: Kettler Brothers, Inc.
Managing Director: James Coulter.
General Manager: John Scanlan. **Accommodations:** 230 1- to
3-bedroom units, most with fireplace. **Rates:** $120–$180 per
couple, special ski packages available. **Minimum stay:** None.
Added: $15–25 each additional guest, 6% tax. **Payment:** Major
credit cards. **Children:** Allowed, 12 and under free. **Pets:** Not
allowed. **Smoking:** Nonsmoking rooms available. **Open:** All
year.

Where singles and younger people buy passes at Seven Sisters
Ski Resort, families flock to Hidden Valley in the Laurel
Mountains of southwestern Pennsylvania, 60 miles east of
Pittsburgh.

While skiing is a major draw, with 17 slopes and trails and
a 610-foot vertical drop, Hidden Valley has myriad other activities for all seasons and ages: a par 72 championship golf
course; 30 miles of groomed and patrolled cross-country ski
trails; 12 tennis courts, some lit for night play; eight restaurants; a Racquet Club with extensive fitness equipment, four
courts, steam room and sauna, and tanning; two lakes for
fishing and boating of all kinds; and an unusual under-21 club
called Club Soda.

Hidden Valley developed around a stone farmhouse built in
the 1850s. A century later, George and Helen Parke bought
the farmhouse and 106 surrounding acres as a weekend escape from their Pittsburgh home — all for $12,500. They
began welcoming guests in 1953 and by 1958 had added three
ski slopes. In 1977, the Parkes joined family friends the Kettler brothers in a venture that brought townhouses to Hidden
Valley. By 1983, Kettler Brothers, Inc. owned the entire facility, adding tens of millions of dollars in improvements in
road, ski, and snow-making facilities, as well as in accommodations.

Overnight guests have access to hotel accommodations in Four Seasons or in the Summit, Vista, and Fairway condominiums along the mountain. The decor is contemporary and extremely tidy; most units have fireplaces, some have stocked kitchens. Guests are given many dining options, including formal fare in the chestnut-walled Hearthside, where Helen Parke first served her country cooking in 1953, and California cuisine in the new cathedral-ceilinged Clock Tower. Several lounges feature nightlife for adults, while kids escape to Club Soda, with its two stereo systems, fog machines, and strobe lights.

> **The 2,000 acres of Hidden Valley are tucked between three state parks, giving a visitor access to 30,000 acres of Pennsylvania forest. With 17 alpine slopes and trails, skiing is a compelling activity; but it's only one of dozens at Hidden Valley.**

Carved into the 3,000-foot summit of Laurel Mountain, Hidden Valley's golf course offers beautiful views from more than 6,000 yards of greens. The 85 acres of skiable terrain receive an average of 150 inches of snow each year, supplemented with extensive snow making. The ski school offers children's and adult programs.

Throughout, Hidden Valley is an informal, active, friendly place. Though contemporary in design, the buildings are spread around the acreage so as not to seem overwhelming or disruptive.

SOUTH STERLING

French Manor

Huckleberry Road, Box 39
South Sterling, PA 18460
717-676-3244
800-523-8200

*A romantic
mini-chateau
in the Poconos*

Proprietors: Ronald T. and Mary
Kay Logan. **Innkeepers:** Michael
and Jennifer Logan. **Accommodations:** 5 rooms and 2 suites.
Rates: Rooms $170, $200 MAP; suites $220, $250 MAP. **Included:** Breakfast and dinner with MAP. **Minimum stay:** 2
nights on most weekends. **Added:** $55 each additional guest,
15% gratuity, 6% tax. **Payment:** American Express, Visa,
MasterCard, Discover. **Children:** Not allowed. **Pets:** Not allowed. **Smoking:** Allowed in common room. **Open:** All year.

This beautiful stone house looks like a miniature fairy-tale
castle. The mini-château was built during the Depression by
industrialist and art collector Joseph Hirshhorn as a country
home — for his art collection. Sixty artisans labored on the
house, constructed of thousands of fieldstone blocks quarried
on the original 600 acres and trimmed inside with oak, cedar,
and pecky cypress woodwork. The two-story-high Spanish
slate roof is interrupted by copper turrets inlaid with small
panes of leaded glass and tiny dormers poking out at odd
angles. The front door is set in a dramatic terra cotta archway.
    The Manor was acquired in December 1990 by Ron and
Mary Kay Logan, proprietors of the 54-room Sterling Inn
down the road. As the Logans slowly make their mark on the
house, some decor choices seem inconsistent; but the owners
are so kind and the property so sophisticated that it would be
a shame to skip a visit just because the Versailles Room is
hung with Williamsburg prints. In an unspoiled part of the
Poconos, near Lake Wallenpaupack and Tobyhanna State
Park, the setting is glorious, with stunning views of Skytop
Mountain from the manor's 38 acres.
    Besides the Versailles Room, guest rooms include the Turret Suite, which includes a sitting room with couch and offers
three spectacular vistas, and the Venice, Monte Carlo, and
Florence rooms, each with an extraordinary king-size bed. A

small common room is a considerate addition. The house feels like a castle inside too, as the ceiling folds and bends around one's head and passageways reveal themselves just steps ahead of one's path. Recently, the Logans refurbished a neighboring residence and added the deluxe San Remo and Geneva rooms.

George Pelepko-Filak, French Manor's highly acclaimed chef, is fortunate to have such a breathtaking dining room in which to serve his French cuisine. The two-story cathedral ceiling reveals oak beams, and the room is warmed by enormous

> **With copper turrets, Spanish slate, leaded windows, and a terra cotta doorway, the French Manor is a diminutive castle. Art lover Joseph Hirshhorn built this wonder in the Depression as a gallery for his collection. The dining room is also a work of art.**

fireplaces at either end. A cold first course may feature a sole mousse with cucumber and dill sauce, a warm one a wild mushroom crêpe with apples and hazelnuts. A choice of two soups may be followed by hearts of palm salad and fresh sorbet. Entrées, all more than $20, may include beef tenderloin with truffled demiglace; breast of chicken with morels, sundried tomatoes, and asparagus; or lobsterettes, scallops, and lobster in three-pepper sauce. Thursdays, a prix fixe eight-course meal is offered for $40. The wine list is quite versatile, and the array of desserts is daunting.

Breakfast should be taken on the large slate porch at the top of the hill, overlooking the mountains and the estate.

STARLIGHT

The Inn at Starlight Lake

P.O. Box 27
Starlight, PA 18461
717-798-2519
Fax: 717-798-2672
800-248-2519

A lakeside setting in Pennsylvania's northeast corner

Proprietors: Jack and Judy McMahon. **Accommodations:** 26 rooms (20 with private bath, 6 rooms share 4 baths): 14 in main inn, 12 in 9 outbuildings, including 1 suite with double whirlpool tub. **Rates:** $127–$154 per couple MAP. **Included:** Breakfast and dinner. **Minimum stay:** 2 nights weekends, 3 nights holiday weekends. **Added:** $49–$54 each additional adult, $37 each additional child age 7–12, 6% tax. **Payment:** Visa, MasterCard. **Children:** Welcome, under 7 free. **Pets:** Not allowed. **Smoking:** Not allowed in dining room. **Open:** All year except first two weeks of April.

In the far northeast corner of Pennsylvania, the Inn at Starlight Lake rests in the lovely unspoiled Appalachians. While certainly removed from civilization, the inn does not seem remote. Its intelligent, personable, professional innkeepers have created an air of comfort and sophistication about this place during their tenure since 1975. They raised a family here and remain very visible fixtures, greeting guests, socializing, and offering interesting local lore.

The inn was built in 1909, encouraged no doubt by the now

abandoned railroad depot several hundred feet away, which made this undiscovered area suddenly accessible to New Yorkers. The main building is of green clapboard with a welcoming front porch; an adjacent tennis court forms a kind of courtyard for the three outbuildings. The inn has canoes, sailboats, and rowboats with which guests can explore the 45 spring-fed acres of Starlight Lake, one of more than a hundred lakes in this area, known as Pennsylvania Lake Country.

The closest big town to Starlight is Binghamton, New York, but somehow, adrift in the Appalachians, the Inn at Starlight Lake feels closer to Canada. This place will bring out the pioneer in you, particularly in winter, when you explore this northern lake country on cross-country skis.

The large lobby of the Main Inn has heart pine walls and highly varnished floors scattered with small Oriental rugs. The huge stone hearth houses a wood-burning stove that casts warmth onto mission furnishings. Through French doors is the informal Stovepipe Bar; beyond are the two dining rooms, one in an enclosed section of the inn's front porch with views of the lakefront. Dinner is both elegant and rustic, ranging from $20 (if you're not on the meal plan) for Continental entrées such as *jaeger schnitzel*, a breaded pork cutlet served with bordelaise sauce and mustard; or pasta of the sea, with scallops, shrimp, lobster over homemade linguine. Sunday brunch includes brioche French toast with nuts and raisins and raised dough waffles.

Upstairs in the main inn are 14 guest rooms, cozy and comfortable, some with brand-new baths and recently refurbished cheery decor, all with silk flowers, plants, and a commendable reading library. Prints, ink drawings of American primitives, and Victoriana art decorate the walls, and there are occasional period antiques. Be sure to request a room with a lake view, as the rates in the main inn are all the same.

Two of the three units in the unfairly named "motel" have great cathedral ceilings. Adjacent are a two-unit cottage and a two-story, three-room house, offering the inn's most elegant accommodation, a two-room suite with a whirlpool bath. Above is an unusual room with two sleeping alcoves on the porch. The family house has three guest rooms, its bottom floor with a capacious bunk room.

The Inn at Starlight Lake is a great place for families as well as for couples seeking a romantic retreat. Golf and horseback riding are nearby, and fishing is optimal at the Upper Delaware trout fishery five miles away. The McMahons have forged 18 miles of cross-country trails in the surrounding area. Downhill skiers venture only 15 minutes away to Mt. Tone, 30 to Elk Mountain, the state's largest.

STATE COLLEGE

The Nittany Lion Inn

200 West Park Avenue
State College, PA 16803
814-231-7500
Fax: 814-231-7510
800-233-7505

> *An elegant center to a thriving college community*

Proprietor: Pennsylvania State University. **General Manager:** James Purdum. **Accommodations:** 262 rooms including 7 suites. **Rates:** $85–$160. **Minimum stay:** None. **Added:** $10 each additional guest. **Payment:** Major credit cards. **Children:** Welcome. **Pets:** Not allowed. **Smoking:** Nonsmoking rooms available. **Open:** All year.

As one approaches the two-story portico of the Nittany Lion, a visitor immediately conjures up images of football weekends, tailgate picnics, and fall foliage; or perhaps black gowns flowing against a background of late-spring blossoms. The regal old inn looks like a country club, a place befitting the distinguished and gregarious alumni who return to Penn State. Built in 1931, 80 years after the university was founded, the Nittany Lion completed an exciting and massive renovation in early 1993.

In this college setting, the Nittany Lion has recently come of age. A generous investment has provided for a bright future for this hotel, which is vastly improved and very deluxe. It sits in the middle of this town in the middle of Pennsylvania's central mountains like the Penn State mascot.

State College is a thriving community in a beautiful setting overlooking the Seven Mountains of wooded central Pennsylvania. The Nittany Lion sits conveniently in the middle of the Penn State Campus. The three-story whitewashed brick building has the air of a colonial mansion, topped with a gambrel roof studded with dormer windows. Rows of small-paned windows are stacked two stories high, trimmed with blue shutters. Several wings radiate from the long center portion of the inn, lined with single-story porches with lattice railings. The landscaping is fastidious and colorful, a big part of the atmosphere at the Nittany Lion, which continues on the walkways throughout the property and the garden areas on the interior.

The grand two-story lobby is bordered by an eight-sided balcony and centered around an enormous chandelier. Additions to the Nittany Lion include the Alumni Ballroom, which easily accommodates 500 people and opens to a skylit area and garden courtyard; the Whiskers Lounge, overlooking the courtyard; ample meeting space; and a new health club and Jacuzzi room. The common areas are generous at the Nittany Lion, including two galleries where guests may read at fireside. The dining room is a high point, led by chefs William Laychur and David Quinn. American cuisine may include homemade lobster bisque or Maryland crab cakes. Entrées range from $12 to $21.50.

The three floors of guest rooms were entirely redecorated in a new version of their traditional colonial design. Rooms have either two-poster king-size beds or two doubles, with televisions, telephones, and bright new baths. The furnishings are a reproduction Williamsburg design, with wallpaper appropriate to the period.

There is a sprightly new air about the Nittany Lion that is quite evident in the staff, who seem thrilled with their new environment. Recreational facilities abound, not just in the Nittany Lion's fitness center but at the two championship golf courses within walking distance, indoor and outdoor tennis, and swimming pool.

WILLIAMSPORT

The Thomas Lightfoote Inn

2887 South Reach Road
Williamsport, PA 17701
717-326-6396

*A historic home
on the
Susquehanna*

Proprietors: Jim and Rita Chilson. **Accommodations:** 5 rooms, 3 with private bath. **Rates:** $55 on weekdays, $60 on weekends. **Included:** Full breakfast. **Minimum stay:** On some weekends. **Added:** 6% tax. **Payment:** Master-Card, Visa. **Children:** Over 5 welcome. **Pets:** Not allowed. **Smoking:** Not allowed in rooms. **Open:** All year.

A city of 33,000 on the Susquehanna River, halfway between Wilkes-Barre and State College, Williamsport is the door to Pennsylvania's north-central mountain ranges and also home to the Little League World Series. Settled in the late 18th century by German Quakers who shared the community with valley Indians, Williamsport became, a century later, one of the world's largest lumber centers and home to a goodly number of millionaires.

Named for the town's surveyor and erected by his Quaker kinsmen, the Thomas Lightfoote Inn was built in 1792 by the Updergraff brothers. The two-story brick and stone house rests on the part of the Susquehanna that the Indians called the Long Reach, across busy Route 220 from downtown Williamsport and "millionaire's mile," West Fourth Street.

The 1783 log cabin across the street was a granary on the Susquehanna canal, and the Updergraff house served as the inn for those loading from the granary. Updergraffs farmed the surrounding acreage for 162 years. The house was once a stop on the Underground Railroad.

The Chilsons bought the faded property in 1986 and restored it over eight months of labor. It took a great deal of work to repair the plumbing and electricity, save the historic structure, and also get the building up to the standards of Jim Chilson, owner and town fire chief. The doors and first-floor shutters are done in Williamsburg blue, and the house is lifted up from the road by a flat lawn and a stone wall. All the rooms are original, except for the back porch and dining room. The Chilsons used stone from a wall knocked down when they extended the house to build a huge fireplace in the new dining room.

> As you drive down South Reach Road, look for a 1783 log cabin on the banks of the Susquehanna River. Right across the street is the Thomas Lightfoote Inn, built a few years later. The house is in tremendous shape, having been restored by the owners, Rita, a consummate hostess, and Jim, the town fire chief.

Four original rooms are at the front of the second floor; a new room is at the back. Three of the front rooms are quite large, with sitting areas, lots of lamps and tables adorned with fresh flowers, lovely period antiques, and some original mantels — as well as televisions and phones. The linens are lovely, with down comforters and heavy sheeting.

The large dining room and English tap room downstairs are open on weekends, and weekday dinner guests have the pleasure of eating in the cozy fireplace room. Dinner might include a delicious corn and chicken chowder and an entrée of chicken and shrimp in champagne cream sauce over wild rice. The breakfasts are also generous, with a hot dish of choice accompanied by homemade biscuits.

Guests will leave remembering the lovely house and the fine food, but most of all cheerful and informative Rita Chilson, a woman of boundless energy and enthusiasm who sincerely enjoys her guests.

Rural Southeast
Pennsylvania

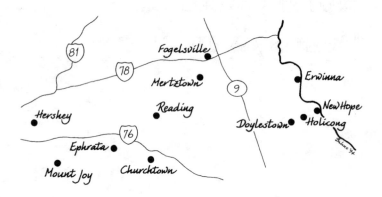

Best Romantic Retreats

Ephrata
  Historic Smithton
Erwinna
  Isaac Stover House
Reading
  The Inn at Centre Park

Best Gourmet Getaway

Erwinna
  Evermay on-the-Delaware

Best Resort

Hershey
  The Hotel Hershey

Best Country Bed-and-Breakfasts

Doylestown
  Highland Farms
  The Inn at Fordhook Farm
Ephrata
  Clearview Farm
Holicong
  Barley Sheaf Farm
Mertztown
  Longswamp Bed and Breakfast

Best Country Inns

Foglesville
  Glasbern
Mt. Joy
  The Cameron Estate Inn and Restaurant
New Hope
  The Inn at Phillips Mill

Best Village Bed-and-Breakfasts

Churchtown
   Churchtown Inn
Ephrata
   The Inns at Doneckers
New Hope
   Wedgwood Collection of Historic Inns

Best Village Inns

Holicong
   The Golden Plough Inn
New Hope
   The Logan

Named for the shire from which William Penn came (Buckingham), Bucks County is a beautiful stretch of land shouldering the Delaware River northeast of Philadelphia. New Hope and Doylestown are the focal points of the county, with the Bucks County Vineyards, the Moravian Pottery and Tile Works, and the Mercer Museum, with more than 60 crafts and 40,000 tools and named for the master craftsman who lived and worked here at the turn of the century. Mercer's home, Fonthill Museum, is also open to the public.

A thoroughly scenic drive is along 60 miles of River Road, which follows the winding path of the Delaware from **New Hope** to Bethlehem. During the 1920s and 1930s, Bucks County was an artistic haven, a kind of Greenwich Village weekend retreat. The country's finest intellectuals, artists, writers, and musicians vacationed here.

This area is replete with history and culture, home most famously to the Amish and Mennonites, who are very much in evidence. Wheatland is here, home of President James Buchanan, as are the Hans Herr House, one of the country's oldest Mennonite meeting houses, and the **Ephrata Cloister,** an intriguing 18th-century German monastic settlement.

For a shopping sojourn, take a side trip to the outlets of **Reading,** which has one of the loveliest bed-and-breakfasts in the region, at Centre Park.

On the banks of the Susquehanna River, Harrisburg has been the state's capital for nearly 200 years, featuring the wonderful State Museum of Pennsylvania since 1905.

Twelve miles east is **Hershey.** By 1900, a young entrepreneur named Milton Hershey was selling his singular chocolate recipe around Lancaster County out of his horseless electric carriage. Hershey built his chocolate factory from 1903 to 1905 and built a town around it that soon adopted its founder's name.

HersheyPark has 45 rides including three roller coasters; Carousel Circle, one of the oldest such carousels in use in the country, hand-carved in 1919 by Italian craftsmen; a 17th-century village called Tudor Square; an 18th-century village called Pennsylvania Dutch Place with crafts and foods; Kid Stuff, with activities and games for children; and Rhine Land, an 18th-century German village.

There are countless activities in the Hershey complex including ten acres of ZooAmerica. The Hershey Museum of American Life, opened by Milton Hershey in 1933, is devoted to the cultures of Native Americans, Eskimos, and Pennsylvania Germans.

The Hershey Gardens are quite extensive. Milton Hershey introduced a rose garden in 1936 on 3.5 acres, in which 12,500 roses in 112 varieties were planted. Today the gardens sprawl over 23 acres and are planted with 120,000 plants, shrubs, and trees, including 700 varieties of roses and 30,000 tulips.

York and Gettysburg are a short jaunt south, including the 3,500-acre Gettysburg National Military Park and a history book's worth of Civil War sites.

CHURCHTOWN

Churchtown Inn

2100 Main Street
Narvon, PA 17555
717-445-7794

A theme-filled B&B set in Amish country

Proprietors: Stuart W. and Hermine Smith and Jim Kent. **Accommodations:** 8 rooms, 6 with private bath; Honeymoon Carriage House. **Rates: Rooms** $49–$95, Carriage House $125. **Included:** 5-course breakfast. **Minimum stay:** 2 nights on weekends, 3 nights on holidays and special weekends. **Added:** 6% tax. **Payment:** Visa, MasterCard. **Children:** Over 12 welcome. **Pets:** Not allowed. **Smoking:** Allowed in designated areas only. **Open:** All year except Christmas.

Recluses beware: the Churchtown Inn is an inescapably sociable place. Owner Stuart Smith was born to be an innkeeper. He loves his business and loves his guests. His wife, Hermine, and his partner, Jim Kent, are energetic and friendly. Summers are always busy with vacationers, and a good time for the gregarious to visit is during one of Stuart's well-planned special-event weekends, from November through May. As a former choir director, Stuart has adopted music into the household: theme weekends may include a violin concert of Christmas music, a sock hop, a New Orleans jazz jam session, or square dancing. Other weekends might feature a Victorian ball, California wine tasting, kite flying, or perhaps a murder mystery. Twice a year, Stuart accompanies guests to an Amish wedding feast; and each Saturday night, the innkeepers join guests for a dinner at a local Amish home.

> With exacting attention to detail, the Churchtown Inn delivers the quintessential bed-and-breakfast experience to its guests. It's not just in the antiques and the atmosphere but in the social activities. Special weekends fill the winter calendar: perhaps a sock hop, a murder mystery, New Orleans jazz, or even kite flying.

Churchtown is a historic hamlet on a hill in rolling countryside about a half hour east of Lancaster. The fieldstone house is the town's cheerful center on a mossy green plot of land in Amish country. Built in 1735 by Welsh settlers, it was later owned by state legislator Edward Davies, who added a section in 1810. The innkeepers added the Carriage House and a glassed-in breakfast room in 1990. It's a pretty place; the two parlors in front are quite elegant.

There are five rooms on the second floor, all with private baths, and three on the third floor that share two baths. Throughout are handmade pieces by Mennonites including flower baskets, quilts, lace doilies, and specially designed television cabinets. The antique beds are cushy and lavishly dressed. Jim Kent created the huge crown canopy over an American Victorian sleigh bed in the David Jones Room.

On the third floor, as with any good garret, visitors should not be taller than six feet. The Henry Shirk Room has eaves that have bowed over time and an art deco walnut bed. Guests are given robes for the shared bath, which has only a tub and a European shower, but the rooms that share it are quite a value for $49 and $55. The Eleanor Fausset Room has a queen-size walnut Victorian high-back bed and a twin French sleigh bed as well, with skylights in a cathedral ceiling. The Carriage House is more contemporary than the senior rooms in the main house, though some may like the clean new lines, canopy bed, ballroom floor, and privacy. The heavy silk curtains were made from women's concert gowns after the Stuart W. Smith Singers performed at Carnegie Hall.

The garden breakfast room is contemporary in design, with a lovely view of the Welsh Mountains and Stuart's English herb gardens. Stuart cooks elaborate breakfasts, serving five courses, which may include peach or Grand Marnier French toast or oatmeal-granola pancakes and local sausage and ham.

DOYLESTOWN

Highland Farms

70 East Road
Doylestown, PA 18901
215-340-1354

A celebration of music and Bucks County bohemia

Proprietor: Mary Schnitzer. **Accommodations:** 4 rooms, 2 with private bath, including 2 suites. **Rates:** $125–$175. **Included:** 4-course breakfast, afternoon refreshments. **Minimum stay:** 2 nights on weekends, 3 nights on holidays. **Added:** $19.50 each additional person, 6% tax. **Payment:** Visa, MasterCard. **Children:** Over 12 welcome. **Pets:** Not allowed. **Smoking:** Permitted in the library. **Open:** All year.

Musicians adore Highland Farms. Oscar Hammerstein and his wife lived here from 1941 to 1961, a part of the cultural migra-

tion to Bucks County from New York City. Stephen
Sondheim and James Michener were among their many well-
known guests. Under the grape arbor out back, Henry Fonda
was married to Hammerstein's daughter.

The unusual 21-room house was built in 1840, three stories
of gray stone and stucco, with a flat roof, black shutters, and white trim. The second-floor wrap-around porch is supported by straight columns, giving the house the look of a riverboat. The Schnitzers, an interior designer and a contractor, bought the home in 1986, and their 13 months of renovations have earned the house a place on the National Register of Historic Places. While their own antiques contribute to the

> **Highland Farms pays homage to Oscar Hammerstein, who once lived in this architectural treasure. Rooms are named for and inspired by Hammerstein productions; sheet music awaits willing and able guests at the grand piano; even the swimming pool pays its tribute.**

elegance, the house holds some lovely original treasures —
leaded glass windows, chandeliers, and a stunning Louis Koch
limewood wall unit from 1740, taken from a castle in England. The glorious mantel in the living room is from the same
period, found in an old house nearby. There is quite a bit of
Hammerstein memorabilia here, including a good deal of
sheet music on the piano in the living room and records,
which guests are free to use.

The four rooms, three on the third floor and one on the second, are named for Hammerstein productions. The Carousel
room is large and playful, with wide-planked whitewashed
floors and a large hand-painted pony in its private bath; Show-
boat is smaller, its Tiffany lamp sitting on an antique table
near a 19th-century mahogany dresser; Oklahoma is a small
room with lace and linens more than one hundred years old.
The King and I is most deluxe, the only room with a fireplace
and hand-painted paper in the private bath. The second-floor
library, with a fireplace, is an informal alternative to the elegant living room. The classic blue wallpaper is, of course,
Highland plaid, with lots of books for guests to read in comfortable sofas.

In the formal dining room, Mary uses her Lenox goldware

every day for her lavish four-course breakfasts, which may feature her highly lauded seven-layer crêpes.

On the five acres of hilltop grounds outside charming Doylestown, the landscape is complete with a tennis court, a 60-foot swimming pool set in stone, and a refreshing view of the surrounding hills. Hammerstein's original outdoor speakers still pump appropriate music to the pool area. Even those underwater can appreciate "The Sound of Music," painted in fancy script on the pool's floor.

The Inn at Fordhook Farm

105 New Britain Road
Doylestown, PA 18901
215-345-1766

> *A garden
> of delights*

Proprietors: Blanche Burpee Dohan and Jonathan Burpee. **Innkeeper:** Elizabeth Romanella. **Accommodations:** 7 rooms (5 in the main house, 3 with private bath; 2 in Carriage House with shared bath). **Rates:** Main house $93–$135, Carriage House $175–$250. **Included:** Full farm breakfast, afternoon tea. **Minimum stay:** 2 nights on weekends. **Added:** $20 each additional person, 6% tax. **Payment:** Visa, MasterCard. **Children:** Over 12 welcome. **Pets:** Not allowed. **Smoking:** Permitted only on terrace. **Open:** All year.

W. Atlee Burpee was a teenage salesman of fancy poultry. By 1876, he realized that he could make more money on feed than on birds. In 1888, the young entrepreneur decided he needed a plot of land in which to test plants for his blossoming 12-year-old mail order seed company, based in Philadelphia. He bought what is now the Inn at Fordhook Farm, and it was here that Burpee's seeds were first planted. His family built and summered in the Victorian cottage at the entrance to Fordhook Farm and renovated the 18th-century fieldstone farmhouse at the turn of the century. The property was the home of the Burpees for three generations until 1985, when grandchildren Blanche Burpee Dohan and Jonathan Burpee decided to share their legacy with others.

The present imposing stone structure, which is on the National Register of Historic Places, was built in three stages from east to west: the kitchen in the 1760s, the center portion, which once served as a boys' school, in the 1830s, and the west wing during the Burpees' turn-of-the-century renovation. The separate Carriage House was erected in 1868. The 60 acres are lovely and well-groomed. The view from the terrace over the sloping lawns will take one's breath away almost as quickly as will a good game of badminton, the sport of choice for those not playing croquet.

> **W. Atlee Burpee was king of a seed dynasty. The roots of his fortune date back to the late 19th century and Fordhook Farm, where he planted his first seed trials. For three generations until 1985, Fordhook Farm was the family's summer retreat; the 60 acres of lawns and gardens are still a joy to behold.**

Some of the rooms in the main house overlook the endless front lawns, others have a shaded view of the seed building and the carriage house. Books about flowers are in every room. The Burpee and Atlee rooms are especially grand, each with its own terrace and fireplace. The Simmons and Torrance rooms are a bit smaller but appointed with lovely antiques, and the third-floor Curtiss Room is a bit more modest than the others. Museum-quality Mercer tile decorates the fireplaces and foyers throughout the house.

The Carriage House is a short walk across the gravel drive; it is very private, with two rooms and a common room on the second floor. While the guest rooms are private, they are less impressive than those in the main house; the attraction is surely the 20-by-30-foot Great Room, with chestnut beams supporting a cathedral ceiling and Palladian windows overlooking the trial gardens.

In the sunny dining room, guests are served a full breakfast, which may consist of oatmeal buttermilk pancakes or an egg strata. In winter, afternoon tea is served in the living room, in the warmer months on the great stone terrace under 200-year-old linden trees. Nearby Doylestown and the Mercer Tile Museum are terrific options for a free afternoon.

EPHRATA

Clearview Farm Bed and Breakfast

355 Clearview Road
Ephrata, PA 17522
717-733-6333

*An outstanding
B&B amid
200 acres of
Lancaster farmland*

Proprietors: Glenn and Mildred Wissler. **Accommodations:** 5 rooms, all with private bath. **Rates:** $89. **Included:** Full breakfast. **Minimum stay:** 2 nights weekends. **Added:** $25 each additional guest, 6% tax. **Payment:** Major credit cards. **Children:** Over 10 welcome. **Pets:** Not allowed. **Smoking:** Not allowed. **Open:** All year.

Bed-and-breakfasts are about as easy to find as horses and buggies in Lancaster County. Yet for a place fairly teeming with small establishments, there are relatively few good ones. Clearview Farm is one of the finest. Clearview was the Wisslers' beloved home for 35 years before they transformed it into a bed-and-breakfast in October 1989. Glenn still runs the 200-acre farm, growing corn and soybeans, and for part of the year retains many cattle. For fun, there are also four peacocks, a pair of swans, and their cygnets.

The grounds are idyllic, with a picturesque pond separating the house from its vast farmland. The huge farmhouse, built in 1814, is of blanched stone with red shutters, and a sunny old porch on one side is decorated with wicker and white wrought-iron furniture. Inside, all the papering, linens, window treatments, and creative bathrooms — two are recent additions — are the result of the Wisslers' hard work. Glenn labored at exposing a lot of the two-foot-thick stone and brick, opening ceilings to reveal hand-pegged beams.

The common spaces are pleasant but old-fashioned, and Mildred concedes that she focused her talents on the guest rooms. The dining room is a display for her good china and crystal, which guests use at elaborate breakfasts that might include ham and cheese soufflé with hollandaise sauce.

> It really shows when owners love their home as the Wisslers do. Clearview Farm has been their livelihood for 35 years and is still a working farm; but in 1989, it became a bed-and-breakfast, too. Glenn and Mildred have reconceived every room, and it's a great success.

Two third-floor rooms, Lincoln and Washington, are especially romantic. Here Glenn exposed the stone and brick walls and fireplaces and the hand-pegged beams in the ceilings. Both rooms have quilts draping four-poster pencil post beds; the Washington room has other quilts draped on a ladder leaning against the chimney. Glenn made the wardrobes from old green shutters; they look like French country decorator items. The random-width floorboards are as wide as 16 inches. The new baths seem old, with wainscoting, exposed beams, and unusual classic detail.

Each of the second-floor rooms is beautifully decorated. The Garden is a bouquet of chintz, with a gilded crown canopy above a brass and iron bed; the Princess Room has a lace-covered curved canopy bed and two pink tufted Victorian chairs. Since these rooms share a bath, each has a basket filled with neatly rolled towels. The Royal Room is a memorable chamber, with an elaborately carved Victorian acorn bed and matching marble-top vanity. Regal red and gold tapestry curtains hang in the windows. The enchanting long and narrow bath has an original clawfoot tub and a shower under a quirky sloped roof.

Guests rejuvenated by this peaceful setting may want to visit the Ephrata Cloister or the charming antiquing town of Lititz on the way into Lancaster.

The Inns at Doneckers

251, 318–324 North State Street
301 West Main Street
Ephrata, PA 17522
717-738-9502
Fax: 717-738-9554

*The name to
remember in
historic Ephrata*

Proprietor: H. William Donecker.
Manager and Innkeeper: Jan Grobengieser. **Accommodations:**
40 rooms in 6 historic homes, all but 2 with private bath, including 13 Jacuzzi suites, 7 of which also have fireplaces.
Rates: $59–$175. **Included:** Continental buffet breakfast.
Minimum stay: 2 nights holiday weekends. **Added:** $8 additional guest, 6% tax. **Payment:** Major credit cards. **Children:**
Welcome. **Pets:** Not allowed. **Smoking:** Allowed except at the
Homestead. **Open:** All year; restaurant closed Wednesdays.

In the historic town of Ephrata near Lancaster, famous for its
fascinating 18th-century cloister, the Donecker family
opened a clothing store about 30 years ago. Patrons came from
all over to spend the day shopping. Eventually, Bill Donecker
answered more of their needs by providing a restaurant,
overnight accommodations, a complex of art galleries and studios, and most recently, a farmers' market offering produce,
foods, and specialty items from 20 vendors around the region.

Today, the Doneckers community rather dominates the
commercial aspects of Ephrata, though 18
in a sensitive and complementary way. The overnight accommodations at the Guesthouse are in several connecting
buildings: a restored Queen Anne Victorian, three residential
brick houses, and the newest addition, the Homestead — a
1910 home for nonsmokers. The colonial 1777 House is several blocks away. The well-received French Restaurant at Doneckers is across the street from the Guesthouse, on the edge
of town near Artworks, a gallery for local artisans in a renovated 1920s shoe warehouse.

Each room is unique. At the Guesthouse, some roomy
suites are in large parlors, and other cozy rooms are tucked
away in gabled attics. A favorite is the luxurious Wheatland
Suite in the house's former foyer, with original inlaid floors,
stained glass windows, lovely bay windows, a satin-draped
crown canopy bed divided from a sitting area by pillars, and a
Jacuzzi. The rooms are decorated with lovely and varied an-

tiques and reproductions, with primitive detailing and stenciling. All have marble washstands and separate baths, except two rooms that share a bath.

While the Guesthouse feels like an inn, the 1777 House seems like a smaller bed-and-breakfast. It was built by clockmaker Jacob Gorgas for his family and shop. Gorgas was a

> Food, clothing, shelter, and art: these necessities are beautifully provided by the Donecker family in historic Ephrata. In addition to its fine French restaurant, popular clothing boutique, and collection of historic homes, Doneckers also offers a complex of art galleries and studios for local artisans.

member of the Ephrata Cloister, and rooms are named for some notable members. The entry is done in turn-of-the-century Mercer tiles, as are some of the working fireplaces, though the one in the Gorgas Suite is original green marble. All the rooms have Alsatian armoires or German *kasses* and are decorated in antiques from several centuries. The Conrad Biessel Suite has a 19th-century tiger's-eye maple table, the Prioress Maria Suite has an 1828 dower chest. Quite outstanding are the two triplex suites in the Carriage House with bedrooms and fireplaces on the first floor, stepping up to a whirlpool, and a sitting area on the third floor. The Homestead, a former Donecker family home built in 1910, contains four more suites.

At the Restaurant at Doneckers, chef Chuck Eichmann presides over several dining areas. Dinner entrées range from $8 to $24, from a French-American menu. Specialties include Dover sole in strawberry butter sauce; pheasant with vegetables, foie gras, and a truffle dumpling; or Châteaubriand for two. A full menu of appetizers is astounding, as are the soups and desserts. A lighter supper menu is also available nightly, from $9.

Historic Smithton

900 West Main Street
Ephrata, PA 17522
717-733-6094

> *The Penn-*
> *sylvania Dutch*
> *experience in*
> *historic Ephrata*

Proprietor and Innkeeper: Dorothy Graybill. **Accommodations:** 8 rooms including 1 4-room suite, all with private bath. **Rates:** Rooms $65–$135, suite $140–$170. **Included:** Full breakfast. **Minimum stay:** 2 nights with Saturday and holiday stay. **Added:** $35 each additional guest, $20 each additional child, 6% tax. **Payment:** MasterCard, Visa, American Express. **Children:** Well-behaved children welcome by prior arrangement. **Pets:** Will consider. **Smoking:** Not allowed. **Open:** All year.

The town of Ephrata in northern Lancaster County is famous for its Cloister of medieval German buildings, the home of an 18th-century Protestant monastic society who called themselves Seventh-Day Baptists, led by charismatic Conrad Beissel. One of the Cloister's ardent members was Henry Miller, who later invited the wrath of Beissel and was barred from worship. Miller, however, maintained his allegiance to the sect and in 1762 built a fieldstone house overlooking the monastery. A year later he opened an inn and tavern for visitors to the Cloister. His descendants owned this large stone house until the 1970s, when they sold it to Dorothy Graybill. Dorothy labored for years and opened the Historic Smithton Inn in 1983, a pristine bed-and-breakfast filled with beautiful Pennsylvania Dutch crafts and artwork.

The inn sits just above the Cloister Museum, on the edge of Ephrata's main street, the old main road to Scranton. Despite its busy location, the inn is a peaceful refuge and a wonderful place in which to immerse oneself in Lancaster lore. Dorothy is a charming, accomplished historian of the Amish and Mennonites as well as of the Ephrata Cloister.

> **An authentic, immaculate, artistic bed and breakfast, Historic Smithton is known for upholding the highest standards in the B&B industry. Dorothy Graybill is the reason why: her exquisite taste and extensive knowledge of the Pennsylvania Dutch make a stay at Historic Smithton a wholly fulfilling travel experience.**

The Amish and Mennonite influence begins in the breakfast room, decorated with quilts hanging on the walls as well as red tablecloths and red velvet curtains. The common room is often lit by a welcoming fire; behind it is a cluttered, comfortable library. Nearly all the immaculate house is original to 1763, including the wide-planked floors.

The furniture has been handmade by local craftspeople. The step-up trundle beds and four-poster canopy beds are dressed with down pillows, feather beds upon request, and Mennonite quilts. Rooms are lit with handcrafted lampshades and pewter sconces. Hand-painted blanket chests, leather wing chairs, and sofas adorn the rooms, and on the Shaker tables flanking the beds are controls for the piped-in classical music. A pair of matching nightshirts, flannel in winter and cotton in summer, are available upon request. Dorothy has stocked every room with books, classics and short stories. Favorite rooms are the first-floor Gold Room and one on the third floor, with four skylights and a Franklin stove. The separate suite is a wonderful space, with a traditional leather-furnished living room and fireplace, a snack area, a new bath with a whirlpool tub and shower, and, upstairs, a headboard canopy and tree of life quilt.

Breakfasts are part of the romance at Smithton. In the plush breakfast room, guests eat a full gourmet meal by candlelight, which might include blueberry waffles or two-inch-thick cinnamon French toast.

ERWINNA

Evermay on-the-Delaware

River Road
Erwinna, PA 18920
215-294-9100
Fax: 215-294-8249

A gourmet's delight on the Delaware

Proprietors: Ronald Strouse and Fred Cresson. **Innkeeper:** Dawn M. Smigo. **Accommodations:** 16 rooms, all with private bath, including one 2-bedroom suite (12 rooms in main house, 3 in Carriage House, 1 in Cottage). **Rates:** Rooms $85–$160, suite $175; weekday discounts. **Included:** Breakfast, afternoon tea, bedside cordial, fresh fruit and flowers. **Minimum stay:** 2 nights with Saturday stay. **Added:** 8% tax. **Payment:** Master-Card, Visa. **Children:** Over 12 welcome. **Pets:** Not allowed. **Smoking:** Not allowed in dining rooms. **Open:** Year-round except Christmas Eve.

Of the dizzying number of country inns in Bucks County, Evermay on-the-Delaware is the easy choice for those in search of formal Victorian elegance, a supremely romantic setting, and the finest of dining. Owners Ronald Strouse and Fred Cresson made extensive renovations on the manor house in 1981, and after two years of success with their rooms introduced their superb restaurant in 1983.

The hamlet of Erwinna sits just across a narrow bridge from Frenchtown, one of New Jersey's charming antiquing villages; Erwinna is also a memorable 13-mile drive north of New Hope on winding River Road, which shoulders the Delaware. No matter what the approach, Evermay on-the-Delaware rests in rural seclusion, with a proximity to the river that few hostelries in the area can claim. The inn has views of the Delaware through trees and past a towpath that attracts a good number of walkers.

The Evermay was built in the 18th century and significantly remodeled in 1871. Listed on the National Register of Historic Places, it stands today behind a row of trimmed hedges and a circular drive, a regal, cream-colored building six windows across, trimmed with brown shutters. The first of its three stories is shaded by a Victorian porch that runs along the facade. The main house is the setting for 11 guest rooms and the dining area, and two outbuildings contain guest rooms with added privacy.

Room names read like a Round Table guest list of noted figures who lived in the area: Oscar Hammerstein, Edward Hicks, Josephine Herbst, S. J. Perelman, Henry Stover, James Michener, Dorothy Parker. The owners decorated the rooms with antiques, refinished and reupholstered with luxurious results. Victorian floral wallpaper is a fitting background for the carved headboards, marble-topped dressers, and converted kerosene lamps on pretty mismatched end tables. It is wise to invest in one of the larger rooms. Though the outbuildings are beautifully decorated in Victoriana, the main house is more authentic.

> The whole is often greater than the sum of its parts — in Evermay on-the-Delaware, this is quite an endorsement. With its picturesque setting right on the Delaware River, its romantic Victorian decor, and its outstanding cuisine, Evermay is a gem in Bucks County.

Guests relax in one of two beautifully decorated Victorian parlors, preparing for dinner with a glass of champagne or brandy. Owner Ronald Strouse is also the accomplished chef, specializing in creative contemporary American cuisine. The six-course prix fixe dinner is served on the enclosed back porch in one seating at 7:30. While the menu changes nightly, a guest might expect the following: hors d'oeuvres of smoked trout salad, sun-dried tomato crostini, and country pâté with green peppercorns; cioppino with saffron croutons; a Mediterranean vegetable tart; a salad of Boston lettuce and mache with violets and toasted walnuts with balsamic vinaigrette; grilled yellowfin tuna with lime-caper hollandaise served with poached asparagus and gingered baby carrots; and cheeses followed by dessert and coffee.

After the glorious meal, you'll be glad you're staying overnight. In the morning, you'll be treated to fresh fruit, croissants, pastries, granola, and a selection of cheeses. If you feel the need, you can walk off these elegant meals on the towpath.

Isaac Stover House

Box 68, Bucks Country
Erwinna, PA 18920
215-294-8044

> *A precious place
> and a designer's
> dream*

Proprietor: Sally Jessy Raphael.
Innkeeper: Susan Tettemer. **Accommodations:** 7 rooms, 5 with
private bath; 1 2-bedroom suite. **Rates:** With private bath
$175, with shared bath $150; suite $250. **Included:** Full
gourmet breakfast, afternoon refreshments. **Minimum stay:** 2
nights; 3 nights on holidays. **Added:** 6% tax. **Payment:** American Express, MasterCard, Visa. **Children:** Over 12 welcome.
Pets: Not allowed. **Smoking:** Only downstairs. **Open:** All
year.

The great majority of B&Bs are run by homeowners trying to
make a living; an intriguing few are owned by wealthy people
who love entertaining and decorating. The Isaac Stover House
is one of the latter, a life-size dollhouse owned by talk show
hostess Sally Jessy Raphael. It's a pricey, romantic place for
those who want to be surrounded by expensively refinished
antiques, lavish linens, and collectible Victoriana. The quiet
setting is ideal: just across a towpath from the Delaware
River, 13 miles north of New Hope.

Raphael and her husband, Karl, bought the 1837 Federal
brick mansion in February 1988. The only evidence of Victoriana outside is the gingerbread porch that extends the length
of the building, but it is from this era that Raphael chose to
decorate her inn. The Isaac Stover House opened after just
three months of nonstop renovation, during which time one
side of the listing house was raised four inches, ceilings were

torn down and rebuilt, and the extraordinary faux marble work was restored.

The strong arm of the decorator is evident: vibrant wall coverings in chintz or commanding patterns are accented by daring window treatments, often lace curtains framed by bold valances or balloon shades. Collectibles such as Scandinavian porcelain, 1920s *Vogue* covers, and quilted throw pillows are placed with a perfectionist's exacting touch in the right spots. Among the pieces are damask-covered slipper chairs hung with antique antimacassars, tassels on newel posts, a Victorian hat above a gilded French mirror, and tiny carved tables. There are dolls from around the world, Indonesian shadow puppets, and the owner's favorite — stuffed animals. The decorator often used simply draped material instead of moldings in the guest rooms.

> Set across the street from the Delaware River in the heart of quiet Bucks County, the Federal facade of the Isaac Stover House with its Victorian porch looks elegant and demure. Owner and talk show hostess Sally Jessy Raphael has made it something more: a gallery for decor, playfulness, and romance.

The Emerald City room has Wizard of Oz memorabilia and stuffed animals in a cradle; Loyalty Royalty is done in splashes of red and blue, with a stuffed toy fox dressed for the hunt, a fireplace, and a chart of the kings and queens of England. The bridal suite on the second floor has a white iron double bed facing the fireplace with views of the Delaware, and dozens of Norman Rockwell prints on the wall.

The third floor has four smaller rooms: Shakespeare and Company displays prints depicting scenes from his plays; the Amore Room has a mahogany bed and scenes of Italy; Cupid's Bower has a bas-relief of cherubim floating above the French bed on pink floral wallpaper.

Innkeeper Sue Tettemer is a great cook, fastidious housekeeper, and tasteful hostess who loves the home and respects her guests. Breakfasts are vast, including home-baked goods and an egg dish, and afternoon refreshments in an admirable variety are always just out of the oven. Be sure to book far in advance for dinner at neighboring Evermay on-the-Delaware.

FOGELSVILLE

Glasbern

2141 Packhouse Road
Fogelsville, PA 18051
215-285-4723

*A country inn
with creature
comforts*

Proprietors: Beth and Al Granger.
Accommodations: 23 rooms, all
with private bath, 11 with fire-
place, including 13 suites with whirlpool tub (in the Gate
House, the Carriage House, and the Farmhouse). **Rates:**
$100–$230. **Included:** Full country breakfast. **Minimum stay:**
2 nights with a Saturday stay. **Added:** $15 each additional
guest, 6% tax. **Payment:** Visa, MasterCard. **Children:** Welcome over 10. **Pets:** Not allowed. **Smoking:** Allowed. **Open:**
All year.

Glasbern's foundation is a 100-acre early-19th-century farm,
but guests today visit a country inn of contemporary comforts. When Beth and Al Granger bought the property in 1985,
it included the oversize barn (now the Gate House), a tractor
shed (the Carriage House), and a farmhouse (yes, the Farmhouse). A renovation of
two buildings combined
the feeling of the old with
the look of the new; and a
restoration of the modest
two-story Farmhouse at
the entrance of the prop-
erty retained a sense of
history.

**Glasbern is both a terrific
place for corporate retreats
and a fine place for
romantics, offering con-
temporary comforts in
historic buildings and fine
French cuisine. A unique
and successful inn, it's
worth a trip in itself.**

The Gate House exte-
rior is a vertical clapboard
reminiscent of barn sid-
ing, but the interior is all
contemporary sophistica-
tion. Half the building is
a bi-level dining area, divided in the middle by a stairway that
leads to two levels of rooms in the other half of the inn. Outside, form follows function, and a white spire interrupts the
plain wooden siding. The dining room is modern open space,

with a cathedral ceiling and plenty of windows and wood. The 14 rooms here are more modest than in the other two buildings, in informal Victorian or traditional decor, some with whirlpool tubs, all with televisions and VCRs, hair dryers, and phones — a far cry from clawfoot tubs, double brass beds, and log cabin quilts. Six rooms have outside entries.

The Carriage House has four rooms, including two suites on the first floor, all with fireplaces and whirlpools. These overlook the kidney-shaped swimming pool. Following the split rail fence, one reaches the Farmhouse, with three two-room suites, all with fireplaces and whirlpool tubs.

Chef Mark Shields is given free rein by the Grangers in his French country preparations, which range from $18 to $30. Appetizers might include carpaccio, thin slices of beef tenderloin, or escargot provençale, along with several soup and salad choices. The menu of six entrées changes weekly: possibly Norwegian pink salmon poached in champagne court bouillon or roast duckling stuffed with apples, pecans, and walnuts under a Grand Marnier and plum-cranberry glaze.

Glasbern has a bit of a formal atmosphere, owing in part to the large and important business clientele, who expect a certain sophistication and efficiency in their leisure.

HERSHEY

The Hotel Hershey

Box 400
Hershey, PA 17033
717-533-2171
800-533-3131
800-HERSHEY
800-437-7439

*A classic resort
for families,
romantics, and
chocoholics*

General Manager and Vice President: Patrick J. Kerwin. **Accommodations:** 243 rooms and suites, plus VIP guest cottage. **Rates:** April–November: from $252 per couple MAP and AP; rest of year: from $198 per couple MAP and AP. **Included:** Breakfast and dinner MAP; three meals a day AP; full use of Hershey Country Club. **Minimum stay:** Flexible 3 nights on holidays. **Added:** $54–$69 each additional adult, $24–$30 each child 4–9 years, $39–$49 each child 9–18 years, 6% tax, gratuities. **Payment:** Major credit cards. **Children:** Welcome, under 4 free. **Pets:** Not allowed. **Smoking:** Nonsmoking rooms available. **Open:** All year.

The Hotel Hershey is a grand resort of intriguing contradictions: a living part of a make-believe world; a luxury hotel adjacent to amusement parks, a zoo, and streetlights shaped like chocolate kisses; a town that makes world-famous chocolate set in rural Pennsylvania Dutch farmland; a sophisticated refuge for adults and a wondrous place for children. Over a million and a half people visit Chocolate World every year, but the Hotel Hershey accommodates overnight guests in a gracious, unhurried manner.

> **Travelers to Hershey may be surprised at the beauty of its grand resort hotel. Hotel Hershey was built in the 1930s, its plans drawn after Mediterranean hotels admired by Milton and Kitty Hershey. Offering more holes of golf per square foot than any resort in the world, Hotel Hershey is an elegant base from which to explore the town and HersheyPark.**

Many years after Milton Hershey's company had become successful and the reputation of the world's greatest chocolate bar was well established, Hershey decided to build a world-class hotel. In 1930, he showed his architect plans for the Heliopolis Hotel in Cairo, which he and his wife Kitty had greatly admired, but the endeavor proved too great. Instead, plans for the hotel were drawn from a postcard of a similar Mediterranean property.

The Depression-era structure gave employment to 800 workers and was finally completed in 1933. The five-story brick building has an extensive verandah that opens like outstretched arms. Its cream-colored brick is lined with Spanish arches, under a green tiled roof and twin bell towers. Its grand lobby has Mediterranean tiled floors and a mosaic. European reflecting pools adorn sculpted gardens, seen through the stained glass windows of the circular dining room.

The guest rooms are traditionally furnished, with reproduction furniture, classic fabrics, and all the expected amenities of a luxury property. The feeling is that of a country club, where guests dress for dinner and enjoy an indoor and outdoor swimming pool, fitness facilities, lawn bowling, shuffleboard, four tennis courts, and putting greens. There are no surprises inside the hotel, since all the surprises rest in the 76 acres of family entertainment at Hershey.

The vast holdings include HersheyPark, with 45 amusement rides; Chocolate World; 10 acres of ZooAmerica; the Hershey Museum of American Life; and 23 acres of flora and fauna at the lavish Hershey Gardens. Of the nonchocolate activities in town, golf is perhaps the most attractive, with 72 holes in the vicinity. Three championship 18-hole courses are at the Country Club and Parkview, and the Hotel Hershey Golf Course and Spring Creek add another 18 holes.

While many grand old resorts have a rather formal nature, the Hotel Hershey is an overwhelmingly friendly place. Milton Hershey's love of chocolate, children, community, and business is evident in every facet of his property.

HOLICONG

Barley Sheaf Farm

Box 10, Route 202
Holicong, PA 18928
215-794-5104

A classic B&B evoking Bucks County history

Proprietors: Don and Ann Mills; Don Mills, Jr. **Innkeeper:** Heather Knight. **Accommodations:** 10 rooms including 2 suites, all with private bath, 1 with fireplace (7 rooms in the main house, 3 rooms in cottage). **Rates:** $95–$175. **Included:** Full farm breakfast, Swiss chocolate truffles, sales tax. **Minimum stay:** 2 nights on weekends, 3 nights on holidays. **Added:** $17 each additional person. **Payment:** Major credit cards. **Children:** Over 8 welcome. **Pets:** Not allowed. **Smoking:** Allowed. **Open:** Closed Christmas week.

Before lyricist George Kaufman owned this stone farmhouse and entertained such notable guests as Lillian Hellman, S. J. Perelman, and the Marx Brothers from 1937 to 1954, Julianna Forge was the proprietress. An avid collector of Delaware Impressionists and first director of the Whitney Museum, she established an arts consciousness at the stone farmhouse, and it was she who built the elegant pool on the back lawns in 1927. There is a long tradition of creativity and entertaining at Barley Sheaf Farm which the Mills family gallantly continues today.

Inspired by English and Continental bed-and-breakfasts, Don and Ann Mills brought the concept to Bucks County in 1979. They have shared their home ever since, and they are in good company: Lyricist George Kaufman and art collector Julianna Forge were former owners of this wonderful 18th-century farmhouse.

A visit to Barley Sheaf is a step into history, both culturally and architecturally. There are two quite distinct parts to the house: the yellow stone part toward the back of the house was built in 1740, and the grander stone part from 1800. The guest cottage was built over the old ice house in 1910, and the 1820 barn was rebuilt after a fire in 1878.

During the 31 years that Don Mills worked in the perfume business, he and his family often vacationed in England and other parts of Europe. They were inspired by their travels to open a bed-and-breakfast and in 1979 introduced Bucks County to Barley Sheaf Farm. Ann Mills decorated each room in English country elegance from her own observations. A wonderful antique wallpaper called Aviary, a cream and rose pattern of several different birds, enlivens the entrance hall and the second- and third-floor hallways. Up the private stairs from the library, Room 6 has cheery floral wallpaper and window treatments and a fully furnished dollhouse. An antique doll family lives in a glass cabinet in Room 2. Room 1 is a suite with a queen-size brass sleigh bed, from which one can look over a wrought-iron balcony to the pool or enjoy the working fireplace in the sitting area. Room 4 has a bathroom as large as its sleeping area, with a glorious clawfoot tub in the center, bordered by pine wainscoting.

The cottage is a charming retreat, with three rooms centered around a common area with a large fireplace. The Hanora Coffee Room is named for its folk art wallpaper. A favorite room is Field of Flowers in a unique space under vaulted ceilings, brilliantly papered in a design of flowerets. It's suitable for those under six feet two.

In the morning, guests gather in the airy brick-floored breakfast room for a full meal of fresh fruit, zucchini muffins, ginger scones, bacon, and blueberry pancakes. On the vast acreage is a wonderfully shaped fishing pond stocked with catfish and wide-mouthed bass. For those who would rather cast their hooks in stores, Peddler's Village is just down the road.

The Golden Plough Inn

Peddler's Village,
    at Routes 202 & 263
Lahaska, PA 18931
215-794-4004
Fax: 215-794-4008

A small luxury hotel in Bucks County

Proprietors: Earl Jamison. **Manager:** Jerrod Godin. **Accommodations:** 60 rooms and suites (22 in main building, 15 in Merchants Row, others in Wagon House, Carriage House, and Carousel). **Rates:** $95–$300. **Included:** Continental breakfast, room refreshments, discount shopping coupons. **Minimum stay:** None. **Added:** $15 each additional guest, 6% tax. **Payment:** All credit cards. **Children:** Welcome. **Pets:** Not allowed. **Smoking:** Allowed. **Open:** All year.

There is plenty of history in Bucks County with B&Bs recalling its colonial days, the Victorian era, and the Algonquin Round Tablers who frequented the area in the 1930s. Those who enjoy history by day but prefer contemporary comforts by night may want to stay at the Golden Plough Inn. The setting is 30-year-old Peddler's Village in Lahaska, several miles from New Hope, where more than 70 shops, six restaurants, and an upscale inn were built by local developer Earl Jamison in 1989. Though the construction is nearly all new, Peddler's Village has an old feel: dinners in a colonial kitchen, quilt competitions, light tavern fare in a pedestrian setting.

The atmosphere at the Golden Plough is that of a luxury hotel, with formal service. Guest rooms are scattered throughout the complex, about half in the hotel, the rest in small numbers throughout the historic-looking complex, lending a bed-and-breakfast feel. The rooms are impressively decorated with Henredon reproductions and lovely Waverly fabrics.

> **Set amid history, farmland, and quaint hostelries, the Golden Plough Inn offers a contemporary perspective on Bucks County. It also offers Peddler's Village, for shoppers a destination in itself. Yet, however modern, the decor at the Golden Plough is traditional and includes local folk art and crafts.**

Much attention has been focused on art at the Golden Plough, with folk art and crafts, primitive cupboards, decoys, and dried flower wreaths and arrangements that make the rooms seems intimate and personable. All rooms have televisions hidden in armoires and refrigerators hidden in closets; one-third have fireplaces, and some have Jacuzzis.

Guests are offered an overwhelming selection of dining possibilities: the Cock 'n' Bull, with family-style colonial cooking, ranging in price from $11 to $22 for dinner; Jenny's, for country elegance with a French influence; and informal pub fare at the Spotted Hog, Peddler's Pub, and Hart's Tavern. There are endless activities in New Hope, Doylestown, and Bucks County, as well as ongoing seasonal activities at Peddler's Village.

MERTZTOWN

Longswamp Bed and Breakfast

RD 2, Box 26
Mertztown, PA 19539
610-682-4884

*A meticulous
B&B lost in
Pennsylvania
farmland*

Proprietors: Elsa and Dean Dimick. **Accommodations:** 10 rooms, 6 with private bath, 4 sharing 2 baths (6 rooms in main house, 3 rooms in cottage, 1 room in guest house). **Rates:** Main house $70, guest house $75; cottage $150. **Included:** Full breakfast, refreshments on arrival. **Minimum stay:** None. **Added:** $30 each additional adult, 6% tax. **Payment:** MasterCard, Visa. **Children:** Welcome. **Pets:** Not allowed. **Smoking:** Not allowed. **Open:** All year.

Near the small working-class village of Mertztown outside Allentown, Longswamp Bed and Breakfast is a huge 18th-century clapboard farmhouse accompanied by a barn and cottage, with walking trails throughout its five acres. After raising five children here, the Dimicks, a couple of boundless energy, interest, and talent, decided to open a bed-and-breakfast in 1983. When Dean is not tending to his private medical practice, he is on call at the bed-and-breakfast. The ubiquitous presence, however, is Elsa: full-time innkeeper and a half-time practicing psychiatrist. Even more notable than her sophisticated skills as host are her talents as an innovative cook, to be sampled at breakfast.

The farmhouse, more than 200 years old and at one time the post office and general store, was creatively remodeled by the Dimicks with huge airy common rooms. The double-sized living room is a delightful space, with a fireplace, two plush couches, a sitting area in front of a picture window overlooking the fields, and three walls stacked with books accessible by a rolling library ladder. Even more extensive than their reading collection is their listening library: Dean is the classical connoisseur and Elsa the jazz enthusiast. Just across the hallway from the living room is the dining room, with lovely vistas to the fields. Elsa loves having fresh flowers, vegetables, and fruits from the gardens around the house.

Signs of a fastidious innkeeper are everywhere: only the best queen-size mattresses, ample reading lamps, lots of prop pillows and current magazines. Elsa stripped and refinished every piece of antique furniture in the house, as well as the highly polished hardwood floors. The two rooms on the second floor are the Colonel's Room, named for Colonel Trexler, who built the house, and large Rachel's Room, done in blues. The four third-floor rooms share two baths; the largest rooms are the ones over the living and dining rooms.

> **Longswamp is a relaxing escape outside Allentown, near Doe Mountain ski area and not much else. The farmland is soothing and serene, and what better way to enjoy this landscape than with a stay in a 200-year-old farmhouse.**

More guest rooms are in the cottage, the first structure on the property, formerly a stop on the Underground Railroad. The Hideaway, on the first floor, is a private one-room guest house with a fireplace. The upper story, the Guest Cottage, is a magnificent space for families or couples traveling together: three rooms with an enormous open-beamed living room and stone fireplace, a private bedroom, and another bedroom under the eaves with a skylight and dressing area. The classic barn, built later, is inhabited by cats and has a full-size basketball court for guests to enjoy.

Allentown is just minutes away, antiquing is available nearby along the short route to Reading, and the Doe Mountain ski area is less than a five-minute drive.

MOUNT JOY

The Cameron Estate Inn and Restaurant

1895 Donegal Springs Road
Mount Joy, PA 17552
717-653-1773
Fax: 717-653-9432

A historic estate neighboring 18th-century Donegal Church

Proprietors: Abe and Betty Groff. **Innkeepers:** Stephanie Seitz, Larry Hershey, Mindy Goodyear. **Accommodations:** 18 rooms, 16 with private bath, 7 with fireplace. **Rates:** $60–$110. **Included:** Continental breakfast. **Added:** $10 each additional person, 6% tax. **Payment:** Major credit cards. **Children:** Over 12 welcome. **Pets:** Not allowed. **Smoking:** Allowed. **Open:** Closed Christmas Eve and Christmas Day

Eleven miles west of Lancaster and 13 miles from Hershey, the Cameron Estate Inn is a country haven with an air of faded Federal elegance. It has the scale and grandeur of a southern plantation, set on 15 acres of groomed and wooded grounds. Visitors can take advantage of the many hiking paths throughout the grounds, as well as a stocked trout stream. The large three-story brick house is set apart from civilization by a series of often unmarked country roads. On the lane approaching the estate is the landmark Donegal Church, built in 1721, which earned its way into history books through the Witness Tree made famous in the Revolutionary War.

The house was built in 1805 and was most importantly the home of Simon Cameron, Lincoln's first secretary of war. Abe and Betty Groff bought the estate in August 1981. Oriental scatter rugs and runners cover the hardwood floors. The rooms on the three floors reflect the traditional Federal decor in both antiques and reproductions. The rooms vary significantly in size and grandeur. The seven rooms with fireplaces, especially those at the front of the house, are quite regal; those under the eaves or dormers are more cozy. The rooms are comfortable, with restful views, leather wing chairs and good reading lamps, writing desks, and interesting artwork; but the baths need some updating.

> **Named for Simon Cameron, President Lincoln's Secretary of War, this early Federal mansion has an impressive exterior surrounded by 15 acres of lovely grounds. Be sure to take a meal at the owner's nearby restaurant, Groff Family Farm, renowned for its hearty American and Pennsylvania Dutch cooking.**

One dining room is warmed by a big fireplace; the other, in a glass-enclosed portico, is the setting for lunches and Sunday champagne brunch. For dinner, chef David Ritchey may prepare an appetizer of crab-stuffed mushrooms, followed by chicken and shrimp Versailles over wild rice, or veal Cameron sautéed with white wine and lemon. Dinner entrées range in price from $13 to $24, and Sunday brunch is very reasonably priced, with entrées from $4 to $9.50, including seafood crêpes and French toast with Grand Marnier sauce.

Be sure to make a pilgrimage to the Groff Farm Restaurant, four miles away. In a 1756 stone farmhouse, the Groffs' son Charlie prepares highly acclaimed American country food in two sittings Tuesday through Saturday. The meals are presented à la carte or family-style, all you can eat, at one price per entrée, from $13.50 to $23.50 per table, and include local vegetables and fresh bread. Betty Groff, who has written several successful cookbooks, masterminded the country recipes for prime rib, home-cured ham, and chicken Stoltzfus, with chunks of chicken in cream sauce served over flaky diamonds of butter pastry.

NEW HOPE

The Inn at Phillips Mill

2590 North River Road
New Hope, PA 18938
215-862-2984
Restaurant: 215-862-9919

A gristmill from 1750, now an enchanting inn

Proprietors: Joyce and Brooks Kaufman. **Accommodations:** 5 rooms, including 1 suite, plus Stone Cottage with large stone fireplace. **Rates:** $75 for rooms, $85 for suite, $125 cottage. **Minimum stay:** 3 nights recommended during holiday weekends. **Added:** 8% tax, $3.50 for Continental breakfast served in a basket. **Payment:** No credit cards. **Children:** Over the age of 10. **Pets:** Not allowed. **Smoking:** Allowed. **Open:** All year except January.

The town of New Hope offers a bewildering number of restaurants and bed-and-breakfasts. You can mix and match the two into a successful vacation, but an easy answer to the dilemma is the Inn at Phillips Mill, a delightfully romantic place to stay with equally wonderful food.

Joyce and Brooks Kaufman bought the property in 1972 and undertook an extensive renovation, marrying their formidable talents — he is a renowned architect, and she has an eye for European interior design. The property itself is a captivating stone structure that was built in 1750 as a barn abutting Aaron Phillips' gristmill across the road, which operated as such under four generations of this prominent Bucks County family.

The early colonial structure has low ceilings, wide-planked floors, and cavernous fireplaces. The rooms are made airy by wide, mullioned windows and doors that Brooks designed in jade-colored iron. There are two halves to the L-shaped building, reached by separate staircases. In one wing, two of the five rooms flank the second-floor dining area and are afforded privacy through castle-thick walls that bend away from the public spaces. One room has a cheerful green gingham bath with a clawfoot tub; another, above the main dining area, has a small sitting area in wicker and a rose-hued bedroom overlooking the back gardens. Room 3, an attic hideaway not for those over six foot five, has a Victorian cottage bed and Pierre Deux fabrics.

Joyce Kaufman very modestly describes her taste as "old barn," but it seems the essence of country formal. Small, cramped spaces have been turned into private havens. Room 4, in shades of rose and Pierre Deux fabrics, is ingeniously cozy, with its bed recessed into the wall and enclosed by drapery. Room 5 is a suite overlooking the backyard.

A special treat is the cottage, just steps away from the main inn's patio. It looks like a hamlet from an English fairy tale, with modern touches: the slate floors are heated, and the indigenous-looking fireplace was installed by Brooks. The upstairs bedroom is lovely, with a monastic look.

> North of town, just as the village disappears into the woods lining the Delaware, the Inn at Phillips Mill stands at a crook in the road. This architectural wonder could only be owned by an architect; its warm atmosphere could only be created by gracious hosts.

A brick walkway laces around the back gardens and kidney-shaped pool, viewed from the back dining room. A brilliant feature is the wood-burning stone fireplace here that may be removed in the warmer months so guests can dine al fresco.

The food at the inn is lovely, prepared by chef Richard Rohal, whose entrées range from $13 to $22. A sampling might include an appetizer of wild mushroom ravioli in a béchamel sauce, tender roast loin of pork in Calvados, and dessert of frozen blond mousse with bits of chocolate and nuts, Alsatian apple tart, or a heavenly Ilona torte, chocolate with a buttercream frosting.

The Logan

Ten West Ferry Street
New Hope, PA 18938
215-862-2300

> *The oldest building in New Hope, built in 1727*

Proprietors: Logan Inn Associates. **Innkeeper:** Gwen Davis. **Accommodations:** 16 rooms, all with private bath. **Rates:** $60–$150. **Included:** Full breakfast. **Minimum stay:** 2 nights on weekends April–November, 3 nights on holidays. **Added:** $17 each additional person, 8% tax. **Payment:** Major credit cards. **Children:** Welcome. **Pets:** Not allowed. **Smoking:** Allowed. **Open:** All year.

In a county abounding with bed-and-breakfasts, the Logan is a diverting change of pace. The only downtown hostelry in New Hope, the Logan is set right in the middle of town, enjoying the bustle of its busiest street. With 16 rooms, the Logan seems more like a hotel than an inn, especially because of the traffic in the dining rooms at mealtime. But the rooms are furnished with lovely antiques and thorough colonial decor, in a manner unique to a true country inn.

Built in 1727, the Logan is New Hope's oldest building and looks every bit its age, albeit well preserved. The first of its three stories is exposed fieldstone bordered by an overhanging green porch. Its next two stories are stucco over fieldstone, trimmed with green. It looks like an old stagecoach stop, as indeed it was, one of the first between Philadelphia and New York on the Shore Swift Line and one of the five oldest inns in the country.

Gwen Davis, the manager since the renovation and a member of the New Hope Chamber of Commerce, has set consistently high standards for her guest rooms: they have all-cotton sheets, down quilts, fresh flowers in warmer months replaced by plants in winter, remote televisions hidden in cabinets, and telephones. Rosemont reproduction pencil post queen-size canopy beds are reached by wooden steps, and some rooms have old and valuable antiques — especially Room 6, which features a Victorian armoire from the 1890s and a carved mahogany bed. The interesting prints on the wall are for sale, as are some antiques and works by local artists. The front rooms are far preferable to those in back (numbers 1, 2, 12, and 14), which are small and comparatively uninspiring.

The tavern, set in the oldest part of the inn, has an imposing stone fireplace and a true colonial feel of heavy ceilings and thick walls. The fascinating murals were painted in the 1930s and restored by a local artist. There are two dining rooms, a formal Gallery Room and an enclosed glass atrium where guests take a full breakfast, the latter featuring a stained glass wall made by local artist Val Sigstedt. Chef Alviero Faschi may prepare chicken Valdostana, Logan crab cakes, or other Continental foods, ranging from $12 to $20. In warmer months, meals are served on the tented slate patio.

> **Long before Washington crossed the Delaware, the Logan Inn stood on its banks, on the main road through New Hope. A drink in the tavern — the inn's oldest section — will give a traveler a sense of what life was like before our country was born.**

Wedgwood Collection of Historic Inns

111 West Bridge Street
New Hope, PA 18938
215-862-2570

A Victorian perspective in New Hope

Proprietors: Nadine Silnutzer and Carl Glassman. **Innkeepers:** Wedgwood Inn, Arlene and Tim Stephan; Umpleby House, Kirk and Tracy Wentzel; Aaron Burr House, Mary Gerdes and Larry Weber. **Accommodations:** 18 rooms, including 6 suites (6 rooms in each house, plus a 2-story Carriage House with kitchenette and fireplace). **Rates:** $70–180. **Included:** Continental breakfast served in a basket, afternoon tea, evening turndown. **Minimum stay:** 2 nights with Saturday reservation. **Added:** $20 each additional person, 6% tax. **Payment:** No credit cards. **Children:** Check with innkeeper. **Pets:** Check with innkeeper. **Smoking:** Not allowed. **Open:** All year.

While many people retire to the industry of innkeeping, it was a first career for Carl and Dinie Glassman. They started with the Wedgwood House in 1982 as young innkeepers and newlyweds, restoring the three-story 1870 Victorian clapboard guest house to a six-room bed-and-breakfast. They painted it Wedgwood blue with their large pottery collection in mind, and business took off. When the neighboring house went up for sale in 1985, Carl and Dinie bought the 1833 Classical Revival stone house. This time their restoration took only three months, resulting in the six-room Umpleby House. The trilogy was completed in 1990 with the acquisition of the Aaron Burr House across Bridge Street, several houses toward town. Built in 1854 by the same unknown author of the Wedgwood House, it was named for the vice president who sought refuge in Bucks County fresh from his duel with Alexander Hamilton. All three houses retain that feeling of safe haven.

> **The three Wedgwood bed-and-breakfasts are not quite modern, but they are about a hundred years newer than the other inns of this historic region. The Wedgwood inns pay homage to 19th-century architecture and antiques.**

The main house has six guest rooms, four with private baths. The house is marked by a historic carriage on the front lawn painted the same Wedgwood blue, maroon, and white. Just steps away is a historic Victorian gazebo, the original wellhouse, a lovely setting for the extensive weekend afternoon teas.

The adjacent Umpleby House is a cream-colored Federal stucco with maroon shutters and arguably offers the nicest accommodations. Dinie's antique-hunting has yielded some spectacular pieces and old light fixtures.

Across the street and down the block, the Aaron Burr is a yellow clapboard house with arched Wedgwood blue shutters. Several of the six rooms have fireplaces, and two have king-size beds. The second-floor sitting area has a lavish fireplace and lovely Empire furniture set on random-width black walnut floors. The third-floor rooms under the gables are particularly charming. Guests who want extra privacy may want to consider the Carriage House.

All guests can expect a breakfast basket with homemade granola, broiled grapefruit, capuccino chocolate chip bread, freshly baked muffins or danish, croissants, homemade jams, and fresh juice and fruit; afternoon refreshments; evening turndown; lovely Victorian common rooms and parlors centering around stoked fireplaces; fresh flowers and handmade quilts; original artwork, most by Dinie's great-aunt Sara Winston; and, of course, ubiquitous Wedgwood pottery.

Service is personal and never intrusive, with two innkeepers per home and the ever-present Glassmans overseeing new projects with zeal and knowledge. An added blessing is the proximity to a town sorely lacking in parking — horse-drawn carriage rides are offered to town. The town park is across the street.

READING

The Inn at Centre Park

730 Centre Avenue
Reading, PA 19601
610-374-8725

> *A breathtaking mansion in Reading*

Proprietors: Andrea and Michael Smith. **Accommodations:** 4 rooms with private bath, including 3 suites, of which 2 have fireplaces. **Rates:** $130–$220. **Included:** Full breakfast, basket of fruit on arrival. **Added:** 6% tax, $22 additional guest. **Payment:** MasterCard, Visa. **Children:** Check with innkeeper. **Pets:** Not allowed. **Smoking:** Not allowed. **Open:** All year.

The Inn at Centre Park could not be built today — not only would costs be prohibitive, but many of the rare materials simply cannot be found. Andrea and Michael Smith, natives of Reading, had their eye on the old Wilhelm mansion for years and bought it in early 1989 when the property went up for sale. Five months of restoration transformed this three-story mansard-roofed stone house from a spooky mansion into one of the grandest properties in the region.

The city's only original Gothic mansion was built in 1877 across from Centre Park. The unbelievably beautiful original artistry includes ornate plaster ceilings and elaborate crown moldings where cherubim play, stained glass in most of the windows, a two-story curved bay addition in copper, quarter-sawn oak floors, built-in sideboards in the formal dining room, eight fireplaces (five working) with faux or real marble mantels, including one that is seven feet high, and unusual Mercer tile designs that decorate the entire back of the exterior first floor exterior.

> **Even its magnificent exterior won't prepare the visitor for what's in store inside Reading's only Gothic mansion. Elaborate crown moldings frame ornate plaster ceilings hung with cherubim clothed in vines; the windows are vibrant with stained glass; one of the eight fireplaces is seven feet high; and Mercer tile decorates the entire room. Save the Inn at Centre Park for a special occasion.**

The drama begins with a step into the foyer, finished in elaborate Bradbury and Bradbury wallpapers. To the left is a sitting room with beautiful Victorian antiques, above which hover some of the plaster angels in the moldings. To the right are an informal dining area and a living room with overstuffed couches on a Bokhara rug. Straight ahead is the magnificent dining room with a barrel-vaulted ceiling.

Guests are greeted with a basket of fruit, and every room has a stocked refrigerator. The Green Room has a sitting area separated from the bedroom by a wide archway, above which is a transom of elaborate leaded and stained glass. A little sitting area in the bedroom rests within the copper bay addition, with three floor-to-ceiling windows. At the foot of the bed is a working fireplace, above which hangs a huge carved mirror. The grand and rare Old World bath has geometric tiles, the original clawfoot tub with a new shower, and an arched beveled window that admits light from a hallway. Terry robes are provided so guests may step out onto the balcony accessible from the bath, which also rests over the copper bay.

The most magnificent room rests in the back of the mansion. The sitting room has a carved wood fireplace seven feet high inset with a mantel of red Austrian marble. A hallway is trimmed with more carved wood, with an archway decorated with wooden cherub faces supported by wooden columns. The bedroom has a white wood sleigh bed, teal plaster trim, and, most rare, a Mercer tiled fireplace and ceiling. The bath is another beautiful Old World room with star-shaped tiles, a marble sink, and a window seat with wood shutters.

The stone Carriage House behind the mansion, larger than many a house, was built in 1890 for the drivers and horses. The two-bedroom suite here has wonderful stained glass dormer windows.

Andrea cooks a sumptuous breakfast, a finishing touch for a fantasy-filled stay. The Smiths have plans to open an intimate restaurant at the inn. The inn is in the heart of Reading, a short walk to restaurants and sights.

Philadelphia and Environs

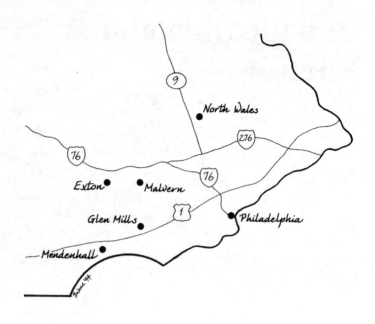

Best Romantic Retreats

Glen Mills
Sweetwater Farm
Mendenhall
Fairville Inn

Best for Urban Intimacy

Philadelphia
Independence Park Inn
Thomas Bond House

Best for Metropolitan Magnificence

Philadelphia
Four Seasons Hotel
Hotel Atop the Bellevue
Omni Hotel at Independence Park
The Rittenhouse
The Ritz-Carlton, Philadelphia

Best Country Inns

Exton
Duling-Kurtz House
Malvern
Historic General Warren Inne
North Wales
Joseph Ambler Inn

There was a great deal of excitement and refurbishment in **Philadelphia** for the 200th anniversary of the Constitution, and the city still shows its pride. Having served almost continuously as the nation's capital from 1774 to 1800, the city still retains a great sense of importance to historic America. Bordered to the east by the Delaware River and to the west by the Schuylkill River, Philadelphia was designed by William Penn to be a "greene countrie town," with five pastoral commons. Independence National Historic Park, in the eastern part of the city, would fill a week's worth of activity. Betsy

Ross, Edgar Allan Poe, and Norman Rockwell have histories tied to Philadelphia, and their respective museums are open to the public. The Rodin Museum has the largest collection of the artist's work outside France; the Franklin Institute Science Museum and Planetarium is an interactive museum; and, of course, the Philadelphia Museum of Art is internationally renowned. The 8,700-acre Fairmount Park is the world's largest landscaped city park, with 100 miles of jogging paths and America's first zoo, from 1874.

To the north and west of town, you will find nice retreats in **Malvern, Exton,** and **North Wales;** to the southwest is the beautiful countryside of the Brandywine River Valley. Winterthur Museum and Gardens and the Nemours Mansion and Gardens are museums of homes established by the Du Pont family; Longwood Gardens is a world-renowned horticultural display on 350 blissful acres; the Brandywine River Museum celebrates the geniuses who were inspired by this landscape, including three generations of Wyeths; and finally, a traveler must stop at the Chaddsford Winery.

EXTON

Duling-Kurtz House

146 South Whitford Road
Exton, PA 19341
610-524-1830
Fax: 610-524-6258

A cozy country inn between Philadelphia and Lancaster

Proprietors: Michael Person. **General Manager:** Tish Marescalchi. **Accommodations:** 12 rooms, all with private bath, including 3 suites. **Rates:** $80–$120 weekends, $50–$70 weekdays. **Included:** Continental breakfast. **Added:** $15 each additional guest, 6% tax. **Payment:** Major credit cards. **Children:** Over 2 welcome. **Pets:** Not permitted. **Smoking:** Allowed. **Open:** All year.

Many historic properties are named for the founding fathers who lived there; the Duling-Kurtz House is named for mothers. Former owners Raymond Carr and David Knauer proudly passed on their mothers' maiden names to their pride and joy. In 1982, the business partners began to revive the 1830 clapboard farmhouse to its present use as a restaurant and also restored the neighboring stucco barn to house 18 guest rooms. Some of the guest rooms were expanded to two-room suites and now number 12.

> **Philadelphia's suburbs go on forever. As you drive west on Route 30, the traffic never seems to subside even though the farmland gets richer and flatter. A turn off this main artery transports you to the real countryside and the Duling-Kurtz House, known for its lovely dining and pretty accommodations.**

Duling-Kurtz House is about halfway between Philadelphia and Lancaster, just off commercial Route 30. Once you turn off the highway onto South Whitford Road, the setting abruptly changes to the serene 12 acres of manicured lawns, with a rose garden and gazebo and an audible brook. The inn is best known for its dining, with seven dining rooms in the original 1830 house, a curious working beehive oven, and seven Palladian windows across the back of the house that provide views of the gardens and fields. The bar and waiting area is a charming spot, with two plaid couches before a huge fireplace. Some dining rooms are decorated in simple period antiques; the second-floor bar and informal dining area is sunny and preppy, with white wicker and green carpeting. The restaurant, directed by chef Gilles Moret, has been favorably received. His Continental and American menu, around $20 for entrées, may offer rack of lamb or fresh lake trout.

The Duling-Kurtz House solves a problem that many country inns encounter by providing private space for overnight guests so they will not be disturbed by evening diners. Guests approach the barn via covered brick walkway. All the rooms have interesting configurations, with odd shapes and nooks and crannies where one finds an unexpected wing chair. Rooms are traditionally furnished in good reproductions, in Williamsburg rusts and blues, and in English toile, with spotless new baths. All rooms have televisions, and five have fireplaces. Even standard rooms are generously sized.

Sweetwater Farm

50 Sweetwater Road
Glen Mills, PA 19342
610-459-4711

A remarkably romantic refuge in the Brandywine Valley

Proprietors: Jonathan Propper. **Innkeeper:** Leigh Hunt. **Accommodations:** 6 rooms, 3 with private bath; 5 cottages, some with fireplaces. **Rates:** Rooms $145–$165, with weekday discounts; cottages $150–$225. **Included:** Full breakfast. **Minimum stay:** Some weekends. **Added:** Saturday dinner with advance notice, 8% tax. **Payment:** Visa, MasterCard, American Express. **Children:** Welcome. **Pets:** Small pets allowed. **Smoking:** Allowed outside. **Open:** All year.

Like a Wyeth painting, Sweetwater Farm captures the untouched nature of the Brandywine River Valley and the warmth of the homestead, looking more like a memory from the past than a picture from the present. This 1734 fieldstone structure is just 35 minutes from Philadelphia and 20 from its airport and Wilmington, Delaware. From the rural, wooded 50-acre setting, to the gracious innkeepers, to the colonial and Federal architecture and the elegant, Old World rooms, this is one of the bed-and-breakfast properties in the Mid-Atlantic.

The circular drive from the wooded country road is a majestic introduction to Sweetwater Farm. In early spring, magenta and bright pink azaleas bloom along the drive and around the fieldstone manor house with its white trim and red shutters (slate blue in the back of the house).

Guests enter through the 1815 Federal half of the manor. The halls and rooms are wide and grand, and all the Federally austere wood and plaster work is original. To the right is a large double living room with some elegant antiques and dentil-carved fireplace (one of nine in the house); to the left is an informal library with an enormous collection of books and a hidden television for viewing old movies. The dining room displays a formidable china collection and an 1865 hunt print on the wall. This is the setting for Leigh's elaborate cuisine: breakfast could be an egg dish or chocolate waffles.

> **Halfway between Philadelphia and Wilmington is heaven on earth: Sweetwater Farm is as close to perfection as a country bed and breakfast can get. Its 50 acres — with horses and sheep and endless flowers — are home to a 250-year-old fieldstone manor house. Andrew Wyeth could have painted here.**

Each of the four rooms on the second floor Federal side of the house has a fireplace and candles on the mantel: the Georgian, the Nursery, the Master Bedroom, and the Calabrese (with private bath). The Nursery is typically lovely, with butter-yellow walls and tulip stenciling, embroidered white antique linens, and a settee in front of the fireplace, over which hangs a Wyeth print. All the beds are gorgeously dressed, if not with antique linens then with Laura Ashley prints and patterns.

The older, three-story part of the building was built by Quaker farmers in 1734. It's a smaller, low-ceilinged version of its Federal partner, with a convivial kitchen with hanging baskets and an early American primitive table. The second floor has the enchanting Garden Room with a curtained four-poster bed, three Williamsburg windows overlooking the back fields, and a huge bath.

The five cottage rooms are good for families or romantics and are very private. The Window Box has a practical bent, with kitchenette and washer and dryer. The Greenhouse, with a glass atrium ceiling, has two bedrooms. The Gardener's Cottage is intimate and lovely, with a sitting room, corner stone fireplace, and a pretty floral bedroom. Attached by a front porch is the Herb Room, tiny and cute, with an adorable little bath. A favorite is the Hideaway, a two-story cottage with views to the fields through leaded windows, featuring a marvelous beehive fireplace and loft bedroom.

In warmer months there is an airy sense about this house; a generous back porch with white wicker furniture overlooks the big oval pool, one of the cottages, and the groomed grounds. Several horses are boarded in the pastures.

MALVERN

Historic General Warren Inne

Old Lancaster Highway
Malvern, PA 19355
610-296-3637
Fax: 610-296-8084

A landmark of hospitality for 250 years

Proprietors: Jim Creed and partners. **Innkeeper:** Karlie Davies. **Accommodations:** 8 suites, all with private bath. **Rates:** $85–$135. **Included:** Continental breakfast. **Minimum stay:** None. **Added:** 6% tax, $10 for additional guest. **Payment:** Major credit cards. **Children:** Over 12. **Pets:** Not allowed. **Smoking:** Allowed. **Open:** Closed Christmas Eve and Christmas Day.

Built as an inn in 1745 to serve the stagecoach line from Lancaster to Philadelphia, the Historic General Warren Inne serves hearty food in colonial dining rooms and offers unusual two-room suites for overnight guests. It's an austere gray stucco building, two full stories under a third dormer story, just off the hectic intersection of Routes 202 and 30 a short drive west of Philadelphia. First named the Admiral Vernon Inn after a British naval officer, the inn was purchased by William Penn's grandson, John, during the Revolution. Penn was a British sympathizer, and the inn became a Tory watering hole. After the war, assuredly to gain a new clientele, Penn renamed the inn after Bunker Hill hero General Joseph Warren.

In 1981, Jim Creed and partners restored the inn with the intention of making it a restaurant. In 1985, the second- and third-floor rooms were renovated as guest rooms and a two-story addition housed a third dining room and more guest rooms. In 1990, the rooms were transformed into two-room suites.

There are five suites on the second floor and three on the third on an intimate scale. All rooms are furnished with Williamsburg reproductions. Stencils dance on the walls over period prints, and trim is painted in Williamsburg colors. Little steps lead up to beds, some with fishnet canopies and quilts. The more authentic rooms have dark-stained floors with scatter Oriental rugs, and those in the new wing have muted wall-to-wall carpeting. All the rooms have private baths, small but well appointed. Three of the suites have working fireplaces, and all have televisions, VCRs, and telephones.

The main dining room is in the recent addition, though it looks as colonial as possible, with spindleback chairs, tables covered in modest white cloths, and scatter Oriental rugs over the dark-stained floor, warmed by an original fireplace. Dinners are served every night but Sunday and range from $17 to $24, with entrées such as beef Wellington and roast duckling. With chef Thomas Estak in charge, the General Warren features tableside preparation of its specialty dishes, such as Dover sole and, for two, rack of lamb and Château-briand. Lunches, served weekdays, are reasonably priced under $10 and include broiled filet mignon with béarnaise sauce and the specialty, Wiener schnitzel General Warren. The brick patios in the back of the house are a lovely addition to the inn.

> **Travelers have come to the Historic General Warren Inne for hearty colonial fare since colonial times. The guest rooms have probably changed most over the years and have recently received a great deal of attention. The addition of Williamsburg furnishings, colors, and stenciling has resulted in very appealing accommodations.**

MENDENHALL

Fairville Inn

Route 52, Kennett Pike, Box 219
Mendenhall, PA 19357
610-388-5900
Fax: 610-388-5902

*A pinnacle
of beauty
and comfort
near Winterthur*

Proprietors: Patricia and Ole Retlev. **Accommodations:** 15 rooms, all with private bath, 7 with fireplace (5 rooms in Main House, 4 rooms in Barn, 6 rooms in Carriage House, including 2 suites with fireplaces). **Rates:** $100–$175. **Included:** Afternoon tea, Continental breakfast. **Minimum stay:** 2 nights on most weekends. **Added:** 6% tax. **Payment:** Major credit cards. **Children:** Over 10 welcome. **Pets:** Not allowed. **Smoking:** Allowed. **Open:** All year.

However daunting the sprawl and congestion may be between suburban Philadelphia and Wilmington, the Fairville Inn has escaped it all. Set back like a country estate from wooded Route 52 near Chadds Ford, the Fairville Inn is a picturesque stone and clapboard manor house 10 minutes north of Wilmington and about 30 minutes west of Philadelphia in the heart of the Brandywine Valley. Longwood Gardens, Winterthur, and the Brandywine River Museum are nearby, as well as horse-racing. It is a tasteful retreat, immaculate, quiet, and private. There is an overwhelming sense of comfort in the large rooms, most with fireplaces, balconies, telephones, televisions hidden in highboys, and large and elegant baths.

After owning an inn in Vermont and working as ski instructors, Patricia and Ole Retlev wanted a property that would keep them busy all year. They fell in love with the hamlet of Fairville, its proximity to the two major cities and wonderful museums, and the wonderful 1820s manor house. In 1986, they restored the butter-colored stone farmhouse, with its five guest rooms, a large common living room, and comfortable breakfast area. They built the Carriage House and redid the Barn behind to provide 10 additional guest rooms, which some may prefer for added space and privacy. Ole commissioned a local artist to do the oil paintings hung throughout the inn. These copies of Dutch master prints are all for sale.

The rooms are done in reproduction Queen Anne furniture, with traditional color schemes. Patricia is always redecorating, with perfect details that give the effect of a showroom.

Preferable rooms are in the two charming outbuildings, white vertical clapboard trimmed in dark green, with serene views of the dale behind the property and trees framing a pond set in gently sloping pasture. The two-story Carriage House is more elegant: all of its six rooms have balconies, three have fireplaces, and some have cathedral ceilings, exposed beams, and canopy beds. The bathrooms are very large, with copper fixtures and separate wash areas. The Barn has four extremely large rooms in two stories, with two-poster king- or queen-size beds, fireplaces, and ample sitting areas.

> **Ten miles north of Wilmington, with hints of Longwood Gardens wafting in the air, Fairville Inn sits in a wooded knoll. This is a superior bed and breakfast. Every aspect has been beautifully prepared by the tireless innkeepers.**

Tea is elaborate and sociable at Fairville, with cold and hot drinks and plates of little homemade cakes and cookies in the breakfast room. Ole and Patricia are almost always present with helpful details of where to dine and what museums to see. Breakfast is a freshly baked Continental affair, featuring Patricia's truly memorable muffins.

NORTH WALES

Joseph Ambler Inn

1005 Horsham Road
North Wales, PA 19454
215-362-7500
Fax: 215-361-5924

> *A handsome country inn north of Philadelphia*

Proprietor: Richard Allman. **Innkeepers:** Steve and Terry Kratz.
Accommodations: 28 rooms, all with private bath (13 in the Barn, 9 in the Main House, 6 in Corybeck Cottage). **Rates:**

$95–$140. **Included:** Full breakfast. **Added:** $15 each additional guest, 8% tax. **Payment:** Major credit cards. **Children:** Welcome. **Pets:** Not allowed. **Smoking:** Allowed. **Open:** All year.

A half hour's drive north of downtown Philadelphia, the Joseph Ambler Inn is fairly lost in its rural setting yet surprisingly close to urban sprawl. The inn opened in 1983 as a 15-room bed-and-breakfast. Today, after renovations and the addition of the restaurant in 1989, the Joseph Ambler has evolved as well into a successful dining spot and corporate retreat.

> **The Joseph Ambler Inn admirably straddles the line between corporate and romantic retreat. Just 13 miles north of Philadelphia, the inn is enveloped by 13 bucolic acres. Old and new are both uniquely represented.**

There are two distinct faces to the Joseph Ambler Inn, one for corporate guests and one for casual weekenders. The Main House is for romantics, dating to 1734 with additions in 1820 and 1929. Its nine rooms have a distinct colonial feel, decorated with some period antiques and faithful reproductions. There are three common rooms downstairs in simple Williamsburg decor, including the 18th-century living room and the schoolroom with its walk-in fireplace. Of the four rooms on the second floor, the Penn Room is the earliest, with sloping ceilings, warped random-width floorboards, and tiny low windows overlooking the front fields. The Roberts Room is perhaps the nicest, with a yellow canopy atop the queen-size bed, matching curtains and chairs, and a separate sitting area. The three charming rooms on the third floor have dormer windows set under the eaves and exposed beams and brickwork. Even the smallest, the Wright Room, is an adorable hideaway with soft floral Victorian wallpaper and upholstered window seats.

The 1820 Barn has the same color scheme as the Main House, fieldstone with cheery butter yellow and barn red trim. The 1820 Barn was completely renovated in 1987, and the only testament to the past is its thick stone shell, which is nicely exposed on the interior in the guest and dining rooms. The restaurant, opened in March 1989, is decorated with colonial reproductions, handmade cherry tables, and Windsor chairs on random-width floors. An airy wooden stairway leads to the 12 guest rooms on the second and third floors. Rooms here are more contemporary than in the Main House, furnished with useful reproductions, modern baths, televisions in highboys, desks, and telephones.

The clapboard tenant farmer's house was built in the 1920s and named Corybeck for the crows and blackbirds that migrated to the farm yearly. The seven rooms here are small and cute, with canopy beds and stenciling. All rooms have access to the front porch or private patios. Here, as elsewhere, the baths are all new and fresh.

Dinners range from $17 to $24, with emphasis on seafood and beef. Rack of lamb is the house specialty, served with Dijon mustard and bread crumbs or with apple and jam sauce.

PHILADELPHIA

Four Seasons Hotel

One Logan Square
Philadelphia, PA 19103
215-963-1500
Fax: 215-963-1439
800-332-3442

> *A grand
> contemporary hotel*

Proprietor: JMB Urban Development Co. **General Manager:** John Indrieri. **Accommodations:** 371 rooms, including 91 suites. **Rates:** Rooms $260–$650. **Included:** Complimentary shoeshine, morning paper, use of fitness facilities. **Added:** $20 each additional guest, 13% tax. **Payment:** MasterCard, Visa, American Express. **Children:** Welcome. **Pets:** Allowed. **Smoking:** 7 of 8 floors nonsmoking. **Open:** All year.

Although the Four Seasons Philadelphia has a contemporary facade, it is one of the city's senior properties. Philadelphia's hotel boom occurred in the mid-1980s, beginning with the opening of the Four Seasons in 1983. The majority of its guest rooms and the public spaces have a superb view of Logan Square's Swann Memorial Fountain — recently restored after a $2 million fundraising effort — fashioned by Alexander Stirling Calder and installed in 1924. The fountain, also referred to as Three Rivers, represents the Delaware, Schuylkill, and Wissahickon rivers.

This eight-story gray granite structure takes up an entire city block. The trademark Four Seasons wide hallways are finished in polished rose marble, the walls a light wood.

> **Superior service is a hallmark of Four Seasons properties, but this hotel is memorable for its guest rooms. Most have a view of the Museum of Art; but guests need only look as far as their own rooms for a special exhibit. Furnishings have been copied from Philadelphia Federal pieces in the museum.**

The decor of the guest rooms is historically appropriate, with colors of blue-cocoa and ivory-rust. The well researched wallpapers are unusually patterned. Some rooms have interesting pieces like an English wing chair in a toile print or perhaps an armoire with delicate inlay. All the rooms have stocked mini-bars. Bathrooms are furnished with a plush terry robe, scale, telephone, and hair dryer.

The popular Fountain Restaurant is formal, with tapestry chairs and geometric carpeting. Three meals are served under the supervision of chef Jean-Marie Lacroix; dinners range from $20 to $30. The Swann Lounge is a cushy, plush place for afternoon tea, intimate conversations, and a Viennese dessert buffet on evening weekends, accompanied by the Tom Lawton jazz trio. In the outdoor Courtyard Café, a lovely alternative in warmer months, visitors enjoy light-fare dining under umbrellas to the music of a cascading fountain on a backdrop of flowers and greenery.

The complete Health Spa offers an indoor swimming pool, Jacuzzi, sauna, fitness classes, and an exercise room with universal equipment. Swedish, shiatsu, and sport massages are available.

Families are happy at the Four Seasons. Children are treated to milk and cookies upon arrival, child-size terry robes, special menus, Nintendo and children's movies, as well as the Swann Lounge brunch, with stuffed animals and toys and edibles like Jell-O squares, M&M cookies, chicken fingers, mini-pizzas, and bite-size hot dogs.

Hotel Atop the Bellevue

1415 Chancellor Court
Philadelphia, PA 19102
215-893-1776
215-732-8518
800-221-0833

> *A classic
> French Renaissance
> revival*

Proprietors: Cunard Hotels and Resorts. **Managing Director:** Chris Van Der Baars. **General Manager:** Ruedi Bertschinger. **Accommodations:** 173 rooms, including 28 deluxe and 50 junior suites. **Rates:** Rooms $210–$250, suites $275–$400, presidential suites from $850. **Included:** Daily newspaper, shoeshine. **Added:** $20 each additional guest, 12% tax. **Payment:** Major credit cards. **Children:** Welcome. **Pets:** Not allowed. **Smoking:** Nonsmoking rooms available. **Open:** All year.

The Bellevue rivals the finest property in any American city. This grand architectural landmark, just three blocks from City Hall, was reworked during three years for more than $100 million and reopened in March 1989.

The original Bellevue Hotel was owned by George Boldt in 1881 and sat across Walnut Street from its present locale. Boldt's reputation as an unsurpassed hotelier prompted the Astor family to request his presence at their Waldorf-Astoria in 1898. Four years later, in 1902, Boldt returned to Philadelphia and built the Bellevue-Stratford with $8 million. The massive French Renaissance edifice opened in 1904, with immense curved stairways, lavish plaster crown moldings, and lighting fixtures designed by Thomas Alva Edison. Each of the 529 guest rooms was heated with its own fireplace. A rose garden on the rooftop was transformed in winter to a skating rink.

While heeling faithfully to the original grande dame, the recent renovation created quite interesting spaces: the first 11 floors now contain offices and shops including Gucci, Ralph Lauren, Dunhill of London, Pierre Deux, and Tiffany. The guest rooms are on floors 12 through 17, surrounding a seven-story indoor atrium and the informal Conservatory Restaurant.

> **The Hotel Atop the Bellevue sits on the top six floors of a 17-story architectural masterpiece. The top floor is the home of two magnificent restaurants.**
> **Linked to a 95,000-square-foot fitness club and a European spa, the Bellevue is a city resort.**

In 1986, the interior design firm of Tom Lee, Ltd., led by Sarah Tomerlin Lee, was hired to mastermind the decor. Since little remained of the original hotel but the Edison fixtures, Mrs. Lee created an imaginary period landscape. The decor of the 19th floor and reception areas is described as late Victorian verging on Edwardian, with belle époque playfulness. The guest rooms are done in American Empire. The side street entrance and lobby were inspired by the London Ritz.

The Conservatory atrium is a serene space, overlooked by half the guest rooms. The creamy white tones of the 3,600-square-foot piazza feel warm in winter and cool in summer. The light wicker furniture, lush plantings, green and white tiled floor, fountains, and glowing lanterns all rest under a 75-foot mural of clouds, supported by four columns.

The elevation of the Bellevue reveals two domes atop the building — the Barrymore Lounge and Founders restaurant, with a small library tucked between. The Barrymore Lounge, introduced by a portrait of the eponymous actress, is the setting for afternoon high tea, evening cocktails, and hors d'oeuvres. The room looks like an inverted Wedgwood teacup, with seven shades of pale blue offset by white plaster molding, culminating in a ceiling mural painted with tassels and swags on a background of stars — the theme echoed in the upholstery and the carpet.

Across the hall at Founders, the dining areas look more like parlor sets, observed by cast-iron statues of influential Philadelphians from each corner of the room. American regional and Continental cuisine is served to the music of a trio, a preamble to Friday and Saturday night dancing. The Philadelphia Library Lounge rests between, where guests enjoy a fireside drink while browsing through a thousand books by or about Philadelphians.

The guest quarters are unusually large at the Bellevue, averaging 460 square feet, decorated with reproduction and antique American Empire furnishings and period wall coverings and borders. All have stocked mini-bars, cherry armoires with televisions, VCRs, and stereos, executive desks, and three telephones. The marbled baths are luxurious, with a separate vanity area, hair dryer, makeup mirror, bidet, scale, telephone and television, terry robes, and slippers. At turndown, a report of tomorrow's weather is propped next to chocolates.

It is rare for a city hotel to have a fitness center, and near to impossible to have one like the Bellevue's. In the connecting building is the Philadelphia Sporting Club. Though it has an outside membership, Bellevue guests have unlimited use of this 95,000-square-foot facility, which fills several floors in utilitarian, neoclassic elegance. Among its features are 125 Nautilus machines, a jogging track, a five-lane junior Olympic indoor pool, and racquetball, handball, squash, and basketball courts. There are also Jacuzzis, saunas, and steam rooms, a sports medicine center with cardiovascular conditioning, massage therapy, and a health bar and café.

For pampering after exercise, the luxurious Pierre and Carlo European Spa Salon is in the Bellevue Shops. Its experts are trained in complex hydrotherapy, application of mineralized body masks, facials including aromatherapy, body scrub, algae hand and foot treatments and reflexology, as well as thorough massage.

Service is to the Bellevue as beauty is to its setting: integral, quiet, classic, and elegant.

Independence Park Inn

235 Chestnut Street
Philadelphia, PA 19106
215-922-4443
800-624-2988.
Fax: 215-922-4487

A cozy inn overlooking Independence Park

General Manager: Thierry Bompard. **Accommodations:** 36 rooms, all with private bath. **Rates:** $120–$155; weekend and corporate rates available. **Included:** Continental breakfast, afternoon tea. **Minimum stay:** None. **Added:** $10 each additional guest, 12% tax. **Payment:** Major credit cards. **Children:** Welcome. **Pets:** Small pets welcome. **Smoking:** 2 of 4 floors nonsmoking. **Open:** All year.

Business travelers on a budget or who prefer an intimate, informal environment will adore the Independence Park Inn. Weekend visitors will appreciate the personal service and proximity to Philadelphia's Independence Mall.

The elegant granite building was built in 1856 as a dry goods store for a wealthy merchant named John Elliott, designed by architect Joseph C. Hoxie to reflect the grandeur of the owner's accomplishments. In this century, the building served as a baby furniture warehouse before it was bought and restored in 1988 by the present owners, whose efforts put the building on the National Register of Historic Places.

The exterior is five attenuated stories tall, with five high and narrow double-arched windows across the front of the six-columned exterior. The lobby is lovely, with grand floor-to-ceiling windows and tufted leather couches in front of a working fireplace. Wood floors are covered with a large Oriental rug. Guests are treated to a lavish afternoon tea in this elegant setting. Toward the back of the lobby is a long, narrow, sunny atrium where the Continental breakfast is served.

There are nine rooms on each of the upper four floors, each one decorated slightly differently. The front queen and king parlor rooms are preferable for their lovely views of Independence Park seen through long three-quarter windows hung with

> **This elegant granite building was revived in 1988 to its original 1856 condition, putting it on the National Register of Historic Places — a fitting honor in a neighborhood replete with historic significance. Casual and friendly, Independence Park Inn is a very pleasant stay.**

heavy striped curtains tucked behind brass tiebacks. All rooms are furnished with two-poster beds and reproduction Chippendale furniture. The rugs are a bright green, and the walls are hung with historic Philadelphia prints. Televisions are hidden in large armoires, and two telephones are provided in each room. The baths are nice but unexceptional. The smaller rooms that overlook the atrium are good for the budget-minded; the friendly service is the same for all rooms at the Independence Park Inn.

This is a casual place in an exceptional piece of architecture. While the innkeeper may be dressed in suit and tie during the week, the inn relaxes quite nicely on weekends to a leisurely pace. Convenient to historic sites, the Independence Park has the same professional virtues as the many luxury hotels nearby, on an intimate, friendly scale.

Omni Hotel at Independence Park

Fourth and Chestnut Streets
Philadelphia, PA 19106
215-925-0000
800-THE-OMNI
Fax: 215-925-1263

> *A luxury hotel on
> Independence Park*

Proprietor: Omni Hotels. **General Manager:** David J. Colella.
Accommodations: 155 rooms on 12 floors. **Rates:** $205, weekend specials. **Minimum stay:** None. **Added:** 12% tax, $20 additional guest. **Payment:** Major credit cards. **Children:** Yes.
Pets: Yes. **Smoking:** 3 nonsmoking floors. **Open:** All year.

With this comparatively intimate full-service hotel, Omni put a new face forward in 1990, introducing its first small European-style luxury hotel. The location directly across from Independence Park is perfectly suited to the new image.

The building nicely complements the historic structures of eastern Philadelphia. Its 13 brick stories, with abundant windows, rest above a two-story limestone base. The gabled peaks at the roofline have clerestory windows. Common rooms include a formal area and a more contemporary space for socializing and music, including a jazz trio on weekends. Large windows have views to the park and street.

> **Visitors to Independence Park will want to consider this terrific new hotel, Omni's flagship European-style property. Not only does it offer a terrific location and elegant public spaces, the Omni's signature restaurant, Azalea, has received enthusiastic reviews for its regional American food.**

On the second floor is Azalea, which has lovely treetop views of Independence Park through floor-to-ceiling Palladian windows. The room, like the lobby below, is light and airy, softly furnished in light wood and pastel colors. The chefs are proud of their reliance on local farms for fresh herbs and vegetables, creating dishes like brook trout with cornmeal crust topped with smoked bacon, or tea-smoked duck breast with honey and chestnut purée and walnut-stuffed figs.

There are about a dozen rooms on each of the 13 floors above — all facing Independence Park. While the color schemes of brown and beige are muted, the rooms are capacious, with large windows and lovely marble baths.

Below ground is a lap pool with serene indirect lighting. The enthusiastic staff is helpful and excited about its new role in Philadelphia.

The Rittenhouse

210 West Rittenhouse Square
Philadelphia, PA 19103
215-546-9000
800-635-1042

> *The most
> luxurious hotel
> in Philadelphia*

Proprietors: Amerimar Realty Company and General Electric Pension Trust. **General Manager:** Paul E. Seligson. **Accommodations:** 98 rooms, including 12 suites. **Rates:** Rooms $235–$260 weekdays, $130–$150 weekends; suites $300–$350. **Added:** $25 each additional guest, 12% tax. **Payment:** Major credit cards. **Children:** Welcome. **Pets:** Small pets allowed. **Smoking:** Every other floor nonsmoking. **Open:** All year.

Philadelphia is lucky to have two quite different consummate luxury properties, in the Hotel Atop the Bellevue and the Rittenhouse, which received its first five-diamond award from AAA in 1992. In addition to housing 98 beautiful guest rooms, the Rittenhouse has a deluxe health club and spa, two highly rated restaurants, nonpareil views of Rittenhouse Square, and the exclusive Nan Duskin women's boutique.

The Rittenhouse sits on the west side of Rittenhouse

Square, one of William Penn's five original city squares. Despite surrounding history, the Rittenhouse is a modern piece of architecture, a glass trapezoid that looks like a very wide staircase standing on its side. The lobby is a beautiful array of olive, taupe, teal, and cream, featuring ash wood millwork, pine Louis XIV bergères, smooth round columns supporting a coffered ceiling with massive ceiling sconces and polished golden marble underfoot.

> **The 6.5-acre commons were named for David Rittenhouse, who in 1792 was named first director of the United States Mint, and yes, Rittenhouse Square feels like old money. The hotel represents the square's elegance beautifully: tasteful, interesting, sumptuous, and unsurpassed in this city.**

The Cassatt Tea Room and Lounge rests beyond the columns, named for the family whose mansion graced this site. The lounge is the setting for afternoon tea, cocktails, and piano music amid the tapestried French chairs and huge potted trees. In the warmer months, the arched French doorways open to a trellised garden café.

Rittenhouse accommodations are oversized and beautiful, reputed to have the finest baths in Philadelphia. Half of the guest rooms have not only wonderful views of Rittenhouse Square but interesting interiors with 90-degree alcoves. The staterooms are decorated in country French themes, navy blues and camels, with striped bergères, Queen Anne chairs and writing desks, and border paper matching the striped drapes. Each room has three phones (one in the bath), a VCR and two televisions (one in the bath), and a mini-bar. Other suites are done in Laura Ashley pink chintz, with an upholstered king-size headboard under a gathered crown canopy. The beige and light brown marble baths have a hair dryer and terry robes. Even the hallways are graced with original art, among which are paintings by Joe Barker, who was discovered selling his paintings outdoors by the Rittenhouse's developer, David Marshall.

Award-winning Restaurant 210 offers contemporary cuisine at lunch and dinner in a high-tech elegant setting overlooking the square. Neoclassic mahogany chairs and millwork, black and beige upholstery, black silk banquettes, and silver linen on the walls and columns make a muted back-drop for colorful abstract art. Executive chef Gary Coyle came from New York's La Côte Basque. His entrées, all above $20, include grilled magret of duck with smoked apple and jimaca torte and green peppercorn sauce; preceded perhaps by Maine lobster medallions with tarragon roe quinoa and lobster dress-ing; or Savoy, leek, and oyster pot pie.

TreeTops is a floor below, a pleasant café decorated with rattan chairs, pastel yellow walls, and terra cotta floors that shares the view of Rittenhouse Square. The jumbo lump crab cakes have been highly praised around town. The woody Boathouse Row Bar is the home of the *Liz Ann,* a scull that John B. Kelly, Grace's father, rowed to a gold medal in the 1920 Olympics.

The Toppers Spa and Fitness Center opened in August 1990. The facilities include a pool, sauna, steam room, row-ing and cycling machines, Stairmasters, and Cybex exercise equipment. The Esthetique Spa features massage, aromather-apy facials, seaweed body wraps, body scrubbing and polish-ing, and hydrotherapy baths.

The Ritz-Carlton, Philadelphia

17th and Chestnut Streets at
  Liberty Place
Philadelphia, PA 19103
215-563-1600
800-241-3333

> *A landmark
> in Philadelphia
> at Liberty Place*

Proprietors: Liberty Place Hotel As-sociates. **General Manager:** Jim Beley, under the Ritz-Carlton Hotel Company. **Accommodations:** 290 rooms, including 17 suites. **Rates:** Rooms $195–$265, suites from $425; weekend rates from $149. **Included:** Five complimentary meal presen-tations on the Club level. **Minimum stay:** None. **Added:** $35 each additional guest, 12% tax. **Payment:** Major credit cards. **Children:** Welcome. **Pets:** Not allowed. **Smoking:** Nonsmok-ing rooms available. **Open:** All year.

Ritz-Carlton hotels represent the finest in sophisticated Old World hospitality, inspired by the Ritz of London. With rich wood paneling, extensive art collections, lavish antiques, and elegant and comfortably furnished public spaces, all of the Ritz-Carlton properties emulate stately mansions and English country manors.

The Philadelphia Ritz opened in November 1990. To get here, look for the city's version of the Chrysler Building. Liberty Place is two twin glass skyscrapers, one of which pierces the sky with its needle tip. A 15-story adjunct rests between them, containing the Shops at Liberty Place, with about 70 boutiques and specialty stores, and the Ritz-Carlton, Philadelphia.

> One of Philadelphia's newest luxury hotels already feels like a classic.
> With 18th- and 19th-century oils, Italian marble floors, classic molding, and handwoven carpets, the interior of this elegant place belies its postmodern exterior — a gleaming skyscraper that has made its mark on Philadelphia's skyline.

Guests enter a foyer at ground level from the busy street front and take an elevator to reception, a floor above. Such is the Ritz-Carlton way, ridding the lobby and reception area of the street's bustle. When the elevators open, all is as it should be: the trademark Italian marble floors gleam, handwoven carpets muffle one's step, fine paintings are kind to the eye, and the softspoken staff is eager to assist.

The common spaces on the reception floor are lovely and civilized. The Dining Room serves formal French cuisine under the direction of starred Michelin chef Philippe Reininger. In this American Federal room, guests dine under crystal chandeliers on bone china and the Ritz-Carlton trademark cobalt blue glasses, with Waterford crystal oil lamps on each table. The Grill and the Grill Bar serve lighter fare in a dark, clubby atmosphere, with rich wood molding and ceilings. The walls are covered in green damask, lit by the flame in a wood-burning French fireplace. The Lobby Lounge serves morning coffee, afternoon high tea, and cocktails in the evening, with a relaxing backdrop of live classical music or a jazz trio.

The guest rooms are reliably lovely. The wallcoverings are gray damask, the furnishings traditional. The baths are entirely marble, with two terry robes. The two top floors of guest rooms are under the tutelage of the Ritz-Carlton Club, with their own concierge and lounge and five complimentary meals a day. The beautiful red Oriental hall carpet is modeled after one in the original London Ritz.

The fourth-floor Fitness Center has a Nautilus and a rowing machine, two bikes, a dry sauna, Jacuzzi, and massage therapy upon request, all in a pristine marble setting.

Thomas Bond House

129 South Second Street
Philadelphia, PA 19106
215-923-8523
800-845-2663

*A city B&B
and a historic
landmark*

Proprietors: National Park Service. **Innkeeper:** Jerry Dunne. **Accommodations:** 12 rooms, all private baths. **Rates:** $80–$150. **Included:** Full breakfast weekends, continental breakfast weekdays, wine and cheese in evenings. **Minimum stay:** None. **Added:** 12% tax, $15 additional guest. **Payment:** Visa, MasterCard, American Express. **Children:** Yes. **Pets:** No. **Smoking:** Yes. **Open:** All year.

Visitors to Independence National Historic Park in Philadelphia can extend their daily walk through the 18th century with an overnight stay at the Thomas Bond House. Though the neighborhood is in transition, visitors may appreciate the inn's proximity to the Visitors' Center Welcome Square and the nearby Customs House, Penn's Landing, and Society Hill.

This three-story brick brownstone, the home of Ben Franklin's personal doctor, is within walking distance of Independence Park. Built around 1769, it has been restored by the National Park Service.

The narrow front of the building, three mullioned windows across, faces South Second Street. Inside are two dining areas, informal and formal, with vivid blue toile wallpaper. During the week, Continental breakfast is served, expanded to a full breakfast for leisurely weekend guests who dine at colonial tables handmade by a local artisan. To the left is the formal parlor, furnished with Williamsburg antiques, where guests enjoy wine and cheese in the early evening.

There are four guest rooms on the second floor, six on the third floor, and two tucked into the fourth floor. Decorated in colonial simplicity, the rooms are comfortable and quite clean, with reproduction Williamsburg furniture and twin, double, or queen beds covered with pretty white lace over blue duvets. Electric candles sit on windowsills, and old Philadelphia prints decorate the walls. Each room has a television tucked in a highboy, and businesspeople will appreciate the desk and telephone. The baths have new brass fixtures and oxford stripe skirts below the sinks.

Below the Thomas Bond House is the Key and Quill Shop, established in 1976, which sells reproductions of 18th-century colonial furniture, accessories, and antique maps.

Central and Western Pennsylvania

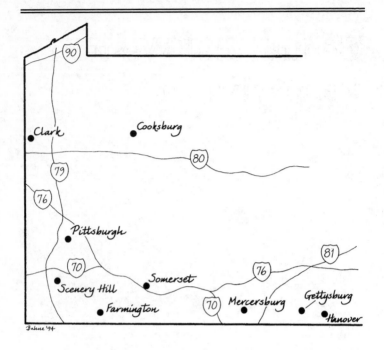

Balne '94

Best Romantic Retreats

Clark
Tara – A Country Inn
Mercersburg
The Mercersburg Inn

Best Remote Refuge

Cooksburg
Gateway Lodge Country Inn and Restaurant

Best Resort

Farmington
Nemacolin Woodlands Resort

Best for Urban Intimacy

Pittsburgh
The Priory – A City Inn

Best for Metropolitan Magnificence

Pittsburgh
Pittsburgh Vista
Westin William Penn

Best Village Bed-and-Breakfasts

Gettysburg
The Brafferton Inn
Hanover
The Beechmont Inn

Best Village Inn

Scenery Hill
Century Inn

About an hour's drive from Wheeling, West Virginia, and from Youngstown Ohio, **Pittsburgh** sits in the southwest part of its state at the confluence of the Ohio, Monongahela, and Allegheny rivers — the Golden Triangle. George Washington surveyed the land, named Fort Pitt in 1758, the history of which is detailed at Fort Pitt Museum. Just east of the Golden Triangle is Three Rivers Stadium in Oakland, also home of the Carnegie, which houses the Museum of Art and the Museum of Natural History, and the Frick Art Museum. And be sure to pay homage at the new Andy Warhol Museum.

Erie sits 100 miles north of Pittsburgh, the only bit of "coast" in the state, on the Great Lake of its name. In the city's center is the Old Customs House, and the Erie Art Museum within this Greek Revival monument. On the city's outskirts is a wonderful recreational facility in Presque Isle State Park, a peninsular spit of beach and greenery.

Western Pennsylvania is the home of dramatic and wild forests: on your way to the Cook Forest in **Cooksburg** and the Clarion River, under the Allegheny Forest, make a pilgrimage to luxurious living at one of the state's most civilized of hostelries, Tara in **Clark.**

CLARK

Tara — A Country Inn

3665 Valley View Road
Clark, PA 16113
412-962-3535
800-782-2803

An antebellum mansion in northwest Pennsylvania

Proprietors: Jim and Donna Winner. **General Manager:** Deborah DeCapua. **Accommodations:** 27 rooms, all with private bath. **Rates:** $198–$318 MAP; 20% less on weekdays. **Included:** Breakfast, dinner, and afternoon tea; use of spa facilities. **Minimum stay:** None. **Added:** 6% tax. **Payment:** Visa, MasterCard, Discover. **Children:** Not allowed. **Pets:** Not allowed. **Smoking:** Limited. **Open:** All year.

After the novel came the movie, then the sequel — then the inn! True romantics erring on the side of fantasy will love

Tara. Few successful hostelries have a theme, and even fewer execute their ideas as tastefully as does Tara, an elegant country inn in northwest Pennsylvania done in the style of Scarlett O'Hara's family plantation. Jim and Donna Winner have owned this 1854 mansion since June 1986. They recently completed an addition that includes 14 rooms and spa facilities with mineral baths. A second AAA four-diamond award proves that their hopes for Tara have not gone with the wind.

The two-story white brick house has a double-story portico supported by six Ionic columns. The many common rooms have the generous scale of a plantation house, furnished with Civil War–

> It's no small surprise to run across the majestic, awe-inspiring sight of Scarlet O'Hara's home an hour north of Pittsburgh. When greeted by staff in hoop skirts, surprise turns to incredulity — and then sheer pleasure. While some may object to the theme, they will be easily outnumbered and assuredly convinced by fans of Tara.

era antiques. To complete the antebellum illusion, the female staff members are dressed in hoop skirts. All is genteel, chivalrous, and elegant. Guests are greeted at the door with smiles and in their rooms by a basket of wine and cheese.

Named either for characters from the book or Civil War themes, the guest rooms at Tara are thoroughly and beautifully decorated. Donna has seen *Gone With the Wind* at least 20 times, vows her niece and sales director Laura Shaffer, simply to garner more ideas for the inn. Throughout are precious antiques, majestic armoires, and lovely bed and window treatments in sweeping silks and tapestries. Gas fireplaces add to the romance in many rooms. There are whirlpool baths in many rooms. The Victorian Room has a lace-draped canopy bed; Master Gerald's room is done in dominating regal reds; Rhett's Room has an intriguing gathered canopy; and Belle's Room is a lovely boudoir with a white satin canopy bed. Breakfast is brought to the rooms on a tray, with fresh banana bread, a coffee cake muffin, coffee, juice, and a fruit cup with raspberry sauce.

Dining at Tara is equally lavish. A piano player sets the formal tone in Ashley's Gourmet Dining Room, a stunning setting for a six-course meal prepared tableside and executed with white glove service. The Old South Restaurant serves family-style. Stonewall's Tavern serves semiformal Continental cuisine in a fabulous cozy grottolike setting among the thick stone walls of Tara's foundation. The wine list is one of Pennsylvania's largest, with more than 150 bottles in the award-winning cellar.

The spa facility was conceived when the Winners discovered that the well underneath their property has a mineral content nearly as high as that of White Sulphur Springs. The impeccable staff is anticipatorily attentive. The Winners are extremely enthusiastic and manage to keep an intimacy about this emerging property.

COOKSBURG

Gateway Lodge Country Inn and Restaurant

Cook Forest, Box 125, Route 36
Cooksburg, PA 16217
814-744-8017
800-843-6862 in Pennsylvania and
    Maryland

> *A hearty neighbor of Cook Forest State Park*

Proprietors: Joe and Linda Burney.
Accommodations: 8 rooms in lodge, 3 with private bath; 8 1- to 4-bedroom cottages, all with fireplace and kitchen. **Rates:**

Rooms $85–$165, cottages $95–$125. Range reflects choice of meal plans: guests may choose from EP, B&B, and MAP for 4- and 7-course meals. **Included:** Use of lap pool for lodge guests only. **Minimum stay:** 2 or 3 nights in cottages. **Added:** 6% tax, 15% service gratuity. **Payment:** MasterCard, Visa, American Express. **Children:** Must be over 8 to stay in the lodge; all ages welcome in cottages. **Pets:** Permitted; $15 per day. **Smoking:** Allowed. **Open:** All year.

The rustic Gateway Lodge looks more like an Adirondack cabin than a northwestern Pennsylvania country inn. This charming lodge was built in 1934 of hemlock and pine logs, with walls and trim in wormy chestnut and oak flooring. Guests enter from the fabulous rough-hewn front porch, with exposed beams and log railings, decorated with a handmade rope swing and wicker chairs. The lounge looks like a movie-set version of a log cabin. The walls are made of heavily chinked pine and hemlock logs, the enormous weathered stone fireplace crackles and snaps at

> Hemlock and pine, wormy chestnut and oak — that's what country inns are made of in this neck of the woods. Gateway Lodge and its cottages are remote, nestled a quarter of a mile north of the Clarion River and the 6,500 acres of Cook Forest State Park.

readers lounging on country plaid sofas, and weighty wood beams support the low log ceiling. Through a low doorway is the dining room, also with chinked log walls as well as a wagon wheel chandelier and tables dressed in country gingham for breakfast and reset with formal pewter and kerosene lanterns at dinner.

The eight lodge rooms are quite small but charmingly cozy. They are furnished with hand-hewn wormy chestnut or brass double beds covered with calico or Amish antique quilts, quaint antique furnishings, and braided oval rugs. The cottages are so rustic that guests must bring their own towels, linens, and kitchen supplies.

Abundant dinners are served in four or seven courses, with soup or salad, two relishes, a loaf of homemade bread and honey butter, mashed potatoes and vegetables, and ice cream or sherbet. The menu includes hearty country recipes like filet mignon with herbed butter; rock Cornish game hens with apple and sausage stuffing and apple glaze; pork chops with bread stuffing, rock Cornish game hens with sausage stuffing, chicken cordon bleu, or baked trout filled with crabmeat, ranging from $14 to $32. Homemade gourmet pies are among the desserts. Afterward, guests can socialize in the old Tap Room.

When Joe and Linda Burney bought the Gateway Lodge and its cottages in 1980, they added an indoor swimming pool, four feet deep and heated to 92 degrees. They also added a country store, which sells some of the crafts displayed throughout the inn, including Amish quilts and rope swings. They and their staff are kind and ever-present at this unpretentious woodsy retreat. Seventeen miles of cross-country ski trails are maintained through the Cook Forest State Park; visitors may rent skis, skates, and snowshoes at the Lodge. Among other park activities along the Clarion River are fishing, tubing, canoeing, and horseback riding.

FARMINGTON

Nemacolin Woodlands Resort

Box 188
Farmington, PA 15437
412-329-8555
Fax: 412-329-6198
800-422-2736

The state's finest new resort and spa

Proprietors: Pete and Maggie Hardy Magerko. **General Manager:** Charles F. Inglasbee, Jr. **Accommodations:** 163 rooms, including 98 rooms in the main inn, with 8 suites; and 65 1- and 2-bedroom accommodations in three condominium units. **Rates:** $139–$250, with seasonal variations. **Included:** Use of all facilities except greens fees. **Minimum stay:** None. **Added:** 6% tax, $15 additional guest, $20 additional guest in condominiums. **Payment:** Major credit cards. **Children:** Welcome in condominiums. **Pets:** Not allowed. **Smoking:** Allowed. **Open:** All year.

The rural town of Farmington, 12 miles southeast of Uniontown, is near the reckoning spot between Pennsylvania, Maryland, and West Virginia. This remote setting is home to Pennsylvania's most luxurious new resort. Named for a Delaware Indian guide, Nemacolin Woodlands is an exclusive property set on 1,000 acres in the Laurel Mountains, renowned for its top spa facilities and award-winning golf academy. The contemporary Tudor buildings were designed by Craig Johnson. Flags fly from the gabled

> **In the midst of the lush Laurel Mountains in southwestern Pennsylvania, the state's finest new resort has made a quiet home for itself. An award-winning spa makes this an enticing, exciting destination.**

rooftops of the main buildings, their Tudor themes echoed in varied structures that dot the vast landscape like outbuildings on a plantation.

The property was once used in 1959 as a hunting preserve for the Rockwell family. Joe Hardy bought the land in 1987 and after stunning embellishments — including a copper roof on the Woodlands Spa and a 4,000-foot airstrip — opened Nemacolin Woodlands in 1988. Inside, visitors will find a surprisingly cosmopolitan interior designed by Amy Storrs, with varied and colorful marble underfoot and classic archways and moldings done in rich mahogany. The Hardys — and now the Magerkos — worked hard to amass their eclectic collections of painting and sculpture. The traditional furnishings are covered in richly patterned materials. The Inn Manor has guest rooms as well as an upper and lower lobby, group facilities, a library, the Club Room, Joseph's, Café Woodlands, the Rose Garden, Fables Lounge, the large wine cellar, and acclaimed dining in Allures and the Golden Trout.

The guest rooms on four floors are exceptionally lovely,

with an intriguing European influence. All rooms, from resort doubles to deluxe penthouse suites, are individually decorated, with brass or canopy beds or rich wood headboards, plush club chairs, and original art. The classic architecture rendered interesting interior spaces set under eaves, with oblique angles and unusual configurations. The furnishings are traditional reproductions in dark wood, with colorful wallpaper and rich fabrics. Some rooms have balconies overlooking the mountains and whirlpools, and all have minibars.

Facing the inn at the base of a circular drive is the three-story Woodlands Spa, reputed to be one of the country's most luxurious. Gloriously appointed in several marbles and rich inlaid wood, the spa has three large, varied floors. The ground level has an indoor pool (heated to 90 degrees), aerobics studios, and a Keiser weight room. The main level has whirlpools, lockers, a boutique, and a lounge and juice bar. The upper level houses the beauty salon and facial treatment and massage facilities. The grassy croquet court is on one side of the spa, and a plethora of activities is nearby: tennis, badminton, and shuffleboard courts, the outdoor swimming pool, the Woodlands Activities Center, and Misty Gardens, the greenhouse with an on-staff botanist who provides the wonderful fresh arrangements seen throughout the rooms and property.

The par 71 golf course is 6,643 yards, and from the Gazebo Snack Shop golfers have views of Maryland and West Virginia. PGA pros teach at the Golf Academy with state-of-the-art equipment and on a specially designed short game at the super range. Playing the links on the Nemacolin course is a great way to tour the property. The fairways run past Lakes Louise, Dottie, and Carol, named for the women in the Hardy family, and past the condos at the Links and Fairway Villas line. Outer fairways run past the riding stables. In addition, a Pete Dye course is planned for the near future.

The staff has been thoroughly trained in a team effort that prompts professional, efficient, and friendly service. Guests venturing outside the groomed grounds of Nemacolin will want to go whitewater rafting at the neighboring Ohiopyle State Park or visit Frank Lloyd Wright's Fallingwater or the Laurel Caverns.

GETTYSBURG

The Brafferton Inn

44–46 York Street
Gettysburg, PA 17325
717-337-3423

*A historic home
in the heart
of Gettysburg*

Proprietors: Jane and Sam Back. **Accommodations:** 8 rooms, all with private bath, including 2 suites.
Rates: $70–$95. **Included:** Full breakfast. **Minimum stay:** None. **Added:** $10 each additional person, 6% tax. **Payment:** MasterCard, Visa. **Children:** Over 8 welcome. **Pets:** Not allowed. **Smoking:** Restricted to Atrium and Garden areas. **Open:** All year.

Those visiting Gettysburg College and those exploring history will love this eclectic bed-and-breakfast and its charitable hosts. The Backs are newcomers to innkeeping from Connecticut academia, close friends with the Agards who ran this hostelry for nearly a decade. In a town of such historic importance, an inn is somewhat obliged to cater to the past, and the Brafferton does so easily. Part of its convincingly historic atmosphere is a Union bullet, lodged in a mantel during the July 1, 1863, Gettysburg battle.

The Brafferton's stone facade looms over the sidewalk, trimmed in Williamsburg blue. In the living room are a player piano and various top hats, part of a vast collection dispersed throughout the house. Down a step is the breakfast room, an addition built in the 1860s, exceptional for the primitive mural painted by local artist Virginia McGloughlan depicting 18 historic Gettysburg landmarks and scenes. While guests study the scenery, they are treated to a vast breakfast that may include peaches and cream French toast, all prepared by Jane and Sam.

The main house has four rooms upstairs and a room in the back: of these, the Master Bedroom, at the front of the house, is the largest, and the Child's Room is the smallest. These rooms are decorated with spare colonial simplicity. The stencilwork is a highlight; it was copied by Virginia McGloughlan from 17th-century designs.

> A stay at the Brafferton Inn really gets a visitor in the mood to experience history. Its new owners have revived the wonderful elements of this great old house and retained its integrity. Most enjoyable is breakfast, surrounded by four walls of a primitive mural depicting Gettysburg scenes.

The six rooms downstairs are the more luxurious. These rooms all have private baths, some antique brass beds, quilts, and stencilwork, and they overlook the herb garden out back. The Garden and New rooms are most desirable, with a pretty view of the flower and herb gardens. The Atrium, which connects the old stone house and its brick addition stretching off the back, is a lovely common space for guests, with exposed brick walls lighted by the greenhouse roof.

High tea is served to Brafferton guests and to the public three afternoons weekly. The delicacies include chocolates, scones, tarts, and finger sandwiches.

HANOVER

The Beechmont Inn

315 Broadway
Hanover, PA 17331
717-632-3013

*A friendly B&B
in a Federal town*

Proprietor/Innkeepers: William and
Susan Day. **Accommodations:** 7
rooms, all with private bath, including 3 suites and 2 with
fireplace. **Rates:** $70–$125. **Included:** Full breakfast, afternoon
tea. **Minimum stay:** 2 nights in suites on weekends. **Added:**
6% tax, $10 additional guest. **Payment:** MasterCard, Visa,
American Express. **Children:** Over 12 welcome. **Pets:** Not allowed. **Smoking:** Not allowed in guest rooms. **Open:** All year.

Any street named Broadway would signify a certain amount
of hubbub, and the Beechmont Inn certainly is in the thick of
things in Hanover. It's a period piece of 1834 Federal elegance,
as is the entire town itself, which saw a battle during the War
between the States. Today the town is a sleepy destination for
weekend shoppers and antiquers heading to nearby New
Oxford and Abbottstown.

The Days recently bought the barn-red Beechmont Inn
from former longtime owners Terry and Monna Hormel, who
fully restored the property in 1986. The Days are keeping up
the same fine standards as their predecessors, including their
fine breakfasts, which feature cheese tarts, breads, and homemade granola.

There are three common rooms, including a formal sitting
area with Federal reproduction furniture and green swag cur-

tains, a game room, and a dining room with hints of the modern day in its parquet floor. The sideboard was built in the 19th century, along with the grand corner cupboards.

The Diller suite is the largest accommodation, with a marble fireplace and a whirlpool bath. The Hershey Suite has a separate entrance and a fireplace. The grand wallpaper mural along the front stairway is from a Chinese silk motif. Among the prettiest rooms upstairs are the Farnsworth, with lovely reproduction Victorian wallpaper and a street view; the Custer, with a blue antique quilt on the wall; and the Stuart, with a "marriage bed" for particularly close couples. The Hampton Suite has a private porch and a full kitchen from its days as a private apartment.

> Twelve miles west of Gettysburg and midway between Harrisburg and Baltimore, pretty Hanover is a transition town. But for antique-lovers, admirers of Federal architecture, Civil War buffs, and for those who have visited the Beechmont Inn, Hanover is a destination in itself.

The back gardens are lovely and tranquil, with a 200-year-old pink-flowering magnolia that hangs over the wrought-iron furniture like an umbrella. On the slate patio sits a bench from which one can admire the restored trellis draped with an orange trumpet vine and the bird bath, where doves splash.

MERCERSBURG

The Mercersburg Inn

405 South Main Street
Mercersburg, PA 17236
717-328-5231
Fax: 717-328-3403

> *A majestic
> mansion in the
> Tuscarora
> Mountains*

Proprietor: Fran Wolfe. **Innkeeper:** John Mohr. **Accommodations:** 15 rooms, all with private bath. **Rates:** $110–$180. **Included:** Breakfast. **Minimum stay:** 2 nights on October weekends and on holidays during ski season. **Added:** $25 each additional person; 6% tax. **Payment:** Major credit cards. **Children:** Welcome. **Pets:** Not allowed. **Smoking:** Allowed on porches. **Open:** All year.

The Tuscarora Mountains roll through the confluence of Maryland, Pennsylvania, and West Virginia, old hills that remain fairly unpopulated and quite rural. Nestled in the hills is charming Mercersburg, Pennsylvania, best known as the birthplace of President Buchanan and the site of a fine boys' preparatory academy. Atop a hill is a regal house called the Mercersburg Inn.

In 1909, a tanner named Harry Byron built this grand brick Georgian Revival house for his wife and three sons. From Mercersburg's main street in the valley, the four-columned, two-story portico is quite visible. When asked about the size of her 20,000-square-foot house, Mrs. Byron is reported to have said, "I don't know how many rooms we have, but I have 40 closets."

Fran Wolfe bought the mansion in December 1986 and opened it as an inn nearly a year later after massive restorations. Guests enter at the drive behind the house. The overwhelming foyer is formalized by elaborate faux marble pillars. The highly polished original floor is white oak with walnut inlay. On one side is the formal ballroom with a large brick fireplace; next to that is the Arts and Crafts–style billiard room, which opens through French doors to a wraparound porch that overlooks the Tuscarora range.

> **In the beautiful landscape of south-central Pennsylvania, the Mercersburg Inn is breathtaking. The Georgian Revival mansion has a ballroom, an Arts and Crafts–style billiard room, a mahogany-paneled dining room, and wraparound porches — all on an extraordinarily grand scale. Make a romantic weekend of it.**

One dining room is paneled in mahogany, its rich, gleaming surfaces warmed by the blaze in a green marble fireplace. Another is in an enclosed porch facing the academy. Six-course dinners are served here from Thursday through Sunday at a fixed price of $45; the French-inspired regional American cooking is prepared by chef John Marshall. You might begin with an appetizer of crab, escargot, and caviar in pastry shell, or cream of wild watercress soup. Entrée choices might include roast lamb with juniper berries and spaetzle; lobster tail wrapped in pastry with saffron beurre blanc; or grilled veal loin chop with Madeira sauce.

The full breakfast the next morning will likely include home-baked sticky buns, sausage, grits, and cheese casserole.

Several second-floor guest rooms have porches with glorious mountain views, and some have working fireplaces. A favorite is Room 2 at the top of the stairs overlooking town, the mountains in the background. The rooms are nicely but sparely furnished. All the rooms have reproduction king-size canopy beds. Some of the private baths are original, with monumental fixtures and elaborate tiling; others have been cleverly transformed from the ample closet space. The rooms are quiet except for the 43-bell carillon that peals out from Mercersburg Academy.

PITTSBURGH

The Priory — A City Inn

614 Pressley Street
Pittsburgh, PA 15212
412-231-3338
Fax: 412-231-4838

A spiritual and sophisticated urban B&B

Proprietors: MaryAnn and Edward Graf. **Innkeeper:** Joanie Weldon.
Accommodations: 24 rooms, including 2 large suites and 1 small suite, all with private bath. **Rates:** $85–$150. **Included:** Continental breakfast. **Minimum stay:** None. **Added:** 11% tax, $10 each additional person, $10 for a roll-away. **Payment:** Major credit cards. **Children:** Welcome; children under 7 are free. **Pets:** Not allowed. **Smoking:** Allowed. **Open:** All year.

Across the Ninth Street Bridge, which spans the Allegheny River, a small hotel of supreme elegance and refinement overlooks the city of Pittsburgh. The Priory was built in 1888, a refuge for Benedictine priests and brothers serving the adjacent St. Mary's Parish. The luxurious Austrian stained glass windows were added to St. Mary's in 1912 once the property was safe from anti-Catholic sentiments of a group called the Know-Nothings.

Less than a century later, in 1981, the life of the church was again threatened, this time for secular reasons, as the Transportation Department planned to route a new part of the interstate through the site. At the last minute, however, the highway was moved back 40 yards, and the Priory was rescued and put up for sale. The Graf family bought the church and Priory and completed a restoration of the latter in 1986. Today it stands as a monumental brick structure, with three stories of arched windows and an air of otherworldly beauty.

> **When the Grafs saved the Priory from destruction, they preserved one of the few examples of Italian classical architecture in Pittsburgh. Sited just across the Allegheny River, it is an exceptionally nice urban bed-and-breakfast.**

Those interested in architecture will be fascinated with the elevation drawings on the walls of the Priory detailing its construction. The building centers on a stunning octagonal staircase, around which radiate common rooms and several guest rooms on the first floor and the more deluxe guest rooms of the second and third floors.

The guest rooms are furnished differently but share themes of high, narrow windows trimmed simply in lace, deep oak moldings, and Victorian antiques and furnishings. Each room has a television, phone, and a new bath. While the rooms in the front of the Priory are quite grand, with tapestried Victorian chairs, precious writing desks, original faux marble mantels inset with fire screens, and antique brass, wood, or iron beds, the smaller rooms are just as nicely appointed.

In the evening, guests are welcome to relax and enjoy a drink in one of two Victorian parlors and cozy up to the working fireplace. In the morning, the delicious aromas of baking waft from the Priory's beautiful original kitchen. Continental breakfast is served in two informal breakfast rooms, where guests enjoy fresh muffins and coffee cake. In warmer months, guests may gather in the wrought-iron courtyard at the back of the Priory.

Most impressive is the warmth of the staff, who are friendly and helpful in this rather formal environment, happy to advise about dining, museums — particularly the new Andy Warhol Museum — and local events.

Pittsburgh Vista

1000 Penn Avenue
Pittsburgh, PA 15222
412-281-3700
800-FOR-VISTA
Fax: 412-281-2687

*The city's most
luxurious hotel*

Operators: Hilton International. **General Manager:** Paul Kelly. **Accommodations:** 615 rooms and 42 suites. **Rates:** $162–$182, suites from $225, weekend packages from $85. **Minimum stay:** None. **Added:** $25 additional guest. **Payment:** Major credit cards. **Children:** Yes. **Pets:** Yes. **Smoking:** 4 nonsmoking floors. **Open:** All year.

The designers of Liberty Center, which houses the Vista Hotel, made sure not to compete with the wonderful landmark of the William Penn hotel. Instead, they built a gleaming glass tower, which opened in the last days of 1986. The hotel is a small part of Liberty Center, which takes up an entire city block from 10th to 11th Streets, from Penn and Liberty Avenues. The striking landmark is one of the three points of the Golden Triangle, with the B&O Railroad as the second point and Point State Park as the pinnacle.

The four-story atrium lobby is filled with greenery and sunlight, linking the interior to the groomed exterior landscape. Under the glass roof are smooth, clean surfaces in contemporary design: the floor is Greek marble, over which rests the specially designed English Axminster carpeting. The interior is lit with elaborate Venetian crystal chandeliers throughout the hotel. Four center columns lead the eye upward.

The lobby is a gallery for local artists. The five-foot terra cotta sculptures at the entrance were made by Jerry Kaplan; the centerpiece bronze sculpture was crafted by Ron Bennett; the four black and white paintings behind the desk are the work of Douglas Cooper. Other works include a wall hanging textured in sand by Adrienne Heinrich on the stairs of the atrium; and six commanding Japanese-style works by artist Donna Bolgrem. Other Pittsburgh artists display works of pottery and ceramics in a neoclassic cabinet by the elevators.

The Liberty Grill is Edwardian in style, paneled in cherry and lit with brass and glass sconces and chandeliers. Local artist John Terzian's oil paintings in the space are Impressionist in style, in keeping with the Old World elegance.

The Orchard Cafe feels like an outdoor garden, with clusters of seating in terraces, walls of yellow and cream, and rattan furnishings. Artist Donna Groer contributed her Pennsylvania forest watercolors to the light setting. The Vista also has a nightclub, called Motions.

> **The Vista is a contemporary glass monolith that scrapes the sky of Pittsburgh and, at Liberty Center, forms one of the three points of the city's Golden Triangle. Its lobby is unusually attractive — bright, airy, and filled with greenery. Special tribute is paid in public spaces and even the guest rooms to local artists.**

The V-shaped guest tower has about 30 rooms on each floor; the top three are Executive Room floors with special amenities. All of the rooms are enlivened by the work of local artist Peter Contis, depicting scenes of the city. The decor is contemporary and unsurprising. The furnishings are mahogany with touches of burl oak, and bronze occasional tables. Nearly all the rooms have views of the Pittsburgh and Allegheny rivers, thanks to the shape of the building — request a corner room.

The Fitness Center on the fourth floor has a whirlpool, sauna, steam room, Keiser exercise equipment, a lap pool, and even aerobics classes. Liberty Center is a thriving business world unto itself — its flagship hotel works efficiently and busily.

Westin William Penn

530 William Penn Place
Pittsburgh, PA 15219
412-553-5239
800-228-3000

> *The grande dame*
> *of Pittsburgh*

Proprietors: Servico Management Corporation. **General Manager:** Karen Marasco. **Accommodations:** 595 rooms, including 47 suites. **Rates:** Rooms from $170, suites from $275; lower rates weekends. **Included:** Continental breakfast, tea, valet parking on weekends. **Minimum stay:** None. **Added:** $20 each additional person, 11% tax. **Payment:** Major credit cards. **Children:** Welcome. **Pets:** Small dogs and cats permitted. **Smoking:** 1 of 9 floors nonsmoking. **Open:** All year.

The Westin William Penn, nearly 80 years old, is a Pittsburgh patriarch. The 1,000-room hotel was built in 1916, a later work of the renowned architect Henry Clay Frick. Soaring a majestic 23 stories above the city's center, the E-shaped brick, terra cotta, and limestone building was most recently renovated in 1984. It has lived through Pittsburgh prosperity and poverty, the Depression and Prohibition, and has hosted 12 U.S. presidents. The Westin William Penn has been named a National Historic Landmark.

The hotel was shockingly modern when it was built: every one of the thousand rooms had a private bath with hot and cold running water; the private telephones required the attention of 30 hotel operators; and with the addition of an electric clock in every room, the William Penn contained the largest collection of timepieces in the world. Thirty miles of carpet lined the walnut paneled and green marbled corridors, done in Italian Renaissance style. The smallest room went for $2.50 a night, and the 15th floor was reserved for bachelors. When the Grant Street annex added 600 more rooms in 1929, the William Penn became the second largest hotel in the world, after the Chicago Conrad Hilton.

> **Renowned architect Henry Clay Frick built Pittsburgh's doyenne for $6 million in 1916. Today it stands as a National Historic Landmark. The William Penn's public spaces are galleries in themselves: the Palm Court sits under a coffered medallion ceiling; and the Urban Room was designed in high art deco in 1927 by Ziegfeld Follies Theater set designer Joseph Urban.**

During its 1984 restoration, archives were consulted to find authentic moldings, wall coverings, fixtures, and carpeting. The only original pieces were the brass doorknobs. Many of the grand common rooms recall the history of the hotel. Visitors are awed by the Fontainebleau ceiling of the Georgian lobby. The grand piano belonged to André Previn when he led the Pittsburgh Symphony Orchestra. On the top two floors of the hotel, the Grand Ballroom shows off three antique crystal chandeliers purchased from a Cannes casino, each crafted from 7,000 Baccarat crystals. The Terrace Room, in rich walnut paneling, is decorated with a mural of George Washington at Fort Pitt: here chef Vince Sanzotti prepares three meals daily, ranging up to $26.

The suites are decorated in two basic styles of Colonial Williamsburg and Italian neoclassic. Standard guest rooms have classic mahogany furnishings, two-poster beds, a desk and wing chair, all done in light or rosy hues. The marble baths are clean and modern. Managed by the ever-efficient Westin Hotels and Resorts, the hotel manifests no hint of the chaos that might accompany a 600-room property.

SCENERY HILL

Century Inn

Route 40
Scenery Hill, PA 15360
412-945-6600
412-945-5180

> *A historic inn
> on the
> National Pike*

Proprietors: Megin and Gordon Harrington. **Accommodations:** 7 rooms.
Rates: $75–$125. **Included:** Breakfast. **Added:** 6% tax. **Payment:** No credit cards. **Children:** Welcome. **Pets:** Not allowed. **Smoking:** Allowed. **Open:** Mid-March–mid-December.

A nice stop between Pittsburgh and Morgantown, Scenery Hill is a minuscule village outside Washington, Pennsylvania. The Century Inn, a fieldstone brick house, is on the National Register of Historic Places. It was built in 1794 on the Nemacolin Indian Trail, which was traversed by a pre-presidential George Washington and his militia during the French and Indian Wars. The road became better known as the National Pike (today's U.S. 40), which joined the eastern seaboard to the open western frontier. The Monongahela Valley still feels hardy and untrodden, with glimpses of villages every 20 miles or so.

The stone inn looks as if it has been blanched by winds over the years. The first floor is protected by an overhanging porch supported by six pillars, five small windows peek out from the second floor, and three dormer windows are cut into the slate roof. Inside are three dining rooms: an intimate room with a fireplace hung with ancient kitchen utensils, a cozy main dining room with exposed fieldstone walls, and a back porch protected by a green awning with vistas to hilly backyards. Breakfast is available to guests only, but lunch and dinner are served daily, with dinner entrées ranging from $10 to $24. A good appetizer choice is the inn's famous peanut soup; the list of entrées includes turkey Devonshire, chicken croquettes, Virginia ham with raisin sauce, and chicken Jackson, a breast stuffed with scallops and lobster.

> The southwestern part of Pennsylvania still feels a bit undiscovered and exposed to the elements. Partly because of the starkness of Scenery Hill, a hamlet on a hilltop, the Century Inn feels like a refuge from the harsh outdoors. A cozy interior and hearty food make this a memorable place.

While waiting for a table, be sure to visit the parlor to see the flag from the Whiskey Rebellion and Monongahela glasswork. The walls throughout the inn have become a canvas for tracings designed by Moses Eaton, one of the most famous stencilers of the early 19th century.

The seven rooms upstairs are charming, decorated in colonial simplicity, with memorably papered walls and a variety of antiques from different periods collected over the years by Dr. and Mrs. Gordon Harrington, who bought the inn in 1945 and are the parents-in-law of owner Megin Harrington. Tom the Tinker is an especially charming room with two impossibly small twin beds covered in different blue-patterned antique quilts and Williamsburg prints on the walls. The Dolley Madison Room is always open to public view, a toy museum teeming with dolls and their furniture, antique toys and carriages.

Virginia

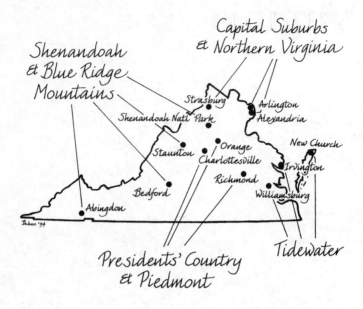

Capital Suburbs
& Northern Virginia

Shenandoah
& Blue Ridge
Mountains

Strasburg

Shenandoah Nat'l Park

Arlington
Alexandria

New Church

Staunton

Orange
Charlottesville

Irvington

Richmond

Bedford

Williamsburg

Abingdon

Behne '94

Tidewater

Presidents' Country
& Piedmont

Virginia is most assuredly a southern state. More than 6 million people live in 41,000 square miles of incredibly varied landscape: from mountains that peak over 4,000 feet, to sandy beaches, to river-soaked marshland, to fairly cosmopolitan cities, to the homes of Presidents. Those who know Virginia's history know American history; this state has more than 1,500 historic sites. The English enclave of Jamestown was the country's first settlement in 1607, and the state was divided formally from West Virginia in 1863. And even while he served as President, Thomas Jefferson's heart remained in Charlottesville. From the Barter Theater in Abingdon to the Pentagon, and from Hot Springs bordering West Virginia to the Chincoteague National Wildlife Refuge, Virginia covers a great deal of historic and beautiful ground.

For Virginia travel information, call 800-VISIT-VA.

Capital Suburbs and Northern Virginia

Best Romantic Retreats

Alexandria
 Morrison House
Fairfax
 The Bailiwick Inn

Best Gourmet Getaways

Paris
 The Ashby Inn & Restaurant
White Post
 L'Auberge Provençale

Best for Metropolitan Magnificence

Arlington
 The Ritz-Carlton, Pentagon City
Tysons Corner
 The Ritz-Carlton, Tysons Corner

Best Country Bed-and-Breakfast

Millwood
 Brookside Bed and Breakfast

Best Country Inns

Middleburg
 Red Fox Inn and Mosby's Tavern
Middletown
 Wayside Inn

Best Village Inn

Strasburg
 Hotel Strasburg

Between Front Royal, the gateway to the Skyline Drive, and Washington, D.C. is horse country. Along Route 50 is lovely scenery, antiquing in **Strasburg,** and great overnighting in **White Post, Millwood, Paris,** and **Middleburg.** Mount Vernon, George Washington's home, is only 16 miles south of Washington, D.C., one of the country's most visited sights. Three miles away is Woodlawn, the house Washington built for his nephew. It was designed by William Thornton, who built the Capitol. Another several miles south is Gunston Hall, home of George Mason, who is best known for having refused to sign the Constitution because it did not prohibit slavery. A wonderful place for an overnight from here is **Alexandria,** established in 1749, a great village for walking and perusing dozens of historic 18th-century homes.

ALEXANDRIA

Morrison House

116 South Alfred Street
Alexandria, VA 22314
703-838-8000
Fax: 703-684-6283
800-367-0800
800-533-1808 in Virginia

> *The finest inn in Old Town Alexandria*

Proprietor: Robert Morrison. **Accommodations:** 45 rooms, including 5 suites. **Rates:** $175–$210, suites from $295. **Included:** Continental breakfast, afternoon tea. **Minimum stay:** None. **Added:** $20 each additional guest, 9.5% tax. **Payment:** Major credit cards. **Children:** Welcome. **Pets:** Not allowed. **Smoking:** Nonsmoking rooms available. **Open:** All year.

The deluxe Morrison House is an impressive undertaking for a private venture. Robert and Rosemary Morrison, longtime Washington residents, wanted to open an inn after years in real estate development and chose their site in Old Town Alexandria, five blocks from the waterfront. In 1983, they presented quite a challenge to James M. Goode, curator of architectural history at the Smithsonian, when they asked him to oversee the design that would replicate a Federal manor house. It would nestle between carefully preserved 18th-century buildings, and any inconsistencies in style would be simply out of place.

The result is quite convincing, a five-story brick house with a beautiful marble portico supported by four pillars, accessible by two curved stairways a half story above the ground. A fountain encircles a marble sculpture by local artist Miles Stanford Rolph — the only modern touch. The house sits regally behind a gold-tipped black wrought-iron fence and brick courtyard. Palladian windows and dentil molding are among the convincing details.

> **The construction of Morrison House in 1983 was overseen by the Smithsonian's curator of architectural history, who made sure that the new building would authentically replicate a Federal manor house.**

The faithful Federal design continues throughout the interior. Guests enter the foyer of gray and white polished marble. Dentil crown molding runs throughout the house, echoed in fireplace mantels. The formal parlor has Chippendale detailing above the threshold and fireplace, lit by a crystal chandelier and sconces. The clubby library has luxurious mahogany paneling and plush red damask window treatments. Reproduction Federal furniture, hall tables, sofas, and chairs are perfectly placed in front of a backdrop of gray-green and off-white.

Upstairs, each of three floors has eleven rooms and a suite, decorated with lovely floral arrangements. The smallest are the red and rose Federal rooms; the Alexandria rooms have a small sitting area, four-poster king-size bed, and nonworking fireplace. All rooms, including the suites, have mahogany armoires with terry robes, remote control televisions, and telephones. The opulent baths are tiled in imported Italian marble, with double vanities and hair dryers, and nicely presented amenity baskets. Rooms are serviced with nightly turndown and chocolates, newspaper in the morning, and 24-hour room service.

The Grill is much like an English club, with red leather chairs, mahogany tables, Brazilian cherry floors, and original art. Entrées, under $35, are American regional cuisine with a Tidewater influence, including Carpetbagger steak, tenderloin stuffed with Chesapeake Bay oysters wrapped in Amish bacon with an oyster cream sauce, and Powtowmack paella with game sausage, Virginia ham, lobster, fish, mussels, oysters, shrimp, and scallops in saffron rice and peas — all prepared under the watchful eye of chef James Cobren.

The staff works very hard to maintain the superb service that brought excellent ratings from Mobil and AAA. Outside is the wonderful living exhibit of 18th-century Old Town Alexandria; and at the waterfront is the Torpedo Factory, which houses a gallery of studios of more than 200 working artists and craftspeople, as well as a laboratory of urban archaeology.

ARLINGTON

The Ritz-Carlton, Pentagon City

1250 South Hayes Street
Arlington, VA 22202
703-415-5000
800-241-3333

A luxury hotel across the Potomac from Washington

Proprietor: The Melvin Simon Co. **General Manager:** Robert Warmon and the Ritz-Carlton Hotel Company. **Accommodations:** 345 rooms, including 41 suites. **Rates:** Rooms $170–$210, Ritz-Carlton Club $240, suites from $400. **Included:** Five meal presentations at Club level. **Added:** $15 each additional guest, 9.75% tax. **Payment:** Major credit cards. **Children:** Welcome. **Pets:** Not allowed. **Smoking:** 13 of 17 floors nonsmoking. **Open:** All year.

The Ritz-Carlton, Pentagon City opened in May 1990, just across the Potomac from Washington, D.C. Among its other virtues, the hotel is quite proud of its chef, Gérard Pangaud, who has earned two stars from Michelin.

Pentagon City is a surreal place, with a spare landscape and clusters of gleaming postmodern skyscrapers. On South Hayes Street, an 18-story light stone monolith puts its narrow face forward, like a brick placed sideways, between a vault-like Nordstroms, which looks like the National Gallery, and the expansive Pentagon City Fashion Centre, with 140 shops. All the telltale signs of the Ritz-Carlton are visible: parquet marble floors, vast Oriental carpets, 19th-century oil paintings and portraits hanging on gleaming paneling, dentil crown molding, and beautifully upholstered parlor sets.

> **The Ritz-Carlton, Pentagon City publishes a booklet to guide visitors through a tour of its $2 million art collection. Perhaps it won't be necessary to venture to the National Gallery after all.**

In addition to these public spaces, two restaurants and a lounge are on the ground level. The Grill, with lovely tapestried chairs, is the setting for three daily meals. The large 18th-century fireplace mantel framed in carved wood and green marble was found in a French château. Visitors gather in the Lounge for the civilized occasion of afternoon tea, evening cocktails, and piano entertainment.

The Restaurant, which holds about 75 guests within its silk-covered walls, is the sublime setting for an intimate dinner. Meals are served on Rosenthal china, accompanied by the Ritz-Carlton signature cobalt blue goblets. Chef Gérard Pangaud might offer turnip ravioli with duck confit; black radish cake with sweetbreads, truffle, wild mushrooms, and fava beans; and from the entrées one might select a cold salmon soufflé with wine sauce or poached lobster in ginger lime sauce. The prix fixe menu for four courses is $62; for five courses, $75. Sommelier David Howard is from the Inn at Little Washington.

The traditionally decorated guest rooms are typical of the Ritz-Carlton. In addition to damask chairs and sofas, stocked honor bars, televisions hidden in armoires, and floral bedding with matching drapes, guests can expect marble baths with vanity mirrors, hair dryers, and terry robes. The Club Floor offers all these amenities in addition to a lounge, concierge, and five meal presentations throughout the day, from a Continental breakfast to chocolate and cordials after dinner.

While city properties scramble to find fitness facilities, the Pentagon City location has a large Fitness Center on the third floor, with a lap pool, plenty of the latest exercise equipment, and steam, Jacuzzi, and sauna rooms. The Fitness Center Bar features juices, fruits, and vegetables.

FAIRFAX

The Bailiwick Inn

4023 Chain Bridge Road
Fairfax, VA 22030
703-691-2266
Fax: 703-934-2112
800-366-7666

> *A supremely romantic and sumptuous B&B*

Proprietors: Anne and Ray Smith. **Accommodations:** 14 rooms, including 1 suite, all with private bath, 5 with fireplace. **Rates:** $105–$275. **Included:** Full breakfast, afternoon tea. **Minimum stay:** None. **Added:** 6.5% tax. **Payment:** Visa, MasterCard, American Express. **Children:** Welcome. **Pets:** Not allowed. **Smoking:** Not allowed. **Open:** All year.

One of the loveliest bed-and-breakfasts in the region, the Bailiwick opened in January 1990 after a $3 million restoration by owners Anne and Ray Smith and the efforts of a handful of creative decorators. This three-story Federal brick house was built in the early 1800s by county sheriff Joshua Coffer Gunnell, across the street from the courthouse of the same period. It was expanded in 1832 and used as a hospital during the Civil War.

The Oliver family bought the house from Gunnell's descendants in 1899 for $2,500, and after a series of owners, it was placed on the National Register of Historic Places in 1987. Many of the original Federal architectural details are present: side and transom lights around the solid front door,

since refinished in faux graining by an English expert; fireplaces with Federal and Greek Revival mantels; architraves over doorways and windows; and a portico with a second-floor porch.

> The 15-mile drive out of Washington is long enough to render that all-important feeling of distance, but short enough to be convenient. Don't despair at the strip malls and traffic: the extraordinarily tasteful Bailiwick Inn is in the charming historic section of Fairfax.

The rooms are named for famous Virginians and decorated according to the period in which they lived: the Thomas Jefferson Room is a replica of his Monticello chamber, with gold-trimmed tassels on the canopy, the drapes, and the bathroom shower curtain. The Lord Fairfax Room is named for the 18th-century absentee English landlord who owned more than five million acres in Virginia, decorated in the Charles II style of Leeds Castle, his English home. The James Madison Room repeats themes from the Montpelier mansion, and the front corner George Mason Room reflects his original Gunston Hall mansion, where he drafted the Bill of Rights.

Whatever the period of the room, the antiques are quite lavish and authentic, and some of the rugs were even custom-made using specified colors and patterns. Four rooms have fireplaces, and several have whirlpool baths.

The common rooms, including the double parlors, are decorated in the height of Federal elegance, with boldly colored walls, inset curio cabinets, and original moldings. A large 1984 addition built onto the back of the house has since been gutted and made into a sunny, two-tiered breakfast area. The several-course breakfast is quite lavish. Guests may also eat in their rooms or on the brick patio out back.

A new feature at the inn is fine dining for guests — candlelight dinners are prepared by chef Charles Bruce, served Wednesday through Sunday, and priced at $45 ($55 Fridays and Saturdays). Your meal may include a first course of red snapper marinated with citrus and herbs, followed by salad, then a choice of grilled shrimp with capers and scallops, sautéed marinated duck breast with a caramelized shallot sauce, or roast loin of pork with apple and cranberry chutney. To finish, you might try summer fruits with Sabayon sauce, chocolate tarte, or Amaretto cheesecake.

The luxurious air of the Bailiwick is carried throughout by the innkeepers, who are quick to offer discreet, sophisticated service.

MIDDLEBURG

The Red Fox Inn & Mosby's Tavern

2 East Washington Street
P.O. Box 385
Middleburg, VA 22117
703-687-6301
Fax: 703-687-6187
800-223-1728 outside Virginia

> *One of the country's oldest original inns*

Proprietor: Turner Reuter, Jr. **Accommodations:** 24 rooms, including 8 suites (6 in the Main Inn, 8 in Stray Fox, 5 in Mc-Connell House, 1 in Night Fox, 4 in Middleburg Inn). **Rates:** $135–$225. **Included:** Continental breakfast served in room. **Added:** $25 for a cot, $10 for a crib, 6.5% tax. **Payment:** Major credit cards. **Children:** Welcome. **Pets:** Not allowed. **Smoking:** Allowed. **Open:** All year.

This favorite retreat for Washingtonians, an hour's drive west, is best known for its wonderful food. Built by Joseph Chinn in 1728, the Red Fox is one of the oldest original inns in the country. It was a convenient stopping point between Alexandria and Winchester, and such a valuable and strategic plot of land that it was sold to the town for $2.50 an acre in the late 18th century. While always an inn, what was then called the Beveridge House served as a hospital and temporary headquarters for the Confederates during the Civil War. The pine service bar here was made from a field operating table used by General Stuart's cavalry.

The inn comprises three buildings, as well as the new Mosby's Tavern for groups and functions. The main building is an important-looking four-story blanched fieldstone. Bay windows on either side of the entrance portico overlook the street. The fourth floor has four dormer windows cut into

> **Washington insiders know the Red Fox offers unique and delicious colonial fare in a quintessentially authentic setting, and great overnight accommodations as well. The beautiful drive, through horse country out to Middleburg, will transport you back hundred of years.**

a tin roof. Behind the Red Fox, the Stray Fox was built in the early 1800s as an inn — familiarly referred to as the Stray Shot for the time during the Civil War when an errant cannonball hit its foundation. Across the path, the McConnell House is a robin's egg blue pill box home, built for a dentist at the early part of this century and adopted into the Red Fox complex in 1985.

Rooms in the Red Fox are decorated in a spare colonial style. While all have televisions, telephones, and private baths, most have working original fireplaces and four-poster canopy beds. The original flooring is charmingly warped. Rooms in the Stray Fox are preferable for their decor and lack of street noise. Here the walls and floors are stenciled and the rooms have more of a country feel. The McConnell House rooms are a little larger and more contemporary. Three of the five rooms have fireplaces and canopy beds, and most have hand-held showers.

There are seven dining rooms throughout the Red Fox, two on the ground level and five on the second floor. Roaring fires are kept going in deep, original stone fireplaces. The exposed hand-hewn beams on the ceiling, thick plaster walls, and spindle-back chairs contribute to the authentic colonial atmosphere. Lunch and dinner are served daily, the latter a bustling affair. Entrées range from $15 to $23 for hearty colonial meals, including grilled medallions of elk with fresh pear sauce and foie gras, grilled venison loin with cinnamon cream sauce and wild rice pancakes, or, for a change of pace, Louisiana bayou gumbo. Don't miss the Red Fox peanut soup, a Virginia tradition, or the pub Cheddar soup.

The former Stray Fox stables were rebuilt in 1983 to serve as the Red Fox Fine Art Gallery, which displays 19th-century paintings and sculpture, some of which are on permanent display on the dining room walls in the inn. The charming town is in the heart of horse country, so try to slate a stay at the Red Fox during show season.

MIDDLETOWN

Wayside Inn

7783 Main Street
Middletown, VA 22645
703-869-1797

A 250-year-old inn in Virginia horse country

Proprietor: Richard Bernstein. **Manager:** William Hammack. **Accommodations:** 24 rooms, all with private bath, including 6 deluxe rooms. **Rates:** $70–$125. **Added:** $10 each additional guest, 6.5% tax. **Payment:** All credit cards except Discover. **Children:** Welcome (under 16 free). **Pets:** Not allowed. **Smoking:** Allowed. **Open:** All year.

One can't help but be reminded of the Red Fox at the Wayside Inn — even the names of the towns are similar. Here, Larrick's Tavern dates to 1724, though most of the inn was built in 1740, finally opening as a stop on the stagecoach route from Winchester down the Shenandoah Valley in 1797. Like the Red Fox, the Wayside served as a hospital during the Civil War, though it sided contrarily with Union troops and served as Union headquarters in 1862 and 1864. The Bernsteins, who bought the property in 1960, are avid antiques collectors. They also own the Strasburg Emporium of Antiques, the state's largest antiques market. Their wide-ranging, fine taste is displayed throughout the Wayside Inn, and most of the pieces are for sale. The inn's decor is an eclectic mixture of colonial, Chippendale, Victorian, and European pieces with a museum of results, all set on Oriental carpets.

The rooms, on the second and third floors, are accessible from two stairways. Some are smaller and cozy, while some of the state rooms and suites are expansive and decorator-designed. All rooms have lovely antiques from different periods: one has a neoclassic French armoire and bedroom set with Egyptian influences;

> **The owners of the Wayside Inn are avid antique collectors. While the inn itself is a remarkable representative from 1740, its furnishings come from colonial through Victorian times and from America to Europe.**

another has Queen Anne chairs in pink damask. There are four-poster colonial beds as well as king-size reproductions, and both Victorian and art deco lamps. Amid all the antiques, each room has a remote control television and private phone.

The three dining rooms are wonderful, open spaces. A favorite room is the low-ceilinged slave quarters, chock full of colonial utensils and relics from the inn's early days around the stone hearth. Lunch and dinner are served daily from a faithful country Virginia menu, with ham, peanut soup, and game in informal family style.

The staff is very personable and welcoming at the Wayside. The short distance from Washington is enough to slow down the pace impressively. Several miles away is Front Royal, the gateway to Skyline Drive and the Shenandoah Valley. Farther south are the Luray Caverns and the George Washington National Forest, with endless hiking and skiing activities. A short drive east to Strasburg off I-81 will please any antiques buff.

MILLWOOD

Brookside Bed and Breakfast

Millwood, VA 22646
703-837-1780

> *An idyllic B&B
> in a mill town*

Proprietors: Gary and Carol Konkel. **Accommodations:** 3 rooms, 1 cabin, all with private bath and fireplace. **Rates:** $95–$125. **Included:** Full breakfast. **Minimum stay:** Selected weekends. **Added:** 6.5% tax. **Payment:** Visa, MasterCard. **Children:** Not allowed. **Pets:** Not allowed. **Smoking:** Not allowed. **Open:** All year.

Those inclined to bed-and-breakfast travel will love Brookside, about 90 minutes west of Washington D.C., in the softly rolling hills of Virginia's horse country. Brookside has an abundance of virtues, a rarity in bed-and-breakfasts, which often require a certain flexibility from their guests. Gary and Carol Konkel are intelligent, friendly, discreet hosts. All rooms have working wood-burning fireplaces; the furnishings are consistently beautiful antiques from the 18th and 19th centuries; and nearby are three highly acclaimed restaurants — the convivial Ashby Inn, the four-star L'Auberge Provençale, and the colonial Red Fox Tavern.

Millwood is a nearly forgotten working mill town transformed in recent years to an informal gallery of antiques shops. Brookside is in the village, just a few feet from the old Burwell-Morgan Mill on which the township was founded, but the B&B is set on five quite rural acres abutting the millrace and a trickling tributary from the nearby Shenandoah

River. The three-story cream-colored clapboard house was built in 1780 by Nathaniel Burwell, the grandson of Robert "King" Carter, a famous colonial Virginian. The Konkels, veteran Washingtonians, retired early from administration jobs and bought Brookside in 1985, opening their B&B two years later. The Konkels have also created a forum for their interest in antiques in an outbuilding on the property, which houses beautiful furniture and an impressive print collection. Most of the formidable pieces in the house are for sale.

Brookside is a natural. The manor house was built in 1780 and is now a virtual gallery for American country and primitive furniture, art, and crafts. If you listen carefully, you can hear the trickle of the mill-race abutting the town mill.

Though the second-floor rooms, the Cranberry and Blue rooms, are lovely, most guests prefer the third-floor Garret Room, the Burwell children's nursery. A subtle childhood theme plays throughout the room. The curiosities displayed include a tiny linen nightgown, an antique doll bed and quilt, an antique toy sleigh, and intriguing children's games. The large bathroom, set under the eaves, has one wall of exposed stone from a chimney, a clawfoot tub, a restored washstand, and a ladder for a towel rack. Most prized about Brookside are the canopied featherbeds: a Sheraton field bed under a fishnet canopy in one room, a structured crewel canopy in another. A generous, romantic touch is the welcome basket with a nightcap and fresh fruit. The log cabin is a particularly romantic retreat.

Guests will need a lot of activity after the large breakfasts made by Gary and Carol. The mill still chugs away from May to November, and visitors can buy fresh-ground flour and cornmeal. Nearby are wonderful bike routes, hiking and fishing at Sky Meadow State Park, and some of Virginia's finest vineyards.

PARIS

The Ashby Inn & Restaurant

Route 1, Box 2/A
Paris, VA 22130
703-592-3900
Fax: 703-592-3781

> *An understated escape for the Washington elite*

Proprietors: John and Roma Sherman. **Managers:** Tara Welty and John and Roma Sherman. **Accommodations:** 10 rooms, 8 with private bath, including 4 suites in Old School House. **Rates:** $90–$200. **Included:** Full breakfast. **Minimum stay:** $20 extra for Saturday-only stay in 4 rooms. **Added:** $20 each additional guest, 4.5% tax. **Payment:** Visa, MasterCard. **Children:** Over 10 welcome. **Pets:** Not allowed. **Smoking:** Allowed in Tap Room and library only. **Open:** All year except New Year's, Independence, and Christmas days.

There are two magnificent gourmet country inns in the northeast part of Virginia: the Ashby Inn and L'Auberge Provençale (see page 516). Quite unusual is the personable nature of the Ashby Inn: the service is natural and friendly, the food is wonderful, the accommodations are lovely. Set breathtakingly in the foothills of Skyline Drive, right on the Appalachian Trail, the Ashby Inn is a white colonial farmhouse with green shutters. The hamlet of Paris is an hour's drive west of Washington, D.C., in the rolling hills of horse country. It's an understated but sophisticated gathering spot for Washington elite as well as for locals with boots muddied from the horse races — surely the place to go in the area.

John is a speechwriter, Roma is an excellent chef, and their staff, headed by Tara, is a happy, interesting group devoted to this convivial refuge. The active, intelligent Shermans came here in 1984 to share Roma's wonderful cooking with the world, offering rooms for enthusiastic guests who simply would not leave.

The guest rooms at the Ashby's main inn are elegantly spare, dressed in primitive Shaker decor. Most desirable is the Fan Room, with breathtaking views of the distant Blue Ridge foothills, as seen through the French doors leading to the porch. The East Dormer Room shares this view from the third floor. Roma and John have collected wonderful artwork and displayed it throughout the inn (some is for sale), including an-

> **The Ashby Inn is a place of warmth and casual sophistication. National legislators and local horse-racers sit at colonial tables and wooden banquettes. They order from a selective wine list tailored to this hearty and seasonal menu, and they sleep in Shaker rooms that frame stunning views of the Shenandoah Mountains.**

tique decoy prints in the New England Room, with its gorgeous green star quilt, painted furniture, and beautiful fireboard painted with a primitive mural. The four new suites in the School House are quite deluxe in their period decor.

After a drink beside a roaring fire in the library, guests enjoy meals in one of four dining rooms. The enclosed porch has mountain views, and another room has wooden banquettes and booths. Most gregarious is the fabulous Tap Room on the lower level, with a grottolike coziness. There is a bit of the hunt theme in several stuffed animal dioramas.

Keith Korn's creative menu changes daily and is priced from $14.75 to $21.50. A winter menu might begin with grilled quail with mushroom risotto or pan-roasted sweetbreads with artichokes and sage. Entrées may include an Atlantic fisherman's stew with tuna, mussels, and scallops in tomato saffron broth with basil aioli and garlic mashed potatoes; or sautéed local venison with candied walnuts, butternut squash, leeks and bacon ragout, in sour cherry sauce. John takes great care in selecting a small but varied wine list.

STRASBURG

Hotel Strasburg

201 Holliday Street
Strasburg, VA 22657
703-465-9191

> *An inn for antiques lovers in a historic village*

Proprietor: Gary and Carol Rutherford. **Accommodations:** 27 rooms including 7 suites, all with private bath (4 in Taylor House). **Rates:** Rooms $69–$149. **Included:** Continental breakfast on weekdays, full breakfast on weekends. **Added:** $10 each additional guest, 4.5% tax. **Payment:** Visa, MasterCard, American Express. **Children:** Welcome. **Pets:** Check with innkeeper. **Smoking:** Nonsmoking rooms available. **Open:** All year.

In the northwest corner of Virginia at the top of the George Washington National Forest, the town of Strasburg is the oldest settlement in the Shenandoah Valley, a fitting place for the state's largest antiques emporium. It's a strategic tourist spot in an untouched historic town, near Skyline Drive and Luray Caverns. Seeing a growing need for Strasburg accommodations, Leo Bernstein, owner of the historic Wayside Inn in nearby Middletown, decided to buy and restore the four-story Queen Anne Victorian in 1977. The property was recently upgraded and reopened in July 1990, still somewhat of a sleeper deserving of much attention.

The four-story white clapboard, black-shuttered building is a rectangular box on a main corner in the center of town. Columns support a second-story wraparound porch. It was built in 1895 as a hospital and took on its present role as a place of dining and lodging in 1915, with many incarnations during this century. The hotel serves as a display for the Strasburg Emporium. All the formidable antique furnishings throughout the common and guest rooms are for sale, collected by the Bernstein family with care and expertise.

The guest rooms are on the second and third floors and in the adjacent colonial Taylor House, which was acquired in 1990. Each room has a list of the furnishings for sale and a description and history of the pieces. There is a wide variety of carved wood and brass beds, Victorian fringed lamps, gilded mirrors, and tufted slipper chairs. The wallpapers and borders are done in bold, heavy Victorian patterns under ten-foot ceilings. Though the rooms are roughly the same size, the third-floor rooms are set under eaves, rendering a particular coziness. Half the rooms have televisions, and six suites have Jacuzzis, including the four at Taylor House. These rooms are particularly interesting, with bathrooms overlooking the Shenandoah Mountains and large sitting rooms and highly decorated bedrooms.

> Virignia's largest antiques emporium is in Strasburg, which is also the oldest settlement in the Shenandoah Valley. The Hotel Strasburg is a showcase for the emporium's treasures: if you like your bed, you can take it home with you.

Lunch and dinner are served daily, the latter ranging in price from $10 for chicken breast in lemon beurre blanc to $17 for tournedos Zinfandel, prepared by chef Frank Asaro. The dining rooms are rather rustic and informal, a friendly, bustling place with colonial spindle chairs and bare wood floors.

TYSONS CORNER

The Ritz-Carlton, Tysons Corner

1700 Tysons Boulevard
McLean, VA 22102
703-506-4300
Fax: 703-506-2694
800-241-3333

*A top luxury
hotel amid 125
shops, boutiques,
and restaurants*

Proprietor: The Ritz-Carlton Hotel
Co. **General Manager:** Lawrence
Sternberg. **Accommodations:** 399 rooms, including 33 suites.
Rates: Rooms $139–$210, suites $325–$1,400. **Included:** 5
meal presentations at Club level. **Added:** $30 each additional
guest, 6.5% tax. **Payment:** Major credit cards. **Children:** Welcome. **Pets:** Not allowed. **Smoking:** Nonsmoking rooms available. **Open:** All year.

Halfway between Dulles and National airports, this extensive
new Ritz-Carlton at Tysons Corner has an urban convenience
to the capital, 14 miles east, and easy access to rural and historic Virginia. With a hotel on DuPont Circle in Washington,
D.C., and a new property in Pentagon City, it seems odd that
the Ritz-Carlton Company would open yet another satellite
hotel outside of the capital — especially one with 400 rooms.
However, the deluxe Tysons Corner Ritz-Carlton debuted in
November 1991, built for business travelers and Washingtonians who want to get away for romance, for Virginia sightseeing, and especially for shopping.
    The hotel sits adjacent to the Tysons II Galleria, with 125
shops, restaurants, and boutiques, including Neiman-Marcus,

Saks Fifth Avenue, and Macy's. Close by is the Fairfax Square Mall, with Fendi, Hermes, and Louis Vuitton; and Tysons Corner Center, with more than 300 shops.

Many of the amenities and virtues of this hotel mirror those at the Pentagon City location. Guests can expect all-day Continental dining at the Restaurant, with entrées beginning at $20 prepared by chef Uffe Mikkelsen. Cocktails and high tea are served in the Lounge. The decor of the guest rooms is similar to that at the Pentagon City Ritz, with 18th-century reproduction furnishings, lots of damask, mahogany molding, chintz drapery, and original art. The uppermost floors feature the

> **The Ritz-Carlton, Tyson's Corner is a study in contrasts. Inside, it is a classic hotel of grand Old World proportions. Outside, it is a postmodern monolith in Virignia's toniest shopping mall. Consider it for a luxury weekend getaway.**

upscale Ritz-Carlton Club with its own concierge, lounge, and five complimentary food presentations daily. There is also a state-of-the-art fitness center, with a 40-foot lap pool, cardiovascular equipment, and steam and sauna rooms.

The staff is on its toes, solicitous and courteous. While Washington hotels might be weary with competition, the Tysons Corner Ritz-Carlton sits confidently apart from the crowd. Mt. Vernon Plantation is a short drive, as is the Wolf Trap Farm for the Performing Arts.

WHITE POST

L'Auberge Provençale

Box 119
White Post, VA 22663
703-837-1375
Fax: 703-837-2004
800-638-1702

*A culinary
treasure
in horse country*

Proprietors: Alain and Céleste Borel. **Innkeeper:** Céleste Borel. **Accommodations:** 10 rooms, 5 with fireplace, including 1 suite (1 suite and 2 rooms in the Manor House, 4 rooms in La Petite Auberge, 3 rooms with fireplace in Les Chambres des Amis). **Rates:** $145–$185. **Included:** Full breakfast; fruits, pastries, and chocolates in room. **Minimum stay:** None. **Added:** $25 for Saturday and holiday stay, 4.5% tax; $30 additional guest. **Payment:** MasterCard, Visa. **Children:** Well-behaved children over 10 welcome. **Pets:** Not allowed. **Smoking:** Restricted. **Open:** All year; restaurant closed Mondays and Tuesdays.

In the foothills of the northernmost part of the Blue Ridge Mountains, north of Front Royal, is some of Virginia's finest French cuisine, at L'Auberge Provençale. The owners, Alain and Céleste Borel, are quite young, energetic, and enterprising — much like their good neighbors at the Ashby Inn. Their accommodations resulted from Alain's formidable skills as a chef, which beckoned crowds from a good distance away.

L'Auberge Provençale, however, is a thoroughly country French experience, from the magnificent menu to the charming rooms.

Alain and Céleste came to the countryside outside White Post in 1981 to buy a 1753 stone farmhouse on eight acres of rolling fields. Two years later, after Alain's restaurant had received its rave reviews, they introduced guest rooms. Part of the house was expanded in 1890, and again by the Borels a century later, in low single-story units to one side of the stone house.

> **Chef Alain Borel is truly a master. The French country cuisine he prepares at this beautiful inn, at the foot of the Blue Ridge Mountains, has been widely and loudly praised. While the dinners are well worth the relaxing hour's drive from Washington, the lovely guest rooms are a great draw too.**

The several rooms in the main house above the dining rooms are large and sunny, offering views of the surrounding fields, furnished with interesting antiques provided by Alain's father, a dealer from Avignon, France. The rooms in the addition are reached by a walkway bordering Alain's herb garden. They have unique Italian chandeliers accented with pineapples, daisies, or lemons; the fireplaces are lined with traditional country French tiles, and the baths are enlivened by wonderful Mexican tile. Wrought-iron beds, wicker furniture, and varied antiques fill the rooms, which are bright with sunshine and have valley views.

The main house has three dining areas, two of which are done in simple country French decor, and the Peach Room, with five French doors in a semicircular addition at the side of the house, filled with interesting curios from Europe. Alain's menu changes monthly, with a prix fixe five-course menu for $52. Appetizers might include duck breast with pasta and port sauce, lobster and chicken sausage with spring onion purée, or sautéed foie gras with fresh mango and ginger or wrapped in Norwegian salmon with sherry and crème fraiche. Chef Alain may feature applewood-smoked rabbit with pasta and fresh morels; roast venison with fresh huckleberries, vintage port, and basil potato purée; Norwegian salmon with light black bean sauce; or roast pheasant with spiced pear and Zinfandel. Alain and Céleste have established a commendable wine list to complement the menu. Naturally, desserts are quite wondrous, including white chocolate mousse cake with dark chocolate glaze and raspberry brown butter tart with sabayon.

Amazingly, Alain is up to prepare breakfast for his guests: a lavish, full event that begins with homemade croissants and jams, café au lait, and fresh juice, followed by eggs en cocotte with crab saffron crème and baked herb tomatoes; or perhaps fresh fruit crêpes with crème fraiche and maple syrup. Those who have not been so lucky as to have stayed at the inn can come for Alain's Sunday brunch. This is offered from spring through fall, for $11 to $18.

Alain and Céleste are quite proud of their home and enamored of the surrounding countryside, which offers antiquing, fox hunts, and visits to Skyline Drive and local vineyards.

Tidewater Virginia

Best Romantic Retreat

Williamsburg
  Liberty Rose

Best Gourmet Getaway

New Church
  The Garden and the Sea Inn

Best Resorts

Irvington
  Tides Inn
  Tides Lodge
Williamsburg
  Kingsmill Resort and Conference Center
  Williamsburg Inn

Best Village Bed-and-Breakfast

Williamsburg
  Colonial Houses

Fredericksburg, 50 miles south of Washington, D.C., shoulders the Rappahannock River on its south shore. One of the town's finest sights is the Kenmore estate, built by George Washington's sister Betty. From here, travelers may explore the flat, marshy plantation land of the Northern Neck, a peninsula that has the Rappahannock on the south and the Potomac to the north, ending at Chesapeake Bay. The 538-acre George Washington Birthplace National Monument is here. North of **Irvington,** at the end of the neck, take a ferry to Tangier Island and farther to the Eastern Shore; or to Smith Island and Crisfield, Maryland.

  The ferry to Crisfield takes a traveler to the Delaware-Maryland peninsula and its south-pointing peninsula of Virginia's eastern shore. Just below the Virginia border is **New Church**. A drive east brings one to the Eastern Shore's busiest town, Chincoteague, which sits in its own bay west of the Assateague Island National Seashore. This protected park stretches up to Maryland, a 37-mile vertical strip of protected beach on the Atlantic Ocean that is best known as the home of a herd of wild ponies.

The peninsula, never more than several miles wide, stretches for about 60 miles from Chincoteague down to Cape Charles and is linked to Virginia Beach by a 20-mile scenic highway. As well as having wonderful beaches on the Atlantic, the Eastern Shore has a great deal of history, with 17th-century communities and Victorian enclaves, as well as quaint Tangier Island, where cars are prohibited. From here, the drive south down the peninsula on its main vein, Route 13, takes one past lovely Onancock, 18th-century Eastville, and 19th-century Cape Charles.

The base of the eastern shore connects to Tidewater Virginia via the Chesapeake Bay Bridge-Tunnel. Here, bustling Virginia Beach, Norfolk, and Hampton cluster around the beaches at the confluence of the James, Elizabeth, and Nansemond rivers.

Upriver from Newport News is the state's most popular tourist attraction, Colonial **Williamsburg**. The history of Williamsburg began in the late 1600s, when the town called Middle Plantation replaced Jamestown as the capital of the British crown colony of Virginia until 1780. A more recent chapter of Williamsburg's history commenced in 1926 when W.A.R. Goodwin and John D. Rockefeller, Jr., undertook a $79 million effort to resurrect an authentic colonial town. Within 3,000 acres of protected land along the James River in Virginia's southwestern corner, Colonial Williamsburg is a 173-acre window to the past, one mile long and five blocks wide, home to 88 original 18th- and early-19th-century buildings, with 50 more resurrected buildings and more than 90 acres of authentic period gardens.

In addition to the historic buildings and streets, there are 20 studios of craftspeople working at the art of colonial survival: binders, yarnmakers, milliners, coopers, and blacksmiths, among others. For sightseeing, the National Park Service maintains the scenic Colonial Parkway to Jamestown and Yorktown.

IRVINGTON

The Tides Inn

King Carter Drive
Irvington, VA 22480
804-438-5000
800-TIDES IN

A southern resort at the base of Virginia's Northern Neck

Proprietors: The Stephens family. **Resident Manager:** Randy Stephens. **Accommodations:** 110 rooms. **Rates:** Per person AP, rooms $120–$130, suites $137–$143; weekends, $155 (lower rates with 3-night weekend stay). **Included:** Three meals per day. **Minimum stay:** None. **Added:** $40–$60 each additional guest, gratuities, 4.5% state tax. **Payment:** Major credit cards. **Children:** Allowed, under 4 free. **Pets:** Small pets (under 50 pounds) allowed. **Smoking:** Allowed. **Open:** Mid-March to early January.

The Tides Inn is quite an anomaly in a business of hungry corporations whizzing with marketing strategies. Reputed to be one of the East Coast's toniest resorts, the Tides has been family-run since 1947. E. A. Stephens felled the cypress for the Dining and View rooms from a nearby swamp and salvaged the roof tile from the Army's Langley Field. Mrs. Stephens decorated with a traditional eye. The property, much expanded but entirely faithful to its origins, is now run by a younger generation of Stephenses. The refined southern hospitality of the Stephens family resort remains like a relic from the past: cherished, rare, and timeless.

The Tides Inn floats on the southern reaches of Virginia's marshy Northern Neck, where the two-mile-wide Rappahannock River meets the Chesapeake Bay. Carter's Creek dissolves off the Rappahannock, surrounding at one point a subtle 25-acre peninsula that serves as the home of the Tides Inn.

Water flows in and out of the flat lowland fields, as the coastline is lost at every turn.

The architecture is traditional and classic: three stories of white clapboard and whitewashed brick, topped with a red tile roof. The Main House undulates along the shoreline, housing two common rooms, the Chesapeake Club and the Dining Room, both with water views that evoke the feeling of a houseboat. In the Main House, the East Wing guest quarters are the only ones without outdoor spaces. A few steps across a path from the Main House, with views of the other side of Carter's Creek, are the Windsor House, consisting of deluxe suites and porches, and the Lancaster House, built in the 1950s, with balconies.

> A captivating small resort with a devoted following, the Tides Inn is the quintessence of refined southern hospitality. Its otherworldly setting on the shoreline of the Rappahannock is mesmerizing, isolated at the marshy end of Virginia's Northern Neck.

All the guest rooms are decorated very traditionally, with long drapes matching bedding, and complementary colors in the wallpaper, lampshades, and club chairs. All rooms have telephones and televisions. Though some of the rooms are a bit on the small side, even these have dressing areas outside the bath. Guests with early tee times will appreciate the coffeemakers in the rooms.

Carter's Creek, a formidable 25 to 30 feet deep in most places, is explored by the classic *Miss Ann*, which embarks on daily cruises, and the *High Tide II*, which offers smaller luncheon cruises.

The staff is extremely solicitous at the Tides. Employees not only are kind and helpful, but seem quite proud; many have been at the Tides Inn for generations. The Tides Inn has unusually authentic southern cooking, and Sunday seafood brunches are legendary.

The Summer House has one of the two outdoor pools at the inn, this one filled with saltwater. In addition to swimming, the inn has four tennis courts and a 9-hole par 3 golf course. The Tartan Course and the Golden Eagle Course, one of Virginia's finest, are within several minutes' drive.

The Tides Lodge

Irvington, VA 22480
804-438-6000
Fax: 804-438-5950
800-248-4337

> *A golfing haven
> at the base of the
> Northern Neck*

Proprietors: E. A. Stephens, Jr. **Accommodations:** 60 rooms in three wings, including 14 suites, 1 golf cottage, and 1 executive suite. **Rates:** $115–$234, with seasonal variations; add $40 per person for MAP rates. **Included:** Use of tennis, game room, and pool facilities. **Minimum stay:** 3 nights on holidays. **Added:** $20 additional guest, gratuities, 4.5% tax. **Payment:** Major credit cards. **Children:** Free under 4 and all ages on weekdays. **Pets:** Small pets allowed. **Smoking:** Smoking and nonsmoking rooms. **Open:** Mid-March–December.

The Tides Inn and Tides Lodge are entirely different properties, each run by a Stephens brother. The choice for Old World southern elegance is the Tides Inn; the informal choice with immediate access to golf is the Tides Lodge. While the Tides Inn is decorated in the manner of a formal parlor, the Lodge is done in the manner of a casual family room. Kids have a great time at the Lodge, which offers a youth program during the summer for children ages 5 to 12.

> **Water and land keep meeting at the southern tip of Virginia's Northern Neck, as the Rappahannock River prepares to converge with the Chesapeake Bay. It's here that the Tides Lodge — the casual sister of the tonier Tides Inn — plays host to two terrific golf courses and much more.**

Across Carter's Creek from the Tides Inn, the Lodge was built and is operated by E. A. Stephens, son of E. A. the elder who built the Tides Inn. The Tides Lodge is a contemporary, geometric series of two-story flat-topped buildings of weathered shingle and wood.

The Scottish theme at the Tides Lodge is a tribute to Sir Guy Campbell, the architect and designer of the first nine holes on the Tartan Course, which begins at the front door.

Campbell died while building the course, and the tartans are everywhere, from the drapes to the rugs running through the public and dining areas.

All the rooms have private balconies and are decorated in a casual, unsurprising hotel style. A 60-foot yacht takes daily cruises around Carter's Creek, and the Lodge also has a 41-slip marina. There are two swimming pools (one saltwater) and three tennis courts. While the Tartan Course begins at the Lodge steps, the Golden Eagle Course is a shuttle away, but as one of Virginia's top courses, it's worth the trip.

NEW CHURCH

The Garden and the Sea Inn

Box 275, 4188 Nelson Road
New Church, VA 23415
804-824-0672

> *A culinary wonder within reach of Chincoteague*

Proprietors: Victoria Olian and Jack Betz. **Accommodations:** 5 rooms with private bath, some whirlpool tubs and porches (2 rooms in Victorian House, 3 in Garden House). **Rates:** $85–$145 (seasonally). **Included:** Fresh-baked Continental breakfast. **Minimum stay:** 2 nights on weekends from Memorial Day to Columbus Day. **Added:** $15 each additional guest, 6.5% tax. **Payment:** All credit cards. **Children:** Well-behaved children welcome. **Pets:** Not allowed. **Smoking:** Allowed in parlor and porches only. **Open:** April through October.

Virginia's eastern shore floats like a tail underneath eastern Maryland and Delaware. Approaching the peninsula from the north, the first town one hits is New Church, home of a new and sophisticated culinary refuge called the Garden and the Sea, which opened in the spring of 1989. Ever since, this inn and restaurant has been getting tremendous reviews from those few who have actually found it.

> **Way over on Virginia's eastern shore, inspired by European inns and Provençale cuisine, a Victorian inn pays tribute to the fruits of the garden and the sea. Victoria Olian's cooking has been widely praised, as have this inn's creative and beautiful guest rooms.**

After traveling extensively throughout Europe and having been inspired by accommodations and Provençale food, Victoria Olian and Jack Betz made plans to buy an inn. They were quite familiar with Virginia's eastern shore, having spent many summers in Chincoteague. In 1988, they discovered that what had been known as Bloxom's Tavern was up for sale. The three-story 1802 clapboard building had been Victorianized in the early 1900s to its present shape with twin gables and a long single-story front porch. Victoria and Jack spent months restoring the inn, which would be a focal point for Victoria's culinary skills. More recently, they restored the nearby Garden House — the oldest house in New Church — complete with three guest rooms and a library and music room.

The guest rooms are unusual, magnificent, and romantic. In the Victorian house, the rooms are on the second floor flanking the center staircase. Victoria and Jack tried to give their large baths an air of European luxury, with skylights, bidets, a pair of sinks, and plush terry robes and towels.

Giverny has a fabulous rare bedroom suite of Victorian wrought-iron furniture painted green; the suite includes a large bed with a richly patterned canopy (a testament to Victoria's prior experience as a decorator), matching a vanity and stool, two end tables, and an armoire. Victoria's window treatments are luxurious and inventive. Across the hall is Chantilly, dominated by a French wicker sleigh bed with accents in teal green and pink, with a Louis XV–style dresser in stenciled pine. Both have sitting areas tucked into three-windowed bays. The Garden House is home to Vaucluse, with a stunning cherry and cane bed, skylights, and a whirlpool tub. Arlesienne has a country look, with stenciled oak furnishings, and Champagne is the inn's most luxurious, with a double whirlpool, a Victorian wrought-iron canopy bed, skylights, and original art.

The dining room is the antithesis of Victoriana. Light pine chairs are covered in salmon-colored fabric, the fireplace is painted a minty color with a flowered tile, and the walls are light and simple. Victoria, whose French country menus change every three weeks and feature only fresh local seafood and produce, wanted an atmosphere evocative of the garden and the sea, in natural, sandy beach tones. Entrées range from $14 to $22. A sampling of the incredibly creative cuisine might include grilled duck breast with duck confit, with apples, plums, and wild and white rice; boneless chicken breast stuffed with goat cheese, roasted peppers, toasted pine nuts, and cumin butter sauce; Chincoteague oysters sautéed with leeks, shiitake mushrooms, spinach, and seasoned cream; or perhaps her specialty, Marseille-style bouillabaisse.

Victoria and Jack are great promoters of local art, crafts, and music. Once a month on Sundays, they host a dinner concert with eastern shore musicians. They also display crafts, sculpture, art, and jewelry.

WILLIAMSBURG

Colonial Houses & Taverns

Post Office Box 1776
Williamsburg, VA 23187-1776
1-800-HISTORY
Fax: 804-220-7729

*An authentic
way to visit
Williamsburg*

Proprietors: Colonial Williamsburg Foundation. **Manager:** John T. Hallowell. **Accommodations:** 84 rooms in 23 colonial houses and 3 taverns, each with from 1 to 4 bedrooms. **Rates:** $99–$145 low season, $125–$325 high season. **Added:** 8.5% tax, $12 additional guest. **Payment:** Major credit cards. **Children:** Welcome. **Pets:** Not allowed. **Smoking:** Nonsmoking rooms available. **Open:** All year.

There is nothing like Colonial Williamsburg, an unreal mixture of historically accurate 17th-century and corporate 20th-century America. More than a million visitors each year travel to this magical place and peruse the 800 acres of history. Its varying accommodations total more than 250 rooms from a budgetary $29 to around $200 for five-star treatment.

Colonial Houses and Taverns is the most authentic place to stay in Williamsburg. The 84 rooms in 26 buildings around the historic complex successfully create a B&B environment in the restored and reconstructed houses of Colonial Williamsburg.

Despite its endless attention to historic accuracy, Williamsburg is a mastery of artifice. The graveled drives, the one hundred men and women who ply more than 30 trades here — from blacksmith to leather tanner — all look convincingly old but suspiciously new. It

> **While it's one thing to be able to spend your days at the resurrected colonial village of Williamsburg, it's another to be able to spend your nights there. That's the unique opportunity available at the 26 buildings comprising the Colonial Houses & Taverns.**

seems that either a wand was waved over the town, putting it to sleep for 300 years, or you were transported back in time. However, just as a visitor begins to believe the magic, it's back to the hotel room, with remote television, king-size beds, room service, and showers.

The Colonial Houses contain these modern amenities, but in the context of the historic houses themselves — cottages with wide-planked flooring, canopy beds, fireplaces, traditional furniture, and decor — so the feeling of colonial life is somewhat continued into the evening. The houses range in size to accommodate from two to twelve people in rather enchanting properties mixed into the historic setting. Some are adorable two-story suites for two, some larger taverns, some with fireplaces and full kitchens. All are decorated meticulously, with antiques and faithful Williamsburg reproductions. Interestingly, the reproduction furniture is not taken from an Ethan Allen warehouse: each piece is hand-crafted by a historically trained artisan, upholstered by another, and placed in a room with paint matched to the history books and wallpaper designed after its ancient cousin.

Of course, guests can enjoy all the wonders of Williamsburg: two golf courses, one designed by Robert Trent Jones, one completed in 1991; the acclaimed food; tennis, pool, and exercise equipment; and the endless perks of resort living.

Kingsmill Resort and Conference Center

1010 Kingsmill Road
Williamsburg, VA 23185
804-253-1703
Fax: 804-253-3993
800-832-5665

> *A luxury resort on the James River near Busch Gardens*

Proprietor: Anheuser-Busch, Inc.
General Manager: Terri Haack. **Accommodations:** 352 units, including 180 suites. **Rates:** Guest rooms, $120–$220, Riverside Villas $173–$599. **Included:** Par 3 golf, use of extensive fitness facilities. **Minimum stay:** None. **Added:** $20 each additional guest, 6.59% state tax. **Payment:** Major credit cards. **Children:** Welcome. **Pets:** Not allowed. **Smoking:** Allowed. **Open:** All year.

A short drive south from Colonial Williamsburg to the contemporary Kingsmill Resort reveals three miles of unadulterated James River coast. Kingsmill is part of the huge enterprise of Anheuser-Busch, with its base and Busch Gardens a short drive away on private, patrolled roads. The property is best known as a conference center, but Kingsmill attracts a goodly number of golfers who play on the two 18-hole championship and par 3 golf courses. It's also the home of the Anheuser-Busch Golf Classic.

Named for English colonist Richard Kingsmill, who settled here in 1736, the resort has nearly 3,000 acres of protected forest and wildlife. Anheuser-Busch bought the property in 1974 to develop private homes and opened the resort a decade later. The groomed grounds, radar-patrolled roads, and contemporary architecture give Kingsmill Resort the feeling of a private country club.

Although conferences are a huge part of Kingsmill's market, transient guests will not feel overwhelmed because the accommodations are rather independent. Guests stay in one of 32 villas clustered in four groups around the conference center. There are two sets of Riverside Villas overlooking the James River and two sets of Sports Villas set on the golf courses, one added as recently as 1991. A villa contains about ten rooms on three floors, from singles to units with three bedrooms. Some of the units have fireplaces and kitchens and all have balconies. All the rooms are bright and are traditionally furnished in light wood, chintz fabrics, and modern comforts.

> **Kingsmill is a destination in itself, with Busch Gardens a short drive away. But if you enjoy golf, you won't want to leave the resort: two championship courses include the River Course, which has continuous water views and annually hosts the PGA, and the Arnold Palmer–designed Plantation Course.**
> **There's a par-3 course, too.**

The championship golf courses include the River Course and the Plantation Course, designed by Arnold Palmer. The Bray Links par 3 course was completed in 1990. The Riverview Dining Room at the Golf Club has a lovely water view and formal dining.

In addition to golf, Kingsmill has 15 tennis courts — two all-weather, and two lit for night play. The Sports Club, completed in May 1988, is a particularly airy building with a cathedral ceiling, a wall of sliding glass doors surrounding the indoor pool, and racquetball courts, Nautilus, aerobics, saunas, and whirlpools.

During the summer months, children may participate in the Kingsmill Kampers program, a supervised day camp with organized activities, sports, and arts and crafts.

Though the resort is contemporary, the architecture has classic influences, with gabled roofs, green roofs, and whitewashed brick. The many activities are within easy reach, and historic sites are just around the corner.

Liberty Rose

1022 Jamestown Road
Williamsburg, VA 23185
804-253-1260
Reservations: 800-545-1825

> *A perfect,*
> *romantic B&B in*
> *Williamsburg*

Proprietors: Brad and Sandra Hirz.
Accommodations: 4 rooms, all
with private bath, including 2 suites. **Rates:** $105–$165. **Included:** Full breakfast, afternoon sweets. **Minimum stay:** 2 nights most weekends. **Added:** $40 each additional guest, 8.5% tax. **Payment:** MasterCard, Visa. **Children:** Over 12 welcome. **Pets:** Not allowed. **Smoking:** Not allowed. **Open:** All year.

Liberty Rose is a beautiful, meticulously cared for bed-and-breakfast, a credit to the industry. A mile from historic Williamsburg, half that from the campus of William and Mary, Liberty Rose is outstanding for its gorgeous bedding and blissful owners, Sandra and Brad Hirz.

Though innkeepers' lives need not enter into a bed-and-breakfast, Sandra and Brad's history played a large role in the creation of this romantic hostelry. They were friends for years, Sandra a decorator in southern California and Brad a farmer in Washington state. Brad had often encouraged Sandi to open a bed-and-breakfast. In 1986, when Sandi bought this 1920 Virginia house, Brad came along to help her with handiwork. They fell in love during the restoration, married on a Wednesday, and opened to a full house of guests that Friday. Somehow, the bed-and-breakfast substituted for a honeymoon, and the property is infused with that same romance.

Liberty Rose is a product of their partnership: Sandra does the sewing and decorating, and Brad cooks the full breakfast and afternoon sweets.

The simple exterior belies the lavish interior: a two-story white clapboard flanked by brick additions and topped by four dormers in the slate roof. The living room has several lovely pieces of furniture, some Victorian in lavish upholstery, a baby grand piano, and a fireplace. It opens through French doors onto the windowed breakfast wing seating eight people for Brad's breakfast, which could be cinnamon bread with strawberries or perhaps French toast stuffed with cream cheese.

A wing unto itself, the Rose Victoria Room is possibly the grandest. To

> If you've come to Williamsburg with a Land Rover full of kids, chances are you'll have a full agenda. If, however, you've come for relaxation, indulgence, and romance, Liberty Rose is for you. With plush linens and lavish boudoirs in beautiful taste, this B&B is as good as it gets.

top the queen-size French canopy bed, Sandi designed elaborate tasseled curtains that replicate 18th-century drapes enclosing the Sheriden down duvet. A large cherry armoire sits across from a tapestry couch, all under a pressed tin ceiling. The bath is exquisite; one of its walls is hidden by a rowhouse oak closet front from 1890. Romantics will use the clawfoot tub; the practical will use the free-standing glass-enclosed shower.

The three bedrooms upstairs are also appointed with lavish and thick bedding in silk and tapestry. Magnolia Peach has a rice bed with a fishnet canopy draped in silk and down bedding, and a cherry armoire. Its private bath has black marble. An adjunct is the Blossom Room, tucked into the dormer, with an antique mahogany twin bed framed by a Regency red swag to match its coverlet. Suite Williamsburg has a wood-burning fireplace, yet another lavish four-poster canopy bed draped in copies of hundred-year-old fabrics, and a lavish bath. All the guest rooms have televisions, VCRs, and access to a library of movies.

In a town dominated by the industry of Colonial Williamsburg, Liberty Rose is a refreshing and luxurious alternative.

Williamsburg Inn

P.O. Box 1776
Williamsburg, VA 23187-1776
1-800-HISTORY
Fax: 804-220-7729

*A luxury resort
in a living
museum of
colonial America*

Proprietors: Colonial Williamsburg Foundation. **General Manager:** John Hallowell. **Accommodations:** 232 rooms including 16 suites (102 in main house, 43 in Providence Hall, 84 rooms in Colonial Houses). **Rates:** $260–$365 (seasonally); special packages available for meal plans. **Minimum stay:** None. **Added:** $12 for roll-aways. **Payment:** Major credit cards. **Children:** Welcome. **Pets:** Not allowed. **Smoking:** Nonsmoking rooms available. **Open:** All year.

In 1926, John D. Rockefeller, Jr. undertook a $79 million effort to bring colonial America to the 20th century. The result is one of the country's most popular tourist attractions, the living museum of Colonial Williamsburg, set on 173 acres in southeastern Virginia. Plans for the Williamsburg Inn were set forth in the mid-1930s with much discussion between Rockefeller and architects who decided that the town needed a European-style luxury hotel.

It was agreed that the inn would not compete architecturally with the colonial themes that were done so authentically. Rather, the grand scale of the West Virginia resort "springs" hotels was adopted, all built in the formal Georgian, Federal, and Regency styles of the early 1800s. Rockefeller and his architects agreed that the Regency style was most fitting, with its lighter colors, whitewashed brick, bright flat plaster walls, Greek Revival pediments, arches, and columns. The ground floor is a grand colonnade, above which floats a two-story portico supported by four Ionic columns and a classic pediment.

The inn was furnished in symmetrical simplicity. The East Wing, housing guest rooms, was added in 1950, and the Regency Dining Room was built in 1972, along with two contemporary Providence Hall wings a short walk from the inn. Everything in the Williamsburg Inn is created by the local artisans. Carpenters, upholsterers, and designers must maintain historical accuracy — in the colonial style as well as in the Regency style of the inn.

Rooms are furnished in exacting authenticity, redecorated in a continual process that turns the rooms around every five years. Each is different, but all the rooms in the main inn are furnished in formal Regency style.

> As an ambassador to colonial America, the Williamsburg Inn is a glamorous, elegant, and outstanding resort. Much has been invested in the integrity and authenticity of this property, which was built in the 1930s as the pinnacle of Rockefeller's restoration of colonial America.

So thorough is the design of the Williamsburg Inn that even the surrounding grounds are interesting, an incredibly diverse horticultural display. Those who come twice yearly will notice different furnishings in the grand reception hall, which has a different decor for winter and summer. The Regency Dining Room, which opens to the gardens behind the inn, is the setting for formal dining.

Second to the outdoor museum of Colonial Williamsburg, guests are apt to concentrate on golf, which is formidable at the Williamsburg Inn. The original championship Golden Horseshoe Course was designed by Robert Trent Jones in 1963, as was the nine-hole Spotswood. In October 1991, Jones's son Rees Jones introduced the Green Course, with a new clubhouse.

Fitness facilities are found at the neighboring Williamsburg Lodge in the Tazewell Club Fitness Center. In addition, there are eight tennis courts — four of them Har-Tru surfaces — lawn bowling, croquet, shuffleboard, and two swimming pools.

Colonial Williamsburg is a busy place. The service is extremely professional, as is every aspect of the organization.

President's
Country
and the Piedmont

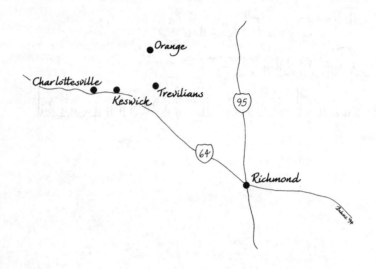

Best Romantic Retreats

Charlottesvlle
   Clifton, The Country Inn
Keswick
   Keswick Hall
Trevilians
   Prospect Hill Plantation Inn

Best Resort

Charlottesvlle
   The Boar's Head Inn & Sports Club

Best for Urban Intimacy

Richmond
   The Berkeley Hotel
   The William Catlin House
   Linden Row

Best for Metropolitan Magnificence

Richmond
   The Jefferson Sheraton
   Commonwealth Park Suites Hotel

Best Country Bed-and-Breakfast

Orange
   The Shadows B&B

Best Country Inns

Charlottesvlle
   Silver Thatch Inn
Orange
   Willow Grove Plantation

Best Village Bed-and-Breakfast

Charlottesvlle
200 South Street

En route to Richmond from Williamsburg, visit Petersburg, a major railroad hub and stronghold of the Confederacy. Seventy-five miles up the James River from the state's first settlement, **Richmond** was settled more than a century after, in the 1730s. The buildings of the capital were designed by the governor at the time in 1785, near the house where he and Mrs. Jefferson lived. It's quite fun to tour the James River by boat. Also, be sure to visit St. John's Church, where Patrick Henry made his "Give Me Liberty" speech in 1775. Additional sights in the area are the Edgar Allan Poe Museum, the Lewis Ginter Botanical Gardens at Bloemendaal Farm, the largest collection of Confederate memorabilia at the Museum and White House of the Confederacy, home to Jefferson Davis during the Civil War, and the world's largest film projector at the Science Museum of Virginia. Of the many plantations in the area, Berkeley Plantation is perhaps the best known, the setting for the first Thanksgiving in 1619, a year before the Pilgrims gave thanks in Massachusetts.

Charlottesville is 71 miles northwest of Richmond and about 30 miles east of Waynesboro. After meticulously constructing the masterpiece of his home, Monticello, from 1769 to 1804, Thomas Jefferson founded the University of Virginia down the hill in Charlottesville in 1819. Other sights in this lovely town are Ash Lawn, modest home to James Monroe, and historic Michie Tavern. Several wineries are within a half hour's drive, and in September and April the area is home to the Foxfield steeplechase.

A short jaunt northeast of Charlottesville takes a visitor to **Orange** and another presidential territory, that of James Madison and Montpelier.

CHARLOTTESVILLE

The Boar's Head Inn & Sports Club

Route 250 West, Box 5307
Charlottesville, VA 22905
804-296-2181
800-476-1988

*A small resort
with a devoted
following*

Proprietors: University of Virginia
Real Estate Foundation. **General
Manager:** Sandie Greenwood. **Accommodations:** 174 rooms,
including 14 suites, 10 rooms with fireplace. **Rates:** $110–
$200. **Minimum stay:** Graduation weekend only. **Added:** $10
each additional guest, 6.5% tax. **Payment:** Major credit cards.
Children: Welcome, under 18 free. **Pets:** Not allowed. **Smoking:** Nonsmoking rooms available. **Open:** All year.

A recent $4 million renovation, completed in August 1991,
has revitalized the Boar's Head Inn, best known for its extensive tennis and racquet facilities. This clubby, surprisingly
traditional resort sits in the Ednam Woods two miles west of
Charlottesville, a fitting retreat for the elite families visiting
the University of Virginia. Despite its size and recent additions, the Boar's Head feels intimate and old school. The property centers around a 19th-century gristmill, around which
classic pitched-roof wings were gradually added.

The Boar's Head opened in 1965, though its interesting history dates to 1834 when the gristmill was built on the banks
of the Hardware River near Monticello. The mill survived the
years, including a torching during the Civil War, squelched by
a rainstorm. In the early 1960s, John B. Rogan bought the
gristmill and took it apart piece by piece to transport it to its
present site where it was rebuilt. The dining room flaunts the
features of the old mill: the large hearth was built from the
mill's fieldstone foundation, and still present are the 40-foot
heart pine beams, warm planked walls, and original scarred

flooring. One common room sits in the old mill — the rest is all new. A downstairs Tavern offers nightly entertainment.

The 53 acres of the Boar's Head are well groomed, with a manmade lake, adjacent to the university's 18-hole par 72 championship Birdwood golf course. The old mill stretches toward the lake, fronted with a new garden room available for special functions and dinners, with wrought-iron furniture and trellis wallpaper. Behind the dining room, the reception area has a clubby, 19th-century feel, with wood-paneled walls, hunting pictures, and forest green rugs.

> Elegant and understated, the Boar's Head is an admirable combination of a 150-year-old gristmill and complementary expansions ever since. Its 53 acres of groomed grounds abut the championship Birdwood golf course; its Sports Club is perhaps its own championship offering.

Several floors of guest rooms are above the reception area, though the majority rest in two new wings between the parking area and the lake toward the Sports Club. They were redecorated in 1991 with bright pile carpeting, chintz spreads and window treatments, and upholstered benches at the foot of the beds. Coffeemakers have been added too. Most have balconies, and most of these face the lake. The Hunt Club rooms on the other side of the mill are the most deluxe, with king-size beds (or two doubles), hair dryers and telephones in the bath, and fluffy terry robes. Original art includes hunt and equestrian themes. These rooms overlook the outdoor pool and sundeck.

The Sports Club has 20 tennis courts: 3 indoor-outdoor Max-cushioned courts, 3 indoor Grasstex courts, 10 clay courts, 4 all-weather Grasstex courts, as well as 2 platform tennis and 4 squash courts. Additional exercise facilities include a large fitness center and three outdoor swimming pools. Finally, the Sports Club offers spa facilities including massages, facials, saunas, and aerobics. There's even hot-air ballooning.

Clifton, The Country Inn

Route 13, Box 26
Charlottesville, VA 22901
804-971-1800
Fax: 804-971-7098

> *The essence of antebellum southern elegance*

Proprietors: Mitch and Emily Willey. **Innkeepers:** Craig and Donna Hartman. **Accommodations:** 14 rooms, all with private bath, including 7 suites (6 rooms in main house, 3 in Carriage House, 2 in Law Office, 3 in Livery). **Rates:** $155–$198. **Included:** Full breakfast, afternoon tea. **Minimum stay:** 2 nights September to mid-November. **Added:** $20 each additional guest, 4- and 5-course dinner on weekends, 6.5% tax. **Payment:** Major credit cards. **Children:** Well-behaved children are welcome. **Pets:** Not allowed. **Smoking:** Not allowed in house. **Open:** All year.

The way of life around Charlottesville is a continuing tribute to the vivid presence of Thomas Jefferson. A wonderful way to visit the area and still be immersed in history is with a stay at Clifton.

Clifton's graceful circular drive, bordered by flowers and tall trees, is most authentically approached by carriage or horseback. Six tall columns stretch up two stories to support the overhanging red roof shading the elegant facade. The shutters are painted a formal black. What was once a tobacco plantation is now home to 45 wooded acres soaring above the Rivanna River. While Martha spent much time as her father's hostess at nearby Monticello, her husband was a rather reclusive lawyer who would retreat for weeks in his books at Clifton — an activity that has a great appeal today.

Despite its formidable appearance and role in history, Clifton remains an informal country retreat. The heart pine floors, paneled walls, and fireplaces in every room are original to the manor house. Six of the eight guest rooms are suites, with working fireplaces and large baths with colonial-style painted parquet floors. Several rooms have canopies that fall grandly from the ceiling moldings.

> **Clifton is an unsurpassingly graceful place. It was built in 1799 on a portion of Jefferson's Shadwell estate, a home to his daughter Martha and son-in-law Thomas Mann Randolph, an early governor of Virginia. From these lofty beginnings, the beauty of this stunning plantation estate has only improved.**

Though the two-story Carriage House was built in 1985 when the owners bought the property, the floors, windows, and banister were taken from the neighboring Meriwether Lewis house, a contemporary of Clifton. Whitewashed walls and a cathedral ceiling lend the feel of a summer cottage, as do the French doors that open at either side of the living room. The Law Office, with two rooms, is even more wonderful as the original building on the premises. The Livery, also original to the property, was recently restored to house three suites with lovely views of the lake.

Craig is a terrific chef who makes good use of his industrial kitchen with six-course dinners. A Jeffersonian harpist/historian joins in on weekends. Guests may ask for a gourmet platter of homemade hors d'oeuvres to start or may sit down to the feast, a fixed price of $38 during the week and $48 on the weekend. Your meal might proceed as follows: a duo of Virginia jumbo lump crab and poached prawns with roasted garlic and shallot sauce; potage lyonnaise with herb croutons and scallions; an organic mixture of baby greens with champagne and tarragon vinaigrette; passion fruit ice; and an entrée of pan-seared yellowfin tuna with sun dried tomato and olive compote with beurre blanc. Dark chocolate rosettes with Rémy Martin and berry coulis will cap off the evening. Rest assured that breakfasts are quite full as well, with delicacies like apple walnut pancakes, seafood omelette, frittata with three cheeses and shiitake and chanterelle mushrooms.

The grounds at Clifton are landscaped as would befit a governor, with a new pool with waterfall and spa, clay tennis court, gravel paths, a sundial, gardens, sculptures, croquet pitches, and unexplored woods. Mountain bikes are available. The innkeepers are extremely professional, enthusiastic, and quite knowledgeable about local history and activities.

Silver Thatch Inn

3001 Hollymead Drive
Charlottesville, VA 22901-7422
804-978-4686
Fax: 804-973-6156

A pretty
country inn
just north
of Charlottesville

Proprietors: Rita and Vince Scoffone. **Accommodations:** 7 rooms, all with private bath (3 in main house, 4 in Cottage). **Rates:** $110–$125. **Included:** Expanded Continental breakfast. **Minimum stay:** 2 nights on some spring and fall weekends. **Added:** 6.5% state tax. **Payment:** Visa, MasterCard, Diner's Club. **Children:** Well-behaved children welcome. **Pets:** Not allowed. **Smoking:** Not allowed. **Open:** All year except Christmas Eve and Christmas Day.

Silver Thatch Inn is a classic country inn several miles north of the University of Virginia on a rolling country road just off horrific Route 29. Though the inn has been a strong town presence for years, the property has been nicely revived since its new and hospitable owners, Vince and Rita Scoffone, took the helm in the spring of 1992 and brought along accomplished chef Gordon Carlson.

The common room is the original part of the house, one of the county's oldest structures, built in 1780 by Hessian soldiers imprisoned on the plot during the Revolutionary War. Various additions elaborated on the white clapboard and black shutter theme in 1820, creating a panoply of undulating weathered shingle rooftops that range from one to three stories. Today the inn sits easily on a manicured courtyard, near an enormous holly tree befriended by magnolias and dogwoods, with a brick walkway in the middle.

> For years the food of the Silver Thatch was its greatest attraction. Then, its rooms received the bulk of the attention. Now, this well-balanced inn is at its best: a place of warmth and hospitality, good food, and pretty rooms.

Each of the three dining rooms has a different feel. The colonial tavern room is furnished in early American primitives; the middle room is elegantly dressed, with plush maroon chairs and floral wallpaper; the third dining room is a large enclosed porch with a more contemporary but still traditional setting. Gordon Carlson's contemporary American cuisine ranges from $16 to $23. One might begin with grilled eggplant with roasted peppers, potatoes, gorgonzola, and walnuts, and move on to sauté of lobster Mojita, with black beans and rice and roasted red pepper onion sauce; or perhaps grilled venison loin chops, with chipotle pepper molasses glaze served with mango red onion confit.

The guest rooms are immaculate and sweet, in early American antiques and reproductions, with authentic Williamsburg trim, stenciling, and playful country wallpaper borders, all spotlessly maintained. As a result of the varied height of the rooftops, the rooms all have surprising eaves, clever window seats, shelves, or desks built into the pitch. The James Madison Room in the main house has a wallpaper border of melons echoed in several pictures, an antique school bench, and a log cabin quilt over crisp white linens on a pencil post canopy bed with matching skirting. The bathrooms have a generous variety of Caswell and Massey amenities. Homemade treats or cookies greet guests, and all rooms have healthy plants.

The Scoffones are extremely enamored of their inn and are

happy to share their knowledge of the area and love for the Silver Thatch. The inn has a swimming pool and tennis courts, as well as hiking and biking trails nearby.

200 South Street: A Virginia Inn

Charlottesville, VA 22901
804-979-0200
Fax: 804-979-4403
800-964-7008

> *An elegant B&B
> in two properties,
> right downtown*

Innkeeper: Brendan Clancy. **Accommodations:** 20 rooms, all with private bath, 9 with fireplace, including 3 suites (11 rooms in mansion, 9 in Cottage). **Rates:** $90–$170. **Included:** Continental breakfast, afternoon tea and wine. **Minimum stay:** 2 nights on special college weekends. **Added:** $20 each additional person, 8.5% tax. **Payment:** Major credit cards. **Children:** Welcome. **Pets:** Not allowed. **Smoking:** Allowed. **Open:** All year.

In 1985, a group of five investors, devoted alumni of the University of Virginia, bought a pair of houses in Charlottesville's historic district with the intent of opening a bed-and-breakfast for visitors of refined tastes. The two adjacent houses — the mansion and the Cottage — are both lemon-colored, trimmed in white, both three stories, but quite different architecturally. The mansion was built in 1856 for Thomas Jefferson Wertenbaker, son of the first librarian at the University of Virginia, a close friend of its brilliant founder and president.

While the restoration was completed in April 1986, the matter of furnishings had to be settled. Two of the owners traveled to Europe to consult with British art dealer Keith Bycroft, who helped procure the glorious English and Belgian antiques that fill the guest and common rooms, as well as the paintings and antique Turkish rugs.

The square brick mansion is the main gathering spot for guests, with dormer windows facing four different directions from the mansard roof. A neoclassic verandah wraps around three sides of the house and descends in the back to a brick breakfast patio. The adjacent Cottage is an early Victorian that recedes from the street in four sections like an accordion, with a broad front porch.

> **The magnificent English and Belgian antiques, Turkish rugs, and the work of Virginia artists were compiled by a group of University of Virginia alumni who wanted a Charlottesville B&B. The result is elegant and tasteful, simple and eclectic.**

The interior of the old mansion is formal and grand, with beautiful Oriental and Turkish rugs covering wood floors. The walls are hung with paintings by Virginia artists as well as with historic Holsinger photos of Charlottesville. The cozy Library is the only congregating spot for guests; it's a small common room for a bed-and-breakfast of 20 rooms. A plentiful Continental breakfast is served here or on the outdoor patio.

Every room has a book describing its artwork and furnishings. Most pieces date from the 18th and 19th centuries, like an armoire from northern France circa 1800, a 1789 armoire from Austria, or a beautiful painting of an elephant dating from about 1865. The beds are quite stunning, with rails extended to accommodate queen-size mattresses. Of the four rooms with twins, one features rare tiger maple sleigh beds. Other beds are canopied with lace or draw curtains, Victorian or Eastlake or elaborately inlaid or carved wood, or have upholstered headboards. Some rooms have whirlpool baths, and nine have gas fireplaces.

Memory and Company, the restaurant, is on the other side of the mansion, with distinctive new American cuisine peppered with influences from southern France, embellished by a rich wine list.

The inn is only one mile from the campus. Veteran innkeeper Brendan Clancy is extremely professional and provides guests with all the local advice and information needed.

KESWICK

Keswick Hall

701 Country Club Drive
Keswick, VA 22947
804-979-3440
Fax: 804-979-3457
800-ASHLEY-1

*An exquisite
English country
house near
Charlottesville*

Proprietor: Sir Bernard Ashley.
General Manager: Grant Howlett.
Accommodations: 48 rooms, all with private bath. **Rates:** $195–$395, suites $395–$645. **Minimum stay:** Graduation weekend only. **Included:** Full country breakfast, afternoon tea, and evening refreshments, use of Club facilities. **Added:** 10% service charge; 6.5% tax. **Payment:** Major credit cards. **Children:** Welcome. **Pets:** Not welcome. **Smoking:** Nonsmoking rooms available. **Open:** All year.

A sister property to the Inn at Perry Cabin on Maryland's Eastern Shore, Keswick Hall, which celebrated its opening in the fall of 1993, is Sir Bernard Ashley's second contribution to American hospitality. While the highest standards of service and beauty unite the two properties, Keswick Hall is otherwise unique. Set on 600 acres in the rolling fields of horse country several miles outside Charlottesville, against a backdrop of the Blue Ridge Mountains, Keswick Hall is just about as impressive a sight as one will behold in this region.

Keswick Hall is actually a combination of three creations of Sir Bernard Ashley: the 48-room Country House hotel, the private Keswick Club, and private Keswick estates. While they share the same acreage, make no mistake: overnight guests are treated like visiting dignitaries, with use of the top-notch dining, exercise, and country club facilities.

The cornerstone of the mansion is in the original 1912 Villa Crawford manor house, a three-story Italianate, its Mediterranean influence evident in the butter-colored stucco exterior and red-tiled rooftop. To realize Keswick, the architect constructed a replica of the original manor house across the grounds, and then joined the twins with a long connecting wing known as the Great Hall. The result is a breathtakingly beautiful U-shaped castle, three stories high at its entrance, topped by a symphony of dormers and chimneys, flanked by grand porches and formal gardens.

In the Great Hall, a museumlike space of grand proportions set on tiled floors that were actually transported from castles in the Loire Valley, guests are immediately enveloped in the tastes and hospitality of Sir Bernard Ashley. His art and antiques collections, his sumptuous fabrics and breathtakingly beautiful designs, and his favorite color schemes contribute to the elegant and very personal interior design. The intimate details to which guests are privy are touching, even disarming — from family photos to jewelry boxes of the late Laura Ashley, to family china collections, to decorator pillows and hand-me-downs, even to the draperies in the Tea Room, which were hand-sewn by Laura Ashley herself. Public rooms unfold naturally, as in a family's home: from the Living Room with its creamy walls and couches, oriental rugs, working wood fireplaces, and china cabinets to the Morning Room overlooking the vast and undulating grounds, and the clubby Snooker Room and Crawford Lounge.

> It is a remarkable achievement of hospitality that such a formal, opulent, and sophisticated estate as Keswick makes a visitor feel comfortable, relaxed, and like a specially invited house guest of Sir Bernard and Lady Ashley.

The 48 guest rooms on two upper floors spanning the breadth of the Country House are showrooms in themselves. Every detail of each room is perfectly executed: color is echoed throughout, from wallpapers to window treatments to upholstery. Furnishings — astoundingly well-preserved armoires, romantic four-poster beds, precious ottomans and end tables — seem plucked from museum displays. The hand-picked art and decoration, including books, musical instruments, flowers, and clocks, is unusual. Not only are the rooms wonderful to behold, but they are exceptionally comfortable, with plush linens and plenty of room for luggage and belongings. Most impressive are the baths at Keswick Hall. Spacious and luxurious, they are studios in themselves, complete with bath leaves, ultra thick terry robes, fragrant amenities, heated towel racks, and enormous tubs with temperature settings. Keswick Hall manages to accomplish the contradictory: offering an experience of Old World, timeless elegance combined with new world comforts and tastes.

Afternoon tea, with scones and fresh jams, is taken in the Morning Room. Before dinner, guests may enjoy drinks and canapés in the Great Hall; afterwards, all may retire to the Snooker Room for port fireside.

The cuisine at Keswick Hall is particularly superlative and an integral part of the entire sybaritic sensory experience. For a fixed price of $55, one can dine in a supremely elegant setting on the ground level of the Country Home, overlooking the porch and groomed grounds through grand Palladian arches. Dinner might include a light lobster and tarragon essence, followed by beef carpaccio with pesto and marinated vegetables. The entrée might be blackened monkfish tails southern style, followed by a Keswick cheese plate, pithiviers with apricot coulis, and coffee with mignardises.

Guests of Keswick have use of the exclusive Keswick Club, right down the hill from the Country House. The decor of the Pavilion mirrors the elegance of the hotel's public spaces, lending the air of a sophisticated English country home. Its many offerings include an indoor-outdoor pool, clay tennis courts, steam rooms, saunas, and spa and fitness facilities, as well as a championship Arnold Palmer signature 18-hole golf course. This supremely luxurious experience is easily accessible and within a short drive of Charlottesville's wonderful offerings.

ORANGE

The Shadows B&B

14291 Constitution Highway
Orange, VA 22960
703-672-5057

*A rare Arts and
Crafts home
near Montpelier*

Proprietors: Barbara and Pat Loffre-
do. **Accommodations:** 6 rooms all
with private bath, including two 1-
bedroom cottages. **Rates:** $80–$110. **Included:** Full breakfast,
refreshments on arrival. **Minimum stay:** 2 nights in autumn
and on special-event weekends. **Added:** $20 each additional
guest, 6.5% tax. **Payment:** MasterCard and Visa. **Children:**
Over 12 welcome. **Pets:** Not allowed. **Smoking:** Not allowed.
Open: All year.

In the rolling hills of central Virginia are endearing incon-
gruities at the Shadows that make it a memorable and lovely
retreat. Nestled among the Georgian and Federal mansions of
Virginia's heartland, the Shadows is a stone and cedar shingle
farmhouse built in 1913 in rare and authentic Arts and Crafts
style. The generous Loffredos greet visitors warmly at the
door, not with lilting southern drawls but with a hint of New
York City: Pat was a Staten Island policeman, and Barbara
worked on Wall Street. They are touchingly thrilled with
their life here, with their unusual house (home of Virginia's
first female lawyer), and with their lovely antiques and expansive grounds. Their long search for a bed-and-breakfast ended
with the Shadows, but their move was delayed for a year and
a half. A friend painted a picture of the Virginia countryside
to sustain them during the wait — and the Loffredos point
fondly to this picture, which hangs in the hallway.

The house is embraced and shaded by 200-year-old cedar trees, part of the original grove that played a great role in the naming of the house by its first owner, horseman Manley Carter. Barbara and Pat spent a year restoring their home, and where they had to replace old shingle they tried to match new cedar as exactly as possible. The true impact of the Arts and Crafts movement doesn't hit a visitor until he or she enters the house at the common room, which runs the front length of the house, with a grand stone fireplace at one end. A half staircase leads to a landing where one can continue to the back half

> From the wonderful architecture, a highly unusual and beautiful example of Arts and Crafts style built in 1913, to the innkeepers, a kind couple who give their hearts to their guests, the Shadows is a memorable experience.

of the house or up more right-angled steps to the four second-floor rooms.

The rooms are spacious and tastefully done, with heart pine floors in wonderful condition and private baths. The most desirable room must be the Rose Room at the front of the house; it's not too large, but it opens out to a grand front porch along the length of the house. The Blue Room is the largest; Pat created its bath from a room-size cedar closet. The Victorian and Peach rooms have views of the gazebo, fish pond, and Barbara's structured gardens.

The Loffredos are unusually sensitive hosts, and guests are afforded the utmost privacy. For those desirous of more than utmost, there are two cozy cottages that are original to the property. The Cottage and the Rocking Horse Cabin each have a full living room, bedroom, and sitting porch.

Pat cooks quite a full breakfast, beginning with fresh fruit garnished with flowers from the garden or pears poached in Grand Marnier, an entrée perhaps of stuffed French toast or giant ham biscuits with cream sauce — and always fresh eggs. With advance notice, Pat can cook dinners: his specialty is chicken cutlets in a mushroom wine sauce, and a New York–style cheesecake for dessert.

Guests will surely venture on to Montpelier, the neighboring home of James and Dolley Madison, or farther to Monticello and Charlottesville, Skyline Drive, and local vineyards.

Willow Grove Plantation

Route 15 North
Orange, VA 22960
703-672-5982
703-256-1976 in Washington, D.C.

*An authentic
plantation home*

Proprietor: Angela Mulloy. **Accom-
modations:** 5 rooms including 2 suites, all with private bath
and some with fireplace. **Rates:** $95–$155; $195–$250 AP rate
includes three meals. **Included:** Full southern farm breakfast.
Added: 6.5% tax, $20 additional guest. **Payment:** No credit
cards. **Children:** Welcome. **Pets:** Check with innkeeper.
Smoking: Allowed. **Open:** All year.

Willow Grove Inn, on the National Register of Historic Places
and a Virginia Historic Landmark, is set on 37 acres of fields
near Montpelier. The house, a sunny presidential yellow with
black shutters and white trim, sits grandly at the end of a
slightly winding drive, a few miles from the bustling village
of Orange. Several outbuildings remain in good standing on
the plantation, including the first schoolhouse in Orange
County. Masterminded by friendly Angela Mulloy, Willow
Grove Plantation is an informal social place and a famous
gathering spot for Sunday brunch.

The back part of the inn was built in the 1770s by Joseph

Clark as a small Federal farmhouse. Clark's son William, a surveyor for Thomas Jefferson, created the grand addition in 1830. The house is typical of Jefferson's classical revival style, with four white brick pillars two stories high supporting a third floor with a semicircular window carved into the cornice. As in a Palladian villa, stairs flank the formal first-floor entrance. Generals Wayne and Muhlenberg used the house as a camp during the Revolutionary War, and a Civil War–era cannonball was found in its eaves.

> **You'll feel somewhat presidential at the Willow Grove, a Jeffersonian Palladian villa near Montpelier. But there's nothing pretentious or overdone at this country inn. The rooms and the food are hearty, authentic, and robust.**

The rooms on the second floor and under the third-floor eaves are named for Virginia presidents born on the Constitution Trail and are decorated according to the period in which they governed. Across the hall from the Madison Room and Taylor Monroe Suite is the Washington room, featuring a grand antique four-poster bed with an upholstered tester and a working fireplace. This room has access to the front porch behind the columns, overlooking the grounds. Here one notices the explicit Jeffersonian influence, as the huge brick pillars remain unattached to the porch front.

Under the eaves of the third floor, the Harrison Room has a small velvet child's fainting couch at the foot of the antique Jenny Lind bed, all in Empire style. The pretty two-bedroom Wilson Suite features two distinct rooms with wicker sitting areas, a pink quilt over an antique iron and brass bed in one room and two cottage twin beds in another in front of the semicircular Jefferson window.

Once the old root cellar, the ground floor is home to Clark's Tavern, an informal gathering spot with exposed hand-hewn beams. There are two full dining rooms on the first floor, with weekend piano and vocal entertainment. Dinners by chef Doug Gibson range from $18 to $23 and feature terrific, creative, and hearty regional southern food. An appetizer might be country pâté of fallow fields venison and Texas wild boar, or Rag mountain smoked trout, Virginia ham, and corn chowder; entrée choices could be Napoleon of roasted duck breast and leg confit with orange, port, and pomegranate sauce, or grilled medallions of pork with chestnut gravy and braised red cabbage. The three-course Sunday brunch is a local tradition. A sampling might be smoked trout with dill mayonnaise followed by plantation toast royale with blackberry sauce and a meat or fish course of Virginia country ham baked with honey bourbon sauce served with fried tomatoes, and grits with cheddar cheese and creole sauce.

RICHMOND

The Berkeley Hotel

Twelfth and Cary Streets,
   Box 1259
Richmond, VA 23210
804-780-1300
Fax: 804-343-1885

> An intimate
> luxury hotel in
> Richmond

Proprietors: 12th and Cary Street Associates. **General Manager:** C.T. Rogers. **Accommodations:** 55 rooms, some with terraces, including one deluxe Governor's Suite. **Rates:** $124–$154, Governor's Suite $350. **Added:** $15 each additional guest, 9.5% tax. **Payment:** Major credit cards. **Children:** Welcome. **Pets:** Not allowed. **Smoking:** Nonsmoking rooms on all floors. Open: All year.

The Berkeley is an extremely handsome postmodern structure built in 1988 in the heart of Richmond's restored Shockoe Slip neighborhood. When Richmond was burned by Confederate troops in the Civil War, the tobacco warehouses of Shockoe Slip were the first to be destroyed, and the first to be rebuilt. Today they stand, preserved in time, on either side of cobblestoned streets, housing charming shops and businesses. The Berkeley Hotel is a sensitive addition to the area, incorporating the facade of an old townhouse in part of its exterior with historic lines echoed throughout the newer structure.

> **Shockoe Slip is an appealing section of Richmond near the Rivanna riverfront, the first section of the town to be rebuilt after it was burned in the Civil War. The post-modern Berkeley Hotel has the prime view of the cobblestoned neighborhood; inside, it's all luxury.**

Sitting on the corner of Twelfth and Cary streets, the center portion of the Berkeley Hotel culminates in a six-story brick and mortar tower, flanked by similar four-story townhouses, with its three-story inspiration tacked on near the Cary Street entrance. The substantive part of the hotel rests just behind the brick facade, unseen from the street, terraced on each floor providing balconies for about a third of the guest rooms.

Under the green awning, guests enter an antique-filled foyer, with dark wood molding, traditional wing chairs, and a lovely swirling-patterned deep Victorian carpet underfoot. The cozy Berkeley Restaurant has received four diamonds from AAA and fine local reviews.Chef Jay Frank prepares dinner entrées ranging from $16 to $26. Three meals are served here daily in a dressy, intimate setting with lacy Roman shades, cherry paneled walls illuminated by tiny brass wall sconces, and dark beamed ceilings. Nightingales Lounge is next to the restaurant.

Cartographers will be interested in the original maps used as artwork throughout the hotel. Across from the elegant elevator banks on each of six floors are prints of old maps detailing the progress of the Civil War from Cornwallis's campaign to the surrender in Yorktown. The guest rooms are nicely decorated in traditional luxury hotel themes, with chintz bedding matching floor-to-ceiling drapes and complementary tones in sitting areas. If televisions aren't hidden in armoires, they are mounted on stands. Most of the beds are king-size, and robes are available upon request. The baths have coffee-makers and telephones. Rooms are serviced twice daily, including European turndown. Fitness facilities are available at a nearby club.

New hotels not sponsored by a major chain are exciting properties in the hotel industry — especially when done as professionally and beautifully as the Berkeley. With only 55 rooms and the stunning Governor's Suite with its 30-foot vaulted ceiling, the Berkeley is small enough to offer personal service with the feeling of a large, luxury hotel.

Commonwealth Park Suites Hotel

Ninth and Bank Streets, Box 455
Richmond, VA 23203
804-343-7300
800-343-7302

*An all-suite hotel
at the foot of
Capitol Square*

Proprietors: Jonathan Ruben and Marvin Bush. **General Manager:** Wendy Swain. **Accommodations:** 59 rooms, including 56 suites. **Rates:** $150–$250. **Added:** $15 each additional guest, 9.5% tax. **Payment:** Major credit cards. **Children:** Welcome. **Pets:** Not allowed. **Smoking:** Nonsmoking rooms available. **Open:** All year.

Two qualities of the Commonwealth Park Suites beckon the traveler: its location, at the foot of dogwood-flecked Capitol Square, designed by Thomas Jefferson after the Maison Carrée in Nîmes, France; and the highly regarded Assembly restaurant, with a romantic setting and much-appreciated cuisine.

Originally, this historic site was owned by Robert E. Lee's brother Charles. In 1845, he sold the land to the Ruegers family, who erected a hotel in their name that was eventually burned, with much of Richmond, at the hands of Union troops (although the Capitol, farther upwind, escaped without a blemish). The present structure went up in 1912, a conservative limestone exterior onto which an 11th floor was added in 1956. What was then the Raleigh became the Mark Raleigh, and finally, by 1983, the Commonwealth Park Suites came into its own after two years of renovations. All was gutted but the marble floors, and the exterior was restored. In early 1991, the hotel was bought by Jonathan Ruben and his partner Marvin Bush, son of the former president.

The Raleigh Hotel once offered 130 guest rooms. The same space is shared today by 56 suites and 3 rooms, with only five or six suites per floor. The result is the privilege of having one's own private apartment at one of Richmond's finest addresses, under a trademark wine-colored awning at the foot of the Capitol. The guest rooms are furnished in

Its location in the heart of Richmond is nothing short of dramatic, at the base of Capitol Square, the lawn for the Capitol designed by Thomas Jefferson. The Commonwealth Park Suites is a formal business hotel, discreet, conservative, and upscale.

18th-century mahogany reproductions, decorated in a rather predictable luxury-hotel style, with thick pile carpeting, blond walls, and rosy chintz spreads and matching curtains. The suites have stocked mini-bars, and the elegant baths have terry robes, towel warmers, marble floors, heat lamps, bidets, and oversize tubs. The hotel has a very small exercise room and a whirlpool tub that may be reserved. Given the level of luxury elsewhere, the spare condition of the elevators is rather surprising.

Despite the lack of public space, the dining rooms are quite lovely. Maxine's is a wonderful garden of an interior, which looks through huge windows onto Capitol Square. Caned chairs and chintz cushions lighten the room, along with the sunny yellow walls and marbled floor. Downstairs dining is quite formal at the Assembly, a plush room limited to 48 patrons. The setting is sumptuous with red silk wallcoverings and red upholstered booths and chairs. The food of chef Doug Brown has been raved about by local reviewers. Entrées, from $16 to $25, might include twin fillets Felix, topped with artichoke bottoms filled with crabmeat and sauce béarnaise, or roasted rack of Wyoming lamb served with minted fresh fruit chutney, finished with a Grand Marnier soufflé.

Service is purposefully invisible at the Commonwealth Park Suites, which has the feeling of a Fifth Avenue apartment building in New York City.

The Jefferson Hotel

Franklin and Adams Streets
Richmond, VA 23220
804-788-8000
Fax: 804-344-5162
800-424-8014

> *A beaux-arts masterpiece, magnificent inside and out*

Proprietor: CCA Industries, Inc., Historic Hotels of America. **Managing Director:** Prem Devedas. **Accommodations:** 274 rooms, including 26 suites. **Rates:** Rooms $150–$190, suites $275–$825. **Included:** Morning newspaper, nightly turndown. **Minimum stay:** None. **Added:** 9.5% tax, $15 additional guest. **Payment:** Major credit cards. **Children:** Welcome. **Pets:** Not allowed. **Smoking:** Nonsmoking rooms available. **Open:** All year.

The Jefferson has a history as rich and grand as the Old South that it so well represents. The hotel was masterminded by Major Lewis Ginter, a mogul who made his fortune as a fabrics merchant and again as a tobacco tycoon in the late 19th century. Having traveled across the Atlantic 30 times and circumnavigated the globe on several occasions, Ginter wanted his hometown of Richmond to have a world-class hotel. His extensive knowledge of art and architecture prompted him to seek out the New York architectural firm of Carrere and

Hastings in 1892. Having produced such marvels as the Henry Frick House and the New York Public Library, the architects designed a classic beaux-arts monolith, with Renaissance elements and classic Greek aspects of the Doric and Corinthian order, at times reminiscent of the Villa Medici and 18th-century French châteaux.

After three years and $2 million, the hotel opened on Halloween 1895 in a social extravaganza. Ginter named the property for the prototypical American Renaissance man, Thomas Jefferson. Ginter went to great lengths to obtain from the University of Virginia the statue of the president that today welcomes guests in the Palm Court. Six years later, half of the hotel was destroyed by fire. By 1907 and with another $1.5 million in improvements, the hotel reopened with elaborate rococo additions. The Jefferson Hotel survived for several more decades until 1980, when a gradual decline in business forced it to close.

> It is rumored that the carpeted staircase in the Jefferson was the model for that in Tara in *Gone With The Wind.* Whether this is fact or myth, the Jefferson certainly represents the quintessence of southern elegance and grandeur.

The hotel remained vulnerable for three years until Richmond developer George Ross and investors bought the property and invested $34 million in its resurrection. Under the management of the Sheraton Corporation, the hotel opened to accolades in May 1986. The restoration process was exhaustive. Original art, fixtures, furnishings, and sconces were found in storage; layers of paint and plaster revealed mahogany paneling in the Flemish Room; the plaster moldings and carvings were cleaned; nine of the twelve original Tiffany stained glass windows in the domed ceiling of the Palm Court and Rotunda were restored and replaced; and the faux marbling of the columns and capitals in the Rotunda was restored.

Today, guests stroll through the vast common spaces of the Jefferson in awe. The two-story Palm Court has a magnificent stained glass domed ceiling 35 feet in diameter. Fan-shaped stained glass arches hover above the gilded capitals of columns supporting the airy ceiling. A statue of Jefferson overlooks this public space.

The guest rooms are generously sized and brightly decorated in rose and green hues, with creamy thick pile carpeting. The custom-made furniture is traditional dark wood, and the bed and window treatments are bright. There are three telephones, including one in the bath. Televisions are hidden in cabinets, the mini-bars are stocked, and rooms with sitting areas have classic wing chairs and couches. A majority of the suites have fireplaces, whirlpool baths, and wet bars.

There are two restaurants at the Jefferson: informal dining at T.J.'s, and formal new American cuisine by chef Lal De-Silva in a series of seven rooms at Lemaire, named for the maitre d'hôtel during Jefferson's presidency. The rooms in Lemaire are extraordinarily beautiful, one of which is the Library, with a solid African mahogany fireplace and original tomes from Jefferson's own library.

Service is happy, friendly, replete with southern charm and pride. A tour of the hotel is highly recommended.

Linden Row

First and Franklin Streets
Richmond, VA 23219
804-783-7000
Fax:804-648-7504
800-348-7424

A place of infinite hospitality

Proprietors: Winthrop Hotels and Resorts. **General Manager:** Jeannette Weir. **Accommodations:** 70 rooms, including 6 parlor suites and 30 Garden Rooms, all with private bath. **Rates:** $74–$152. **Included:** Continental breakfast, wine and cheese reception, use of YMCA, morning newspaper. **Minimum stay:** None. **Added:** $10 each additional guest, 9.5% tax. **Payment:** Major credit cards. **Children:** Welcome, under 18 free. **Pets:** Not allowed. **Smoking:** Nonsmoking rooms available. **Open:** All year.

There are two reasons why a stay at Linden Row is unavoidable: no one can walk by the magnificent row of architecture on East Franklin Street, between First and Second, without peeking inside — and once inside, no one can resist the charm of its hostess, Jeannette Weir. In this strikingly proud southern town, nearly everyone except a native will feel like an outsider — except for French-born Ms. Weir, and everyone on whom she smiles.

> The seven Greek Revival townhouses of Linden Row were built between 1847 and 1857, when the neighborhood was Richmond's toniest. Fully restored, they stand now as the finest example of its kind in the nation. The same superlatives apply to Innkeeper Jeannette Weir.

The row of seven Greek Revival townhouses is the finest example of its kind in the nation. Thanks to the preservation efforts of noted local architect and oral historian Mary Wingfield Scott and the Historic Richmond Foundation, the buildings were saved from destruction and kept alive. Thanks to the 1988 restoration efforts of Winthrop Hotels and Resorts, visitors may stay overnight in lovely accommodations in the architectural marvel. And thanks to the legendary hospitality of Jeannette Weir, guests will extend their visits and return again and again. It's not an understatement. Ms. Weir has left a trail of admirers around the world, most recently in Washington, D.C., as the manager of the Embassy Row Hotel. Her staff is quite smitten, as guests can tell the moment they walk in the door and for a memorable while after they leave.

The antebellum address of Linden Row was Richmond's most exclusive. Built between 1847 and 1857 in the height of Georgian elegance as private homes, the rowhouses numbered ten altogether. Two of the rowhouses were razed in 1922, and the remaining eight were threatened in 1950 when Mary Wingfield Scott bought up the land. The 1988 restoration was greatly aided by the Historic Richmond Foundation, which painstakingly researched period details such as furniture, wall coverings, and carpeting.

Seven of the eight original townhouses belong to Linden Row, containing 38 guest rooms with seven extremely large parlor suites. Every room has a writing desk, a queen-size or two double beds, some interesting period antiques, remote televisions, and telephones. The baths are quite large, with elegant old tiling.

Behind the facade is a lovely brick courtyard with café tables, umbrellas, and manicured gardens — as well as three two-story brick buildings that served as the original kitchen and carriage houses to the antebellum town houses. Along the brick paths and pretty gardens, the Garden Quarters have 35 smaller rooms decorated in French country with furniture commissioned for Linden Row, double beds covered with wedding ring quilts, and private phones and televisions.

Ms. Weir greets guests each evening in a rather extensive wine and cheese party, with a fireside presentation of appetizers in the original parlor. Guests have only to walk several steps to the dining room, in an intimate boutique setting. Lunch and dinner are served daily, under the care of Alain Vincey, with dinner entrées ranging from $15 to $22 for coquilles St. Jacques, sea scallops encased in duchess potatoes, Chesapeake crabcakes, or steak aux poivres served with French mustard and white wine. The ambience shifts away from romance in the sunlit breakfast area in the morning, with a bottomless Continental breakfast consisting of hot oatmeal, cereals, and fresh muffins and fruit.

With its courteous, likable staff and exceptional hostess, Linden Row feels like a European boutique hotel. The service is that of an attentive full-service property with bed-and-breakfast friendliness.

The William Catlin House

2304 East Broad Street
Richmond, VA 23223
804-780-3746

*A charming B&B
across from
St. John's Church*

Proprietors: Robert and Josephine Martin. **Accommodations:** 5 rooms, 3 with private bath, 4 with fireplace. **Rates:** $70–$90. **Included:** Virginia tax and room tax, full breakfast, gratuities. **Minimum stay:** None. **Payment:** Visa, MasterCard. **Children:** 12 and over welcome. **Pets:** Not allowed. **Smoking:** Allowed. **Open:** All year.

Among the most significant of Richmond's many landmarks is St. John's, atop the Historic Church Hill District, the church where Patrick Henry requested liberty or death. Weary patriots will find refuge right across the street at the William Catlin House. After two years of preparation, Robert and Josephine Martin left careers in newspaper photography and the police force to open a bed-and-breakfast. They took with them some pretty antiques, a strong work ethic, and great hopes for their property.

In 1990, the Martins bought this established B&B and changed its name from Catlin Abbott to the William Catlin House, after its contractor William Catlin, who erected the three-story brick house in 1845. The masonry was done by his servant William Mitchell, the father of the country's first African-American bank president and founder of the first African-American–owned bank — who was also a woman.

The house is nearly twice as deep as it is wide. After the Civil War, during which more than 800 Richmond homes were burned, an addition was built to house some of the homeless. The Martins live in the addition, which shares lovely porches with the old section of the house, overlooking the old carriage house and gardens.

> **Perhaps if you lean out from your second-floor room and strain to hear the winds of history, you can hear Patrick Henry gallantly declaiming, "Give me liberty or give me death." For it was right across the street from the William Catlin House at St. John's Church that his famed speech was delivered.**

The traditional double parlor, with its working fireplace, is nicely decorated with high Victorian and late Empire antiques collected by the Martins over the years. The two guest rooms on the second floor have fireplaces, traditional furniture including wing chairs, and queen-size canopy beds with lovely bedding. The unusual third-floor room is quite large, tucked under the eaves, with two deep dormer windows and a quilt rack in an odd alcove — the only room without a fireplace. The English basement has two cozy rooms, each with a fireplace, good for families as they share one bath. The room features a separate front entrance, a back porch and garden, and a full kitchen.

Guests enjoy a full breakfast in a rather formal setting around the reproduction Chippendale dining table, with hot meats, eggs, and pancakes, as well as fresh fruit and juice. The meal provides sustenance for a leisurely drive to see the plantations along the James River on Route 5 toward Williamsburg. Robert and Josephine are hard-working, sincere professionals who love their change of life.

TREVILIANS

Prospect Hill Plantation Inn

Route 3, Box 340
Trevilians, VA 23093
703-967-0844
Fax: 703-967-0102
800-277-0844

*A glorious
country inn near
Charlottesville*

Proprietors: The Sheehan family.
Innkeeper: Michael and Laura Sheehan. **Accommodations:** 13 rooms, including 3 suites (5 rooms in main house, 8 rooms in 7 cottages). **Rates:** $195–$295 per couple, MAP; some week-day discounts. **Included:** Full breakfast and dinner, afternoon tea. **Minimum stay:** Two nights with a Saturday stay. **Added:** $35 each additional guest, 4.5% tax. **Payment:** Visa, Master-Card. **Children:** Welcome in cottages. **Pets:** Not allowed. **Smoking:** Allowed. **Open:** All year except Christmas Eve and Christmas Day.

Prospect Hill is one of the most unusual accommodations in the Mid-Atlantic states. Fifteen miles east of Charlottesville, this country inn is set on ten acres of a resurrected southern plantation. Guests stay in several rooms in the warm manor house and in seven outbuildings, including the slave quarters, a log cabin (built in 1699), the overseer's house, a summer kitchen, a smokehouse, a carriage house, and the groom's quarters. While guests share the social warmth of a country inn, they have the romantic advantage of private cottages.

The manor house is a beautiful, pristine yellow clapboard with white trim and black shutters, completed in 1732 by Roger Thompson. Slaves were brought over as early as 1796, and the other buildings were erected under the ownership of Richard Terrill. Years later, the plantation was owned by William Overton, who returned from the Civil War like Scarlett to Tara only to find ruin and despair. The Overtons began taking in guests, expanded the manor house, and renovated the slave quarters. Sheehan expanded on Overton's hospitality ideas, bringing to the plantation a sense of sophistication, luxury, and romance.

A great part of Prospect Hill's appeal rests in the elegant dining experience. Guests gather in the colonial common rooms for a drink fireside and sit down to dinner at the signal of a bell. The meal, prepared by host Michael, is a four- or five-course French Provençale meal, the menu of which changes nightly. A sample might be a potage fermier cream and potato soup, a house salad, supèmes de volailles Beaugency with artichokes, and a Genoise chiffon cake, chocolate with mocha buttercream. Guests dine intimately by candlelight. The five-course dinners are part of the overnight rate; they are $40 for outside guests.

> The manor house and many of the seven outbuildings of Prospect Hill plantation were constructed in the 18th century — the earliest in 1699. The southern inn is now beautifully restored and serves wonderful French Provençale dinners by candlelight.

The drive, stretching grandly toward the picturesque manor house, is flanked by the unique cottages, which are connected by walkways covered with white trellises, and bordered by trimmed bushes and picket fences. The Overseers, the Little Boys, and Uncle Guy's cabins are on one side of the drive; on the other, two cottages: the Kitchen and the Carriage House, above the Groom's Quarters. Most luxurious are the Carriage House and Sanco Pansy's cottage, a short walk behind the manor house. The former has a tiled floor, sweeping Palladian windows, a full sitting area, and an 1840s cherry four-poster bed. The cottages are furnished with antiques, and all have working wood-burning fireplaces, refrigerators, stereos, private porches, and views of the rolling countryside. Some have whirlpool baths. Guests are welcomed by a bottle of wine, fruit and cheese basket, and homemade cookies.

Rooms in the manor house are decorated in traditional Williamsburg style, authenticated by sloping original flooring, window sashes, doors, and mantels.

Service at Prospect Hill is discreet, pampered, and genteel. Full breakfasts are brought to one's room in a charming presentation on a silver tray. Guests may pass time with an idle walk in the fields to pet the horses or with a swim in the pool.

Shenandoah Valley and the Blue Ridge Mountains

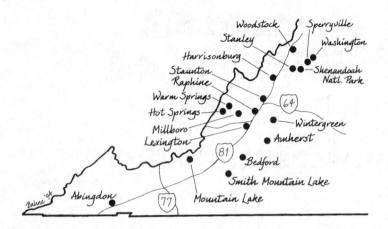

Best Gourmet Getaway

Washington
  The Inn at Little Washington

Best Remote Refuges

Bedford
  Peaks of Otter Lodge
Millboro
  Fort Lewis Lodge
Shenandoah National Park
  Skyland Lodge & Big Meadows Lodge
Warm Springs
  Meadow Lane Lodge

Best Resorts

Hot Springs
  The Homestead
Mountain Lake
  Mountain Lake Hotel
Wintergreen
  Wintergreen

Best Country Bed-and-Breakfasts

Amherst
  Dulwich Manor Inn
Raphine
  Oak Spring Farm and Vineyard
Smith Mountain Lake
  The Manor at Taylor's Store
Sperryville
  The Conyers House Inn and Stable
Wintergreen
  Trillium House
Woodstock
  The Inn at Narrow Passage

Best Country Inns

Lexington
   Maple Hall
Stanley
   Jordan Hollow Farm Inn

Best Village Inns

Abingdon
   Martha Washington Inn
Harrisonburg
   Joshua Wilton House
Staunton
   The Belle Grae Inn
Warm Springs
   The Inn at Gristmill Square

The Shenandoah National Park is 80 miles long, composed of 200,000 acres, and averages between 2 and 13 miles wide between Front Royal and Waynesboro. It averages 2,000 feet above sea level, with spectacular views from **Skyline Drive.** South of Waynesboro, Skyline Drive becomes the Blue Ridge Parkway, 470 miles long with 217 miles of drive in Virginia.

Driving due west from Washington, D.C., for an hour and a half will bring you to Skyline Drive: but please, don't miss the overnight of your life at the Inn at Little Washington, the country's most fulfilling inn experience. The gateway to Skyline Drive is around **Woodstock,** Luray, **Stanley,** and Front Royal, where antiquing and caverns can sidetrack you for days.

Finally you arrive at Skyline Drive, only to be diverted by the wonderful towns nestled in the valley between Shenandoah National Park and the one million acres of the George Washington National Forest, which forms a natural border with West Virginia. **Harrisonburg** is a bustling town, home to James Madison University and Mennonite College. **Staunton** is a San Francisco of the Mid-Atlantic, with flashy Victorian architecture amid steep hills. Though settled as early as 1731, the city was chartered in 1870 in the heyday of Victoriana and became a large intersection of the Chesapeake-Western and the Chesapeake and Ohio railroads. It is home to Mary Baldwin College and the Woodrow Wilson Birthplace and has a great resource in the Museum of American Frontier Culture. The next college town after Staunton is **Lexington,** home of the Virginia Military Institute and Washington and Lee University, as well as the Virginia Horse Center.

Farther west a traveler will arrive at **Hot Springs,** home of the Homestead Resort and some of the state's finest golf and skiing. The natural mineral springs discovered here in the 18th century have attracted followers over the centuries. Five miles north of the Homestead are the original **Warm Springs** Pools, heated naturally by underground springs to a steady 98 degrees year-round. The men's pool, built in 1761, is said to have been designed by Thomas Jefferson; the women's pool was added in 1836.

The Blue Ridge Parkway begins here. About 15 miles south of Lexington is a wondrous sight in Natural Bridge, a limestone arch 215 feet high and 90 feet long, supporting U.S. 11. Roanoke is the gateway to Virginia's southwest, a hardworking town strong in fine arts. **Smith Mountain Lake,** an endless recreation area, is about 20 miles southeast of Roanoke, not far from Booker T. Washington National Monument. Just north is the wonderful estate of Poplar Forest, the summer retreat of Thomas Jefferson between 1806 and 1813, an octagonal Palladian tribute.

With tickets in hand to an event at the Barter Theater, visitors will find a side trip to **Abingdon** quite rewarding. The theater was named because barter was accepted as payment for tickets when it opened in 1932.

ABINGDON

Martha Washington Inn

150 West Main Street
Abingdon, VA 24210
703-628-3161
Fax: 703-628-8885
800-533-1014

> *A lavish mansion across from the Barter Theater*

Proprietors: United Co. **General Manager:** Deborah J. Bourne. **Accommodations:** 61 rooms, 11 suites, some with fireplaces, whirlpools, steam showers. **Rates:** $85–$250, suites $145–$250. **Included:** Afternoon tea, nightly turndown service with chocolates, use of nearby fitness facility. **Added:** $10 each additional guest, 8.5% tax. **Payment:** Major credit cards. **Children:** Welcome, under 12 free. **Pets:** With management approval. **Smoking:** Nonsmoking rooms available. **Open:** All year.

People come to Abingdon from April through December to see performances at the famous Barter Theater, the country's longest-running Equity theater. It is so named because during the Depression, when the theater was founded, the price of a ticket was "35 cents or the equivalent in produce." When people come to the Barter Theater, they can stay at the historic Martha Washington Inn, conveniently across the street.

It's quite fascinating to find this bastion of culture here in Virginia's southwest corner. Abingdon is nestled in a narrow but lofty valley with an elevation of 2,000 feet, between the Appalachian and Blue Ridge mountains.

The inn was built in 1832 as a lavish private residence. In 1858 Martha Washington College bought the building, which doubled as a hospital during the Civil War. The Depression took its toll and the college was closed in 1932, but the building was reopened as a hotel three years later, given the new popularity of the Barter Theater.

Wallpaper murals in the grand foyer are replicas of those used by Jacqueline Kennedy in the White House. They depict colonial scenes and national sights including nearby Natural Bridge.

The First Lady's Dining Room is a stupendous space, its pressed-tin ceiling supported by faux wood-grain columns. The wooden bar is gorgeous, set off by the green Queen Anne chairs. The silver dining table in the center, found in a box during the 1986 restoration, is 50 years old. There are twelve Waterford crystal chandeliers, bought originally for $11 each. The other dining room, the Epicurean Club, serves dinner only, Tuesdays through Saturdays. Chef Lisa Mullen prepares classical and regional fare for these two dining rooms, with dinners ranging from $12.50 to $22.

> The Barter Theater, founded in the Depression, is the country's longest-running Equity theater. Overlooking it is the Martha Washington Inn, a dramatic architectural vision built in 1832. In 1936 wings were added to mirror the Greek Revival facade of the theater. You'll give it a standing ovation.

While all the rooms are configured differently, they have a unique and very pleasing decor for a luxury hotel: the beds are dressed with plain duvets with printed skirts matching curtains, with a distant Chinese influence. The furniture is a mixture of reproductions and excellent antiques, and the baths are beautifully appointed with green marble. Amenities include nightly turndown and room service.

Nearby outdoor activities are found in Mount Rogers National Recreation Area (which peaks at 5,700 feet), Holston Lake, or the ubiquitous Appalachian Trail nine miles south. The Virginia Creeper Trail, once a railway between Abingdon and Whitetop Mountain, is now a 34-mile-long scenic pathway, good for hiking, biking, and skiing.

AMHERST

Dulwich Manor Inn

Route 5, Box 173A
Amherst, VA 24521
804-946-7207

> *A Greek Revival mansion three miles from Sweet Briar*

Proprietors: Bob and Judy Reilly. **Accommodations:** 6 rooms, 4 with private bath, 2 with shared bath. **Rates:** $65–$85. **Included:** Full breakfast. **Added:** 4.5% tax. **Minimum stay:** Some college weekends. **Payment:** No credit cards. **Children:** Welcome. **Pets:** Not allowed. **Smoking:** Restricted. **Open:** All year.

A half-hour drive east of the Blue Ridge Parkway and north of Lynchburg brings a visitor to the doors of Dulwich Manor, a grand three-story brick mansion in the countryside just three miles from Sweet Briar College. Sweet Briar was founded in 1901, several years after Dulwich Manor had been completed. The house, built on more than 1,000 acres of farmland, belonged to a single family for 60 years, It was purchased by Bob and Judy Reilly in 1988. The Reillys are quite thrilled with their relatively new endeavor, settling on five acres of rural bliss after years in New York City, during Bob's career as an actor and Judy's as a theater public relations officer.

Despite its proximity to Sweet Briar, Dulwich Manor seems lost in rural farmland, reached by a winding quarter mile of gravel drive. A 300-year-old oak tree and new privet hedges line a brick walkway that leads to the majestic entrance. The front porch is shaded by a double-story portico with four massive Ionic columns holding up a triangular third-floor pediment. Oversize picture windows with Palladian treatments flank the entrance, allowing light to filter into the library and parlor on either side of the foyer.

Good traditional furnishings, antiques and reproductions, fill the original library, which has a fireplace, the big double parlor, which has pocket doors, and the formal dining room. On the second floor are five large guest rooms named for British counties and furnished with pretty antique beds lengthened to queen size. A third-floor room was recently added, with beautiful exposed wood floors and lovely views through a triad of dormer windows, tucked under the eaves of the high rooftop. There are five working gas fireplaces throughout the house, three of which are in guest rooms. The Scarborough Room has a whirlpool bath as well as a reproduction curved fishnet canopy bed and a beautiful mirror-back Victorian settee. The Coventry Room has a graceful Victorian bedroom suite in pine and walnut. Guest rooms are freshened with flowers and potpourri. The baths, though rather plain, have travel-size generic amenities. Robes are provided in each room so guests may use the outdoor hot tub in the gazebo.

> **This turn-of-the-century manor house is a stunning sight at the end of its quarter-mile driveway, in the valley between Lynchburg and the Blue Ridge Parkway. You can view the 1,000 acres of undeveloped farmland from your pretty guest room: there's simply nothing in sight but trees and grass.**

Judy cooks a very full breakfast, served in the formal dining room or on the long verandah, consisting of fresh muffins and breads, a hot entrée like stuffed French toast or crêpes, and country sausage or bacon. A day's activity apart from a visit to Sweet Briar or the seven colleges surrounding Lynchburg might consist of a trip north to Wintergreen for four seasons of activities, or a trip across the Blue Ridge Parkway to Lexington, the Virginia Horse Center, and Natural Bridge.

BEDFORD

Peaks of Otter Lodge

Box 489
Bedford, VA 24523
703-586-1081

> *The only inn
> right on the Blue
> Ridge Parkway*

General Manager: Don Humphreys. **Accommodations:** 62 rooms, with 3 suites in main lodge. **Rates:** Winter, rooms $75, suites $85; rest of year $65 (no meals). **Included:** Weekday dinner and breakfast; weekend dinner only. **Added:** $4 each additional adult, 6.5% tax. **Payment:** MasterCard, Visa. **Children:** Welcome. **Pets:** Not allowed. **Smoking:** Allowed. **Open:** All year.

The Peaks of Otter Lodge is propped up on the Blue Ridge Parkway, halfway between Roanoke and Lynchburg. The magnificent mountainside, lakeside property is leased from the National Park Service; and the Lodge, built in 1964, is privately owned. Accommodations, therefore, are a tad fancier than average National Park fare, at extremely reasonable rates.

The peaks are two neighboring mountains providing majestic views: Flat Top, just over 4,000 feet, and Sharp Top at 3,875 feet. Three theories have evolved around the naming of this scenic place: the appellation could have derived from the Indian word *ottari*, meaning "high places"; the peaks might have been named by Scottish settlers after a mountain in their homeland that resembles Sharp Top, called Ben Otter; or they may have been directly named for nearby Otter River.

The Lodge hovers at a lowly 2,560 feet, dominated by a busy public restaurant that serves three meals daily, as well as a famous Sunday buffet. Overnight units are set apart from the Lodge in a contemporary two-story structure. Yet most important, the Peaks of Otter rest around the one-mile perimeter of Abbott Lake, 24 acres of crystal waters stocked with smallmouth bass.

> You won't believe the setting: on the Blue Ridge Parkway at 2,560 feet, with Flat Top and Sharp Top peaks looming overhead, right on Abbott Lake.
> The food and rooms are quite good, and its location is simply remarkable.

Each room is furnished in motel-style simplicity. They are quite clean, with two double beds and sensible furniture, including a writing desk and ample reading lamps, all looking toward a picture window with an expansive lake view. The baths are new, clean, and spare. Happily, all the rooms at Peaks of Otter have balconies or patios overlooking Abbott Lake and Sharp Top Mountain.

Most commendable are the reasonable rates for this groomed lakeside property with mountain views. Dinner entrées range from $8 to $14 in the sociable dining hall. The Peaks of Otter is an active recreational hub for appreciative visitors to the Blue Ridge Park. Guests have the double pleasure of the Lodge, which is fairly bustling during high season, and the privacy of clean, comfortable rooms with mountain-view balconies.

HARRISONBURG

Joshua Wilton House

412 South Main Street
Harrisonburg, VA 22801
703-434-4464

A Victorian inn serving Harrisonburg and two colleges

Proprietors: Roberta and Craig Moore. **Accommodations:** 5 rooms, all with private bath, 2 with working fireplace. **Rates:** $85–$95. **Included:** Full breakfast. **Minimum stay:** None. **Added:** $25 each additional guest, 6.5% tax. **Payment:** American Express, MasterCard, Visa. **Children:** Over 10 welcome. **Pets:** Not allowed. **Smoking:** Not allowed. **Open:** All year.

Harrisonburg, a bustling town west of Shenandoah National Park, is home to two large student populations, at James Madison University, established in 1908, and at Eastern Mennonite University, founded nine years later. A visitor driving down Main Street will undoubtedly notice an impeccably restored Victorian house, brightly painted in roses and mauves, called the Joshua Wilton House. This fancy Victorian is home not only to five lovely guest rooms but also to great dinners served in a formal, elegant setting.

Craig Moore was a well-established Harrisonburg chef before he and his wife Roberta opened their own inn in 1988. The goal for this creative couple was to create the town's most elegant dining spot, a luxurious setting with beautiful food and a full wine list. After restoring the house to its original 1883 condition, the Moores had the Joshua Wilton House placed on the National Register of Historic Places.

The first floor is devoted to the elegant dining experience. Guests enter the magnificent foyer, where the light falls on the floor in a spectrum of color fractured by the elaborate beveled glass around the front door. Before dinner, guests await their table in a mahogany-paneled lounge, with tufted leather chairs and banquettes, in front of an antique oak and carved soapstone bar. Of the four dining areas, one has a bay window, another a turret, another is a cozy and private nook, and the last is an enclosed sun room. The front two dining rooms have working fireplaces with original oak mantels. Guests also dine outdoors under kiss-shaped umbrellas on the patterned brick patio.

> **Two colleges, a bustling town, and tourism from the Appalachian and Shenandoah mountains provide a varied business.**
> **The Joshua Wilton House responds well to the needs of this diverse community, offering romance, elegance, dignified comforts, and acclaimed food prepared by owner Craig Moore.**

Upstairs, each of the five guest rooms was decorated by a different member of the Moore family, in Victorian elegance with varied design, some feminine, others reserved and stately. Roberta and Craig parted from heavy Victorian colors and lightened the walls and window treatments. The pleasing art on the walls is for sale, a gallery for the Shenandoah Watercolor Society. Room 2 has a working fireplace, a brass and white iron bed, an armoire with a mirror, and a pair of ladies' slipper chairs. Room 3 is the smallest, featuring a lovely rosewood rocker, and a window seat nestled in a four-windowed bay. Room 5 has the other working fireplace and a four-poster pencil post bed. The antique pieces, including the beds, are in the finest taste, and the chairs are upholstered in precious silk and damask.

It is no surprise that a full breakfast is integral to a stay at the Joshua Wilton House, with specialties of jumbo lump crabmeat asparagus omelettes or poached eggs with smoked salmon or smoked duck.

HOT SPRINGS

The Homestead

Post Office Box 2000
Hot Springs, VA 24445
703-839-5500
Fax: 703-839-7544
800-336-5771
800-542-5734 in Virginia

> *The state's finest
> grand old resort*

Proprietors: Club Resort Inc. **President:** Gary K. Rosenberg. **Accommodations:** 518 rooms, including 81 parlor suites. **Rates:** $215–$306 per couple MAP, with higher rates Thanksgiving and Christmas. **Minimum stay:** 3-day minimum during Christmas week. **Added:** $81 each additional guest MAP, $7.50 daily housekeeping, 4.5% tax, 15% service charge. **Payment:** Major credit cards. **Children:** Allowed, 12 and under free. **Pets:** Not allowed. **Smoking:** Nonsmoking rooms available. **Open:** All year.

A quintessential grand old resort, the Homestead is a gracious property steeped in tradition, 2,500 feet up in the Allegheny Mountains of western Virginia. Chesapeake and Ohio Railroad president M. E. Ingalls bought the property with a group of associates in 1891, and the resort was run by his family for four generations. Although the family tradition has now been passed to a private management company, the Homestead has a small-town warmth that is highly unusual in a 500-room resort. In fact, it looks rather touchingly like an enormous — albeit quite luxurious — schoolhouse.

Hot Springs was settled in 1721. By mid-century, the curative nature of its mineral waters was well known. George Washington visited in 1761, five years before the land was sold to Thomas Bullitt, who built the first Homestead. A modern building was erected in 1846, and it was expanded in the 1890s when the resort opened formally. The Casino, the Cottages, the Bathhouse, and the first tee of the Homestead golf course were laid out in 1892. It wasn't until 1901 that the recognizable Georgian exterior was built of red Kentucky brick, then expanded to the west in 1903, and again to the east in 1914 when the Ingalls family bought a controlling interest in the property. The trademark Homestead Tower, completed in 1929, was recently placed on the National Register of Historic Places.

> **For more than 100 years, the Ingalls family ran the Homestead, a staggering feat of endurance. Though the resort was recently bought by a private company, the Homestead retains the sense of community endowed by the Ingalls during their reign.**

A visitor won't believe that such an extensive property is nestled so inconspicuously into the hills. On its 1,500 acres are three championship golf courses, 19 tennis courts (4 all-weather), a spa and an indoor pool naturally heated by mineral waters, two outdoor pools, four skeet and two trap fields, rifle and archery ranges, 100 miles of trails cut for hiking and horseback riding, some of Virginia's best trout fishing, an Olympic skating rink and eight ski slopes, two lawn bowling greens that date to colonial times, an eight-lane bowling alley, croquet, badminton, horseshoes, and putting greens.

Guests enter from the long verandah to the 200-foot-long Great Hall, supported by 16 magnificent Corinthian columns, the setting for afternoon tea and a classical concert. The common rooms are elegantly appointed with antiques and lavish floral arrangements, and guest rooms fill the wings that radiate from the Great Hall. The rooms, redecorated in a recent multimillion-dollar effort, are traditionally furnished in dark wood reproductions in several schemes, all extremely classic and understated.

Swiss-born executive chef Albert Schnarwyler has been at the Homestead since 1962, his legendary skills admired in the elegant and formal main dining room. Guests have a number of other less formal dining options, including Sam Snead's Tavern in the village. Upscale shops line one of the main wings. The Cottages below the Homestead, rebuilt in the 1920s to resemble the original 1890s structures, house boutiques and the Café Albert.

The original bathhouse, built in 1892, is an architectural marvel and a vision from the past. As well as the naturally heated indoor pool, built in 1903, guests enjoy two outdoor pools, full spa amenities, and hydrotherapy in mineral waters that range from 102.5 to 106 degrees.

The three golf courses at the Homestead are among the East Coast's finest. The original first tee of the Homestead course, built in 1892, is the oldest in the country in continuous use. Three miles south is the Cascades course, designed by William S. Flynn in 1923, said to be one of the country's best mountain courses. Robert Trent Jones designed the Lower Cascades Course in 1963, the resort's longest. Sam Snead, a member of the Homestead staff since 1975, grew up a mile and a half from the resort and used to caddy here as a youngster.

Guests who opt for a more golf-oriented or value-oriented stay might want to inquire about the 50-room Cascades Inn three miles away near the Homestead and Lower Cascades courses, a low white clapboard building with a country club look.

Skiing has been a Homestead feature since 1959, with three trails and eight slopes. With a base elevation of 2,500 feet and a vertical drop of 700 feet, it's a great place to learn how to ski. For those few who might disagree, the Olympic-size outdoor skating rink offers figure skating instruction.

Younger guests at the Homestead have an indoor and outdoor playground. Summers offer even more to 7- to 10-year-olds, who can receive instruction in golf, tennis, fishing, swimming, hiking, and target archery.

While the atmosphere is the same formal one that greeted the country's wealthiest moguls and eight presidents over three centuries, there is a genuine friendliness among the generations of staff who make the Homestead a grand family resort.

LEXINGTON

Maple Hall

Historic Country Inns
  of Lexington
Route 11 and Interstate 81
Mailing address:
11 North Main Street
Lexington, VA 24450
703-463-2044
Fax: 703-463-7262

> *A beautiful estate*
> *near Lexington*
> *and its two colleges*

Proprietors: The Peter Meredith family. **Innkeeper:** Don Fredenberg. **Accommodations:** 21 rooms with private bath, including 5 suites and 10 with gas fireplace (12 rooms in Manor House, 3 rooms in Guesthouse, 6 rooms in Pond House). **Rates:** $95–$155. **Included:** Continental breakfast. **Minimum stay:** 2 nights on some college weekends. **Added:** $15 each additional guest, 6.5% tax. **Payment:** Visa, MasterCard. **Children:** Welcome. **Pets:** Not allowed. **Smoking:** Not allowed in Pond House and Guesthouse. **Open:** All year.

Maple Hall is one of the three Historic Country Inns of Lexington, a commendable restoration project undertaken by the Peter Meredith family of Norfolk in 1978. Two less formal properties are in the historic section of Lexington, while elegant Maple Hall is six miles north, just off the interstate. In 1984, the Merediths bought the distinguished Maple Hall from the descendants of John B. Gibson, who built the plantation house in 1850.
  While within view of the interstate, the stunning three-story Georgian and Palladian brick structure is surprisingly removed on its 56 acres. The formal guest entrance is ap-

proached by a dual staircase in true Palladian fashion, leaving a separate ground-floor entrance underneath for the dining areas and two handicap-accessible rooms. Large black-shuttered windows on two floors flank four white pillars.

The inn is decorated with period reproductions and Federal antiques. The first and second floors have three queen bedrooms and one twin bedroom, each with a fireplace and television, four-poster reproduction bed, a desk, wing chairs, and a newly appointed bath. Each room features several good antiques. These rooms are much preferable to the two double-bedded rooms in a wing off the first floor. The common room is on the first floor, with a gas fireplace.

> Set in the southern countryside, several miles from Lexington, Maple Hall is a terrific find. The three-story Georgian and Palladian brick manor house is a stunning sight. Teamed with the property's 1828 Federal home and a contemporary replica, a pool, and 56 acres of countryside, Maple Hall is an ideal getaway.

Maple Hall forms the third of a trio of brick buildings on the property set tidily around a courtyard of greenery. The middle building, just off the outdoor dining terrace, is the Guesthouse, the first on the property, built in 1828 by the Gibson family as it settled on the 257-acre plantation. Adjacent is the Pond House, completed in April 1990, a replica of its older cousin except for some modern details and porches. Both are two stories, decorated in Federal simplicity; some rooms have gas fireplaces and balconies overlooking the stocked fishing pond, the swimming pool, and the tennis court. There are several miles of trails maintained and mapped for active guests.

Dinner is served in three dining rooms, most pleasantly in the enclosed brick porch. The menu is specialized and seasonal, and entrées range from $15 to $21. A favorite appetizer is lobster bisque or angels on horseback — large gulf shrimp and oysters wrapped in bacon and broiled. The chef's offerings might include chicken Suzanne sautéed with Virginia ham and topped with cheese sauce; filet mignon, wrapped in bacon with béarnaise sauce on the side; or grilled quail.

Innkeeper Don Fredenberg may be found at the McCampbell Inn in town, though the large Maple Hall staff is helpful and happy. Despite the genteel plantation atmosphere at

Maple Hall, it is a busy place given its proximity to Washington and Lee University and the Virginia Military Institute.

MILLBORO

Fort Lewis Lodge

HCR 3, Box 21A
Millboro, VA 24460
703-925-2314

A wilderness destination in southeastern Virginia

Proprietors: John and Caryl Cowden. **Accommodations:** 13 rooms, all with private bath, including 3 silo rooms; and 2 historic Log Cabins. **Rates:** $130–$145 MAP; 2-bedroom family suite $150; Log Cabins $180; hunting packages available. **Included:** Breakfast and dinner. **Minimum stay:** None. **Added:** $25 each additional guest, $15 each child age 5–12, 4.5% tax. **Payment:** Visa, MasterCard. **Children:** Welcome. **Pets:** Not allowed. **Smoking:** Not allowed. **Open:** Closed January through March; seasonal hunting.

Fort Lewis Lodge and little else rests in a 3,200-acre dell in the Allegheny Mountains and lower reaches of the George Washington National Forest, along a five-mile stretch of the Cowpasture River. The mountain farm had been known for two centuries as Fort Lewis Plantation, named for Colonel Charles Lewis, who built a stockade on this land in 1754 to protect his family from the Indians. Today, the five square miles of untouched wilderness belong to John and Caryl

Cowden, who transformed their crop and cattle farm into an overnight lodging place in 1986.

John built the lodge as a modern testament to the traditional structures of barn and silo. The lodge is sided with three stories of western red cedar, incorporating a 40-foot stone silo at one end that houses three guest rooms with mountain vistas in every direction. John then restored the 1850s gristmill, two floors of open-beamed wooden ceilings and walls, with a dining room, common area, and a gift shop. A swimming hole was created from a dammed section of the old millrace.

> In the spring and fall, this 3,200-acre valley draws hunters and fishers; in the summer, naturalists flock here. The lodge and 40-foot stone silo hold the hearty, comfortable accommodations; family-style meals are served in the restored 1850s gristmill.

The lodge has a great beam-ceilinged common room, with plaid couches and comfortable traditional rockers and wing chairs warmed by a brick fireplace. The wallpaper borders are country patterns of animals and a great *Field and Stream* magazine cover motif. The skills of a local taxidermist display the whitetail deer, bobcat, turkey, and other creatures of the wild frozen in time. The 15 guest rooms are decorated in Virginia Shaker simplicity. The furniture was made by local craftswoman Beth Brokaw from such diverse woods as locust, butternut, walnut, cherry, and oak. The yellow pine floors are covered in woven rugs, and the beds are draped with red and black plaid blankets in the winter and quilts in the warmer months.

The Log Cabins are recent additions to Fort Lewis. They were moved from West Virginia to the site and are wonderful historic buildings, built in 1870 and 1892. Romantics will love the large stone fireplaces.

Fort Lewis Lodge is a popular spot for hunting and fishing in the spring and late fall, and in the months between for leisure guests. Spring brings trout and bass fishermen to the Cowpasture River, and wild turkey hunters from mid-April through mid-May. Hunting resumes in mid-October through December. Leisure guests come more quietly from mid-May through mid-October's foliage season.

Rates include a country breakfast of home-baked muffins, egg and sausage casseroles, and oatmeal pancakes, as well as

Caryl's bountiful dinners, signaled by the ringing of a bell across the fields. The family-style buffets include hearty dishes like barbecued chicken and ribs, harvest roast, and Cowpasture River trout, all served with garden vegetables. On the vast acreage, guests enjoy exploring wildflowers, bird-watching, tubing, swimming, trout and bass fishing, and 18 miles of hiking trails.

MOUNTAIN LAKE

Mountain Lake Hotel

Route 700
Mountain Lake, VA 24136
703-626-7121
Fax: 703-626-7172
800-346-3334

> *A breathtaking
> lakefront resort
> on 4,000-foot
> Salt Pond Mountain*

Proprietor: Mary Moody Northern Foundation. **General Manager:** H. M. Scanland. **Accommodations:** 92 units (45 in main lodge, 16 in Chestnut Lodge, 31 in 19 cottages) **Rates** (MAP): Rooms $130–$165, suites $190–$245, family suites $255–$265, Chestnut Lodge $180. **Included:** Breakfast and dinner. **Minimum stay:** 2 nights on weekends. **Added:** $35 each additional guest, children age 5–12 $20 (under 5 free), 6.5% tax, $5.50 service charge per person daily. **Payment:** Major credit cards. **Children:** Allowed. **Pets:** Not allowed. **Smoking:** Non-smoking rooms available. **Open:** All year; open only on weekends November 1–May 1.

Mountain Lake is one of the most remote resorts in the region, wedged in the Potts Mountains of Jefferson National Forest on the lower border of the Virginias. A winding, narrow, seven-mile drive up Salt Pond Mountain offers spectacu-lar, ever-changing perspectives on the mountainous setting. At the summit, just under 4,000 feet, is the beautiful stone lodge, a series of log cab-ins, and the stunning vista of sparkling Mountain Lake, one of only two natural freshwater lakes in Virginia. The resort remains a secret, and its 2,600 acres and 15 miles of trails a rare treat for naturalists. If the place looks rather familiar, it's because *Dirty Dancing* was filmed here in 1986.

> Seven miles straight up a mountain may convince you that you're lost, but when you arrive at the summit to behold a glorious 1936 stone manor house and the sparkling lake, you'll feel triumphant. Even though *Dirty Dancing* was filmed here, Mountain Lake Hotel's 2,600 acres remain a secret.

There are three faces to Mountain Lake: the elegant stone manor house, with its nicely appointed rooms, some with Jacuzzis; the less formal, contemporary Chestnut Lodge, in which rooms have fireplaces and bal-conies; and the very rustic cottages. Resort days at Mountain Lake date to 1857 and a white wooden boarding house that became vastly popular at the turn of the century. William Lewis Moody from Galveston, Texas bought the property in the early 1930s and erected the stone lodge in 1936.

Couples may want to spend time in the main lodge or Chestnut Lodge, the former with 45 rooms on two floors fur-nished in deluxe, traditional reproduction furniture, the latter in a more contemporary style, built in 1985, with 16 rooms. Families tend to gather in the many informal log cabin cot-tages scattered around the property. The main lodge remains the focal point of a stay at Mountain Lake. The public rooms on the first and ground levels seem rather fortresslike, with thick stone walls, low ceilings, and cozy, library-inspired sit-ting areas leading to tranquil porches overlooking the lake. The dining room is wonderful, with romantic fireside and lake views, its ceiling supported by stone pillars.

Though couples will love long walks, the fireplaces, car-riage rides, golf, tennis, and cross-country skiing, families with children will be overwhelmed by the dozens of activities organized daily by a full-time staff. Cookouts, clambakes, steak fries, storytelling, dancing, and other events take place in the recreation barn and loft. Mountain Lake is stocked with trout, largemouth bass, blue gill, and sunfish. For above-water pleasure, there are canoes, paddleboats, and rowboats. A pontoon boat makes daily runs to the Boat House at the end of the lake. There is a casual, Old-World elegance about Mountain Lake, and while hosting all activities of a large resort, the management maintains a small, intimate scale. The staff seems like a large family, helpful and genuinely happy to be in this setting and part of a great hospitality tradition.

RAPHINE

Oak Spring Farm and Vineyard

Route 1, Box 356
Lexington, VA 24472
703-377-2398

A vineyard and ideal B&B near Natural Bridge

Proprietors: Pat and Jim Tichenor. **Accommodations:** 3 rooms, all with private bath. **Rates:** $63–$73. **Included:** Extensive Continental breakfast. **Minimum stay:** Some college weekends. **Added:** 6.5% tax, $15 in Victorian room only. **Payment:** Visa, MasterCard. **Children:** 16 and over welcome. **Pets:** Not allowed. **Smoking:** Not allowed. **Open:** All year.

Seasoned bed-and-breakfasters will appreciate this idyllic, professionally run property. After 26 years in the army, 16 of which were spent overseas, Jim and Pat Tichenor opened their first bed-and-breakfast, Fassifern, in Lexington, Virginia. A means of retirement for two very active, organized people, the bed-and-breakfast became a quick success. The Tichenors discovered that they wanted to spend more time with guests, sold Fassifern, and bought Oak Spring Farm, in the countryside halfway between Lexington and Staunton, in 1989.

> An 1826 farmhouse, 35 acres of fields, five acres of vineyards, and Shetland ponies from the Natural Bridge petting zoo: these are some of the wonderful elements of Oak Spring Farm bed and breakfast.

The original four-room white brick house was built in 1826 by a family with nine children. The back ell was added to the house in 1840. Today, the surrounding 40 acres of land remain nearly untouched but for the burros, miniature cow, and Shetland ponies from the Natural Bridge Petting Zoo, which leases part of the land.

The guests have their own living room with a working fireplace, and Pat has decorated the house with pretty period border papers, antiques, and beautiful Oriental rugs. Many of the artifacts around the house were collected from Pat and Jim's worldwide travels and years in Korea. Perhaps the most striking aspect of Oak Spring is its cleanliness, the result of Pat's standards, which are as high as the retired colonel's.

At the front of the house, the original 1826 section, are two large guest rooms and a sitting area done in late Empire. The Art Deco Room has two twin rose-colored velvet tufted beds, a fireplace, beautiful Bukhara rug, and an old washstand made into a sink. The Victorian Room is notable, with an 1840 queen-size bed and a twin brass bed covered in an antique log cabin quilt. The bath is very large, with black and white parquet tiles and a double-size shower. The Regency Room in the back 1840 addition has two southern exposures and a small sitting area in the ell hallway. The Tichenors are very conscious about having good bed-and-breakfast touches such as current magazines, good reading lamps, drinking glasses, fresh flowers and plants, and soft towels. Though it should be a surprise, they offer the nice touch of chocolates on pillows.

They bake their own muffins, grow their own berries, and pick their own flowers and fruit — apples, peaches, pears, plums, and cherries. These will surely be featured at breakfast, when guests are given fruit soup, cherry cream scones, and fancy French toast. The farm has been a vineyard for more than a decade, and in 1990 Jim harvested more than 13 tons of grapes from the vines on five acres. Nearby is Natural Bridge, as well as the Virginia Horse Center.

SHENANDOAH NATIONAL PARK

Skyland Lodge
Big Meadows Lodge

Skyline Drive
Shenandoah National Park,
  Virginia
Mailing address:
Box 727, Luray, VA 22835
Skyland: 703-999-2211
Big Meadows: 703-999-2221
800-999-4714

> *The only lodges
> on 105-mile
> Skyline Drive*

Proprietors: ARA Virginia Sky-Line Co., Inc. **General Manager:** Mike Slowinski. **Accommodations:** 186 rooms in lodge units and cabins at Skyland Lodge; 103 rooms in Big Meadows Lodge in 25 lodge units and cabins, some with fireplaces. **Rates:** $48–$140 (highest on weekends and in October). **Minimum stay:** None. **Added:** 6.5% tax. **Payment:** Major credit cards. **Children:** Welcome. **Pets:** Not allowed. **Smoking:** Allowed. **Open:** Skyland: Late March through November; Big Meadows: Early May through October.

Ten miles apart on Skyline Drive, just outside of Stanley, Skyland and Big Meadows are the only two lodging facilities on the 105-mile-long scenic mountain pass. Owned by the ARA Virginia Sky-Line Company, which runs the concessions along the Drive, these two lodging spots combine the rustic excitement of camping and the comfort of a hotel in one of the country's most beautiful National Parks.

The Skyland Lodge is the northern property, at milepost 41.7. It is slightly more private than Big Meadows. At 3,680 feet, Skyland is one of the highest points on the Drive, offering inspirational views. The property consists of 186 rooms spread among 26 buildings, from contemporary two-room suites to motel units to rustic two-room cabins. Lodge rooms have balconies or patios looking westward to the glorious landscape of the Shenandoah Valley. The large dining room, which shares its menu with Big Meadows, serves hearty mountain food and Virginia cooking, such as roast prime rib, country ham with spiced apples, or southern fried chicken served with corn fritters and local honey. The specialty dessert is blackberry ice cream pie, enhanced with blackberry syrup and meringue.

> **Those coming to explore the wonders of Shenandoah National Park, including its 500 miles of hiking trails, will surely stay at Skyland or Big Meadows Lodges. At around 3,700 feet, they offer breathtaking views, fine rooms, private cabins, and unlimited access to a national treasure.**

Big Meadows (at milepost 51) offers a little more beauty in its architecture. Its main lodge, built in 1939, is introduced by a flagstone patio looking 3,640 feet down the Shenandoah Valley. While the grand dining room shares this view, it is in itself a most glorious sight, with a cathedral ceiling of open-beamed wormy chestnut. Some rustic guest rooms are in the lodge, others are spread throughout the lodge units and five rustic cabins with fireplaces.

Each property hosts its own nightly entertainment. As the accommodations are furnished sparely with average decor, the consensus at Big Meadows and Skyland is that the splendor rests in the outdoors.

A visitors center at Big Meadows details the dizzying number of outdoor activities in the park: more than 500 miles of marked hiking trails, including a 95-mile segment of the Appalachian Trail, horseback riding, bird-watching of more than 200 species in the park, family camping, and dozens of naturalist programs.

SMITH MOUNTAIN LAKE

The Manor at Taylor's Store

Route 1, Box 533
Smith Mountain Lake, VA 24184
703-721-3951, 800-248-6267

*A lively B&B
near Smith
Mountain Lake*

Proprietors: Lee and Mary Lynn Tucker. **Accommodations:** 6 rooms with 4 private baths, and 3-bedroom 2-bath Christmas Cottage. **Rates:** $80–$125. **Included:** Full breakfast. **Minimum stay:** 2 nights with Saturday stay, from April through October. **Added:** 6.5% tax. **Payment:** MasterCard, Visa. **Children:** Welcome in the Christmas Cottage. **Pets:** Not allowed. **Smoking:** Permitted in Christmas Cottage. **Open:** All year.

The Manor at Taylor's Store is three miles from wondrous Smith Mountain Lake, an active boating and state recreation center in Virginia's southwestern frontier. The 20,000-acre lake has 500 miles of shoreline, is about 40 miles long, and is well loved by fishermen looking for landlocked striped and largemouth bass. The lake's overwhelming beauty is best — and uniquely appreciated from the basket of a hot-air balloon, an undertaking that innkeepers Lee and Mary Lynn Tucker will be most happy to arrange — you'll be picked up right on the inn's front lawn.

Fifteen miles east of Roanoke and the Blue Ridge Mountains, the Manor at Taylor's Store is named for a famous merchandise trading post established on this site in 1799 by Skelton Taylor, an introduction to the unexplored West on the

Old Warwick Road. Most of what stands today is an elegant three-story white clapboard manor house set back from Route 122 by lovely lawns, built in the early 19th century as part of a tobacco plantation, rebuilt in the 1890s, and restored by its current owners over two years starting in 1986 when they were newly-weds. Lee, a pathologist, and Mary Lynn, a former nurse, are consummate hosts with contagious enthusiasm for their home and surroundings.

> **There's a surprise in this 19th-century manor house. Hosts Lee and Mary Lynn Tucker are hot-air balloonists. From this, you may surmise that this lovely 120-acre property is not your average quaint B&B.**

The Tuckers have collected some beautiful antiques over the years, including a Victorian living room set with several velvet tufted chairs and a mirror-back couch. The imposing tall case clock in the corner was designed in 1903 by Stanford White for a wealthy Long Island family. Through a threshold are the dining room and enclosed sun porch with views to some of the 120 acres, home to two Newfoundlands, several horses, and six spring-fed ponds, which are wonderful for fishing, swimming, and canoeing; the largest has two swimming docks. There's also a swimming pool and a creative and rare colonial garden, with geometric brick walkways, raised beds, antique plantings, and a Gazebo from which to take it all in.

Lee and Mary Lynn devoted much space for guests' common use: the lower level Great Room has a slate floor with a big-screen television and a fitness room with rowing and cross-country ski machines, an exercise bike, and weights. Adjacent to this is an enclosed hot tub and a kitchen for guest use. The cozy Garden Room shares the ground floor, with a private entrance and sun porch.

A favorite is the first-floor Plantation Suite, with a working fireplace and two antique handmade double beds in rich carved walnut, under canopies whose linens match bedskirts and window treatments. Among the preferred second-floor rooms are the Colonial Room, past the well-stocked hall library, with a queen-size fishnet canopy bed and a private balcony; the Toy Room, with antique quilts and toys, opening through French doors to a dramatic view of the back pastures; and the Castle Suite, with a queen-size canopy bed, mountain views, and a new bath featuring a sunken tub. Mary Lynn prefers the comfort of flannel sheets year-round and is meticulous about her rooms.

The Booker T. Washington National Monument is four miles away on the route to Smith Mountain Lake.

SPERRYVILLE

The Conyers House Inn and Stable

Slate Mills Road, Route 1, Box 157
Sperryville, VA 22740
703-987-8025, 703-987-8709

An English country B&B in the Blue Ridge foothills

Proprietors: Sandra and Norman Cartwright-Brown. **Accommodations:** 9 rooms, including 2 suites (1 in Sperryville Village) and 2 cottages, all with private bath. **Rates:** $100–$195. **Included:** Full breakfast, afternoon refreshments. **Minimum stay:** 2 nights on autumn weekends and holidays. **Added:** 4.5% tax. **Payment:** No credit cards. **Children:** Welcome. **Pets:** Welcome in the Cellar Kitchen and the Springhouse. **Smoking:** On exterior porches only. **Open:** All year.

Though American bed-and-breakfasting has been fashionable for more than a decade, the Conyers House shows no trace of such an influence. In the remote countryside in the eastern foothills of the Blue Ridge Mountains, this farmhouse seems lifted from the English countryside. It's a bed-and-breakfast in true European style: without bric-a-brac, solicitous hostmanship, matching chintzes, or marble baths — just Old World heirlooms and antiques. The only American thing about Conyers House are the rates, which are steep for the area. But in true old-money fashion, no one speaks of such things here.

The Cartwright-Browns came to Sperryville, at the valley's north end in Rappahannock County, from Chevy Chase, Maryland. Their bed-and-breakfast is geared for their horsey tastes, and those of their former neighbors, the capital's elite in search of an unadorned country retreat. Sandra and British-born Norman bought the house as their own weekend retreat in 1979, installed plumbing, and opened it to guests in 1981. The oldest part of the house is the stone section, built by Hessian mercenaries around 1790, moved here and attached to Bartholomew Conyers' new house in 1810, when it became known as Conyers' Old Store. Most notably, the house features ten working fireplaces.

Guests have to duck their heads when descending the stairs to the room called the Cellar Kitchen, with a huge fireplace, painted stone walls, exposed beams, and a waist-high antique double bed. The largest of the three rooms on the second floor is Uncle Sim's Suite, with a long porch overlooking the narrow country road, an 1840 high canopy bed, an antique secretary, and a sitting room with a hanging French tapestry, and a television and VCR. Helen's Room also has a private porch, a fireside sitting area, and lots of windows; and the very cozy Grampie's Room has a fireplace also. Of the two attic rooms, one under the eaves has a clawfoot tub positioned in the middle of the room, either romantic or a nuisance; but either way the room has lovely views of the fields and horses. Choice accommodations are the cottages, romantic hideaways several paces up the hill from the house. The walk can be a bit muddy, but once there, guests may not want to leave since each cottage has a Franklin stove, television, VCR, and tape player, and a small, stocked refrigerator: the Hill House has a double jacuzzi, and the Spring House has a private sleeping loft.

> This English country home is filled with Old World heirlooms and antiques. Horses — English saddle only — complete the picture at this informally formal country retreat.

A satisfying breakfast may include pancakes with sausage-apple filling. Also of note is the Cartwright-Browns' Fox & Grape teahouse in Sperryville, where Valerie Clark serves American cuisine for $135 per couple: a dinner entrée might be venison with lingonberry-wine sauce or smoked trout.

En route from Washington, having driven through horse country, some travelers may get the equestrian bug. Sandra is an avid horsewoman and has eight horses on the property. She will be quite happy to arrange for trail rides lasting several hours through beautiful scenery ($35), lessons (from $35 to $50), or, you can participate in a fox hunt.

STANLEY

Jordan Hollow Farm Inn

Route 2, Box 375
Stanley, VA 22851
703-778-2285
Fax: 703-778-1759

*Horseback riding
and mountain
views*

Proprietors: Marley and Jetze Beers.
Accommodations: 21 rooms with
private bath (1 Farm House suite, 16 rooms in Arbor View
Lodge, 4 rooms in Mare Meadow Lodge). **Rates:** $140–$180.
Included: Full breakfast and dinner. **Minimum stay:** None.
Added: 6.5% tax. **Payment:** Major credit cards except American Express. **Children:** Welcome. **Pets:** Not allowed. **Smoking:** Allowed. **Open:** All year.

At Jordan Hollow Farm, 25 horses wait to be ridden — or simply observed — against the backdrop of the Blue Ridge Mountains. Just west of Skyline Drive near cavern-famous Luray, Jordan Hollow Farm is one of the few inns along the Shenandoah National Park possessing such a magnificent view from its 45 acres.

Marley and Jetze Beers met in West Africa. As newlyweds, they spent weekends renovating their 1790 weekend farmhouse with the intention of drawing conference groups who wanted unique meeting facilities to the country. On Memorial Day weekend 1981, the group that booked the entire property canceled hours before arrival time. As the weekend's food was cooking on the stoves, the Beerses asked local hotels to send them their overflow. They had such fun that they geared their entire market toward individual travelers, many of whom return today.

Jordan Hollow Farm is a series of buildings. First is the 150-year-old stable; the Arbor View Lodge (built in 1984) and the Mare Meadow (finished in 1990) flank either side of the drive; and at the end is the old farmhouse, a blond two-story clapboard building with stacked porches. The latter is the main gathering spot, with one second-floor suite and four dining rooms serving breakfast and dinner. (Box lunches are provided on request.)

The 16 rooms in the Arbor View Lodge are on two floors

and overlook the pasture, riding rings, meadows, goat houses, and Chinese chickens. Second-floor rooms have better views from the rocker-filled porch. These rooms are cozy and clean and country-decorated, with handmade furniture and interesting pieces such as tapas from the South Pacific or Africa and Mennonite quilts.

> **Near Luray, famous for its caverns and access to the Shenandoah National Park, is a unique country inn that specializes in many enjoyable things, but mostly horses. On Jordan Hollow's 45 acres, you can ride one of 25 horses and enjoy magnificent mountain views.**

The rooms are more luxurious in the Mare Meadow Lodge, with gas fireplaces, whirlpool tubs, and private porches overlooking the meadows. The handmade furniture is cedar, and the quaint animal or country decor includes some nice quilts. Mare Meadow Lodge has its own common room, also with a fireplace.

The dining rooms offer unusual settings: the two 1790 log cabin rooms, the fox room with a hunt theme, and the exotic African room with artwork from the Beerses' travels. Dinners are part of the overnight rate: they are all served with soup, salad, vegetables, and fresh bread. Specialties are sautéed chicken topped with white wine and cream sauce, served on wild rice or quinoa pilaf; rainbow trout amandine with crab stuffing; and vegetarian dishes that promises to convert even the most devoted steak lover.

The Beerses offer trail rides for all levels and pony rides for children. They are proud of their extremely rare Norwegian Fjord horses, one of the oldest breeds known, ridden and worked by the Vikings. For nonequestrians, there are trails for walking and carriage rides, swimming and fishing at Lake Arrowhead 10 minutes away, nearby caverns, and skiing at Massanutten and Bryce resorts.

STAUNTON

The Belle Grae Inn

515 West Frederick Street
Staunton, VA 24401
703-886-5151

*A pretty and
unusual inn in
historic Staunton*

Proprietor: Michael Organ. **Accommodations:** 21 rooms in five houses
(8 rooms in main house, 4 suites in
Jefferson House, 3 rooms and 1 suite in Townhouse, 2 suites
in Bishop's Suite, 3 rooms in Bungalow). **Rates:** $55–$90,
suites $95–$200. **Included:** Full breakfast. **Added:** $2 per person daily service, 15% tax. **Payment:** Major credit cards. **Children:** Well-behaved children welcome. **Pets:** Not allowed.
Smoking: Limited. **Open:** All year.

This inn is a successful compilation of many aspects of hospitality, the result of the inexhaustible efforts of owner
Michael Organ. He bought the Belle Grae in 1983 and has
been hard at work continuously, expanding, restoring, decorating, antiquing. In addition, he is a consummate host, providing a thorough library of local history and activities for
guests, the author of a brochure of day trips from the inn and
a flyer detailing Staunton's ten formidable restaurants
(including his own). Daily from 5 to 6 P.M., he hosts an
innkeeper's social in the parlor where he meets his guests;
and he is always present at breakfast. He is paternally close
with his staff, who happily and busily roam about this mansion like family members — an aspect of innkeeping that
guests notice only when it is absent.

Staunton is a beautiful town that has been successfully restored during the last several years, a Virginian San Francisco
with Victorian architecture on hilly streets. Mary Baldwin
College and the Woodrow Wilson Birthplace are among the
many sights. The Belle Grae Inn sits atop a hill in the Newtown Historic District, an elegant three-story Federal brick
house built in 1873, expanded in the latter part of the century
to 19 rooms with an Italianate wraparound porch. Eight
rooms are on two floors of the main house, with wonderful
antique spool, brass, and sleigh beds and lovely Victoriana.
The Bistro, serving Continental food, offers spectacular views

of Staunton through large picture windows. The full breakfast is served here. Light-fare dining is available on the sunny patio behind the Bistro.

The four satellite houses vary in decor. The Bishop's House was built in the 1880s for the Episcopalian bishop of the diocese and is now home to two suites, adjacent to the registration office and decorated in period antiques. Built in the 1880s for workers at the local pajama factory, the Jefferson House is the newest property to be restored and has the most daring, romantic decor, mixing traditional Victoriana and lovely antiques with creative patterns, colors, and crown canopies. The old Townhouse is at the front of the Belle Grae and connects to the Bistro by a footbridge. It was built in the 1860s as a traditional valley home and has three rooms good for business travelers, with desks, televisions, and phones, and one contemporary suite. The Bungalow has three bedrooms suitable for families.

> **Staunton is a beautiful, hilly town just west of the Blue Ridge Mountains. A high point in its historic section is the Belle Grae Inn, recognizable by its Italianate wraparound porch. The inn sits as if on a throne overlooking the Victorian town.**

An hour's drive provides dozens of local activities: to the west, Hot and Warm Springs in the Allegheny Mountains and the Homestead Resort; to the south, Natural Bridge and historic Lexington, with the Virginia Military Institute and Washington and Lee University; to the north, James Madison University in Harrisonburg and Endless Caverns in New Market; or a drive across Skyline Drive east to Charlottesville and Monticello.

WARM SPRINGS

The Inn at Gristmill Square

Box 359
Warm Springs, VA 24484
703-839-2231

> *A charming village inn set over a millrace*

Proprietors: The McWilliams family. **Innkeeper:** Bruce McWilliams. **Accommodations:** 16 rooms, all with private bath, 8 with fireplace in five separate buildings. **Rates:** $80–$95 per couple; MAP rates also available, per couple. **Included:** Continental breakfast in room; use of the tennis courts, swimming pool, and sauna. **Added:** $10 each additional person, $32.50 each additional person MAP. **Payment:** Visa, MasterCard, Discover. **Children:** Welcome. **Pets:** Not allowed. **Smoking:** Allowed. **Open:** All year.

Warm Springs was named for its 98-degree natural pools. The hamlet is only several miles north of Hot Springs, home to the legendary Homestead Resort. Both springs sit on Route 220, the westernmost road along this mountainous stretch, which winds along the valley of the Jackson River through breathtakingly beautiful farmland, overlooking the lush thicket of the George Washington National Forest.

The village of Warm Springs consists of a post office, several municipal buildings, a church, and the Inn at Gristmill Square. The Square is a lovely composition of four preserved 19th-century buildings clustered around a gristmill, which served as the town's main industry for more than 200 years. The present mill was built in 1900 and functioned until 1970, when it was transformed into the Waterwheel Restaurant. This forms a triad across a white gravel walkway with the Blacksmith Shop (home to two guest rooms and the Office) and the Hardware Store, which today houses six guest rooms.

> **Warm Springs is a pretty hamlet. Besides its church, post office, and municipal buildings, the only other structures are the four historic buildings of Gristmill Square, straddling Warm Springs Mill Stream.**

Adjacent is the Miller's House, which has four guest rooms; and across the narrow street that spans Warm Springs Mill Stream sits the elegant Steel House with its four guest rooms.

The McWilliams family has been a proud fixture in Warm Springs since 1981, when they bought the inn from Phil Hirsch, who restored and opened Gristmill Square in 1972 (he now owns the nearby Meadow Lane Lodge). All the rooms are completely different, some with a sense of independence, like the outer rooms in the Steel House and Miller's House, and some with a sense of community, like those in the old hardware store. The four Steel House rooms are lovely and traditional, furnished with antiques, telephones, televisions, and refrigerators. The Jenny Payne Room is especially pretty, with a queen-size bed, a working fireplace, and a separate room with a tub overlooking the mountains. The Quilt Room has four antique quilts on an antique rack with a spinning wheel tucked into the corner.

Favorite rooms in the Square are the Silo Room and the Tower Apartment, with entirely round walls in their common rooms, giving it a feeling of being in the interior of a barrel. Bedrooms in each radiate off the circular living rooms, and the Tower Apartment has the advantage of a tin-roofed turret that is much fun in the rain.

Behind the Steel House are three tennis courts, an outdoor swimming pool, and a sauna.

The Waterwheel Restaurant is a popular attraction. The wheel was a working part of this gristmill for more than half a century and today is a functioning part of the restaurant, used to display more than 96 varieties of wine, which rest in its gears and picks. The dining rooms are intimate and dimly lit, with open-beam ceilings. Entrées range from $15 to $20 for roast duckling with oranges, tenderloin en croûte with Marsala served in a pastry shell. The smoked mountain trout is an area specialty, smoked over hickory chips and served with horseradish cream. After dinner, the impossibly small and charming Simon Kenon Pub lures the gregarious.

Meadow Lane Lodge

HCR 01, Box 110
Warm Springs, VA 24484
703-839-5959

A wilderness retreat with regulation croquet

Proprietors: The Hirsh family. **Innkeepers:** Cheryl and Steve Hooley. **Accommodations:** 11 rooms. **Rates:** $85–$130. **Included:** Full breakfast. **Minimum stay:** 2 nights on October weekends. **Added:** $25 each additional guest, 4.5% tax. **Payment:** Visa, MasterCard, American Express. **Children:** Over 6 welcome. **Pets:** May be allowed with prior approval. **Smoking:** Allowed in rooms only. **Open:** All year.

Meadow Lane Lodge is secluded on 1,600 acres of protected farmland, four miles west of historic Warm Springs in the dells of the Allegheny Mountains. Visitors fish for trout along two private miles of Jackson River, hike, splash in a six-foot swimming hole, or simply bask in the peaceful nature of this glorious retreat.

Meadow Lane dates to 1750, when William Warwick bought the plot from Charles Lewis, who had received it as a land grant from King George III. The impending threat of the

French and Indian Wars prompted Warwick to build a stockade-type fort on this property in 1754, known as Fort Dinwiddie, named for the state's governor. The second building on the property was built by Warwick's son Jacob in 1805. The only remaining historic building is the Slave Cabin, which dates from the late 18th or early 19th century.

> **Meadow Lane Lodge is where you come to escape everything except civility. Its 1,600 acres have access to two trout-filled miles of the Jackson River and unlimited views of the Allegheny Mountains. Outdoor activities include trail hiking, tennis, golf, swimming, and six-wicket croquet.**

Innkeeper Cheryl cooks full southern breakfasts, which include a soufflé-like batter bread, grits, and greens. With advance notice, Cheryl will also cook dinners on weekends from April to October. For $25 per person, visitors will sample tenderloin aux poivres or grilled rainbow trout.

Lodge accommodations are filled with antiques and have porches and fireplaces. The lodge's Great Room is a fine gathering spot with twin stone fireplaces over a country plaid rug; and the Breakfast Room features a 1710 oak sideboard. Contemporary accommodations are also in the Ice House, Craig's Cottage, and the Car Barn, formerly the Carriage House. In the Warm Springs Historic District, the Francisco Cottage is a two-bedroom cabin built in 1820 of hand-hewn square logs and furnished with antiques. It has a modern kitchen and a shady porch.

Wonderful activities abound at Meadow Lane. Seven trails, from one to three miles, provide not only magnificent views but sightings of bald eagles, osprey, fox, mink, bobcat, deer, and an occasional bear. A favorite walk is only an eighth of a mile to the Deck, with spectacular views of the verdant plateau against the backdrop of the Alleghenies. Residents of the barns are Nubian goats, donkeys, peacocks, ducks, geese, and Chinese chickens.

The Jackson River divides the acreage. While its natural inhabitants include smallmouth and rock bass, blue gill, pickerel, and fall fish, the river is stocked with rainbow and brown trout for recreational fly-fishing. In addition, guests may use the Dynaturf tennis court, the pool, and the Homestead's Upper and Lower Cascades golf courses.

Meadow Lane is a member of the United States Croquet Association and has a regulation-style court. For equally posh diversions, visit the Warm Springs thermal pools, which stay at a constant 98 degrees year round.

WASHINGTON

The Inn at Little Washington

Middle and Main Streets, Box 300
Washington, VA 22747
703-675-3800
Fax: 703-675-3100

*A masterpiece
of dining
and overnighting*

Proprietors: Patrick O'Connell and Reinhardt Lynch. **Accommodations:** 12 rooms, including 3 suites, all with private bath. **Rates:** $240–$480. **Included:** Breakfast, afternoon tea. **Minimum stay:** None. **Added:** $40 each additional guest, 7% tax. **Payment:** MasterCard, Visa. **Children:** Not allowed. **Pets:** Not allowed. **Smoking:** Allowed. **Open:** All year.

Of all the superlatives associated with this property since its inception in 1978, none is too strong and none is quite adequate. The Inn at Little Washington, 67 miles west of the capital nearing the Shenandoah National Park, has been lauded for years by the most esteemed critics as a place of absolute perfection from its food to its accommodations. In 1991, the Inn was the first American property in the history of the Mobil guide to receive a five-star rating for both food and accommodations — and it has kept this exceptional status ever since. With only 12 rooms and just 65 dining tables, the Inn at Little Washington requires its guests to reserve far in advance and pay a good deal for the honor of a meal and a room. Still, a lifetime of luxury is not complete without a night at the Inn at Little Washington.

> The Inn at Little Washington ought to be a national landmark, for when it opened in this tiny farming community in the Blue Ridge foothills in 1978, the hospitality industry was transformed. Since then, people have been coming by the limo-ful to this culinary paradise — and leaving with an experience that will never be forgotten.

Perhaps what makes the inn such an inspiring accomplishment is that owners Patrick O'Connell and Reinhardt Lynch built the property from scratch, with $5,000 and undaunted determination. The two met in 1970 in Washington, D.C., where Patrick worked as a chef and Reinhardt at a hospital. They were able to buy a 100-acre farm in the foothills of the Blue Ridge Mountains, where they started a catering business. After six years, Reinhardt and Patrick had a faithful following who pledged frequent countryside pilgrimages, and they opened a restaurant. They rented a garage for $200 a month in the rural community of Washington, transformed the mechanic's pit into Patrick's kitchen, and slowly refurbished the premises. In January 1978, they served their first dinners to 70 thrilled guests. By 1984, they provided eight oft-requested guest rooms and, several years later, two duplex suites. Today, amid deafening accolades, the Inn at Little Washington is one of only 19 independent American properties in the elite and prestigious Relais & Châteaux.

The guest rooms, which were designed by English stage set designer Joyce Conwy-Evans, are nothing short of stunning. She is famous for her use of rich fabrics and combinations of lavish patterns. The antiques, fabrics, and wallpapers were imported from England; the extensive faux wood graining and marbling throughout the inn was done to her specifications by artist Malcolm Robson.

Each of the nine guest rooms is thoroughly insulated and a world unto itself: one is a cozy alcove dressed in floral wallpaper; another is a successful hurricane of patterns, with a blackberry wood headboard crowned by a yellow floral canopy with a reverse in rose floral material over a plaid spread; yet another has a Chinese influence with a pagoda-style canopy over a rosewood headboard. The two third-floor duplex suites are identically furnished with regal baths with Jacuzzis, separate showers, heated towel racks, and Greek marble countertops (the only real marble in the inn). Each has two balconies with mountain views.

The staff of 55 at the Inn is highly polished and trained, the definition of discreet and solicitous service. Guests enter a wood-paneled reception area whose stained glass ceiling is a collage of 5,000 hand-drawn gilded and painted blocks. The dining areas are to the right, so thoroughly draped, festooned, swagged, and tapestried as to conjure images of the inside of a genie's bottle: cushioned, exotic, lavish, and plush.

Samples from the winter menu include preludes of sesame pastry filled with shiitake mushrooms, Jarlsberg, and leeks; a steaming puff of French poppy bread; or applewood-smoked trout. These might be followed by an appetizer of skewered rabbit sausage with sauerkraut; or half-seared peppered tuna, shrimp, and scallops. Entrées might include mignonettes of lamb, beef, and Virginia venison in a potato nest with wild mushrooms and lingonberry sauce; or rockfish roasted with mushrooms, pine nuts, and ruby grapes on wild rice pilaf. While the desserts choices are baffling, a fine solution is to request the Seven Deadly Sins, a sampling of seven of the offerings presented in a Mondrian design of dripped sauces on the canvas of the plate. This for a fixed price of $78 per person.

Breakfast is prepared with similar elegance and European understatement: freshly baked croissants, muffins, picture-perfect fruits, coffee, and juices, and homemade lemon curd and raspberry jam. Weather permitting, guests might dine in the brick garden furnished with rattan chairs and tables, lattice and trelliswork, gazebos, fountains, and sculptures.

Now approaching its third decade, the Inn at Little Washington is still a breathtaking and groundbreaking property, constantly updated and refreshed.

WINTERGREEN

Trillium House

Wintergreen, Box 280
Wintergreen, VA 22958
804-325-9126

Proprietors: Betty and Ed Dinwiddie. **Accommodations:** 14 rooms including 2 suites, all private bath. **Rates:** Rooms $85–$105, suites
$120–$150. **Included:** Full buffet breakfast. **Minimum stay:** 2 nights on most weekends, 3 nights on some holidays. **Added:** $35 for additional guest, 4.5% tax. **Payment:** MasterCard, Visa. **Children:** Well-behaved children welcome. **Pets:** Not allowed. **Smoking:** Not allowed in dining room. **Open:** Closed Christmas Eve and Christmas Day.

> *An intimate way to visit the Wintergreen resort*

For those who love the modern conveniences of resort life and a traditional country inn atmosphere, Trillium is a great find, on the peak of Wintergreen resort. The resort, though rather contemporary in design, is unusually appreciative of its surrounding wilderness. Guests at Trillium House have access to the very best of Wintergreen: extensive natural history programs, snowmaking, a pair of award-winning golf courses, some 20 miles of marked hiking trails, horseback riding, spa, and tennis courts.

> **Wintergreen is a magnificent, expansive resort, but you won't notice its huge proportions in the context of 11,000 acres of wilderness 3,800 feet high in the Blue Ridge Mountains. Trillium House is its country inn, a cozy experience on the 17th hole of the Devil's Knob golf course.**

Trillium was built on the 17th hole of Wintergreen's mountaintop Devil's Knob golf course by Ed and Betty Dinwiddie in 1983. The gray clapboard house is an interesting combination of traditional two-story, dormer-windowed saltbox and contemporary structure, with Palladian windows, set at oblique angles. Quite generous with its common space, Trillium House is blessed with a large center section with a cathedral ceiling, into which was built a library loft filled with four walls of books. Below, a comfortable sitting area surrounds a Vermont stove. Around the center chimney is a sunny porch with a view of the golf course.

Single-entrée dinners, prepared by chef Ellen English, are served at a 7:30 seating in the dining room on Friday and Saturday nights only — a sociable, informal event. The first floor of the inn has eight rooms; the second floor has four. These are furnished sparely, with occasional antiques, done in simple winter resort style with little clutter.

The Dinwiddies are kind, family people, with a great passion for their unique location at Wintergreen and their profession as innkeepers. Try to visit Wintergreen's nature center, staffed with highly informed professionals who impart a great appreciation for the environment in this mountain resort.

Wintergreen

Box 706
Wintergreen, VA 22958
804-325-2200
Fax: 804-325-6760
800-325-2200

A wondrous resort in the Blue Ridge Mountains

Proprietors: Wintergreen Partners Inc. **General Manager:** Gunther Muller. **Accommodations:** 320 mountain villas (including studio, 1- to 4-bedroom condominiums, and 2- to 6-bedroom homes). **Rates:** Seasonal, with mini-week and weekly rates available, tennis, golf, ski, family, and romance packages available. Studios $110–$140, lodge rooms $125–$155, condominiums (1 to 4 bedrooms) $135–$375, houses (2 to 6 bedrooms) $200–$530. **Included:** Use of Wintergreen Spa. **Minimum stay:** 2 nights on weekends. **Added:** 6.5% tax. **Payment:** American Express, Visa, MasterCard. **Children:** Welcome. **Pets:** Not allowed. **Smoking:** Allowed. **Open:** All year.

It would be easy to say that the most special aspect of Wintergreen is its location, 3,800 feet high in the Blue Ridge Mountains, a mile from the scenic Blue Ridge Parkway; but there are so many other features of life at Wintergreen that make it a wonderful, unique, and commendable new resort.

Even more important than its two golf courses, 25 tennis courts, six swimming pools, and indoor spa; even better than its ski facilities — Virginia's best — including snowmaking and 17 ski runs (10 lit for night skiing) on a mountain with a 1,000-foot vertical drop; most notably, Wintergreen has a clear environmental conscience and one of the finest nature programs in the Mid-Atlantic region.

> A sensitive development in the Blue Ridge Mountains, Wintergreen is a haven for naturalists. Of its 11,000 acres of mountain wilderness, 6,700 have been set aside as undisturbed forestland. Wintergreen offers an extensive natural history program in addition to its full resort facilities.

Wintergreen is owned by its shareholders. The property includes condominiums, homes, and hotel units, with a great architectural range of more than 20 communities, all built below tree level and approved by an architectural review board, so as not to disrupt the landscape. It may sound busy, but accommodations at Wintergreen are spread over 11,000 acres — so even if the resort is booked to its capacity of 1,300, each guest has about nine acres to himself or herself. The interior decor is contemporary, deluxe, and quite varied.

There are six restaurants throughout Wintergreen, ranging from snack shops to a Lobby Cappuccino Bar, country cooking and formal dining; two lounges; nightly entertainment; and a gallery of shops. The fantastic Wintergarden Spa has an indoor lap pool, three hot tubs, saunas, and an exercise room.

The resort has set aside 6,700 acres as undisturbed forestland, overseen by naturalist Doug Coleman. He and his staff of five conduct guided field trips, maintain more than 25 miles of marked trails, and give lectures about the area's natural history — from 8,000-year-old artifacts to the 400 species of wildflowers to wildlife at Wintergreen.

The children's programs at Wintergreen are nationally acclaimed. Four-day summer camps focus on study of ecology, botany, archaeology, and animals. Teen camps are designed with a more adventurous spirit, offering canoeing down the rapids, ropes courses, horseback riding, hiking, and scuba diving at Lake Monocan. Nighttime activities and ski season activities are also available.

Wintergreen is home to two award-winning golf courses: uppermost Devil's Knob, the highest in the state at 3,800 feet with 50-mile vistas, and Stoney Creek in the foothills, providing incredible views of two very different foliage seasons, at their different altitudes. In fact, since Stoney Creek is kept open year-round, guests may move from the links in the morning to the slopes in the afternoon. Its new golf school, introduced in 1991, boasts a four-to-one student-teacher ratio.

The Skyline Pavilion, completed in 1990 for $3.5 million, is the base for the state's best ski facilities and rental equipment, with 1,800 pairs of skis. Of the 17 ski slopes with runs up to 4,500 feet, ten are lit for night skiing and improved by advanced snowmaking. The Wintergreen Ski School offers beginning through advanced instruction, as well as racing facilities at Diamond Hill.

WOODSTOCK

The Inn at Narrow Passage

Route 11 South
Woodstock, VA 22664
703-459-8000

*A colonial B&B
at the gateway to
the Shenandoah
Valley*

Proprietors: Ed and Ellen Markel. **Accommodations:** 12 rooms, 10 with private bath, 7 with fireplace. **Rates:** $55–$95 per couple. **Included:** Full breakfast. **Minimum stay:** 2 nights on autumn weekends and holidays. **Added:** 4.5% tax. **Payment:** Visa, MasterCard. **Children:** Welcome. **Pets:** Not allowed. **Smoking:** Not allowed in rooms. **Open:** All year except Christmas Eve and Christmas Day.

The Shenandoah Valley is replete with written and oral history dating back to colonial times. When Ed and Ellen Markel wanted to open a country inn with historic significance and undertake a restoration project, they were fortunate enough to find the Inn at Narrow Passage in 1982, two miles south of the town of Woodstock at the valley's northern end. After much restoration and construction, the Markels opened their inn in 1985 on a very lovely plot of land facing Massanutten Mountain and the north fork of the Shenandoah River, which is famous for its fly-fishing (lessons and classes are available from local Harry Murray).

> Route 11 is the scenic route along the western valley of the Massanutten Mountains; it really opens up after Woodstock. The Inn at Narrow Passage is a great launching point — it was for Stonewall Jackson, who headquartered here. There's legendary fly-fishing in the Shenandoah River behind the Inn.

The Inn was built in the 1740s as a refuge from raiding Indians and became a stagecoach inn for the Valley Turnpike (now Route 11). Stonewall Jackson used it as his headquarters for the Valley Campaign in 1862 and 1864. Daisy Stover McGinnis later turned it into a girls' boarding school and summer resort.

The Markels' restoration was very involved because the Inn had been abandoned for a number of years and one of the original wings had been destroyed by fire nearly a century ago. The Markels breathed life back into the first structure, exposing much of the original logwork and hand-hewn beams of the older log cabin, and restored its five rooms to their colonial character. From independent research and oral histories from Woodstock natives, the Markels reconstructed the eastern wing as faithfully as possible, allowing all five rooms to open onto porches with mountain and river views.

The five rooms in the original building, including the Stonewall Jackson Room, are on the second floor, all simply furnished with reproduction colonial furniture, handmade queen-size pine beds, and standard comfortable baths. The 1880s wing and the new wing have pine furniture carved by a Pennsylvania woodworker in colonial simplicity. Most rooms throughout the property have working fireplaces.

The common room has a grand limestone fireplace, exposed original pine beams, and 1780s pumpkin pine flooring. Ellen makes a hearty breakfast, which guests enjoy by the dining room fireplace at colonial tables. Narrow Passage is not a fluffy place, bedecked with ruffles and trinkets; rather it's a hearty stopover, good for fishing, foliage, and country mountain air.

West Virginia

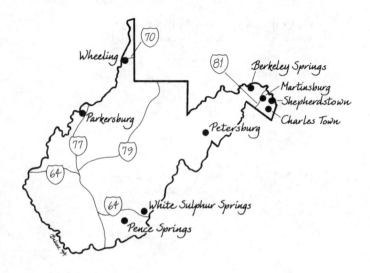

Berkeley Springs
The Country Inn and Renaissance Spa, 622
Charles Town
Hillbrook Inn on Bullskin Run, 624
Martinsburg
Boydville: The Inn at Martinsburg, 626
Parkersburg
Blennerhassett Hotel, 628
Pence Springs
Pence Springs Hotel, 630
Shepherdstown
Bavarian Inn and Lodge, 632
Thomas Shepherd Inn, 634
Wheeling
Wilson Lodge at Oglebay Resort and Conference Center, 636
White Sulphur Springs
The Greenbrier, 638

Best Romantic Retreats

Charles Town
  Hillbrook Inn on Bullskin Run
Martinsburg
  Boydville: The Inn at Martinsburg

Best Resorts

White Sulphur Springs
  The Greenbrier
Wheeling
  Wilson Lodge at Oglebay Resort

Best Country Inns

Pence Springs
  Pence Springs Hotel
Shepherdstown
  Bavarian Inn and Lodge

Best Village Inns

Berkeley Springs
  The Country Inn and Renaissance Spa
Parkersburg
  Blennerhasset Hotel

Best Village Bed-and-Breakfast

Shepherdstown
  Thomas Shepherd Inn

With a population just under 2 million spread over 24,000 square miles, West Virginia has a lot of room for visitors, more than any other Mid-Atlantic state. While New Jersey has about 1,000 people per square mile, West Virginia has 77. With eight ski resorts, 36 state recreation areas, and the vast Monongahela National Forest, West Virginia is a naturalist's paradise. Early explorers of the largely ignored half of Virginia were Daniel Boone and George Washington, the latter visiting the restorative springs in the southeastern part of the state. This vast tract of mountains and forests became autonomous during the tussle of the War Between the States, and was finally named West Virginia in 1863.

The eastern panhandle is the part of the state that looks most like the other states in the Mid-Atlantic, with rolling hills along the banks of the Chesapeake and Ohio Canal and the Potomac River. Several charming towns rest in the easternmost hook of the state. Harper's Ferry National Historical Park rests at the confluence of the Potomac and Shenandoah rivers, in the Blue Ridge Mountains. This town, which earned its wealth from water power, was the site of the nation's first armory, ordered at the behest of President Washington in 1790. It thrived well into the mid-1800s with the C&O Canal presence and the B&O Railroad, though the Civil War destroyed any industrial potential it had.

Charles Town is an adorable village nearby, on the way to **Martinsburg** and **Shepherdstown.** On the bluffs above the Potomac and just across the border from western Maryland's Antietam Battlefield, Shepherdstown is the state's oldest settlement. Originally named Mecklenburg and dating to 1762, it bills itself as the birthplace of the steamboat at the hands of West Virginian John Rumsey. Last, **Berkeley Springs** attracted wealthy Victorians with its curative mineral springs. Built in 1875, Berkeley Castle is an incongruous stone edifice cut into the hill above town, and is worth a special visit. The town's state park features warm, bubbling mineral springs all year, and nearby Cacapon State Park features an 18-hole golf course designed by Robert Trent Jones, among other outdoor activities.

The drive from the eastern panhandle to **Parkersburg,** bordering Ohio, is quite dramatic. There is a good deal to do in this small town, which once hosted the country's oil, lumber, and gas moguls. It was for them that the Blennerhassett Hotel was built in 1889. The property was named for Harman Blennerhassett, a West Virginian folk hero of sorts. He was born in Ireland and was ostracized from his family after marrying his niece, Margaret Agnew. They moved to America and bought an island in the middle of the Ohio River, about two miles south of Parkersburg. In 1798, the couple built a mansion which they called Eden, a 7,000-square-foot regal retreat of white clapboard, which was burned in 1811.

Before this, however, Blennerhassett's life was touched by

tragedy when Aaron Burr visited him on his island and so-licited support to fund his conspiracy. Blennerhassett was twice arrested for his part in the Burr affair and remained imprisoned until after Burr's release. His life never returned to normal, and he finally returned to Ireland where he died in 1831. There is a happy ending of sorts to the Blennerhassett tragedy: in 1980, the West Virginia legislature formed the Historic Blennerhassett Commission, which reconstructed the mansion. The Blennerhassett Island Historical State Park is a wonderful site to visit after a short riverboat ride. The Middleton Doll Company in Ohio and the Fenton Art Glass Company are interesting jaunts, each a short drive away.

From the capital, Charleston, to White Sulphur Springs is a magnificent drive on unbelievably mountainous and remote roads, with a stop near breathtaking Beckley for a visit to the Pence Springs Hotel, once a pilgrimage destination for the wealthy who flocked here on the railroads that stopped a dozen times daily during the Roaring Twenties. While here, be sure to visit the Exhibition Coal Mine and the Riverside Inn for wonderful food.

No West Virginia visit is complete without a trip to its finest attraction, the Greenbrier resort in **White Sulphur Springs**.

For West Virginia tourist information, call the Tourism Authority at 800-CALL-WVA.

BERKELEY SPRINGS

The Country Inn and Renaissance Spa

207 South Washington Street
Berkeley Springs, WV 25411
304-258-2210
800-822-6630

> *A fine inn with
> spa facilities*

Proprietors: Jack and Alice Barker.
General Manager: Jim Kell. **Accommodations:** 69 rooms, including 3 suites, 12 rooms share baths (33 rooms in old building, 36 rooms in new building). **Rates:** $35–$145. **Added:** $10 each additional guest, 9% tax. **Minimum stay:** 2 nights on most weekends. **Payment:** Major credit cards. **Children:** Welcome. **Pets:** Not allowed. **Smoking:** Allowed, nonsmoking rooms available. **Open:** All year.

The town of Berkeley Springs is located in the eastern panhandle of the state, six miles from Hancock, Maryland. Its mineral springs have summoned the healthy and wealthy for centuries. George Washington is noted to have bathed in the springs in 1748, and he returned to plant an elm tree that remains standing today. Present-day visitors can enjoy these same waters with some modern conveniences at the Country Inn and Renaissance Spa.

The regal main building of the Country Inn was built in 1932, a colonial design of red brick and black trim whose entrance rests under a two-story portico six columns across. Jack Barker bought the property in 1972, after he retired from his position as teacher of a boys' school and director at a boys' camp. He has made vast improvements over the years, to everyone's delight.

Quite wonderfully, the first-floor common room also serves as an art gallery. Here the work of local artists is displayed, and one can view them, in true salon form, from many comfortable couches and chairs. A fellow visitor might know how to play the 18th-century melodeon, fixed like a museum piece near the center of the room, while the less accomplished tinker on the baby grand.

The rooms on the second and third floors of the main inn are all different. The hallways are emboldened by bright red carpeting, and some of the rooms adopt the dash of color in wallpapers and upholstery, resulting in a preppy good taste. The majority of rooms have been recently redecorated to include traditional reproduction furnishings. The annex behind the main inn is a new three-story building with large hotel-style rooms with cable TV and roomy baths, all decorated with locally made oak furnishings.

Cut into the hill behind the inn is the pride of the property, the Renaissance Spa. Echoing the rotunda shape of the dining room, the spa seems to hover above the property like a glass and stone flying saucer — albeit an inconspicuous one. Inside, guests will find stress relief in three whirlpool tubs, as many massage rooms, and a beauty salon, all decorated with marble tiles in high-tech cleanliness.

> **Good food and immaculate accommodations are attractions of the Country Inn; a bonus are its spa facilities. With so many outdoor wonders in the area, including Cacapon State Park, a massage at the end of the day is a gift from the heavens.**

The Garden and round West Virginia dining rooms are the workplace of chef Douglas Praskach. His American cuisine ranges from $12 to $20, using local West Virginia products and regional wines. Locals love the Country Inn, a telling aspect of its hospitality, which hosts entertainment and dancing on weekends. A preamble to dining is found in an intimate lounge that looks like a speakeasy, its booths gleaming in highly lacquered wood.

Nearby Cacapon State Park has a lovely 18-hole golf course designed by Robert Trent Jones, as well as tennis, hiking, and horseback riding. A short hike up the mountain is Berkeley Castle, which bills itself as the only English Norman Castle in this country.

CHARLES TOWN

Hillbrook Inn on Bullskin Run

Route 2, Box 152
Charles Town, WV 25414
304-725-4223

*An architectural
wonder in
West Virginia's
eastern panhandle*

Proprietor: Gretchen Carroll. **Assistant Innkeeper:** Nadia Hill. **Accommodations:** 5 rooms including 1 suite, 2 with fireplace. **Rates:** $120–$190; $35 additional on Saturdays and holidays. **Included:** Full breakfast. **Minimum stay:** 2 nights on weekends. **Added:** 9% tax, 15% gratuity, 7-course dinner $55 with wine. **Payment:** MasterCard, Visa. **Children:** Welcome. **Pets:** Not allowed. **Smoking:** Limited. **Open:** Year-round; dinner served Thursdays through Sundays.

In the green, flat farmland of West Virginia's panhandle, six miles from Harper's Ferry National Historic Park, where Maryland and Virginia meet, an exquisitely beautiful country inn lies on the outskirts of Charles Town. Hillbrook nestles in a dreamlike setting on acres of undulating hills divided by a spring-fed stream and a Chinese footbridge, speckled with more than two dozen ducks who have the run of the place.

Most captivating is the architecture of this 1922 Tudor-style manor. While only one room wide — about 20 feet — the half-timbered home is quite long, descending the hill on which it is built with the sensitivity of Frank Lloyd Wright's Fallingwater. The gabled peaks of the second story punctuate the skyline like treetops, rising and falling while following the slope of the land. The dark wood beams and white stucco of the exterior make a striking contrast to the bright flowers that decorate the ground.

The beauty of the interior quite matches that of the exterior. Several rooms are in loft areas on the gabled second floor, while others are found in nooks along narrow passages on the first floor. The house faces west and receives spectacular sun through its thousands of tiny windowpanes. The wallpapers, sometimes a dark paisley, sometimes a gilded pattern, absorb or reflect the sunlight with ever-changing results.

This stunning piece of architecture is made complete by the sophisticated creativity and the impeccable taste of its innkeeper. Gretchen Carroll has owned the Hillbrook Inn since 1985, opening in the spring after months of restoration. An extremely enthusiastic woman, Gretchen came to Hillbrook after a lifetime of international travel. Her experience fills the rooms figuratively and literally: precious antiquities such as South Pacific tapas, Mayan sculpture, a Thai spirit house, and a Scottish teapot. Antique Oriental scatter rugs decorate the original flooring. While some furnishings may be Victorian, the flavor is uniquely European and eclectic. The Locke's Nest, the Lookout, the Point, the Bamford Suite, and the Cottage have designer linens on antique beds, some with fireplaces or patios. Chocolates at turndown and fresh flowers add to the pampered luxury of Hillbrook, though the baths are a bit too spare. Guests enjoy a full breakfast in the beautiful dining room, perhaps pecan pancakes with ginger butter.

The seven-course European dinner changes with the whims of the talented chef. Twenty-five guests sit in the magical setting of the dining room at intimate tables during the several hours of this romantic interlude. The woody Bull-Skin Tavern rests quite separately at the bottom portion of the Tudor building, the setting for live music on the weekends.

> **It is difficlt to describe Hillbrook in words, but its statistics may suffice: 15 fireplaces, 2,000 panes of leaded glass (360 in the living room alone), countless gables, seven-course meals, home to dozens of ducks. This 1922 Tudor marvel is as enchanting a place as you'll ever find.**

MARTINSBURG

Boydville: The Inn at Martinsburg

601 South Queen Street
Martinsburg, WV 25401
304-263-1448

*An early
19th-century manor
offers antebellum
hospitality*

Proprietor: LaRue Frye. **Innkeepers:** LaRue Frye, Bob Boege, Carolyn Snyder, Pete Bailey. **Accommodations:** 6 rooms, 4 with private bath; 2 rooms have fireplaces. **Rates:** $100–$125. **Included:** Expanded Continental breakfast. **Minimum stay:** 2 nights on weekends in May and October. **Added:** $25 each additional guest, 9% tax. **Payment:** MasterCard, Visa. **Children:** Over 12 welcome. **Pets:** Not allowed. **Smoking:** Not allowed. **Open:** Closed August.

A plaque on Martinsburg's Queen Street describes the historic house that belonged to General Elisha Boyd, hero of the War of 1812. A turn here will head a visitor down a beautifully manicured drive flanked by gorgeous trees introducing the manor house at the end. Its generous two stories are built of native limestone, in some cases five feet thick, covered in stucco, now painted white with green shutters. It is a truly elegant southern plantation house, a place for American royalty. It's also a fitting place for Proprietor LaRue Frye, whose family has been part of Virginia and West Virginia history since the early 1700s.

The house is an architectural gallery, and really is its own display: the foyer is an incredible display of faux graining, made in France in 1811, which is carried up the stairs to the second-floor hallway. The paint on paper successfully mimics elaborate inlays of burl, walnut, and tiger mahogany in huge panels. In addition, all the brass and Waterford chandeliers, interior woodwork, and window glass, including the English fan Palladians, are original to the house. The five rooms of inlaid flooring and bronze ormolu chandeliers were brought from Europe to the house by General Boyd's daughter, whose husband was minister to France.

As with any grand old mansion, the common rooms are wide, airy, and generous. There is a music room, a formal living room, and a dining room. All the mantels are original and hand-carved. The

> As you approach this beautiful home, built for General Elisha Boyd, a hero of the War of 1812, you will be transported back 150 years. The genteel southern plantation has maintained its integrity, authenticity, and 14 acres of groomed grounds right in the center of busy Martinsburg.

house is furnished in English and American period antiques, and some treasure-like heirlooms. In addition, a huge, sprawling sun porch stretches off the back of the house with an engulfing stone fireplace and library of books. Guests may stroll the 14 acres and explore the original outbuildings or simply survey the property from the elegant verandah that stretches along the entire front of the house, furnished in original rockers and swings.

One of the two first-floor guest rooms has a working fireplace. The elegant General Adam Stephen Room features a mural of scenic America that was hand-painted in France in the 19th century and a solid African mahogany bookshelf from floor to ceiling.

Four rooms on the second floor are more traditionally formal. The Senator Charles Faulkner Room has a four-poster bed; the General Elisha Boyd Room has an 1800s cherry cannonball bed and a cherry single bed; and the Belle Boyd Room is named for the infamous Confederate spy. Even the baths are unusual, clean with Old World charm, some oversize fixtures and old octagonal tiling, with considerate amenities.

Breakfast includes fresh fruits and freshly baked coffee cakes.

PARKERSBURG

Blennerhassett Hotel

Fourth and Market Streets
Parkersburg, WV 26101
304-422-3131
Fax: 304-485-0267
800-262-2536

> *A grand turreted*
> *mansion near*
> *the Ohio River*

Proprietor: United Properties, Inc.
General Manager: Lawrence S. Demme. **Accommodations:**
104 rooms, including 4 suites. **Rates:** Rooms $57-$67, suites
$140–$160. **Included:** Nightly turndown, morning coffee and
newspaper. **Payment:** Major credit cards. **Children:** Welcome.
Pets: Small pets permitted. **Smoking:** Nonsmoking rooms
available. **Open:** All year.

The fortresslike five-story, turreted brick mansion is the
grandest building in Parkersburg. It's named for Harman
Blennerhassett, a folk hero during his West Virginia tenure in
the early 19th century. The hotel was built over a period of
six years for the influx of Ohio oil magnates to the area, and
it opened in 1889. Almost a century later, the hotel was
entirely renovated and expanded during a year's labor, reopen-
ing in 1986. The red brick of the lavish facade was cleaned
and brightened, the enormous dentil trim painted a gleaming
white, and the arched windows refitted. An addition was
tacked invisibly onto the back, adding twice as many guest
accommodations.
  Guests enter under a green awning to the reception area to
the left and Harman's restaurant to the right. The latter is a

convivial place; with paneled walls and high ceilings, it's dimly lit and has the feel of a 1920s tavern. Chef Yancy Roush has a loyal local following, with American entrées reasonably priced from $10 to $30. His beef is shipped in from a Chicago purveyor and is featured in specialty dishes such as prime rib, served with Yorkshire pudding and fresh horseradish, or filet mignon Aida, served on a bordelaise sauce, topped with shrimp scampi and béarnaise sauce. The Friday seafood buffet and Sunday Jazz Brunch are exhaustive, fun occasions that attract a good crowd.

> Just several miles from the Ohio River, Parkersburg is a gateway to Ohio from West Virginia. It's hard to miss the Blennerhassett, built in the oil boom of the 1880s. Its fortresslike Richardson Romanesque facade is a grand sight, recalling the town's Victorian heyday.

A bit more than half the rooms are in the newer part of the hotel, decorated in four historic color schemes of red, green, blue, and maroon trim and upholstery. The furniture is reproduction Chippendale, and English and American Audubon prints hang on the walls. While the rooms are not luxurious, they are pleasant and comfortable, with beds covered with floral quilts, desks, sitting chairs, and modern baths with the bonus of Krups coffeemakers. The newer rooms are built around the perimeter of a three-story atrium/courtyard with a stone floor, which has a nice patio feel. Most preferable are the three turret rooms, built into the curved corner of the hotel.

The staff are outgoing and warm, and the common areas at the Blennerhassett are delightful, with antique furnishings and dark Victorian decor. Among the many activities surrounding Parkersburg are a visit to the Middleton Doll Company in Ohio and the Fenton Art Glass Company a short drive away. Most exciting is a visit to Blennerhassett Island and the reconstructed 1789 estate of the same name, reputed to be one of the finest mansions in its day.

PENCE SPRINGS

Pence Springs Hotel

Box 90
Pence Springs, WV 24962
304-445-2606

> *A Georgian Revival
> mansion with
> a rich history*

General Manager: O. Ashby Berkley. **Assistant Innkeeper:** Rosa Lee Miller. **Accommodations:** 30 units, each with 2 bedrooms sharing a bath. **Rates:** $45–$65, suites $75–$150. **Included:** Breakfast. **Minimum stay:** None. **Added:** $15 each additional person, $10 for children under 12, 9% tax. **Payment:** Major credit cards. **Children:** Welcome. **Pets:** Allowed in basement. **Smoking:** Allowed. **Open:** All year.

Pence Springs Hotel, on the National Register of Historic Places, has perhaps one of the most unusual histories in this book. It went from being a grand resort in the Roaring Twenties to a state prison for women as recently as 1983, with various incarnations in between. This incongruously elegant country Georgian structure is 20 miles from I-64 and 40 miles from I-77, along a beautiful stretch of Route 3 near Beckley, West Virginia. Rough mountains stretch up either side of the wild Greenbrier River, leading to an enormous mansion atop a hill in the hamlet of Pence Springs.

Built in 1918 as a resort, the 60-room hotel had a 9-hole golf course, mineral spa, and a staff of 100. At $6 a day for full American plan, it was a truly elegant place to be, almost a sister property to the nearby Greenbrier. The C&O Railroad would stop here 14 times a day by 1926, and summers were booked to the capacity of 125. During Prohibition, several secret rooms reached by tunnel under the massive porch held stashes of alcohol. The Depression came, and the resort was turned into a girls' school, only to be shut down in the early '40s. Soon after, it became a women's state prison, holding from 13 to 60 women at a time. In 1983, it was shut down again and remained abandoned until 1986. O. Ashby Berkley bought the place, put more than $1 million into its renovation, and reopened it in November 1988.

The main house has a three-story portico, four columns

across, with two wings stretching off on either side. One enters the hotel from the back. The foyer abuts a lovely, large common room at the hotel's center portion. The room is eight-sided, with a piano, working fireplace, and many windows that open up to a generous porch overlooking the holly trees out front. Downstairs is the Cider Press Lounge, whose gorgeous marble bar was in the movie *Matewan*.

The guest rooms on the second floor are small and rather boxy, with small windows, double beds, private phones, and spare, simple decor. There are also two spacious suites. Baths, like the rooms, are clean and a bit barren.

Some may want to avoid the third floor, and others will certainly request to see it, but everyone ought to know about it. At the end of one guest wing, four of the original solitary-confinement cells remain. The locks were taken out when the jail closed, but the bars, the battleship gray floors, and even the inmates' graffiti remain. Without direct light, set in the center of the room with an exercise corridor around the perimeter, it's a haunting place, and innkeeper Rosa has some eerie stories about some of its infamous inmates.

> **If walls could speak, the Pence Springs Hotel would be a world-renowned orator. This grand structure on a hill high above the Greenbrier River in the West Virginia wilderness was by turns an incredibly exclusive resort, a watering hole in Prohibition, a girls' school, and a women's prison; and now, it's a fascinating place to stay.**

The dining room looks like a ballroom, with hardwood floors and white walls and ceilings. The country-style restaurant serves three meals, including hearty suppers such as chicken with cornbread stuffing and gravy, old Virginia chicken and peanut pie, and baked ham with pineapple, ranging from $9 to $18. For fancier fare, guests should visit Mr. Berkley's Riverside Inn, a gourmet supper club about a mile down the road. Built by the late Governor Hatfield, a member of the infamous Hatfield-McCoy feud, it was at one time a state-sanctioned watering hole and was used by Pretty Boy Floyd as a summer retreat.

SHEPHERDSTOWN

Bavarian Inn and Lodge

Route 1, Box 30
Shepherdstown, WV 25443
304-876-2551
Fax: 304-876-9355

> *A letter-perfect country inn on the C&O Canal*

Proprietors: Erwin and Carol Asam.
Accommodations: 42 rooms, all with balcony and private bath, including 18 deluxe rooms with fireplaces, Jacuzzis, and balconies (3 in main lodge, 39 in 4 chalets). **Rates:** $75–$100 weekdays, $85–$145 holidays and weekends. **Minimum stay:** 2 nights on some holidays. **Added:** $10 each additional guest, 9% tax. **Payment:** Major credit cards. **Children:** Welcome, under 12 free. **Pets:** Not allowed. **Smoking:** Some nonsmoking rooms available. **Open:** All year.

Those seeking an old restored house with creaky floors and well-used antiques and a Robert Frost communion with nature ought to look elsewhere. This is a place for couples who want privacy, fireplaces, deluxe accommodations, a river view from a private balcony, and hearty German food.

Owners Erwin and Carol Asam moved to the area from Washington, D.C., in 1977 with the intent of opening a small country restaurant. Four years later, they expanded their services to include overnight accommodations, in the form of four chalets built, as Erwin Asam describes, in a Bavarian Alpine motif on the steep cliffs of the Potomac. For about a decade, the inn has consistently received four diamonds from AAA and four stars from Mobil — every year since 1984 — much to the credit of the innkeepers and their staff.

Separated from Maryland by the scenic Potomac River, Shepherdstown is located in West Virginia's eastern panhandle, a lovely historic place and a college town with more than 4,000 students. It was founded in 1730 as Mecklenburg and was home to the state's oldest settlement, comprising mostly Germans. This influence is rekindled at the Bavarian Inn, which sits on 11 acres just outside of town.

The old building, built in 1930, serves as the restaurant and is also the home of three of the guest rooms. It is a charming fieldstone house with a steeply pitched roof punctuated by three dormer windows.

A bastion of Bavaria, this inn is convivial, luxurious, and immaculate. It is at once a 1930 fieldstone manor house, a restaurant serving fine Bavarian and Continental cuisine, and a setting for four contemporary Bavarian-Alpine chalets with great views of the Potomac.

The restaurant serves three meals daily and is fairly bustling, a great place for groups. The menu is extensive, with dinners ranging from $11 to $20. Specialties are sauerbraten marinated for a week in vinegar and spice brine, served with red wine ginger sauce; *geschmorte rindsroulade*, a roll of roast beef stuffed with bacon, onions, and pickles; and wiener, paprika, or jaeger schnitzel. Two dining rooms are sociable and expansive, another is quaint with Bavarian memorabilia and history decorating the walls, warmed by firelight.

The upstairs rooms are decorated quaintly with feminine linens and pretty antiques. The four nine-room chalets are on the riverfront, clad in light stucco with dark beams and brightened with Bavarian stenciling and artwork. Each has a large bath (some have a Jacuzzi) and a private balcony providing terrific views of the Potomac and the C&O Canal National Historic Park in Maryland. The furnishings are traditional and hotellike, with reproduction canopy beds, good lighting, hidden televisions, sitting areas, and some fireplaces. Guests are sure to find rooms spotless.

On the grounds is a pool, a tennis court, and a putting green. The Cress Creek Golf Course is within walking distance, the C&O Canal has scenic paths for walkers and joggers, and the Antietam Battlefield is less than a mile away, over the Potomac into western Maryland.

Thomas Shepherd Inn

German and Duke streets
Box 1162
Shepherdstown, WV 25443
304-876-3715

A sweet B&B in West Virginia's oldest community

Proprietor: Margaret Perry. **Accommodations:** 6 rooms, all with private bath, plus a cottage. **Rates:** $75–$105. **Included:** Full breakfast. **Minimum stay:** 2 nights on holidays and weekends with Saturday stay. **Added:** 9% tax, $20 additional guest. **Payment:** Major credit cards. **Children:** 12 and over welcome. **Pets:** Not allowed. **Smoking:** Not allowed. **Open:** All year.

Shepherdstown is its state's oldest community, settled more than 100 years before West Virginia was deemed a state in the Union in 1863. A literal stone's throw from Maryland and the Antietam Battlefield (site of the Civil War's bloodiest fight), Shepherdstown rests on the western banks of the Potomac River. It is home to a college that shares its name, founded in 1871. The historic town looks more like a refined New England outpost than a part of wild and wonderful West Virginia, with its main street a gallery of Federal and Victorian architecture. The Thomas Shepherd Inn greets visitors at the town's main junction, an introduction to charming Main Street and a block's walk to the college.

Built in 1868 as a Lutheran parsonage, the inn was transformed from a private residence to a B&B in 1984. The owners restored the inn to its original pristine Federal condition, a two-and-a-half-story whitewashed brick building with a modest single-story portico. Margaret Perry came from New England seeking a suitable bed-and-breakfast and found her ideal property here in September 1989. She is quite devoted to her innkeeping tasks, enthusiastically hosting tea every afternoon, cooking large morning breakfasts, gardening, and packaging soaps and potpourri for the guests. Margaret will also prepare picnic lunches for $12, and dinners with advance notice (for $20–$30).

The scale of the inn is intimate. To the right of the foyer is the double parlor, which has a working fireplace and is furnished with both antique and reproduction Federal pieces and trimmed in colonial colors. In the two dining rooms, similarly decorated in meticulous Federal style, Margaret serves her full breakfasts, which include fresh muffins and a hot dish such as sour cream blueberry pancakes with Vermont maple syrup, or sautéed pears in sherry sauce. An edible flower will complete the presentation.

> **A former Lutheran parsonage, built in 1868, the Thomas Shepherd Inn sits on the lovely main street of this historic town. This sweet bed-and-breakfast is within walking distance of the college: en route, note the admirably restored Federal and Victorian architecture at every turn.**

The three guest rooms in the front section of the house are preferable to those in the back, which are less formal. The most deluxe room is at the front of the house, with a Pierre Deux crown canopy, maroon wing chairs, and an antique hope chest. A pencil post canopy sits across the hall and a sleigh bed in a room behind, topped with an elaborate antique quilt. Guests use the library at the back of the house, which overlooks the gardens and yard beyond. Beyond Shepherd College is Harper's Ferry National Historic Park; and within sight on the Maryland banks of the Potomac is the C&O Canal and Towpath for hiking and biking enthusiasts.

WHEELING

Wilson Lodge at Oglebay Resort and Conference Center

Oglebay
Wheeling, WV 26003
304-243-4000
Fax: 304-243-4070
800-624-6988

> *A great family resort in northern West Virginia*

Proprietor: Wheeling Park Commission. **General Manager:** G. Randolph Worls. **Accommodations:** 204 rooms in lodge, 35 cabins, 3 chalets with 24 rooms. **Rates:** Wilson Lodge $115–$125, $130–$150 with living room; 2-, 4-, and 6-bedroom family cabins $145–$220 overnight, $545–$865 weekly; seasonal overnight and weekend packages $58–$188 per couple. **Minimum stay:** 2 nights on weekends. **Added:** $5 for roll-away, 9% tax. **Payment:** Major credit cards. **Children:** Welcome. **Pets:** Not allowed. **Smoking:** Allowed. **Open:** All year.

In the narrow northern neck of West Virginia, wedged between Pennsylvania and Ohio, Wheeling offers a wonderful family resort and park called Oglebay. In 1926, philanthropist and industrialist Colonel Earl W. Oglebay willed his summer estate, Waddington Farm, to the citizens of Wheeling to be used for recreation and education. The 1,500 acres are maintained by a private board, the only self-sustaining municipal park in the country. As a result, accommodations and activities are a bit more reasonably priced than at a private organization. Oglebay's identity is more a nature sanctuary than a full-service resort, though it does enjoy two wonderful golf courses, 14 tennis courts, an indoor and outdoor pool, and full fitness facilities.

Accommodations for Oglebay guests are in three contemporary wings of the main Wilson Lodge set high above the acreage, three satellite chalets, as well as 35 family cabins scattered through the lower reaches of the park. The three wings in the Lodge are Kline, built in 1966 with rustic paneled walls; Allen, the original wing built of knotty pine; and Byrd, the favorite because of its breathtaking mountain views. The rooms are furnished identically in the comfortable style of a moderate hotel, with remote television and private phones, balconies, coffeemakers, and some fireplaces. The chalets are a bit more luxurious and private. The cabins all have fireplaces and stocked kitchens.

> **Oglebay is the only self-sustaining park in the country, with a museum, an arboretum, a zoo, nature and garden centers, a science theater, a three-acre lake, and wonderful Waddington Gardens. It also features a great family resort, with a myriad of activities, great golf, and skiing in winter.**

However pleasant, the guest rooms are a small part of life at Oglebay. At the entrance to the park is the Mansion Museum, Colonel Oglebay's former residence, a majestic piece of Greek Revival architecture with a two-story portico supported by six columns. The museum, furnished in Federal formality, contains a substantial glass collection and changing exhibits. The Good Children's Zoo, in the valley just below the Wilson Lodge, is a 65-acre natural habitat home to bison, elk, and the endangered red wolf. Visitors take a mile-and-a-half adventure ride on a vintage 1863 miniature Huntington train that runs the perimeter of the zoo, through the bison range, and over a waterfall. The Benedum Science Theater shows films and seasonal laser shows. A miniature golf course prepares kids for a bright future on the Oglebay links.

Three-acre Schenck Lake is stocked with trout, catfish, and bass. Nonfishermen will enjoy the paddleboating. Naturalists appreciate the vast horticultural efforts of the Oglebay group. The Brooks Nature Center offers lectures, guided walks, and workshops. The Wheeling Civic Garden Center and Oglebay

Greenhouse are at the entrance to the park. The Wigginton Arboretum offers miles of paths through some of Oglebay's most breathtaking scenery. The park's most recent project is the Waddington Gardens, which opened in 1992.

Oglebay's greatest attraction may be the two golf courses set in the hills, offering magnificent views. The Crispin Course sits at the foot of Wilson Lodge; and the tougher Speidel Course, designed by Robert Trent Jones, is where the West Virginia LPGA was held for 11 years. The driving range and the 40-acre par 3 course are lit for night golfers, the latter becoming a ski center from December through March, complete with snowmaking, poma lift, and rentals.

Guests dine in the tiered Ihlenfeld dining room, expanded in 1990 to encompass wonderful views through picture windows of Schenck Lake and the hills beyond. The Continental cuisine is quite reasonably priced, with special family and fitness menus.

WHITE SULPHUR SPRINGS

The Greenbrier

White Sulphur Springs, WV 24986
304-536-1110
Fax: 304-536-7834
800-624-6070

The Mid-Atlantic's greatest grand old resort

Proprietors: CSX Corp. **President and Managing Director:** Ted J. Kleisner. **Accommodations:** 650 guest rooms, including 49 suites and 69 cottages. **Rates:** Rooms $132–$273 per person MAP, other packages available; suites from $231–$322 per

person (up to 14 guests) MAP; cottages $180–$305 per person
(4–8 guests) MAP. **Included:** Breakfast and dinner in most facilities. **Minimum stay:** 2 nights on weekends. **Added:** 6%
tax, $110 additional guest MAP, $14.25 service per person per
day. **Payment:** Major credit cards. **Children:** Welcome. **Pets:**
Not allowed. **Smoking:** Nonsmoking rooms available. **Open:**
All year.

The magnificence of the Greenbrier is simply overwhelming.
To appreciate the scale and the 200-plus years of history at
the Greenbrier, a visitor ought to take a tour of the grounds
conducted daily by the on-staff historian. As old and historic
as the Greenbrier is, it is also one of the most consistently
updated properties in the region.

In 1987, millions were invested in the glorious spa and
mineral baths. The rooms and public spaces are continually
being redecorated by Car-
leton Varney, president of
the Dorothy Draper Com-
pany of New York. The
6,500 acres provide more
activities than one visitor
can possibly accomplish,
from the usual fun on the
three golf courses, the 20
tennis courts, and the
Olympic-size swimming
pools, to trap and skeet
shooting, bowling, horse-
back riding, ice skating,
sleigh rides, and croquet.

> While one day would be
> memorable enough for a
> lifetime, you could — if you
> could — spend months at
> the Greenbrier and its
> 6,500 acres in West Virginia
> mountain wilderness. Its
> two centuries of history
> require the employ of a staff
> historian, whose tours are
> well worth the wait.

As early as 1778, af-
flicted souls began com-
ing to White Sulphur Springs for its curative mineral waters.
In 1808, a tavern to accommodate 60 guests was built on the
site, which now serves as a croquet lawn. The first cottages
were built as early as 1810. By 1858, the Grand Central Hotel
was erected, fondly referred to as Old White because of its
whitewashed brick. From 1861 to 1865, the resort was tugged
between the Union and Confederate armies, the former win-
ning out as West Virginia seceded from Confederate rule in
1863.

After the Civil War, Old White became one of the country's
most elite gathering spots. It was bought by the Chesapeake

& Ohio Railroad in 1910 for $150,000, and architect Frederick Junius Sterner was commissioned to design a fireproof addition, resulting in the herculean Greenbrier. An indoor pool inspired by Roman baths was added in 1912, the largest in the world at the time, measuring 100 by 42 feet. In 1913, Charles Blair McDonald designed the Old White golf course, though by 1922 the building for which it was named was dismantled. During World War II, the Greenbrier became the Ashford General Hospital, closing for two years before it reopened as a splendid resort once again in 1948. Various wings were added in 1930, 1954, and 1962, and further renovations included the Greenbrier's first tap room in 1970 in the Old White Club. In 1977, the Greenbrier golf course was added to the grounds under the supervision of Jack Nicklaus.

The long, formal driveway ends in a loop under a colonnade at the front entrance. The grand hallways, leading to the 30 lobbies and public spaces, are outfitted with extensive floral arrangements and open to terraces, sculpted gardens, and to the 80,000-bulb tulip garden.

The mastery of the Greenbrier's aesthetics is the product of legendary Dorothy Draper, who first decorated the resort in 1946. Her vision lives on today through Carleton Varney. While the furniture is always traditional, from wing chairs to Queen Anne settees and mahogany tables, the fabrics, from the upholstery to the bedding and drapes, are boldly colored in swatches of red, yellow, blue, or green or dramatically patterned in floral and chintz, recalling the Greenbrier theme of the rhododendron, West Virginia's state flower.

The guest rooms, the majority of which have twin beds, might have a wide-striped pink and white wallpaper, with royal blue pile carpeting, red club chairs, and pink chintz drapes; or perhaps canary yellow drapes, bright red carpeting, blue club chairs, and wild floral bouquets papering the walls. The variety and audacity is highly successful.

In addition to the hundreds of guest rooms in the main building, the ten rows of cottages are a unique option in accommodations. Set around the perimeter of the groomed Greenbrier commons, most are historic and original, some have fireplaces, and all have porches and private patios, and stocked kitchens.

The new Spa wing is not only functional as it houses the new coffee shop and salon, pool and Spa, but simply beautiful, with its green and pink inlaid marble floor, pastel walls, and white trimmed archways leading to the Spa and the original 1912 pool. This pool is a most tranquil setting, the walls tiled in an intricate mosaic, the pool itself flanked by colonnades, resting under a softly canopied ceiling. Among facilities using mineral waters are soak tubs, whirlpools, Swiss showers, Scotch sprays, and saunas. Beauty treatments and therapy massage are also available.

The food is one of the highlights at the Greenbrier, prepared by a team of chefs trained in its own Culinary Apprentice Program, under the direction of head chef Walter Scheib. The six-course formal dinner is served in the three-room dining salon. Amateurs might inquire about week-long cooking school packages, conducted by Ann Willan of La Varenne in Paris.

For a complete luxury experience, Greenbrier guests may arrive and depart as they did a century ago, in a plushly appointed passenger train. The Greenbrier Limited is the first privately operated sleeper car since the Broadway Limited, which discontinued service in 1967. The stunningly beautiful route from Chicago to New York City makes stops at major cities. Guests dine on silver, crystal, and linens in a car of Honduran mahogany and sleep amid lavish French fabrics.

Recommended Guidebooks

For help in compiling this reading list I would like to thank the Travellers Bookstore, an invaluable resource. Owner Diana Wells also offers a mail order catalog with close to 800 practical and eclectic listings, available for $2 by calling 212-664-0995 or by writing 22 West 52nd Street (75 Rockefeller Plaza), New York, NY 10019.

General Travel and Mid-Atlantic Region

Smithsonian Guide to Historic America. Stewart, Tabori, and Chang, $17.95. Three pertinent volumes include New York, New Jersey, Pennsylvania; Virginia, the Capital Region; the Carolinas and Appalachian States, West Virginia. Thoroughly researched, wonderfully written history and cultural almanac, including original maps, photographs and prints, and architectural notes.

The Discerning Traveler's Guide to the Middle Atlantic. David and Linda Glickstein, St. Martin's, $16.95. A personally researched and tenderly written guide with ten itineraries including where to go, stay, and dine, and what to do.

Romantic Weekend Getaways, Mid-Atlantic. Larry Fox and Barbara Radin Fox Wiley, $12.95. Creative, manageable itineraries for amorous couples.

Getaways for Gourmets. Nancy Webster and Richard Woodworth, Wood Pond, $14.95. Well-researched, thorough itineraries for culinary-minded travelers.

Travel with Your Pet USA. Artco, $9.95. A must-have almanac for those intending to vacation with a furry family member.

Away for the Weekend. Eleanor Berman, Clarkson Potter, $12.95. Thoughtful, trusted itineraries within 250 miles of Mid-Atlantic cities.

Daytrips, Getaway Weekends, and Vacations in the Mid-Atlantic States. Patricia and Robert Foulke, Globe Pequot, $13.95. Easy, varied itineraries around six states.

Civil War Sourcebook. Chuck Lawliss, Harmony, $18. A detailed history of the war within the context of travel. Sightseeing tours of Virginia and points north, including historic, battlefield, and monument sites.

The Complete Guide to Music Festivals in America. Carol Price Rabin, Berkshire Traveler Press, $10.95. More than 250 listings and descriptions of classical, opera, jazz, ragtime, pop, dixie, folk, Cajun, bluegrass, and country music festivals.

The Amusement Park Guide. Tim O'Brien, Globe Pequot Press, $12.95. Comprehensive descriptions and interesting histories of amusement parks, first popularized in Coney Island and Pennsylvnaia.

National Park Guide. Michael Frome, Prentice Hall, $14.95. Listing and descriptions of national, Washington, D.C., area, archaeological, historic, and natural/recreational parks.

Pat Dickerman's Adventure Travel North America. Pat Dickerman, Adventure Guides Inc, $15.95. Detailed information on hiking, mountaineering, canoeing, ballooning, sailing, and cycling trips.

Family Sports Adventures. Megan Stine, Time Life Inc. From *Sports Illustrated for Kids*, geared for parents and children to use together.

Wine Routes of America. Jan Aaron, E. P. Dutton, $15.95. A wonderful reference guide for beginners or advanced, in a thick volume detailing vineyards and wineries, as well as terminology and cultural activities in the area.

Great Vacations with Your Kids. Dorothy Jordon and Marjorie Adoff Cohen, E. P. Dutton, $12.95. An expert guide with itneraries for cities, resorts, skiing, and farming, with advice on modes of travel, babysitting, and surprising other topics.

Where the Old Roads Go: Driving the First Federal Highways of the North East. George Cantor, Harper & Row, $10.95. An interesting history and guide to U.S. routes, such as the 319-mile stretch of U.S. 11 between Champlain and Binghamton, or U.S. 20 between Cardiff and Ripley, New York — in the vein of *On the Road.*

Waterside Escapes: Great Getaways by Lake, River, and Sea. Betsy Wittemann and Nancy Webster, Wood Pond Press, $13.95. Detailed waterside itineraries in the Mid-Atlantic states.

A Seasonal Guide to the Natural Year. Scott Weidensaul, Fulcrum Publishing, $15.95. A monthly guide to natural events, including when ducks migrate, when the Blue Ridge Mountains wildflowers blossom, and when the wild blueberry hunts are staged.

Short Bike Rides . . . Globe Pequot. Fun, friendly format, with a naturalist's bent. By various authors. Titles include **New Jersey,** $8.95; **Long Island,** $8.95; **in and around Washington D.C.,** $9.95; and **Eastern Pennsylvania,** $9.95.

50 Hikes . . . Backcountry Publications. With very good maps and mileage breakdowns, a background section of every area, and access. By various authors. Titles include **in Central New York,** $12; **in Central Pennsylvania,** $12; **in Western Pennsylvania,** $11; **in Western New York,** $13; **in New Jersey,** $10; and **in New Jersey's Kittaninies,** $13.

25 Bicycle Tours . . . Backcountry Publications. With maps and mile-by-mile guides to the areas. By various authors. Titles include **in the Hudson Valley,** $10; **in the Finger Lakes,** $10; **in Eastern Pennsylvania,** $10; **in and around Washington D.C.,** $10; **on the Delmarva,** $10; **in New York City,** $10.

Walks and Rambles . . . Backcountry Publications, $11. By various authors. Guides to the ecology and history of the regions. Titles include **on the Delmarva Peninsula; in Dutchess and Putnam Counties;** and **in Westchester and Fairfield Counties.**

The Factory Outlet Guide to the Mid-Atlantic States. A. Pennypincher & A. Tightwad, Globe Pequot, $8.95. A state-by-state guide, cross-referenced with a product index, profiles, and maps.

National Geographic Guide to the Civil War National Battlefield Parks. National Georgraphic, $12. Profiles of the sites and histories, with photos, on battlefields in Maryland, Pennsylvania, Virginia, and West Virginia.

Flashmaps. Fodor, $8.95.

Delaware

Canoeing the Delaware. Gary Letcher, Rutgers University Press, $25. A timeless book written by an expert.

District of Columbia

Washington, D.C. Access. Harper Collins, $12.95. An impeccably organized, detailed, all-in-one guide to architecture, history, culture, events. Wonderful maps.

Gault-Millau Washington D.C. $16.95. Stocked with information and opinion about every aspect of the capital.

Zagat Restaurant Survey. Zagat Publishing, $12.95. A highly respected insider's guide to restaurants, with considerate cross-referencing, in a handy size.

Michelin Green Guide to Washington, D.C. $14.95. The reliable standby.

Fodor's: Washington, D.C. Random House, $11. A thorough handbook on every aspect of everyday travel in the capital — with a handy alternative in ***Pocket Washington, D.C.,*** for $8. Features detailed maps.

Places to Go with Children in Washington D.C. Judy Colbert, Chronicle Books, $9.95. Good, sensible advice and plans for parents for the activity-filled capital.

Kidding Around, Washington D.C. Anne Pedersen, John Muir, $9.95. A children's guide, written for young readers.

Let's Go Washington D.C. 1994. St. Martin's, $11.99. A down-to-earth guide that includes information on Arlington, Alexandria, historic Virginia, Baltimore, and Annapolis; with a fresh bent, including sections on ethnic foods and music.

Detours: Washington D.C. Joseph Downtown, Detours Publishing, $13.95. A gay and lesbian travel guide, with a guide to neighborhoods, nightlife, shopping, and resources.

Frommer's City Guides: Washington D.C. Prentice Hall, $13. Tried and true.

Washington D.C. Ethnic Food Guide. Jonathan Stein, Open Pon Publishers, $9.95. 125 great spots in D.C., northern Virginia, and Maryland for Peruvian, Lebanese, Greek, Ethiopian, and other ethnic food.

The Unofficial Guide to Washington D.C. Bob Sehlinger, Joe Surkiewicz, with Eve Zibart, Prentice Hall, $13. A terrific idea: an extremely honest guidebook that offers constructive warnings, not just niceties.

Maryland

The Chesapeake Bay Book: A Complete Guide. Allison Blake, Berkshire House, $14.95. A wonderful and comprehensive guide about the region, its history, culture, recreational information, and much more.

Adventuring in the Chesapeake Bay Area. John Bower, Sierra Club Travel Guide. A terrific companion to the Tidewater Regions of Maryland, Virginia, D.C., and Virginia Cape. Well written, with appendixes, including information about the weather, wildlife, and terrain.

Maryland: Off the Beaten Path. Globe Peqout, $8.95. One in a series of thin, friendly, down-to-earth books filled with creative suggestions.

Zagat Restaurant Survey: Baltimore. Zagat, $9.95. A well-respected insider's guide to restaurants, with considerate cross-referencing, in a handy size.

New Jersey

New Jersey: Off the Beaten Path. Globe Pequot, $8.95. One in a series of thin, friendly, down-to-earth books filled with creative suggestions.

Guide to the Jersey Shore: From Sandy Hook to Cape May. Robert Santelli, Globe Pequot, $11.95. A detailed, eclectic guide to activities along the shore, including boating, fishing, antiquing, concerts, horse racing, casinos, and Victorian, tulip, and film festivals in Cape May.

New Jersey Day Trips. Barbara Hudgins, Woodmont Press, $10.95. Short outings in New Jersey and neighboring states.

Fodor's: Atlantic City and New Jersey Shore. Random House, $8.95. A thin, useful guide to the gambling and beach attractions, with detailed maps.

Fodor's: Vacations on the Jersey Shore. Random House, $11. A great, detailed primer for the state's great sites, with terrific maps.

Guide to Shipwreck Diving in New York and New Jersey. C. Henry Keatts, Pisces Books, Gulf Publishing, $16.95. A fascinating book for divers and others about maritime history on the historic shipping route, including details on 55 wrecks since 1614.

Best Hikes with Children in New Jersey. Arline and Joel Zatz, Mountaineers, $12.95. 75 child-oriented hikes, including where to stop for "tired feet" and safety tips.

New Jersey Parks, Forests, and Natural Areas: A Guide. Michael P. Brown, Rutgers University Press, $14.95. This book has won no beauty prizes, but it's a good reference guide to 250 natural places around the state.

New York City

Access New York City. Richard Saul Wurman, Harper Collins, $16.95. Impeccably organized, detailed all-in-one guide for architecture, history, culture, events for the five boroughs.

Blue Guide New York. Carol von Pressentin, Wright Norton, $19.95. The cultural landscape of New York City, rich in history and good writing.

Gault-Millau New York. Prentice Hall, $16.95. Stocked with information and opinion about every aspect of a traveler's New York.

New York, Cadogan City Guides. Vanessa Letts, Globe Pequot, $14.95. A tour of the city via eight neighborhood walks, with information on history, art, cafés, dining, shopping, and day trips.

American Express Pocket Guide: New York. Herbert Bailey Livesey, Prentice Hall, $10.95. A handy at-your-fingertips book.

Michelin Green Guide to New York City. $14.95. A reliable standby.

AIA Guide to New York City. Elliot Willensky and Norval White, Harcourt Brace Jovanovitch, $21.95. Encyclopedic listing and description of important architectural landmarks in five boroughs by neighborhood.

Fodor's City Guides: New York City. Random House, $13. Highly detailed maps and thorough research make this a great all-around guide; includes 25 walking tours.

Museums in New York. Fred W. McDarrah, St. Martin's Press, $13.95. A long-standing, much-needed reference guide to the city's art world.

Born to Shop. Suzy Gershman and Judith Thomas, Bantam Books, $8.95. A budget hunter's almanac.

Shopping Manhattan. Corky Pollan, Penguin, $12.95. *New York* magazine's Best Bets columnist reveals where to find anything in New York.

Art Walks in New York. Marina Harrison and Lucy D. Rosenfeld, Michael Kensend, $14.95. Guide to public art and gardens in and around Manhattan.

The Complete Guide to Ethnic New York. Zelda Stern, St. Martin's Press, $8.95. An interesting breakdown of the original melting pot.

Zagat Restaurant Survey New York. Zagat Publishing, $12.95. A highly respected insider's guide to restaurants, with considerate cross-referencing.

Kidding Around, New York. Sarah Lovett, John Muir, $9.95. A children's guide, written for young readers.

New York Times Guide to Restaurants in New York City. Bryan Miller, Random House, $15. A trustworthy guide from the *Times*'s regular reviewer. Honest, wonderfully written, up-to-date.

The Greenwich Village Guide. Fred W. and Patrick J. Mc-Darrah, A cappella Books, $11.95. Sixteen historic walks through SoHo, TriBeCa, and the Villages.

Frommer's Walking Tours of New York City. Rena Bulkin, Prentice Hall, $12. Thirteen routes with detailed maps.

Gitters 24-hour New York. Gitters Publishing, $9.95. An unusual reference book for the city that never sleeps: where to go all night, from dry cleaning to gourmet dining.

New York Walks. 6 Walking Tours by the 92nd Street Y. Edited by Batia Plotch, Henry Holt, $12.95. From Brooklyn Heights to Battery Park to Millionaire's Mile, walking tours from the cultural center at the 92nd Street Y.

Brooklyn: Where To Go, What To Do, How To Get There. Ellen Freudenheim, with Daniel P. Wiener, St.Martin's Press, $12.95.

A Walker's Guidebook: Serendipitious Outings Near New York City. Marina Harrison and Lucy D. Rosenfeld, Michael Kensend, $12.95. A friendly guidebook with maps, descriptions of the walk as well as after the walk.

New York State

New York Walk Book. The New York, New Jersey Trail Conference, Doubleday, $15.95. Professionally prepared field guide, quite brass tacks.

Best Hikes with Children in the Catskills and Hudson River Valley. Cynthia C. and Thomas J. Lewis, Mountaineers, $12.95. 50 child-oriented outings, including where to stop for "tired feet" and safety tips.

Zagat Restaurant Survey, Suburban New York City. Zagat Publishing, $12.95. A highly respected insider's guide, with considerate cross-referencing, in a handy size.

The Hudson Valley and Catskills Mountains: An Explorer's Guide. Joanne Michaels and Mary-Margaret Barile, Countryman Press, $15. A comprehensive guide, with what to see, special events, green spaces, driving and scenic tours.

The Hudson River Valley. Tim Mulligan, Random House, $12. Highly recommended guide to this varied area.

New York: Off the Beaten Path. Globe Pequot, $8.95. One in a series of thin, friendly, down-to-earth books filled with creative suggestions.

One Day Adventures by Car: Daytrips from New York City. Lida Newberry, updated by Joy Johannessen, Hastings House, $12.95.

Country Walks near New York. William G. Scheller, Appalachian Mountain Club, $8.95. Handy pocket book detailing 20 rural walks.

Short Nature Walks on Long Island. Rodney and Priscilla Albright, Globe Pequot, $8.95. Twenty-five walks on beaches, in towns, in woods, and on great estates.

Short Bicycle Rides on Long Island. Phil Angelillo Globe Pequot, $8.95. 30 well-mapped, conversationally described rides in a down-to-earth format.

Fodor's: Vacations in New York State. Random House, $14.95. An everything-in-one, personally researched book with history, culture, practical advice, and wonderful maps.

The Adirondack Book: A Complete Guide. Elizabeth Folwell, Berkshire House, $14.95. A wonderful and comprehensive guide about the region, its history, culture, recreational information, and much more.

Great Camps of the Adirondacks. Harvey H. Kaiser, David Godine, $50 hardcover, $35 paperback. Fascinating, wonderfully written cultural and architectural history of the playgrounds of the wealthy at the turn of the century, with great maps and more than 200 pictures.

Guide to Adirondack Trails: Highland Parks Region. Edited by Tony Goodwin, Adirondack Mountain Club. A thorough, technical guide with extensive maps.

Favorite Short Trips in New York State. Harriet Webster, Yankee Books. A good friend to escort you around, with insights into areas and regions, written by a true Yankee.

Let's Take The Kids! Great Places To Go with Children in New York's Hudson Valley. Mary Barile and Joanne Michaels, St. Martin Press. A happily written guide with advice on travel and ideas from farms to history to rodeos to museums.

Pennsylvania

Guide's Guide to Philadelphia. Julie P. Curson, Curson House, $11.95.

Zagat Restaurant Survey Philadelphia. Zagat Publishing, $12.95. A highly respected insider's guide to restaurants, with considerate cross-referencing in a handy size.

Philadelphia Access. Harper Perennial, $18. Impeccably organized, detailed all-in-one guide for architecture, history, culture, events. Color-coded. Wonderful maps.

Insight Guide: Philadelphia. Edited by John Guttuso, Houghton Mifflin, $19.95. Colorful, comprehensive guide, with a vivid presentation and large pictures.

Frommer's Philadelphia 93-94. Jay Golan, Prentice Hall, $13. Informative and accessible, the all-in-one pocket guide.

Philadelphia with Children. Elizabeth S. Gephart and Ann S. Cunningham, Starrhill Press, $11.95. A great value: colorful and easy-to-comprehend book, with history, museums, nature, performing arts, and so much to keep kids going.

Pennsylvania: Off the Beaten Path. Globe Pequot, $8.95. One in a series of thin, friendly, down-to-earth books filled with creative suggestions.

Guide to Amish Country. Bill Simpson, Pelican. A full-service book that is highly useful, with eclectic information such as where to find farmer's markets and covered bridges.

Virginia

Virginia: A History and Guide. Tim Mulligan, $10.95. A rich history and culture of the state and its major cities.

Sierra Club Guides to the National Parks: East and Middle West. Stewart, Tabori, and Chang, $14.95.

Virginia: Off the Beaten Path. Globe Pequot, $8.95. One in a series of thin, friendly, down-to-earth books filled with creative suggestions.

Hiking the Old Dominion. Allen DeHart, Sierra Club, $12.95. Commendably researched by a writer who loves his subject.

West Virginia

Hiking the Mountain State and Trails of West Virginia. Allen DeHart, AMC Books, $14.95. A much-needed book by a caring professional.

What's What

Where's the best place for *you* to stay? Following is a cross reference to accommodation types and special interests.

Good Places for Families

Maryland
Wades Point Inn on the Bay, 106
New Jersey
The Chalfonte Hotel, 146
New Jersey
The Queen Victoria, 151
New York
Bear Mountain Inn, 273
Beaverkill Valley Inn, 281
Canoe Island Lodge, 180
Danfords Inn on the Sound, 358
East Hampton Point Cottages, 348
Four Seasons Hotel (New York City), 307
Gideon Putnam Hotel, 218
Gurney's Inn Resort & Spa, 354
The Hedges, 173
Hemlock Hall, 175
The Inn at Starlight Lake, 396
Lake Placid Lodge, 184
Mirror Lake Inn, 187
Mohonk Mountain House, 286
Montauk Yacht Club Resort and Marina, 356
Otesaga Hotel and Cooper Inn, 209
Paramount, 320
The Sagamore, An Omni Classic Resort, 177
Taughannock Farms Inn, 262
Pennsylvania
Four Seasons Hotel (Philadelphia), 455
Hidden Valley, 392
The Hotel Hershey, 424
Nemacolin Woodlands Resort (condominiums), 476
Pittsburgh Vista, 487
Skytop Lodge, 390
Woodloch Pines, 384

Virginia
  The Boar's Head Inn & Sports Club, 541
  Fort Lewis Lodge, 587
  The Homestead, 582
  Jordan Hollow Farm Inn, 599
  Kingsmill Resort and Conference Center, 530
  Linden Row, 562
  Maple Hall, 585
  Mountain Lake Hotel, 589
  Peaks of Otter Lodge, 578
  Skyland and Big Meadows lodges, 593
  The Tides Inn, 523
  The Tides Lodge, 525
  Williamsburg Inn, 534
  Wintergreen, 611
Washington, D.C.
  Hotel Washington, 27
  The Mayflower–A Stouffer Hotel, 30
West Virginia
  The Greenbrier, 638
  Wilson Inn at Ogleby Resort and Conference Center, 636

Good Value

New Jersey
  The Chalfonte Hotel, 146
New York
  The Algonquin, 300
  Bear Mountain Inn, 273
  Hotel Wales, 311
  Paramount, 320
  Radisson Empire Hotel, 326
  Sagamore – Historic Adirondack Great Camp, 192
Pennsylvania
  Independence Park Inn, 460
  The Settler's Inn at Bingham Park, 382
  Thomas Bond House, 467
Virginia
  Peaks of Otter Lodge, 578
  Skyland and Big Meadows lodges, 593
Washington, D.C.
  Hotel Washington, 27
West Virginia
  Wilson Inn at Ogleby Resort and Conference Center, 636

Suitable for Groups

Delaware
  Hotel du Pont, 13
  New Devon Inn, 6
Maryland
  Admiral Fell Inn, 55
  Antrim 1844, 77
  The Doubletree Inn at the Colonnade, 60
  Harbor Court Hotel, 63
  Henderson's Wharf, 65
  Historic Inns of Annapolis, 51
  Imperial Hotel, 91
  Inn at Perry Cabin, 102
  Peabody Court, 67
New Jersey
  Hilton at Short Hills, 130
  The Inn at Lambertville Station, 124
  Inn at Millrace Pond, 120
  Marriott's Seaview Golf Resort, 140
New York
  The Algonquin, 300
  Bear Mountain Inn, 273
  Beaverkill Valley Inn, 281
  Beekman Arms, 292
  The Carlyle, 303
  Danfords Inn on the Sound, 358
  East Hampton Point Cottages, 348
  Elk Lake Lodge, 189
  Essex House, 305
  Four Seasons Hotel (New York City), 307
  Garden City Hotel, 353
  Geneva on the Lake, 247
  Gideon Putnam Hotel, 218
  Gurney's Inn Resort & Spa, 354
  The Harry Packer Mansion, 386
  The Hedges, 173
  Hôtel Plaza Athénée , 310
  The Inn at Quogue, 360
  The Mark, 315
  The Mayfair Hotel Baglioni, 316
  Mirror Lake Inn, 187
  Mohonk Mountain House, 286
  Montauk Yacht Club Resort and Marina, 356
  The Otesaga Hotel, 209

Swimming Pool

Delaware
  The Towers Bed and Breakfast, 8
Maryland
  Antrim 1844, 77
  Chanceford Hall Inn, 108
  The Doubletree Inn at the Colonnade, 60
  Harbor Court Hotel, 63
  Henderson's Wharf, 65
  Inn at Perry Cabin, 102
  Tyler Spite House, 71
New Jersey
  Hilton at Short Hills, 130
  Marriott's Seaview Golf Resort, 140
New York
  The Adelphi Hotel, 216
  Beaverkill Valley Inn, 281
  Canoe Island Lodge, 180
  Centennial House, 345
  East Hampton Point Cottages, 348
  The Garden City Hotel, 353
  Geneva on the Lake, 247
  Gideon Putnam Hotel, 218
  Gurney's Inn Resort & Spa, 354
  The Inn at Quogue, 360
  Mirror Lake Inn, 187
  Montauk Yacht Club Resort and Marina, 356
  Otesaga Hotel, 209
  The Peninsula, 322
  The Pink House, 351
  The Sagamore, An Omni Classic Resort, 177
  Troutbeck, 271
  U.N. Plaza–Park Hyatt, 335
  The Village Latch Inn, 367
Pennsylvania
  Barley Sheaf Farm, 426
  Four Seasons Hotel, 455
  Gateway Lodge Country Inn and Restaurant, 474
  Glasbern, 423
  Hidden Valley, 392
  Highland Farms, 409
  Hotel Atop The Bellevue, 457

Tennis

Horseback Riding

Golf

Fishing

Cross-Country Skiing

Fitness Facility

State or National Park Nearby

Pets Welcome with Permission

No Smoking

Index

Best Places Report

Authors of the Best Places to Stay series travel extensively in their research to find the best places for all budgets, styles, and interests. However, if we've missed an establishment that you find worthy, please write to us with your suggestion. Detailed information about the service, food, setting, and nearby activities or sights is most important. Finally, let us know how you heard about the place and how long you've been going there.

Send suggestions to:

> The Harvard Common Press
> Best Places to Stay Suggestions
> 535 Albany Street
> Boston, Massachusetts 02118

NAME OF HOTEL _____

TELEPHONE _____

ADDRESS _____

_____ ZIP _____

DESCRIPTION _____

_____

_____

_____

_____

_____

_____

YOUR NAME _____

TELEPHONE _____

ADDRESS _____

_____ ZIP _____